World Music
Traditions and Transformations

Second Edition

Michael B. Bakan
The Florida State University

Mc Graw Hill

Connect
Learn
Succeed™

The McGraw·Hill Companies

McGraw Hill — Connect Learn Succeed™

WORLD MUSIC: TRADITIONS AND TRANSFORMATIONS, SECOND EDITION

Printed in the United States of America.

3 4 5 6 7 8 9 0 QDB/QDB 1 0 9 8 7 6 5 4 3 2

ISBN 978-0-07-352664-5
MHID 0-07-352664-9

Vice President & Editor-in-Chief: *Michael Ryan*
Vice President EDP/Central Publishing Services: *Kimberly Meriwether David*
Publisher: *Christopher Freitag*
Editorial Coordinator: *Marley Magaziner*
Executive Marketing Manager: *Pamela S. Cooper*
Senior Project Manager: *Joyce Watters*
Design Coordinator: *Margarite Reynolds*
Cover Designer: *Carole Lawson*
Cover Image Credit: *Mike Redig, photographer*
Senior Photo Editor: *Natalia Peschiera*
Photo Researcher: *Toni Michaels, PhotoFind, LLC*
Media Project Manager: *Sridevi Palani*
Buyer: *Susan K. Culbertson*
Compositor: *Laserwords Private Limited*
Typeface: *10/12 Fairfield Light*
Printer: *Quad/Graphics*

Library of Congress Cataloging-in-Publication Data

Bakan, Michael B.
  World music: traditions and transformations / Michael B. Bakan. — 2nd ed.
    p. cm.
  ISBN 978-0-07-352664-5 (alk. paper)
  1. World music—History and criticism.   I. Title.
  ML3545.B24 2011
  780.9—dc22
                                          2010050752

www.mhhe.com

To my family, my students, and all who love to learn.

"Good-bye," [said the little prince].
"Good-bye," said the fox. "Here is my secret.
It's quite simple: One sees clearly only with the heart.
Anything essential is invisible to the eyes."

Antoine de Saint-Exupéry,
The Little Prince

Michael B. Bakan is Professor of Ethnomusicology and Head of Ethnomusicology/World Music in the College of Music at Florida State University, where he also directs the university's Balinese gamelan ensemble and the Music-Play Project, a program for children on the autism spectrum and their families. He has been the recipient of numerous awards and honors, including two Florida State University Undergraduate Teaching Awards (1998, 2010). His first book, *Music of Death and New Creation: Experiences in the World of Balinese Gamelan Beleganjur* (University of Chicago Press, 1999), was selected to the *Choice* Outstanding Academic Titles list for the year 2000 and was recognized as one of the two "most significant publications on Balinese music in almost half a century" in *The Times* (London). The first edition of *World Music: Traditions and Transformations* (McGraw-Hill, 2007) has been adopted at more than 100 universities and colleges worldwide. Bakan's many other publications encompass topics ranging from Indonesian music and world percussion to electronic music technology, early jazz history, film music, multicultural music education, and the ethnomusicology of autism. He is also the series editor of the Routledge Focus on World Music Series.

As a percussionist, Bakan has performed with many renowned world music, jazz, and Western classical music artists and ensembles, including the Toronto Symphony Orchestra, the Music at Marlboro Festival Orchestra, John Cage, A. J. Racy, Phil Nimmons, I Ketut Sukarata, and the championship beleganjur groups of Batur Tengah and Tatasan Kaja in Bali, Indonesia. He is also an active composer, with traditional and experimental works for Balinese gamelan, world music/jazz fusion pieces, film scores, and modern dance compositions to his credit.

Bakan has been a visiting professor or invited lecturer at numerous institutions, including Harvard, Yale, Indiana, and Boston universities; the universities of Chicago, Colorado, Illinois, Maryland, and Washington; and the Berklee College of Music. He previously served as president of the Society for Ethnomusicology's Southeast/Caribbean Chapter. He and his family live in Tallahassee, Florida.

brief contents

contents

preface

World Music: Traditions and Transformations, second edition, is an introductory-level survey of diverse musics from around the world. It assumes no prior formal training or education in music and, with the exception of a single illustrative example, avoids the use of Western music notation entirely. It is written primarily for undergraduate nonmusic majors, but is equally appropriate for music majors, and is therefore ideal for courses enrolling both music and non-music students. The text is supported by a four-CD set of musical examples and by extensive online supplements and interaction opportunities.

In writing this book and producing its accompanying resources, I have tried to create an engaging, clear, and accessible work that college and university instructors from a variety of backgrounds can use to make world music a vehicle of exploration, discovery, intellectual stimulation, and fun for their students. For me, the world's diverse and ever-changing forms of music are entryways into joyful experience, intellectual growth, compassion and empathy, intercultural understanding, and a deep appreciation for the inherent qualities of creativity, resilience, resourcefulness, and shared humanity that connect people everywhere. I teach music because I want to share what music has taught me. Even more importantly, I teach because I believe that experiencing and learning about music from a global perspective can inspire my students to find within themselves valuable resources and opportunities for growth, engagement, commitment, and the cultivation of humanitarian ideals. Getting inside of music and seeing how it works, how it lives, and what makes it meaningful enables students to expand their horizons and better appreciate diversity and multiculturalism in the contemporary world. It also holds the capacity to enrich their sense of who they are and what truly matters. In offering this book to my fellow teachers of world music and to our students, I hope that I can contribute something of value to our shared aspirations in these pursuits.

Organization, Content, and Approach

This book is organized in two parts. Part I, consisting of the first six chapters, provides an inviting and nonthreatening introduction to the elements of music that is global in its inclusivity, encompasses cultural as well as purely musical elements, and is written with the explicit goal of being readily accessible to readers with no background in music. The depth of coverage in these chapters is geared specifically to preparing students for the materials they will encounter in Part II and is accordingly limited and focused.

Chapter 1 examines the fundamental question, What, in the world, is music? Chapter 2 looks at how music lives as a phenomenon of culture and explains the book's core concept of *musicultural tradition*. Chapters 3–6 explore how music works as a medium of organized sound, with discussions of rhythm (Chapter 3), pitch (Chapter 4), dynamics, timbre, and instruments (Chapter 5), and texture and form (Chapter 6). These four chapters (3–6) have been significantly streamlined and revised in the second edition to ensure optimal clarity and accessibility, especially for nonmusic majors.

The various elements introduced in Part I, both musical and cultural, are brought to life and made accessible via a combination of musical examples and illustrative materials of four kinds:

- Participatory activities based on songs that will likely be familiar to most students ("The Alphabet Song," "Mary Had a Little Lamb," "The Star-Spangled Banner").
- Recorded selections on the CD set representing diverse music traditions from around the world.

- Online Musical Illustrations that exemplify specific musical elements (these are located at the Online Learning Center at www.mhhe.com/bakan2e—see p. xxv).
- User-friendly visual aids that are closely integrated with the musical examples discussed.

The world music recordings serve a dual purpose. Beyond providing illustrations of specific music elements (syncopation, melodic contour, call-and-response, etc.), they also initiate the global musical journey that then continues on a different plane in Part II of the book. Collectively, the Part I recordings give students both a musical preview of traditions that are explored more fully in later chapters and an introduction to numerous other traditions that are not: Native American traditional music and First Nations rock (the latter being an exciting new addition to the second edition), Aboriginal Australian and contemporary didgeridoo music, Greek folkloric music, Zimbabwean world beat, Roma brass band music, Mongolian and Tuvan-style multiphonic singing, Fijian church hymnody, and American blues, to list a few examples. A number of musicultural traditions introduced in the Part I chapters that received relatively little attention in the first edition are the subject of more comprehensive coverage in the second edition (see "What's New in the Second Edition," pp. xxv–xxvii), providing for a more balanced treatment of global musical diversity overall.

Building upon the broad foundations of Chapters 1–6, the seven chapters of Part II offer more focused studies of specific traditions originating in Indonesia, India, Ireland, West Africa, Latin America, the Middle East, and China. Each chapter first establishes a central topic of musical focus and links it to a central topic of cultural focus. This yields a productive lens through which to view the musicultural matrix as the chapter moves from traditional, to neo-traditional, to post-traditional domains, all in close integration with examples on the CD set. This orientation defines the book's *focused, musicultural approach*.

To better explain this approach, let's examine Chapter 7. In the chapter, the primacy of interlocking parts in a particular type of Balinese gamelan music, beleganjur, is paralleled to the primacy of communal interdependence in Balinese society, as well as to the interlocking worlds of Hindu-Balinese cosmology: demonic, earthly, and divine. The Balinese interlocking principle, defined in these holistic terms, serves as the basis for a wide-ranging musicultural journey that takes readers from the royal courts of Central Java to Balinese cremation processions and music competitions, and ultimately to contemporary Indonesian and American musical domains in which elements of gamelan, rock, jazz, funk, hip-hop, and country music are creatively fused and juxtaposed.

As with Chapter 7, the other chapters in Part II similarly examine a clearly defined musicultural tradition as it relates to diverse and intersecting planes of geography, history, identity, and cultural worldview and practice. This synthesis is made possible by the core concept of *tradition* that guides the book as a whole. In this conception, tradition is defined as *a process of creative transformation whose most remarkable feature is the continuity it nurtures and sustains.* This definition emphasizes the fact that traditions, wherever they are found—which is in fact everywhere that human communities exist—are dynamic rather than static, flexible rather than fixed, resilient yet adaptable to change.

Applying a focused, musicultural approach to this dynamic and flexible perspective on tradition allows for modes of teaching and learning that are at once broadly encompassing of global musical diversity, conducive to a significant depth of exploration, manageable in scope for students at the introductory level, and potentially inclusive of all forms of music in the world, from the most archaic and resolutely traditional to the most modern, familiar, commercial, or radically experimental. The following content overview of Chapters 8–13 provides some sense of this range.

Chapter 8 centers musically on the Hindustani raga tradition of northern India, placing that tradition in context through an emphasis on processes of *barhat* (growth/transformation) that encompass a myriad of musical and cultural domains. An exploration of the life, artistry, lineage, legacy, and international influence of Ravi Shankar guides the chapter's narrative. Other Indian/South Asian classical, folk, and popular traditions besides Hindustani raga are introduced, including Karnatak music, bhajan, bhangra, and qawwali. The second half of the chapter explores a diversity of raga-inspired Indian-Western musical encounters of the modern era—Ravi Shankar and Yehudi Menuhin, John Coltrane, the Beatles, John McLaughlin and Shakti—and concludes in Bollywood with a section on the music of celebrity Indian film composer A. R. Rahman.

Chapter 9 takes Irish traditional dance tunes as its main point of focus. The chapter weaves an intricate tapestry of musicultural tradition and transformation from the rural Irish country-side to Dublin and New York City, and from the uilleann pipes to Irish-jazz-rock fusion. Examples on the CD set that were not included in the first edition, including a beautiful example of *sean nós* singing by Lillis O'Laoire and a classic 1973 recording by Planxty, add an important new dimension to the chapter in its coverage of Irish vocal traditions.

In Chapter 10, a specific West African instrument, the kora, is the central musical topic in an exploration of polyvocal musical and cultural expression in Africa that also encompasses drum speech and drumming-based dance music of Ghana, the musical art of jeliya, endongo music of Uganda, Central African vocal polyphony, and the world beat pop balladry of Angé-lique Kidjo. A new boxed feature on South African *isicathamiya* music, along with a new CD track featuring the legendary isicathamiya group Ladysmith Black Mambazo, are included among the exciting additions to the chapter in this edition.

Chapter 11 looks at Latin American music and the development of pan-Latino identity mainly through the lens of a single song, "Oye Como Va," tracking its prehistory, genesis, and transformation from West Africa, Spain, Cuba, and Puerto Rico to New York City (Tito Puente), San Francisco (Santana), and Miami (Tito Puente Jr.). New to the second edition is an expansive survey of other Latin American music traditions, which covers Brazilian samba, bossa nova, and tropicália; tango, mariachi, and steel band; and Andean traditional and folkloric musics. Several new corresponding examples are included on the CD set. Increased coverage of salsa and Latin jazz is another notable feature of the revision.

The primary subject of Chapter 12 is Middle Eastern women's dance and its music, with an emphasis on traditions and dance rhythms of Egypt and their transformations in contexts ranging from the Egyptian commercial film industry to the cosmopolitan, international world of contemporary belly dance. A substantive section on Arab instrumental art music (*taqsim*, *maqam*, *takht*) that was not a part of the first edition is included here, along with new coverage of traditions and musical artists from Arab countries beyond Egypt, such as Iraq and Lebanon.

Chapter 13, like Chapter 10, has as its musical focus a particular instrument, in this case the Chinese *zheng*. The cultural focus is on music and politics. The zheng's history in China from antiquity to the present offers rich opportunities to examine topics and issues including Confucian philosophy, socialist ideology, minority rights and resistance, censorship, and music as protest, all of which are explored. Also notable in Chapter 13, and new to this edition, is a relatively substantial treatment of Japanese music. It focuses on the tradition of the koto, an instrument historically related to the zheng, through which several historical and contemporary Japanese genres—gagaku, koto, sankyoku, and J-pop—are examined. New coverage of Chinese and Chinese American rock has been added as well.

Key Features

Beyond its unique treatment of the elements of music (Part I) and its focused, musicultural approach (Part II), this text and its accompanying resources offer a number of other valuable and attractive key features. These are described below.

Expanded and Improved Four-CD Set

The original three-CD set accompanying the first edition has been expanded to a four-CD set in this new edition. The new compilation includes 107 tracks constituting a full five hours of music, with more than an hour's worth of new music in all. The same emphasis on high-quality, professional recordings by the likes of Ravi Shankar, John Coltrane, Tito Puente, Santana, Shakti, Angélique Kidjo, The Chieftains, Eileen Ivers, and Yo-Yo Ma that defined the first edition has carried over to the second edition, and the compilation has been enhanced by the addition of 19 brand new tracks (see list of new tracks, pp. xxvi–xxvii). Most of the new tracks represent cultures, genres, and styles that were either not covered in the first edition or that were covered only marginally, but that receive substantial coverage here. These include five new Latin American examples (samba, tropicália, tango, salsa/Latin jazz, and Andean music), among them the classic 1968 recording of "A Minha Menina" by the Brazilian band Os Mutantes; a new selection of First Nations rock; gamelan-jazz-rock fusion; Bollywood film song; Indian-techno fusion; Irish sean nós; South African *isicathamiya*; Middle Eastern art and popular musics; Japanese koto and J-pop; and Chinese American zheng rock. A complete raga performance by Ravi Shankar is another exciting new addition.

Beyond the many new tracks, the four-CD format of the second edition accommodates a large number of complete tracks and extended excerpts in place of the shorter excerpts that were included with the first edition. For example, in Chapter 8, you can now listen to the complete soprano saxophone solo by John Coltrane on "India" and the complete John McLaughlin guitar solo on Shakti's "Joy." Additionally, you can now hear the entire recording of Jasbir Jassi's catchy bhangra tune "Kudi, Kudi" in all its glory rather than just the brief excerpt of the first edition.

As with the first edition, a high level of integration and synergy between the music on the CD set and the content of the text is a hallmark feature of the second edition. A "music first" priority, in which the music drives the text rather than the other way around, is emphasized throughout.

Getting Inside the Music Features

In keeping with its "music first" priority, *World Music: Traditions and Transformations*, second edition, offers a number of features to help students comprehend and enjoy the musics they encounter, both musically and culturally:

■ Guided Listening Experience narratives linked to the main musical examples of Part II chapters highlight key elements of music sound and cultural meaning as they unfold. They are written to be accessible and engaging for nonmusic majors, while improving students' listening skills and taking them deeply into the music without becoming overly technical.

■ Boxed Guided Listening Quick Summaries immediately follow each of the main Guided Listening Experience narratives. These timeline boxes concisely summarize the principal features emphasized in a format that is easy to follow during listening.

- Musical Guided Tours take students inside the music in a different way. These brief and straightforward audio-recorded lecture demonstrations (which also appear in transcribed form in the text) enable students to hear and understand how music works from the inside out, step by step and part by part. They will learn, for example, how the multiple layers and interlocking patterns of Balinese gamelan music are structured and organized (Chapter 7), how Irish traditional dance tunes are melodically ornamented and combined to form medleys (Chapter 9), and how polyrhythms are generated in West African drum ensemble music (Chapter 10). There are seven Musical Guided Tours, one for each of the chapters in Part II of the text (Chapters 7–13).

- The Making Music Exercises included in some chapters provide another avenue of access to music's inner workings. Here, students are given simple, step-by-step instructions on how to actually *perform* on some level the musics they are learning about, either on their own or interactively with the recordings. They get to keep tal with Ravi Shankar, mark out Egyptian drum patterns with Hossam Ramzy, and actually *experience*, rather than just learn in the abstract, the meanings of key musical terms like melody, rhythm, and tempo. These exercises also work well as in-class group activities when directed by the course instructor.

- Finally, there are 26 Online Musical Illustrations that demonstrate key elements and features discussed in the text, from scales and instrumental timbres to the paired tuning of Balinese gamelan instruments and traditional, neo-traditional, and post-traditional treatments of a single melodic figure in an Irish dance tune.

Maps and Timelines

Chapter maps and timelines are located at the beginning of each chapter in Part II. These highlight key geographical locations and historical and musical developments. They are designed to facilitate efficient, organized reading strategies and are valuable study resources as well. The maps are color coded so that the principal area or areas of focus in the chapter are the most boldly colored, with the secondary areas being slightly lighter and the tertiary areas lighter still.

Lists of Key Terms, Pronunciation Guidance, and Glossary

Foreign and technical terms are kept to a minimum in the text but are inevitable to some degree due to the subject matter. The following features are included to assist both students and instructors:

- Key terms, which are highlighted in boldface, generally at the point of their first appearance, and are listed at the end of each chapter to facilitate studying. Foreign terms that are not key terms are italicized.

- "Commonsense"-style phonetic pronunciation guidance in the margins for key terms and other words or names that may present pronunciation difficulties.

- A glossary that includes both definitions and pronunciation guidance for key terms, as well as reference to the main chapter or chapters in which the term appears.

Photographs, Visual Aids, and "Insights and Perspectives" Boxes

This book is enriched by abundant photographs, figures, tables, and other illustrative materials that bring the music and text vividly to life and enrich the clarity and enjoyment of the reading and music-listening experience. "Insights and Perspectives" boxes, which supplement or provide alternate points of view on the main text, are another important feature.

Study Questions, Discussion Questions, and "Applying What You Have Learned" Sections

A list of study questions is included at the end of each chapter, along with discussion questions and suggestions for student projects and assignments that build upon or extend from chapter materials ("Applying What You Have Learned"). Students are also directed to the Online Learning Center at www.mhhe.com/bakan2e for additional resources and study aids at the conclusion of each chapter.

Flexibility

The text is designed to be flexible and adaptable to varied teaching situations and instructor needs and interests. This is the case for both Part I and Part II.

Though designed as an integrated unit, the six preliminary chapters that constitute Part I may be approached in a variety of ways. Different student backgrounds (e.g., nonmusic majors versus music majors), pedagogical aims (e.g., greater "music" emphasis versus greater "culture" emphasis), or course settings (size of class, semester versus quarter) may inspire instructors to approach the teaching of these chapters in different ways (a number of suggestions are included in the Online Instructor's Manual at www.mhhe.com/bakan2e). Some instructors may even elect to teach the chapters in an alternate order, for example, beginning with the elements of music sound addressed in Chapters 3–6 before addressing the more conceptual and cultural issues of Chapters 1–2.

As for Part II, there is a great amount of flexibility. The chapters may be taught in any order. Though cross-references between certain chapters do occur and there are overarching themes that can be productively developed across chapters (e.g., music and nationalism, music and gender), each chapter is ultimately a stand-alone unit. Some instructors may opt to cover all seven chapters, while others may prefer to select just five or six to allow time for more in-depth study. Some may follow the book's order of chapters; others may prefer a different organizational strategy, for example, moving from "near to far" geographically, starting, say, with the Latin American and Irish music chapters (Chapters 11 and 9) before tackling Indonesia or India (Chapters 7 and 8). Again, the Online Instructor's Manual provides suggestions on possible approaches.

Consistency of Presentation and Authority in a Single-Authored Text

In contrast to several other introductory world music texts, *World Music: Traditions and Transformations*, second edition, is a single-authored work rather than a collaboration of multiple authors contributing individual chapters in their respective areas of specialization. Single authorship allows for a level of consistency of presentation in both the conception and writing of a work of this scale that is difficult, if not impossible, to achieve in a multi-authored textbook.

As for the accuracy and authority of the text, each chapter has benefited from a rigorous peer review process. All of the chapters of Part II have been reviewed by leading ethnomusicologists who specialize in the areas covered.

Supplementary Features

This text offers helpful online resources for both instructors and students. The Online Learning Center, Student Edition, at www.mhhe.com/bakan2e, provides students with a wealth of materials for course preparation and study, including chapter overviews, sample multiple-choice quizzes, sample music-listening quizzes, exam study guides, Internet links, annotated lists of resources and references for further study and research (books, articles, recordings, videos and DVDs, Web sites), guidance on pronunciation of foreign language terms (beyond that included in the main text), and an image bank. Downloadable mp3 files of five of the book's seven audio Musical Guided Tours are located at the Online Learning Center (the other two Musical Guided Tours are included on the four-CD set). So, too, are the 26 audio Online Musical Illustrations, which are likewise downloadable (with the exception of one).

The Online Learning Center, Instructor Edition, also located at www.mhhe.com/bakan2e, gives instructors access to all of the materials of the student edition plus much more. The most notable component of the instructor edition is the aforementioned Online Instructor's Manual. This includes lesson plans, ideas for in-class participatory activities, supplementary information on chapter topics that can be used to enliven and enrich lectures, additional lists of resources for research and class use, sample syllabi and course schedules tailored to different course contexts (e.g., single semester, quarter, nonmusic major, music major), and a test bank including hundreds of questions. The Online Learning Center also provides a link to my personally maintained and regularly updated Web site at www.michaelbakan.com, where lists of links to hundreds of online videos organized by chapter and topic may be found, along with many other valuable teaching and learning resources for instructors and students. See the "New Online Resources" section on page xxvii for additional information on the Web site.

What's New in the Second Edition?

This new edition of *World Music: Traditions and Transformations* has been completely revised and updated. Among other improvements, it includes significant coverage of a large number of musical traditions, genres, and cultures that were either not covered at all in the first edition or that were covered only tangentially. New sections on the following topics have been added:

- Brazilian music, including samba, bossa nova, and tropicália
- Japanese music, including gagaku, koto, sankyoku, and J-pop
- Bollywood
- First Nations/Native American traditional music and rock
- Tango
- Steel band
- Andean music
- Mariachi
- Salsa and Latin jazz
- South African isicathamiya
- Sean nós and other Irish vocal traditions

- Chinese and Chinese American rock
- Middle Eastern art music (taqsim, maqam, takht)
- Javanese gamelan, Balinese gamelan gong kebyar, and Indonesian popular music

Other changes to the text include:

- Extensive revision of Chapters 3–6, which cover the elements of music, and of the Guided Listening Experience narratives and summaries of Chapters 7–13; these revisions facilitate greater clarity, accessibility, and reading enjoyment, especially for nonmusic majors.

- Expansion of the Latin American music chapter, Chapter 11, to include new sections on samba, bossa nova, tropicália, tango, steel band, Andean music, and mariachi, as well as additional coverage of salsa and Latin jazz.

- Addition of new sections to the Indonesian music chapter, Chapter 7, including both a comparative discussion of Central Javanese gamelan and Balinese gamelan gong kebyar and an introduction to the innovative gamelan-jazz-rock fusion of Balinese electric guitar virtuoso I Wayan Balawan.

- A major revision of the chapter on Indian music, Chapter 8, which now incorporates a complete Hindustani raga performance by Ravi Shankar and a substantive section on Bollywood film music.

- Supplementation of the chapter on Irish music, Chapter 9, with new examples and discussions emphasizing Irish vocal genres including sean nós and influential bands like Planxty.

- A new boxed feature in the chapter on African music, Chapter 10, which focuses on South African isicathamiya and is linked to a new example on the CD set by Ladysmith Black Mambazo.

- Increased attention to instrumental art music of the Middle East in Chapter 12, including a new Guided Listening Experience exploring the artistry of Iraqi 'ud master Ahmed Mukhtar and his takht ensemble.

- The scope of the chapter on Chinese music, Chapter 13, has been expanded through the addition of new materials on Chinese and Chinese American rock, as well as by the aforementioned coverage of Japanese traditions with significant historical or contemporary ties to Chinese musical culture (gagaku, koto, J-pop).

- The first edition's chapter on music and Jewish mysticism (Chapter 14) is now available online for adopters of the second edition.

New Tracks on the Four-CD Set

The following tracks on the *World Music: Traditions and Transformations* four-CD set were not included on the first edition's three-CD set. All of these new selections, with the exception of one ("Monsoon Malabar"), are complete tracks:

- "A Minha Menina," Os Mutantes (Brazilian tropicália)
- "Dance," Eagle & Hawk (First Nations rock)
- "Iraqi Café," Ahmed Mukhtar (Iraqi takht)
- "Tori no Yo ni," Sawai Tadao (Japanese koto)
- "Country Beleganjur," I Wayan Balawan (Balinese gamelan-jazz-rock fusion)

- "Monsoon Malabar," Bombay Dub Orchestra (Indian-techno fusion)
- "Raga Sindhi-Bhairavi," Ravi Shankar (Hindustani raga)
- "Barso Re," A. R. Rahman, Shreya Ghoshal (Bollywood)
- "Ag an Phobal Dé Domhnaigh," Lillis O'Laoire (Irish sean nós)
- "Song for Ireland," Noel McLoughlin (Irish)
- "Bean Pháidín," Planxty (Irish)
- "Unomathemba," Ladysmith Black Mambazo (South African isicathamiya)
- "Evolução de Samba," Jacaré Brazil [Florida] (Brazilian samba de batucada)
- "Fueye," Trio Hugo Diaz (tango)
- Ceremonial julajula panpipe music from the Bolivian Andes
- "Nena," Francisco Aguabella (salsa/Latin jazz)
- "Hou Hou Hou," Emad Sayyah (contemporary belly dance music, Lebanese style)
- "Sakitama," Rin (J-pop with koto and other traditional Japanese instruments)
- "Hot Thursday," Bei Bei He and Shawn Lee (Chinese American zheng rock)

New Online Resources

The book's Online Learning Center has been updated, revised, and improved while retaining all of the outstanding features of the first edition version, including the Musical Guided Tours, Online Musical Illustrations, Online Instructor's Manual, and other valuable teaching and learning resources. An author-maintained Web site (www.michaelbakan.com) has been created to supplement the text, CD set, and Online Learning Center for the second edition. The signature feature of this Web site is its regularly updated lists of links to hundreds of online videos that support and enhance the text. Also included are field video recordings from my personal archives, course lecture notes, lists of supplementary music recordings for class use, and informational posts and announcements related to book content and effective teaching and learning strategies. The Web site is additionally linked to a *World Music* Facebook page that offers opportunities for direct interaction with me and with world music instructors and students worldwide.

CourseSmart eTextbooks

This text is available as an eTextbook from CourseSmart, a new way for faculty to find and review eTextbooks. It's also a great option for students who are interested in accessing their course materials digitally and saving money. CourseSmart offers thousands of the most commonly adopted textbooks across hundreds of courses from a wide variety of higher education publishers. It is the only place for faculty to review and compare the full text of a textbook online, providing immediate access without the environmental impact of requesting a print exam copy. At CourseSmart, students can save up to 50 percent of the cost of a print book, reduce their impact on the environment, and gain access to powerful Web tools for learning, including full text search, notes and highlighting, and e-mail tools for sharing notes between classmates. For further details contact your sales representative or go to www.coursesmart.com.

McGraw-Hill Create www.mcgrawhillcreate.com

Craft your teaching resources to match the way you teach! With McGraw-Hill Create you can easily rearrange chapters, combine material from other content sources, and quickly upload content you have written like your course syllabus or teaching notes. Find the content you need in Create by searching through thousands of leading McGraw-Hill textbooks. Arrange your book to fit your teaching style. Create even allows you to personalize your book's appearance by selecting the cover and adding your name, school, and course information. Order a Create book and you'll receive a complimentary print review copy in three to five business days or a complimentary electronic review copy (eComp) via email in about one hour. Go to www.mcgrawhillcreate.com today and register. Experience how McGraw-Hill Create empowers you to teach *your* students *your* way.

Acknowledgments

I am grateful to the many reviewers, colleagues, friends, and loved ones who have contributed to this work. My thanks, first, to the following reviewers for their insightful and helpful comments, criticisms, and suggestions: Julia Chybowski, *University of Wisconsin, Oshkosh*; George Dor, *University of Mississippi*; Andrew Eisenberg, *Northwestern University, SUNY-Stony Brook*; Thomas George Caracas Garcia, *Miami University*; Jeremy Grimshaw, *Brigham Young University*; Nancy Gunn, *Southern Maine CC*; James Hall, *Marshall University*; William Hearn, *Clayton State University*; Adriana Helbig, *University of Pittsburgh*; Morgan Jenkins, *Pennsylvania State University, Mont Alto*; Michael Kaloyanides, *University of New Haven*; Susanna Reichling, *Missouri State University*; Noraliz Ruiz, *Kent State University*; Peter Schimpf, *Metropolitan State College of Denver*; Ted Solis, *Arizona State University*; Robert Stevens, *University of Connecticut*; David Such, *Spokane Community College*; Sarah Tyrell, *Johnson County CC, Blue River CC*; and Daniel Wyman, *San Jose State University*.

Thanks also to David Knapp for his outstanding work in editing and mastering the four-CD set that accompanies this new edition; Trevor Harvey and Bret Woods for their valued input and consultation on a variety of matters both technical and substantive; Jade Stagg, Todd Rosendahl, Stephanie Thorne, Plamena Kourtova, Matt Morin, Elizabeth Clendinning, and my other graduate assistants and students at Florida State University for their contributions, feedback, and inspiration; Michael Redig for his fine photographs; Deng Haiqiong and Lynnsey Weissenberger for their Musical Guided Tour performances; and Anne Prescott, Sean Williams, Lillis O'Laoire, Henry Stobart, Larry Crook, Welson Tremura, Vince Fontaine, Ahmed Mukhtar, I Wayan Balawan, Andrew T. Mackay, Nalini Vinayak, Carlos Odria, Carlos Silva, Brian Hall, Katelyn Wood, Lisa Beckley-Roberts, Carolyn Ramzy, Peter Hoesing, Jane Scott, Meg Jackson, Ross Brand, Jeff Jones, Pacho Lara, Mariano Rodriguez, León Garcia, Brittany Roche, Elizabeth Timan, Melinda Cowen, Jim Cox, Richard Zarou, Damascus Kafumbe, Rachel Harris, Roderic Knight, Roger Vetter, Bryan Burton, Jennifer Post, Jay Keister, Margaret Puente, Tito Puente Jr., Joe Conzo, Ted Levin, A. J. and Barbara Racy, Aisha Ali, Steve Stuempfle, Allan Marett, Katherine Hagedorn, Michelle Kisliuk, Li Xiuqin, Jane Sugarman, Michael Frishkopf, Peter Manuel, Eric Charry, Stephen Slawek, Jonathon Stock, Charles Atkins, Jen Brannstrom, Alec McLane, Daniel Avorgbedor, Joe Williams, Steven Loza, Ellen Koskoff, Michael Tenzer, I Ketut Gedé Asnawa, I Ketut Sukarata, I Ketut Suandita, Sherry Simpson, Henry Hall, Min Tian, David Bellamy, Cal Melton Jr., Jill Braaten, Latricia Hudson, Caren-Alexandra Entwistle,

Jon Entwistle, Atesh Sonneborn, Andrew Jervis, Bei Bei He, Mana Yoshinaga, Michael Serena, Chris Wilkey, David Frasure, Michael McFadin, Patrick Kelly, and Megan, Isaac, Leah, and Paul Bakan for their various forms of assistance and support.

My colleagues in the College of Music at Florida State University have been extraordinarily supportive, and I especially want to thank Douglass Seaton, Frank Gunderson, Benjamin Koen, Dale Olsen, Denise Von Glahn, Charles Brewer, Jeffery Kite-Powell, Don Gibson, Jon Piersol, Clifford Madsen, Jane Clendinning, Pamela Ryan, Patrick Meighan, Jerrold Pope, Barbara Ford, Leo Welch, Seth Beckman, Wendy Smith, Meghan MacCaskill, Sally Gross, Jennie Carpenter, Dee Beggarly, and Brian Gaber for their help. Numerous undergraduate and graduate students of mine beyond those already acknowledged—as well as many students, world music course instructors, and ethnomusicologists at other institutions who are likewise not mentioned by name here—also have played an essential part in this work; my heartfelt appreciation goes out to all of them.

The editorial and production team at McGraw-Hill has been consummately professional and a joy to work with. Special thanks to the editorial team of Chris Freitag and Marley Magaziner; development editor Nadia Bidwell; copyeditor Alyson Platt; designer Margarite Reynolds; project manager Joyce Watters; photo research coordinator Natalia Peschiera and buyer Susan K. Culbertson. Special thanks, too, to Tom Laskey at Sony BMG Music Entertainment; Sunitha Arun Bhaskar and Erika Jordan at Laserwords Maine; and Toni Michaels at PhotoFind for their outstanding efforts on behalf of this project.

Finally, I would like to express my deep appreciation to the many musicians who are discussed in the pages of this book and whose recordings are featured on the CD set. Some I know personally, others I do not; most are still with us, others have passed on. This work is a tribute to all of them, and also to musicians and people everywhere who create, appreciate, support, and find meaning and inspiration in music.

Michael B. Bakan
The Florida State University

about this book: an introduction for students

". . . the value of a piece of music as music is inseparable from its value as an expression of human experience."

John Blacking

World Music: Traditions and Transformations, second edition, is an introductory-level survey of diverse musics from around the world. It assumes no prior formal training or education in music of any kind. You do not need to have taken music lessons or classes to understand this book; nor do you need to know how to read music or play an instrument. The only real prerequisite is your willingness to explore music as the global phenomenon of human expression and experience it truly is, and in turn to approach the diversity of music you encounter with an open mind, open ears, thoughtfulness, and active engagement.

Throughout this text, you will be invited to listen deeply to music, think broadly about what it means and why it is significant in human life, and even perform it yourself in some instances. The purpose of this multifaceted, experiential approach is not just to increase your understanding of what music is and how it works, but also to increase your appreciation and enjoyment of music overall. Experiencing, learning about, and taking pleasure in music go hand in hand; at least they ought to. Each of these interrelated ways of engaging with music enriches the other. All of them together have the capacity to enhance our appreciation of cultural diversity, intercultural tolerance, human creativity and resourcefulness, and the common spirit of humanity that unites us all.

World Music

"World music" is a slippery term. It is broad enough to encompass any and all music that exists or has ever existed in the world, yet it lacks the precision to accurately apply to any *specific* music tradition; it is open to many interpretations. A *raga* from India is neither more nor less deserving of the designation "world music" than a Mozart piano sonata. Yet most Westerners, if asked, would classify the former as an example of world music but not the latter; and most connoisseurs of Indian music would strongly disagree with this type of a classification scheme altogether.

Here, our approach will be to conceive of the study of world music simply as an exploration of selected music traditions from *throughout* the world. Each of the traditions chosen is traced from its point (or points) of beginning to wherever its multidirectional pathways of continuity and transformation may lead. The geographical and cultural "hubs" of given musics—the places identified with their origins, the communities and societies with which they are connected, the musicians recognized as their leading exponents—are most certainly accounted for, but so too are the complex, intersecting webs of geography, culture, technology, and sound that situate these hubs in more broadly global frameworks. All manner and forms of musical expression, from the most resolutely traditional and geographically specific to the most commercially oriented, cross-culturally diverse, and radically experimental, are included.

A Focused, Musicultural Approach

This text is organized in two main parts. Part I, comprising Chapters 1–6, offers a general introduction to music as a phenomenon of sound and a phenomenon of culture. Drawing upon a combination of simple, familiar songs (such as "The Alphabet Song") and an eclectic range of music from around the world for its examples and illustrations, the six Part I chapters collectively address three fundamental questions:

- What is music?
- How does music live in people's lives?
- How does music work?

These chapters establish the basic foundation and framework for what follows in Part II.

Each of the seven chapters of Part II (Chapters 7–13) offers an exploration of a single *musicultural tradition*. The merging of the words "music" and "cultural" into the compound term *musicultural* is intended to emphasize the inseparability of music as sound and music as "an expression of human experience" (Blacking 1995:31). Each chapter links a central topic of musical focus to a central topic of cultural focus. Together, these provide the principal musicultural lens through which the music tradition as a whole is then viewed. For example, in Chapter 7, a standard approach to rhythmic organization used in music from the island of Bali, Indonesia, is linked to fundamental cultural values and practices relating to Balinese concepts of social interdependence. This link then becomes the basis of an exploration of Balinese music traditions and transformations covering everything from ritual music played at Hindu-Balinese cremation ceremonies to pieces that combine traditional Balinese *gamelan* music with elements of rock, jazz, funk, and hip-hop.

Traditions and Transformations

Looking at relationships between established world music traditions and the processes of transformation that challenge and redefine them is central to this work. Every chapter in Part II builds around this issue of tradition and transformation in one way or another, and in each case a conception of *tradition as a process,* specifically, *a process of creative transformation whose most remarkable feature is the continuity it nurtures and sustains,* is at the heart of the discussion.

We encounter a series of first traditional, then neo-traditional, and finally post-traditional musical examples as each chapter unfolds (these are included on the text's accompanying four-CD set—see p. xxxiii). On one level, key similarities and connections between the different examples are highlighted. This is done in order to illustrate how foundational features of style and meaning endure even in the face of far-reaching musical and cultural change. Examining the music on this level offers insights into what defines a tradition at its core, regardless of the eclectic musical surfaces that may become attached to it along the way. It helps us to comprehend, for example, how a single song like "Oye Como Va" can be transformed and adapted to many different musical styles, acquiring new sounds along the way but never losing its core cultural identity and meaning (Chapter 11); or how a popular song in a Bollywood film can be interpreted as an extension of the classical *raga* tradition of India (Chapter 8).

On a second level, contrasts and departures from convention that *distinguish* the different musical examples of each chapter one from the other—in terms of both their musical content and cultural meanings—also are emphasized. These serve to demonstrate the creative range and possibilities for transformation that are inherent in the flexibility of the tradition itself. As I try to show in each chapter, it is this flexibility that enables traditions to retain their vitality and relevance as they move through time across history, are transported to diverse locations around the globe, absorb and influence elements of other traditions, and become important and meaningful to different people for different reasons in different situations.

Depth versus Breadth: A Difficult Balancing Act

Many students reading this text will be contending with not just one but *two* rather complex subjects for the first time: the study of music and the study of culture. The focused, musicultural approach described earlier is intended to guide you toward appreciating the richness and depth of both—and of the fascinating domains of interaction that arise between them—without overwhelming you in the process. I have learned over the years that the richest appreciations, deepest understandings, and most enjoyable experiences of world music come not from trying to "cover everything" in a single course (an impossibility in any case, as I will discuss shortly), but rather from a more narrowly defined approach that explores a relatively small number of diverse traditions and topics.

That said, trade-offs and compromises are inevitable. In the present work, certain traditions and topics are included at the exclusion of many others that are every bit as interesting, important, and worthy of our attention. For example, there is a chapter on Chinese music (Chapter 13), but no chapter on Japanese or Korean music (though sections of Chapter 13 do cover some types of Japanese music). Moreover, the Chinese music chapter focuses mainly on the tradition of a single instrument (the *zheng*), with only brief accounts of a handful of the thousands of other instrumental, ensemble, vocal, popular, and theatrical traditions encompassed under the massive umbrella of "Chinese musical culture." In the chapter on Latin American music (Chapter 11), a particular lineage of musical tradition and transformation is traced from its West African and Spanish roots to Cuba, Puerto Rico, and the United States, with relatively less coverage of musics of, for example, Mexico and South America. The single chapter devoted to musics of Africa (Chapter 10) focuses almost entirely on traditions originating in West Africa, with only brief discussion of musics from other regions of this enormous and musically rich and diverse continent.

In Part I, I have tried to account for at least some world music areas and traditions not covered in the main chapter case studies of Part II. Recordings representing Native American, First Nations, African American, Aboriginal Australian, Mexican, Brazilian, Andean South American, Japanese, Mongolian, Tuvan, Polynesian, Micronesian, Romanian, Greek, and Spanish musics, as well as traditions from several regions of Africa (i.e., southern, central, and eastern) are to be found among the selections on the CD set linked to the Part I chapters. Yet even if I were to add an entire chapter on each of these, we would still be just scratching the surface of what the universe of world music actually contains in all its comprehensive breadth. Our planet is host to thousands—indeed hundreds of thousands—of distinct music traditions and cultures, each fascinating and important in its own right.

A variety of factors guided my choices of what topics and areas to include in the seven chapters of Part II. In opting to include chapters on music traditions originating in China and India, for example, I was definitely swayed by the fact that these two nations together account for more than one-third of the world's entire population. At least as significant, though, was my interest in two particular musicians, Deng Haiqiong from China and Ravi Shankar from India. I felt that their musical odysseys, both in their native lands and internationally, offered wonderful opportunities for exploring tradition and transformation in world music. My interest in the individual musician as a focal point for exploring musical tradition and transformation also influenced my decision to build the chapter on Latin American music (Chapter 11) largely around the iconic figure of Tito Puente, and, more specifically, around his most famous composition, "Oye Como Va."

There is no one ideal, or even one best, rationale for deciding what to include and what not to when approaching a topic as vast as "world music." Practical considerations (What can one reasonably expect to cover in a single course?), representational considerations (including a range of musics that are diverse, cover a wide geographical range in their totality, and represent a number of the world's major music-culture regions), thematic considerations (choosing musics and topics that lend themselves well to a tradition-and-transformation approach), and personal considerations (areas of research specialization, interest in specific musicians) all entered into my decision-making processes. Above all else, though, my priority has been to make choices that collectively yield an introduction to world music that students will find accessible, enlightening, and exciting.

Getting Inside the Music

The *World Music: Traditions and Transformations*, second edition, four-CD set is in many respects the heart of this entire work. The book is driven by the music, rather than the other way around. Each chapter has been conceived and written "from the music up." The musical examples *themselves* tell the stories of musicultural tradition and transformation illuminated by the text. The main purpose of the text, then, is to help you hear those stories better, to get you inside the music on multiple levels and to provide a contextual framework to better understand and appreciate it.

The four-CD set, which was produced by Sony BMG Music Entertainment, includes more than a hundred selections (a combination of excerpts and complete tracks). Most of these are drawn from professional, commercial recordings. Among the many artists and groups represented are some of the most well-known, highly respected, and influential in the world of music, past and present: Ravi Shankar, Tito Puente, Santana, Shakti, Angélique Kidjo, Taj Mahal, John Coltrane, The Chieftains, Eileen Ivers, Yo-Yo Ma, Os Mutantes, Ladysmith Black Mambazo, A. R. Rahman.

For each of the main musical examples of Part II included on the CDs, Guided Listening Experience narratives followed by concise, bullet-style Guided Listening Quick Summaries help you to explore how the music is organized *as* music and how key musical elements reflect larger musicultural issues. To get the most out of the Guided Listening, I suggest the following general approach:

- First, listen to the example, without reading the accompanying text.

- Second, read the Guided Listening Experience narrative to learn how the music is organized and how it reflects key cultural themes of the chapter.

- Third, listen to the example *at least* one more time, following along with the Guided Listening Quick Summary timeline and attempting to identify as many of the musical features highlighted as possible.

- Fourth, view related videos online, which you can find by doing your own searches or by consulting my personal Web site at www.michaelbakan.com (see the next page for more information on the Web site).

Musical Guided Tours in each of the Part II chapters provide another opportunity for getting inside the music and understanding how it works. These take the form of brief, audio-recorded lecture demonstrations (which also appear in transcribed form in the text) that break down particular styles of music explored into their constituent parts, then put them back together again. Through these tours, you will hear how the interlocking parts in Balinese music are organized, how multiple rhythmic patterns are layered in West African drumming performances, and how Irish musicians "decorate" their dance tunes with musical ornaments.

The Musical Guided Tours are interesting and instructive in and of themselves, but they also are useful for developing listening skills that can be productively applied to the Guided Listening Experiences.

Five of the seven Musical Guided Tours are located at the *World Music: Traditions and Transformations* Online Learning Center, Student Edition (www.mhhe.com/bakan2e), where they are available as downloadable mp3 files; the other two are included on the four-CD set (the text directs you to the appropriate location in each chapter). Also available at the Online Learning Center are 26 Online Musical Illustrations, which provide audio-recorded examples of key musical elements and features discussed in the text. These, too, are downloadable (with the exception of one). The Online Learning Center additionally offers a wealth of other materials for enhancing your learning and study experience: chapter overviews, sample multiple-choice quizzes, sample music-listening quizzes, exam study guides, Internet links, guidance on pronunciation of foreign language terms (beyond that included in the main text), an image bank, and annotated lists of reading, listening, viewing, and Internet resources. Beyond the Online Learning Center, the author-maintained Web site mentioned earlier, www.michaelbakan.com, offers many additional valuable resources. At the Web site, you will find links to hundreds of online videos (YouTube, etc.), organized by chapter and chapter topic, which relate directly to the content of your book and CD set. The Web site is also linked to the *World Music* Facebook page, where you can connect with me and with world music students and instructors worldwide to ask questions, find out about interesting musical events and opportunities, and share ideas and thoughts about the music you are listening to and learning about.

A final way of getting inside the music to better understand, appreciate, and enjoy it is to actually *perform* music yourself. Many chapters include simple performance exercises that allow you to experience how music works firsthand by either making it or interacting in specific ways with the recordings. These kinds of "hands-on" experiences can be tremendously helpful in increasing your understanding of how music works. They also can be a lot of fun, especially when you team up with friends or fellow students—or even your whole class—to try them out.

Welcome to the wonderful world of world music. Learn well and enjoy the journey!

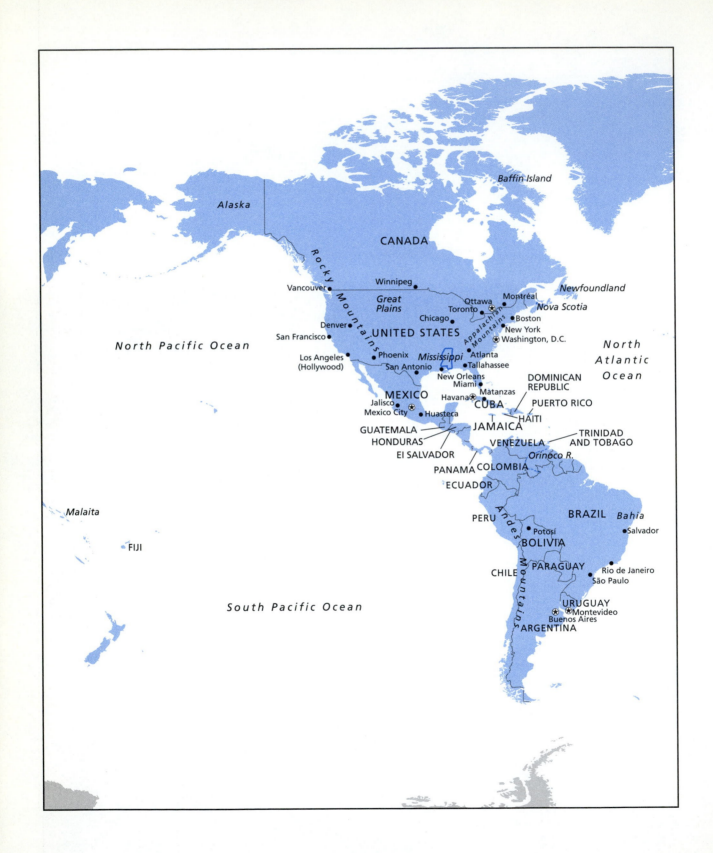

Baffin Island

Alaska

CANADA

North Pacific Ocean

Rocky Mountains

Vancouver
Winnipeg
Great Plains
Ottawa
Montréal
Newfoundland
Toronto
Nova Scotia
Chicago
Denver
Boston
UNITED STATES
New York
San Francisco
Appalachian Mountains
Washington, D.C.
North Atlantic Ocean
Los Angeles (Hollywood)
Phoenix
Mississippi
Atlanta
Tallahassee
San Antonio
New Orleans
Miami
Matanzas
DOMINICAN REPUBLIC
MEXICO
Havana
CUBA
PUERTO RICO
Jalisco
Mexico City
Huasteca
HAITI
GUATEMALA
JAMAICA
HONDURAS
TRINIDAD AND TOBAGO
EI SALVADOR
VENEZUELA
PANAMA
COLOMBIA
Orinoco R.
ECUADOR

Malaita

PERU

FIJI

Andes Mountains

Bahia
BRAZIL
Potosí
Salvador
BOLIVIA
CHILE
PARAGUAY
Rio de Janeiro
São Paulo

South Pacific Ocean

URUGUAY
Montevideo
Buenos Aires
ARGENTINA

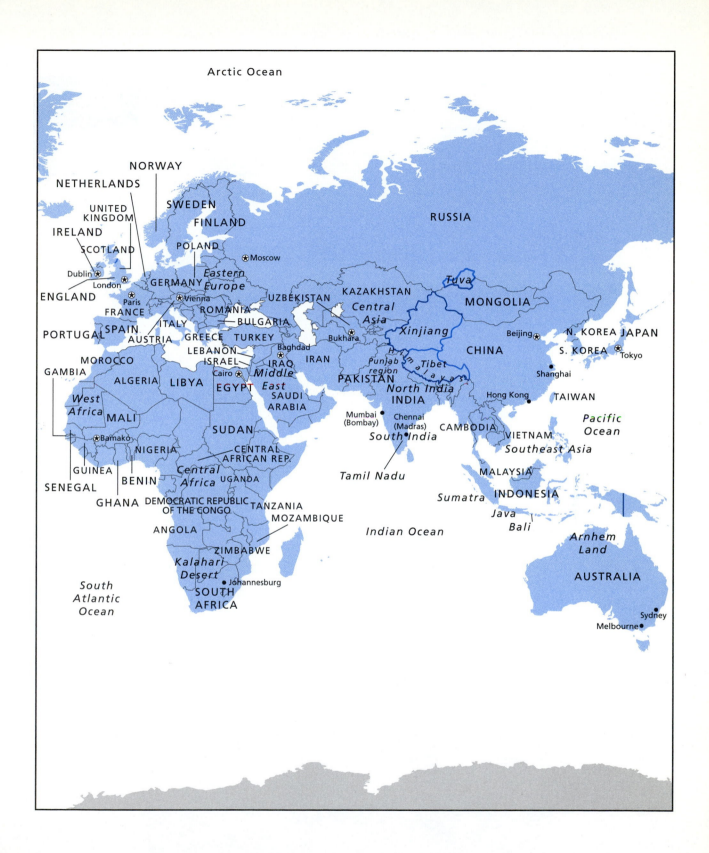

Arctic Ocean

NORWAY
NETHERLANDS
UNITED
KINGDOM
IRELAND
SCOTLAND
SWEDEN
FINLAND
POLAND
Dublin
London
ENGLAND
GERMANY
*Eastern
Europe*
Moscow
RUSSIA
*Central
Asia*
KAZAKHSTAN
Tuva
MONGOLIA
Paris
FRANCE
Vienna
ROMANIA
UZBEKISTAN
Xinjiang
Beijing
N. KOREA JAPAN
PORTUGAL
SPAIN
ITALY
AUSTRIA
BULGARIA
GREECE
TURKEY
LEBANON
ISRAEL
Baghdad
IRAQ
IRAN
Bukhara
Himalayas
Tibet
CHINA
S. KOREA
Tokyo
Shanghai
MOROCCO
GAMBIA
Cairo
*Middle
East*
EGYPT
*Punjab
region*
PAKISTAN
North India
INDIA
Hong Kong
TAIWAN
ALGERIA
LIBYA
SAUDI
ARABIA
*West
Africa*
MALI
Bamako
SUDAN
NIGERIA
CENTRAL
AFRICAN REP.
Mumbai
(Bombay)
Chennai
(Madras)
South India
CAMBODIA
*Pacific
Ocean*
GUINEA
BENIN
*Central
Africa*
UGANDA
Tamil Nadu
VIETNAM
Southeast Asia
SENEGAL
GHANA
DEMOCRATIC REPUBLIC
OF THE CONGO
TANZANIA
MALAYSIA
Sumatra
INDONESIA
ANGOLA
MOZAMBIQUE
Indian Ocean
Java
Bali
*Arnhem
Land*
ZIMBABWE
*Kalahari
Desert*
AUSTRALIA
*South
Atlantic
Ocean*
Johannesburg
SOUTH
AFRICA
Sydney
Melbourne

what, in the **world,** is **music?**

The piano recital is about to begin. The first piece listed on the program is *4'33"* (*four minutes, thirty-three seconds*), by a composer named John Cage.

The pianist is greeted by warm applause as she steps out onto the stage and bows to the audience. She sits down at the piano, puts a musical score up on the stand, and clicks a button on a stopwatch. Closing her eyes and gracefully placing her hands over the piano keys, she appears poised and ready to play. But she doesn't play anything. Thirty seconds go by, then a minute. Nothing but silence. She reaches up and turns a page. Still no music. Two minutes go by. Another page turn; *still* no music. The "silence" becomes almost overwhelming. Every sound in the concert hall—the muffled coughs, the squeaking seats, the whirring of the air-conditioning system—seems as though it is coming through an amplifier.

Finally, four minutes and thirty-three seconds after sitting down at the piano, the pianist reaches over, turns off the stopwatch, stands up, and bows, never having played a note. Some members of the audience applaud enthusiastically. Others do not seem to know quite what to do.

This is music?

Shift the scene now to a mosque. A passage from the **Qur'an,** the holy book of Islam, is being recited. The words flow forth in melodious tones: beautiful, profound, elegantly crafted—in a word, musical. Yet this is categorically *not* music according to the Muslim people who have gathered at the mosque to pray. In fact, to refer to it as such is not just wrong from an Islamic perspective, but offensive.

Is *this* music?

A third scene now. A teenage boy sits in his room on a Saturday afternoon listening to his favorite recording, *Wrecking Everything,* by the thrash metal band Overkill. The music is turned up loud, very loud. The boy's father is downstairs working on his taxes. He is tired and has a headache. After a while, he loses his patience, charges up the stairs, and storms into his son's room. "Turn that garbage off!" he shouts. "How can you listen to this junk? It's nothing but noise. It's not even music!"

Not to him perhaps, but it certainly is to his son.

Is this music?

And one last scenario. The year is 1968. The scene: the Third International Festival of Song in São Paulo, Brazil. Os Mutantes (The Mutants), a controversial local rock band from São Paulo, come onstage to join the master Brazilian musician Caetano Veloso in a performance of Veloso's song "É proibido proibir" (It's forbidden to forbid). The members of Os Mutantes wear bizarre plastic outfits and are eyed with suspicion by the large crowd. They launch into what is perceived as "an amplified barrage of distorted noise that immediately elicits a hostile response from the audience," which boos loudly and hurls tomatoes, grapes, and wads of paper at the band (Harvey 2001:107).

History will be kinder to Os Mutantes. They are ultimately hailed as "the Brazilian Beatles" by rock music journalists, and their discovery in the 1990s by influential progressive/alternative rockers like Kurt Cobain (Nirvana), David Byrne (Talking Heads), and Beck leads to profound transformations on the landscapes of popular music and pop culture worldwide. A song from the band's classic, self-titled 1968 album *Os Mutantes* even finds its way into a 2008 television commercial featuring cute kids playing soccer and eating McDonald's Happy Meals. That song, "A Minha Menina" (My Girl), is included in its entirety as the first selection on the CD set accompanying this book, **CD ex. #1-1.** Listen to it now. It's a catchy tune—innovative, danceable, and fun to listen to. No wonder McDonald's saw fit to use it in their global efforts to sell hamburgers and fries (somewhat ironic given that the band's rise to prominence occurred within the context of a Brazilian social movement inspired by resistance to multinational corporate hegemony, but more on that in Chapter 11).

The Brazilian rock band Os Mutantes in concert during a recent reunion tour.

Returning to the moment of Os Mutantes' now-legendary performance at the 1968 international song festival in Brazil (which, in fairness, was considerably more brazen than "A Minha Menina"), it would appear that what the band was up to was decidedly *not* received as music by many in attendance, the tomato and grape hurlers for starters. Rather, as reported, it was heard as something quite different—"distorted noise," "a sonic assault" (Harvey 2001:107). That something was apparently not at all appreciated at the time, but it would come to be greatly appreciated, and appreciated *as* music specifically, later on, both in Brazil and internationally.

So, was it music? Or was it not?

■ ■ ■

A Point of Departure:
Five Propositions for Exploring World Music

Determining when you are experiencing "music" and when you are experiencing something else is not always a straightforward matter. One person's music may be another person's noise, prayer recitation, or even silence. The question "What is music?" can yield radically different responses even within a single family or tight-knit community. Expand the scope to a global scale and the range of answers multiplies exponentially.

All of this raises at least two interesting questions:

1. What factors account for people's many and vastly different views of what music is, and what it is not?

2. Given that there is not even general agreement about what music is in the first place, how might we establish a reasonable, common point of departure from which to begin our exploration of music—world music—as the global and extraordinarily diverse phenomenon of humankind that it is?

The **five propositions** that follow address these questions in both direct and indirect ways. In the process, they collectively provide a point of departure regarding what music is—and what it is not—that underscores the approach of this text as a whole. This approach is based on the idea that it is important to have an open-minded and inclusive perspective on what music is when exploring world music. In keeping with this idea, these five propositions represent perspectives that are widely shared among people interested in the study of music as a worldwide phenomenon. The propositions are by no means definitive or closed to debate, however. They are presented here mainly to establish a common ground for our musical journey, but also will hopefully stimulate you to think about and discuss your own, possibly different, ideas about what music is.

Proposition 1: The basic property of all music is sound

Music is made up of sounds. To distinguish music sounds from other kinds of sounds (noise sounds, speech sounds, ambient sounds, etc.), we will use the term **tone** to designate a music sound. A tone, then, is *a sound whose principal identity is a musical identity, as defined by people (though not necessarily all people) who make or experience that sound.*

Every tone possesses four basic physical properties: duration (length), frequency (pitch), amplitude (loudness), and timbre (quality of sound, tone color). We will learn more about these four properties of tones in Chapters 3–6.

timbre (TAM-ber)

Additionally, tones are defined by the musical environments that surround them. Each tone gains musical meaning through its relationships with other tones. It is through these relationships between tones that the building blocks of music—melodies, chords, rhythms, textures, all of which will be topics of Chapters 3–6 as well—are formed.

Tones also acquire *cultural* meanings from the symbolic associations that people attach to them, associations that extend far beyond the domain of music sound itself. A tone with a particular set of physical properties may be used in one instance to summon deities in a religious ritual. But that exact same tone also may appear in a commercial jingle for a fast-food restaurant, where the purpose is to convince people to buy the new combo meal. How any given tone is understood, then, has at least as much to do with what people make of it as with the physical properties of the sound itself.

Any and all sounds have the potential to be tones, that is, to be music sounds. This includes obvious candidates such as notes that are sung or played on a piano, guitar, or violin, but it also includes the sounds of slamming shutter doors, pig squeals, water rushing in a stream, or anything else. As we shall explore later in the chapter, the classification of sounds as music sounds (tones) or as nonmusic sounds is principally a product of people's intentions and perceptions

John Cage.

regarding sounds. Theoretically, at least, there are no limits, but people do make decisions about what they will and will not accept as a music sound, just as they make decisions about what they will and will not accept in most other areas of life. That is why some people identify the sounds of Qur'anic recitation or of thrash metal as music sounds, while other people categorically do not.

But what about John Cage's 4′33″, a work in which the most basic property of music—that is, that it be based in sound—seems conspicuously absent? Surely here, in what is often referred to as "Cage's silence piece," we have crossed the line of what any reasonable human being might justifiably classify as music. Or have we?

Perhaps not. Actually, there *are* sounds—many sounds—in every performance of 4′33″. There are the sounds of the performers' footsteps as they walk onto the stage, of the audience applauding, of the clicking on and off of the stopwatch, of the turning of pages at prescribed time intervals, of the random assortment of coughs, chair squeaks, heating and air-conditioning system hums, and whatever else may emerge during a given performance. It is not an absence of sounds, then, that makes 4′33″'s status as a piece of music controversial. It is, rather, the fact that most people are not accustomed to hearing the types of sounds that occur in a performance of the piece *as* music that mainly accounts for the controversy it has generated for over a half century since its premiere performance (by the Pianist David Tudor) in 1952. Indeed, one of the main "points" of 4′33″ is that it creates a framework for music listening that compels people to reorient their hearing, to hear "the music" inherent in a range of sounds and silences whose musical qualities are conventionally ignored or go unnoticed by music listeners.

Proposition 2: The sounds (and silences) that comprise a musical work are organized in some way

One marker of difference between music sounds and other types of sounds is that music sounds always emerge within some kind of organizational framework, whereas other sounds may or may not. Music, then, is a form of *organized sound*. This is plainly evident when we listen to a well-known Western classical music work such as Ludwig van Beethoven's Symphony #9 (**CD ex. #1-2**), but the organizational element is no less significant in music that seems, at least to many Western listeners, to defy recognizable principles of organization. This latter category may include music from a foreign culture that is based on unfamiliar organizational schemes, such as the Japanese *gagaku* music heard in **CD ex. #1-3** (see the photo, p. 5). It also may include music originating in our own culture that intentionally *subverts* the common and familiar organizational principles that make music recognizable, things like conventional types of melodies, rhythms, and instrumental sounds. Much of the late John Cage's music fits this description.

gagaku
(gah-GAH-koo)

Proposition 3: Sounds are organized into music by people; thus, music is a form of humanly organized sound

The baseline assertion that helps us begin to distinguish between music sound and a great many other types of organized sound is that *music is a human phenomenon:* it is a form of "humanly organized sound" (Blacking 1973). There is no doubt that many animals express themselves and even communicate using organized systems of sound that have music-like qualities. It may even be true that some animals (e.g., whales, dolphins) conceptualize certain types of sounds they create in ways that are closely akin to how people conceptualize music. Research suggestive of such possibilities already exists, and it is likely that future research will be even more revealing.

For our present purposes, however, it is proposed that music, understood as such, is essentially a human invention. It is something that people either make, hear, or assign to other kinds of sounds. Birds and whales did not "sing" until human beings saw fit to label their distinctive forms of vocalization with that musical term (which, again, is not necessarily to say that they do not have a well-defined concept of what they *are* doing when *we* say they are singing—a good subject for research, speculation, and debate). Moreover, birds and whales do not necessarily "make music" any more than pigs do, but the "songs" of birds and whales seem to have been more amenable to musical interpretation *by people* than the grunts of pigs (see also Nettl 2006:23).

In short, returning to a point made earlier, any and all sounds have the *potential* to be employed and heard as musical sounds. However, only when a human being uses a given sound for musical purposes, or perceives or describes that sound in musical terms, does the sound actually enter into the domain of "music." Once again, it is not what a sound is per se, but rather what people make of it, that is the main criterion.

Proposition 4: Music is a product of human intention and perception

Expanding on another premise alluded to earlier in the chapter, there are two basic processes of human cognition involved in determining what is and what is not music: intention and perception. When any sound, series of sounds, or combination of sounds is organized by a person or group of people and presented as "music"—that is, with the *intention* that it be heard as music—our point of departure will be to treat it as music. Similarly, when any person or group of persons *perceives* a sound, series of sounds, or combination of sounds as "music," our point of departure will be to treat that as music too.

The value of this approach—which I refer to for convenience as the **HIP (human intention and perception) approach**—is that it (1) privileges inclusiveness over exclusiveness and (2) emphasizes the idea that music is inseparable from the people who make and experience it.

John Cage created 4′33″ with the intention of making a piece of music; musicians who perform the work approach it as a piece of music; and at least some members of the audiences who hear it performed are likely to perceive it as music. Thus, it fits the criteria of "music" in the HIP model. Granted, a performance of 4′33″ may be interpreted as many things other than a music performance—for example, as a philosophical statement *about* music, a commentary on the experience of music listening, or a challenge to conventional expectations of music listeners—but these other points of view only enrich how 4′33″ may be understood and appreciated *as* music.

Islamic Qur'anic recitation, an example of which may be heard on **CD ex. #1-4,** can be treated as music because its melodic and rhythmic organization is likely perceived by you (if you are not a Muslim) in musical terms. The undeniably "musical" quality that Qur'anic recitation suggests to Western listeners—and indeed the close similarity of such recitation to forms of organized sound that Muslims themselves *do* recognize as music (see Chapter 12)—makes the question of why it is not considered music by Muslims all the more interesting. The answer is that many Muslims believe music to be essentially a profane art that has no place in religious observance: if it is part of worship, it is not music, regardless of what it sounds like. In this case, religious and cultural principles take priority over ostensibly musical properties of sound. (As we will see in Chapter 12,

Japanese gagaku orchestra.

Muslim men praying together inside a mosque in Alexandria, Egypt.

attitudes in Islamic societies concerning the relationship between worship and music are considerably more varied and complex than the present discussion suggests.)

As for the example of the father dismissing his son's favorite thrash metal recording as being "not even music," the HIP approach favors the idea that this *is* indeed music. The musicians created it with the intention that it be heard as music, and the teenage boy heard it as music. It thus meets the basic criteria of music status. This does not mean that the father's opinion on the matter should not be part of the discussion, however. Examining *why* different people in the same situation accept or reject something as music is one of the best paths to understanding the roles and functions of music in human life. In this case, differences in age and generational status between the boy and his father would seem to be decisive factors in explaining their very different views on what is, and what is not, music.

In the case of the 1968 performance by Os Mutantes at Brazil's Third International Festival of Song, cultural factors having to do with ideas about music's symbolic relationship to Brazilian national identity were key to the initially hostile, "not music" judgment of the band's performance. As cultural attitudes on such matters changed over time, so too did Brazilian assessments of the *musical* value and significance of this historic performance.

Proposition 5: The term *music* is inescapably tied to Western culture and its assumptions

We can now say that music is a category of humanly organized sound that takes its core identity from the musical intentions and perceptions of its makers and listeners. That would be a solid point of departure for our journey were it not for the fact that many of the world's peoples do not even have a word equivalent to *music* in their languages. Furthermore, even in languages that do possess a term closely akin to *music,* such as Arabic, the term may not always apply where we would expect it to, as the example of Qur'anic recitation illustrates.

And so we are left with a dilemma: even though every human culture in the world has produced forms of organized sound that we in the West consider music, many of these cultures do not categorize their own "music" as music at all. It seems that our concept of music, however broad and open-minded we try to make it, cannot transcend its Western cultural moorings. We are apparently doomed to a certain measure of **ethnocentrism;** that is, we cannot help but impose our own culturally grounded perspectives, biases, and assumptions on practices and lifeways that are different from our own.

What options do we have for confronting this dilemma? We can

1. Avoid dealing with these problematic phenomena of sound in musical terms altogether.

2. Impose Western musical concepts on them, in essence "converting" them into music on our terms (for example, treating Qur'anic recitation as music regardless of the Muslim claim that it is not music).

3. Try to find some way to integrate and balance our own perceptions of what we hear as "music" with the indigenous terms and concepts used by other people when describing the same phenomena.

The third of these options is the one that for the most part guides the approach of this text, both in relation to the fundamental question of what is and is not music and in terms of two closely related issues that we address in the forthcoming chapters: how music lives and how music works.

Summary

This chapter began with the question posed by its title: *What, in the world, is music?* Following a series of four brief scenarios that challenged conventional notions of what music is, five propositions about music were offered to provide a conceptual framework for addressing this question. These propositions posited that

1. The basic property of all music is sound.

2. The sounds (and silences) that comprise a musical work are organized in some way.

3. Sounds are organized into music by people; thus, music is a form of humanly organized sound.

4. Music is a product of human intention and perception.

5. The term *music* is inescapably tied to Western culture and its assumptions.

In addition to providing a basic framework for exploring the question of what is and what is not music, these five propositions also were presented, collectively, as a general point of departure for exploring world music from open-minded and broadly inclusive perspectives.

Key Terms

Qur'an (Qur'anic recitation)
five propositions (about music)
tone

HIP (human intention and perception) approach
ethnocentrism

Study Questions

- What were the five propositions for exploring world music presented in this chapter?
- What is the HIP approach, and why is it important in the study of world music?
- Why do Muslims not consider Qur'anic recitation music, even though it sounds like music to other people?
- What is ethnocentrism?
- Why can John Cage's *4'33"* be categorized as a piece of music even though it does not seem to sound like one?

Discussion Questions

- Do you think John Cage's *4'33"* should be classified as music or not? On what grounds might you argue for or against its musical status?

- Do you think animals make music, or is music specifically a human phenomenon? How would you support an argument for either side of the debate?

- Do you agree with the five propositions for exploring world music presented in the chapter? Are there any you think are open to challenge? If so, why, and how? Can you think of any alternate or additional propositions that would help to clarify what is—and what is not—music?

Applying What You Have Learned

- Go to the quietest place you can find: a secluded forest, a remote mountainside, an isolated room. Sit or lie down, close your eyes, and listen to the "silence." What sounds do you hear? Is there a sense in which they take on a musical character after a while? Describe the experience as a *musical* experience.

- Create a list of different kinds of sounds, classifying them into "music" and "nonmusic" categories. Use your own subjective criteria to decide what to include on each list. Are there instances where the types of sounds that you think of as music would not qualify as music according to the criteria of this chapter (e.g., animal sounds), or where sounds that you categorize as nonmusic would be classified as music using the HIP approach? If so, what do you think accounts for these "discrepancies"?

Resources for Further Study

Visit the Online Learning Center at www.mhhe.com/bakan2e, as well as the author's personally maintained Web site at www.michaelbakan.com, for additional learning aids, study help, and resources that supplement the content of this chapter.

how **music lives:**
a musicultural approach

In the first chapter, we were introduced to the idea that music is defined not only by its sounds, but also by the environments in which it lives and the meanings people attach to it. This chapter explores that idea in more detail.

Music becomes significant mainly in the context of human life: in what people do, who they think they are, what they believe, what they value. When we explore what people do, think, believe, and value as members of groups and communities, we are exploring what is known in the social sciences as *culture*. Music is a phenomenon of culture, and, as such, it is best understood in relation to culture, more specifically, in relation to the *cultural context*—or contexts—in which it lives.

Understanding music as a phenomenon of culture is always important, but is perhaps especially so when dealing with music from a global perspective.

Often, it is the beliefs and practices of cultural life that are embedded in music, rather than the sounds themselves, that reveal the most profound insights into what makes music meaningful and significant in people's lives. **Ethnomusicology**—an interdisciplinary academic field that draws on musicology, anthropology, and other disciplines in order to study the world's musics—makes a first priority of engaging music in ways that reveal such insights. Ethnomusicologists are interested in understanding music as a **musicultural** phenomenon, that is, as a phenomenon where *music as sound* and *music as culture* are mutually reinforcing, and where the two are essentially inseparable from one another. Our purpose throughout this text will be to understand and appreciate the musics we encounter in this way, and this chapter, therefore, lays the groundwork for examining how music lives in human life, not just as sound, but as culture as well.

■ ■ ■

Culture in Music

In 1871, Edward Tylor, a seminal figure in the history of anthropology, defined **culture** as "that complex whole which includes knowledge, belief, art, law, morals, custom, and any other capabilities and habits acquired by man [humankind] as a member of society" (quoted in Barnard 2000:102). Scores of other definitions of the term *culture* have been proposed since, yet Tylor's classic formulation has proven extraordinarily durable. It still provides a good baseline for comprehending the concept of culture in our modern world.

As the Tylor definition implies, the study of culture encompasses most everything having to do with people's lives as members of human communities: their religions and political systems; their languages and technologies; their rituals and dances; their modes of work and play; the things that make them laugh and cry; what they wear and what they eat; and, of course, the music they make and listen to.

But what is the community, or what are the *communities,* that define a culture? Throughout human history, cultures have always been changing, merging, overlapping, malleable, in flux; and that is likely more true today than in any previous era. Globalization, mass media communications, the Internet, multinational entertainment industry corporations, easy access to international travel, and other forces of modernity often make it difficult, if not impossible, to draw a clear line in the sand distinguishing one culture from another, musically or otherwise. An example: What is "the culture" of residents of Germany who are of Turkish descent but who define and express themselves mainly through an African American-derived style of hip-hop music, with lyrics that alternate between Turkish and German (Jackson 2010)? There is no clear answer to such a question; indeed, there is no clear best point of departure from which to begin to address it.

Yet despite such complexities, cultures—and the cultural traditions through which they become manifest—are real and they do endure, even as they transform. Certain groups of people—tribes, clans, religious sects, ethnic groups, societies, nations—do indeed behave, think, and believe differently than others on the whole, and the degrees of difference and similarity between different cultural groups vary: the musical cultures of Egypt and Lebanon are in many ways distinct, yet they clearly have more in common than the musical cultures of Egypt and Finland.

Music is a mode of cultural production and representation that reveals much about the workings of culture, from the resilience of traditional ways to people's remarkable capacities for cultural adaptation, innovation, and transformation. In the collective sounds and meanings of the world's musics lies a remarkable pool of resources for comprehending what unites and separates us as individuals, as communities, as musicultural beings, and as members of the global culture of humanity to which we all belong.

Meaning in Music

Music comes into existence at the intersection of sound and culture. It is not until some kind of *meaning* is connected to sounds—sounds that might otherwise be heard as random or arbitrary—that these sounds come to be perceived as music. Meaning, then, is the essential glue that binds together sound and culture to form music.

As was mentioned briefly in Chapter 1 (p. 3), the tones of music are meaningful in at least two ways. First, they have meaning relative to one another. For example, the familiar children's song "Mary Had a Little Lamb" consists of a series of tones, or *notes* (a common term used to refer to the specific tones in a piece of music), that occur in a particular order. Each of these notes acquires meaning relative to the others: the first note sounds "higher" than the second, the second note sounds higher than the third. The relative highness or lowness of these three notes (a function of the musical element of *pitch*, which we will explore in Chapter 4) invests each with a particular meaning in the context of that song. This kind of meaning is essentially limited to the sounds themselves, in other words, to music solely as a phenomenon of sound.

At the second level of meaning, the one that concerns us here, musical sounds acquire meaning in relation to things beyond themselves. Imagine being raised in a culture where the exact same melody that we associate with "Mary Had a Little Lamb" was the basis of a funeral lament instead of a children's song. Hearing the melody would cause you to have entirely different feelings, memories, and thoughts. The song's meaning would be completely transformed.

This example illustrates what is so often true of music: that its meaning is determined as much or more by matters of context as by "the notes" themselves. This is musical meaning at the level of a phenomenon of culture, not of sound alone. Musical meaning as a phenomenon of culture accounts for why shamans (traditional healers) among the Warao, an Amerindian people of Venezuela, believe that there are certain kinds of songs that have the power to heal people and other kinds of songs that have the power to make people sick or even cause them to die (Olsen 1996: 262–63). It also accounts for why the singing style heard in **CD ex. #1-5,** an example of a Chinese opera song (see Chapter 13, pp. 330–331), is perceived as beautiful by its Chinese admirers but may be perceived quite differently by people who do not share their culturally informed points of view regarding music.

Identity in Music

How people make and perceive meaning in music is inextricable from how they think about and represent themselves and one another. Conceptions of music throughout the world are closely tied to conceptions of **identity,** that

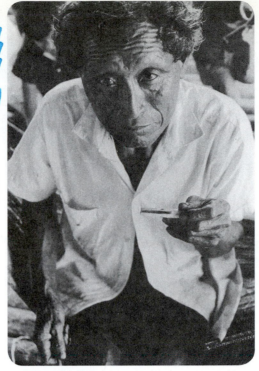

The late Jaime Zapata, a powerful Warao shaman.

Costumed Beijing Opera performer.

Mongolian khoomii singer Amartuwshin Baasandorj, who is featured on CD ex. #1-6.

is, to people's ideas about who they are and what unites them with or distinguishes them from other people and entities: individuals, families, communities, institutions, cultures, societies, nations, supernatural powers.

To a significant degree, music always provides partial answers to two fundamental questions: *Who am I?* and *Who are we?* If you are a hip-hop DJ or enthusiast, your involvement with that music will inevitably contribute to your conceptions of who you are—the "I" portion of your identity. It also will cause you to identify and socialize with certain individuals, groups, and communities more than others—the "we" portion of your identity. On the "I" level, connecting yourself to hip-hop and its musicultural world (or worlds) may impact your self-esteem, your fashion sensibilities, your approaches to expressing yourself and communicating with others. On the "we" level, it may lead to new friendships with like-minded listeners, or to a shift away from spending time with old friends and acquaintances who do not share your passion for hip-hop.

Music also frames identity in regards to a related pair of questions: *Who is she (or he)?* and *Who are they?* When you first encounter a Mongolian singing performance like the one featured on **CD ex. #1-6,** or a Central Javanese *gamelan* performance from Indonesia such as that heard in **CD ex. #1-7,** you tend to immediately begin forming ideas about what the people making the music are like and what kind of a culture they come from. If you go a step further and study the music and the culture in some depth, you may discover that some of your initial impressions were on track, but that others were misguided.

gamelan (gah-muh-lahn)

Go deeper still and you are likely to encounter a host of interesting music-culture parallels, but also an abundance of contradictions and ambiguities revolving around the interrelationships of music, culture, and identity. Disparities exist between how musicians represent themselves and their culture versus how they are represented by others. Misleading stereotypes relating to ethnicity, gender, and race abound, distorting musical and cultural meanings while shaping them at the same time. You also may find your own assumptions about the music you hear—your notions about whether it is traditional or modern, authentic or inauthentic—turned upside down in the face of historical and contextual realities.

A Central Javanese gamelan.

Listen to **CD ex. #1-8,** which features the opening portion of a Rabbit Dance song performed in a style that is identified with Native American (U.S.) and First Nations (Canada) music cultures of the Great Plains region of North America (spanning westward from Manitoba, Canada, and the Mississippi River to the Rocky Mountains). With its evocative title, descending vocal lines, intense singing style, and percussive accompaniment, "Rabbit Dance" sounds very traditional. Hearing this opening portion of the song and knowing its title, you might assume it is being sung in an unfamiliar Native American language, and that the performers belong to a culture that is rather isolated from your own and far removed from the modern Western world generally. Or you might assume that the words deal specifically with the subject of rabbits, whether through literal or figurative representations of the animal's speed, agility, and cleverness or in terms of traditional American Indian spiritual beliefs highlighting the essential harmony between the human, natural, and spirit worlds.

But listen now to **CD ex. #1-9,** which includes the complete song rather than just the opening part. Beginning at 0:34, focus your attention on the words. You will notice immediately that they are sung not in a foreign language, but in English: "Hey, sweetheart, I often think of you. I wonder if you are alone tonight. I wonder if you are thinking of me." If you added a guitar part and a different rhythmic accompaniment, this could well pass as a country-and-western tune on the trials and tribulations of love, longing, and heartache. It turns out, then, that this is a different kind of song than you initially thought it was, and this suggests that the identities of the people singing it—that is, who they are—may also be quite different than you presumed. Their world and their culture are likely to be much closer to your own than you first imagined.

Returning now to the opening section of "Rabbit Dance" (0:00–0:33), you may be wondering what language the vocalists were performing in *before* they started singing in English. The answer: no language. They were singing in **vocables,** a generic term used by musicologists to describe nonlinguistic syllables that are used in vocal performances (singing, rapping, etc.). Vocables are employed in many different types of music worldwide: jazz scat singing, "beat boxing" in hip-hop, and the all-vocal *gamelan* "orchestras" of the Balinese Kecak dance-drama (Chapter 7, pp. 97–99; **CD ex. #2-13**) are three good examples.

In Native American and First Nations cultures, vocables are a very common feature of many musical styles, from Alaska to California and Baffin Island to Florida. One musical domain in which vocables are particularly prominent is in songs that accompany the dance performances and competitions presented at intertribal celebrations called *powwows,* which originated in the Great Plains region and now are produced throughout North America. This powwow style of singing in vocables forms the basis of **CD ex. #1-10,** the song "Dance," by the First Nations rock band Eagle & Hawk (see the photo, p. 14). But though "Dance" is rooted in traditional powwow song style, it is by no means a traditional powwow song (**CD ex. #1-25** is such a song, if you wish to compare). Rather, it is a powwow song recontextualized in a modern, rock-oriented musical setting. Its blending and juxtaposition of rock, folk-rock, and traditional First Nations musical elements is key to its effectiveness as a powerful expression of the complex multidimensionality of contemporary First Nations identities, for example, the identities of the band members themselves.

Eagle & Hawk is widely recognized as one of the leading bands on the current First Nations/Native American rock scene. Based in the Canadian city of Winnipeg, Manitoba, they have won numerous awards for their songs and albums, including a Juno Award, seven Canadian Aboriginal Music Awards, two Native American Music Awards, and nine Aboriginal Peoples Choice Music Awards including Best Group and Best Rock Album of 2009. Their concert tours have taken them throughout North America and around the world, from regional powwows and other intertribal events to European concert tours and guest appearances with classical music organizations such as the Winnipeg Symphony Orchestra. The group's members include electric guitarist and vocalist Vince Fontaine (who directs and founded the group and is the principal songwriter), lead vocalist and acoustic guitarist Jay Bodner, traditional singer and hand drummer Ray "Coco" Stevenson (also known as Walking Wolf), bassist Lawrence "Spatch" Mulhall, and drum set player Marty Chapman.

"Dance" has been one of Eagle & Hawk's most popular and critically acclaimed hits, accounting for several of the group's many awards and accolades. It does not contain a single, actual word; rather, its "text" consists entirely of vocables. And yet, through its compelling fusion of diverse musical and cultural elements—from powwow song to

Eagle & Hawk, featuring (left to right) Lawrence "Spatch" Mulhall, Vince Fontaine, Ray "Coco" Stevenson, Jason Bodner, and Marty Chapman.

contemporary rock—"Dance" delivers a powerful message of First Nations cultural pride and a vital sense of what it means to "live Indian" in the present while embracing the past. In Fontaine's assessment, expressed to me during a 2009 phone interview, "'Dance' captures the signature sound of Eagle & Hawk, which is a combination of modern and traditional elements."

The traditional aspect of "Dance" is to be found principally in the tune itself, which is sung by Stevenson, an accomplished traditional powwow singer who, like Fontaine, is of Ojibwa descent. The tune and its vocables-based text were composed by Fontaine. He describes them as being "pure, traditional powwow" in style. His compositional process began with the jotting down of the song's vocables on a piece of scrap paper:

way ya hey ya hey ya hay

way ya hey ya hey ya hay

way ya hey ya hey ya hay

way ya hey ya hey ya hay

ya hey ya hey ya hey ya ho

ya hey ya hey ya hey ya ho

After writing the vocables out, Fontaine, who is not trained in traditional powwow singing, handed the paper to Stevenson and sang him his "best approximation" of what he had in mind. Stevenson took this as his point of departure, adding embellishments and nuances that converted Fontaine's tune into a genuine-sounding powwow song.

Next, this powwow song was merged with folk-rock musical style and instrumentation (guitars, fiddle, electric bass, drum set, etc.). But even in its rock-like elements, there remains a conscious adherence to traditional First Nations musical foundations. For example, the drumming part combines a traditional hand-drum beat with a drum set groove (from 1:33 forward) that sounds very much like a standard rock beat. As Fontaine explains, however, even this "rock beat" is really a converted powwow dance song rhythm, the *crow hop,* translated to the Western drum set. He further explains that this is essentially the same rhythm one would hear played by multiple players performing together on a single, large powwow drum (like the drum heard earlier in the "Rabbit Dance" examples–see also the photo on p. 47) in a powwow Grass Dance or Women's Fancy Shawl Dance competition. The fact that this crow hop rhythm maps so readily onto a rock beat is a nice bonus given the intercultural musical style, but it is important to observe that Fontaine emphasizes that the rhythm is, first and foremost, crow hop rather than rock.

Similar ideas pervade Fontaine's discussion of some of the instruments used. The fiddle (violin) is an instrument of European origin, but it was long ago adopted both as a musical instrument and an identity emblem by certain First Nations/Native American groups. Thus, as Fontaine explained to me, the use of the fiddle in this performance is an identifier of the music's "Indianness" more than anything else. Such ways of creating, processing, and interpreting identity and meaning in the music of Eagle & Hawk are aptly encapsulated in Fontaine's description of the group's essence. "We're a band that's known for having that Native element," he asserts. "I'm trying to keep that, but from my own perspective, and really that's what art's about."

The examples of "Rabbit Dance" and Eagle & Hawk's "Dance" described point to the fact that identities—of people, of groups, of types of music—are very complex. They consist of many different components. Some of these components are mutually reinforcing; others seem contradictory; many of them overlap. I think of myself as a Canadian, though I reside in and have spent more than half of my life in the United States. As a musician, I conceive of myself mainly as a jazz drummer, though I am much better known in my profession as a Balinese gamelan musician (this despite the fact that I have not an ounce of Balinese blood in me). To some people, I am a teacher; to others, an ethnomusicologist and book author; to still others, a father and husband. The music I compose and perform contains elements of all these different aspects of my identity, and often reflects the complex relations that exist between them.

If you think about who you are—as an individual, as a cultural being, and in terms of your impressions of who *other* people think you are—you will realize that your identity, too, is complex and multifaceted. You also may discover that it is intimately bound up with the way music functions in your life. Music reflects and embodies the social realities and ideals of the people who make and listen to it in significant ways. It can tell us much about who these people are and what matters to them, but we need to know how to listen in a culturally informed way to get the message.

Identity is located in music at many different levels. Societies, cultures, nations, transnational communities, and other large-scale social units fundamentally define people's conceptions of who they and others are, at home and throughout the world. It is these large-scale units of social organization that provide the broad frameworks, or outlines, for the shaping of identity through music, and to which we now turn our attention.

Native American dance performance. This dancer is participating in the Men's Fancy Dance competition at a powwow.

Societies

A **society** may be defined as *a group of persons regarded as forming a single community of related, interdependent individuals.* When we study the relationship of music and society, our interest is in how music functions among the members of such a group of persons to foster their sense of community, and sometimes to challenge it.

While the term *society* may be applied to communities of virtually any size, it is most often used in connection with large-scale social entities, such as nations. Because of their size, societies are usually *imagined communities* (Anderson 1991). This means that they are unified as communities not because all of their members actually know each other on a "face-to-face" basis, but rather because they share a connection to one another through certain ideas and **social institutions.**

All societies are built around aggregates of intersecting social institutions. These may be governmental, economic, legal, religious, family-centered, activity- or interest-based, service-oriented, or purely social in nature. Sororities and fraternities, churches and synagogues, political parties and village councils, banks and corporations, hospitals and schools, marching bands and rock bands, dance clubs and sewing clubs are all examples of social institutions.

Social institutions function and take on meaning within and across a range of different family-based, administrative, and political spheres of a society: families, peer groups, tribes, clans, neighborhood organizations, villages, towns, cities, counties, states and provinces, large regional areas, nations. They also may take on significance in interactions between different societies, for example, in a cultural exchange program for high school orchestras from the United States and Taiwan. At every level of society, music may serve to mark the society's identity in significant ways, whether through the performance of a family rock band at a local dance hall or an international concert tour of a national music-and-dance troupe.

The study of music and society focuses on how musicians and musical institutions act and function relative to their societies. It explores how they enter into, are affected by, change and are changed by, and contribute to the interplay of, the social institutions that keep the engine of a society running, or that may in some instances cause it to stall.

Looking at the domain of gamelan music in Bali, Indonesia (which is explored again in greater detail in Chapter 7), offers key insights into the relationship of music and society. A gamelan consists of a large number of instruments—mainly percussion instruments such as gongs, drums, cymbals, and xylophone-like bronze **metallophones**—played by a large group of musicians in an intricately coordinated way. We earlier heard an example of gamelan music from the island of Java (**CD ex. #1-7**). Gamelan music from Bali, Java's neighboring island to the east, tends to have a strikingly different sound and character, as can be readily heard by comparing the Balinese gamelan selection of **CD ex. #2-12** to its Javanese counterpart. A detailed comparison of these pieces is included in Chapter 7 (see pp. 90–95). Though employing similar types of instruments and based on related histories and musical principles, they represent very different musicultural worlds.

The principal social institution linked to musical performance in Bali is the *sekehe gong,* or gamelan club. A sekehe gong is typically made up exclusively of people from a particular *banjar,* or village ward; strict rules prohibit individuals from other banjars from joining. The sekehe gong has an important function within the banjar, furnishing gamelan music for important Hindu-Balinese religious ceremonies and other occasions. It also represents the banjar in music competitions against clubs from neighboring banjars.

Traditionally, all of the members of a sekehe gong were male. Western influences on Indonesian national policies in recent decades, however, have led to changing conceptions of women's roles in Indonesian society, and one outcome of this has been the advent of women's

**metallophones
(meh-TAL-lo-phones)**

**sekehe gong
(SUH-kuh ["uh" like
"oo" in "look"])**

banjar (BAHN-jahr)

Sekehe gong performing during a religious ceremony.

sekehe gong in the banjars of Bali. The women's clubs tend to perform in a much more limited range of contexts than their male counterparts: while they may be featured at political rallies and other events of a nationalistic bent, they rarely play during traditional Balinese religious rituals. The women's groups also have generated much controversy in different sectors of Balinese society, being championed by some as icons of progressive modernity while being chastised by others as a threat to the integrity of traditional cultural values.

Through this brief portrait of the social institution of the Balinese sekehe gong as a nexus of Balinese musical life and society, we begin to see the fruitful lines of inquiry that the study of music in its relation to society can reveal, whether our interests lie in the areas of gender, nationalism, religious ritual, or social relations.

Cultures

We have already examined *culture* as an overarching concept for exploring the subject of music in context. In this section, we explore culture at a more specific level of meaning, looking at it as a particular kind of social entity that at once complements, overlaps with, and is distinct from society. Whereas a society is defined principally in terms of its social institutions and their operations and interactions, *a culture is defined mainly by a collective worldview shared by its members.* Put another way, societies are rooted in social organization, whereas **cultures** are rooted in ideas, beliefs, and practices that underscore social organization: religions, ideologies, philosophies, sciences, moral and ethical principles, artistic creations, ritual performances. To illustrate the distinction, we will continue with our profile of the Balinese sekehe gong, now emphasizing its links to Balinese culture rather than Balinese society.

An important duty of every banjar's sekehe gong is to perform on a set of processional gamelan instruments called the *gamelan beleganjur* during cremation processions (see Chapter 7, pp. 95–97 and 99–103). Music played on this type of gamelan (**CD ex. #2-14**) is believed to possess special powers that ward off evil spirits, spirits who endeavor to capture the souls of the dead and drag them to the underworld of the Balinese cosmos. Only men are thought to have the requisite strength to harness the power of the gamelan beleganjur and properly

**beleganjur
(buh-luh-gahn-
YOOR)**

Balinese women's sekehe gong.

Balinese musician
I Wayan Beratha.

direct it musically, thus ensuring deflection of the demons and safe passage of deceased souls from the earthly world to the upper world of gods and deified ancestors. The cultural importance of the correct gender identity of beleganjur performers (i.e., male) is therefore great: the very sanctity of human souls in the afterlife depends on it. For this reason, beleganjur music has conventionally been performed exclusively by men, even outside of traditional ritual contexts. This practice is consistent with a Balinese cultural worldview.

In the mid-1990s, however, the Balinese arm of the Indonesian national government, responding to the call of a politically motivated *emansipasi* (women's emancipation) agenda for the nation, sponsored the formation of women's beleganjur groups in several Balinese banjars. As a Balinese societal phenomenon, this development represented merely an extension of an existing social institution, the banjar-based sekehe gong. As a Balinese *cultural* phenomenon, it was considerably more radical and problematic. While some Balinese viewed it as progressive in a positive sense, others, such as the venerable musician I Wayan Beratha, found it reprehensible. "[T]he proper spirit of [beleganjur] music is masculine and courageously bold (*berani*)," explains Beratha, echoing a Balinese cultural conviction that is shared widely among both men and women, "and to have girls play it both cheapens the music and puts the girls in an awkward and inappropriate situation" (quoted in Bakan 1999:248).

**emansipasi
(ee-mahn-see-
PAH-see)**

berani (buh-rah-nee)

The case of women's beleganjur groups in Bali illustrates how examining music in relation to society, on the one hand, and in relation to culture, on the other, offers different kinds of insights into how music lives in the lives of people and the communities to which they belong. It is from the blending of these different yet complementary perspectives that *sociocultural* understandings of music emerge. Cultivating such understandings is central to the approach of ethnomusicology and to the musicultural approach of this text.

Nations and nation-states

Societies and cultures are often defined in relation to nations. Moreover, the idea of nation figures prominently in how many music traditions of the world have been developed, conceptualized, and even self-consciously invented over the course of history, from ancient kingdoms and empires to modern nation-states.

It is important when dealing with the relationship of music to nationhood to recognize a distinction between two terms: **nation-state** and **nation.** The members of a nation-state share a national society and culture *and* a national homeland. Canada is a nation-state. Its people, the Canadians, are unified by a national government and a network of other social institutions (society), by shared ideas about and expressions of what constitutes Canadian identity (culture), and by the geographical landmass of Canada itself (homeland). Palestine, by contrast, is a nation but *not* a nation-state. The Palestinians share a society, a culture, and a strong sense of nationhood, but they do not (as of this writing) have political autonomy over the geographical area they claim as their homeland. Palestine is thus a nation without a state.

Nation-states and nations without states alike are catalysts for nationalist music traditions and musical nationalism. **Nationalist music** is often promoted by governments and other official institutions to symbolize an idealized "national identity." The range of raw materials from which nationalist musics are constructed is very broad—some are rooted in rural folk music forms, others in contemporary popular music styles, still others in centuries-old classical music traditions. Some embrace Westernization and modernization as symbols of national progress, while others eschew all outside influences in their efforts to promote a "pure" notion of national ideals inscribed firmly in indigenous musical soil.

But all nationalist musics share the common feature of a nation-building or nation-consolidating agenda, and typically emerge and develop through some form of collaboration between musicians and political authorities. The Indonesian nationalist-inspired incorporation of women's beleganjur groups into the local musical culture of Bali is an example of this. In later chapters, we will witness the close interaction of music and nationalism in the musical cultures of China, Egypt, and elsewhere.

On the flip side of nationalist musics are often to be found musics of resistance, protest, and subversion. As surely as music has the power to reinforce national solidarity and ideals, it also has the power to profoundly challenge and undermine them. The Civil Rights movement in the United States and the anti-Apartheid struggle in South Africa were two instances where music played a central role in articulating and bringing to mass public attention the plights and aspirations of peoples who had long been marginalized and oppressed. Directly and indirectly, African American and Black South African musicians such as James Brown and Miriam Makeba contributed significantly to overturning the laws, policies, social institutions, and public attitudes in which the racist infrastructures of U.S. and South African nationhood had historically been grounded. It is noteworthy, too, that these same musicians and their music have been absorbed into the mainstream of national imagery symbolism in the United States and South Africa in contemporary times. This kind of transformation of meaning, where musics of protest and resistance are essentially recast as nationalist musics in different times and circumstances, has been a common feature of the dynamic relationship between music and the construction of nationhood in many countries.

The late South African singer Miriam Makeba.

Diasporas and other transnational communities

The term **diaspora** refers to an international network of communities linked together by identification with a common ancestral homeland and culture. People in diaspora exist in a condition of living away from their "homeland," often with no guarantee, or even likelihood, of return. The term dates back to the original Diaspora, the Jewish diaspora, in which the Jewish people of ancient times were expelled from their ancestral homeland (present-day Israel) millennia ago and began a centuries-long odyssey of dispersal (i.e., diaspora) throughout many parts of the world. Wherever they went—Persia (Iran), Morocco, Spain and Portugal, Poland, Russia, Ukraine, Bukhara (in Uzbekistan), North America, South America, Melbourne and Sydney, Australia—Jewish people preserved and transformed their religious and cultural traditions in relation to the other peoples, societies, and cultures among whom they came to live. They both influenced and were influenced by these other cultures. Jewish musical traditions like *klezmer* richly embody such processes of diasporic, cross-cultural experience.

Diasporic communities are found around the globe. The African diaspora, which was initiated by the insidious institution of the Euro-American slave trade centuries ago, ultimately led to the establishment of large diasporic communities and cultures in the Americas—in Cuba, Brazil, the United States. More recent waves of diasporic movement from the African continent have occurred since the 1950s in Africa's postcolonial era. These have led to the growth of sizable diasporic cultures in Europe, especially in major urban centers such as London and Paris. The vast geographical and cultural expanse of the African diaspora today encompasses all of these diverse communities. Their collective contributions to the global landscape of musical culture cannot be overestimated. From American jazz and hip-hop, to Brazilian samba (**CD ex. #3-19**) and Cuban rumba (**CD ex. #4-4**), to popular recordings by contemporary African emigré music stars like

Brazilian samba group performing in a Carnaval (Carnival) parade. Samba is discussed in Chapter 11 (pp. 228–229).

emigré (e-mi-gray)

Angélique Kidjo that are produced in the major studios of Paris, London, and New York (**CD ex. #3-18**), music of the African diaspora has defined and influenced global music making at just about every conceivable level for a half century and more.

The Irish diaspora also has had a profound historical and modern impact on the world of music. This diaspora began with the Irish potato famine of the 19th century, when the threat of starvation led Irish people to leave their homeland by the thousands to seek refuge in foreign lands such as the United States and Canada (see Chapter 9, p. 161). Since that time, a series of subsequent transnational waves of migration have continued to redefine and recast the dynamic relationship between the Irish homeland and its diasporic outreach. Musicians such as the Irish-American fiddler Eileen Ivers have crystallized the richness and multidimensionality of Irish diasporic music in highly innovative and globally influential ways. An example of Ivers' creative, transnational approach is featured in **CD ex. #3-11,** which we will explore more fully in Chapter 9, pp. 184–187.

Diasporic communities also might be regarded as belonging to a larger class of *transnational communities,* overlapping with other immigrant communities, migrant worker communities, and a diverse range of social groups whose geographical diffusion around the globe defies ready categorization in terms of conventional notions of society, nation, and culture. **Virtual communities,** that is, communities forged in the electronic sphere of cyberspace rather than in more conventional ways, represent the latest chapter in the complex story of transnational identity formation. Through electronic technologies such as the Internet, established notions of what constitutes a community, a social group, a society, a culture, a nation, or a diaspora are being radically transformed. The dissemination of music via these electronic media is in many cases proving to be a major piece of the puzzle in new forms of transnational identity formation.

The Individual in Music

Cultures, societies, nations, and transnational communities provide important frameworks for understanding identity through music. They do not, however, actually do or think *anything,* let alone make music. Rather, it is individual people, flesh-and-blood human beings operating alone

Do You Belong to a Virtual Music Community?

Do you download music files on the Internet, surf the Web for information about your favorite musicians, or correspond with friends via e-mail, instant messaging, or social networking software about music-related matters? If so, you are part of the vast world of virtual music communities. The Internet has radically transformed the world of music and musical communities, making it possible to be a part of informal or formal global networks of people—communities, in essence—bound together wholly or in part by their shared musical activities, tastes, interests, and listening experiences.

or as members of groups, who make and listen to music and who find meaning and define their identities in relation to it.

In a certain sense, all individuals may be viewed as communities unto themselves. Each of us is an ever-evolving repository of multiple identities, and we bring the full range of these varied identities to all that we experience in music and all that we express through it. This is why the music of an individual like the late salsa and Latin jazz superstar Tito Puente is best understood in relation to the multifaceted identity he brought to his musical career (see Chapter 11). Puente, whose classic original recording of his signature song, "Oye Como Va," is heard on **CD ex. #4-7,** was a native and lifetime resident of New York City. He nonetheless identified himself ethnically as a Puerto Rican, while claiming that Cuban music formed the foundation of his *musical* identity (Loza 1999). This complex of identities sheds light on the character of Puente's music, since he was a true master of **musical syncretism,** the merging of formerly distinct styles and idioms into new forms of expression. His multidimensional identity is also relevant when we consider his *family* legacy as a musical patriarch, since his son, Tito Puente Jr., has made significant contributions to the continuing development of Latin dance music (see Chapter 11, pp. 266–270).

Tito Puente.

Ethnomusicologists in recent decades have become increasingly interested in focusing their studies on particular musicians rather than on the cultures or societies to which they belong more broadly. Timothy Rice, in his important book *May It Fill Your Soul: Experiencing Bulgarian Music* (1994), traces the lives in music of two Bulgarian musicians, the *gaida* (Bulgarian bagpipe) player Kostadin Varimezov and his wife, the singer Todora Varimezova. He also devotes considerable attention to what he experienced personally and musically while conducting **fieldwork** in Bulgaria. Fieldwork is a hallmark of ethnomusicological research. It involves living for an extended period of time among the people whose lives and music one researches, and often learning and performing their music as well. In chronicling the stories of Kostadin, Todora, and himself, Rice offers many insights into Bulgarian culture, society, and nationhood, but he does so while maintaining a consistent focus on the individual musician as the primary location of musical identity and meaning. Many of the later chapters in this text reflect a similar philosophy in their focus on individual musicians.

**gaida (GUY-dah
["gai" rhymes
with "high"])**

Spirituality and Transcendence in Music

In most world cultures and societies, music plays an integral role in worship, religious ritual, and the expression of faith. It may serve as a bridge between the earthly world and worlds beyond, bringing people closer to invisible realms or into communion with supernatural forces. In such instances, music facilitates *transcendence*. Examples of music-related transcendence are found in many cultures. During Balinese cremations, it is believed that the soul of the deceased ascends to the upper world of the cosmos on a "ladder" of beleganjur music (Chapter 7, pp. 102–103). The legendary Jewish mystic known as the Baal Shem Tov is said to have risen through music to heaven and finally to have *become* music following his death. Practitioners of the Afro-Cuban Santería, or Regla de Ocha, religion employ specific drum rhythms such as those heard on **CD ex. #4-3** as a form of invitation to deities (orishas) to temporarily descend to the earthly world and participate in sacred rituals presented in their honor. When the summoned orishas descend, they become manifest through ritual dances of spirit mediums, people who undergo *transubstantiation* (transformation into altered states of being) when "possessed" by the visiting orishas (Chapter 11, p. 244).

Music also may reflect spiritual beliefs about the order of the cosmos and the cycle of life. As we will explore in more detail in later chapters (i.e., Chapters 7 and 8), music in Hindu cultures such as Bali and India is often built over *musical cycles*, which are patterns that are repeated over and over again during the course of a performance while other aspects of the music change and evolve around them. These cycles in the music reflect core Hindu *cultural* ideas and beliefs about the design of the universe. Each musical cycle symbolically encompasses a process of birth, preservation, and death leading to rebirth, from which the cycle is regenerated again and again, ad infinitum. This is a musical correlate of the Hindu belief in reincarnation, and in turn of the cyclic, divine convergence of the "Three Shapes" (Trimurti) of

Santería (San-te-REE-yah)

orisha (o-REE-sha)

Dancing for the orishas during a Santería (Regla de Ocha) ritual to the accompaniment of batá drums (see Chapter 11, p. 244).

(*Note:* This photograph originally was published by The Associated Press. The taking of photographs at ceremonies such as this one is generally proscribed, but photojournalists sometimes negotiate terms under which it is permissible.)

the Hindu godhead—Brahma, the Creator; Vishnu (Visnu), the Preserver; and Shiva (Siva, Siwa), the Destroyer—who together facilitate a balanced and stable cosmic order.

Music's spiritual importance also resides in its unique capacity to bring members of communities together in social solidarity and in a single, unified expression of their faith. When people make music together, they are often "at their best" in terms of displaying a sense of common purpose and endeavor in their worship. **CD ex. #1-11,** a performance of a Christian hymn from the island of Fiji, captures this spirit of the communal expression of faith with poignance and power.

Church choir, Fiji.

Music and Dance

Music may move people to transcendent states, but it also has the capacity to move them in a more literal way by inspiring them to dance. The integral connection of music and dance is a feature of music cultures worldwide. In many instances, in fact, music and dance are regarded as mutual reflections of one another, the one expressing itself in organized sound, the other in organized movement. The myriad forms and contexts of dancing accompanied by music occur in just about every kind of social and cultural situation imaginable, from the most sacred of religious rites to the most secular spectacles of revelry. In the musical journey of this text, we will encounter dancing and dance music in several musicultural traditions: Irish dance tunes (Chapter 9), Latin dance music (Chapter 11), traditional women's dance in Egypt and international belly dance (Chapter 12). Each case offers a unique scenario of dance as a sociocultural phenomenon and as an activity through which people define identity and meaning in their lives.

Dance, and the music that accompanies it, may serve as a lens through which to view social celebration, community solidarity, the physical expression of culture, and the performance of identity. It also may provide revealing and sometimes troubling insights into how people treat and classify each other in terms of issues of gender, race, and ethnicity. In the Middle East, professional female dancers who dance publicly in the company of men are generally accorded low social status. Their artistry—and their art—is marginalized due to the social stigma attached to it. Indeed, the historical association of music with women's dancing in Islamic societies has been a major factor in music's reputation as a profane art that must be kept separate, physically and conceptually, from the sacred practices of Islamic worship (see Chapter 12, p. 298).

Rationalizations for racism and racist social policies levied against African peoples and people of African descent in the Americas were historically supported by theories of racial inferiority that were tied to dance and music as well. The purported "natural rhythm" of Africans and people of the African diaspora, together with their integral use of dance to express core values of cultural identity and faith, were turned against them. African rhythm and African dance were cast by Western exploiters as symbols of African "primitiveness," and in turn were used to justify the inhumanely oppressive institutions and policies of the European colonization of Africa and the Euro-American slave trade. The vestiges of such attitudes are still with us today in cultural and ethnic stereotypes relating to music and dance.

Racist stereotyping of "African" dancers.

The communal performance of music, often presented in conjunction with some form of dramatic or dance presentation, is a prominent feature of **rituals** in many world cultures. Rituals are special events during which individuals or communities enact, through performance, their core beliefs, values, and ideals. They often take the form of communal performances of myths, legends, epics, or sacred texts or stories that are foundational to a culture's identity. As a result, rituals reveal a great deal about the *worldviews* of the people who perform them, that is, about the ways in which these people conceive of their world and their place and purpose within it. Rituals have been a major focus of attention for anthropologists and others interested in the study of culture, including ethnomusicologists, who have long been fascinated by the prominent role of music in ritual performances.

Rituals may be sacred or secular. They are used to mark important life-cycle events and rites of passage in all cultures. They play a prominent role in healing practices the world over. They have long served to legitimize the authority and power of political leaders and social institutions, or alternatively to subvert and challenge them. Even when rituals are not explicitly spiritual or religious, they tend to have a transcendent quality to them, since they are, by definition, events that are set off from the regular course of everyday life. This separation is frequently symbolized by the presence of music in the ritual space, which marks that space as special.

zaar (zahr)

The Egyptian *zaar* (zar) is a healing ritual in which music functions prominently (see Chapter 12, pp. 289–293). During a zaar, specific kinds of rhythms like the ones heard in **CD ex. #1-12** are played on drums and other percussion instruments. These rhythms accompany a dance performed by a woman who is believed to have fallen ill as a result of being entered, or

asyad (ahs-sigh-yed)

"possessed," by an *asyad,* a type of supernatural being. The afflicted woman's dancing, which is

A zaar ritual.

driven by the powerful percussive rhythms of the music, is performed with the intention of convincing the intruding asyad to depart. If the woman returns to a state of health, this is taken as an indication that the ritual has succeeded, that the patient has been liberated from her affliction and the asyad has moved on. The entire event may be viewed as a performance of worldview and belief, one that, like many rituals, moves its participants from one state of being and perception to another.

Alan Maralung.

Music as Commodity and the Patronage of Music

Support and ownership of music are major factors that influence how music lives in communities, cultures, and societies. Some music is regarded as the property of a family lineage (e.g., in India) or an entire village community (e.g., in Bali). Other music is not regarded as property at all, rather being thought of as an integral facet of communal life that is absorbed into the broader fabric of culture. Ownership of music by individuals is also common. We in the West are very familiar with the idea of a song or other musical composition being privately owned. The laws of copyright protect musical works as a form of intellectual property. A songwriter or composer who holds the copyright to a piece of music holds the exclusive legal right to sell, market, and distribute that music as he or she sees fit. In this context, the music is a commodity.

The idea of private music ownership is by no means limited to the modern West. In some Aboriginal Australian and Amerindian cultures, songs bequeathed to particular individuals in dreams or visions are regarded as their exclusive property. No one else may perform these songs, with the possible exception of people who receive them as gifts from their original owners.

Different models of ownership of music become complexly intertwined when cultural representatives of different societies join forces. **CD ex. #1-13,** "Ibis," is a case in point. This is a song that was owned by the late Alan Maralung, who was a revered Aboriginal Australian singer of Arnhem Land in Australia's Northern Territory. Arnhem Land is the traditional heartland of Aboriginal culture, including music. "Ibis" is one of a large number of *wangga* songs that Maralung claimed as his own on account of reportedly having received them directly from supernatural beings in dreams.

In his singing of "Ibis," Maralung is accompanied by two instruments: a pair of wooden sticks that are struck together (clapsticks) and a *didgeridoo* (didjeridu). The didgeridoo is a truly remarkable instrument. In its traditional form, it is constructed of a long branch of eucalyptus wood—usually 1 to 1.5 meters in length—which has been hollowed out by termites. (More modern adaptations sometimes use PVC pipe or other materials in place of eucalyptus.) By blowing into the didgeridoo in a variety of ways, the player is able to produce a wide range of sounds, as can be heard in the example. (The didgeridoo is discussed further in Chapter 5, pp. 59–60.)

Didgeridoo being played by Benjamin Koen.

According to the rules of his culture, Maralung exclusively owns this song and all others that were likewise bequeathed to him during his lifetime. No one else may perform or claim these songs, at least not without having received his explicit endorsement. But how does the status of the song and its ownership change in light of the fact that it has been made available commercially by an American record company (Smithsonian Folkways), and that it has in turn been presented to you—in excerpted form—on the CD set accompanying this text? As Ronald Radano and Philip Bohlman assert in the book *Music and The Racial Imagination,* "The condition of ownership has . . .

been stripped from world music, for anyone able to buy CDs or turn on the radio or television can possess it" (Radano and Bohlman 2000:9). Their claim is debatable, but the issues it raises are significant. Now that "Ibis" has been commodified and Maralung has passed away, does Smithsonian Folkways or McGraw-Hill (or do I) have specific *ethical* responsibilities regarding the song's use and distribution? Did Maralung himself act appropriately in allowing the song, a gift from a supernatural being, to be distributed internationally in the ways it has been? These are complicated questions, but ones worth considering.

Closely aligned with issues of music ownership and commodification is the matter of music patronage. Music patronage involves the support of musicians and musical institutions, whether that support be financial, social, institutional, educational, or of some other type. In former times (and still sometimes today), kings, queens, princes, and princesses were leading music patrons, supporting musicians and even entire musical cultures in their royal courts and music ministries (see, for example, Chapters 10 and 13). Churches and other religious institutions also have been important music patrons historically.

But the tradition of patronage of musicians by brothel owners, country dance hall proprietors, and the like probably dates back at least as far as royal patronage. Different musical traditions have always been closely linked to different social classes, and sources of musical patronage—who pays the piper, in essence—have always borne directly on connections between music, class, and social status. Sources of musical patronage also have had important implications on how different musical traditions and styles are classified relative to one another. They have as much or more to do with the use of designations like folk music, popular music, religious music, art music, court music, classical music, entertainment music, and commercial music as the musical styles linked to those terms themselves. The same style of music—even the same piece—is likely to be classified quite differently and take on different meanings and identities if it is played in a concert hall than if it is heard as part of the soundtrack for a television sitcom.

Today, government arts agencies, university music departments and conservatories, private arts funding organizations, music industry corporations, Internet music providers, radio and television advertisers, nightclub proprietors, music festival producers, book publishers, and

Sting performing with Algerian *rai* music star Cheb Mami. The two collaborated on the hit song "Desert Rose."

makers of films and television shows, music videos, cell phones, and video games all have a role to play in the complex networks of local, national, and international finance that constitute the contemporary universe of music patronage. So too do lawyers, rock star world music producers (Paul Simon, Peter Gabriel, Sting), journalists, music critics, and general music consumers who attend concerts and download music from the Internet. The global culture of music patronage is highly complex, and nowhere more so than in the world of "world music."

Technology itself is also a key player in the patronage of music. The technologies used to produce, record, transmit, and disseminate music largely shape and determine what kind of music gets heard and by whom, who supports that music, and indeed what music actually sounds like. Humans are ultimately the source of all musical production, even of computer-generated music; it is human intention and perception put into practice that constitutes the lowest common denominator of music, as we saw in Chapter 1. But technologies—from the didgeridoo, to the multitrack recording studio, to the iPod—largely shape both musical sound and the cultural frameworks and attitudes that give that sound meaning and identity.

The Transmission of Music and Musical Knowledge

Music is a social fact. One way or another, it becomes meaningful by entering the realm of social life. Once there, it moves among people and communities, sometimes locally, sometimes globally. The processes by means of which music moves from one person to another, from one generation to another, from one community to another, and potentially throughout the whole world, are processes of *music transmission.*

Music may be transmitted directly from one person to another, "face-to-face" in the context of a performance or some kind of a music lesson. It also may be transmitted via music notation (e.g., as sheet music) or in some other graphic form. Additionally, music can move from person to person and place to place through electronic media—recordings, films and television shows, radio, the Internet. And transmission of knowledge and information *about* music—through books, articles, Web sites, documentary films, and other media—plays an integral role in the transmission of music itself, influencing what music does and does not get heard (and by whom) and how that music is produced and received.

Production and reception

All forms of music transmission share two basic features: the production of music and the reception of music. Sometimes the roles of music maker and music receiver are clearly separated, as in a Western classical recital in which a pianist (the performer) performs a piece of music written by someone other than herself (the composer) and plays it for a gathering of people who sit and listen quietly and do not participate actively in the performance other than to applaud at the end of it (the audience). The performer in this case is a *music specialist*—often a professional, a virtuoso, a "musical artist." The audience is made up of music consumers—often paying customers—who are there to be entertained, or perhaps to be enlightened, or just to be seen.

In other instances, distinctions between the processes of music making and music reception are much less clear. In many African societies, for example, recognized distinctions between "performer" and "audience" do not exist to nearly the extent that they do in the West, at least in some contexts; all members of the community are expected to participate actively (perform) *and* to encourage and appreciate the performances of their fellow community members (i.e., to be part of their "audience").

The way in which music is taught and learned constitutes one of the most important domains of music transmission. Sometimes the passing on of music and musical knowledge implicit in the teaching-learning interaction is informal and unstructured. Musical knowledge, ability, and experience are acquired in the normal course of communal life; musicality develops through a kind of osmosis, as a product of being in and being a part of musical environments as one grows up and "learns" one's culture. In other cases, music learning is highly formal and structured.

Western concert performance. Notice the physical separation of the musicians of the symphony orchestra on the stage and the people in the audience.

East African communal performance. This photo is of a Sukuma post-harvest masked dance event in western Tanzania. Here, the distinction between performers and audience members is much less clearly defined than in the Western concert setting.

An Indian music lesson.

Students of Indian classical music (see Chapter 8) are expected to devote themselves to their *gurus* (musical mentors) with total and unwavering commitment for a period of many years as they learn the intricacies of their demanding art. In contrast to their counterparts in the classical music worlds of the West or Japan, whose learning methods include the use of music notation (a musical score of some kind that is "written out"), Indian musicians trained in the traditional manner usually rely almost exclusively on memorization and performance models provided by their gurus to cultivate their musical artistry.

Music creation processes

The issue of transmission in music also is informed by what kind of musical material is actually transmitted. Different types of music creation processes turn musical ideas into musical works and performances in different ways. Among the most important of these processes are the following four: composition, interpretation, improvisation, and arranging.

The process of **composition** involves planning out the design of a musical work prior to its performance. This may be done by an individual (the composer) or by a group of musicians working collectively. The transmission of composed music may occur via a notated score, a live performance, a recording, or a computer-generated sound file. The traditions of Balinese gamelan (**CD ex. #2-12**), the Japanese shakuhachi flute (**CD ex. #1-14**), and Western symphonic music (**CD ex. #1-2**) all emphasize the process of composition, that is, they are traditions in which the content of a piece of music is typically planned and worked out quite precisely before the piece is ever performed.

Interpretation is the process through which music performers—or music listeners—take an existing composition and in a sense make it their own through the experience of performing or listening to it. Interpretation is present to some degree in all music performances, even of works in which composers provide performers with very precise instructions on how to approach the piece. Interpretation accounts for why no two performances of Beethoven's Ninth Symphony (**CD ex. #1-2**) are exactly alike, even though all of them are generated from essentially the same original musical score.

Improvisation involves composing in the moment of performance. In certain musical idioms—jazz, Indian raga (Chapter 8; **CD ex. #2-23**), Arab taqsim (**CD ex. #1-15** [0:00–1:35]; see also Chapter 12, p. 283)—the quality of improvisation, rather than of composition per se, is the principal criterion for assessing musical artistry. While the process of improvisation is sometimes characterized as a form of spontaneous musical invention, this is for the most part misleading. The majority of improvisatory traditions are grounded in highly systematic and rigorous conventions. Though the improvised performance *is* spontaneous, it is also the product of much disciplined training and practice.

Arranging is the craft of taking an existing musical work and transforming it into something new, while still retaining its core musical identity. The Beatles song "Yesterday" exists in thousands of arrangements, which may use different combinations of voices and instruments and have a variety of other distinctive features as well. Blending of elements from diverse musical traditions can result in particularly interesting arrangements, such as the Scottish bagpipes-and-drums arrangement of the Christian hymn "Amazing Grace" of **CD ex. #1-16** and the Egyptian rhythm-anchored take on the Mexican song "La Cucaracha" of **CD ex. #4-22**.

Music in the Process of Tradition

In much the same way that music exists at the intersection of sound and culture, tradition exists at the intersection of culture and music. It is through tradition, and within the contexts of *music traditions,* that musics become culturally meaningful, socially functional, and representative of individual and communal identities at all levels.

Tradition, like culture, is a term that can mean many different things. For some, it suggests that which is old, stable, entrenched, static, of the past. That is not the sense in which the word tradition is used in this text, however, at least not the primary one. Rather, as was mentioned briefly in the Introduction to this book, **tradition** is here conceived of as a *process,* in particular *a process of creative transformation whose most remarkable feature is the continuity it nurtures and sustains.*

This concept of tradition as process is well articulated by the ethnomusicologist Henry Spiller. "To my mind," writes Spiller, "what qualifies music as traditional is not how old it is, but rather how well it teaches, reinforces, and creates the social values of its producers and consumers. Traditional music is not something that is stuck in the past; it grows and changes, just as the people who make and listen to it grow and change, just as the values they share with those close to them change (albeit a bit more slowly). Truly traditional music, then, exploits new resources, acknowledges new requirements, and responds to new situations. It provides a place for people to try out new approaches to their existing values, to experiment with new ideas, and to synthesize the new with the old" (Spiller 2008:4).

I agree with everything Spiller states in the above passage, though I prefer to describe what he identifies as "traditional music" as *music of tradition* instead. Music of tradition can be very modern, radical, and experimental. It can draw upon a great variety of different kinds of music and the resources of many different cultures. It can embody multiple meanings and levels of meaning and may reflect, embody, and inform many different identities. It also can be ancient and archaic, very specific in its cultural meanings, or deeply conservative in the values it expresses. Or it can represent the synthesis of a host of seemingly incongruous elements, from the most resolutely traditional to the most ultramodern.

Two related examples of blues music will help to illustrate the concept of music of tradition, a concept that is integral to the development of every chapter in Part II of this text. Listen to **CD ex. #1-17,** a classic performance of the song "High Water Everywhere" by the seminal Mississippi blues musician Charlie Patton. Patton lived from around 1891 until 1934 (some sources place his birth date as early as 1881) and is often described as the founding father of the Mississippi Delta blues tradition. This performance, then, might be characterized as an example of "traditional blues" in a quite literal sense—music that is old and "authentic," that takes us back to the roots of the blues tradition.

Now listen to **CD ex. #1-18,** "Kargyraa Moan," by the modern blues musician Paul Pena. This piece represents a synthesis of two great traditions. The first is American blues, which was Pena's musical home base, as it were. (Pena died in 2005.) The second is *khoomei,* which comes from the distant land of Tuva, in Central Asia. Tuvan khoomei is closely related to the Mongolian style of singing known as *khoomii* that we listened to earlier, in **CD ex. #1-6.** Like their Mongolian counterparts, the various types and subtypes of Tuvan khoomei rely upon the ability of a singer to manipulate his or her vocal apparatus in such a way that *multiple* tones, rather than just a single tone, are produced at once (see Chapter 5, p. 60).

Through an amazing musicultural odyssey (chronicled in the equally amazing, Oscar-nominated documentary film *Genghis Blues*), Paul Pena, who was both blind and plagued by numerous health challenges, discovered Tuvan khoomei, mastered one of its main substyles (called *kargyraa*), developed a unique musical synthesis of khoomei and blues, traveled to Tuva, competed in the Tuvan national khoomei competition, and emerged a winner of the contest. The version of "Kargyraa Moan" featured here was recorded live, in Tuva, during Pena's triumphant performance in that competition. The prize for his victory was a horse.

khoomei (khoo-may)

khoomii (khoo-mee)

Paul Pena.

On the surface, Pena's combining of blues and khoomei elements in "Kargyraa Moan" seems quite radically innovative, and it is. Yet Pena viewed his bridging of these seemingly disparate musical worlds less as a departure from his deep blues heritage than as a tribute and a return to it. When he first encountered the multitone style of Tuvan *kargyraa,* with its distinctive, guttural, "growling" sounds, Pena was certainly drawn in by the novelty of what he heard. But his attraction to kargyraa also came from the fact that it strongly reminded him of the singing styles of Charlie Patton and other "rough-voiced" blues greats like Tommy McLennan and Howlin' Wolf who had been his original inspirations. This profound sense of connecting back to the roots of his own musical past *in* blues *through* khoomei proved key in Pena's impassioned and tenacious pursuit of a new and unique musical vision.

Whatever form or forms it takes, music of tradition always comes out of a particular musical, social, and cultural history that prefigures it and that is at some core level inscribed in the sound and meaning of the music itself. It always expresses something essential about who people are and what matters to them. Music of tradition tells us about the people responsible for the music's creation, and for its preservation and sustenance. Indeed, it has the capacity to tell us something important about the members of *all* communities for whom it comes to have meaning and significance. In an earlier publication, I defined ethnomusicology as "the study of how music lives in the lives of people who make and experience it, and of how people live in the music they make" (Bakan 1999:17–18). In essence, that is what this book is about, too, as it explores diverse traditions of world music and the process of tradition that runs through all of them in unique and compelling ways.

Summary

In exploring how music lives, this chapter focused on the intersection of music as sound and music as culture that gives rise to meaning, identity, transmission, and creation in music. It is at this intersection of sound and culture that music exists as a musicultural phenomenon.

We began by situating this chapter and this text more broadly in relation to the discipline of ethnomusicology. An anthropological (and in turn ethnomusicological) definition and concept of culture was then introduced. From there, we distinguished different types of musical meaning (sound-based versus cultural context-based) and explored how identity becomes tied to music and musical expression on many levels: society, culture, community, nation, diaspora, the individual. We then looked at how diverse musics and identities come together and create new forms of musical and musicultural expression through processes of syncretism. We also explored important connections that exist between music and spirituality, dance, ritual, commodity, and patronage; and surveyed musical transmission and processes of music creation (composition, interpretation, improvisation, and arranging).

The final section of the chapter focused on music as tradition, positing that tradition is a process of creative transformation whose most remarkable feature is the continuity it nurtures and sustains. Transformation, even radical transformation, is very much a part of musics of tradition worldwide, as later chapters of this book will explore in myriad ways.

Key Terms

ethnomusicology
musicultural
culture (Tylor definition)
identity
vocables
society
social institutions

cultures (as social entities distinct from societies)
nation-state
nation
nationalist music
diaspora
virtual communities
musical syncretism

fieldwork
rituals
composition
interpretation
improvisation
arranging
tradition (as a process)

Study Questions

- What is ethnomusicology? What does it mean to study music from a musicultural perspective?

- What is Edward Tylor's definition of *culture*? When was it first published?

- How did the Native American/First Nations examples included in this chapter illustrate the richness and complexity of cultural identity as it is made manifest in music?

- What distinguishes societies from cultures? What different kinds of insights do societal and cultural approaches to the study of music reveal? How was the Balinese example of this chapter used as an illustration?

- What are some of the principal types of social institutions we might look to if we wished to gain an understanding of music and society?

- Why are some nations *not* nation-states? How do nationalist musics develop and contribute to concepts of nationhood?

- What is a diaspora? What can we learn about diasporic processes and phenomena from studying music? Give examples.

- What is musical syncretism?
- What is involved in doing ethnomusicological fieldwork?
- What were the main processes of music creation and transmission discussed?
- What is music of tradition, and what examples were used to illustrate this concept?

Discussion Questions

- How is music as a phenomenon of society distinct from and/or related to music as a phenomenon of culture? Draw from examples in this chapter and either real or hypothetical examples of your own to explore and discuss this question.

- How do the Internet and other mass media influence the ways in which people conceive of their identities and the identities of others relative to music? What kinds of virtual music communities do you belong to (or could you belong to), and why? Does today's high-tech world make the potential for building community through music greater or less great than it was in the past? Why, and in what ways?

- What are some of the principal social institutions that are involved in music production and reception in your world? How do these various institutions contribute to the ways in which you experience, understand, and value the musics that are a part of your life?

- This chapter introduced numerous themes and issues for exploring music as a phenomenon of culture. There are a great many more that one might consider: children's music, music and the elderly, music among people with disabilities. How might one go about examining these areas, and what others can you think of that could lead to deeper understandings of music and human experience?

Applying What You Have Learned

- Think of a song or other piece of music that has been a part of your life for a long time. Has the significance or "meaning" of that song changed over the years? If so, what has changed in your perception of the song, and what factors in your life—personal, cultural, or other—might have contributed? Write a brief account chronicling your personal history of this song, focusing specifically on what it means to you today and what it has meant to you at different points in the past.

- Draft a chart listing all of the different kinds of music you listen to, indicating when you usually listen to them and for what purposes. What do you listen to when you're trying to relax, or when you're working out, or studying? What do you like to dance to? What music makes you feel romantic, nostalgic, happy, sad, patriotic, subversive? Are there specific kinds of music that you identify with your ethnicity, or with your cultural or national identity? On the basis of this chart, create a "music identity profile" of yourself, considering how music in your life contributes to your sense of who you are on multiple levels.

- Do your own ethnomusicological fieldwork project. Get to know some musicians in your local community and spend time observing, taking part in, and documenting their musical lives. This may involve attending rehearsals and performances in which they are involved (or other musical events), spending time with them socially, conducting interviews and engaging in informal conversations, and learning about the music they play and why it is important to them. Keep a journal of your observations, impressions, and experiences over a period of several weeks, then write a brief ethnomusicological report on your findings.

Resources for Further Study

Visit the Online Learning Center at www.mhhe.com/bakan2e, as well as the author's personally maintained Web site at www.michaelbakan.com, for additional learning aids, study help, and resources that supplement the content of this chapter.

how **music works,** part I:
rhythm

Having explored the questions of what music is and how music lives in Chapters 1 and 2, we turn our attention in this chapter, and also in Chapters 4–6, to another fundamental issue: how music works. Collectively, this set of four chapters provides a general introduction to music sounds and to the way they are organized; in other words, to the basic *elements of music*. We want to know what the building blocks of musical sound, structure, and form are; to develop a shared vocabulary for describing and comprehending them; and to be introduced to them in a way that is accessible yet prepares us well for the diverse world music journey ahead.

Moreover, we want to engage with the elements of music not as mere abstractions, but rather as identifiable components of sound that we are able to *actually hear.* In working toward this goal, we employ examples of two kinds to illustrate the main terms and concepts introduced. These are:

- Well-known songs that are likely to be familiar, such as "The Alphabet Song," "Mary Had a Little Lamb," and "The Star-Spangled Banner" (the national anthem of the United States).
- Recordings covering a wide range of world music traditions and cultures.

With respect to the first of these two categories, some of the examples (especially the children's songs) may strike you as overly simplistic, even a bit silly, but they have the advantage of being straightforward and recognizable. With regard to the world music recordings, the main emphasis is not on learning and memorizing all of the different names of cultures, styles, and instruments that come up. Rather, it is to become acquainted with general aspects of how music works with the aid of examples that will likely *not* be familiar to you. In the process, you will have an opportunity to sample some of the world's rich musical diversity as a prelude to the more focused case studies of the chapters in Part II.

This chapter explores the element of rhythm specifically, but we begin on a more general level with a brief introduction to the four basic properties of tones that were first mentioned in Chapter 1.

■ ■ ■

The Four Basic Properties of Tones

Every sound we hear in a piece of music—and indeed every sound we hear in our world—is defined by four basic properties: duration, frequency, amplitude, and timbre. **Duration** relates to *how long or short* a tone is. It is the basis of *rhythm* in music. **Frequency,** which becomes manifest in music as *pitch,* corresponds to *how high or low* a tone is. **Amplitude** relates to *how loud or soft* tones are. The relative loudness and softness of different tones (with silence at one extreme of the loudness-to-softness continuum) are what define *dynamics* in music. **Timbre** is analogous to the *actual sound quality or "tone color"* of tones, to what they "sound like": tones played on a trumpet are timbrally distinct from tones played on a saxophone, even if both instruments are heard playing the same frequency (pitch) for the same duration (rhythm) at the same amplitude (dynamic level).

Duration, frequency, amplitude, and timbre, then, are the four basic properties of tones, the building blocks of musical sound. Their musical correlates—rhythm, pitch, dynamics, and tone color, respectively—are the foundational elements of music. (See Table 3.1.)

Rhythm

When we speak of **rhythm,** we are dealing with *how the sounds and silences of music are organized in time.* In understanding rhythm, two terms used in Western music provide a good

TABLE 3.1	The four basic properties of tones and their musical correlates.
Property of Tone	**Musical Correlate**
Duration	Rhythm
Frequency	Pitch
Amplitude	Dynamics
Timbre	Tone color, sound quality

Mozart and "The Alphabet Song"

"The Alphabet Song" may be known to you only as a simple, children's song that was used by your parents or kindergarten teacher to help you learn the alphabet, but it has a rather interesting history. The tune of "The Alphabet Song" is identical to that of at least two other popular children's songs, "Baa, Baa, Black Sheep" and "Twinkle, Twinkle, Little Star." This tune descends from a very old French children's song that the great Viennese composer Wolfgang Amadeus Mozart used as the basis of a piano piece he composed in 1778. The piece is usually referred to today as Mozart's *Variations on "Twinkle, Twinkle, Little Star"* and remains a popular work for solo piano.

starting point: note and rest. An individual musical tone may be referred to as a *note*. A pause between notes is a *rest*.

Try performing "The Alphabet Song" by tapping it out on your desk, *without* actually singing "the tune." The result is a performance of *the rhythm of that song*. You will notice that some of the notes are longer than others; in other words, that the notes have different *durations*. The notes for the first few letter names—"a, b, c, d, e, f"—are shorter by half than the note on the letter "g" which follows them. A little further on, you get to "l, m, n, o," which turn out to be twice as short as "a, b, c, d, e, f" were, and four times shorter than "g" was. (See Figure 3.1.)

Thus, we find that there are three different lengths of notes in the opening section of "The Alphabet Song." In Western music terminology, the faster-moving notes are usually called **sixteenth notes,** the medium-speed ones **eighth notes,** and the slower ones **quarter notes.** Figure 3.2 shows how these different-length notes appear in Western music notation.

Many types of music in the world, including several explored in this text, use rhythms that "translate" quite well into sixteenth, eighth, and quarter notes. These terms will therefore be used in connection with the discussions of musical rhythm in various chapters, though it should be understood from the outset that they do not necessarily reflect how people in other cultures conceive of or describe their *own* rhythms.

FIGURE 3.1

Notes of different duration in "The Alphabet Song."

| a | b | c | d | e | f | g |

| h | i | j | k | l | m | n | o | p |

FIGURE 3.2

"The Alphabet Song" rhythm in Western notation.

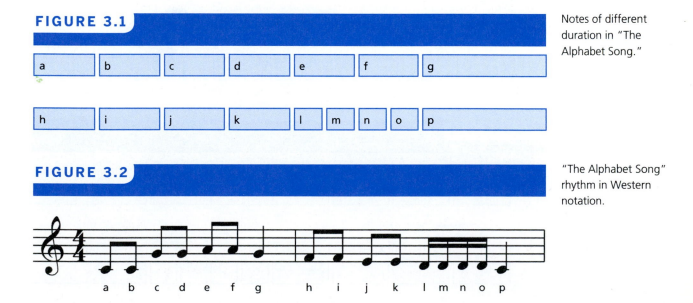

a b c d e f g   h i j k l m n o p

Beat

In "The Alphabet Song"—and, indeed, in much music—the lengths of the different notes are organized in relation to a steady, underlying pulse known as the **beat.** The beat is what you tap your foot to when you listen to a song, or what you move your feet to when you dance. The beat in "The Alphabet Song" is defined by a steady stream of quarter-note pulses. Each one of these pulses is called *a* beat, while the continuous stream of quarter-note pulses that underlies the entire performance is called *the* beat.

To make the relationship between a song's beat and its rhythm concrete, sing "The Alphabet Song" while clapping the beat in steady quarter notes (Figure 3.3).

The beat of a piece of music may be marked out explicitly in sound (as when you sang "The Alphabet Song" while clapping along) or it may just be implied, that is, felt but not actually heard (as when you sang the song earlier without clapping). Either way, it provides the foundation upon which all other rhythmic aspects of the music are organized.

Subdivision

In most music, the individual beats are divided into smaller rhythmic units. This results in rhythmic **subdivision.** Two evenly spaced notes per beat create *duple subdivision.* This is what we hear in the opening of "The Alphabet Song," in which the first two letters sung—"a" and "b"—subdivide the first beat, and the next two letters—"c" and "d"—subdivide the second beat. Four evenly spaced notes per beat create *quadruple subdivision,* as in the "l-m-n-o" portion of "The Alphabet Song," where all four notes are squeezed into the space of just a single beat. (See Figure 3.4.)

Triple subdivision is also common. The song "Row, Row, Row Your Boat" is an example. Sing the line "Mer-ri-ly, mer-ri-ly, mer-ri-ly, mer-ri-ly" while clapping out the beats (see p. 37, Figure 3.5, line 3) and you will notice that each syllable occupies exactly one-third of a beat; this yields triple subdivision of each beat. In the next line, "Life—is but—a dream," the triple subdivisions continue, but the middle "note" of each beat's group of three notes is essentially

"The Alphabet Song," with beats marked out.

FIGURE 3.3

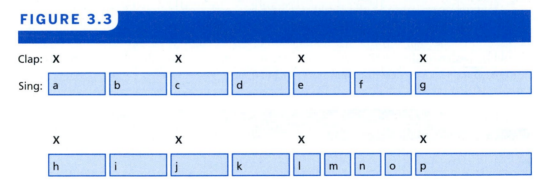

Clap:	X		X		X		X	
Sing:	a	b	c	d	e	f	g	

	X		X		X		X	
	h	i	j	k	l	m n o	p	

Examples of duple and quadruple subdivision, "The Alphabet Song."

FIGURE 3.4

Clap:	X				X				X				X			
Sing:	a		b		c		d		e		f		g			

	X				X				X				X			
	h		i		j		k		l	m	n	o	p			

left out (Figure 3.5, line 4), resulting in a rolling or swinging type of rhythm that is actually a signature element of popular dance rhythms in many world music traditions, such as the blues shuffle (**CD ex. #1-19**) and the Celtic hornpipe (**CD ex. #3-6**). (See Figure 3.6.)

Many other kinds and levels of subdivision occur in music as well, some of them quite complex. Familiarity with the basic duple, triple, and quadruple forms will serve our purposes well, however, so we can now proceed to our next key element, meter.

Meter

Just as individual beats can be subdivided into smaller rhythmic units, they may also be grouped together to form larger units. In Western music, such a grouping of beats is called a **measure** (or *bar*), and the number of beats in a measure defines the music's **meter.** Meters of two (duple), three (triple), and four (quadruple) beats per measure are the most common in the West and in many other parts of the world as well. More complex meters—with 5, 7, 11, or 13 beats per measure—also occur, and there are even instances where the meter *changes* from one measure or section of a piece of music to the next. For now, though, it will be sufficient for us to focus on the simpler types of meters.

"The Alphabet Song" is in a meter of four. A consistent, four-beat pattern of strong (**S**), weak (w), and medium (M) beats is repeated continuously throughout the entire song. The first two measures are charted out in Figure 3.7 on page 38. Try singing this portion while marking the individual beats of each measure with handclaps, using loud claps for the "**S**" beats, soft claps for the "w" beats, and medium claps for the "M" beats.

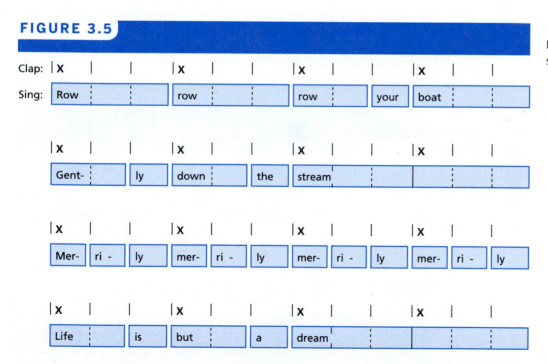

FIGURE 3.5

"Row, Row, Row Your Boat," a song with triple subdivision.

FIGURE 3.6

Shuffle/hornpipe triple subdivision rhythm.

Four-beat (quadruple)
meter in "The Alphabet
Song."

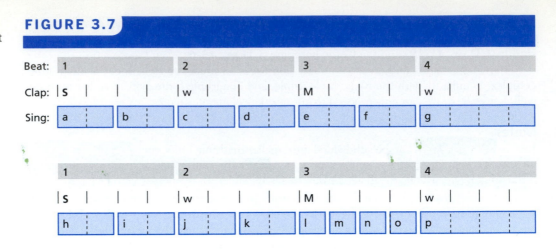

FIGURE 3.7

"The Star-Spangled Banner" is in a meter of three. Here, each measure follows a consistent, recurring, strong-weak-weak (**S**-w-w) triple-meter beat pattern. Figure 3.8 charts out the first four measures. Try singing it now, again marking the meter with loud and soft handclaps.

Let us now turn our attention to a couple of recorded world music examples in which the meters are relatively straightforward and easy to identify. The Egyptian dance rhythm heard on **CD ex. #1-12** is in a duple meter; each of the low-pitched "Dum" strokes on the drums marks one beat; higher-pitched "tek" strokes fall in-between the main beats (i.e., subdividing the beats) at different points (Figure 3.9). Try marking out the main "Dum" beats with handclaps as you listen to this piece.

The famous Mexican *mariachi* tune "Cielito Lindo" (Beautiful Cielito, or Beautiful Sweetheart), featured on **CD ex. #1-20,** is a triple-meter song with the characteristic **S**-w-w beat

**"Cielito Lindo"
(See-el-ee-toe
Lin-doe)**

Triple meter in "The
Star-Spangled Banner."

FIGURE 3.8

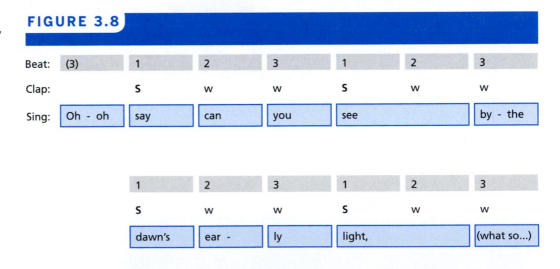

Egyptian dance rhythm
in duple meter.

FIGURE 3.9

FIGURE 3.10

Beat:	1		2		3		1		2		3		1
Clap:	**S**		w		w		**S**		w		w		**S**
Music:	**Bass**		strum		strum		**Bass**		strum		strum		**Bass**

pattern. Each strong (**S**) beat is marked by a low, bass note; each weak (w) beat by a strummed guitar chord (we will learn about chords in Chapter 4), as is charted out in Figure 3.10.

insights and perspectives

Clap on 2 and 4: Backbeats

In styles such as rock, blues, funk, and hip-hop, the second and fourth beats of four-beat measures (or *backbeats,* as they are called in such contexts) typically are given *more* emphasis (strength) than the first and third beats. This entirely changes the feel of the rhythm, that is, the music's *groove.* You can get a sense of this difference by performing "The Alphabet Song" as you mark out the meter in a way that emphasizes the backbeats. Use a soft clap to mark each weak beat (w) and a loud clap to mark each strong beat (**S**).

Charles Atkins.

Beat:	1				2				3				4			
Clap:	w				**S**				w				**S**			
Sing:	a		b		c		d		e		f		g			

	1				2				3				4			
	w				**S**				w				**S**			
	h		i		j		k		l	m	n	o	p			

Just with this simple shift of emphasis on beats, the groove acquires a bit of a rock music feel.

In rock, funk, and blues (the latter exemplified by **CD ex. #1-19,** "A Funny Way of Asking," by Charles Atkins), a "thwack" on the high-pitched snare drum of the drum set is often used to emphasize the backbeats.

Mariachi band. The instruments being played, from left to right, are the guitar, accordion, vihuela, violin, and guitarrón. Mariachi music is discussed in Chapter 11 (pp. 239–243).

insights and perspectives

Three Beats or Seven?

In Eastern European countries like Bulgaria and Romania, music with meters of 5, 7, 11, or 13 beats is common. **CD ex. #1-21** features a Roma brass band from Romania playing a dance tune with a meter of seven fast beats per measure (2 + 2 + 3). That is how Western music analysts describe this meter, in any case. Roma themselves would say this is essentially a *triple* meter, with two "short" beats followed by a "long" beat every measure. The "shorts" and "longs" correspond to different dance steps.

This is a good example of the difference between cultural insiders' and outsiders' perceptions of music (or between *emic* and *etic* perspectives, respectively, in anthropological terms). In this case, as in many (e.g., the music versus nonmusic status of Qur'anic recitation discussed in Chapter 1), there is validity to both perspectives. Each sheds light on the subject at hand in a different way.

As you listen to "Cielito Lindo," try to mark out the pattern of the meter with loud claps on the strong (**S**) beats and soft claps on the weak (w) beats. We will learn more about this song in Chapter 11 (pp. 240–241).

In musical traditions of India, Indonesia, China, the Middle East, and other parts of the world, meters are sometimes very long and complex. Rather than consisting of two, three, or four beats, or even five or seven beats, a "measure" may consist of as many as 108 or 256 beats! For these longer types of meters, we usually speak of a **metric cycle** rather than a measure or bar when describing how the beats are grouped and organized. In later chapters, we will encounter examples of metric cycles.

Accent and syncopation

The notes of rhythms that are given special emphasis and a little extra "oomph" during a musical performance are called **accents,** or accented notes. Usually an accent is produced by simply playing one note more loudly than the notes surrounding it.

Accents often fall directly with the main beats, but they may fall in-between the beats as well. An accented note that falls between beats is called a **syncopation.** Some music features little syncopation (the Beethoven's Ninth Symphony excerpt of **CD ex. #1-2**) or none at all (a conventional rendition of "The Alphabet Song"). Other music features an abundance of syncopation, in which case it may be described as highly syncopated music (James Brown's "I Got You [I Feel Good]"). Listen to **CD ex. #1-22,** focusing on the rhythm of the vocal shouts. This is an example of *bhangra* music from India, to which we will return in Chapter 8. The rhythmic accompaniment of the drums outlines a strong, steady beat. Against this, the shouts of "Hoi!" create syncopated accents between the main beats.

The term *syncopation,* like most Western music terminology, is culturally loaded. Much West African music (see also Chapter 10) is described by Western listeners as "highly syncopated" (for illustrations, listen to **CD ex. #2-7** or **CD ex. #3-14**), but the majority of West Africans do not think of it that way at all. From their perspective, the "syncopation" designation is simply not relevant because they hear and feel the music in a different way.

West African drum ensemble.

bhangra (BHAHNG-rah)

Tempo

The element of **tempo** is one of the easiest aspects of rhythm to comprehend. The word *tempo* (Italian for time) simply refers to *the rate at which the beats pass in music.* Tempos range from very slow, to slow, medium-slow, medium (moderate), medium-fast, fast, and very fast. Try singing "The Alphabet Song" at several different tempos (just alter the speed of the beats to change the tempo). Note how the feeling and character of the music seem to transform as the tempo changes. Tempos may be *constant* (steady, unchanging, metronomic) or they may be *variable* (speeding up and/or slowing down within the course of a performance). They may *accelerate* or *decelerate,* suddenly or gradually.

A gradual acceleration in tempo is used as a device to heighten musical excitement in many music traditions. An example of this effect may be heard in the excerpt of the song "Zorba the Greek" on **CD ex. #1-23.** As you listen to the selection, try clapping along with the beat and notice how dramatically the tempo increases.

Free rhythm

Thus far, our discussion of the elements of rhythm has related specifically to music in which there is a discernible beat, and, in turn, usually a discernible meter and tempo as well. Such music is called *metric music*

The Athenians, the group featured on CD ex. #1-23.

A South Indian music performance, featuring vina (right) and mrdangam.

(i.e., measured music). Not all music is metric, however. Much of it is *nonmetric*, or in **free rhythm.** Music in free rhythm does not have a discernible beat. It tends to float across time rather than march in step to it. **CD ex. #1-24** begins with music played in free rhythm on an instrument from South India called the *vina*. Then, just before the drum (called a *mrdangam*) enters, a beat is established and the drum part marks out a metric cycle (of eight beats). Note the difference between the nonmetric and metric sections, and see if you can "find the beat" once the drum part begins. We will learn more about this type of music in Chapter 8 (pp. 122–124).

vina (VEE-nah)

mrdangam (mir-DUNG-ahm)

Summary

Rhythm was the focus of this chapter. Our examination of rhythm followed a brief overview of the four basic properties of tones—duration, frequency, amplitude, and timbre—with rhythm defined as the fundamental musical correlate of duration. We explored rhythm through both participatory exercises based on familiar songs and discussions of recorded examples representing diverse world music traditions. Elements of rhythm including beat, subdivision, meter, metric cycle, accent, syncopation, tempo, and free rhythm were introduced.

Key Terms

duration	eighth notes	metric cycle
frequency	quarter notes	accents
amplitude	beat	syncopation
timbre	subdivision	tempo
rhythm	measure	free rhythm
sixteenth notes	meter	

Study Questions

- What are the four basic properties of tones and how is each defined?
- What is rhythm?
- What are quarter notes, eighth notes, and sixteenth notes?
- How is the rhythm of a piece of music defined by its relation to elements such as beat, subdivision, meter, accents, syncopation, and tempo?
- What musical examples used in this chapter were in duple meter? Triple meter? Other meters? Which illustrated duple subdivision? Triple subdivision?

- What is a backbeat, and in what types of music are you likely to find backbeat accents?
- How do backbeat accents change the rhythmic feel, or groove, of music?
- What is the difference between metric music and music in free rhythm?

Applying What You Have Learned

- Listen to a variety of songs and pieces from your personal music collection (focusing especially on ones with which you have the greatest familiarity) and try to identify different elements of rhythm present in each of them. Locate the beat of the song, then see if you can determine the level of subdivision (e.g., duple, triple, quadruple, other) and the meter (again, duple, triple, quadruple, other) by using the listening skills you have developed in this chapter.

- Listen to two or more pieces of music from your personal collection that are representative of the same musical style (e.g., two hip-hop tunes) and identify as many elements of rhythm as you can; next, listen to one or two other pieces in a contrasting musical style (e.g., a pop ballad) and do the same. Compare your findings. What does this reveal about *general* similarities and differences in rhythmic approach between the two styles?

- Take a familiar song ("Mary Had a Little Lamb" will do) and sing it several times in a row, each time at a different tempo—slow, medium, fast, very fast, variable. How does changing the tempo change the feeling and spirit of the song overall? What does this tell you about the significance of tempo in music?

- Get together with a friend or two and play a rhythm game. Clap out the rhythm of a familiar song (e.g., "The Alphabet Song," "The Star-Spangled Banner") without actually singing the tune and see if your friend(s) can identify the tune on the basis of that rhythmic performance alone. Then switch roles and have someone else clap out tunes while you try to identify them.

Resources for Further Study

Visit the Online Learning Center at www.mhhe.com/bakan2e, as well as the author's personally maintained Web site at www.michaelbakan.com, for additional learning aids, study help, and resources that supplement the content of this chapter.

how **music works,** part II:
pitch

Pitch is the element of music that pertains to *the highness and lowness of musical tones.* In terms of the four basic properties of tones (duration, frequency, amplitude, timbre), pitch is related specifically to *frequency.*

Musical tones, and indeed all sounds, result from vibrations (usually in air) that create *soundwaves.* The rate of vibration in a soundwave varies from one tone to another. Tones with many vibrations per second have high frequencies. Those with fewer vibrations per second have lower frequencies. Correspondingly, high-frequency tones have higher pitches than low-frequency tones.

To track the pitch of a song is to track how the notes go "up" and "down" from one to the next. The particular sequence of pitches that unfolds is what we hear as the song's **melody.** Every melody has its own distinctive features:

- *Melodic range:* the distance in pitch from the lowest note to the highest note.
- *Melodic direction:* the upward (ascending) and/or downward (descending) movement of the melody as it progresses from note to note.
- *Melodic contour:* the overall "shape" of the melody, which is a product of its range, direction, and other features.

Pitch and melody in "Mary Had a Little Lamb" and a Native American Eagle Dance song

Hum the tune of "Mary Had a Little Lamb," leaving out the words. This is the *melody* of the song. Now go back and start again and add in the words, but sing just the first five notes. Notice how your voice—or, more specifically, the *pitch* of your voice—first moves down two steps ("Ma-ry had"), then comes back up two steps ("a lit-"[tle lamb]), arriving back at the starting pitch on the fifth note (Figure 4.1). This descending-ascending arc of pitches is immediately identifiable as the beginning of the melody of "Mary Had a Little Lamb." Its *melodic direction* is a distinctive feature of the song's *melodic contour*.

Now sing through "Mary" from start to finish. Notice that the pitches never get very much higher or lower than the pitch of the starting note. This is because it is a song with a limited, or narrow, *melodic range*.

The melodic range of the song heard in **CD ex. #1-25** is considerably larger than that of "Mary Had a Little Lamb," and other characteristics of the melody are different in distinctive ways as well. This is an Eagle Dance song of the Northern Arapaho people. Such songs are frequently played in accompaniment of competitive dance performances at Native American and First Nations powwow celebrations (see also Chapter 2). Arapaho traditional songs, like those of other music cultures of the Great Plains region (e.g., Ojibwa, Sioux, Omaha, Pawnee, Cheyenne), have a signature pattern of melodic contour: they usually unfold as a series of *descending melodic phrases*. An approximation of the contours of the three descending phrases of the "Eagle Dance" excerpt included on the CD is charted out in graphic form in Figure 4.2 on the next page.

Arapaho (Ah-RA-pa-ho)

Names of pitches in Western music

In order to distinguish between different pitches, the Western music system assigns letter names to them, from A to G: A B C D E F G. There are also some pitches that fall "in the cracks" between the ones with just plain letter names. There is, for example, a pitch that falls exactly halfway between C and D. If we identify that pitch as being a bit higher than a regular C, it is referred to as C-sharp (C♯). If, alternatively, we identify it as being a bit lower than D, it is called D-flat (D♭). In the always metaphorical language of music terminology, "sharpening" a note means making it a bit higher, while "flattening" it means making it a bit lower. Notes that are neither sharpened nor flattened are called "naturals" (e.g., C-natural, D-natural).

Melodic contour of the opening notes of "Mary Had a Little Lamb."

FIGURE 4.1

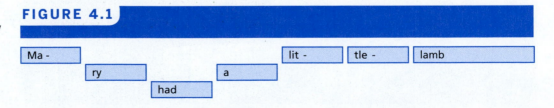

FIGURE 4.2

Melodic contour in "Eagle Dance" (CD ex. #1-25).

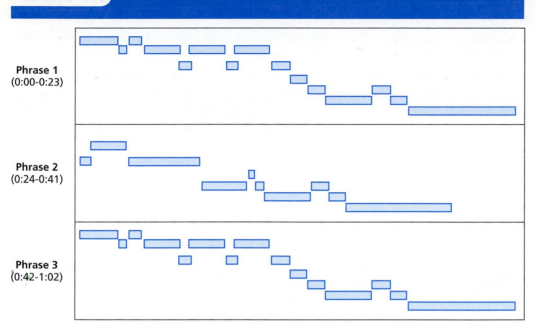

Phrase 1 (0:00-0:23)

Phrase 2 (0:24-0:41)

Phrase 3 (0:42-1:02)

Labeling the pitches of tones with letter names only works in certain cases, such as for voices and for instruments like the piano, guitar, violin, flute, trumpet, and xylophone, all of which are described as having *determinate pitch*. The tones produced on other instruments—shakers, cymbals, triangles, most kinds of drums—cannot be identified by a single-pitch letter-name. These are instruments of *indeterminate pitch,* which means that rather than being dominated by just one pitch, the individual tones they produce generate many different pitches that compete for the ear's attention all at once, with no clear "winner" among them. The difference between determinate and indeterminate pitches can be seen visually in computer graphics of their respective soundwaves, as illustrated in Figure 4.3 on page 48.

Song performance at a powwow. All of the singers are seen playing together on the large powwow drum at the center of their circle as they sing. This is the customary mode of performance.

The melodic direction of a song may have important *cultural* ramifications. Earlier (Chapter 2, p. 11), we learned that Warao shamans in Venezuela use certain types of songs to cure illnesses and other kinds of songs to *cause* illnesses. Research on the music of the Warao by the ethnomusicologist Dale Olsen convincingly demonstrates that the shamanistic curing songs consistently have descending melodies, while the shamanistic "inflicting songs" (the ones performed with the intent of causing illness or even death) consistently conclude with ascending melodies (Olsen 1996: 262–63). This is a clear instance of music as sound and music as culture integrally informing one another.

octave (OCK-tiv)

The Western pitch system and the octave

The pitch system for most Western music is based on the series of 12 determinate pitches that are laid out as the white and black keys on a piano keyboard (Figure 4.4). Playing all 12 notes in sequence from low to high or from high to low yields what is known as the *chromatic scale*. A **scale** is *an ascending and/or descending series of notes of different pitch*. Songs and other pieces of music are typically "built" from the notes of particular scales, much as words, sentences, and stories are built from the letters of the alphabet.

Computer-generated images of indeterminate and determinate pitch soundwaves.

FIGURE 4.3

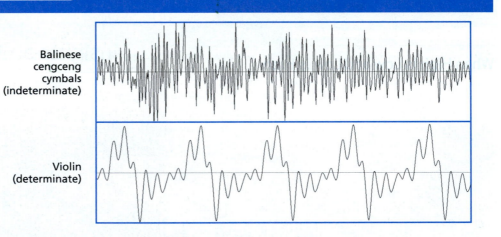

Balinese cengceng cymbals (indeterminate)

Violin (determinate)

Labeled pitches on the piano keyboard.

FIGURE 4.4

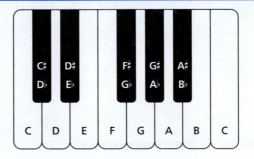

Scale versus Mode

Related to but broader than the idea of a scale is that of a **mode.** Whereas a scale essentially comprises a "raw" sequence of pitches, a mode is something more comprehensive and multidimensional. The rules of the mode tell the musician not only *what* pitches can be used in a given piece or performance, but also offer instructions on *how* to use each of those pitches. Rules pertaining to how certain notes of the mode's scale are to be ornamented, how to move from one pitch to another in an appropriate manner, and which notes should receive relatively more or less emphasis are built into the melodic system of a mode. So too are a variety of features that might be classified as *extramusical.* Particular modes may be identified with certain emotions, times of the day, or seasons of the year, or with specific episodes of dramatic performances or rituals. We will encounter examples of modal systems in later chapters.

Listen to the ascending chromatic scale illustration of **Online Musical Illustration #1** (located at the Online Learning Center at www.mhhe.com/bakan2e). It has all 12 notes of the scale, yet it sounds incomplete. Now listen to **Online Musical Illustration #2.** This one has a more satisfying conclusion because it adds a 13th, final note that is actually of the same pitch as the *first* note: both the first and last note have a pitch of C (Figure 4.4).

This may be a bit confusing, since the last note is clearly higher in pitch than the first one. How can they be "the same"? The answer: they are the same pitch an **octave** apart. The octave

When High Is Low and Low Is High

In our discussion of aspects of pitch like the octave, pitch ranges, and melodic direction in this chapter, there has been an implicit assumption that we all know what the difference is between "high" and "low" where pitch is concerned. It is part of our "commonsense" knowledge in this culture that the voice ranges of women are generally *higher* than the voice ranges of men, or that a relatively small instrument like a flute plays higher pitches than a very large instrument like a tuba.

Yet ethnomusicological research reveals that such seemingly basic, common-knowledge "facts" about musical sound—known to nonmusicians and musicians alike—may be more culture-specific, indeed more arbitrary, than they first appear to be. The 'Are'are (Ah-ray Ah-ray) people of Malaita (Solomon Islands, Micronesia) recognize that there are different pitches in their music, and that the musical tones range in pitch from low to high. However, their cultural conception of pitch is completely the reverse of ours. What they refer to as low pitches are what we in the West think of as high pitches; what they identify as high pitches are what we call low pitches (Zemp 1979). Therefore, from an 'Are'are perspective, the most "commonsense" assumptions that Westerners have about pitch are turned, quite literally, upside down.

is a musical phenomenon that is nearly universally recognized in the world's music traditions (though it is known by many different names in different cultures and languages). Its existence explains why a man and a woman can sing the exact same melody together even though the woman's voice produces much higher pitches than the man's. Men and women sing in different octave **ranges** (or *registers*). The phenomenon of the octave also explains why a version of a tune played on a tuba (an instrument with a very low pitch range) is recognizable as having the same melody as a version played on a flute (an instrument with a much higher pitch range). It is the same melody in both cases, but played in different octave ranges.

Common scales in Western music: Major, pentatonic, minor, and blues

In the conventional pitch system of Western music, the octave is divided into the 12 evenly spaced pitches of the chromatic scale, and this sequence of pitches climbs higher and higher (or descends lower and lower) as it spans across different octave ranges. In some styles of music, all 12 pitches are employed and have more or less equal "status." More often, however, songs and other pieces are constructed from the notes of musical scales that use only certain, select pitches out of the 12 available ones. These include the major scale, pentatonic scales, minor scales, and the blues scale. Though these scales are specifically linked to the Western music tradition and its particular system of pitch organization, there are at least two reasons why they nonetheless provide a viable point of departure for understanding what musical scales are and how they work in the world's musics more generally. The first reason is that Western scales (and pitch-related aspects of Western music overall) have either influenced or been fully adopted into many music traditions worldwide during the modern era. The second reason is that by examining how some common Western scales work, we can develop a set of basic terms, concepts, and listening skills that will serve us well in exploring the scales and pitch systems of other world music traditions we encounter, even ones that have no direct relationship to Western music.

MAJOR SCALE The **major scale** can be produced using the white keys of the piano only, starting on the pitch C (Figure 4.5). It has seven pitches per octave. Each represents one *scale degree*, or "step." For example, in the C-major scale shown in Figure 4.5, the pitch C is the first scale degree, or **tonic;** D is the second scale degree; E, the third scale degree; and so on. **Online Musical Illustration #3** provides an illustration of a C-major scale, moving through all seven scale degrees and ending with the pitch C an octave above the starting note. Major scales can be created with any of the 12 chromatic pitches as the tonic, but only the C-major scale can be produced with the white keys only.

Many songs in the Western music tradition are built predominantly or even exclusively from the notes of major scales (e.g., "The Alphabet Song," "Mary Had a Little Lamb"). Such songs are described as being in a major **key.** Music in major keys tends to have "happy" connotations for Western listeners, mainly because people in the West have been *culturally conditioned* to perceive major-key music in this way.

C-major scale pitches on the piano keyboard.

FIGURE 4.5

PENTATONIC SCALE A **pentatonic scale** has only five pitches per octave. Many varieties exist, in Indonesia, China, Japan, Uganda, and elsewhere. The most common pentatonic scale in Western music is essentially a major scale minus the fourth and seventh scale degrees. Thus, with a tonic of C, it includes the notes C D E G A (Figure 4.6). You can hear this scale in **Online Musical Illustration #4,** while **Online Musical Illustration #5** illustrates the same type of scale, but with D as the tonic (i.e., D E F♯ A B). The identical form of pentatonic scale with a tonic pitch of F♯ is played using only the black keys of the piano keyboard (Figure 4.7).

MINOR SCALES **Minor scales,** like major scales, employ seven pitches per octave. They come in a couple of different varieties. **Online Musical Illustration #6** provides an illustration of, first, a major scale; second, a type of minor scale called the *harmonic minor scale;* and third, a type of minor scale called the *melodic minor scale.* Notice how the last of these uses a different set of pitches when it ascends than when it descends.

The most important distinction between major and minor scales has to do with the distance in pitch between the second and third scale degrees of each. The distance between any two notes, whether in a scale or a melody, is called an **interval.** The interval between the second and third degrees in a major scale is always a bit (i. e., a half-step) larger than that between the second and third degrees of a minor scale. This small difference has a big effect on how we perceive music in major and minor keys. It alone can account for conventional Western distinctions between a melody that sounds "happy" (major key) and one that sounds "sad" (minor key). You can hear this in the comparison of two different versions of "Mary Had a Little Lamb" performed by the saxophonist Patrick Meighan in **Online Musical Illustration #7.** The first version is in a major key; the second, in a minor key. Notice how much "sadder" this normally "happy" song becomes merely on account of the lowering of a single pitch (i.e., the third scale degree) in the version based on the minor scale.

FIGURE 4.6

Comparison of pitches of the C-major scale and the C-pentatonic scale.

Scale degree	1	2	3	4	5	6	7
Pitch	C	D	E	F	G	A	B
Pentatonic scale	■	■	■		■	■	
C-major scale	■	■	■	■	■	■	■

FIGURE 4.7

"Black key" pentatonic scale starting on F#.

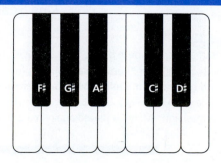

FIGURE 4.8

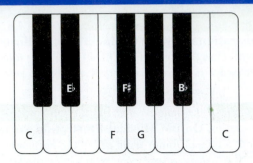

BLUES SCALE The **blues scale** combines features of major, minor, pentatonic, and traditional African scales. Starting on the pitch C, it essentially includes six main pitches: C E♭ F F♯ G B♭ (**Online Musical Illustration #8**). Three of these—E♭, F♯, and B♭ (along with variant versions of each that defy simple letter-name identification)—may be described as the "blue notes" (Figure 4.8). These largely account for the "bluesy" sound of music based on this scale.

The blues scale is used not just in blues per se. It also is present in many other styles of music around the world that have been influenced by blues and other African American traditions. In bluesman Charles Atkins' "A Funny Way of Asking," the melody, sung by Atkins (**CD ex. #1-19,** starting at 0:21), is fully rooted in the blues scale.

Pitch and scales in non-Western musical systems

slendro (slen-djroh)

pelog (PAY-lawg)

The Western pitch system is but one of a great many such systems in the world of music. In Indonesian *gamelan* music (see Chapter 7), there are two main pitch systems, one called *slendro* and the other called *pelog*. Neither has anything to do with the 12-part division of the octave used in Western music, nor with the major, minor, pentatonic, blues, or other Western scales. Rather, they are unique unto themselves. An example of a slendro-based scale and a pelog-based scale, respectively, may be heard in **Online Musical Illustration #10.** Both of these scales use five notes per octave—that is, they are pentatonic—but neither is the same as the Western pentatonic scale discussed earlier (though the slendro scale does sound something like it!). The notes of these scales may sound "out of tune" to your ears, but this is only because you are unaccustomed to them. Western scales would likely sound equally "out of tune" to you if you had been raised listening only to gamelan music.

Twenty-two distinct pitches per octave are recognized in certain classical music traditions of India. Like their Western counterparts, Indian musicians often build pieces and musical

insights and perspectives

Modulation: Moving from One Scale and Key to Another

In some music, different sections of a piece will be in different keys; that is, they will draw their pitches from different scales and/or have a different tonic, or "home note." Moving from one key to another during the course of a musical work is called **modulation. Online Musical Illustration #9** offers an example of a modulation. First you hear the tune of "Mary Had a Little Lamb" played in the key of C major. Then there is a modulation (i.e., the key changes) and "Mary" is played again in a different key (specifically, F major).

performances from scales comprised of seven ascending and seven descending pitches, but they have many more pitches upon which to draw in generating these scales.

Middle Eastern music in the Arab tradition (see Chapter 12) is also built from systems of tiny intervals, or **microtones.** Instead of 22 pitches per octave, though, the Arab music system has 24. The Egyptian quarter-tone accordion featured in **CD ex. #1-26** is a standard Western-type accordion adapted to produce 24 pitches per octave rather than the customary 12. (**Online Musical Illustration #11** provides a saxophone illustration of a microtonal scale with 24 pitches per octave.) This accordion is also designed with special features that allow for the sophisticated forms of melodic **ornamentation**—that is, "decoration" of the main notes of the melody—that are heard in the example. Intricate ornamentation of melodies is a key feature of Arab music, and of many Indian (Chapter 8), Celtic (Chapter 9), West African (Chapter 10), East Asian (Chapter 13), and other global music traditions as well. The accordion playing here additionally offers excellent examples of diverse styles of **articulation,** such as the short, clipped notes that may be described as having **staccato** articulations and the contrastingly long, sustained ones that are called **legato.** As you listen, try to recognize these distinctive features of pitch, ornamentation, and articulation.

Pitch, Chords, and Harmony

Notes of different pitch may occur either one after the other (sequentially) or simultaneously. Generally speaking, a series of notes presented one after the other yields a melody, whereas a group of two or more notes of different pitch sounded simultaneously yields a **chord.** A chord that "makes sense" within the context of its musical style is called a **harmony.** Western music has its own rules and aesthetics of harmony. Other musical traditions have theirs too, and these often have nothing whatsoever to do with what we in the West perceive as sounding "right" or sounding "wrong."

Chords come in many varieties. Sometimes there is just a single chord underlying an entire piece of music, as is the case, for example, in many hip-hop recordings. Other times, the music moves steadily from one chord to another, creating what is known as a **chord progression.** The guitar part of the first section of **CD ex. #1-27** provides a good and clear example of a chord progression. This is a well-known *bossa nova* song called "Wave," composed by the great Brazilian composer Antonio Carlos Jobim and performed here by a quartet led by alto saxophonist Paul Desmond, who was best known for his work with the Dave Brubeck Quartet. The guitarist on this track is Ed Bickert, an important figure in the history of Canadian jazz. We will return to this recording and to the subject of bossa nova more generally in Chapter 11 (see pp. 229–231).

bossa nova
(bah-sah NO-vah)

Jobim (Joe-BEEM)

In some types of music, each note of the melody becomes the basis of its own chord. This results in what will be referred to in this text as **harmonization.** The vocal parts of **CD ex. #1-2** (from Beethoven's Ninth Symphony) and **CD ex. #1-11** (a Fijian church hymn) provide two beautiful examples of harmonization, each unique in its power of expression.

Chords may also be broken up, with their individual tones presented one after another in sequence rather than all at once. This quasi-melodic type of "broken chord" harmony is called an **arpeggio,** or arpeggiated chord. Spanish *flamenco* guitar music such as that featured in **CD ex. #1-28** includes an abundance of arpeggios, which are a signature element of the music's style.

arpeggio
(ahr-PEH-jee-oh)

As was alluded to earlier, the rules and aesthetics of chords and harmony need not have anything to do with Western music standards or conventions. Listen again to **CD ex. #1-3,** the Japanese gagaku selection from Chapter 1. This, too, might be described as a type of harmonized music with chords—there are even some arpeggios—but the chords and harmonies depend on the logic of a system of pitch organization that is radically different (and much older!) than the one to which we in the West are accustomed. To Western listeners, gagaku harmonies tend to sound "strange," but again, Western harmonies would likely sound just as strange, just as *dissonant,* to someone who had been raised listening only to gagaku music. (Chapter 13 examines gagaku in more detail. See p. 322).

In **CD ex. #1-29,** the prevalence of dissonant chords and harmonies has a different basis. The piece, "Thgirbla .W," is a work for solo *zheng* (see Chapter 13) by the Taiwanese/American composer Chihchun Chi-sun Lee, who did her graduate studies in music composition at the University of Michigan. Though this is a work written for a traditional Chinese instrument, the musical vocabulary is entirely Western; its style and idiom might even be said to trace back in lineage to the works of composers such as Beethoven. The pitch system and the foundational elements of melody, harmony, and rhythm heard here actually share much in common with those of a piece like Beethoven's Ninth Symphony, but they have been transformed and manipulated in a myriad of ways, sometimes to the point of seemingly *defying* the very tradition they reference. Music like this challenges conventions, and in doing so it challenges us, as listeners, to expand our musical horizons as well.

zheng (jung [rhymes with "lung"])

Summary

The musical element of pitch was the topic of this chapter. We learned that the pitch of any given tone is determined by its frequency, or rate of vibration. We also learned that some tones have a determinate pitch whereas others are of indeterminate pitch.

Melody was our point of departure for looking at and listening to how pitch works in actual musical contexts. Melodic range, direction, and contour were shown to be basic features distinguishing one melody from another. From there, we moved on to the pitch system of Western music, common Western scales (major, minor, pentatonic, blues), and pitch systems in other world music traditions that are essentially unrelated to the Western system and build from different principles of organization. Pitch-related elements such as modulation, microtones, and melodic ornamentation also were introduced.

The final part of the chapter was devoted to how pitch relates to chords and harmony. Again, both Western and non-Western systems were examined.

Key Terms

melody
scale
mode
octave
ranges
major scale
tonic
key

pentatonic scale
minor scales
interval
blues scale
modulation
microtones
ornamentation
articulation

staccato
legato
chord
harmony
chord progression
harmonization
arpeggio

Study Questions

- As rhythm is to duration, pitch is to _____.
- What is a melody? What were the three principal features of a melody identified?
- What was distinctive about the melodic direction in "Eagle Dance" (CD ex. #1-25), and how is this musiculturally significant? How is the specific cultural function of a Warao shaman's song revealed by *its* melodic direction?
- What are pitch ranges, and how do they relate to the phenomenon of the octave?
- What does it mean to say that a particular song is "in the key of C major" or "in the key of D minor"?
- What are distinguishing features of the major scale, pentatonic scale, minor scales, and blues scale, as discussed in this chapter?
- What does it mean when we say that there is a modulation in a piece of music?
- What, in general, distinguishes a scale from a mode?
- What is the difference in sound between a chord that is harmonized (as defined in this chapter) and one that is arpeggiated? What is a chord progression?

Applying What You Have Learned

- Listen to several pieces from your personal music collection and try to identify instances where the music is built from major, pentatonic, minor, or blues scale-based melodies and chords. Use the listening skills you have developed in this chapter—as well as your subjective impressions of the music (does it sound "happy," "sad," "bluesy," etc.)—to make your determinations.

Resources for Further Study

Visit the Online Learning Center at www.mhhe.com/bakan2e, as well as the author's personally maintained Web site at www.michaelbakan.com, for additional learning aids, study help, and resources that supplement the content of this chapter.

how **music works,** part III:
dynamics, timbre, and instruments

Dynamics, timbre, and music instruments account for what the different tones of music *sound like*. This, then, is a chapter that explores the characteristics and qualities of music sounds themselves and that also examines the material resources involved in their making.

Dynamics

When we speak of *dynamics* in music, we are referring to how loud or how soft the different tones are; in other words, to their *amplitude*. Music is filled with "small" and "big" sounds covering a continuum from silence at one extreme to potentially deafening loudness at the other. The various gradations along the way (e.g., very soft, soft, medium, loud, very loud) account for dynamics.

The computer-generated image reproduced in Figure 5.1 represents the dynamics of the saxophone tone heard in **Online Musical Illustration #12.** This tone starts soft, then has a **crescendo** (it gets gradually louder), and then a **decrescendo** (it gets gradually softer). Compare this to the tone heard in **Online Musical Illustration #13,** which is represented visually in Figure 5.2. Here, the dynamic level changes quite suddenly—from soft to loud and from loud to soft—rather than gradually. This results in a tone with *terraced dynamics.*

In scientific terms, the amplitude of a tone is measured in *decibels.* The higher the decibel count, the louder the sound. But this kind of "absolute" measurement is less significant for our purposes than thinking of how loud or soft the different notes in a piece of music are *relative to each other.* This is mainly what accounts for what we perceive as dynamics. Dynamic levels may change from loud to soft, suddenly or gradually, as we have seen; there also may be instances in which different instruments are played at different dynamic levels at the same time.

Our perceptions of dynamics are often context-dependent. A "loud" dynamic level in a heavy metal rock band's performance is going to be much louder, in *absolute* terms (i.e., in decibels), than a "loud" dynamic level in a solo flute recital. On the other hand, the **dynamic range**—that is, the range between the softest and loudest notes—in the flute performance will likely be greater than that of the rock band, since Western classical music usually relies more on *dynamic contrast* to achieve its aesthetic goals than does heavy metal music.

Computer-generated image of a tone with crescendo and decrescendo.

FIGURE 5.1

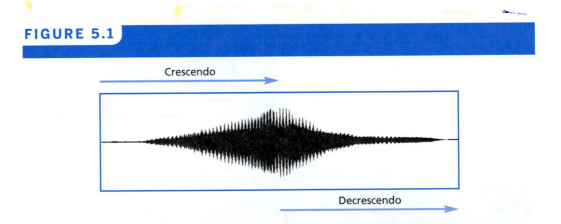

Crescendo

Decrescendo

Computer-generated image of a tone with terraced dynamics.

FIGURE 5.2

To describe timbre is to attempt to account for the *character or quality of a musical tone or tones*. Differences in timbre are primarily what enable us to distinguish between the sounds of a trumpet and a flute, or between those of an **acoustic** (unamplified) guitar and an electric (amplified) guitar. Tones of the exact same pitch, register, duration, and amplitude played on these different instruments sound different. It is their distinct timbres that distinguish them from one another. Different types of **ensembles** (music groups, whether vocal, instrumental, or a combination) also have characteristic timbres. A choir (ensemble of singers) sounds categorically different than a symphony orchestra, which, in turn, has a completely different timbre than a heavy metal band. The *genuinely* "heavy metal" sound of a Caribbean-style steel band like the one heard on **CD ex. #1-30** takes us into yet another timbral universe. Steel band music is discussed in Chapter 11 (see the photo, p. 230).

In **Online Musical Illustration #14,** the first sound you hear is a tone played on a saxophone. The second is a tone of essentially the same pitch, register, duration, and amplitude played on a flute. What differentiates these two tones is their distinct timbres, which can be represented visually using computer-generated images called *spectrograms* (Figure 5.3).

The different shapes of these spectrograms, and in turn the different timbres of the tones they represent, can be explained by the fact that every tone is actually comprised of multiple pitches, not just the single pitch that you generally perceive when a note is played on an instrument such as a saxophone or a flute (e.g., the pitch C, or A, or F♯). Each one of these many pitch components of a tone is called a *partial*. A spectrogram is essentially a snapshot of all of the partials contained in a tone, as well as of the loudness (amplitude) of each of the partials relative to all the others. The actual timbre you hear when a tone is played on a saxophone or flute is the audible equivalent of that snapshot. Just as the flute and saxophone tones look different in computer images, they sound different in terms of their respective timbres.

A tone consists of two types of partials: the fundamental pitch (represented as the darkest part of a spectrogram) and a series of *overtones,* or **harmonics.** The fundamental pitch is often so much louder than the harmonics that it basically absorbs them. We hear the note as having a pitch of F, or of B♭, or whatever the fundamental pitch is. We *do* hear the overtones, too, but not as distinct pitches; rather, they merge together with each other and with the fundamental pitch to generate the tone's distinctive timbre.

In some music traditions, the ability of performers to manipulate the relationship between the fundamental pitch of a tone and its harmonics through techniques that generate

FIGURE 5.3

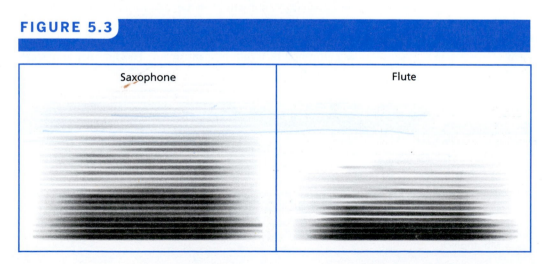

Spectrograms of saxophone and flute tones.

a great variety of timbres has been developed to a very high art. This is certainly the case with the Aboriginal Australian **didgeridoo,** which we heard earlier on **CD ex. #1-13** ("Ibis," by Alan Maralung).

As we learned in Chapter 2, a traditional didgeridoo is constructed from a long wooden branch (usually eucalyptus) that has been hollowed out by termites. A ring of beeswax or eucalyptus gum may be affixed to the narrower end of the instrument into which the player blows, serving as a kind of mouthpiece (see Figure 5.4; see also the photo on p. 25). Using a difficult technique called *circular breathing,* which involves breathing in through the nose and out through the mouth at the same time, the skilled didgeridoo player is able to produce a continuous tone uninterrupted by breath pauses. But while the tone goes on continuously, its timbre is constantly being transformed. Changing the shape and positioning of his or her mouth relative to the instrument and employing a variety of different blowing techniques, the player manipulates the relationship between the fundamental pitch and its harmonics in myriad ways, thereby creating a veritable world of timbral diversity from a single tone.

The marvelous sound and wide timbral scope of the didgeridoo is illustrated in a traditional context in "Ibis" (**CD ex. #1-13**). **CD ex. #1-31** features the instrument in a more contemporary musical setting: a funk-inspired didgeridoo duet called "Axis."

Like the didgeridoo, the human voice is capable of some rather remarkable feats of timbral manipulation through the use of harmonics. Vocal traditions of Central Asian cultures in Mongolia and Tuva display the potential of the voice in this regard to a degree that is almost unfathomable. The Mongolian *khoomii* ("overtone singing") song of **CD ex. #1-6,** to which we were introduced in Chapter 2, is an excellent example. Other than the accompanying instrumental part (played on an instrument called a *tobshuur*), all of the different layers of sound—including the high-pitched "whistling" lines (which are not *really* whistling at all) and the ultra-low-pitched guttural tones—are produced by the voice of a single vocalist, Amartuwshin Baasandorj (he can be seen on p. 12). He manipulates the relationships between the fundamental pitches and harmonics of the tones he sings to yield a dazzling array of timbres. By shaping and positioning his mouth and altering his vocal apparatus in many ways, Baasandorj changes the balance of fundamental pitches and harmonics so dramatically that he not only produces a broad palette of timbres, but actually creates the effect that he is singing not just one but multiple tones *at the same time.* Thus, singing of this type is sometimes described as *multiphonic* singing (i.e., "multiple sound" or "multiple tone" singing).

Differences in timbre enable us to distinguish not only between different types of tones—vocal tones, trumpet tones, flute tones, didgeridoo tones—but also between similar types of tones performed by different musicians. An experienced jazz listener will be able to tell you whether the tenor saxophonist on a particular recording is John Coltrane or Lester Young from hearing just a single note; and even a casual listener will likely be able to pick out the voice of Dave Matthews, Bob Dylan, or Louis Armstrong from a recording with just a few notes to go on.

Online Musical Illustration #15 includes a series of five instrumental and vocal tones, each representing the "same" note performed by a different musician. The first two tones are

Didgeridoo.

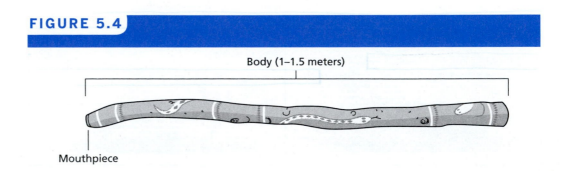

FIGURE 5.4

Body (1–1.5 meters)

Mouthpiece

played by saxophonists with distinctive "sounds." The remaining three are sung by different vocalists (male, male, and female, respectively). What words might you use to describe and compare the distinct timbres of the two saxophone tones? Or to compare and contrast the different timbral qualities of the three vocal tones?

Trying to come up with just the right words to describe and compare different timbres is challenging. This is because the descriptive language associated with timbre in English and other Western languages tends to be rather impressionistic, consisting of a veritable grab-bag of different types of metaphors. The timbres of music are described variously in terms of textures (gravelly, velvety, airy—not to be confused with *musical* textures, to which subject we will return in Chapter 6), human anatomy (nasal, guttural, throaty), metaphysics (ethereal, heavenly, otherworldly), emotions (cheery, somber, melancholy), technological "spheres" (industrial, techno, space-age), socioeconomic classes (rich, majestic), and food (creamy, sweet). The "master metaphor" for timbre is color, by virtue of the fact that timbre is very often *defined* as "tone color." Yet paradoxically, color designations are rarely used in connection with actual timbres: the "blue notes" in blues music and related styles (see page 52) get their name from their pitches, not their timbres; "red hot" music is usually described as such due to its fast tempos and loud dynamics rather than anything to do with its palette of tone colors.

Altogether, the timbral lexicon available to us, in English at least, is anything but precise or objective. (Terms used to describe timbres in some other languages, such as Japanese, are in many respects richer and more exact.) Often, the most distinctive verbal "description" we can provide of a tone's timbre is to identify the name of the *instrument* that produces it. **Online Musical Illustration #16** illustrates this point. In it, you will hear a series of tones played on various world music instruments. No matter how the tones are produced on any one of these, it would be difficult to mistake one instrument for another, since the basic timbre of each is so distinct. A list of the instruments featured in the example is provided in Table 5.1.

Music Instruments

Music comes into being through the sounds of music instruments. A **music instrument** is here defined as *any sound-generating medium used to produce tones in the making of music*. This includes the human voice; all manner of traditional instruments associated with the world's music

TABLE 5.1	World music instruments featured in Online Musical Illustration #16.
Time	**Description**
0:00–0:06	Indonesian angklung
0:07–0:18	Mexican guitarrón
0:19–0:26	Ugandan madinda (amadinda "xylophone")
0:27–0:37	Native American powwow drum
0:38–0:48	Javanese gong
0:49–0:53	Japanese sho (mouth organ)
0:54–0:59	West African axatse (rattle)
1:00–1:07	Appalachian dulcimer
1:08–1:19	Balinese suling (bamboo flute)
1:20–1:24	Andean siku panpipes

traditions (guitar, violin, trumpet, flute, didgeridoo, cymbals, maracas); and the entire spectrum of instruments and devices used in computer-generated and electronic music (synthesizers, digital samplers, sound modifiers—these will be discussed later in the chapter). It also may include the sources of any other natural, "found," or newly invented sounds that music makers use with the *intention* that they be heard as musical tones, or that music listeners *perceive* as music when they hear them: gumballs rattling in a machine, a jackhammer hammering, a bird "singing."

Every music instrument has its own unique timbre and range of timbral possibilities. This is likewise true for every different combination of instruments used in an ensemble. The **instrumentation** employed in any musical work or performance—that is, the types of instruments (potentially including voices) and the number of each—largely dictates the timbral landscape of the music.

Music instrument classification

The world of music instruments is vast and diverse. Thousands upon thousands of instruments are used to make music, and individual instruments may even be used to produce tones in several different ways (plucked violin versus bowed violin, struck tambourine versus shaken tambourine). Instrument classification systems have developed over the course of the millennia and in many parts of the world. These systems have been used to account for both the shared features and unique qualities of particular instruments and types of instruments. In many instances, they also have been employed to link specific instruments to certain rituals, classes of people, or supernatural powers. The oldest documented instrument classification systems come from countries such as India and China and have histories dating back more than 3,000 years.

Elaborate instrument classification systems also have been preserved in oral/aural tradition–based societies (societies that until modern times did not have traditions of writing or literacy). The 'Are'are people of Malaita—whose "inverse" conceptions of pitch we encountered earlier (see p. 49)—have a fascinating system for classifying music instruments. Their principal category of instruments is called *'au.* 'Au means bamboo. Since the primary melodic instruments among the 'Are'are are bamboo panpipes of a type similar to those heard in **CD ex. #1-32** (which actually features Kwara'ae-style 'au music, also from Malaita), the 'Are'are classify *all* instruments capable of producing melodies (other than the voice) as "bamboo instruments" ('au). Modernization has brought an interesting twist. Since electronic devices such as tape recorders and radios are capable of "producing" melodies, the 'Are'are classify them as 'au, that is, as bamboo instruments (Zemp 1978)!

The best-known *Western* instrument classification system employs three main categories: strings, winds, and percussion. The string category includes violin, viola, cello, string bass, guitar, mandolin, and harp. Wind instruments include trumpet, French horn, trombone, tuba, flute, clarinet, bassoon, and oboe. Percussion encompasses all drums, shakers, cymbals, triangle, and xylophone. This system works quite well for most standard Western orchestral and band instruments but has limitations in its ability to logically account for the complexity of music instrument diversity on a global scale.

More flexible and globally inclusive is the **Hornbostel-Sachs classification system** (aka Sachs-Hornbostel), which was originally published in 1914 by two eminent German musicologists. This system identifies four principal instrument categories, with numerous subdivisions for each: **chordophones, aerophones, membranophones,** and **idiophones** (Hornbostel and Sachs 1992 [1914]). A fifth category, **electronophones** (or electrophones), was added later.

CHORDOPHONES Chordophones are *instruments in which the sound is activated by the vibration of a string or strings (chords) over a resonating chamber.* The guitar, harp, violin, banjo, mandolin, hammered dulcimer, Middle Eastern 'ud (**CD ex. #1-15**), South Indian vina (**CD ex. #1-24**), and Indonesian rebab (the two-string fiddle heard at the beginning of **CD ex. #1-7**) are all chordophones. East Asian *board zither chordophones* such as the Japanese *koto* (**CD ex. #2-1**) and the Chinese *zheng* (**CD ex. #1-29**) represent an important chordophone subcategory that has been in existence for many, many centuries (see Chapter 13).

dulcimer
   (DULL-si-mer)

'ud (ood)

rebab (ruh-BAHB)

zither
   (ZI-ther [rhymes
   with "hither"])

koto (KOE-toe)

zheng
   (jung [rhymes
   with "lung"])

Although all chordophones depend on the activation of some kind of "string" (or "strings") to produce sound, the methods of *sound activation* vary. Plucking, bowing, rubbing, or even striking the strings are all possibilities, and various implements—fingertips, plectra (e.g., a guitar pick), bows, or mallets—may be involved. The piano is a chordophone of a rather unique type. When you press down on the piano keys, sound is generated by the setting in motion of small, felt-tipped hammers that strike the strings hidden inside the body (resonator) of the instrument (Figure 5.5, p. 64).

The guitar is a plucked chordophone, meaning that the strings are plucked to activate the sound. Its basic construction is similar to that of many chordophones. It includes a body, or resonator, with a soundhole in the middle of it; a number of strings that are affixed to a *bridge* near one end of the instrument; and a *neck* over which the strings (usually six) pass, attaching to *tuning pegs* on the *head* at the other end. *Frets* placed along the length of the neck of the guitar divide the instrument's multi-octave pitch range into chromatic intervals (all 12 pitches of the chromatic scale) from top to bottom (Figure 5.6, p. 64).

With the possible exception of the guitar, the violin (Figure 5.7, p. 65) is probably the most widely used of all chordophones on a global scale. Like the guitar, it has a resonator (body), a bridge, strings (four), and a head with tuning pegs. The head is usually called a *scroll* on account of its distinctive shape. Instead of a round soundhole in the center of the body, the violin (like its relatives, the cello, viola, and string bass) has two f-shaped soundholes on either side of the strings. Additionally, it differs from the guitar in having no frets. As we encounter chordophones other than the violin and guitar in later chapters, we will frequently come across the same kinds of terms relating to features of their design and construction.

AEROPHONES The sounds of aerophones emerge from vibrations created by the *action of air passing through a tube or some other kind of resonator.* The Western flute, clarinet, bassoon, and oboe are aerophones, as well as Western "brass" instruments such as the trumpet, trombone, French horn, and tuba. The pipe organ (the traditional church organ, that is, not the electronic organ) is also an aerophone, since its sound, too, is activated by the passage of air through tubes (see photo, p. 66).

Internal mechanism of
a piano.

FIGURE 5.5

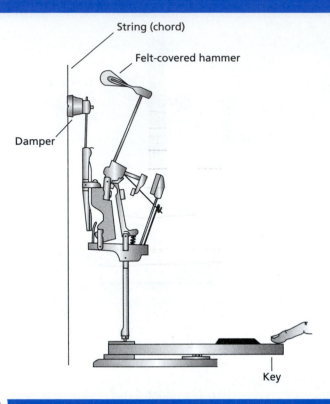

String (chord)

Felt-covered hammer

Damper

Key

Labeled diagram
of a guitar.

FIGURE 5.6

Tuning
pegs

Head

Fret

Neck

Soundhole

Body
(resonator)

Bridge

FIGURE 5.7

Violin.

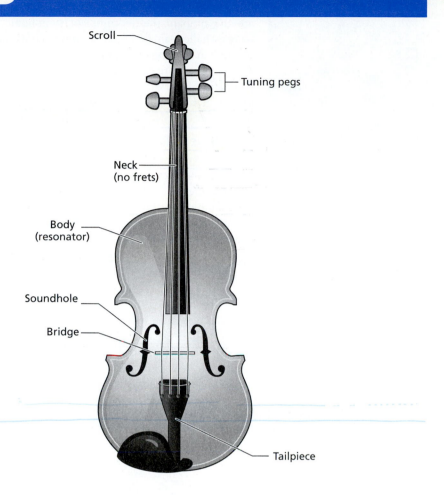

Scroll

Tuning pegs

Neck
(no frets)

Body
(resonator)

Soundhole

Bridge

Tailpiece

Other aerophones include the bamboo panpipes heard earlier on **CD ex. #1-32,** the Japanese *shakuhachi* flute (**CD ex. #1-14**), the Irish tinwhistle (**CD ex. #3-6**), and the didgeridoo (**CD exs. #1-13** and **1-31**). Some aerophones, like the Western flute, are side-blown instruments; others, like the shakuhachi, are end-blown instruments (see photos, p. 66).

shakuhachi
(sha-koo-HAH-chee)

The human voice is also an aerophone. Technically, it differs from other aerophones only because the "tube" and "resonator" of the instrument are within the human body rather than external to it. On cultural levels, however, the difference between the voice and other music instruments is usually perceived as great. Because our voices are inseparable from who we are—as individuals, social beings, carriers of culture—it is counterintuitive for us to classify the voice as just another variation on the aerophone theme. Whether singing opera, blues, or Mongolian khoomii; rapping or reciting poetry over musical accompaniment; or reciting the Qur'an in "melodious" tones, people tend to think about their voices as either representing a separate category of music instrument or as not belonging within the category of music instruments at all.

MEMBRANOPHONES The third class of instruments in the Hornbostel-Sachs system, the membranophones, includes *instruments in which the vibration of a membrane (natural or synthetic) stretched tightly across a frame resonator produces the sound.* Drums are the predominant type of instrument in this category, though there are others, like the kazoo, which are perhaps

Taylor & Boody's "Opus 20," the organ of First Presbyterian Church, Tallahassee, Florida.

less obvious inclusions. The snare drum, bass drum, and tom-toms of the Western drum set are all membranophones, as are the timpani (kettledrums) of symphonic orchestras and bands, shallow-shelled *frame drums* such as tambourines, and the Indian mrdangam drum we listened to earlier in **CD ex. #1-24.** So too are countless thousands of other types of drums originating from all around the globe. Membranophones are played in many ways: with sticks, fingers, the palms of the hands, foot pedals, and even mouths (kazoo).

IDIOPHONES Idiophones are *instruments in which the vibration of the body of the instrument itself* (rather than a string, air tube, or membrane) *produces the sound.* "Idio-phone" literally means "self-sounder." The vibrating material and the resonating chamber are one and the same (though an external resonator may be added to increase the instrument's volume). The idiophone class includes just about all percussion instruments other than drums: gongs, triangles, shakers, cymbals, spoons, castanets, hand claps. Xylophone-type instruments also belong to the idiophone class, including the beautiful *metallophone* instruments featured in Indonesian gamelan orchestras (**CD ex. #2-12**). Other melodic instruments, like pans (steel drums) (**CD ex. #1-30**) and the extraordinary *mbira dzavadzimu* of the Shona people of Zimbabwe heard in **CD ex. #2-2,** are idiophones as well. The mbira is made of rows of tuned metal "tongues"

Western flute (side-blown) and Japanese shakuhachi (end-blown).

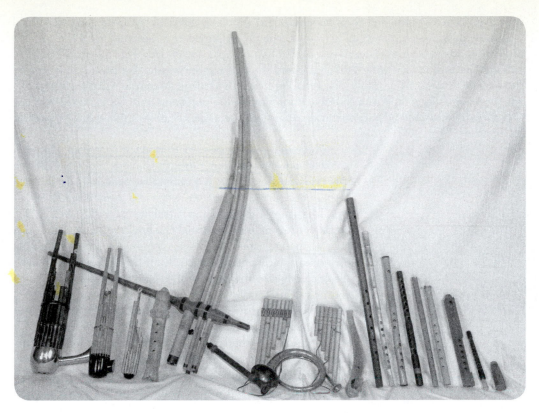

Aerophone instruments.

Membranophone instruments.

**mbira dzavadzimu
(em-BEE-rah
dzah-vah-DZEE-moo)**

Shona (SHO-nah)

lamellae (lah-mel-lay)

(lamellae) that are attached to a wooden board frame. A calabash gourd resonator is held under the instrument to amplify its sound. The player plucks the "tongues" with the thumbs of both hands. Buzzing devices (sea shells, bottle caps) are attached to the instrument to enhance its timbre. The gourd resonator and the buzzing devices have a profound effect on the overall timbre of the mbira. This can be heard in **Online Musical Illustration #17,** which demonstrates, first, the sound of an mbira without a resonator or buzzers; second, the same sound enhanced by a resonator; and third, the "complete" mbira timbre, with resonator and buzzers.

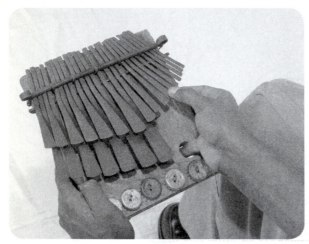

Mbira dzavadzimu (gourd resonator not shown).

There is a great range of performance techniques for idiophones, including striking, rubbing, shaking, plucking (mbira), stamping, and clapping. A tambourine functions as a membranophone *and* an idiophone when the membrane (head) is struck, causing the membrane itself to sound as well as the jingles. If a tambourine is shaken, however, it is heard as a pure idiophone, since the shaking action does not activate the membrane sufficiently to make it audible. This difference is illustrated in **Online Musical Illustration #18,** in which you first hear the tambourine as a combined idiophone/membranophone when it is struck, and then as a pure idiophone when it is shaken.

"Compound" instruments that consist of a number of *separate* instruments conceived of as a *single* instrument may combine a variety of idiophones and membranophones. The most familiar instrument of this kind is the **drum set,** which is common in rock, jazz, and many types of world music. In its most standard, conventional format, the drum set includes a foot pedal-operated *bass drum;* a bright-sounding *snare drum;* several *cymbals,* including a pair called the *hi-hats* that are mounted on a stand controlled by a foot pedal; and two or more *tom-toms* (Figure 5.8). Many of the musical examples discussed in this

Idiophone instruments.

FIGURE 5.8
Drum set.

Tom-toms

Cymbal

Hi-hat cymbal (top)

Hi-hat cymbal (bottom)

Floor tom-tom

Snare drum

Bass drum

Hi-hat pedal

Bass drum pedal

text (e.g., **CD exs. #2-10, 2-17, 3-1,** and **3-11**) include performances on drum sets played in a variety of musical styles.

ELECTRONOPHONES Finally, we come to the electronophones, the newest and by far the fastest-growing category of instruments. There are two main subcategories: the *"pure" electronophones,* such as synthesizers and digital samplers, in which electronics are used to generate the sound *and* to amplify and enhance it; and the *"hybrid" electronophones,* such as the electric guitar, which are basically modified versions of conventional acoustic instruments (i.e., chordophones, aerophones, membranophones, and idiophones) that make use of electronic methods of sound amplification and processing. If you have to plug in an electronophone to make it function as the instrument it was designed to be, it is a pure electronophone; if it can function, at least marginally, without electric power, it is a hybrid electronophone. For example, if you tried to play a song on a keyboard synthesizer (a pure electronophone) without plugging it in, you would hear nothing except the little clicking sounds of the keys being pressed down. But if you tried to play the same song on a solid-body electric guitar (a hybrid electronophone) without plugging it in, you *would* be able to hear the melody, albeit very softly.

Electronically generated music usually emerges from systems or networks of interconnected instruments and devices. For all their complexity and variety, the various electronic music instruments included in such systems can be broken down into two main, interrelated categories: *sound generators* and *sound modifiers.* Sound generators are used to produce sounds; sound modifiers are used to alter and enhance them. Today, technological advances and miniaturization make it possible to contain a complete music production system with software-based sound generators and modifiers on a standard laptop computer. In the past, comparable systems would take up an entire room.

The sound generators category of electronophones includes instruments such as synthesizers and digital samplers (in addition to actual computers). Several different technologies of *sound synthesis* are used to generate tones on these instruments. The technology of **digital sampling** allows for any existing sound to be recorded, stored as digital data, and then reproduced either "verbatim" or in electronically manipulated form (often via a piano-type synthesizer keyboard). The fluid merging of acoustic and electronically generated sound made possible by

TABLE 5.2	Digitally sampled and synthesized tones heard in Online Musical Illustration #19.	
Time	**Description**	
0:00–0:10	Digital sampling (source: Middle Eastern 'ud)	
0:11–0:19	Digital synthesis	
0:20–0:31	Digital sampling (source: viola)	
0:32–0:39	Digital synthesis	
0:41–0:54	Digital sampling (source: brass aerophones [horns])	
0:55–1:03	Digital synthesis	

digital sampling and other advanced technologies has been an important factor in the growth in recent decades of *electro-acoustic music,* which combines sonorities of purely acoustic and purely electronic origin in innovative ways.

While the digital sampling process originates with a sound (or sounds) recorded from an external source, a second technology, *digital synthesis,* creates electronic sounds from scratch, as it were. Computers or other devices (e.g., synthesizers) are used first to *create* an electronic soundwave and then to *process* that soundwave until the desired timbre is achieved. Like digital sampling, digital synthesis has reached a level of extraordinary sophistication. A skilled sound synthesist can generate tones that sound almost exactly like conventional music instruments, or that are so fantastic and otherworldly that you can hardly believe what you are hearing.

Online Musical Illustration #19 features several electronically generated tones and tone sequences, some created through digital sampling, others through digital synthesis. Table 5.2 (see above) identifies which technology was used to generate these sounds.

The sound modifiers, including amplifiers (devices that add volume, or amplitude, to the sound of an instrument) as well as a vast array of what are known as *effects devices,* are used to transform tones through the addition of features such as reverberation (reverb), echo, vibrato (tremolo), and distortion. The amplifier is to an electronic music instrument what the resonator is to an acoustic one; similarly, different "effects" are often to music electronics what different *acoustical spaces* (the physical environments in which music performances take place) are to music that is not electronically processed. Musicians have long recognized the transformative potential of different acoustical spaces, like the echo of a canyon or the hollow reverberation of a large cathedral. The science of musical effects devices aims to simulate such spaces electronically, and, in the spirit of electronic music generally, to do things to and with sound that musicians of the pre-electronic age likely never even imagined.

In **Online Musical Illustration #20,** a "basic" tone with a flute-like timbre is presented and then processed and altered in a variety of ways using electronic sound modifiers. The different types of sound modification employed are outlined in Table 5.3.

Electro-acoustic music production and recording studio.

TABLE 5.3   Examples of electronic sound modification illustrated in Online Musical Illustration #20.

Time	Description
0:00–0:03	Basic tone
0:04–0:08	Basic tone plus reverberation (reverb)
0:09–0:13	Basic tone plus vibrato (tremolo)
0:14–0:18	Basic tone plus echo
0:19–0:22	Basic tone plus reverb, vibrato (tremolo), and echo
0:23–0:29	Basic tone plus reverb, vibrato (tremolo), echo, and distortion

TABLE 5.4   Common music instruments, classified in Hornbostel-Sachs system categories.

Chordophones	Aerophones	Membranophones	Idiophones	Electronophones
Guitar	Flute	Snare drum	Gong	Computer
Harp	Trumpet	Timpani (kettledrums)	Shaker	Synthesizer
Violin	Pipe organ	Kazoo	Hand clap	Digital sampler
Zheng	Didgeridoo	Mrdangam	Mbira	Electric guitar

Perhaps the most important electro-nophone subcategory of all is that which encompasses the full range of *music recording technologies,* past and present. The production of recordings, and the very capacity to create them, has revolutionized the making, reception, perception, and meaning of music on a global scale since the invention of the phonograph (the original music recording machine) by Thomas Edison in 1877. One of the many recording technologies that has had a huge impact on how music is made since at least the mid-1960s is **multitrack recording.** Through the use of multitrack recording machines and computer-based multitrack *sequencers,* it is possible to layer dozens upon dozens of separate musical *tracks* one atop the other. This is called **overdubbing.** Overdubbing technology, combined with an endless variety of electronic and computer technologies that allow for the creation of new sounds and the processing and transformation of existing ones, has changed the very conception of what it means to "make music" in cultures worldwide. Many of the musical selections we will explore in this text, even ones that sound traditional, make extensive use of these advanced production and recording technologies.

Summary

This chapter introduced three important elements of music that collectively make manifest the characteristic sounds and sound qualities of musical tones. These three elements are dynamics, having to do with the relative loudness and softness of tones; timbre, which relates to sound quality or "tone color"; and music instruments, the actual material objects (including the human body) responsible for generating the tones we hear in music.

With respect to dynamics, we learned that dynamic ranges in music may cover a spectrum from silence to deafening loudness, that dynamic contrast is an important aspect of much music, and that the dynamic ranges found in different types and styles of music vary.

Timbre was shown to be an element of music for which the available terminology in the English language is highly subjective: in the absence of precise terms to describe the different qualities of sound in music, we tend to borrow words from other domains—like "gravelly" or "majestic"—to describe musical sounds. Nonetheless, describing timbre is decisively important in terms of distinguishing between different music traditions, styles, instruments, and even performers on the same instrument (including singers). Furthermore, the timbral quality of any given musical work or performance is crucial to its identity and affect. On a technical level, timbre was shown to be a product of relationships between the *partials* that constitute musical tones, that is, between the fundamental pitch and harmonics (overtones).

As the actual physical objects that in a sense give birth to music in performance, music instruments—including the most ubiquitous of all, the human voice—play a crucial role in all music traditions. Our exploration of music instruments was mainly linked to the Hornbostel-Sachs classification system, with its four-part division of chordophones, aerophones, membranophones, and idiophones, and a fifth division, electronophones, that was added after the original Hornbostel-Sachs publication.

Key Terms

crescendo
decrescendo
dynamic range
acoustic (as in acoustic
   instrument)
ensembles
harmonics

didgeridoo
music instrument
instrumentation
Hornbostel-Sachs classification
   system
chordophones
aerophones

membranophones
idiophones
electronophones
drum set
digital sampling
multitrack recording
overdubbing

Study Questions

- As rhythm is to duration and pitch is to frequency, dynamics are to _____.

- What happens to a tone that crescendos? To one that decrescendos?

- How do didgeridoo players and khoomii singers bring out multiple pitches from a single, fundamental tone?

- What are the four principal categories of the Hornbostel-Sachs classification system? What is the important fifth category that was added later?

- What specific features of a tone are revealed by a spectrogram? What do spectrograms tell us, in technical terms, about why different instruments and voices have different timbres?

- In discussing electronophones, what is the basic distinction between a sound generator and a sound modifier? Between a "pure" electronophone and a "hybrid" electronophone? Between sounds generated by digital sampling and sounds generated by digital synthesis?

Applying What You Have Learned

- Select recordings by three of your favorite singers and listen to them, focusing specifically on the timbre of the singer's voice. Write out a detailed description of what each singer's voice sounds like (i.e., its timbre), then compare the three voice timbres and draw distinctions between them. What is it about the timbre of each voice that stands out to you and is appealing? Does this comparison of timbre reveal anything about why you like these particular artists, each for different reasons in different situations?

■ Randomly scan through the various selections on the CD set accompanying this text, listening to a variety of examples. For each example you select, try to isolate and describe at least one instrument you hear (sometimes there will be only one). Indicate whether you think the instrument is a chordophone, aerophone, idiophone, membranophone, or electronophone. Describe its timbre to the best of your ability. Also describe the dynamic range and any other features of dynamics you hear in the music. If possible, create a graphic portrait of the "dynamics landscape" of the piece.

■ Many computers today are equipped with quite sophisticated yet user-friendly music composition and production software packages right out of the box (e.g., Garage Band). If you have such software, try creating some of your own music using it. If not, see if you have friends who use it and listen to and write a brief report on some of the music they have created.

Resources for Further Study

Visit the Online Learning Center at www.mhhe.com/bakan2e, as well as the author's personally maintained Web site at www.michaelbakan.com, for additional learning aids, study help, and resources that supplement the content of this chapter.

chapter six

how **music works,** part IV:
texture and form

Much as the characters in a novel relate to and interact with one another in certain ways, the "characters" in a musical work—the notes, rhythms, melodies, patterns, and vocal and instrumental parts—relate to and interact with one another in certain ways as well. The kinds of relationships that emerge and evolve between them define the element of music called **texture.**

Form is the element of music that pertains to the large-scale dimensions of musical organization. When we study form, we are interested in how musical works and performances develop and take shape from start to finish, phrase by phrase and section by section.

Texture and form will be our final areas of focus as we conclude this general introduction to the inner and outer workings of music.

Many kinds of relationships exist in life, and many types of textures occur in music. **Single-line textures** are the simplest type. They are otherwise known as **monophonic** textures. Music with single-line textures is not limited to performances by a single musician. Two, ten, a hundred, or five thousand individuals can contribute to a monophonic texture, so long as all of them play or sing together in **unison,** that is, performing the same sequence of pitches in the same rhythm.

Textures in which there are two or more distinct parts are called **polyphonic.** Polyphony may result from the playing (or singing) of different parts on different instruments, or it may occur in the part of a single instrument that can play more than one note at the same time, such as a piano or guitar. Even a single human voice can create polyphony, as we heard in the Mongolian khoomii selection of **CD ex. #1-6.**

A melody accompanied by a **drone** is one of the simplest types of polyphonic textures. In a melody-plus-drone texture, the melody unfolds over a sustained, continuous tone, as in the Scottish bagpipe performance of "Amazing Grace" on **CD ex. #1-16.**

Harmonized textures emerge when notes of different pitch occur together to form chords, or "harmonies." Each note of a melody can generate its own chord, as in the Fijian church hymn of **CD ex. #1-11,** or the chords may be supplied by one instrument (e.g., guitar) in accompaniment of a melody played on another (e.g., saxophone), as in **CD ex. #1-27.**

Multiple-melody texture occurs in polyphonic music that features two or more essentially separate melodic lines being performed simultaneously. The Zimbabwean popular music excerpt of **CD ex. #2-3** features a multiple-melody texture, with one group of male vocalists singing a unison melody in a low register and a second group singing a harmonized melody in a higher register. These two layers of vocal melody interweave over an accompaniment of chordal and rhythmic instruments.

Javanese gamelan music of Indonesia, such as that heard in **CD ex. #1-7,** provides profusely rich and varied multiple-melody textures. It typically includes many different layers of melody all being sung and played at once. In the example, both male and female vocalists and musicians performing on a diverse array of instruments spin out melodic layer upon melodic layer. Each of these layers is unique, yet all of them are interrelated.

A very different, yet equally stunning and complex, type of multiple-melody texture is illustrated in **CD ex. #2-4.** This is a traditional elephant hunting song of the BaMbuti people of Central Africa. Here, the different strands of vocal melody seem to flow over each other like the

insights and perspectives

The Debate over Polyrhythms in West African Music

Some types of polyphonic music are characterized as *polyrhythmic*. Much West African music is portrayed in this way (see page 77), but there are some scholars and musicians who suggest that this is misleading. They argue that the term polyrhythmic does not accurately reflect how West African musicians actually conceptualize their music. Rather than perceiving this as music of "many rhythms" (i.e., polyrhythms), it is possible instead to perceive it as music defined by a single, unified rhythmic expression with multiple manifestations.

The technicalities supporting either side of this interesting debate are well beyond our scope here. The controversy is still worth noting, however. It provides yet another good example of how the study of music as sound can rarely, if ever, be appropriately separated from the study of music as culture.

A classic photograph of a BaMbuti ritual performance, Central Africa.

cascades of a waterfall. The relative equality of all the different vocal parts in this music—there are no "soloists" or "accompanists"—is reflective of the high value placed on egalitarianism in BaMbuti culture and society. This is a pervasive cultural value among other so-called pygmy societies of Central Africa as well.

Multiple-part textures need not be built from or even include melodies; two or more distinct *rhythmic* lines performed at the same time can also create polyphony. **Polyrhythm** is the term used to describe music in which there are several different parts or layers, with each defined mainly by its distinctive rhythmic character rather than by melodies or chords. **CD ex. #2-5** is a West African, drumming-based selection with a richly polyrhythmic texture (at least that is one way of describing it—see the "Insights and Perspectives" box on page 76 for an alternate view).

Multiple melodies and multiple rhythmic lines can be stacked one atop the other to create polyphonic textures of many different kinds, as we have seen. Moving in the opposite direction, a *single* melodic or rhythmic line may be *divided* among two or more instruments or voices. When this occurs, the result is textures based on **interlocking.** The opening melody (0:03–0:14) of **CD ex. #2-6** features folkloric music of the Andes mountains of Bolivia, South America. The melody is divided between two Andean panpipes (*siku*), whose parts on the recording are clearly split between the left and right speakers. (This can be best heard through headphones.) Each panpipe has only *half* of the pitches of the complete scale needed for the melody, and each provides about half of the total number of melody notes in the interlocking texture. (This kind of texture, where two or more instruments "split" a single melody between them, is sometimes called *hocket*.) Figure 6.1 on page 78 provides a graphic representation of the interlocking panpipe parts heard from 0:03–0:10 of the CD example. Interlocking textures also figure prominently in the music of Bali, Indonesia, which is explored in Chapter 7, and in musics of many African nations, including Uganda. We will learn more about interlocking panpipe textures in Andean music in Chapter 11.

hocket (HAH-ket)

Graphic representation of interlocking panpipe parts in CD ex. #2-6.

FIGURE 6.1

Left:

Right:

Andean musicians playing on panpipes. These panpipes are called *siku*.

Call-and-response is another very important musical process linked integrally to the subject of musical texture. As its name implies, call-and-response involves back-and-forth alternation between different instrument or voice parts. The conversational element of music present in so many traditions is nowhere more apparent than in call-and-response dialogue. This dialogue may take any of a variety of forms. It can occur between a lead singer and a group of background singers, a singer and an instrumentalist, two groups of instrumentalists, two groups of singers, or any other such combination. **CD ex. #2-7** (the complete track of the West African piece that we heard an excerpt of in **CD ex. #2-5**) features call-and-response singing between a lead vocalist and a group of vocalists. The call-and-response vocal parts are presented over an accompaniment of polyrhythmic percussion at 0:40, following the all-percussion introduction.

Form: The Designs of Musical Works

Understanding how the *form* of a piece of music works has mainly to do with comprehending how it is laid out from beginning to end, with how the music unfolds and develops as it progresses. If no repetition of musical materials occurs and there is an absence of distinct sections in the music's design, the form is described as *through-composed*. In most cases, however, repetition, patterns, and sectional organization are present in music and indeed largely *define* its forms. These are the types of forms that will be our focus here.

Forms based on repetition and patterns

Repetition and *patterning* are key features of most music. Certain elements—melodies, rhythms, chord progressions, metric cycles, even entire large sections of complex musical material—are presented and then recur in the course of a piece or performance, perhaps just once, perhaps many times. The repetition of these materials may be exact or it may be varied from one occurrence to the next. *Varied repetition* is common in many music traditions.

The presence of repetition and recurring patterns in musical forms largely accounts for why when you listen to music, at least in familiar styles, you often have an intuitive sense of what is coming next. Even if you have not been formally trained to do so, you perceive a sense of order, of sequence, in the music's design: you feel when something you heard before is about to come back, or when the catchy "hook" of the song is about to arrive. Of course, this does not always happen. There may be surprises as well, unexpected twists and turns that take the music—and thus you, the listener—in directions unanticipated. Indeed, the effectiveness of a musical work or performance on its audience generally has much to do with how well it achieves a balance between predictability and unpredictability in its formal design, both in and of itself and relative to the stylistic conventions of the musical tradition to which it belongs.

OSTINATO-BASED FORMS Some musical works and performances are built entirely from the repetition or varied repetition of a single musical pattern or phrase. A short figure that is repeated over and over again is called an **ostinato.** The ostinato is typically the smallest unit of organization upon which musical forms are built. An example of an ostinato-based musical form is found in **CD ex. #2-8.** This is a piece entitled "Xai" (Elephants). It comes from the Qwii people (aka Bushmen, San) of the Kalahari Desert of southern Africa. The instrument is an *nkokwane,* a Qwii hunting bow that doubles as a struck chordophone instrument (see the photo, p. 80). The "string" of the bow is struck with either an arrow or a stick. Two different tones (with different pitches) are produced, as well as a wide range of timbres.

The basic ostinato pattern of "Xai" repeats roughly every two seconds (or every six "beats"). As you listen, notice how the ostinato is subtly varied from statement to statement, rarely being repeated exactly the same way twice. The continual presence of the ostinato and its perpetually varied repetition offer both continuity and variety, sameness and contrast.

Ostinato-based forms may gain richness and complexity through a texture of **layered ostinatos.** In this type of texture, two or more ostinatos are "stacked" one on top of the other. An example of a layered ostinato texture may be heard in **CD ex. #2-9** (from "Oye Como Va," by Tito Puente, to which we will return in Chapter 11). First you hear the ostinato melody (or *riff*) of the saxophones being played and then repeated. Next, at 0:15 of the excerpt, a layer of trombone ostinato is laid overtop the saxophones. Finally, a third ostinato layer, featuring trumpet, comes in over the saxophones and trombones at 0:31 (Figure 6.2).

ostinato
(ah-sti-NAH-toe)

"Xai"
(like English "shy")

nkokwane
(en-koh-kwah-nay)

FIGURE 6.2

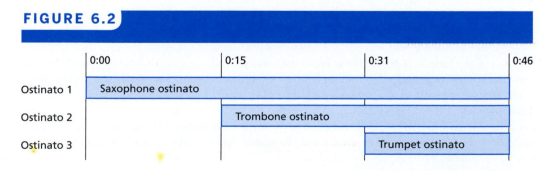

Layered ostinatos in Tito Puente's "Oye Como Va" (CD ex. #2-9).

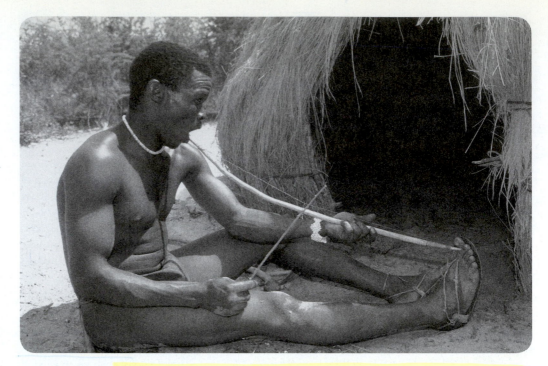

Nkokwane ("musical bow") played by Qwii musician. In this instance, one end of the bow is inserted into the performer's mouth, which serves as a resonator. In other cases, a calabash gourd is used as the resonator.

CYCLIC FORMS Cyclic forms are similar to ostinato-based forms, but the repeated unit of the **cycle** is typically longer than that of an ostinato. The majority of blues songs are in a cyclic form called the **12-bar blues.** Each cycle is 12 measures (i.e., 12 bars) long and has the same basic chord progression as the others. Charles Atkins' "A Funny Way of Asking" (**CD ex. #1-19**) is a 12-bar blues form song. All of the 12-measure cycles are the same length and have the same chords, but they differ in their instrumentation and textures. As you listen, mark the beginning of each of the first four 12-bar blues cycles with a clap and note the contrasting musical features that distinguish one cycle from the next, as outlined in Figure 6.3, page 81.

Forms with contrasting sections

We now shift to forms with multiple, identifiably distinct sections (called *formal sections*). The different sections in such forms often contrast with one another musically. For example, there may be a modulation from one key to another, a change in the chord progression or instrumentation, or a change in the meter or rhythmic structure from one section to the next. Often, multiple changes such as these will occur simultaneously.

One of the most common formal designs featuring contrasting sections is the **verse-chorus form.** The main formal sections in a verse-chorus song are the alternating verses (A sections) and choruses (B sections). Other sections may be incorporated into the form as well, including an introduction, interludes, transitional passages, one or more improvised instrumental solos, and a special ending section (sometimes called a *coda,* from an Italian term meaning "tail"). If the song has lyrics, new words will usually appear in each successive verse, whereas the words of the chorus typically remain constant throughout. Musically speaking, the chorus is normally the part of the form that contains the *hook,* the catchy bit of the song that tends to stick in your head and (hopefully) make you want to hear it over and over again. The words sung to this hook often furnish the title of the song as well, for example, U2's "I Still Haven't Found What I'm Looking For."

"Ingculaza (AIDS)" (**CD ex. #2-10**) is a song with a verse-chorus form by the Zimbabwean *world beat* musician Dumisani "Ramadu" Moyo. (*World beat* is a term used to

"Ingculaza"
(In-cool-ah-zah)

Dumisani "Ramadu" Moyo (Doo-mee-sah-nee Rah-mah-doo Moy-yo)

FIGURE 6.3

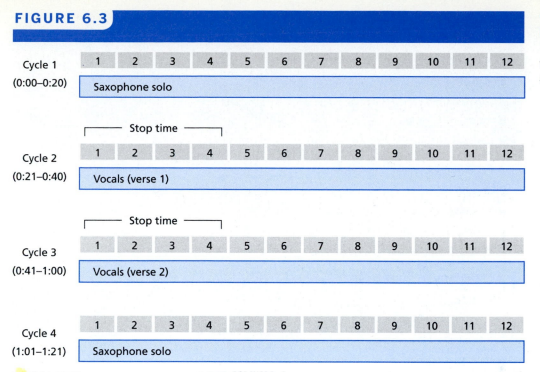

Charles Atkins' "A Funny Way of Asking": 12-bar blues form timeline chart (CD ex. #1-19).

Cycle 1
(0:00–0:20)

| 1 | 2 | 3 | 4 | 5 | 6 | 7 | 8 | 9 | 10 | 11 | 12 |

Saxophone solo

┌──── Stop time ────┐

Cycle 2
(0:21–0:40)

| 1 | 2 | 3 | 4 | 5 | 6 | 7 | 8 | 9 | 10 | 11 | 12 |

Vocals (verse 1)

┌──── Stop time ────┐

Cycle 3
(0:41–1:00)

| 1 | 2 | 3 | 4 | 5 | 6 | 7 | 8 | 9 | 10 | 11 | 12 |

Vocals (verse 2)

Cycle 4
(1:01–1:21)

| 1 | 2 | 3 | 4 | 5 | 6 | 7 | 8 | 9 | 10 | 11 | 12 |

Saxophone solo

identify commercial music styles that blend elements of diverse world music traditions and Western popular music.) This is a social commentary song about the AIDS pandemic in Africa. More specifically, it is about the devastation the disease has wrought in Ramadu's home village. The song is sung in Ramadu's native language, Ndebele. The distinctive "click" sounds that are integral to Ndebele (and to other southern African languages) are heard at several points. The song text, a portion of which appears in translation below, metaphorically personifies the disease and grapples with the problem of how the tragedy of AIDS might be abated:

Ndebele (IN-duh-bel-ee)

> *Everybody in my village is crying about you*
>
> *You have taken away my sisters, brothers and innocent souls including children*
>
> *What shall we do?*
>
> *How should we behave?*
>
> *The answer is simply to "prevent rather than cure"*
>
> *in order to have a healthy community with a good life and a happy future.*
>
> (Moyo and Heller 2002)

The form of "Ingculaza," which is charted out in the box on the following page, includes two sung verses (the A sections) and three sung choruses (the B sections). The last chorus is *looped* (repeated over and over without pause) as it grows progressively more expansive and texturally dense before fading away to silence. The performance commences with an instrumental introduction before the opening verse. There is also an improvised electric guitar solo. Listen to this beautiful song now, following along with the timeline chart and tracking the formal sections and musical features it outlines.

Dumisani "Ramadu" Moyo.

Form Chart: "Ingculaza (AIDS)," by Dumisani "Ramadu" Moyo (CD ex. #2-10)

I (INTRODUCTION)
0:00–0:28

- Single harmonized vocal phrase near beginning.
- Gradual crescendo.
- Layered ostinatos (guitar, percussion).

A (VERSE 1)
0:29–1:00

- Unison male group singing over drone-based harmony.
- Syncopated guitar ostinato.
- Percussion.

B (CHORUS 1)
1:01–1:22

- Chord progression replaces drone-based harmony.
- Vocal parts harmonized.
- Rhythmic accompaniment changes.

A (VERSE 2)
1:23–1:54

- Harmonized vocals contrast with the unison vocal texture of Verse 1.
- Thicker texture than in Verse 1.

B (CHORUS 2)
1:55–2:15

- Essentially the same as Chorus 1.

S (SOLO)
2:16–2:59

- Improvised electric guitar solo.
- This solo section takes the place of a potential third verse in the formal design of the arrangement.
- Electric guitar features a "fuzzy" timbre, created by electronic distortion effects devices.
- Lead vocalist (Ramadu) talks over the electric guitar solo; does not sing.
- Final, transitional passage of solo (beginning at 2:49) builds toward climactic arrival of the final chorus (Chorus 3) at 3:00.

B (CHORUS 3)
3:00–end

- Chorus is looped (repeated) several times to reinforce the hook of the song.
- Texture becomes increasingly dense as music builds.
- Multiple melodic lines: lead vocalist, background vocalists (harmonizing), solo electric guitar.
- Selection ends with music fading away to silence.

Summary

In this chapter, we learned that texture is the element of music that accounts for relationships between the different parts (instrumental and/or vocal) in a musical work, while form is the element that accounts for how musical works on the whole are organized.

A basic distinction between single-line (monophonic) and multiple-part (polyphonic) textures was made, and a variety of different types of multipart textures were defined and illustrated through recorded examples and visual illustrations. Musical processes that generate distinctive textures, such as interlocking and call-and-response, also were introduced.

Several types of musical forms were examined, and a distinction between forms that are through-composed and those that feature repetition, patterns, and sectional organization was set forth. The focus of our discussion then turned to a variety of specific types of forms. Ostinato-based forms, cyclic forms, and forms with contrasting formal sections such as the verse-chorus song form were highlighted.

Key Terms

texture	harmonized texture	layered ostinatos
form	multiple-melody texture	cycle (in a cyclic musical form)
single-line textures (monophonic)	polyrhythm	12-bar blues (form)
unison	interlocking	verse-chorus form
polyphonic	call-and-response	
drone	ostinato	

Study Questions

■ How are the terms *texture* and *form* defined in relation to music?

■ What distinguishes between monophonic and polyphonic textures?

■ What is a drone? What musical example was used to illustrate melody-plus-drone texture?

■ What is the difference between a harmonized texture and a multiple-melody texture?

■ On the basis of the musical examples in this chapter, what musicultural traditions might you look to for abundant examples of polyrhythmic textures? Of interlocking textures?

■ What is an ostinato-based form? In the piece "Xai," was the ostinato figure repeated exactly each time, or with variation from one statement to the next?

■ What is the standard cyclic form of much blues music?

■ In a verse-chorus form song with words, are the words usually the same from one chorus section to the next or different? What about in the successive verses of the song?

Applying What You Have Learned

■ Take a familiar piece of music from your personal collection and write a description of its texture and form. In terms of texture, what kinds of relationships do you hear between the different voices/instruments? Is there unison singing or playing? Harmonization? Call-and-response? Interlocking? Does the form of the piece appear to be ostinato-based? Or does it seem to conform to the model of a 12-bar blues tune, or a verse-chorus tune, or some combination of different types of formal designs? Use your listening skills from this chapter to take you as far as you can go with this exercise, but don't get frustrated if you find that you cannot account for all that you hear. There is much in actual music making in terms of texture and form that goes well beyond what we have been able to accommodate in this brief introductory chapter. Just have fun with this, and try to hear and account for as much as you can.

Resources for Further Study

Visit the Online Learning Center at www.mhhe.com/bakan2e, as well as the author's personally maintained Web site at www.michaelbakan.com, for additional learning aids, study help, and resources that supplement the content of this chapter.

chapter **seven**

Indonesian **gamelan** music: **interlocking** rhythms, interlocking **worlds**

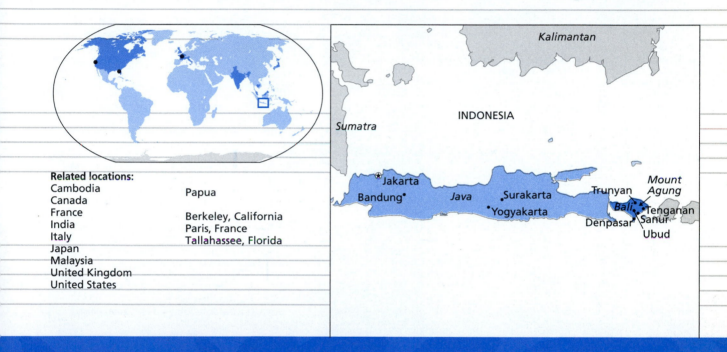

Related locations:

Cambodia
Canada
France
India
Italy
Japan
Malaysia
United Kingdom
United States

Papua

Berkeley, California
Paris, France
Tallahassee, Florida

Bali is a small island located in the Southeast Asian nation of Indonesia. I first ventured there in 1989 while an ethnomusicology graduate student. I have since traveled to Bali many times, and my professional life has come to revolve largely around studying, performing, and teaching Balinese music. Many of my important life lessons—about trust, compassion, and the joys and challenges of experiencing music in a distant land with people whose musical and cultural backgrounds are far removed from my own—I learned in Bali.

Soon after arriving in Bali during my first visit, I headed into town one day to do some shopping. On my way back to my bungalow, I stumbled upon a brick-paved temple courtyard where four teenage boys were sitting

World events		Music events
Hinduism and Buddhism brought to Bali ● from Java, blending together with one another and with earlier Balinese belief systems to form the base of the Hindu-Balinese Agama Tirta religion	**13th century–1906 Pre-colonial era**	● Advanced culture and arts with *gamelan* music as central component of ritual, social, and political life
Frequent warring between rival Balinese ● kingdoms		
	1889	● French composer Claude Debussy hears gamelan at the World's Fair in Paris; influences his compositional approach
Bali colonized by Dutch ●	**1906–1908**	● *Gamelan gong kebyar* and kebyar musical style emerge in the wake of Dutch colonization, sociopolitical transformation
	1933	● German film *Insel der Dämonen* (Island of Demons), featuring *Kecak* performance
Republic of Indonesia declared (though ● full national independence not achieved until 1949)	**1945**	
	1950s–present	● Extensive experimentation on the part of both Indonesian and Western musicians with the blending of gamelan and Western music elements
	1986	● First *gamelan beleganjur* contest, Denpasar
		● New contest musical style, *kreasi beleganjur,* emerges
	1990–1992	● Beleganjur groups directed by composer I Ketut Suandita win three consecutive annual championships in the major Denpasar beleganjur contest
	1997	● Premiere performance of "B.A.Ph.PET," a post-traditional work for gamelan and scratch turntable soloist by Michael Bakan
	2005	● Sony BMG Indonesia releases *Magic Finger,* by I Wayan Balawan and Batuan Ethnic Fusion; includes the track "Country Beleganjur"

around relaxing and chatting. Resting in a haphazard arrangement near the boys were four small knobbed gongs and a bundle of mallets. Apparently some kind of a rehearsal was about to begin. This excited me, for I had heard little Balinese music of any kind since my arrival.

It took a long time—perhaps half an hour—for all of the musicians to arrive and for the rehearsal proper to begin, but it was well worth the wait. I counted 21 musicians in all. The music they played was powerful: loud, brash, and forcefully energetic. It sounded nothing like any of the Indonesian music I had heard before coming to Bali, and nothing like the rather uninspiring "tourist performances" I'd attended since arriving either. It pumped along with a contagious groove and mesmerizing rhythmic drive. The two drummers and eight cymbal players propelled the music forward with dazzling unison figures and continuous streams of interlocking rhythm that unfolded over the anchor of a steady, recurring cycle played on large gongs suspended from ornately decorated stands. Meanwhile, rapid-fire melodies played in interlocking patterns by four musicians on a set of four small hand-held gongs elaborated a two-tone ostinato melody played on a pair of similar instruments an octave below.

The rhythmic complexity, the precise execution, the inventiveness of the musical arrangement with its endless variations and contrasting sections—all of these were breathtaking. I was transfixed, and I listened carefully, transcribing the rhythms in my head as best I could. After a while, the playing stopped. There was some talking among the musicians and the next thing I knew, one of the cymbal players was looking at me, smiling, beckoning me to come over. As I walked toward him, he held out his cymbals.

I took the cymbals and sat down next to a slim, mop-topped member of the group. He appeared to be the leader of the cymbal section. He smiled and introduced himself as Madé. As the drumming introduction started up, I glued my eyes on Madé's hands. He sprang into action and I followed. (At this point, listen to **CD ex. #2-11** as you continue to read.)

CENG - - - CENG - CENG - - - CENG CENG, went the cymbals; then again,

CENG - - - CENG - CENG - - - CENG CENG. Then softer,

ceng - - ceng - - ceng - - ceng - ceng - CENG CENG CENG, leading directly into an

intense passage of interlocking cymbal rhythm,

CENG-ceCENG-ceCENG-CENG-ceCENG-ceCENG-

CENG-ceCENG-ceCENG-CENG-ceCENG-ceCENG-, then, back to unison:

CENG-CENG-CENG-CENG-CENG-CENG-CENG-CENG CENG

Then a repetition of the whole last chunk:

CENG-ceCENG-ceCENG-CENG-ceCENG-ceCENG-

CENG-ceCENG-ceCENG-CENG-ceCENG-ceCENG-

CENG-CENG-CENG-CENG-CENG-CENG-CENG-CENG CENG, and on we went.

CENG ce-CENG (CHAYNG chuh-CHAYNG)

The author (with beard) performing in a contest with a gamelan beleganjur group in Bali, Indonesia, 1990.

What joy! Here I was, halfway around the world, playing a kind of music I had only just discovered with a group of musicians I had never met before and with whom I didn't even yet share a common language. But we were playing together, the music sounded good, and we were having a great time.

When our session ended, I asked the cymbal player, who spoke some English, what kind of music we had been playing.

"Gamelan music," he said.

"Gamelan what?" I asked. "What kind of gamelan music?"

"Gamelan beleganjur," he replied.

I jotted down the unfamiliar name on a notepad. A new chapter of my life had just begun.

gamelan beleganjur (gah-muh-lahn buh-luh-gahn-YOOR)

■ ■ ■

Introduction

This chapter explores musical traditions of Indonesian **gamelan** music, with a particular focus on the **gamelan beleganjur,** the Balinese "gamelan of walking warriors." The term *gamelan* essentially means "ensemble" or "orchestra". It is used in reference to a diverse class of mainly percussion-dominated music ensembles found on Bali, Java, and several other Indonesian islands. Related types of ensembles also are found elsewhere in Southeast Asia, for example, in Malaysia and Cambodia. Though they usually consist of a large number of individual instruments played by multiple performers, each gamelan is conceived of in its entirety as a *single* music instrument. Each is regarded as being unique and distinct from all other gamelans, even from other gamelans of the exact same type. Individual gamelans even have their own proper names, like Gamelan of the Venerable Dark Cloud.

The gamelan beleganjur is a *processional ensemble* (i.e., the musicians walk or march as they perform, as in a Western marching band) consisting of multiple gongs, drums, and cymbals (see the photos, pp. 96, 104, and 106). It has played an integral role in Balinese ritual and ceremonial life for many centuries. Traditionally associated with warfare, battles with evil spirit forces, and rituals for the dead, it has in modern times become the basis of an exciting type of music contest as well. From the interlocking rhythms of its music to the interlocking of worlds it animates—human and spirit, traditional and modern, Balinese and Western—the gamelan beleganjur is an ideal lens through which to view vital processes of tradition and transformation in Balinese music.

Balinese Gamelan Music in Context

Like all music traditions, Balinese gamelan traditions are framed by broader musical, historical, cultural, and societal contexts. In this section, we briefly overview some of these in preparation for the more focused exploration of beleganjur and related gamelan musics that follows in the later portions of the chapter.

Bali and the Republic of Indonesia

Bali is one of more than 17,000 islands in the Southeast Asian nation of Indonesia (Republic of Indonesia), which spans from Sumatra in the west to Papua in the east. Close to 6,000 of Indonesia's islands are inhabited. Bali is very small—you can easily drive around its perimeter in a day—but it is densely populated. More than 3 million people live there, the majority in the fertile rice-growing lands of the southern and southeastern portions of the island. Bali is home to a very large tourist industry, annually hosting hundreds of thousands of visitors from other parts of Indonesia and throughout the world.

The capital of Indonesia is Jakarta, the country's largest city with a population of 14 million. Jakarta is also one of the world's most densely populated metropolises. It is located in the northwestern portion of Java, Bali's neighboring island to the west. More than 120 million people, over half of Indonesia's entire population, live in Java. Surakarta and Yogyakarta are other major Javanese cities. Both are located in the province of Central Java. They are home to the great musical traditions of **Central Javanese court gamelan** (*gamelan kraton*), an example of which we heard earlier on **CD ex. #1-7** (to which we will return). Another major historical and contemporary center of gamelan activity is the city of Bandung, where the distinctive language, culture, and music of the Sundanese people of West Java predominate.

Bandung (Bahn-doong)

Indonesia became an independent nation in 1945, though full national sovereignty was not achieved until 1949. Most of its lands, including Bali, were formerly Dutch colonies or Dutch-occupied territories. Bali did not come under Dutch colonial rule until 1906–1908, much later than Java and many other Indonesian islands. The national language is **Bahasa Indonesia** (Indonesian), a derivative of Malay, though more than 300 other languages are spoken by members of the country's 300-plus ethnic groups, each of which has its own distinctive culture. The Balinese are one of these many ethnic groups, accounting for less than 2 percent of the Indonesian population. Almost 40 percent of Indonesians are of Javanese ethnicity, and another 16 percent are ethnically Sundanese.

Bahasa Indonesia (Bah-HAH-suh Indoh-NEE-see-uh)

Indonesia's national slogan, **Unity in Diversity** (Bhinnéka Tunggal Ika), was instituted to provide a framework for the preservation, development, and nationalization of the country's diverse cultures and cultural traditions. Certain traditions, including various forms of Central Javanese gamelan and Balinese gamelan, have figured especially prominently in the national image of Indonesia promoted under the cultural nationalism agenda of Unity in Diversity, both within Indonesia and internationally. The modern, contest style of beleganjur music, which originated in Bali's capital city, Denpasar, in 1986, has received abundant government support as a musical emblem of Balinese-Indonesian cultural nationalism.

Bhinnéka Tunggal Ika (Bee-nay-kah Toon-gahl EE-kah)

Denpasar (Duhn-PAH-SAHR)

Religion in Bali and Indonesia

Indonesia is the world's largest Islamic nation, both geographically and in population. Almost 90 percent of Indonesians are Muslim, though the religion is practiced in many varied forms that often represent syncretisms with earlier Hindu, Buddhist, and indigenous belief systems. Bali is the only province of Indonesia in which Hinduism is the majority religion. Indeed, Bali is the only world society outside of the Indian subcontinent in which the majority of the population is Hindu.

Agama Tirta (Ah-gah-muh TEER-tuh)

wayang kulit (wah-yahng KOO-leet)

Though historically derived from Hinduism in India and sharing many key features with it—cremation of the dead, belief in reincarnation, entrenchment in great mythic Hindu epics such as the Ramayana and the Mahabharata, a prominent place for music and related arts in religious life—Balinese Hinduism is a unique religion. It is known either as Agama Hindu (Hindu Religion) or **Agama Tirta** (Religion of Holy Water) and is in fact a syncretic faith blending elements of Hinduism and Buddhism (both originally brought to Bali from Java beginning in the 13th century) with earlier layers of indigenous Balinese spiritual belief and practice. Gamelan music always has been central to the practices of Balinese Hinduism and is performed at virtually all religious ceremonies. Most of the major forms of Balinese gamelan and related arts—dances, dance-dramas, shadow puppetry (*wayang kulit*)—trace back historically to the same Hindu-Javanese culture (the Majapahit) that brought Hinduism to Bali many centuries ago.

Gambuh, an ancient Balinese dance-drama.

Not all Balinese are Hindus. In certain Balinese villages such as Tenganan and Trunyan, people follow indigenous religious faiths that have not absorbed the Hindu or Buddhist layers of influence that largely define Agama Tirta. These are the villages of peoples known as the **Bali Aga,** or "Original Balinese." Though there are similarities between the Bali Aga and Hindu-Balinese cultures, there are also profound differences. Certain sacred Balinese gamelans believed to predate the arrival of Hindu-Javanese culture centuries ago, such as the iron-keyed *gamelan selonding* of Tenganan and certain other Bali Aga villages, are regarded with reverence not only among the Bali Aga themselves but by the Balinese population at large.

It is also important to note that though Islam is not nearly as prevalent in Bali as it is elsewhere in Indonesia, there is a sizable Muslim population on the island. A number of villages and towns in northern Bali are predominantly Muslim.

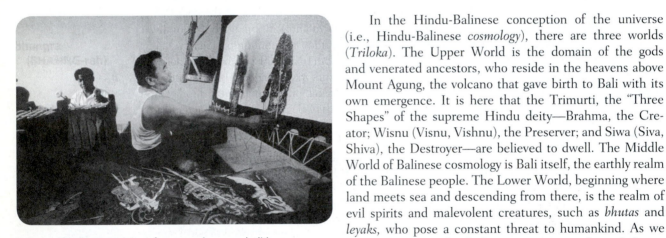

Balinese shadow puppet performance (wayang kulit).

**Triloka
(Tree-LOH-kah)**

**Trimurti
(Tree-MOOR-tee)**

In the Hindu-Balinese conception of the universe (i.e., Hindu-Balinese *cosmology*), there are three worlds (*Triloka*). The Upper World is the domain of the gods and venerated ancestors, who reside in the heavens above Mount Agung, the volcano that gave birth to Bali with its own emergence. It is here that the Trimurti, the "Three Shapes" of the supreme Hindu deity—Brahma, the Creator; Wisnu (Visnu, Vishnu), the Preserver; and Siwa (Siva, Shiva), the Destroyer—are believed to dwell. The Middle World of Balinese cosmology is Bali itself, the earthly realm of the Balinese people. The Lower World, beginning where land meets sea and descending from there, is the realm of evil spirits and malevolent creatures, such as *bhutas* and *leyaks*, who pose a constant threat to humankind. As we will explore, gamelan beleganjur music performed during Hindu-Balinese cremation processions functions in important ways in the battles between the human and evil spirit forces that animate these events.

Gamelan in Bali and beyond

Few world cultures have held so tenaciously to the cultivation of their indigenous musical traditions as have the Balinese, and few musical traditions have inspired such awe among world music connoisseurs as has Balinese gamelan.

Indonesia is a nation of extraordinary musical diversity that goes far beyond gamelan music. Non-gamelan-based religious, folk, and popular traditions of many kinds; regional and national musical styles; and contemporary, experimental music genres blending traditional Indonesian and international elements abound. Resources for exploring some of the fascinating non-gamelan music traditions of Indonesia are included at the Online Learning Center (www.mhhe.com/bakan2). Here, though, we limit our focus exclusively to gamelan.

kebyar (kuh-BYAHR)

BALINESE AND JAVANESE GAMELAN MUSIC: A COMPARISON The best-known Indonesian gamelan traditions are Central Javanese court gamelan and Balinese **gamelan gong kebyar,** examples of both of which we have already heard in connection with earlier chapters (**CD ex. #1-7** and **CD ex. #2-12,** respectively). These two traditions share a common line of historical descent originating with Javanese gamelan traditions of several centuries ago. The following general musicultural features are characteristic of both, and of gamelan musics generally:

■ Related types of instruments (bronze gongs, bronze metallophones, drums, end-blown bamboo flutes, bowed chordophones).

■ A basis in cyclic musical forms.

■ Related tuning systems, scales, and modes.

■ Multipart textures in which the higher-pitched instruments play at faster rhythmic rates than the lower-pitched instruments.

■ Melodic organization in which a main, slow-moving melody played on one or more instruments (the *core melody*) is embellished by faster-moving melodies played on other instruments.

■ Close associations with various forms of dance, dance-drama, and other arts (e.g., shadow puppetry).

■ A common historical foundation in Hindu religious cultures, which is reflected symbolically in the music.

Yet while Central Javanese court gamelan music and Balinese gamelan gong kebyar music exhibit key similarities, they sound very different from one another. This can be heard by comparing the Javanese selection of **CD ex. #1-7** and the Balinese selection of **CD ex. #2-12.** Listen to the first two minutes or so of each and make a subjective comparison, noticing how distinct these pieces are in their styles and in the musical impressions and moods they create. Each might be considered emblematic of its own tradition.

The Javanese piece (entitled "Ketawang: Puspawarna") captures the majestic, expansive, almost ethereal quality of Central Javanese court gamelan. This is music that evokes the royal pageantry and splendor of a time long ago when gamelan instruments and music served as potent symbols of the power, legitimacy, and perceived semi-divine status of Javanese rulers in royal court life. With its many and varied layers of intersecting melody, extremely wide range of instrumental and vocal timbres, and highly stratified polyphonic texture, all of it anchored by a perpetually recurring cycle of gong tones played on impressive bronze gongs of many sizes, this is music that "aestheticizes the structure of the universe" in Javanese terms. Its cyclic form orders time into cycles that mirror the progress of time and space, its "exaggerated musical stratification" symbolizes the extreme *social* stratification of dynastic Java centuries ago, and its musical texture overall reflects, models, and makes manifest in sound the complex relationships that were believed to exist between individuals, the social order, and the cosmos in ancient Java (Spiller 2008:70).

"Ketawang: Puspawarna" ("Kuh-tah-wahng Poos-pah-WOR-nuh")

"Jaya Semara" ("Jah-yuh Suh-MAH-ruh")

Central Javanese gamelan performance.

In contrast, the Balinese piece ("Jaya Semara") captures Bali's signature gamelan sound: resonant bronze gongs, shimmering bronze-keyed metallophones, fast-paced melodies played on metallophone instruments and sets of small tuned gongs, intricate drumming, and a frenetic pace and energy. This is the sound of *kebyar*, a Balinese term that literally means "to flare up" (like a match), though it is sometimes also translated as "lightning." It is fiery, explosive music, born of a time in the early 20th century when Balinese society was in the midst of tremendous social upheaval, moving toward modernity under Dutch colonial rule after some five centuries of Hindu-Balinese monarchies (see Tenzer 1998 [1991], 2000 on kebyar).

Balinese gamelan gong kebyar. Notice the very large gongs at the back of the photo. Such gongs are foundational to *gong cycles* in both Balinese and Javanese gamelan music. The two musicians positioned directly in front of the large gongs (who are facing forward rather than sideways) are playing the *reyong*, a melodic instrument consisting of multiple, small kettle-gongs.

We now take a closer look at these two well-known gamelan compositions, beginning with the Javanese piece, "Ketawang: Puspawarna." The word *ketawang* refers to its cyclic form, which is defined by a *gong cycle* of that name with 16 beats. Each ketawang cycle begins and ends with a stroke on the largest, lowest-pitched gong of the gamelan; the other beats are marked by various smaller gongs of higher pitch. The consistent, recurring pattern of gong strokes that results provides the music's main foundation.

"Puspawarna" is the proper name of the piece, which distinguishes it from all other compositions. It is a word meaning "kinds of flowers" and refers to nine different flowers that metaphorically symbolize the nine principal aesthetic states (*rasa*) in traditional Javanese spiritual philosophy; the sung text makes reference to two of these flowers. The melody and text are attributed to a 19th-century Javanese prince, who reportedly composed the piece to commemorate his favorite wives and concubines.

"Ketawang: Puspawarna" was traditionally performed as an entrance piece for the prince during royal ceremonies. It was used both to herald his arrival and to symbolize in musical sound his exalted status and due reverence. The recording heard here on **CD ex. #1-7** (originally released in 1971) was made at the Paku Alaman royal palace in Yogyakarta, Central Java. It features a famous set of gamelan instruments that is more than 250 years old.

The performance begins with an introduction played on a bowed chordophone with two strings, the *rebab*. Drums (*kendhang*) join the rebab about three seconds in, slowing the tempo slightly and cueing the entrance of the rest of the ensemble a few seconds later. The drummer is always the director of the ensemble, even though the drum parts in Central Javanese gamelan music tend to be subtle and understated.

The first stroke on the largest gong (at 0:07) marks the beginning of the composition proper. The 16-beat ketawang gong cycle commences here, as does a slow and steady-paced core melody played on several metallophone instruments (*saron*). During the course of the first gong cycle (0:07–0:22), all of the instruments of the ensemble enter. Most of the instrumental parts other than the drumming and the gong cycle are melodic. Some of the melodies are played on tuned sets of small bronze kettle-gongs (see photo, p. 91), others on a wooden-keyed xylophone-type instrument, others yet on keyed metallophone instruments or plucked chordophones. Some are quite sparse, steady-paced, and slow-moving, while others move along quickly with a great deal of rhythmic activity, or else seem to float temporarily beyond the confines of the metric rhythmic structure altogether.

The overall effect is of a complex and richly enveloping multiple-melody texture. The various layers of "basic" melody and melodic elaboration seem to weave in and out of each other like the many strands of a most intricate tapestry, with all of them ultimately answering to the authority of the drummer's direction (tempo changes, cueing of new musical sections) and the underlying constancy of the gong cycle.

Beginning with the second gong cycle, its arrival marked by a second stroke on the largest, lowest-pitched gong at 0:22, the vocalists—a male chorus and two female soloists—come increasingly to the fore. The multitiered symbolism of the sung poetic text—flowers, aesthetic philosophy, spirituality, and reflections on life, love, and romance all rolled into one—finds poignant parallels in the rich multidimensionality of the musical texture that frames it.

The historical significance of this recording of "Ketawang: Puspawarna" extends beyond its status as an exemplar of Central Javanese gamelan artistry. It was one of the selections included on the now-legendary Voyager Golden Record, a gold-plated, copper record album that was launched into space onboard NASA's two *Voyager* spacecraft in 1977. NASA's aim in producing the Golden Record was to create for posterity (and for the possible benefit of extraterrestrial life forms yet unknown to us) a compilation of sounds and images that would collectively portray the diversity of life and culture on earth. As of 2008, the two *Voyager* spacecraft had become just the third and fourth human-made objects ever to escape entirely from our solar system. They will presumably fly around in outer space as a time capsule of human cultural achievement for billions of years, or until some intelligent extraterrestrials manage to capture them (and perhaps figure out how to listen to the record as well), whichever comes first.

The Balinese counterpart to "Ketawang: Puspawarna" in our gamelan style comparison is "Jaya Semara" (Victorious Semara) (**CD ex. #2-12**). The piece is named for the god of love in Hindu-Balinese mythology, Semara, who resides in the floating sky and is married to the moon. It was composed by I Wayan Beratha (b. 1924; see the photo, p. 18), arguably the most important and influential Balinese composer of the 20th century. The introductory section of the piece, called the *kebyar* (which gives the ensemble its name), accounts for more than half of the performance's four-minute length. It alternates between explosive unison passages played by the entire ensemble and rapid interlocking passages that highlight individual sections of instruments within the ensemble. The *reyong,* which consists of a set of small kettle-gongs played by four musicians (see photo, p. 92), gets the most features, with especially impressive bursts of interlocking at 0:26–0:32 and 1:01–1:30. The high-pitched **gangsa** metallophones (see photo, p. 95) put their interlocking skills on display in the passage from 0:48–0:58. The two **kendang** drummers get their turn to shine in an extended interlocking duet from 1:51–2:10 (note that the spelling for the Balinese drums, *kendang,* differs slightly from that for the Javanese drums, *kendhang*).

The arrival of the gong cycle at 2:13 marks the beginning of the second main section of the piece, which continues until 3:29. Like its Javanese ketawang counterpart, this Balinese gong cycle has a length of 16 beats, but its sequence and pattern of gong strokes is different. The first beat of each gong cycle is marked by a very large, low-pitched gong (see photo, p. 92). Certain other beats within the cycle are marked by higher-pitched gongs. There is also a small, muffled gong that punctuates every one of the 16 beats of the cycle, providing a steady-beat pulse for the other musicians and for listeners (no instrument of equivalent function is used in the Javanese gamelan). A steady-paced core melody moves along at the same rate of 16 beats per cycle; this is performed on metallophones of relatively low pitch (e.g., the instrument seen at the bottom-left of the photo on p. 95).

A significant contrast to the Javanese piece is in the area of tempo, which in "Jaya Semara" is very fast. Each 16-beat cycle takes only about five seconds to complete (e.g., 2:13–2:18, 2:19–2:24). In "Ketawang: Puspawarna," the first gong cycle is 15 seconds long (0:07–0:22) and the second one, played at an even slower tempo, occupies a full 24 seconds (0:22–0:46).

Drumming is another area of marked contrast between the two pieces, and between Central Javanese and Balinese gamelan generally. In the Balinese case, like in the Javanese, it is the drumming part that directs the ensemble, signaling changes in tempo, cueing new sections of the piece, and so on. But whereas in the Javanese example there is just a single drummer who plays in a relatively understated manner, the Balinese example features two drummers playing fast and complex interlocking patterns in a flashy, virtuosic style. One drum is the "male," the other the "female" (though the two players are typically of the same gender, traditionally, but not always, male).

Complex, interlocking textures dominate the music at many other levels as well: all of the fastest-moving melodic parts result from two or more players performing different patterns that interlock to create an integrated whole. As in the opening kebyar, the different instrumental sections here are featured one after the other in spectacular interlocking displays as the form unfolds (e.g., drums at 2:13, metallophones at 2:31, kettle-gongs at 2:48). In this second section, however, a steady-beat accompaniment grounded in the music's 16-beat gong cycle and core melody provides a firm foundation for the interlocking pyrotechnics that emerge above it.

insights and perspectives

The Paired Tuning of Female and Male Instruments

One of the most striking features of the sound of a gamelan gong kebyar is its shimmering quality. This owes much to the unique **paired tuning** of sets of Balinese gamelan instruments. As noted, the gamelan gong kebyar features a number of melodic metallophone instruments called gangsa, which come in different sizes and octave ranges (see photo, p. 95). There is either one pair or two pairs of gangsa in each octave range. One instrument of each pair is identified as the "female," the other as the "male." The bronze keys of each male-female instrument pair are tuned to produce the exact same sequence of pitches. However, each female note is tuned slightly *lower* than its male counterpart. **Online Musical Illustration #21** illustrates this. First you hear a five-note ascending scale played on a female metallophone; then you hear the same scale played on that metallophone's male counterpart instrument. Notice how all five notes in the "male" scale are slightly higher in pitch.

Listening to these two different versions of the same scale, you might think that the two instruments are simply out of tune relative to each other. This apparent "out-of-tuneness" is intentional, however, for when the male and female notes are played together, the blending of their different pitches creates an acoustical beating effect called **ombak** (OAM-bahk), or "wave," that is the essence of the gamelan's brilliant, shimmering sound. Ombak is illustrated in **Online Musical Illustration #22.** In the example, you first hear a single tone played on the female instrument, then the "same" (slightly higher) tone played on the male instrument, and finally both female and male struck simultaneously to produce the ombak wave effect. After this, you hear the full scale of five notes illustrated earlier, but this time with *all* five notes played together on both the male and female metallophones, producing a series of ombak tones from bottom to top.

Balinese say that it is the ombak effect that breathes life into the sound of a gamelan. Without it, a gamelan is *mati,* literally, dead. Symbolically, then, it is the union of female and male elements that creates life in the gamelan, just as it is through the union of female and male in human life that new life is created. On another symbolic level, the lower-pitched tuning of the female instruments may be interpreted generally as a manifestation of Hindu-Balinese notions about gender, where femaleness is associated with the earth and maleness with the sky. (This is similar to the concept of Mother Earth and Father Sky in certain Native American cultures.)

The piece concludes with powerful, full-ensemble unison passages (3:30-end)—minus the gong cycle and core melody—that are reminiscent of the opening kebyar.

Comparing "Ketawang: Puspawarna" and "Jaya Semara" enables us to see how two different traditions with a shared ancestry and many closely related musical and cultural elements— Central Javanese court gamelan and Balinese gamelan gong kebyar—can yield music of strikingly different sound and character. We now turn our attention to other forms of Balinese gamelan, and ultimately to the gamelan beleganjur in particular.

BALINESE GAMELAN DIVERSITY The gamelan gong kebyar, though it is the best-known form of Balinese gamelan on an international scale by far, is, like its musical relative the gamelan beleganjur, but one of more than two dozen distinct types of gamelan found on the tiny, hyperartistic speck of the earth that is Bali. Each type has its own sound and characteristic style. Some feature bronze gongs and metallophones like those heard in the gamelan gong kebyar. Others do not, relying instead on instruments made with sounding materials of iron, hardwood, bamboo, and other substances. There is even one kind of gamelan, to which we will be introduced later, that uses no instruments per se at all, only voices. The music of some gamelans, like that of the grand and ancient *gamelan gong gedé* ("gamelan of the great gongs"), is in many ways closer in character to the regal Central Javanese gamelan tradition than to the fiery style of kebyar. And other gamelan musics bear little apparent resemblance to either of these. Different types of Balinese gamelan also are distinguished by cultural rather than specifically musical criteria. Each one has a unique, designated role within Balinese culture, being associated with particular rituals, ceremonies, dances, dance-dramas, shadow puppet plays, competitive events, and regional styles.

sekehe (SUH-kuh)

The culture of gamelan in Bali is not only rich and diverse, but also extraordinarily active. There are literally thousands of functioning gamelan clubs (*sekehe gong*) on the island dedicated to the preservation and cultivation of its myriad gamelan traditions. In the most densely populated areas, such as the capital city region of Denpasar and Ubud to its north, one can hear a different gamelan rehearsing on the corner of virtually every square block in the weeks leading up to a major gamelan competition.

Gangsa-type metallophones of a gamelan gong kebyar.

Of all the many different traditions that are carried on by Bali's scores of gamelan clubs, none is more ubiquitous or fundamental to the meeting of ritual and social requirements of Balinese life than the gamelan beleganjur.

The Gamelan Beleganjur: An Introduction

We begin our journey through the world of gamelan beleganjur with our first Musical Guided Tour, in which the following elements are introduced and explained:

- The instruments of the ensemble.
- The basic **gong cycle** (i.e., the recurring sequence of strokes on different gongs that serves as the music's foundation).
- The relationship between the music's core melody and the elaboration of that melody in other instrumental parts.
- The standard rhythms and interlocking rhythmic and melodic patterns employed.
- The stratified structure of the music, in which higher-pitched instruments play at faster rates than lower-pitched ones.

Though specifically intended as an introduction to the gamelan beleganjur and its music, this tour also focuses on musical elements and types of instruments that are characteristic of many other types of Balinese gamelan, including the gamelan gong kebyar. Many of these characteristics are even found in Central Javanese gamelan and gamelan traditions of other islands and cultures.

The text in the box below is a transcript of the audio Musical Guided Tour. As you listen to this tour at the Online Learning Center (www.mhhe.com/bakan2e), follow along with this transcript. Listening through headphones or good quality speakers is recommended.

musical guided tour

The Gamelan Beleganjur

The basic tempo-keeping instrument of the gamelan beleganjur is a medium-small gong called *kajar* (from the root *ajar,* meaning "to line things up"). It keeps a steady beat, like this [♪].

The root foundation of beleganjur music is a *gong cycle* of eight beats called **gilak** (GEE-lahk). It employs two very large gongs called the **gong ageng** (gohng ah-GUHNG), or "great gongs"; plus a medium-sized gong, the *kempur.* Here is the lowest gong ageng, which is identified as the female gong [♪] ; now the slightly higher-pitched male gong [♪]. Finally, here is the kempur [♪] . Combined together with the time-keeping kajar in the context of the eight-beat gilak gong cycle, these instruments sound like this [♪]. An

The instruments of the gamelan beleganjur: bendé, gong ageng (female, male), and kempur in back row, left to right; kendang (drums); reyong (4), kajar, kempluk (optional instrument, not discussed), and ponggang (2) in second row, left to right; cengceng (8 pairs) in front row. Note that the beleganjur version of the reyong consists of just four small kettle-gongs, each hand-held and played by a separate player. The reyong of the gamelan gong kebyar (see photo, p. 92) is a different type of instrument. All subsequent reyong references in the chapter are to the beleganjur type shown here.

additional, clangy-sounding gong called the *bendé* [♪] is usually added to the gilak gong cycle in beleganjur as well. Here is its contribution [♪]. The order of the gong strokes also may be reversed in gilak, which gives the gong cycle a rather different character, like this [♪].

The next musical layer above the gong cycle is the melodic layer. This has two components:

■ A core melody played on a pair of tuned, hand-held gongs (the *ponggang*), which sounds like this [♪]; and

■ Rapid-paced elaborations of the core melody played on a set of four smaller, higher-pitched, hand-held gongs called **reyong.** Each reyong "pot" is played by a different player. Player 1 performs this pattern on the highest pot [♪]. That pattern is then doubled on the lowest pot, like this [♪]. The second-highest pot fills in some of the rhythmic spaces, like this [♪]. Then the third-highest pot fills in the rest [♪]. Here now is the complete reyong part together with the core melody and the gongs [♪].

The third and final layer of the beleganjur musical texture is provided by drums and cymbals. There are two drums, which are called kendang. One is the female drum [♪]; the other, slightly higher in pitch, is the male drum [♪]. They are played in complex interlocking patterns, like this [♪]. The two drummers are the leaders of the beleganjur ensemble.

The rhythms of the crash cymbal parts are closely aligned with the drumming. There are eight pairs of cymbals, called *cengceng* (chayng-chayng), and eight cymbal players. The cymbal section alternates between performing unison rhythmic figures like this [♪] and interlocking patterns like this [♪]. The most common rhythm for cymbal interlocking is a simple pattern that sounds like this [♪]. By having some of the cymbal players play that pattern on the beat [♪], others play it starting just after the beat [♪], and the rest play it starting just ahead of the beat [♪], but all at the same time, a continuous stream of interlocking rhythmic sound is generated [♪]. This pattern of rhythmic interlocking is called **kilitan telu** (kee-lee-TAHN tuh-LOO). It is the basis of a great variety of different interlocking textures in Balinese music, some melodic, others purely rhythmic.

By way of conclusion, here is the complete gamelan beleganjur, played in a traditional style that incorporates all of the elements outlined above [♪].

Kilitan Telu Interlocking Rhythms:
A Musical Symbol of Communal Interdependence

The interlocking texture of the kilitan telu rhythmic patterns, as described and illustrated in the preceding Musical Guided Tour, is interesting not only on a purely musical level, but as a symbol of broader Balinese cultural values as well. Specifically, the kilitan telu and related forms of interlocking are poignant musical symbols of *communal interdependence* in Balinese society. In most every realm of life, from rice cultivation to the meeting of civic duties and religious practice, Balinese people give high priority to working together collectively in pursuit of their communal goals. Individuality and individual expression, so highly prized in Western cultures, tend to be less emphasized among the Balinese. The kilitan telu elegantly symbolizes a Balinese cultural vision of an integrated, interdependent community. Each of its three rhythms is identical to the other two but for its placement relative to the main beat, yet none of these rhythms is considered to be complete by itself; each one *needs* the other two. The kilitan telu whole, as represented sonically by the continuous stream of interlocking rhythm created when all three patterns are played together, is greater than the sum of its individual parts.

Balinese Kecak and the kilitan telu

The rhythmic patterns and interlocking textures of the kilitan telu extend across the full range of Balinese gamelan music, from beleganjur cymbal patterns to the intricate melodic tapestries of pieces like "Jaya Semara" (**CD ex. #2-12**). Another context in which they figure prominently is **Kecak,** a Balinese dance-drama with music provided by a gamelan comprised not of

Kecak (Ke-CHAHK)

A Balinese performance of Kecak.

instruments per se, but exclusively of voices, sometimes upwards of 200 of them! Appropriately, this massive vocal ensemble is called a *gamelan suara,* meaning "voice gamelan."

The musical roots of Kecak are found in an ancient trance ritual called Sanghyang Dedari, in which mesmerizing vocal chanting of the kilitan telu and other rhythmic patterns by a group of men surrounding an oil lamp was used to induce trance in female spirit mediums. During the ritual, these mediums would summon ancestral spirits to aid the village community during a time of crisis, especially if the villagers feared that they were under siege by malevolent spirit beings.

In Kecak, the small vocal group of Sanghyang Dedari is expanded into a huge rhythmic chorus, and gamelan gong cycles, melodies, and textures are recreated vocally, with onomatopoeic or other syllables substituting for the different gamelan instruments (for example, "sirrr" for the large gong and "pur" for the smaller gong called kempur). The interlocking rhythmic patterns of the kilitan telu—performed using the vocal syllable *cak* (chak)—remain central to the music. **CD ex. #2-13** is an excerpt from a Kecak performance that illustrates this spectacular and unique sound.

The Kecak dance-drama involves the enactment of episodes from a grand Hindu epic, the Ramayana. The most popular plot involves the kidnapping of a beautiful princess (Sita) by an evil king (Rawana) and her eventual rescue by her beloved Prince Rama and an army of monkeys. The musicians of the vocal gamelan double as actors, playing the roles of the monkeys in Rama's army.

In Bali, Kecak is promoted as an authentic, traditional Balinese dance-drama. In actuality, it is a modern invention, resulting in large part from a collaboration between Balinese musicians and dancers and an expatriate German painter named Walter Spies in connection with a 1933 German film entitled *Insel der Dämonen* (Island of Demons) (see Bakan 2009, Dibia 1996:6–9). Kecak was eventually developed into a dramatic production for tourist performances, and that is its primary cultural niche to the present day.

Experiencing Balinese interlocking, Kecak-style

To get a sense of how it feels to perform interlocking Balinese rhythms like those heard in Kecak, try performing the kilitan telu rhythms charted out in Figure 7.1 with some of your

	1	2	3	4	5	6	7	8	(1)
Pung	X	●	●	●	X	●	●	●	(X)
Chak 1	X	●	X	X	●	X	X	●	(X)
Chak 2	●	X	●	X	X	●	X	X	(●)
Chak 3	●	X	X	●	X	X	●	X	(●)

friends. Use the sound "chak" to articulate the notes with your voice, and if there are several of you participating, have one person mark out a steady pulse on the syllable "pung" while the others do interlocking "chak" patterns. Repeat the eight-beat cycle of Figure 7.1 multiple times without pause if you can. If you are uncomfortable doing this exercise vocally, you can clap out the rhythms instead.

The Gamelan Beleganjur in Battles of Good versus Evil

Perceived threats from malevolent spirit beings are an abiding concern for Balinese individuals and communities. Beleganjur music often plays a key role in ritual activities enacted to combat the forces of evil. According to Balinese lore, the gamelan beleganjur was originally created by evil spirits of the Lower World. Later, it was transformed into a powerful force for good after coming into the possession of the Balinese people of the Middle World. It has been an important source of mediation between the three worlds of the Balinese cosmos—Lower, Middle, and Upper—ever since.

In ritual contexts such as cremation processions, beleganjur music is performed to intimidate and drive away malevolent spirits who are said to travel to the earthly Middle World in order to cause harm to people and departing souls of the dead and to disrupt the delicate balance of the cosmos. Despite its supposed underworld origin, the imposing sound of beleganjur music is believed to have the power to frighten evil spirits, who it is hoped will be inclined to scatter in fear rather than face human adversaries equipped with such a potent sonic weapon.

Beleganjur music in Hindu-Balinese cremation processions

Beleganjur music is played in many kinds of rituals, but its presence is nowhere more crucial than in the grand processions of Hindu-Balinese cremation rituals (*ngaben*). The act of cremation is regarded as the first essential step that frees the soul, or **atma,** of the deceased from its ties to the earthly world so that it can commence its afterlife journey to worlds beyond. Ideally, this journey leads to the paradise-like Upper World of the gods and ancestors, where the atma goes to await reincarnation and a return to the Middle World in some form, or, in the most sublime of outcomes, to experience liberation from the cycle of reincarnation altogether and gain a permanent home in the Upper World.

First, though, the body or exhumed remains (bodies of the dead are sometimes buried for a lengthy period of time prior to being cremated) must be ritually prepared and taken in a large cremation tower (*wadah*) (see photo, p. 100) from the family home compound of the deceased to the Temple of the Dead at the far end of the village. This journey takes the form of a communal procession. The procession ideally involves the participation of all members of the deceased's **banjar.** The term *banjar* is usually translated as "village ward" or "hamlet," though "neighborhood organization" may be more apt. A banjar typically consists of between 50 and 500 families and is responsible for planning and producing most of the core communal, religious,

ngaben (nya-buhn)

banjar (BAHN-jahr)

Cremation tower being carried in procession.

and social activities of its membership (Eiseman 1990:72–73). The planning and production of cremations and other mortuary rituals represent the highest calling of the banjar community.

The procession to the cremation grounds is thought to be fraught with peril. Deceased souls who have yet to be cremated are considered dangerously vulnerable to the meddlesome practices of bhutas, leyaks, and other evil spirits. It is feared that these forces of evil will abduct the uncremated, unliberated atma and drag it down to the underworld. The banjar community uses all resources at its disposal to ensure that this does not happen. The performance of beleganjur music is among the most important of these. The music is believed to help both the atma of the deceased and the banjar community in several different ways, both during the course of the procession and during the act of cremation itself.

At the start of the procession, the beleganjur group assembles and lines up immediately behind the cremation tower. It maintains this position throughout the procession. Men and women singing sacred verses also gather in close proximity to the tower. Although the singing is entirely unrelated to the beleganjur music, the two together contribute to a rich musical cacophony that helps to generate the desired state of *ramé,* or "crowdedness," that is a hallmark of virtually every Balinese ritual or social occasion. Other types of processional gamelan may contribute to this ramé soundscape as well, and the general rule is that the more kinds of music there are—the more "crowded" and multifarious the soundscape is, in other words—the better.

insights and perspectives

Caste and Class in Bali

As in other Hindu societies such as India, social organization among the Balinese has traditionally relied upon a *caste system.* A caste is a hereditary social class. In caste societies, every individual is born into a specific caste. One's caste may determine anything from educational and professional opportunities in this life to one's spiritual destiny in lives beyond.

The Balinese caste system is different from the caste system of India (where the whole concept of a social system organized around caste is now officially banned by law, though the vestiges of a caste-based social order are by no means entirely gone—see also Chapter 8, p. 125). In the Balinese system, there are four castes: the priestly caste, the warrior caste, the merchant caste, and the commoner caste (*sudra*—literally "outsider"). About 90 percent of Balinese Hindus belong to the commoner caste. There is no "Untouchables" (Dalit) caste in Bali, in contrast to the traditional Indian caste system.

Functionally, caste affiliation in Bali has mainly to do with one's religious life and obligations: temple affiliations, cremation rites, in some cases priestly duties. Beyond the religious sphere, in social and professional life, caste is much less operative, though not necessarily irrelevant. With the exception of certain sectors of the priesthood, Balinese from all castes associate freely with one another in daily life and business and are generally at liberty to pursue the educational and professional paths of their choice and take part equally in civil affairs.

The tower consists of multiple tiers that represent the three worlds of the Balinese cosmos. The body of the deceased is placed near the top of the tower, symbolizing the hope of its ascent to the Upper World. It is wrapped in a long white cloth, symbolizing purity. The number of tower carriers depends on the size of the tower. It may range from a half dozen men for a small tower to upwards of 20—and in some cases many more than that—for a large one. The largest towers are reserved for wealthy and high-caste individuals (see "Insights and Perspectives" box on page 100 regarding caste).

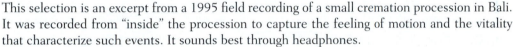

guided listening experience

Beleganjur Music Performed during a Balinese Cremation Procession

- CD Track #2-14
- Featured performer(s)/group: Beleganjur group of Banjar Belaluan Sadmerta, Denpasar, Bali, Indonesia
- Format: Excerpt
- Source recording: Field recording by the author

This selection is an excerpt from a 1995 field recording of a small cremation procession in Bali. It was recorded from "inside" the procession to capture the feeling of motion and the vitality that characterize such events. It sounds best through headphones.

As the recording begins, we find ourselves on a street in Denpasar outside the home of the deceased. The members of the banjar have been summoned to begin the procession to the cremation grounds. A group of women and men sing sacred verses (*kidung*) as poetic offerings to the gods and ancestors, imploring their benevolence to ensure a good cremation and safe passage of the departed soul to a good afterlife. The body of the deceased, adorned in a long white cloth, is being placed in the upper tiers of the cremation tower. We hear clicks and taps as final adjustments are made to the tower and the body is eased into its proper place. The tower bearers stand ready to lift the heavy tower onto their shoulders and prepare themselves for the long march ahead. Procession organizers move about the area, telling people to step backward or forward into proper formation and closing off the street to traffic. The beleganjur group takes its place immediately behind the tower. (*Note:* There is no reyong section in the ensemble in this example, as sometimes occurs in ritual beleganjur performances like this one.)

kidung (kee-DOONG)

At 0:36, the lead drummer (performing on the "male" drum) starts to play, cueing the rest of the musicians to raise up their instruments and "announcing" to the entire congregation that the procession is about to begin. He is joined in a brief interlocking flourish by the second drummer (playing the "female" drum) at 0:40, and this cues the entry of the full ensemble at 0:41. Just as the first gong stroke and cymbal crash are sounded, the tower carriers hoist the cremation tower up on their shoulders and the procession begins, with everyone moving at a quick and energetic pace. Unison cymbal rhythms, reinforced by the drumming, are pounded out over the propulsive gong tones of the gilak gong cycle. The unison rhythms give way to a brief passage of interlocking rhythm at 0:53.

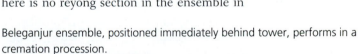

Beleganjur ensemble, positioned immediately behind tower, performs in a cremation procession.

Next, at 0:56, the drums and cymbals lay out momentarily while the gong cycle continues. Interlocking drumming and cymbal rhythms follow, with the cymbal section playing its signature kilitan telu patterns (1:06–1:38). The dynamic level of the cymbals and drums rises and falls at different points, reflecting and influencing the pace and energy of the procession. The lead drummer keeps a careful eye on the proceedings, calibrating and adjusting the musical intensity in accordance with the event's functional needs. At 1:39, the cymbals drop out and the two drummers come to the fore, playing an intricate drum duet. The cymbals sneak back in at 1:50, then launch into their kilitan telu interlocking again at 1:54, rising and falling in dynamics and ending with an emphatic CENG! CENG! at 2:05. The drummers and cymbal players rest as the gong cycle continues through to the fade-out ending.

guided listening quick summary

Beleganjur Music Performed during a Balinese Cremation Procession (CD ex. #2-14)

0:00–0:35

- Sound of crowd assembling, singing of sacred verses (kidung).

0:36–0:55

- Entry of lead drummer (0:36), cueing beleganjur ensemble and signaling beginning of procession.
- Full ensemble enters over gilak gong cycle at 0:41 (as tower carriers hoist tower onto their shoulders and the procession begins); unison rhythms in cymbals.
- Brief passage of kilitan telu cymbal interlocking cymbal at end of section (0:53–0:55).

0:56–1:05

- Gong cycle only (no drums or cymbals), followed by interlocking drumming and return of cymbals.

1:06–1:38

- Long passage featuring kilitan telu cymbal interlocking.

1:39–1:49

- Drum duet feature section.

1:50–end

- Cymbals reenter, more kilitan telu interlocking; excerpt fades out after 2:05 as gong cycle continues.

Crossroad battles and a musical ladder to the Upper World

The beleganjur ensemble's assigned task in the cremation procession is far from over at the point where the music fades out at the end of the preceding musical selection (**CD ex. #2-14**). It plays continuously from the start to the finish of the procession, providing a steady yet dynamic sonic backdrop to the ritual proceedings.

Its role is especially important at crossroads along the procession route. Balinese believe that crossroads are the locations where bhutas and leyaks congregate in greatest abundance. They are very dangerous places, especially for vulnerable, uncremated souls of the dead, upon whom the evil spirits are most likely to prey. At every crossroad the cremation tower is spun around in a circle at least three times, as quickly as possible (see the photo, p. 100). This is done because it is believed that the bhutas and leyaks can only travel in straight lines. Thus, the spinning of the tower is thought to confuse them and prevent them from invading the tower to capture the atma.

The spinning of the tower at crossroads is accompanied by beleganjur music of especially great volume and intensity. This energetic music serves several purposes. First, it is believed that it has power, in and of itself, to frighten and deflect potentially meddlesome bhutas and leyaks. Second, it is used to inspire physical strength and courage among the carriers of the heavy tower, who face a formidable challenge in their efforts to spin the tower with sufficient speed and energy. Third, it is hoped that it will embolden the atma of the deceased itself, who it is believed otherwise may be tempted to flee the tower in fear of the advancing evil spirits, destroying its prospects for a good cremation and a successful afterlife.

At the end of its trek, the processional entourage finally reaches the cremation grounds. The beleganjur group concludes its performance with a climactic passage played just after the tower is lowered to the ground. The body (or its remains) is then removed from the tower, ritually prepared for cremation, and encased in an animal-shaped sarcophagus while the beleganjur musicians briefly rest. Then, as soon as the burning of the sarcophagus begins, they start playing again, performing music of a quieter and more meditative character in a song of farewell that is intended to accompany the departing soul on its journey. This music may be described metaphorically as a ladder upon which the atma, having achieved the first stage of its liberation from the bonds of earthly life and the precarious state of death before cremation, may finally begin its ascent to the Upper World.

Walking Warriors: Worldly Battlegrounds of Beleganjur Music

In exploring the role of beleganjur in Hindu-Balinese cremation rituals, we have seen how it functions as a music of battle, in particular, of battles fought between human communities and their evil spirit adversaries over control of the fates of deceased souls.

Beleganjur music also was performed for battles of a different kind in former times: battles of war fought by the armies of rival Balinese kingdoms. Bali was ravaged by frequent and brutal wars throughout much of its precolonial history. Warfare was glorified. The Balinese kings (*rajas*) were regarded by their subjects as semidivine beings. To fight for one's king and his kingdom was thus to fight on behalf of the deities. The great Balinese warrior was a heroic figure.

Warfare in Bali was accompanied by grand pageantry and ritual, and music played on the gamelan beleganjur, the "gamelan of walking warriors," was key. Balinese armies marched into battle to the accompaniment of beleganjur. The music served to inspire the warriors to bravery and to strike terror in the hearts of their enemies. With a faint hum of gongs advancing like a distant storm before an explosion of lightning cymbals and thunderous drums, beleganjur music heralded the impending doom of battle with foreboding power and force. Human rather than spirit adversaries represented the principal targets of beleganjur's threatening tones in this context, but the basic theme of a music used for battle connects the worlds of beleganjur as a music of cremation rituals and as a historical music of actual warfare.

Lomba beleganjur: The modern beleganjur contest

Though beleganjur's traditional role as a music of warfare has been rendered obsolete in modern times, the revered image of the heroic Balinese warrior of old has by no means disappeared. It is kept alive in many different contexts, from the famous Baris "warrior's dance" (see photo, p. 104) to countless dance-dramas and shadow puppet plays (*wayang kulit*) that chronicle the martial exploits of both the historical and mythical Balinese past.

This heroic warrior's image resurfaced anew in the mid-1980s with the invention of the modern beleganjur contest, or *lomba beleganjur*. In a lomba beleganjur, numerous beleganjur groups representing different banjars, districts, or regions of Bali compete against each other in a formal competitive environment. The first lomba beleganjur was held in Denpasar in 1986. More than two dozen groups from the city and its surrounding region (Badung) competed. The performers were all male, predominantly teenagers and young men in their early 20s.

Badung (Bah-DOONG)

The contest was a great success and within short order had become the model for scores of similar events held all over the island. These contests range from small regional competitions featuring just a handful of groups to islandwide championships played out before audiences of thousands in high-profile, politically charged events. The larger contests are frequently held in

Group performing in a beleganjur contest.

conjunction with election campaigns and political rallies. Many are sponsored by Balinese cultural agencies of the Indonesian government. The synthesis of Balinese cultural pride and modern Indonesian nationalist values that these contests are said to invoke fits well with an idealized, Unity in Diversity–based image of Indonesian cultural nationalism.

Women's and children's beleganjur groups have emerged since the 1990s, though the contest style of beleganjur, in common with beleganjur played in traditional ritual contexts such as cremations, is still mainly identified with men, and indeed with core Balinese conceptions of manhood and masculinity (see also Chapter 2, pp. 16–18).

Kreasi beleganjur: The contest musical style

kreasi
(kray-YAH-see)

The lomba beleganjur contest event has given rise to a dramatic, neo-traditional beleganjur musical style with its own, unique performance aesthetic. This is known as **kreasi beleganjur,** or "new creation beleganjur."

Traditional beleganjur such as that performed in cremation processions is quintessentially *functional* music. Its sole purpose is to support the ritual it accompanies. Kreasi beleganjur is something else altogether. It is flashy, fast, complex, inventive, full of musical contrasts and surprises, and enhanced by elaborate pageantry, colorful costumes, and impressive choreographed movement sequences (see the photo on p. 106). Yet for all of that, it remains strongly rooted in the musical soil of traditional beleganjur.

Contest audiences may be very large; thousands of spectators come to the biggest events. They also can be quite raucous and unruly, pressing forward and encircling the musicians with almost suffocating closeness as the contest officials attempt to push them back out of the performance arena. At a good contest, the energy is electrifying as the musicians and the crowd feed off of each other's excitement and intensity.

The exciting, virtuosic style of a beleganjur contest performance is well illustrated by **CD ex. #2-15.** This is an excerpt from a 1995 field recording made in Bali that features a composition by the great beleganjur composer and drummer I Ketut Sukarata. The group featured is from the Sanur Beach region of southeastern Bali, where the contest was held. We first hear them approaching from the distance. The master of ceremonies builds up anticipation as they near the judging area. Applause from the crowd marks their arrival. All of the instruments except the gongs drop out for a while. Then the full group reenters overtop the continuing gilak gong cycle—first drums and reyong kettle-gongs, then cymbals—and the music becomes highly energetic.

I Ketut Sukarata.

I Ketut Sukarata (Ee Kuh-TOOT Soo-kah-rah-tuh)

Sanur (Sah-NOOR)

This is music in which precision, virtuosity, and originality, not just functionality, are both valued and formally graded. Its main "job" is to impress and entertain the adjudicators and audience rather than serve the functional ritual requirements of a religious ritual. The goal of the performers is to win the contest rather than battles against malevolent spirit adversaries.

Tradition and innovation in kreasi beleganjur: An elusive balance

Kreasi beleganjur differs from traditional beleganjur in the high value it places on the following:

- Compositional originality.

- Ensemble virtuosity (*Note:* not *individual* virtuosity—the group, rather than the musician, is always the "star").

- Emphasis on showmanship, both in the playing of the music itself and in **gerak** (literally "movement"), which are choreographed sequences performed by the musicians (see the "Insights and Perspectives" box, p. 106).

gerak (GUH-rahk)

- Varied textures, in which different sections of the ensemble (drums, cymbals, reyong) are featured in turn.

In all of these priorities, kreasi beleganjur exhibits strong influences drawn from the style of kebyar music, such as that heard and discussed earlier in **CD ex. #2-12** ("Jaya Semara"). Some beleganjur composers also have been influenced by popular music styles. Sukarata, for example, gained notoriety in the late 1980s for his incorporation into beleganjur of rhythms adapted from hip-hop and funk.

The key to creating a successful, prize-winning kreasi beleganjur contest piece is to be found in achieving a balance between beleganjur traditionalism and modernity. On the one hand, a high priority is placed on adhering to key elements of form and style that define traditional beleganjur music: the eight-beat gilak gong cycle, kilitan telu interlocking, conventional beleganjur instrumentation and stylistic features. On the other hand, this traditional base needs to be embellished by elements of novelty, compositional innovation, virtuosity, and showmanship.

Gerak: The Choreographic Element in Kreasi Beleganjur

Gerak are the choreographed movement sequences in kreasi beleganjur performances. They are executed by the musicians themselves as they play. This is one of the highlight features of the beleganjur contest style. The root of gerak is to be found in choreographic sequences that alternately invoke and "comment upon" the central figure of the archetypal traditional Balinese warrior and his *kepahlawanan,* or "heroic," character. Classic poses of battle and martial arts maneuvers are precisely executed by the musicians in their mutually reflective duet of sound and movement. These choreographic images are juxtaposed to others that draw from various beleganjur-related domains, such as the spinning of the cremation tower at a cross-road during a cremation procession. Gerak also may be used to humorous effect. The gerak sequences for Sukarata's "Brek Dan" (Break Dance), for example, caricatured the sometimes comical moves and grooves of nightclub dancers in Bali.

All told, kreasi beleganjur gerak represents a mélange of diverse choreographic and symbolic expression. Lighthearted, satirical moments ebb and flow against the current of more solemn and reverential characterizations. Gerak choreographies offer a poignant commentary on the complex and multidimensional nature of contemporary Balinese-Indonesian identity, one that is completely consistent with the character of kreasi beleganjur music itself.

Gerak maneuver in a beleganjur contest.

The right balance is difficult to achieve. Groups that fail to bring enough creativity and novelty to their performances are met with indifference and may even be ridiculed. But those that stray too far from the style and character of traditional beleganjur in their innovations risk public scorn and possible disqualification.

Achieving the elusive balance: The kreasi beleganjur music of I Ketut Suandita

If there is any figure in the kreasi beleganjur world whose music epitomizes an ideal balance of traditionalism and creative innovation, it is I Ketut Suandita. Suandita grew up playing beleganjur, kebyar, and other styles of gamelan and studied composition with I Ketut Gedé Asnawa and other master teachers. By the age of 23, he had achieved the unprecedented distinction of being the composer of the winning composition in Bali's most prestigious beleganjur contest three years straight (1990, 1991, and 1992). Not only that, but he directed three different groups from three different villages to those championships, and performed as the lead drummer for two of them. Experts like Asnawa describe the early 1990s as a "golden age" of kreasi beleganjur, pointing to Suandita as the exemplary beleganjur composer of that period.

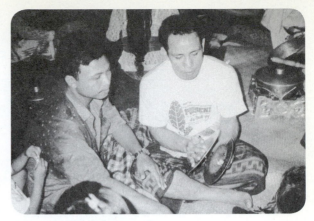

I Ketut Suandita (right).

**Suandita
(Swahn-DEE-tuh)**

guided listening experience

"Wira Ghorava Cakti '95" (Kreasi Beleganjur), by I Ketut Suandita

- CD Track #: **2-16**
- Featured performer(s)/group: Beleganjur group of Banjar Meranggi, Denpasar, Bali, Indonesia
- Format: Excerpt
- Source recording: Field recording by the author

Suandita's distinctive kreasi beleganjur style is well exemplified in the work "Wira Ghorava Cakti" (Friendly and Spiritually Powerful Hero), a prize-winning piece performed here (in an excerpt from a 1995 performance) by the group from the banjar of Meranggi that Suandita directed to the 1992 beleganjur championship. This ensemble is recognized as one of the best beleganjur groups ever.

"Wira Ghorava Cakti" never loses sight of its traditional beleganjur roots, but it pushes the boundaries of tradition with a host of innovations that were highly novel for their time. These include:

**"Wira Ghorava
Cakti" ("Wee-rah
Go-rah-vah
CHAK-tee")**

- Sections in which the gong cycle drops out completely.
- Passages that feature just one type of instrument performing unaccompanied, such as the reyong feature section at 0:19.
- A large variety of melodic and rhythmic variations, all highlighting ensemble precision and virtuosity.
- A wide range of tempos and frequent changes in dynamics.
- More complex styles of interlocking, such as having eight different interlocking cymbal patterns rather than just the three standard patterns of the kilitan telu.

Listen to the example now, following along with the Guided Listening Quick Summary on the next page and trying to hear the musical features identified.

Crossing International Borders

Composers from outside of Indonesia have long held a fascination for gamelan music. Ever since the important French composer Claude Debussy heard a Javanese gamelan at the 1889 World's Fair in Paris, many non-Indonesian composers have been influenced by, and in some cases written works for, Javanese and Balinese gamelan: John Cage, Lou Harrison, Colin McPhee, Benjamin Britten, Philip Glass, Steve Reich, Michael Tenzer, Wayne Vitale, Evan

guided listening quick summary

"Wira Ghorava Cakti '95," by I Ketut Suandita (CD ex. #2-16)

0:00–0:06

■ Excerpt begins with impressive interlocking drumming, syncopated cymbal rhythms; gilak gong cycle provides foundation.

0:07–0:18

■ Brief passage featuring distinctive, eight-part interlocking cymbal texture (0:07–0:09).

■ Reyong, drums, and other instruments come in from 0:10 on.

0:19–0:27

■ Unaccompanied reyong feature (gong cycle drops out); superb example of fast, intricate reyong interlocking.

0:28–1:14

■ Gong cycle returns; talents of full ensemble on display; good examples of more eight-part cymbal interlocking from 0:38.

1:15–1:28

■ Transition to slow-tempoed section of the piece; contrasting musical character.

1:29–2:11

■ Slow section proper begins (over a dramatically slower gilak gong cycle).

■ Unpredictable and dramatic changes in tempo, texture, and rhythm.

2:12–end

■ Drums and cymbals play at double the tempo of the other instruments, creating an effect of two levels of tempo (slow and fast) occurring at once.

■ Excerpt fades out as performance continues (3:00).

Ziporyn, Barbara Benary. Even pop stars like Janet Jackson (on "China Love") and Beck (on "Loser") have used digital samples of gamelan in their music.

Indonesian composers have likewise been influenced by Western and other international musics, both in the popular music arena and in the experimental, avant-garde genre of Indonesian *musik kontemporer* ("contemporary music"), which combines Indonesian and non-Indonesian musical elements in novel ways. A number of prominent Balinese composers, including Asnawa and his brother I Komang Astita, have composed internationally acclaimed musik kontemporer works.

On the popular music side, the contemporary Balinese musician of widest international reputation today is the virtuoso electric guitarist I Wayan Balawan, who leads the innovative band Batuan Ethnic Fusion (BEF). Balawan and BEF were the first Balinese artists to be signed by Sony BMG, one of the largest and most influential multinational record companies. The group's 2005 Sony BMG release *Magic Finger* features a track entitled "Country Beleganjur," which is also included in its entirety on your CD set as **CD ex. #2-17.** This selection combines elements of beleganjur and kebyar music from Bali with elements of American country music, bluegrass, rock, funk, and jazz; there even seem to be some traces of polka in the mix, and the whole production has a lighthearted, tongue-in-cheek quality to it. Balawan's blistering speed on the guitar, a signature feature of his style, is put on fine display in the bouncy, bluegrass-tinged opening section of the track following the introduction (0:15–0:54). The lively, two-beat groove laid down by the electric bassist and the drum set player here is enhanced by kilitan telu-type cymbal patterns furnished by four cengceng players performing in the standard beleganjur interlocking

musik kontemporer (moo-SEEK koan-tuhm-poh-RAYR)

Astita (Ah-stee-tuh)

style. (A video performance, http://wn.com/Batuan, which was available at the time of this writing, has the cengceng players wearing Balinese attire identical to that worn by competitors in Balinese beleganjur contests.) A fun and quirky section from 0:55–1:07 juxtaposes a polka-like melody in the guitar part to kotekan-style melodic interlocking reminiscent of beleganjur reyong parts. The clash of Western and Balinese pitches here creates an effect that is at once intriguing and humorous. The next section of the arrangement is all percussion (plus some percussive, Kecak-style vocals), with the cengceng section playing in precisely the manner they would in a Balinese beleganjur contest (including fine displays of kilitan telu interlocking) and the drum set backing them up with a driving, funk-rock groove (1:11–1:29). The cengcengs and drum set are eventually joined by a pair of Balinese kendang drums (1:30–1:49), which also are played in the beleganjur con-

I Wayan Balawan playing a double-necked electric guitar.

test style. Following the percussion feature, the texture and style change abruptly as Balawan launches into an improvised jazz guitar solo accompanied by the rhythm section (1:50–2:28). Unison figures by the cengcengs, along with vocal parts akin to melodies heard in Kecak and occasional violin riffs, provide an interesting twist to the otherwise straight-up jazz style. Finally, Balawan and the band return to the lively two-beat groove and country/bluegrass/Balinese style of the opening to round out the performance (2:29–end).

guided listening experience

"B.A.Ph.PET," by Michael Bakan

- CD Track #: **2-18**
- Featured performer(s)/group: Charles Tremblay (scratch turntable soloist) with the Florida State University Balinese Gamelan
- Format: Excerpt
- Source recording: From the personal archive of the author (all rights reserved)

Gamelan performance groups are active today in many countries, from the United States and Canada, to the United Kingdom, Italy, and Japan. The majority of these groups specialize in Javanese gamelan traditions, but there are a number of Balinese gamelan ensembles as well. The best-known of the latter is Gamelan Sekar Jaya, based in Berkeley, California. Additionally, there are Balinese gamelan programs at a number of universities, including UCLA, the University of British Columbia, Bowling Green State University, and Florida State University (FSU). The final piece of music we will explore in this chapter, "B.A.Ph.PET," was composed for the student Balinese gamelan group I direct at FSU.

"B.A.Ph.PET" is a post-traditional Balinese gamelan piece scored for gamelan gong kebyar instruments, the four reyong kettle-gongs of a gamelan beleganjur, keyboard synthesizer, synthesized drums and percussion, electric bass, and scratch turntable soloist. The scratch turntable part is improvised; all of the other parts are composed. The turntable soloist is Charles Tremblay, who was an FSU student, gamelan member, and dance club DJ working in the Tallahassee area when this recording was made (1997). Charles, a percussionist by training, performed with the FSU gamelan for several years. He was a standout member of the group, excelling especially in the difficult art of Balinese kendang drumming. For his final concert with the ensemble, we decided to create a work that would highlight his talents as a turntablist while

Florida State University Balinese gamelan, with Charles Tremblay playing kendang (drum).

exploring some new possibilities of intercultural gamelan music. "B.A.Ph.PET," short for "Big Attitude Phat Pet" (in honor of a dog with a rather memorable personality), was the result.

The gamelan aspect of "B.A.Ph.PET" incorporates many conventional Balinese elements: gong cycle, core melody, interlocking parts, a texture that features fast-moving parts in the high-pitched instruments and slow-moving parts in the low-pitched ones. All of these Balinese elements, however, are tied to Western-style chord progressions and synthesizer melodies in some portions of the piece. And they are progressively encompassed by hip-hop/funk drum rhythms, bass lines, and improvised turntabling during the second part of the work, which commences at 1:26.

Many of the rhythms and interlocking patterns of "B.A.Ph.PET," including the opening rhythmic ostinato played on muffled reyong kettle-gongs, derive from a shortened variant of the basic kilitan telu rhythm. Rather than the full pattern of [x-xx-xx-], a truncated pattern of [x-xx--] is used instead (see Figure 7.2). Uncontentional clusters of gamelan pitches (chords) add dissonance to the musical effect.

During the first minute of the piece, the gamelan instruments enter one after another, section by section. Multiple ostinato layers are stacked atop each other as more instruments join in. Many of the parts interlock, until all of the rhythmic spaces are ultimately filled in by a dense texture of interlocking melody and polyphonic richness. To this texture is finally added a synthesizer melody, which arrives at 0:54, supported by low gong tones and an electric bass part.

The second part of the piece commences with a return to the single reyong texture of the opening at 1:26, followed by the entrances of synthesized drums (1:30), electric bass (1:33),

Basic kilitan telu rhythmic pattern compared to truncated "B.A.Ph.PET" rhythmic pattern.

FIGURE 7.2

	1	2	3	4	5	6	7	8	1	2	3	4	5	6	7	8	(1)
Kilitan telu	X	•	X	X	•	X	X	•	X	•	X	X	•	X	X	•	(X)
B.A.Ph.PET	X	•	X	X	•	•	X	•	X	X	•	•	X	•	X	X	(•)

and scratch turntable soloist (1:39) in quick succession. Beginning at 2:29, the gamelan instruments gradually reenter amidst this radically transformed musical enviroment in the same order as before, and playing essentially the same parts. The music builds progressively, both in instrumental layers and in intensity, through to the full ensemble climax near the end (3:55).

Two scratch turntablists. Afrika Bambaataa, the "Godfather of Hip-Hop," is seen in the left-side photo.

guided listening quick summary

"B.A.Ph.PET," by Michael Bakan (CD ex. #2-18)

PART I

0:00–0:13

- The four reyong kettle-gongs come in one after the other, together building a dissonant cluster of notes (chord).
- Ostinato rhythm is a shortened variant of the basic kilitan telu rhythmic pattern.

0:14–0:53

- Large gong enters, followed by metallophones (gangsa).
- Instruments continue to enter, one by one, gradually filling out texture with multiple layers and interlocking ostinato parts.

0:54–1:25

- Synthesizer melody unfolds over steady, slow-moving core melody in lower-register metallophones.
- Sequence of low gong strokes (supplemented by electric bass tones) combines elements of a Balinese-style gong cycle and the bass line of a Western-style chord progression.

Summary

Though it covered a broad range of gamelan and gamelan-based music traditions—Central Javanese court gamelan, Balinese gamelan gong kebyar, Balinese Kecak, and intercultural fusion music—the principal focus of this chapter was the gamelan beleganjur. After situating beleganjur in its broader musical, social, and cultural contexts and following a Musical Guided Tour, we explored the ensemble's multiple roles and functions in traditional Hindu-Balinese cremation rituals (ngaben). From there, we moved on to the modern, contest style of kreasi beleganjur. We concluded with explorations of intercultural fusion music that combines elements of Balinese gamelan and Western popular music styles.

A unifying theme of this entire journey was the principle of interlocking. A specific, ubiquitous set of interlocking rhythms, the kilitan telu, was tracked through virtually all of the music introduced. Sometimes left intact in its conventional form and at other times transformed through various types of manipulations, this enduring component of Balinese musical identity took on many different forms but was always found to be present in one guise or another. Moreover, the interlocking principle underlying the kilitan telu was shown to inform larger cultural practices and values that are central to Balinese life, such as the high priority placed on communal interdependence.

Whether across oceans, between cosmic realms, or between music instruments, the concept of interlocking permeates gamelan music and its culture on many levels. It is a key to understanding both the resilience and vitality of the Balinese musicultural tradition.

Key Terms

gamelan	gamelan gong kebyar	reyong
gamelan beleganjur	gangsa	kilitan telu
Central Javanese court gamelan	paired tuning	Kecak
Bahasa Indonesia	ombak	atma
Unity in Diversity	gong cycle	banjar
Agama Tirta	gilak	kreasi beleganjur
Bali Aga	gong ageng	gerak

Study Questions

- What is a gamelan?

- The best-known gamelan traditions of Indonesia are from what two islands?

- What are some of the basic similarities and differences between Central Javanese court gamelan and Balinese gamelan gong kebyar?

- What kinds of instruments are used in the gamelan beleganjur? Is it usually played from a seated position or in processional style?

- What is the capital city of the Republic of Indonesia? What is the capital city of Bali?

- What are the best-known gamelan traditions of Java and Bali, respectively? (*Hint:* gamelan beleganjur is *not* a correct answer.)

- What were the *general* musicultural features of gamelan music outlined in the chapter?

- What is ombak? Paired tuning?

- How does the kilitan telu set of rhythmic patterns, as well as other sets of interlocking patterns that are pervasive in Balinese music, represent a musical manifestation of important *cultural* values in Balinese society? What other kinds of cultural (including religious) symbolism are present in gamelan music?

- In what ways does beleganjur music function as a "weapon" in the battles against evil spirits that occur during Hindu-Balinese cremation processions?

- In what year was the first beleganjur contest held? Where did it take place?

- What features of musical form and style distinguish kreasi beleganjur from traditional beleganjur (and what common features link the two)?

- What is gerak, and what is its importance in kreasi beleganjur performance?

- What innovations did the composer Suandita introduce into kreasi beleganjur music?

- What famous French composer first heard gamelan at the World's Fair in Paris in 1889 and subsequently was influenced by the experience?

- What Balinese and American popular music styles are combined in I Wayan Balawan's "Country Beleganjur"?

- How does the piece "B.A.Ph.PET" build upon standard musical conventions and instrumentation of Balinese gamelan music? In what ways does it depart from gamelan tradition?

Discussion Questions

- The history of the Balinese dance-drama Kecak provides an interesting example of the kind of complex relationships between tradition and modernity that define many world music traditions. Though it is promoted as a "traditional Balinese genre," it is in fact a product of 20th-century intercultural innovation. Try to think of types of music with which you are familiar that are marketed as "traditional" and "authentic" despite being modern and contemporary in many if not most respects. Discuss these in class.

- In this chapter, "B.A.Ph.PET" is presented as a piece belonging to the tradition of Balinese gamelan. What do you think of this? Should music of this kind be played using gamelan instruments, or is this inappropriate? Is there any point at which musicians should be expected to draw the line in terms of how far they go in their efforts to fuse very different music traditions? On these same terms, what are your thoughts and views on Balawan's "Country Beleganjur"?

Applying What You Have Learned

- Look closely at the kilitan telu rhythmic patterns charted in Figure 7.1 (p. 99). Try to figure out how all three patterns are in fact the "same" rhythm placed at different points relative to the main beat. One of these rhythms is known as the "follower," another as the "anticipator." Can you tell which is which and explain why?

- A metaphor of battle is central to the cultural functions of beleganjur music on many levels. Thinking about what you have learned about the beleganjur tradition in this chapter, create a list of different ways in which this battle metaphor plays out in actual Balinese cultural practice, both in traditional ritual contexts and in modern beleganjur contests.

- Search YouTube for video examples of gamelan and Indonesian popular music. Write a brief report on your findings.

Resources for Further Study

Visit the Online Learning Center at www.mhhe.com/bakan2e, as well as the author's personally maintained Web site at www.michaelbakan.com, for additional learning aids, study help, and resources that supplement the content of this chapter.

chapter eight

from **raga** to bollywood:
developments and **intercultural** crossings
in **Indian music**

Related locations:

Canada
France
Italy
United Kingdom
United States

Boston
London
New York
Paris
San Rafael, California

Music, for the Indian, is the food of his soul. . . . Music, being the finest of arts, helps the soul to rise above differences. It unites souls, because even words are not necessary. Music stands beyond words.

Hafez Inayat Khan,
The Mysticism of Sound and Music

The year: 1965. The song "Norwegian Wood" appears on a new Beatles album called *Rubber Soul*. It features lead guitarist George Harrison playing a solo not on his customary electric guitar, but rather on a plucked chordophone instrument of India called the **sitar.**

One year later, 1966. George Harrison becomes a student of the master Indian sitarist Ravi Shankar. This association with a rock musician breaks new ground for Shankar. He has already made his mark on the Western classical music world through his collaboration with the violinist Yehudi Menuhin and on jazz through his influence on the saxophonist John Coltrane, among others. But the "great sitar explosion" that erupts internationally in the wake of Shankar's sudden and unexpected envelopment into Beatlemania proves to have an unprecedented impact on both his own life and the world of music at large.

World events		Music events
Advanced urban civilization, Indus River Valley (now part of Pakistan)	**c. 3000 BCE**	
Possible time of emergence of distinct northern and southern Indian cultures; key elements of Hinduism (worship of many deities, caste system, Vedas) date from this period as well	**c. 1500 BCE**	
Buddhism and Jainism originate in India	**5th century BCE**	
Islam first introduced to India	**8th century CE**	
Southern expansion of Central Asian Islamic kingdoms into India	**c. 1000 CE**	
Islamic influence begins to exert a strong influence on Hindustani culture in north of India	**13th century**	Beginning of divergence of Hindustani and Karnatak musics into distinct traditions
Spice trade brings significant European presence and influence to India	**15th–16th centuries**	
Sikh religion (Sikhism) is founded	**16th century**	Karnatak and Hindustani music recognized as fully distinct (but historically related) traditions
Turko-Persian Mughals rule much of northern India	**1526–1857**	Mughal influence on Hindustani music is profound
		Sufism important factor in cross-pollination of Hindustani and Turko-Persian music under the Mughals
	1562–1607	Life of Tansen, legendary musician revered as the wellspring of Hindustani musical culture
Britain becomes the predominant colonial power in India	**19th century**	Life of Tyagaraja (1767–1847), master Karnatak composer
India officially becomes part of the British empire	**1858**	
	1920	Ravi Shankar born
	1930s	Ravi Shankar lives abroad and tours internationally with brother Uday Shankar's troupe; meets both future *guru* Allaudin Khan (Baba) and the violinist Yehudi Menuhin during his time in Paris
	1942	John McLaughlin born

sitar (si-TAHR [rhymes with "guitar"])

Ravi Shankar (RUH-vee SHUN-kuhr)

Also in 1966, George Harrison's deepening immersion in Indian music and culture yields the song "Love You To," which is included on the Beatles' next album, *Revolver*. In India, a child is born into a musical family. His birth name is A. S. Dileep Kumar, but he will eventually be known throughout India and the world as A. R. Rahman, the greatest Indian film composer of his generation and a musician whose international influence rivals that of Ravi Shankar.

To 1967, an eventful year on many fronts. John Coltrane dies; his plans for an intensive, long-term course of study with Ravi Shankar will never come to fruition. The Beatles include another deeply

World events		Music events
Led by Mahatma Gandhi, India achieves national independence from Britain	**1947**	
	1950s	Establishment of important musical partnership between Ravi Shankar and Yehudi Menuhin
	1957	*Sounds of India*, by Ravi Shankar, released
	1961	Ravi Shankar collaborates with Bud Shank and other jazz musicians on *Improvisations*
		John Coltrane records "India"; acknowledges his admiration for Ravi Shankar in a published interview that same year
	1964–1965	Coltrane studies briefly with Ravi Shankar (dies in 1967 before having the opportunity to undertake more extensive studies with Shankar)
	1965	George Harrison of the Beatles plays a sitar solo on "Norwegian Wood"
	1966	Harrison studies sitar with Ravi Shankar; subsequent deepening of Indian influence on Beatles; "Love You to" released (*Revolver*)
	1967	Harrison's "Within You, Without You" released on Beatles' album *Sergeant Pepper's Lonely Hearts Club Band*
		Ravi Shankar performs at Monterey Pop festival
		A.R. Rahman born
	1967–1969	Ravi Shankar becomes an unwitting international pop culture icon: enmeshed in "great sitar explosion," hippie counterculture
	1969	Ravi Shankar performs at Woodstock
	1975	Pioneering Indian-jazz fusion group Shakti formed by John McLaughlin
	1976	Release of album *Shakti, with John McLaughlin,* featuring "Joy"
	1990s	A.R. Rahman dominates Bollywood music industry
	2007	Bollywood film *Guru* (including Rahman's song "Barso Re") released
	2008	Rahman wins two Oscars for *Slumdog Millionaire*
	2009	CNN-IBN Indian of the Year awards for Ravi Shankar, A.R. Rahman

Indian-inspired George Harrison song, "Within You, Without You," on their new album, *Sergeant Pepper's Lonely Hearts Club Band,* which will ultimately achieve acclaim as the greatest rock album of all time. Meanwhile, Ravi Shankar's continuing musical collaboration with Yehudi Menuhin gives rise to the groundbreaking recording *West Meets East,* which tops the classical music charts. Shankar also performs a marathon concert of Indian classical music at Monterey Pop, the largest rock music festival ever held up to this point. There, he shares the program with the likes of Jimi Hendrix, Jefferson Airplane, and Simon & Garfunkel. The festival and its offshoot documentary film, *Monterey Pop* (1968), which is seen by millions, catapult Ravi Shankar to superstar pop-culture celebrity status.

But this is as nothing compared to the fame and notoriety achieved by Shankar in the wake of his historic 1969 performance at Woodstock, the grandest rock festival of them all, and his featured appearance in the *Woodstock* film that follows. The sex, drugs, and rock-and-roll world into which he is thrust as an unwitting hero becomes at once a source of fascination and disgust for him. Meanwhile, during this same year, 1969, a talented young British jazz guitarist named John McLaughlin comes to New York to join jazz trumpeter Miles Davis's band. McLaughlin, like Ravi Shankar, Yehudi Menuhin, John Coltrane, and the Beatles before him, will emerge as a leading figure in the fascinating history of Indian-Western cross-cultural musical encounter.

Forty years later. It is 2009. CNN-IBN (India Broadcast Network) is airing its annual Indian of the Year awards show. The show's official Web site touts it as "the biggest and the most credible award of the nation," honoring "Indians whose endeavors stood beyond the ordinary this year and in the process, built brand India." It represents "the pinnacle of Indian achievement, . . . standing resolute for the resilience and trust of a billion free Indian minds." India's prime minister, Manhoman Singh, bestows the honors. Nine awards are handed out in all. Five are in specific categories: politics, sports, business, entertainment, and public service. Two are special awards, one given to a famous filmmaker and actor in recognition of his fifty years in the cinema, the other to the Indian cricket team for achieving top rank in international competition.

But the two supreme awards are reserved for musicians.

The Indian of the Year Lifetime Achievement Award goes to . . . Ravi Shankar.

And the Indian of the Year Award goes to . . . A. R. Rahman.

Hindustani raga (Hin-dus-TAH-nee RAH-gah [or RAHG])

Ravi Shankar playing the sitar (center), accompanied by Alla Rakha on tabla (left) and a tambura player (right).

This chapter explores tradition and transformation in Indian music from two different but closely interrelated perspectives. In the first perspective, we examine the **Hindustani raga** tradition of Indian classical music, especially as embodied in the artistry and wide range of influence of that tradition's leading international proponent, Ravi Shankar. In the second perspective, we survey the modern history of Indian/Western intercultural musical encounter, again mainly through the lens of Ravi Shankar, whose musical innovations and contributions as a performer, composer, teacher, cultural icon, and international ambassador of Indian music have had a profound impact on the shaping of our modern musical world on many levels. This journey ultimately leads to the music of A. R. Rahman, the double Academy Award–winning composer of *Slumdog Millionaire,* whose phenomenal success and popularity in India and internationally have made him the iconic face of Indian music for the new millennium, and whose fervently internationalist musical approach and appeal may be seen to extend the global legacy of Ravi Shankar himself, albeit indirectly.

From Ravi Shankar to A. R. Rahman, John Coltrane to John McLaughlin, and the Beatles to Bollywood, the musicultural journey of this chapter traverses a wide range of traditions and transformations: Hindustani and

Karnatak raga, bhangra, qawwali, Indian film song, jazz, and rock. Underlying the guiding narrative of this journey are processes of growth, expansion, transformation, and interculturality that might be likened to the process of **barhat** that animates how traditional ragas are actually played by musicians like Ravi Shankar.

barhat (bar-hut)

In the terminology of Hindustani music, the Hindi word barhat refers to the note-by-note expansion of the melodic range of a raga during performance. This term derives from a verb meaning to increase, multiply, extend, advance, push ahead, progress, grow. Though barhat is a term that is specific to a particular dimension of melody in Indian music, the concept of barhat is relevant to other matters we will explore as well, some musical, some cultural. Beyond their note-by-note expansion, ragas grow during the course of performance in other ways, through changes in rhythm, tempo, dynamics, and instrumentation. Within the process of raga performance, too, musical forms emerge, and social relationships between musicians, and between musicians and listeners, deepen and take on new meaning. On a social structure level, the **gharana,** the "musical families" that have preserved, cultivated, and developed the different "schools" of traditional raga performance in India and beyond, often over the course of many generations, also are defined in large measure by the ways in which *they* grow, multiply, and advance the raga tradition. Finally, there is the growth, extension, and pushing ahead of Indian classical music that has occurred in connection with the fascinating intercultural history of musical encounter between India and the West for more than half a century. This history, which has largely been defined by the lineage and influences of Ravi Shankar (see Figure 8.1, p. 120) provides a revealing window through which to view key issues explored in this text: tradition, transformation, and intercultural processes in music.

gharana (gha-RAH-nah)

■ ■ ■

Indian Music in Context

The vast Indian subcontinent is both geographically and ecologically diverse, with terrain and ecosystems ranging from tropical jungle to mountain forests. It is bounded by oceans to the east, south, and west, and by the Himalayas to the north. Mountain passes in the northwest served as the main entryway to India for nearly all migrating groups and invaders prior to the first arrival of Europeans in the 15th century. Over millennia, innumerable groups moved into the subcontinent, resulting in a great deal of intermingling among cultures but also much retention of regional distinctiveness.

The Indian population is one of the most diverse in the world—physically, ethnically, linguistically, and culturally. More than 200 languages and 1,600 different dialects are spoken; Hindi and English are recognized as national languages. Although there is great diversity throughout the subcontinent, broad ethnic, linguistic, and cultural distinctions exist between northern and southern India; for example, the languages of northern India belong to a different linguistic group than the languages of southern India.

The origin of this distinction may have been a historical event that occurred about 1500 BCE. Prior to this time, as far back as 3000 BCE, an ancient urban civilization existed in northwestern India, in the Indus River Valley (now part of Pakistan). The high level of development of this civilization was similar to that of ancient Mesopotamia (present-day Iraq). About 1500 BCE, a wave of invaders pushed the indigenous inhabitants south; some experts believe this movement may be the original source of the distinction between northern and southern Indian cultures, though not everyone agrees. Some elements of the **Hindu religion**, the majority faith in India, date to this time. These include the worship of many deities and the caste system of rigid hierarchical levels in society.

Fundamental to the origin of Hinduism were the four **Vedas** (Rig Veda, Sama Veda, Yajur Veda, and Atharva Veda). These ancient, seminal Hindu scriptures in the Sanskrit language (in which the word for musician, *baqawathar*, also means "he who sings the praises of God" [Metting 2001:252]) are believed by Hindus to be of divine rather than human origin. Their texts

Veda(s) (VAY-dah)

Ravi Shankar: Lineage and influences.

FIGURE 8.1

Tansen

Baba (Maihar Gharana)

Uday Shankar

Ali Akbar Khan

Ravi Shankar

Alla Rakha

Yehudi Menuhin

George Harrison

John Coltrane

John McLaughlin

L. Shankar

Zakir Hussain

Shakti

A.R. Rahman

Shreya Ghoshal

Performance of a bhajan. The bhajan tradition is discussed briefly on page 121.

have been carried through the ages to the present in the form of Vedic chants, which feature melodic recitation of the Veda texts. According to Ravi Shankar, Indian classical music evolved from Vedic chant through a centuries-long process of musical transformation (Metting 2001:252). There is no musicological evidence to support the claim of any direct connection between the two, however. The existence of direct historical links between Indian classical music and a body of Hindu devotional songs and hymns known as **bhajan** is more clear. **CD ex. #2-19** is an excerpt of a bhajan devoted to the Hindu deity Krishna sung with instrumental accompaniment (we will discuss Indian instruments later).

In the 5th century BCE, two other religions, Buddhism and Jainism, originated in India. Islam was first introduced in the 8th century CE, and Islamic kingdoms extending into northern India were established by Turks, Persians, Mongols, and other peoples from Central Asia beginning in about 1000. The differences between Hinduism and Islam are profound: "Hinduism recognizes many gods, whereas Islam recognizes only one; Hinduism cherishes religious images, whereas Islam prohibits them; and Hinduism promotes vegetarianism [and venerates cows], but Islam, although it has dietary restrictions, allows the killing and eating of many animals, including cows" (Molloy 2002:180). Another major Indian religion, Sikhism, was founded in the 16th century. Though it incorporates elements of both Hinduism and Islam, Sikhism is a resolutely unique faith. Much of the political unrest within India in modern times—and between India and some of its neighbors—stems from centuries-old tensions among different religious groups, especially Hindus, Muslims, and Sikhs.

Despite their differences, Hindus and Muslims (and Sikhs) in India have in many instances forged synergistic bonds through culture, and music is an area where this has certainly occurred. Such synergy owes much to Sufism, a mystical form of Islam (see also Chapter 12) that has exerted an especially strong influence on Indian culture, including music. Sufism, in contrast to other forms of Islam, shares with Hinduism the belief that music may serve as a pathway to communion with the divine. This has facilitated musical, religious, and cultural syncretism historically. Sufi musicians and musical traditions have had, and continue to have, a great impact on the broader musical culture of the Indian subcontinent. **CD ex. #2-20** offers an example of Sufi song originating from the Punjab region (which is divided between Pakistan and India). The vocalist is Shafqat Ali Khan.

The musical style heard in **CD ex. #2-20,** including the singing and the driving rhythms of the drumming, is related to that of a type of music called *qawwali*. Qawwali, also from Punjab, became a major world music phenomenon through the international popularity of the late singer Nusrat Fateh Ali Khan. In qawwali, the lead singer is joined by an accompanying ensemble of vocalists and instrumentalists. The powerful and emotional singing style of qawwali, combined with the compelling rhythms of the drumming and unison handclapping by members of the group, account for much of the genre's broad appeal internationally.

European influence on India began in the 15th and 16th centuries when the Portuguese, French, Dutch, and

Shafqat Ali Khan.

bhajan (BUH-jin)

Sikh (like "sick," but with an aspirated [breathy] "kh")

qawwali (kah-WAH-lee)

The late qawwali superstar Nusrat Fateh Ali Khan.

English, arriving by sea in pursuit of the spice trade, set up fortified posts and attempted to establish exclusive commercial agreements for their trading companies and countries. Some Europeans tried to import Christianity but met with limited success. In the 19th century, Britain became the predominant colonial power, officially adding India to its empire in 1858. Led by Mahatma Gandhi, India achieved national independence in 1947. With much violence and bloodshed, two primarily Muslim areas in the northwest and northeast became Pakistan and East Pakistan (now Bangladesh). Today, India is officially a secular state, but more than 80 percent of the population is Hindu.

Musical Diversity and Two Great Traditions

Just as there is great cultural, ethnic, and linguistic diversity in India, there is also great diversity in Indian music. Literally thousands of genres, subgenres, and styles of folk, religious, devotional, popular, and film music are found in India and throughout the subcontinent.

Indian film song is the dominant popular music of modern India. There are actually several large and active film industries based in different cities and regions of the country. The biggest by far, and indeed the largest film industry in the world, is centered in Mumbai and is known as Bollywood (the "Bo" portion of "Bollywood" is derived from Mumbai's old name, Bombay). The audience for film songs extends from hundreds of millions of people in India to millions more living in South Asian diasporic communities around the world. The final portion of this chapter will focus on a major hit song by the current king of Bollywood composers, A. R. Rahman.

bhangra
(BHAHNG-rah)

A major component of contemporary music heard in Bollywood productions is **bhangra**, which originated in Punjab. Traditional bhangra features lively Punjabi folk songs and dances accompanied by powerful rhythms played on a large, barrel-shaped drum called a *dhol*. Rhythmic shouts ("hoi!") from the dancers add extra rhythmic punch. Since the 1980s, the folk base of bhangra has been merged with other Indian popular music styles and with everything from hip-hop to reggae. This modern bhangra style has become very popular among South Asian diasporic communities in North America, the United Kingdom, and elsewhere and has achieved a considerable following among non-Indian world music audiences. It is heard on many Indian film soundtracks and on commercial recordings by Indian, Pakistani, and South Asian diasporic musicians. Jasbir Jassi is a leading star of modern bhangra. **CD ex. #1-22** (discussed earlier, in Chapter 3, p. 41) is an excerpt from his catchy hit tune "Kudi Kudi" (Girl, Girl), replete with dhol drumming and electronic drum grooves, abundant use of synthesizers, and energetic, syncopated "hoi!" shouts.

Jasbir Jassi
(Jahs-BEER
JUH-see)

"Kudi Kudi" (like
"curry curry," with
"r" touching roof
of mouth)

Karnatak
(Kar-NAH-tuck)

In the domain of Indian classical music, there are two great traditions: the **Karnatak** (Carnatic) tradition of southern India and the Hindustani tradition of northern India. The Hindustani tradition is the better known of the two outside of the Indian subcontinent, partly because of the global stature of Ravi Shankar and partly because of immigration patterns: historically, most Indian immigrants have come from northern India and have brought this music with them to countries such as the United Kingdom, the United States, and Canada.

The Karnatak and Hindustani traditions have been recognized since the 16th century as distinct music cultures with related but separate histories. Though they share many features, they also exhibit significant differences (Table 8.1). These may be attributed to a variety of factors, including the different political histories, languages, and local cultures of southern and northern India. One important factor of difference was the greater impact of

Scene from a Bollywood film.

Islamic cultures on the Hindustani north beginning in the 13th century. Especially influential on Hindustani music and culture were the Muslim, Turko-Persian Mughals, who ruled over much of northern India from 1526 to 1857. Much cross-pollination between the existing Hindustani music culture and the Turko-Persian music culture brought by the Mughals occurred during this period. (Sufi influence was pervasive under Mughal rule.) Though Islamic invasions did eventually reach and affect southern India, the impact was not nearly as great as in the north, and this is reflected musically.

As for similarities, both Hindustani and Karnatak music build from highly complex and elaborate melodic systems called **raga**, employ systems of rhythm and meter known as **tala** (literally, "time"), and are deeply steeped in the spiritual and cultural traditions of Hinduism. They both belong within larger frameworks of what is known as *sangita* in their respective cultures. Sangita is a term that is often translated as "music," but that also encompasses the music-related arts of dance and drama.

In both Karnatak and Hindustani cultures, singing is regarded as the highest form of musical expression. The sound of the human voice is believed to be the closest possible approximation of **Nada Brahma**, the "Sound of God," the divine source of all sound and

A bhangra performance. The drummer on the right is playing a dhol drum.

tala (TAH-lah [or TAHL])

TABLE 8.1	Comparison of Karnatak and Hindustani music traditions.
Similarities	
■ Raga as basis of melody	
■ Tala as basis of rhythm/meter	
■ Part of larger sangita traditions (encompassing music, dance, drama)	
■ Singing highest form of musical expression	
■ Instrumental traditions closely connected to parallel vocal traditions	
■ Related histories (especially pre-16th century)	
■ Related types of instruments	
Differences	
■ Recognized as distinct traditions since 16th century	
■ Hindustani: Greater influence from Islamic cultures (especially Mughal)	
■ Karnatak: Less influence from Islamic cultures	
■ Hindustani: More international exposure and recognition outside of India	
■ Karnatak: Status of singing more elevated relative to instrumental music	
■ Hindustani: Sitar, tambura (Hindustani), tabla instrumental trio common	
■ Karnatak: Vina, tambura (Karnatak), mrdangam instrumental trio common	
■ The specific ragas, talas, and music terminologies are different in the two traditions	

music. Instrumental traditions in Hindustani and Karnatak music alike are closely connected to parallel vocal traditions. This is especially the case in Karnatak music, but in Hindustani music, too, the merits of instrumental performances are measured largely by how well they accord with singing-derived aesthetic ideals. It is therefore somewhat paradoxical that instrumental music, rather than vocal music, has become iconic of Indian classical music outside of India. This, like so much else pertaining to the international image of Indian music, is largely attributable to the dominant international impact of Ravi Shankar. Whereas instrumentalists such as Shankar have long been the leading international celebrities and cultural ambassadors of Indian classical music (and the principal subjects of introductions to Indian music like this one, which tend to deal almost exclusively with instrumental music), in India itself it is vocalists who reign supreme; instrumentalists occupy considerably lower rungs on the ladder of musical status.

Standard in both Karnatak and Hindustani instrumental music are ensembles consisting of three instruments (trios). Each of the three instruments has a primary responsiblity of contributing one layer to the music's overall texture, which comprises *a single-line melody, a drone, and rhythmic accompaniment.* (Chords and harmony, as such, are not part of traditional Indian classical music textures.) One of the most common trio configurations in Karnatak music features the **vina**, a plucked chordophone, as the solo melodic instrument; the **tambura**, another plucked chordophone, as the principal drone-providing instrument; and the **mrdangam**, a double-headed drum, as the rhythmic accompaniment instrument. This trio of instruments is featured in **CD ex. #1-24,** which we listened to earlier in connection with Chapter 3 (see p. 42).

Listen to that example again now. The name of the piece is "Sarasasamadana." It is a work attributed to Tyagaraja (1767–1847), one of the greatest composers in the Karnatak tradition. The introductory, opening section is in free rhythm and features an improvised melody played on the vina. The accompanying drone (which is the first thing the listener hears at the beginning of the selection) is furnished by the tambura and also by special drone strings with which the vina itself is equipped. Notice that there is no drumming in the introduction. The main, second section of the composition begins with the introduction of Tyagaraja's "Sarasasamadana" melody in the vina part at 0:51. A steady beat at a medium tempo is established here. The vina is joined a few seconds later (at 0:57) by the mrdangam, which marks out and embellishes a metric cycle (tala) of eight beats called *adi tala.* The rest of the performance alternates between composed and improvised passages, all of which are based on the main Tyagaraja melody and all of which unfold over top the perpetually recurring adi tala metric cycle (each cycle is about six seconds long). The vina soloist on "Sarasasamadana" is Karaikudi Subramaniam. His mrdangam accompanist is Trichy Sankaran. Both are widely regarded as leading representatives of the art of Karnatak music performance.

Since this chapter focuses principally on Hindustani rather than Karnatak music, only this brief exploration of the Karnatak tradition can be offered here. (Resources for further study of Karnatak and other Indian music traditions may be found at the Online Learning Center, www.mhhe.com/bakan2e.) On the Hindustani side, one of the most common instrumental trio configurations—essentially the "equivalent" of the Karnatak vina-tambura-mrdangam ensemble discussed above—is that which includes the sitar as the lead melodic instrument, the Hindustani version of the tambura as the drone instrument, and the pair of drums known as **tabla** as the rhythmic accompaniment instrument (see the photo on p. 118). We will learn more about this ensemble shortly.

vina (VEE-nah)

tambura (tum-BOO-rah)

mrdangam (mir-DUNG-ahm)

tabla (TUB-lah [like "tub" in English])

Karnatak instrumental trio: mrdangam, vina, and tambura.

The Hindustani Raga of Northern India

We turn now to a journey through the world of North Indian music from a vantage point specifically linked to the life, career, and influence of Ravi Shankar. In this section, we explore the unique sounds, rhythms, and instruments of Hindustani raga, using recordings that feature Shankar as our main guides. In the next section, we touch on Shankar's encounters and associations with Western musicians, including the Beatles, and we explore a variety of musical examples that reflect richly synergistic products of intercultural encounter along the way. The recordings by John Coltrane, John McLaughlin and Shakti, Bombay Dub Orchestra, and A. R. Rahman that we will examine are all reflective of such synergy.

Ravi Shankar and the Maihar Gharana

As Indian music scholar Gerry Farrell has written, Ravi Shankar is the only Indian musician "to have become a household name in the West" (Farrell 2000:564). He was born Ravindra Shankar Chaudhuri into an upper-class, Hindu family of the priestly Brahmin caste in 1920 (see "Insights and Perspectives" box on the caste system below). His father was a prominent educator, politician, and activist for Indian national independence.

Early on, young Ravi showed prodigious talent as both a dancer and musician. In the 1930s, while still in his teens, he joined an Indian music-and-dance troupe formed by his older brother, Uday, and with that group toured the great capitals of Europe as a sitar player and dancer. He spent extended periods of time in both London and Paris during this early part of his career. While in Paris, he befriended the famous, young English classical violinist Yehudi Menuhin. Years later (in the 1950s), Shankar and Menuhin would form an important intercultural musical partnership that helped bring Indian classical music to widespread international attention, a subject to which we will return.

It was also during his early years in Paris in the 1930s that Shankar met the great raga master Allaudin Khan, otherwise known as Baba (literally, "Father"). A few years later, Shankar would return to India to be initiated as a musical disciple (*sisya*) of Baba. Living with Baba for some eight years and forsaking virtually all in life except musical study under the strict watch of his extraordinarily demanding **guru** (mentor), Shankar was transformed from a precocious musical talent into an inspired and disciplined young master of the art of raga. In becoming a

insights and perspectives

The Caste System in India

Like Hindus in Bali (Chapter 7, p. 100), Hindus in India have traditionally recognized a caste system. Caste divides society into social classes based on family birthright or occupational specialization. The Indian caste system is more highly structured than its Balinese counterpart, though practices and policies based on caste division are officially illegal in modern India. Efforts to eradicate the caste system in India have been largely inspired by concerns about the plight of members of the lowest caste, the Dalit, or "Untouchables," who have been subject to many abuses and severely limited opportunities historically. But while the caste system is legally banned, its vestiges survive in many areas of Indian social and cultural life.

The caste system is supported by ancient Hindu scriptures, which posited that there are different types of people who should perform different roles in society, and that stratification of this kind is essential to the maintenance of a balanced social and spiritual order. There are five principal castes: Brahmin (priest), Kshatriya (warrior), Vaishya (merchant), Shudra (peasant), and Dalit (untouchable). The Brahmin caste, to which Ravi Shankar and his family belong, is the highest of the five. Members of this caste have traditionally been assigned responsibilities and afforded opportunities not available to members of the other castes.

The gharana is the principal social institution through which knowledge of raga is disseminated and legacies of raga performance are transmitted from musician to musician and generation to generation. Although the term *gharana* is sometimes translated as "musical family," the basic criterion of membership in a gharana is not typically blood or marital relations between its members (though such relations often do exist), but rather indoctrination into a particular lineage, or "school," of raga performance. According to raga scholar Stephen Slawek, what unifies the members of a gharana first and foremost is a shared "style or approach to performance practice that sets them apart from other ghārānas" (Slawek 1991:170).

Members of the gharana trace their heritage through their own guru back through the guru's guru and so on through the generations to the founder of the gharana. The gharana's founder, in turn, typically traces his lineage to the legendary 16th-century musician Tansen (1562–1607), who is revered as the wellspring of Hindustani musical culture. Tansen himself is believed to have received his extraordinary musical and spiritual gifts from divine powers.

Like the ragas they preserve and cultivate, gharanas develop through a process of growth. The founder is the seed from which the gharana as a whole blossoms and comes to fruition. Through the collective efforts and devotion of his sucessors, the gharana "musical organism" grows. Each line of succession across the generations, each individual member, becomes a branch or leaf on the gharana "tree"—all grounded in the same trunk and nourished by the same root.

Maihar (MA'EE-har [as in first syllable of "mighty"])

disciple of Baba, Shankar also became a member of the highly famed and influential "family" or "school" of raga study and performance known as the Maihar Gharana, of which Baba himself was the founder.

With the aid of Baba, Ravi Shankar came to be revered as one of the master sitar players, raga performers, and Indian music gurus of his generation. Through his collaborations with Yehudi Menuhin and other Western musical luminaries from the worlds of classical and jazz music, he also became a pathbreaking innovator of intercultural musical experimentation and India's principal musical ambassador to the world. But it was as a result of his relationship with a quiet English rock guitarist, George Harrison of the Beatles, that Shankar was catapulted rather tumultuously and incongruously into the role of global superstar celebrity. As such, he inspired revolutionary changes in rock and world musics, becoming an unwitting pop culture icon of 1960s "hippie" counterculture and ultimately emerging, in Harrison's words, as the "Godfather of World Music."

Beyond all this, Ravi Shankar is famous as a father in the more literal sense. He is perhaps best known among younger music enthusiasts today not for any of his own professional achievements, but as the father of two musician daughters: Anoushka Shankar, who is continuing his Maihar legacy as a sitarist; and singer-songwriter Norah Jones, who might be seen as extending her father's "other" legacy as a force of influence in the worlds of Western popular music and jazz.

Anoushka Shankar playing the sitar.

Anoushka Shankar: Carrying on the Legacy

Anoushka Shankar is a highly accomplished professional musician and has been touted as the only classical sitarist in the world trained exclusively by Ravi Shankar. Her first solo CD, *Anoushka,* was a chart-topper in the world music area. Additional albums have followed (including the acclaimed *Rise,* released in 2005, and 2007's *Breathing Under Water,* with Karsh Kale) and she has frequently appeared both live and on recordings performing together with her father (for example, on the album *Full Circle*). Like Ravi Shankar, Anoushka has charisma, talent, and eclectic musical tastes and interests. She has risen to prominence among the ranks of international Indian classical music artists.

"An Introduction to Indian Music," by Ravi Shankar

For an introduction to the sound of Hindustani raga and a primer on its core features, terms, and concepts, we now turn to a brief recorded lecture demonstration that Ravi Shankar created for the purpose of introducing the art of Hindustani raga to new listeners (**CD ex. #2-21**). We will treat this as the chapter's Musical Guided Tour. Shankar uses some terms that we have not yet discussed in detail, including raga, tala, **alap**, **tintal**, **theka**, and **sam**, but we will explain these terms shortly. For now, just listen to Shankar's explanations and experience the sound of Indian music. Try to hear the various features and characteristics of raga identified: the melodic forms of the raga "scale," the melodic ornaments and microtones, the distinctive sound of the drone, the beat-counts of the talas. A transcript of Shankar's lecture demonstration is included in the box below.

alap (ah-LAHP)

tintal (TEEN-tahl)

theka (TAY-kah)

sam (like English "some")

musical guided tour

"An Introduction to Indian Music" (CD ex. #2-21)

Ragas are precise melody forms. A raga is not a mere scale [♪]. Nor is it a mode [♪]. Each raga has its own ascending and descending movement [♪] and those subtle touches and usage of microtones, and stresses on particular notes, like this [♪]. With the tambura, the drone instrument, in the background [♪], the soloist does a free improvisation known as *alap,* after which he starts the theme based on a rhythmic framework known as *tala.* He can choose from many talas, such as *tintal,* a rhythmic cycle of sixteen beats [♪], or *jhaptal,* having ten beats [♪]. The tabla are the drums, which keeps *[sic]* this framework, just plays the *thekas,* or beats, in the beginning, as you heard just now. Then starts the gradual progression of playing first smaller patterns, then longer ones. In the beginning, the accompanying tabla gives, if I may say so, a reply to the lead instrument, such as the sitar. At times they may play together a long rhythmic pattern, and return with a climax to *sam,* or the "one" [i.e., beat one of the tala's metric cycle], which is the most important thing, like this [♪]. Although the role of the tabla is relatively free, it is the lead instrument [e.g., the sitar] which directs the whole progress of the improvisation.

The Western listener will appreciate and enjoy our music more if he listens with an open and relaxed mind, without expecting to hear harmony, counterpoint, or other elements prominent in Western music. Neither should our music be thought of as akin to jazz, despite the improvisation and exciting rhythms present in both kinds of music.

The sitar-tambura-tabla trio: Instruments and texture

Now that we have had an opportunity to hear what the sitar, tambura, and tabla sound like and how they function together within an ensemble setting, we are ready to take a more detailed look at these fascinating instruments. Though the sitar-tambura-tabla combination is but one of many ensembles employed in Hindustani music, it has in a sense become emblematic of Indian music on an international scale. This has much to do with the influence of Ravi Shankar, whose introduction of Indian music to the West was largely achieved through his international performances and recordings within this ensemble context.

SITAR The sitar, the instrument Ravi Shankar plays, is a long-necked, plucked chordophone (Figure 8.2). Its resonating body (resonator) consists of a half gourd covered over by an artistically decorated wooden "face." The long wooden neck is hollowed out, or *scalloped,* in a way that allows the strings running across it to be pressed in and out with the fingers of the left hand. This "bending" of the strings facilitates the production of many different kinds of melodic ornamentation. Twenty arched metal frets are attached to the instrument's neck. Rather than being fixed in place as on a guitar, they are attached with nylon threads, making it possible to move them to different positions to achieve different pitches. This is an important feature, since Indian music involves a system of tuning that incorporates microtones, requiring very precise pitch intervals that could not be achieved with any single setup of frets as one finds on a guitar.

There are six or seven strings running across the main platform of the sitar's neck. Some of these are designated for melody while others supply drone tones. Additionally, there are 13 thinner strings called *sympathetic resonance strings* running underneath the frets. These special strings magnify certain high overtones emerging from the melody and drone strings. The three different kinds of strings—melody, drone, and sympathetic—combined with certain other design features, account for the unique timbre of the sitar. The instrument is held diagonally across the lap by a player seated cross-legged on the floor. As with a guitar, the right hand is used to pluck the strings and the left to finger the neck (see the photos, pp. 118 and 126).

Labeled diagram of a sitar.

FIGURE 8.2

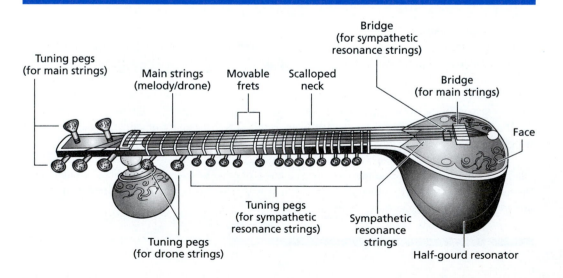

TAMBURA Although the sitar is capable of supplying its own drone tones, another instrument, the tambura, is dedicated specifically to droning and serves no other function. The construction and shape of the tambura's body and neck are similar to those of the sitar. It has four or five strings, which are tuned to the most fundamental pitches from which the sitar melody builds during a performance (including the tonic, known as **vadi**). Thin threads underneath the strings pick up high overtones and contribute to the tambura's distinctive, multidimensional timbre. The tambura is held vertically in the player's lap and plucked continuously to produce a constant, underlying drone.

When one thinks of the word *drone,* a single, monotonous tone being sounded incessantly comes to mind. The drone of the tambura, however, is something else altogether. It swirls and whirls around the fundamental pitch, bringing out different tones and overtones to create a wavelike timbral effect.

TABLA Unlike its southern, Karnatak relative, the mrdangam, the tabla is not a single double-headed drum, but rather a pair of single-headed drums played by one player (Figure 8.3). The higher-pitched, right-hand drum, called the *dahina* (or *tabla*) has a tapering cylindrical shape and is made of thick wood. The lower-pitched, left-hand drum, the *bayan,* has a kettle-like shape and is usually made of metal. Both drums have goatskin heads. To each is affixed a thick and prominent black "weight spot" that largely accounts for the distinctive sound and large range of timbres produced. The heads are attached to the bodies of the two drums by laced leather straps. The intricate tabla tuning method involves adjusting the tension on the straps (and thus on the heads) to change the pitch. The dahina is tuned to produce a clear, ringing tone. The bayan, in contrast, has a deep, resonant tone. Its pitch can be bent up and down by pressing the heel of the hand into the drum head while playing with the fingers. The drums are played with the bare hands from a cross-legged, seated position (see the photos, pp. 118 and 146). The range of hand and finger strokes employed is nothing short of dazzling.

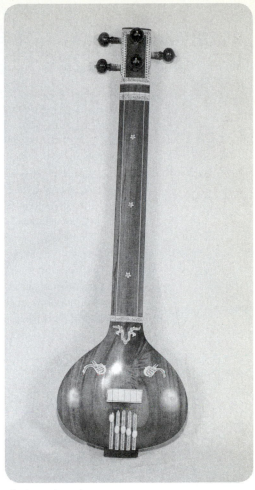

Hindustani tambura.

vadi (VAH-dee)

dahina (DAH-hee-nah)

bayan (BAH-yin [rhymes with "Ryan"])

Tabla drums.

FIGURE 8.3

Black weight spots

Metal body

Tuning straps

Wood body

Bayan **Dahina**

Ravi Shankar has performed with many illustrious tabla players, but none greater than Alla Rakha (AL-lah RUH-khah) (see photo, p. 118). Their decades-long association represented one of the most significant musical partnerships of the 20th century. Rakha's legacy continues through his son, Zakir Hussain (see photo, p. 146), possibly the greatest tabla master of his generation and a maverick intercultural music pioneer in his own right.

Ravi Shankar is a Hindu, whereas Alla Rakha was a Muslim. "Interfaith" musical partnerships such as this are, and long have been, common in the Hindustani musicultural world. Additionally, it is noteworthy that the percentage of Hindustani musicians who are Muslims is disproportionately large relative to the general population of northern India.

It may seem peculiar that the realm of Hindustani instrumental music, in which music is treated explicitly as a path toward spiritual enlightenment, is so heavily populated by followers of Islam, a religion that, in its familiar orthodox manifestations at least, views music as suspect where religious worship is concerned. As with other religions, though, Islam is highly diverse and takes many forms. The kind of Islam that developed in northern India (at least among denizens of the Hindustani music culture) shared with Hinduism a concept of music as a sacred, devotional art. Historically, this was partly the result of its absorption of Hindu influences, and, as was alluded to earlier, partly a product of the fact that Sufism was a major force in the spread of Islam to India. It is noteworthy that A. R. Rahman was raised in the Hindu tradition but converted to Islam as a young man, adopting a form of Islamic faith that is deeply entrenched in Sufism.

Other Hindustani Melodic Instruments

Though it is better known in the West than its counterparts, the sitar, our focus melodic instrument in this chapter, is just one of a large variety of such instruments used in Hindustani raga performance (see photos, p. 131). These include the *sarod*, which is also a plucked chordophone. It has a shorter neck than the sitar, no frets, and a fingerboard made from metal rather than wood. The lower part of the instrument's body is covered with animal hide instead of wood. The most famous player of the sarod in the modern era was the late Ali Akbar Khan, another principal proponent of the Maihar style. He was the son of Ravi Shankar's guru, Allaudin Khan (Baba), and, like Shankar, had a major role in introducing Indian music to the West.

sarod (sa-ROAD)

Baba himself was a specialist on the sarod and also the violin, which was adopted as an Indian concert instrument long ago and is prized for the voice-like quality of its tone. Some Indian violinists hold the instrument in the conventional Western playing position, but most sit cross-legged and hold it in a downward-pointing position so that the scroll (the "head" where the tuning pegs are located) rests on the player's foot. This allows the left hand to slide up and down the fingerboard more freely, which makes it easier to produce the proper melodic ornaments. Other Hindustani melodic instruments include the bamboo flute *bansuri* (also prized for its voice-like timbre), the oboe-like *shahnai,* and the bowed chordophone *sarangi*.

bansuri (BAHN-sree)

sarangi (SAH-rahng-ee)

The sarod and the bansuri are both featured on **CD ex. #2-22.** This is an excerpt from a track entitled "Monsoon Malabar," by Bombay Dub Orchestra. It is from their 2008 album *3 Cities.* Although the playing styles of the sarod and bansuri here are rooted in the musical conventions of Hindustani raga, the track is anything but a classic raga performance. It is, rather, the product of a contemporary cross-cultural fusion project, and as such provides both an opportunity to hear traditional Hindustani instruments in a novel context and a preview of what is to come in the later parts of this chapter that focus on Indian-Western intercultural musical encounters.

Sarod, played by Ali Akbar Khan.

Violin, played by N. Rajam.

Bansuri, played by Benjamin Koen.

Shahnai, played by Bismillah Khan.

Sarangi, played by Ram Narayan.

Besides the featured sarod and bansuri, the instrumentation of "Monsoon Malabar" also includes other Indian instruments discussed thus far, such as the sitar, tabla, and dhol drum (the standard type of drum used in bhangra music). Additional Indian and Western percussion instruments (including drum set), as well as an orchestral string section of the type commonly heard in Bollywood film scores, are employed as well. Additionally, a vast array of electronically generated and processed sounds—from manipulated Indian vocal tracks to synthesizer effects and hard-driving electro-funk grooves—figure prominently in the music's eclectic soundscape.

Bombay Dub Orchestra is the brainchild of two British musicians, Garry Hughes and Andrew T. Mackay, who have worked in close collaboration with some of India's finest musical artists on their innovative recording projects. "Monsoon Malabar" highlights the talents of bansuri virtuoso Ashwin Srinivasan and sarod master Zarin (Zarine) Sharma. Ashwin Srinivasan's first instrument as a young child was the sitar, which he studied with his mother, herself a student of Ravi Shankar. He took up the bansuri at age seven and has risen to the status of one of India's leading performers on that instrument. Based in Mumbai (Bombay), he is sought after as a session musician for Bollywood films and as a solo and ensemble artist in classical, popular, and intercultural music settings. Zarin Sharma has been a true pioneer of the Indian music world. She first rose to national fame on the sarod as the winner of the 1960 All India Radio music competition, which she won at age 13. The following year, she was selected to perform for Queen Elizabeth II during a visit by the British monarch to India. In that same year, 1961, she also embarked upon an illustrious and long-standing career as a musician in the Indian film industry. She holds the dual distinction of being one of the first major female classical artists of the sarod and one of the first women to penetrate the heavily male-dominated world of Indian film music (Booth 2008:126–27). Her husband is the sitar player Ashok Sharma, one of whose principal mentors was Ravi Shankar.

On **CD ex. #2-22,** an improvised melody played on the bansuri by Ashwin Srinivasan is heard over a driving rhythmic groove during the first portion of the excerpt. This is followed directly by an improvisation played on the sarod by Zarin Sharma over the continuing rhythmic groove. The track drives to its conclusion with cascades of electronically processed, highly rhythmic vocal parts taking the foreground.

Raga defined

Having now heard a preview of Indian-Western intercultural fusion music, we return to the subject of classic Hindustani raga. In "An Introduction to Indian Music" (**CD ex. #2-21**), Ravi Shankar explained that ragas "are precise melody forms." More specifically, each raga is *a complete and self-contained melodic system* that serves as the basis for all the melodic materials in any composition or performance created *in* that raga. There are many different Hindustani ragas (the index of the *Garland Encyclopedia of World Music's* India volume lists 58 of them [Arnold 2000:1066]). Each has a distinctive set of features that includes the following five:

- *An identifying set of pitches,* more or less a "scale," which usually consists of seven ascending pitches and seven descending pitches per octave. The main pitches, microtones, and ornaments of the ascending and descending forms of the raga's scale may differ from one another. Also, there may be twists and turns that deviate from a straight, up-and-down presentation of the main pitches.

- *A unique repertoire of melodic ornaments and melodic motives,* many of which incorporate microtonal inflections, that is, subtle melodic figures that employ "the notes between the notes" (pitches located *between* the raga's main pitches) in some systematic fashion.

- *A system of rules and procedures* for dealing with the various pitches, ornaments, and melodic motives of the raga in relation to one another; this system of rules functions like a musical road map that is internalized in the musician's mind after years of study and practice, and that guides the course of improvisation during a raga performance.

- *A repertoire of set (precomposed) compositions* that is unique to that particular raga. The same system of rules and procedures that guides improvisation in the raga is embedded within each of these set compositions as well. Set compositions may have been passed down in oral/aural tradition through many generations or may be of more recent vintage. They may be very short or very long. In the course of a performance, the musicians draw upon their knowledge of the raga's repertoire of set compositions, selecting specific ones to incorporate into the broader framework of their overall improvised performance.

- *A host of extramusical associations,* which may link a given raga to a particular time of day (e.g., a "morning raga," an "evening raga"); season of the year (e.g., a "summer raga," a "winter raga"); ceremonial event; or designated emotional state of mind, or *rasa* (e.g., joy, sadness, peacefulness).

Tala: Meter and rhythm in raga performance

The rhythmic framework of a raga performance, and especially the metric cycle in which the music is grounded, is called the *tala.* Just as there are many different ragas, there are also many different talas. Like meters in Western music, each tala has a specific number of beats. Talas range in length from simple cycles of three or four beats to exceptionally complex ones of over a hundred beats. In "An Introduction to Indian Music," Ravi Shankar mentioned two popular talas, the 16-beat tala called *tintal* and the 10-beat tala called *jhaptal.* We will learn to mark out and "perform" the 16-beat tintal pattern later in the chapter.

**jhaptal
(JUP-tahl ["jhap"
rhymes with
"cup"])**

As with Western meters, the various beats in a tala receive different degrees of emphasis relative to one another; that is, there are strong, medium, and weak beats (and often finer gradations, in addition). As we learned in Shankar's "An Introduction to Indian Music," the first beat of each cycle of a tala (which generally doubles as the *last* beat of the preceding cycle) is called *sam.*

Standard Features of a Tala Summarized

- Each tala has a specific number of beats (e.g., 16 beats for tintal, 10 beats for jhaptal); the number ranges from as few as 3 beats per cycle to more than 100 beats per cycle.
- The metric cycle of the tala has a specific pattern of relatively stronger and weaker beats.
- The basic, "skeletal" drumming pattern that defines the tala is called the *theka*.
- The first beat of each tala cycle—which simultaneously functions as the last beat of the preceding cycle—is called *sam*.

The skeletal drum pattern that outlines the basic structure of the tala cycle is called the *theka*. This pattern is rarely heard unembellished in actual performance, except to some extent when the tabla first enters. After this, the drumming tends to become highly elaborate in its varied rhythmic exploits and improvisations, to the point that the skeletal theka is largely obscured (though it still continues to *function* implicitly as the rhythmic foundation for the piece). Raga is an art of adornment, elaboration, virtuosity, and improvisation, and this applies as much to the tabla player in the treatment of the tala as it does to the sitar player in the treatment of raga melody.

How a raga "grows"

The way a raga is developed in performance, explains Indian music scholar George Ruckert, is described in terms of its *barhat,* or growth. Various metaphors are used, from the growing of a seed to the act of making love (Ruckert and Widdess 2000:84). From the "seed" of the raga itself, a seed containing all of the directions, resources, and methods necessary to bring to fruition a rich and self-contained musical world, the musician grows his unique yet deeply tradition-bound rendering of "the raga," essentially creating it in the very moment of performance. The raga is internalized not as some tangible music entity like a "piece of music" in the Western sense, but as a *template for musical action* that has been developed through many years of devoted study and practice. It is a generating source from which musical ideas and inspirations grow and flow, or, in Ruckert's words, "a map a musician follows in his or her creation of a musical performance: a catalog of melodic movements that the artist unfolds, details, and expands while following a traditional performance format that has been passed down orally from teacher to student," generation after generation (Ruckert and Widdess 2000:66). With a deep awareness of the unique features, rules, procedures, and philosophical and spiritual underpinnings that define the particular raga he is playing—for example, Raga Sindhi-Bhairavi—a master musician such as Ravi Shankar explores the musical, symbolic, and spiritual potential inherent in that raga. He adheres strictly to the raga's dictates while simultaneously pushing it to the limits of its potential, cultivating the achievement of a state of musical and spiritual transcendence for himself and his listeners.

Raga Sindhi-Bhairavi (RAH-gah SIN-dee BHAY-ruv-ee)

The number of paths on which to travel in journeying through a raga's realm of possibilities is essentially limitless. No two performances of a given raga are ever identical, not even two different performances by the same musicians. On the other hand, every path the raga may lead to is carefully marked by the signposts of a standard formal plan that nurtures the growth process inherent in every raga performance. We turn to a discussion of this formal plan next, and after that to a participatory musical activity and then a raga Guided Listening Experience featuring a complete raga recording by Ravi Shankar.

Form in raga performance

According to Ruckert, the overall pattern in the various forms and styles of raga is defined by music that starts with slow and abstract movement and becomes increasingly metrical as it accelerates to a presto [very fast-tempoed] conclusion (Ruckert and Widdess 2000:84). This process of gradually progressing from slow melodic motion in a free and unmetered rhythm at the beginning, to very fast melodic motion that is highly structured rhythmically and metrically by the end (Figure 8.4, p. 135), is symbolic of the growth process that is a general characteristic of raga performance. Most typically, that process occurs within a musical form consisting of four main formal sections that proceed from one to the next without pause: alap, **jor**, **gat**, and **jhala**.

gat (like English "gut")

ALAP The "slow and abstract movement" portion of an instrumental raga performance is contained in its opening section, the alap. As we heard in Shankar's "An Introduction to Indian Music," the alap is improvised by the melodic soloist (e.g., the sitar player) with only a drone accompaniment. It is an exploratory journey through the raga's melodic essence and range of possibility. There is no drumming, no meter, no set compositions. Woven into the alap are successive passages in which each of the principal tones of the raga is introduced and deeply explored. Each one is presented alone, "dressed up" in characteristic ornaments and microtonal nuances, and contributing to distinctive melodic figures and motives that may be developed more extensively later on in the performance. As the various individual pitches are introduced, the broader dimensions of the raga's overall musical organization begin to blossom. The rhythm becomes more and more animated and the melodic range expands and grows as the soloist explores the raga in various octave registers. At the same time, the raga's designated mood-state, its rasa, starts to emerge and grows increasingly clear. Hearing an alap is like going to see a play and being introduced to all of the characters before the play proper begins, in a way that gives a deep sense of who those characters are and how they will act and interact as the play unfolds.

Finally, the alap serves as an introduction not just to the raga but to the soloist playing it as well. Improvisational ability constitutes the true measure of a raga performer, and the alap is regarded as the quintessential test of improvisatory skill in a raga performance. It is in this improvised opening that the true mettle and expertise of the soloist are assessed by the audience.

JOR The jor is an intermediary section that serves as a musical bridge between the introductory alap that precedes it and the main section (the gat) that follows it in a standard raga performance. It is characterized by playing on the solo melodic instrument that is more rhythmically active, steady, and energetic than that heard in the alap. Despite the increased rhythmic regularity and activity of the jor, there is still neither a set metric cycle (tala) nor drumming accompaniment in this section.

GAT The entry of the drums (usually tabla) signals the beginning of the gat. This drumming establishes the tala, which serves as the foundational metric cycle for the music henceforth. Both the skeletal rhythmic pattern of the tala and improvised embellishments of that basic pattern are contained within the drumming part. The gat is also the section of the form in which the raga's main, composed melody is introduced. This melody serves as the principal point of departure for various improvised passages, melodic and rhythmic variations, and new melodic passages that unfold during the subsequent course of the performance.

With the commencement of the gat, a raga performance becomes a brilliant display of musical/social interaction. The sitar player may be the "soloist" and the tabla player the "accompanist," but these labels are frequently eclipsed by the sense of equal partnership that is achieved in their musical dialogue. As the gat unfolds, the drum part may move fluidly between accompanying the solo instrument in some parts, engaging in dialogue with it in others, and playing complex rhythmic unison passages together with it in still others. The intensity and depth of interplay increase as the performance progresses and grows. The gat combines both composed and improvised passages and includes multiple subsections. All of its musical materials emerge from the raga itself and are presented in the established tala (the

Two Kinds of Time

So far, our exploration of raga has focused specifically on how a raga "grows" during the course of a performance. This growth has been depicted as gradual and continuous, a progressive process of development across time. In addition to this kind of time, another kind of time—represented by the tala—is running concurrently. As the raga grows and progresses throughout the gat and jhala, it does so framed against the cyclic regularity of the tala. Thus, the progress of raga growth is "measured" against the constancy of tala time. Just as the growth of a tree is both measured and profoundly affected by the cyclic passage of time from day to day, season to season, year to year, so too is the melodic growth of the raga marked and in large measure determined in reference to the constant, cyclic time of tala.

same raga may be combined with different talas in different performances). As the gat moves forward, two general patterns emerge: first, there is a gradual increase in tempo; second, patterns and sections become longer and increasingly complex (see Figure 8.4). Again, parallels to processes of growth are obvious.

JHALA Raga forms typically conclude with a jhala. The jhala follows the gat directly, driving the performance to an exciting and climactic finish. The commencement of the jhala is usually signaled by a sudden upward jump in tempo and intensity. From here, the tempo continues to accelerate further and the musical energy intensifies progressively right through to the end. An almost percussive style of playing on the solo instrument (e.g., sitar) is characteristic of the jhala, and this is reinforced by motoric rhythms in the drumming part.

The jhala, like the alap, jor, and gat that precede it, belongs to a musical whole—the complete raga performance—that is greater than the sum of its parts. In its overall process of growth, its barhat, the raga grows through the medium of its performance in ways that strive toward an ultimate goal of Nada Brahma, "the Sound of God." At its sublime best, the playing of a raga is more than mere musical artistry; it is also a spiritual practice invested with the expression of deep meaning and devotion.

FIGURE 8.4

Form in raga performance.

Slow, abstract → Fast, metered

Alap/Jor	Gat/Jhala
• Improvised • Progressive introduction of raga's tones, stylistic elements • Gradual expansion of melodic range and increase in rhythmic activity • Jor connects alap to gat	• Arrival of drumming and establishment of the tala announce gat • Progressive intensification through overall increase in tempo, complexity of cycles • Growth of musical interaction between performers • Alternation of composed and improvised sections • Performance builds to climactic finish during the concluding jhala

Keeping tal with Ravi Shankar

Were you to attend a live raga performance in India (or even outside of India), you might be surprised to see members of the audience quietly clapping, touching their fingers together, and moving their hands in the air in time to the music as the musicians play. This patterned method of marking musical time is called **keeping tal** (short for "keeping tala"). In this section, we will learn how to keep tal with selected passages of "An Introduction to Indian Music."

CLAPS, WAVES, AND FINGER TOUCHES Keeping tal is essentially just a more sophisticated version of what we in the West do when we tap our feet to the beat while listening to music. What makes keeping tal a bit more complex than your standard foot tap is that it not only marks the beats, but also provides *a visual system for differentiating their relative strengths and functions within the tala's metric cycle.* For example, for the 16-beat metric cycle called tintal, there is one system of keeping tal in which three different kinds of hand gestures are incorporated into marking out the tala pattern: claps, waves, and finger touches. Beats 1, 5, and 13 are each marked by a handclap. These are the *tali,* or "full," beats of the metric cycle of tintal. Beat one receives a bit of extra emphasis since it marks the all-important principal beat, sam. Beat nine, conversely, is marked by a silent wave (Figure 8.5), which is executed by turning your right hand over from back to front, so that you end up with the palm facing upward. This wave gesture signifies the *khali,* or "empty," beat of the tintal cycle. It arrives exactly halfway through the cycle and essentially represents the *opposite* of the very "full" sam beat, where all the different elements of the music come together (*sam* literally translates as "together"). Hindu cosmology defines the universe largely in terms of balanced opposites, or binary oppositions (light-dark, sacred-profane, male-female, etc.), and this full/empty, clap/wave opposition symbolizes this concept in musical terms.

khali (KAH-lee)

All of the other beats in tintal are marked by finger touches (Figure 8.6), in which you touch your right thumb with the tips of your right ring, middle, and index fingers one after the other on successive beats (i.e., ring finger on beat 2, middle finger on beat 3, index finger on beat 4; likewise for beats 6, 7, and 8; 10, 11, and 12; and 14, 15, and 16, respectively). These are the subordinate beats of the cycle.

In Figure 8.7, the basic hand gesture pattern for keeping tal with tintal is marked out. The claps are marked by an "x," the wave by an "O," and the finger touches by dots. Uppercase "X" is used for beat one, or sam, as a reminder to give that beat extra emphasis.

Khali (silent wave) hand gesture.

FIGURE 8.5

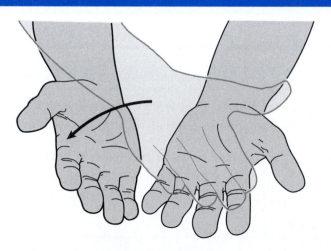

FIGURE 8.6

Finger touches.

FIGURE 8.7

Keeping tal pattern for tintal.

1	2	3	4	5	6	7	8	9	10	11	12	13	14	15	16
X	●	●	●	x	●	●	●	O	●	●	●	x	●	●	●

LEARNING TO KEEP TAL As the first step of learning to keep tal, try to mark out the entire tintal pattern using the appropriate hand and finger gestures while keeping a steady tempo. Repeat the cycle two or three times directly, without pausing between cycles. Practice by "playing along" with the model of **Online Musical Illustration #23.**

Once you are able to mark out the cycle on your own, cue up "An Introduction to Indian Music" (**CD ex. #2-21**) to the tintal musical illustration located at 1:45–2:00. Keep tal along with Shankar's counting of the beats, making sure that your various claps, waves, and touches line up with the correct beats. You will notice that Shankar adds an accent to his verbal counts on each of the main clap and wave beats (1, 5, 9, and 13).

Finally, try to keep tal with the performance demonstration located at 2:58–3:30. Here the tempo is extremely fast, to the point where you probably will not be able to mark all of the subordinate beats with finger counts. Therefore, just focus on executing the claps and waves of the main beats: 1, 5, 9, and 13. See if you can count the number of tala cycles in the performance overall.

In doing this final exercise, be prepared for the possibility that keeping track of the tala may get especially difficult toward the end, where the rhythm loops around and cuts across the main beats in mind-bending ways. The reason for this is that the musicians are finishing their performance with something called a **tihai**, in which the same rhythmic pattern is played three times in succession, with the final statement of the pattern landing precisely on sam to end the piece. The tihai functions as a rhythmic *cadence,* an ending pattern that provides a satisfying sense of closure at the end of a musical performance or section of a musical performance.

tihai (ti-HA-EE ["ti" as in "tip," not "tea"])

insights and perspectives

The Rhythm of Tihai

Because the basic rhythmic pattern of the tihai is of an irregular length, it creates a highly syncopated effect and the sense of rhythmic "dislocation" seems to intensify with each repetition (sometimes varied repetition) of the pattern. This creates an exciting rhythmic tension that is satisfyingly resolved when everything comes back together emphatically on the performance's final, climactic note. The musicians must carefully calibrate the length of the tihai to ensure that it does indeed land back on sam as it is supposed to. Most raga performances end with a tihai, and many of the internal sections within a performance do as well. Listen once more to the final section of the **CD ex. #2-21** performance, from 3:23–3:30. Try to identify the tihai pattern as it recurs three times.

guided listening experience

"Raga Sindhi-Bhairavi" (Hindustani Raga), Ravi Shankar

- CD Track **#2-23**

- Featured performer(s)/group: Ravi Shankar (sitar), Chatur Lal (tabla), N. C. Mullick (tambura)

- Format: Complete track

- Source recording: *The Sounds of India,* by Ravi Shankar (Columbia)

To hear how a Hindustani raga comes to life in performance, we will listen to a recording of Raga Sindhi-Bhairavi (Sindhu-Bhairavi). The performers are Ravi Shankar on sitar and Chatur Lal on tabla (with N. C. Mullick on the tambura). This recording was first released in 1957 and has the status of a classic. The album on which it was originally included, *The Sounds of India,* provided many Western listeners of that period with their first exposure to Indian classical music.

Raga Sindhi-Bhairavi belongs to the Bhairavi family of ragas. Bhairavi ragas are morning ragas. They are identified with the female form of Bhairavi, who is described vividly in ancient writings from India: "The great poets sing of Bhairavi, the consort of Lord Bhairava, worshipping her Lord seated on a carved crystal on the peak of Mount Kailasa with soft leaves of full blossomed lotus flowers. She holds cymbals in her hands, and her eyes sparkle with a yellowish glint" (see Kaufmann 1968:533).

Though classified as a morning raga, Raga Sindhi-Bhairavi is often performed at night, specifically as the closing raga of an Indian classical music concert that begins in the evening. Since such concerts are generally long, extending beyond midnight, this is deemed appropriate—after all, it is morning, technically speaking, by the time Sindhi-Bhairavi is played (Lavezzoli 2006:4).

Sindhi-Bhairavi is further classified as a light classical or semi-classical raga; it is sometimes even described as having a folk-like character. As such, it is never the main, central raga of an Indian classical music concert. Its conventional placement at the end of such concerts has particular functional aims: with its relative simplicity and highly melodic character, Sindhi-Bhairavi serves to calm and relax the audience and the performers alike after the intensity and excitement of the main raga that normally precedes it. It also is presented as a form of penance, a musical statement asking forgiveness for any mistakes or moments of impropriety—musical, spiritual, or otherwise—that may have occurred during the concert.

In sum, then, Sindhi-Bhairavi is generally thought of as a light raga of feminine character that is played to calm and appease. But in this performance (**CD ex. #2-23**), Ravi Shankar plays against type and offers a boldly different interpretation. His Sindhi-Bhairavi is rhythmically intense and muscular—even aggressive at times—and many things about the performance, from the bravura of Shankar's display of technical virtuosity to the melodic ornaments he employs, have the effect of transforming this oft-performed raga into something quite different than it usually is. For some Indian music connoisseurs, such as the sitar player Nalini Vinayak, Shankar comes very close to crossing the line of propriety here. "This is a very different way of playing Sindhi-Bhairavi than I am used to," Vinayak told me as we listened to the recording together during a 2010 interview. "You would never hear Vilayat Khan or Shahid Parvez Khan [two of the other great sitar masters of Shankar's generation] approaching Sindhi-Bhairavi like this. Their performances were for me more true to the spirit of this raga, more subtle, more gentle. This one is an impressive display of technique, but it is more forceful than I would prefer."

Why the arguably excessive exuberance? Perhaps it stems from Shankar's attempt on this recording to make a strong impression on Western listeners new to Indian music. Or maybe it is a product of the same adventurous spirit for striking a balance between traditionalism and innovation that has defined Shankar's life and musical career on so many levels. There are other possible explanations, too, but whatever the case may be, this interpretation of Raga Sindhi-Bhairavi bears Ravi Shankar's unique and indelible musical stamp. It is as powerful as it is controversial, a testament to the restless creativity and willingness to test limits that have long defined who Ravi Shankar is and what he has achieved as a musical artist over the course of more than half a century.

The recording begins with a brief musical demonstration that precedes the raga performance proper. Shankar introduces and then plays the ascending (*aroha*) and descending (*avroha*) pitches of the basic scale of Raga Sindhi-Bhairavi (0:00–0:15). As you can hear, even this "basic" rendition of the scale is quite complex. The sequence of pitches coming down is not just a simple reversal of the sequence of pitches going up. Rather, the ascending and descending versions each have their own unique pitch sequences, microtones, and ornaments on certain notes. This is commonly the case for many ragas, as we learned earlier.

The ascending (aroha) form of the Sindhi-Bhairavi scale is approximately as follows when translated into Western pitch equivalents:

B♭ C E♭ F G E♭ F A♭ B♭ C

Its descending (avroha) counterpart takes this form:

C B♭ A B♭ A♭ G F E♭ G F E♭ D E♭ D♭ C

Note that neither of the above transcriptions accounts for the large variety of melodic ornaments and microtonal nuances on specific notes that define Sindhi-Bhairavi as surely as do the main pitches themselves. Also note that while 10 notes are played in the ascending version of the scale and 15 are played in the descending version, all of these notes derive in one way or another from a rudimentary set of seven pitches in the Indian music theory system: Sa Re Ga Ma Pa Da Ni. In the case of Sindhi-Bhairavi, the raga's "theoretical" scale of Sa Re Ga Ma Pa Da Ni can be approximated to the following sequence of Western pitches:

Sa	Re	Ga	Ma	Pa	Da	Ni
C	D♭	E♭	F	G	A♭	B♭

One of these pitches (Re or D♭) does not even appear in the ascending form of the scale at all, whereas two of the pitches (Da and Re) each appear in *two* variant forms in the descending form of the scale (A♭ and A for Da; D♭ and D for Re). There is much more that we could discuss about the "basic" scale of Sindhi-Bhairavi as well, but even this rudimentary introduction should suffice as an illustration of the depth and multidimensionality of what makes a raga a raga.

Following the scale demonstration that opens the track, Shankar announces that the tala for this performance will be tintal, "a rhythmic cycle of 16 beats." This, of course, is the same tala that we have already learned about. From the point at which the tabla drums enter (about six minutes in) until the end of the track, tintal will define the metric cycle and rhythmic design of the performance overall.

The first two things we hear once the performance proper begins (at 0:27) are the drone of the tambura and a *taraf*, which is a sweeping, downward run (glissando) across the sitar's 13 sympathetic resonance strings that sets those strings in motion and signals that we are now officially underway. From here, the raga's gradual process of barhat, or growth, progressively unfolds, first in the introductory alap, then in the transitional jor, then in the multisectioned gat, and finally in the concluding jhala.

ALAP (0:27–4:52) In the alap, Shankar performs an improvisation in free rhythm on his sitar (with only the drone of the tambura as accompaniment). Following a dramatic opening flourish of ascending notes up the Sindhi-Bhairavi scale, he presents the notes of the raga one by one, step by step, exploring the distinctive character of each and their relationships with one another, as well as the distinctive ornaments, melodic motives, and microtonal nuances that collectively account for Sindhi-Bhairavi's unique musical and emotional character and identity. As the alap progresses, the improvisation extends from a single note at the beginning through to expansive melodies covering multiple octaves of the sitar's melodic range by the end, and from slow and sparse rhythmic motion to relatively fast playing with many notes in quick succession. The increased rhythmic regularity of the last part of the alap (4:24–4:52) brings this opening section of the performance to a close with a foreshadowing of things to come.

JOR (4:53–5:51) The jor is the transitional section that connects the alap to the gat. The word *jor* literally means "link," a term that aptly describes its function within the larger form. The arrival of the jor is marked by steady, driving rhythms played on the two top strings of the sitar (called the *jhala* strings), which serve a specifically rhythmic function. The near-perpetual rhythmic motion created between these rhythmic strings and the melody of Shankar's continuing improvisation effect a change in mood from the opening alap and anticipate the new rhythmic character of the gat section to follow.

GAT (5:52–12:35) The arrival of the gat, or main composition section of the performance (the term *gat* is translated as "composition"), is signaled by the entry of the tabla drums, played by Chatur Lal. Following a virtuosic, introductory flourish by Lal on the tabla and a second taraf glissando on the sitar (5:52–5:54), Shankar plays a series of seven melodic notes with tabla accompaniment before he and Lal land decisively (and momentarily pause) on an eighth melody note at 5:58. This note marks the beginning of the piece's first 16-beat tintal cycle. The cycle continues through to 6:04, at which point a second tintal cycle begins (and so on with the subsequent tintal cycles at 6:11, 6:17, etc.). As you listen, try to mark out the 16-beat tintal cycles using the keeping-tal techniques learned earlier (but be aware that this is quite difficult to do with this recording!).

As the gat takes shape, Shankar engages in what might be described as a call-and-response sitar dialogue with himself. The principal melodic motive of the gat recurs over and over, and in between statements of that motive, Shankar fills in with brief passages of improvisation. The melodic motive is called a *chalan*; the improvised passages are called *toda*.

Starting at 7:04, Shankar moves away from the chalan-toda alternating format momentarily and presents a more extended improvisation over the continuing tabla accompaniment. He returns to chalan-toda alternation at 7:25, initiating a section including some inventive sitar-tabla interplay. The rhythm gets especially complex starting around 8:13, at which point Shankar shifts from duple to triple subdivisions of the beat and is deftly followed in that rhythmic shift by Lal on the tabla. The alternating passages of unison rhythm and rhythmic counterpoint that emerge during this section show off the talents and closely integrated musical sensibilities of these two master Hindustani musicians to fine effect.

The new material introduced in the sitar part at 9:23 marks the beginning of a second section of the gat called the *antara* (literally meaning "between"). This is followed by a return to the earlier melody (chalan) just over a minute later. We hear it three times before Shankar takes off again with a new improvisation. There is a brief reprise of the chalan melody, and then a sudden, dramatic upward jump in tempo, which introduces the final section of the gat, called *drut gat* (fast gat), starting at 11:26. Here new melodic material is introduced once again and the music sets off on a progressive race to the finish, with the increasingly long, complex, and virtuosic improvisational passages of the sitar matched by increasingly active drumming on the tabla.

JHALA (12:36–END) The performance concludes with the jhala, which brings it to an exciting and climactic finish. The arrival of the jhala is marked by another sudden jump in tempo, at 12:36. At this same point, Shankar and Lal team up for a propulsive rhythmic section that features Shankar playing his sitar almost as though it were a percussion instrument. The main rhythmic drive is furnished by the prominence of rhythms played on the sitar's high-pitched jhala strings, which derive their name from this section of the musical form that highlights them.

Once the new, fast tempo and high-spirited rhythmic energy of the jhala are established, Shankar begins to spin out a succession of improvised passages of escalating rhythmic complexity. Meanwhile, the tempo continues to increase progressively, accelerating from one level to another phrase by phrase. It is as though Shankar and Lal are driving a race car and shifting up into higher and higher gears. Once they have reached warp speed, they lock together one last time for a grand tihai at 14:49, which brings this exciting raga journey to a close.

Along the path of the journey, Raga Sindhi-Bhairavi has grown in a multiplicity of ways in Shankar's and Lal's capable hands: from a single note to cascades of melody and rhythm played at blinding speed; from slow, abstract movement to fervent rhythmic energy; from solo introspection on the part of Shankar to virtuosic musical-social interplay between Shankar and Lal. And there is a sense of spiritual growth and transcendence having occurred as well, though this is less easy to identify objectively.

One is left to wonder whether this rather unorthodox approach to a traditional raga, Sindhi-Bhairavi, is boldly innovative, brazenly inappropriate, or something in between. But certainly there can be no question about the extraordinary skill and virtuosity displayed by these master musicians in this compelling demonstration of Hindustani musical artistry.

guided listening quick summary

"Raga Sindhi-Bhairavi," Ravi Shankar (CD ex. #2-23)

OPENING DEMONSTRATION OF RAGA AND TALA

0:00–0:15

- Ravi Shankar introduces and demonstrates the ascending (aroha) and descending (avroha) forms of the "basic" scale of Raga Sindhi-Bhairavi.

0:16–0:26

- Shankar explains that the tala will be tintal, "a rhythmic cycle of 16 beats."

ALAP

0:27–4:23

■ Following the establishment of the tambura drone and a taruf (glissando) across the sitar's sympathetic resonance strings, Shankar progressively explores the notes, contours, and other characteristics of the raga through a free-rhythm sitar improvisation that gradually builds in melodic range, rhythmic activity, and intensity.

4:24–4:52

■ Increasing rhythmic activity and regularity in this last portion of the alap foreshadow the changing rhythmic character of what is to come.

JOR

4:53–5:51

■ Rhythmic strumming on the jhala strings, combined with near-perpetual rhythmic motion overall, characterizes this transitional section linking the preceding alap to the gat that follows.

GAT

5:52–7:03

■ A tabla flourish and another taruf on the sitar (5:52–5:54) mark the arrival of the gat.

■ The 16-beat tintal metric cycle is established starting at 5:58, preceded by seven even-paced melodic notes played on the sitar with tabla accompaniment.

■ The form alternates between statements of the principal melodic motive (chalan) and brief improvised passages (toda) played by Shankar on the sitar.

7:04–9:22

■ Shankar moves away from the chalan-toda alternation format to perform a more extended improvisation, then returns to the chalan-toda format at 7:25; the section at 8:13 adds new levels of rhythmic complexity, including a shift from duple to triple subdivisions of the beat.

9:23–11:25

■ The antara section, in which new melodic material is introduced, commences at 9:23; this is followed by a return to the chalan melody just over a minute later and by passages of improvisation that build the music's intensity.

11:26–12:35

■ The gat concludes with a final section called drut gat (fast gat), which is marked by a sudden increase in tempo, extended passages of improvisation, and increasingly active drumming.

JHALA

12:36–end

■ Another jump in tempo and propulsive rhythmic playing highlighting the jhala strings of the sitar signal the commencement of this closing section of the performance.

■ A series of exciting tempo accelerations and continually growing intensity drive toward the climactic, closing tihai at 14:49.

Intercultural Crossings and Transformations

This second main part of the chapter surveys dimensions of the intercultural musical landscape that has emerged out of interactions of Indian, Western, and other musicultural traditions since the 1950s. Ravi Shankar and the Hindustani raga tradition he represents will serve as our main points of departure for exploring key cross-cultural developments in the worlds of Western classical, jazz, and rock music, and finally for a consideration of the highly cosmopolitan musical world of Bollywood.

It should be be noted that the discussion here represents a very narrow view of the globalization of Indian music in the modern era, and even of Ravi Shankar's own contributions to that phenomenon. A more comprehensive treatment would cover non-Indian music conservatories devoted exclusively to the teaching of Indian classical music (e.g., the Ali Akbar College of Music in San Rafael, California), Indian music performance courses taught at North American and European universities, the stories of scores of non-Indian musicians who have traveled to India to study and become highly accomplished performers of Indian music, and international cultural organizations that sponsor Indian classical music performances. It would also cover the vibrant and vital Indian music scenes that have come into being in large, urban communities of the South Asian diaspora in North America, the United Kingdom, and other places in recent decades. In short, what is presented here represents a small but significant thread in a much larger fabric of Indian music's global outreach.

Early inroads: *West Meets East, Improvisations,* and the music of John Coltrane

By the mid-1960s, Ravi Shankar was a well-known figure in Western classical music circles. The fact that the violin virtuoso Yehudi Menuhin had undertaken serious studies of Indian classical music performance with him beginning in the 1950s had garnered much public attention. And when Menuhin began to concertize and record with Shankar, the art of Hindustani raga, the fruitful potential of cross-cultural musical collaboration, and indeed the singular artistry of Ravi Shankar himself, all came to the prominent attention of Western classical music audiences in one fell swoop. Especially influential was the seminal Shankar-Menuhin recording *West Meets East* (1967), the first of a series of popular recordings featuring the two master musicians performing Indian music together.

Several years before the release of *West Meets East,* Shankar had already extended his musical range into cross-cultural, experimental musical projects with prominent American jazz musicians. Though Shankar resisted facile comparisons between raga and jazz, rightly insisting that they were entirely distinct and historically unrelated musical traditions, he did acknowledge that certain similarities between the two—especially their shared emphases on virtuosity and improvised solos—furnished a fertile meeting ground for musical cross-pollination. In addition, as Gerry Farrell has noted in his book *Indian Music and the West,* Shankar found that jazz musicians "were quick to grasp the rhythmic subtleties of Indian music, in ways that [Western] pop and classical musicians were not" (Farrell 1997:189). A pioneering Indian-jazz fusion album entitled *Improvisations,* featuring Shankar with flutist Bud Shank and several other well-known jazz musicians, was released in 1961 to critical acclaim.

It was also in the year 1961 that a quintet led by the influential jazz saxophonist John Coltrane recorded a Coltrane composition entitled "India" (**CD ex. #3-1**). This piece featured an Indian-inspired style of jazz music with extended passages of improvisation over drone-based harmonies (chords played over an underlying, tonic drone). Over the next few years, this style became the foundation of Coltrane's highly innovative approach to jazz, an approach in which Indian music became, according to Farrell, "a musical reference point in artistic consciousness that also worked freely with influences from Africa and the Middle East, as well as blues, folk, and Western classical music" (Farrell 1997:191).

John Coltrane playing the soprano saxophone.

Prior to recording "India" in 1961, John Coltrane had been devoting much of his time and energy to listening to and closely studying Indian music recordings, especially recordings by Ravi Shankar. Referring to Shankar in a 1961 interview, he commented that "I collect the records he's made, and his music moves me. I'm certain that if I recorded with him I'd increase my possibilities tenfold . . ." (Porter 1998:209).

Alas, Coltrane never did record with Shankar, though he studied with him briefly in the winter of 1964–1965. Recalling their lessons together many years later, Shankar said of Coltrane that he was "amazed by our different system of improvisation, . . . by the complexity of our talas, and more than anything by how we can create such peace, tranquillity and spirituality in our music" (Shankar 1999:178).

When Coltrane and his wife Alice gave birth to a son in 1965, they named him Ravi. Coltrane had planned to undertake more serious studies with Shankar, but the plans never materialized due to his failing health. He succumbed to cancer in 1967 while still a young man.

Ravi Shankar, the Beatles, and the "great sitar explosion"

At about the same time that John Coltrane was engaged in his brief course of study with Ravi Shankar, George Harrison, a musician from a very different world, was embarking upon his own Indian music odyssey. Legend has it that Harrison first happened upon a sitar during filming of the Beatles movie *Help!* The instrument was being used as a prop on one of the stage sets. Harrison picked it up, plucked a few notes, and, liking the sound, began teaching himself to play it.

As mentioned, a sitar solo played by Harrison was featured on the song "Norwegian Wood," which appeared on the Beatles' 1965 album *Rubber Soul.* In that context, the instrument was merely a novel timbre, adding "exotic color" to the song's acoustic, otherwise folk-rock texture. The cultural impact was significant, however. Suddenly, the sound of the sitar was being heard by Beatles fans the world over, reaching and intriguing millions of listeners with no prior exposure to it.

The following year, 1966, Harrison began his formal sitar studies with Ravi Shankar. At first, Shankar was not quite sure what to make of this quiet, humble, English rock guitarist. It was one thing for Shankar to work with a musician like Yehudi Menuhin, who, like himself, was a leading proponent of a long-established classical music tradition. Working with jazz musicians also had proved a reasonably comfortable stretch, due to the fact that jazz shared with raga certain key musical features and priorities. Rock music, however, was completely alien territory for Shankar. He was surprised to encounter a rock musician with aspirations of learning a classical music tradition, and a tradition of a foreign music culture at that. But Harrison seemed serious and motivated, so Shankar agreed to teach him. At the time, he had no idea that this simple decision to take on a new student would contribute to a musical and cultural revolution and to a radical transformation of his own life and career.

By the time Harrison's song "Within You, Without You" was released on the Beatles album *Sergeant Pepper's Lonely Hearts Club Band* in 1967, the imprint of Indian music was firmly embedded in the music's sound, instrumentation, structure, and lyrics. In addition to employing sitar, tabla, and several other traditional Indian instruments, "Within You, Without You" incorporated raga-like features in its melodies and forms and tala-inspired meters and rhythms. Moreover, Harrison's introspective lyrics reflected his growing interest in Hindu philosophy and spiritual practices.

Once the sitar had made its debut on a Beatles record, it was not long before it became a favored "exotic" sound in the live and recorded performances of other leading rock, pop, and folk bands, the Byrds, the Yardbirds, and the Rolling Stones among them. Soon, other signature elements of Indian music—drones, "Indian" vocal effects (slides, slurs, etc.), raga-like scales, mystical or quasi-religious lyrics—also were finding their way into many rock and pop tunes.

George Harrison with Ravi Shankar.

"Sitar rock" had become part and parcel of the rock and pop music landscape, but core principles of Hindustani raga were not exactly being adopted into rock contexts as part of this trend. As Farrell explains, pop musicians of this period had neither the technical ability nor the aesthetic perspectives to work within, say, a genuine raga framework, with the result that "the elements of Indian music that appeared in pop were fragmented, their musical meaning changed through being out of context" (Farrell 1997:182). In the case of the post-1966 Beatles, the appropriation of Indian musical elements was generally approached with seriousness of purpose and a sense of adventurous creativity. In most other instances, however, rock sitar solos and other Indian music markers served as little more than trendy tokens of exoticism (which is not to say that they necessarily lacked effectiveness *within* their own new musical contexts).

Ravi Shankar found the often trite and gratuitous uses to which the sitar and other Indian instruments and musical devices were put by these rock and pop bands of the "great sitar explosion" of the 1960s and 1970s disturbing, though he tried to keep an open mind and maintain an attitude of acceptance. As he wrote in his 1968 autobiography:

> Though the sitar is being exploited now by pop groups on both sides of the Atlantic and will no doubt continue to be used this way for some time, those who sincerely love Indian music as *classical* music should not be upset by this. One instrument can serve many styles of music. (Shankar 1968:93)

Even more troubling for him than the musical effects of the great sitar explosion, though, were its cultural side effects. The sitar and all things Indian came to be equated with drug-induced, altered states of consciousness. Indian music became the vehicle of choice for "tripping out" and "getting high" on LSD and other drugs. For Shankar, this was abhorrent, though once again he tried to find cause for optimism despite his misgivings:

> I have been facing a surprising problem with some of my concert audiences since about 1965, especially in England. I found many young people who were "high"; sitting in the front rows of the hall, they were altogether in another world. Often, too, they sat there in front of me carrying on indecently with their girl friends or boy friends [*sic*], and many of them even lit cigarettes (if that, in fact, was what they were) whenever they pleased. Their conduct disgusted me, for too many people in this dazed stupor send out bad vibrations that are extremely upsetting.
>
> . . . but I am now happy to note that things have changed to such an extent that this problem has practically disappeared. My audiences everywhere are so much more clean and respectful, serious and receptive—especially in the United States. (Shankar 1968:96)

Alas, evidence suggests that this problem actually had not disappeared, or at least that it was still fully in view during Shankar's historic performance at Woodstock in 1969.

A new level: John McLaughlin and Shakti

In the late 1960s, a period that witnessed the untimely death of John Coltrane, the great sitar explosion, and the gradual disintegration of the Beatles, the career of a brilliant young British jazz guitarist, John McLaughlin (b. 1942), was just beginning to take off. Moving to New York in 1969, McLaughlin was hired by jazz trumpet great Miles Davis, who had already helped to launch the careers of many other top jazz musicians, including Coltrane.

McLaughlin brought to his work with Davis an eclectic musical background. As a child, his first love was Western classical music—Beethoven, Schubert, Brahms. But before he had reached his teens, he had come to love many other kinds of music as well: Mississippi Delta blues, Spanish flamenco, jazz, and rock. As he developed into a gifted guitarist and composer, all of these early influences came to shape his unique, hybrid style. So too did his early passion for Indian classical music, though the full impact of that particular tradition would not come to the fore until after his tenure with Davis.

By the early 1970s, McLaughlin had left Davis to pursue other projects. In 1971, he formed an influential jazz-rock fusion band called the Mahavishnu Orchestra. ("Mahavishnu" means "divine compassion, power, and justice" in Sanskrit.) In addition to its jazz and rock elements, the Mahavishnu Orchestra's music showed strong Indian music influences, such as complex, tala-like metric cycles and raga-inspired scales, melodies, and musical forms. During his Mahavishnu period, McLaughlin took music lessons with Ravi Shankar, studied yoga, and became a disciple of the Hindu spiritual teacher Sri Chimnoy, ultimately converting to Hinduism himself. With single-minded devotion, he penetrated deeply into the ways of Indian culture both musically and spiritually. Jazz writer John Ephland has characterized the course of McLaughlin's experiences during that time as "the eventual immersion of one person into another culture, allowing himself to be transformed in the process" (Ephland 1991[1976]:4).

In 1975, McLaughlin's ever-deepening Indian immersion process led him to form a new group called Shakti (meaning "creative intelligence, beauty, and power" in Sanskrit). Indian instrumental sounds and musical features had become quite common in jazz, rock, jazz-rock fusion, and other Western music genres by this time, but Shakti took the idea of Indian-jazz fusion to a new level. Other than McLaughlin himself, all of the players were Indian classical musicians by training. Though Ravi Shankar was not actually a member of Shakti, his presence was strongly felt. The group's violinist, L. Shankar, was his nephew, and the young tabla player, the aforementioned Zakir Hussain, was the son of Shankar's own long-time musical partner, the tabla player Alla Rakha.

The other two members, R. Raghavan and T.H. Vinayakaram, were master percussionists of the southern, Karnatak tradition. Thus, from an Indian perspective, Shakti was actually a fusion group *within* a fusion group, fusing Indian and Western forms to be sure, but also Hindustani and Karnatak traditions.

For his work with Shakti, John McLaughlin developed a special kind of acoustic guitar modified with sitar-like features (scalloped fingerboard, extra strings) that made it possible for

Shakti. John McLaughlin is seen playing the guitar, with L. Shankar (violin) and Zakir Hussain (tabla) to his right.

Mahavishnu (MAH-hah-VISH-noo)

him to closely approximate the kinds of microtonal inflections and timbral nuances required of the group's heavily Indian-rooted fusion style. This unique instrument provided McLaughlin with a distinctive sound that was ideally suited to Shakti's approach.

Shakti was the premiere Indian-jazz fusion group from their founding in the mid-1970s through the 1980s. After disbanding for several years, they reunited as Remember Shakti in the late 1990s and once again become a dominant force in intercultural music making.

guided listening experience

"Joy," Shakti

- CD Track **#3-2**
- Featured performer(s)/group: Shakti, with John McLaughlin (guitar), L. Shankar (violin), Zakir Hussain (tabla), R. Raghavan and T.H. Vinayakaram (mrdangam/South Indian percussion)
- Format: Excerpt
- Source recording: *Shakti, with John McLaughlin* (Columbia/Legacy)

The trademark virtuosity of Shakti is well displayed in a piece entitled "Joy," which was included on the band's debut 1976 recording, *Shakti, with John McLaughlin*. "Joy" is not a raga, but it draws upon raga elements, combining them with jazz-derived forms and structures to create an exciting synthesis.

The main melody of the piece, played primarily in rapid unison rhythms by McLaughlin (guitar) and L. Shankar (violin) over a drone and fiery drumming accompaniment, builds from a scale that is clearly raga-derived. It consists of a series of contrasting melodic sections, most of which are played once and then repeated (sometimes more than once, and sometimes with variations). In its entirety, this melody is almost a full two minutes long (0:29–2:23). The rhythmic structure of the main melody is highly complex. Though everything ultimately fits within a series of tintal-like, 16-beat tala cycles, the individual melodic phrases push and pull against this underlying metric regularity, making it difficult (though not impossible) to keep tal with the music. Some of the melodic phrases sound as though they are half a beat too long, others as though they are half a beat too short. In the end, however, it all averages out.

Impressive improvised solos follow the main melody section on the excerpt included on your CD set. (The full track is more than 18 minutes long.) A brief tabla solo by Zakir Hussain (2:24–2:34) sets the rhythmic mood. Hussain is followed by McLaughlin, who starts his guitar solo in a relatively limited melodic range and with lots of rhythmic space, then builds in a jazz-inspired, raga-like fashion to ever greater levels of intensity. L. Shankar follows with a brilliant violin improvisation at 5:05, which climbs progressively higher up the instrument's range as it unfolds.

guided listening quick summary

"Joy," Shakti (CD ex. #3-2)

0:00–2:23

- Main melody (0:29–2:23) follows spoken introduction by McLaughlin (0:00–0:28).
- Melody, mainly played in guitar-violin unison, is complex rhythmically but is anchored by a 16-beat tala.
- Melody is accompanied by drone, tabla, and South Indian percussion.

Bollywood and Beyond: The Genius of A. R. Rahman

In the mid-1980s, Shakti's tabla player, Zakir Hussain, collaborated with the renowned South Indian violinist Kunnakudi Vaidyanathan on an innovative album entitled *Colours (Golden Krithis)*. *Colours* combined elements of Karnatak, Hindustani, and Western music in a unique synthesis that owed much stylistically to the sounds and textures of Indian film music as well. The ensemble accompanying the two soloists consisted of orchestral strings, South Indian and Western percussion, and keyboard synthesizers. The keyboard player was a talented young musician from Chennai (Madras) named A. S. Dileep Kumar, who would change his name to A. R. Rahman following his conversion to Islam a couple of years later.

"He was barely 19 years old then," Hussain recalls of Rahman, "but [he] had mastered many different styles of music—Western classical, jazz, rock and Carnatic [Karnatak]. Even after his work was done he would stay in the studio, sitting through other musicians' pieces, eyes and ears tuned in, constantly imbibing. Very intelligent, smart and creative" (Srinivasan 2002).

Today, A. R. Rahman stands as arguably the most renowned and influential Indian musician on an international scale since Ravi Shankar. He is the preeminent composer and **music director** in contemporary Indian cinema (the music director is responsible for all of a film's musical components, including background music, songs, and dance compositions) and one of the top-selling musical artists of all time, with a reported total of more than 300 million recordings sold. In India, where film song is dominant over all other genres of music in terms of both mass popularity and broadness of appeal across most every sector of society, Rahman is the reigning king of the film music world.

A. R. Rahman's prominence as an international musical figure is mirrored by the profuse cosmopolitanism of his approach; indeed, it is that very cosmopolitanism that likely accounts in large measure for his immense popularity both within and beyond India. Yet Rahman's global reach rarely exceeds his sure-handed grasp on the firmament of Indian musical tradition that provides his foundation. He has a talent for keeping what is necessarily and essentially Indian about "Indian music" in his music, while at the same time pushing that essential core of Indianness to the outer reaches of global inclusiveness.

A. R. Rahman.

As the Indian music critic Jayanth Deshpande has observed, Rahman's film music "mirrors not only the variegated tapestry that is India, but also the global musical culture. Rahman borrows ever so subtly from American soul or Gospel. He draws generously from rap, disco, folk, reggae, qawaali [qawwali], Hindustani and Carnatic in his rhythms. And the vocal ornaments of Carnatic music are ever present. Orchestral textures and harmonies typical of Western music often grace the background. His is a truly international music with a distinctly Indian feel. He has experimented as perhaps no other Indian composer has before him or does now" (Srinivasan

2002). And the end result is the creation of music of immense and widespread appeal; as another Indian commentator observes, Rahman's music "transcends all barriers—geographic, age or linguistic. Everyone from 6 to 60, Kashmir to Kanyakumari, as the cliché goes, are fans of his music. . . . All in all, quite arguably, no one has influenced Indian music as much as Rahman has in recent times" (Srinivasan 2002).

A. R. Rahman began his professional career in music at the age of nine, when the untimely death of his father—also a film composer—compelled him to capitalize on his prodigious musical talents in order to help support his struggling family. While still in his teens (and even before), he performed as a keyboard player with orchestras directed by legendary South Indian film composers such as M. S. Viswanathan, Ilaiyaraja, and K. V. Mahadevan. Zakir Hussain, another beneficiary of an abundantly musical childhood (as the son of Ravi Shankar's first-call tabla player, Alla Rakha), draws a clear parallel between Rahman's early musical experiences and his later career success: "He started as a young boy working with great composers like K. V. Mahadevan, for example. He knows the public pulse and has given the public a very intelligent combination package. This reminds me of R. D. Burman," Hussain adds, referring to the famed composer and music director who reigned supreme over Bollywood during the pre-Rahman era of the 1970s through the early 1990s, and whose innovations in the integration of rock and jazz with Indian melodies paved the way for Rahman's own musical internationalism. "These guys made it possible to bring together all elements of world music," says Hussain (Srinivasan 2002).

As a teenager, Rahman toured internationally with Zakir Hussain and with other leading Indian concert artists as well, including the violinist L. Shankar, also of Shakti fame. He went on to advanced Western classical music studies, on scholarship, at the Trinity College of Music in England, receiving a degree from that prestigious institution. His self-designed course of Western musical training also came to encompass myriad other forms and styles over time—jazz, rock, soul, hip-hop, reggae, techno, electronica, musical theater—as well as explorations of a variety of musical traditions originating from other world cultures: Japanese, Brazilian, Egyptian, and more. In addition, he immersed himself deeply in the study of an array of Indian musical styles, from classical Hindustani and Karnatak to rural folk dance traditions, bhangra, and qawwali, the latter of which he studied with the great Nusrat Fateh Ali Khan.

Rahman's passion for qawwali was underscored by the centrality of Sufism to his adopted Islamic faith and practice, which has also influenced many of his songs and musical compositions over the years. "I'm a deeply spiritual person," he states. "Sufism is about love—love for a fellow human, love for all-around humanity, and ultimately love for God. For me, it's where music and religion meet. . . . That's my inspiration" (Shubhash 2010).

Indian classical traditions such as Hindustani and Karnatak raga are likewise fundamental to Rahman's musical practice and aesthetic philosophy, even when working in musical idioms far removed from such classical forms. In the following comments about his compositional approach, Rahman implicitly links the organic growth process of music that is definitive of raga's essence, barhat, to the ideal of divine intervention and communion (in this case, from Allah) to which the process of a raga's evolution is ultimately directed in its highest form. For Rahman, composition—whether of a song for a movie, the background music for a cinematic scene, a spectacular dance sequence in a film, or a Sufi devotional hymn—is basically rooted in the same barhat process as a Ravi Shankar raga performance. "Nobody can be completely original," he asserts, "because the notes are already there . . . [F]rom the notes we form a raag [raga] and from the raag a tune . . . it is a process. As far as possible, to my conscience, I try to be original. The rest is up to Allah. . . . Once I complete a composition, a week later, I listen to it[,] and after two weeks, I take it up again. In the process my music grows" (Srinivasan 2002).

Rahman's earliest successes as a composer and music director for films came in the Tamil Nadu film industry of South India, which is based in his native city of Chennai. His first film score, for the 1992 Tamil-language movie *Roja,* received both popular and critical acclaim and launched Rahman to immediate stardom. 1995 witnessed Rahman's next big breakthrough as he "stormed the Bollywood bastion" with *Rangeela,* his first original score for a Hindi-language, Bollywood film. Traditionally, the worlds of Tamil and Hindi film have been largely separate entities, their separation premised on a host of linguistic, geographic, historical, sociopolitical, and cultural barriers. Such barriers and their associated prejudices would normally have ensured that there would be little opportunity for a composer of Tamil origin such as Rahman to break into the exclusive ranks of Bollywood's gargantuan film industry. But with the overwhelming success of *Rangeela,* Rahman not only broke the Tamil-Hindi barrier; he shattered it. By the end of 1995, he was widely recognized as the number-one composer in Bollywood and in the world of Indian film music overall, an unprecedented achievement. He dominated Bollywood and Tamil Nadu alike. The endless stream of successes that followed in the intervening years—musical scores for dozens of top-grossing movies, numerous chart-topping hit songs, hosts of national awards, and unprecedented sales numbering in the hundreds of millions—cemented his iconic stature in India and throughout South Asia and the South Asian diaspora.

Today, Rahman's mega-stardom has gone globally international in the broadest sense. His music for the 2008 international hit film *Slumdog Millionaire*—winner of eight Academy Awards (Oscars), including best picture of the year—garnered Rahman himself two Oscars: one for best original music score, the other for best original song ("Jai Ho"). He has received a slew of other honors in the wake of *Slumdog Millionaire*'s success as well, including being selected to *Time* magazine's "*Time* 100" list of the world's most influential people in 2009 (the magazine referred to him as the "Mozart of Madras") and receipt of the aforementioned CNN-IBN 2009 Indian of the Year Award. Beyond the cinematic world, Rahman has also taken part in other high-profile productions: a concert in Germany with the late Michael Jackson, collaborations with Andrew Lloyd Weber, a project with producer and former Talking Heads lead singer David Byrne. Surely his is a very different musical persona than Ravi Shankar's, yet much like Shankar, A. R. Rahman has redefined Indian music from within and without, and has made an indelible mark on global musical culture at many levels in the process.

guided listening experience

"Barso Re," by A. R. Rahman, Featuring Vocalist Shreya Ghoshal

■ CD Track **#3-3**

■ Featured performer(s)/group: A. R. Rahman (composer/music director), Shreya Ghoshal (vocalist)

■ Format: Complete track

■ Source recording: *The Best of A R Rahman: Music and Magic from the Composer of Slumdog Millionaire* (Sony Legacy)

In 2007, the year before *Slumdog Millionaire,* A. R. Rahman enjoyed a banner year. He composed the scores for a total of six films released that year, including his first mainstream English-language release, *Elizabeth: The Golden Age,* in which he shared composer credits with Craig Armstrong.

The Bollywood film *Guru* (originally released in Hindi) was one of the year's most successful Indian cinematic productions. It garnered five prestigious Filmfare awards (equivalent to the Academy Awards for Bollywood). Two of those went to Rahman himself, for best music director and best background score. The hit song of the film, "Barso Re," composed by Rahman (with lyrics by Gulzar), accounted for two of *Guru*'s other three Filmfare awards: one for Shreya Ghoshal for best female **playback singer** (see next page); the other for Saroj Khan for best choreography. *Guru* also won the best art direction award and was additionally nominated for best film, best director (Rahman's longtime collaborator, Mani Ratnam), best actress (Bollywood cinema goddess and former Miss World beauty pageant winner Aishwarya Rai), best actor (Abhishek Bachchan, in the title role of Gurukant Desai, aka Guru), best male playback singer (A. R. Rahman), best supporting actor (Mithun Chakraborty), and best lyrics (Gulzar).

Guru received international attention and acclaim far beyond the borders of India. Indeed, its premiere showing was not in India, but rather at Toronto's Elgin Theatre, making it the first Indian film to have a mainstream international premiere in Canada. It was favorably reviewed in *Time* magazine, *The New York Times,* and numerous other international publications.

The film offers a rags-to-riches story about a boy from humble beginnings who defies his lowly prospects to become an international business tycoon possessing great wealth and power, but questionable ethics and morals. His unethical ways nearly lead to his downfall, though in the end he manages to escape a completely tragic end. Aishwarya Rai plays the role of Guru's wife, Sujata. It is she who is seen singing "Barso Re," a song celebrating the life-sustaining gift of water and the arrival of long-awaited seasonal rains, as she dances ecstatically atop Hindu temples and in front of waterfalls and such in a display of hyper-dramatic devotion. It is all quite spectacular and grandiose.

In truth, Rai does not actually sing "Barso Re." Most Bollywood stars do not perform the songs they appear to be singing in their films. Rather, they lip-synch them, leaving the vocal artistry to skilled specialists known as *playback singers,* who often become top-selling recording artists and major stars in their own right. The greatest playback singer of all is the legendary Lata Mangeshkar, whose thousands of recordings over six-plus decades have earned her a citation in the *Guinness Book of World Records* as the most recorded musical artist of all time.

The playback singer featured on "Barso Re" is Shreya Ghoshal. Ghoshal is regarded by many as the rightful heir to Mangeshkar's throne as the queen of Bollywood playback vocalists. She received her early musical training in Hindustani classical music and first rose to fame as the singing surrogate for Aishwarya Rai in one of her earlier films, *Devdas* (2000). Ghoshal's performance in *Devdas* yielded her first Filmfare best playback singer award, along with the R. D. Burman Award for outstanding upcoming talent. Since *Devdas,* Ghoshal has been one of Bollywood's most sought-after vocalists, with a plethora of appearances and accolades to her credit. Her "Barso Re" performance brought her unprecedented acclaim, including the aforementioned Filmfare award and just about every other best playback singer award in Bollywood.

Playback singer Shreya Ghoshal.

"Barso Re" is not a raga by any stretch of the imagination; it is basically a popular song with a verse-chorus form. Yet, in the way the music unfolds and grows over the course of the song's arrangement, and in the way that Ghoshal herself shapes the melodies of her vocal part, a barhat-like process of growth emerges. This may be seen to parallel the more extended and expansive processes of barhat that characterize actual raga performances, such as Ravi Shankar's rendition of Raga Sindhi-Bhairavi that we listened to earlier (**CD ex. #2-23**).

The first sound that issues forth in "Barso Re" is not that of an Indian instrument at all. Rather, it is a Brazilian musical bow-type chordophone called a *berimbau* (see also Chapter 11). The berimbau part here is a bit drone-like—somewhat akin to a tambura drone in a raga performance perhaps—but with more rhythmic punch. About four seconds into the track, as the berimbau settles into a drone-esque ostinato groove, we hear

Ghoshal's voice for the first time. She begins with a simple four-note motive on a single pitch ("Na-day-na-day") inflected by very subtle ornamentation. This motive is then taken up imitatively by a bansuri flute. The voice and the bansuri exchange phrases in call-and-response fashion. With each successive phrase, the simple opening motive is progressively developed through increased ornamentation and expanded melodic material; in other words, it grows. This fine and clear example of a barhat process in action takes place within the first half-minute of the track.

The entry of drums and a harmonized bansuri line at 0:33, together with the supplanting of the berimbau ostinato by electronic timbres and rhythmic grooves, set up the opening verse of the song, which arrives at 0:45. The melody of the first part of the verse (0:45–1:00) essentially continues the barhat-like development of the opening melodic motive established from the outset, but now with words (rather than just vocal syllables) and a recognizable tune. At 1:01, the melodic character changes considerably, becoming ever more tuneful and even a bit coy and playful right toward the verse's end (1:20–1:25).

The first chorus arrives dramatically at 1:26. Here, the melody swoops upward in a flight of vocal harmonies against a hard-driving, bhangra-inspired groove of electronically processed dhol drum rhythms and other electronic and electro-acoustic timbres and effects. Digitally sampled male bhangra singers add rhythmic accents for good measure. The chorus concludes at 1:43 and is followed immediately by what initially sounds like the beginning of a second verse. The verse is cut short, however, giving way to a new melody sung by a male vocalist (the well-known playback singer Uday Mazumdar) and then to another new melody of harmonized bansuri parts.

An abrupt change in texture at 2:28 harks back to the opening of the piece with the return of the berimbau. What follows is rather interesting. The expectation is for a second verse that is essentially the same as the first verse heard earlier—same length, same melody, new words. Instead, what we get is an elaborated and extended reconfiguration of the original verse material, replete with improvisational passages and profuse melodic ornamentation in the vocal part, the introduction of new and unexpected melodic and rhythmic materials (as well as jazz-like harmonies), and increased musical interaction between Ghoshal and her accompanying instrumentalists. The net result of all this change and embellishment is a transformed second verse (2:32–3:24) that is more than a quarter-again as long as its first verse counterpart (0:45–1:25). This is evidently another instance of barhat in action, a raga-like process of growth occurring within the context of a verse-chorus form song in a Bollywood film. Yes, it is possible that Rahman merely found ways to extend the length of the second verse in order to make the music fit together with the on-screen action; but in Bollywood, where songs are king, it is just as likely that the film scene was shot to fit the music instead. Either way, techniques of barhat are very much in play in Rahman's compositional process here, and in Ghoshal's vocal approach as well.

"Barso Re" continues directly from its varied and extended second verse to a second chorus that is essentially identical to the first (3:25–3:41). Following an instrumental interlude, a final, third verse arrives at 4:00, leading to a triumphant conclusion as Ghoshal and company vamp out on the final chorus from 4:41 onward. A scintillating, Indian classical music-inspired vocal improvisation by Ghoshal starting at 5:10 adds poignancy and excitement to this closing passage.

guided listening quick summary

"Barso Re," A. R. Rahman (CD ex. #3-3)

INTRODUCTION

0:00–0:44
- A Brazilian berimbau (musical bow) sets the tone for the song with a drone-like rhythmic ostinato.
- A simple motive on a single pitch is introduced by the singer, Shreya Ghoshal, at 0:04.

- The opening motive is extended and developed melodically in call-and-response dialogue between the voice and a bansuri (flute) until 0:32.
- The texture changes in the last part of the introduction (0:33–0:44): voice and berimbau drop out, drums enter, harmonized bansuri melody introduced, electronic groove established.

FIRST VERSE (VERSE I)

0:45–1:25

- First part of verse (0:45–1:00) extends the barhat-like development of the opening motive, but now with words.
- Change to more tuneful melodic character at 1:01. Singing becomes coy and playful in last few seconds before the chorus (1:20–1:25).

FIRST CHORUS (CHORUS I)

1:26–1:43

- The chorus arrives dramatically with ascending, harmonized vocals and a bhangra-inspired electro-acoustic groove (with dhol drum).

INTERLUDE I

1:44–2:27

- An apparent second verse at 1:44 never materializes, instead giving way to new melodic sections featuring, first, a male vocalist, and second, harmonized bansuri.

BRIEF REPRISE OF INTRODUCTION

2:28–2:31

- Abrupt change in texture as the berimbau ostinato of the opening reappears in anticipation of the second verse.

SECOND VERSE (VERSE II)

2:32–3:24

- The second verse becomes an extended and developed variation on the first, with additional improvisation, ornamentation, textural variety, and other new features, as well as an overall increase in length (12 seconds longer). Exemplifies barhat process within the verse-chorus song form.

SECOND CHORUS (CHORUS II)

3:25–3:41

- Essentially the same as Chorus I

INTERLUDE II

3:42–3:59

- Instrumental interlude introduces some new musical materials and links the preceding chorus to the verse to follow.

THIRD VERSE (VERSE III)

4:00–4:40

- This verse is the same length as Verse I (shorter than Verse II).

THIRD CHORUS (CHORUS III)

4:41–end

■ Starts off the same as the earlier choruses, but is extended and varied toward the end; at one point the instruments drop out, leaving just voices; last section (from 5:10) features exciting, Indian classical music–inspired vocal improvisation by Ghoshal.

Summary

The main subjects of this chapter were the Hindustani raga tradition of northern India and Indian-Western intercultural musical encounters. Ravi Shankar was the central figure around whose life, career, music, and wide range of influences the discussion built. Through the story of Shankar, we were introduced to musicians encompassing many musical domains, from Western classical (Yehudi Menuhin), to jazz (John Coltrane, John McLaughlin), to rock (the Beatles), to Bollywood (A. R. Rahman). We were also introduced to several other important musical traditions of India and elsewhere on the South Asian subcontinent, including bhajan, bhangra, qawwali, and music of the Karnatak classical tradition of South India.

Beyond Ravi Shankar himself, another important unifying element of the chapter was the concept of barhat. This term is related specifically to processes of musical growth in the Hindustani raga tradition, but was also shown to be applicable by extension in other musical and cultural contexts. Barhat processes were evident in non-raga musical examples such as the Bollywood song "Barso Re." They also had relevance to the chapter's discussions of growth, development, and transformation in the gharana "musical families" that cultivate specific raga performance traditions and in the global expansion and outreach of Indian music that has largely defined the modern history of Indian-Western musical encounters.

Key Terms

sitar	tala	sam
Hindustani raga	Nada Brahma	vadi
barhat	vina	gat
gharana	tambura	jor
Hindu religion	mrdangam	jhala
Vedas	tabla	keeping tal
bhajan	guru	tihai
bhangra	alap	music director
Karnatak	tintal	playback singer
raga	theka	

Study Questions

■ What are some of the basic features of Hinduism?

■ What are the two great classical traditions of Indian music? How are they related, and how are they different?

■ Which tradition do the sitar and tabla belong to? The vina and mrdangam?

■ Identify three melodic instruments of Hindustani music other than the sitar.

■ What is a gharana? What gharana was Ravi Shankar raised in and who was his guru?

■ Who were the important exponents of the Hindustani raga tradition discussed in this chapter?

■ What instruments do (or did) the following musicians play: Ravi Shankar, Ali Akbar Khan, Alla Rakha, Zakir Hussain, L. Shankar, John McLaughlin, Yehudi Menuhin?

- Beyond their specific musical outcomes, why were Ravi Shankar's relationships with Yehudi Menuhin and George Harrison so significant historically?

- What are the names of Ravi Shankar's two famous musician daughters? Which one plays the sitar?

- What kinds of Indian (and Pakistani) traditional musics other than the Hindustani and Karnatak classical traditions were discussed in this chapter? Describe each.

- What were the five principal features of a raga outlined in the chapter?

- What kinds of metaphors are used to describe the barhat, or growth, of a raga?

- What are the main formal sections of a Hindustani raga (i.e., when it is performed)? Discuss in relation to the Ravi Shankar performance of Raga Sindhi-Bhairavi explored in the chapter.

- What are the different hand gestures used in keeping tal, and which appears where in the 16-beat metric cycle of tintal?

- Which musicians, groups, and recordings discussed in the chapter were historically significant in terms of the fusion of Indian music with Western styles, especially jazz and rock?

- How can the form of the song "Barso Re" be described in terms of the barhat concept?

- What is a playback singer? Who are some of the most famous playback singers?

- What are some of the main features of A. R. Rahman's music that account for its immense popularity?

Discussion Questions

- What *general* principles relating to processes of musical tradition and transformation are exemplified by the discussion and musical examples of this chapter? Do all of the musical examples explored seem appropriate choices for exploring "the Indian music tradition"? Do any of the examples fall outside of the boundaries of that tradition, in your opinion?

- In Indian films, it is generally assumed that playback singers, rather than the on-screen actors and actresses themselves, are the singers of songs in films. In Western films, contrastingly, there is often a stigma attached to actors and actresses who are "exposed" for not having sung their own songs in their films. Speculate on what might account for this fundamental difference in cultural attitudes and values.

Applying What You Have Learned

- Since the time of the Beatles, the sounds of sitars and other traditional Indian instruments (either the actual instruments or digitally sampled versions) have become commonplace in much Western popular music. Recordings of groups and artists ranging from the Rolling Stones and Steely Dan to Metallica and Beck have incorporated sitar sounds and solos and other "Indian" elements. Beginning with keyword searches on the Internet (e.g., "sitar rock"), try to locate several examples of such music and create a list. If possible, listen to the examples you find and describe what Indian music elements you hear and how they function in the music.

- As a paragon of Indian classical music and the "Godfather of World Music," Ravi Shankar has influenced countless musicians around the world on many levels. The artists discussed in this chapter represent just a small (but important) sampling of what might be described as Shankar's "global gharana." Do an Internet search of "Ravi Shankar" and use this search to locate musicians who have collaborated with him, who acknowledge his influence, or who otherwise are identified in connection with him. Create an annotated list summarizing your findings.

- Beyond the synthesis of many different Indian and Western elements in his music, A. R. Rahman draws from a diversity of other musical traditions of the world in his film scores and songs. Research Rahman and write a brief report on his use of musical elements and influences from outside the Indian and Western traditions.

Visit the Online Learning Center at www.mhhe.com/bakan2e, as well as the author's personally maintained Web site at www.michaelbakan.com, for additional learning aids, study help, and resources that supplement the content of this chapter.

chapter nine

'not the same, but just as nice':
traditions and **transformations** in
Irish music

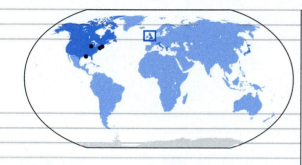

Related locations:

Canada	Appalachian Mountains, United States
Greece	Brittany, western France
Italy	Newfoundland, Canada
Japan	Nova Scotia, Canada
United States	Southwest Louisiana (Cajun region)
	Boston
	Chicago
	New York

Think of Ireland and any of a host of thoughts and media images may come to mind. Rolling green pastures stretching to the sea, a lone shepherd off in the distance herding his sheep, the roar of the surf crashing on a secluded rocky shore. The poetry of William Butler Yeats, the novels of James Joyce, the urban squalor of a gritty industrial town on a gray and rainy day. Four-leaf clovers and leprechauns. Newsreel chronicles of the carnage and suffering of a bitter civil war fueled by religious divisions. Old friends gathering over a pint of stout at the neighborhood pub to tell stories to one another and laugh together.

And music, always music. Music in the home, at the pub, on the street corner, in the concert hall. Music in the Irish homeland and across the seas to

World events		Music events
Earliest period of Celtic culture in Ireland ●	**4th century** BCE	
Beginning of Irish potato famine ●	**1840s**	
Mass starvation and emigrations (to U.S., ● Canada, elsewhere), initiating Irish diaspora		
	1919	● Seamus Ennis born
Political division of Ireland (Republic of ● Ireland, Northern Ireland)	**1920**	
Irish Free State ●	**1921–1949**	● Decline in Irish traditional music (especially after 1930) despite efforts to preserve, promote, and nationalize it
First president, Eamon De Valera ●		
Economic devastation of Irish inner cities ●		● Seamus Ennis emerges as a central figure in preservation, performance, and dissemination of Irish music
	1926	● Radio Éireann established
	1931	● Sean Ó'Riada born
	1930s–1940s	● Irish traditional music thrives and develops in Irish diaspora communities (U.S. and elsewhere)
Republic of Ireland becomes fully ● independent nation	**1949**	
Massive urbanization, shift from ● agricultural to manufacturing-based economy (and industrialization of agriculture)	**1950s**	
Economic upturn for Ireland ●	**1960s**	● First decade of Irish music revival
Irish cultural revival begins ●		● Shift toward neo-traditional musical styles, ensemble rather than solo performance
		● Growing cross-pollination between Irish and Irish diaspora musicians on both sides of the Atlantic

wherever Irish people and people of Irish descent live or have left their mark: in Boston and New York, Liverpool and London, Nova Scotia and Newfoundland, the Cajun belt of Louisiana, the Appalachian mountains of the eastern United States. Irish music is a core emblem of Irish identity in Ireland and beyond, and its influence permeates musical traditions and transformations around the globe. It is there in everything from American country music, to the rock styles of U2 and The Pogues, to the adventurously international Irish-world music fusion approaches of contemporary groups like the Afro Celts, Dropkick Murphys, and Eileen Ivers and Immigrant Soul.

The core of Irish music itself, and of myriad musical styles that claim Irish music as their root, is what is known as **Irish traditional music.** Common to all of the diverse types and styles of music that fall within the Irish traditional rubric—traditional, neo-traditional, and post-traditional—is a basis in rural, Irish folk music tradition. This tradition can only be traced back a couple of centuries with any authority, though its roots are widely presumed to date back much farther.

World events		Music events
	1960	● Sean Ó'Riada forms the group Ceoltóirí Cualann, ushering in a transformation of Irish traditional music
	1963	● Founding of the iconic Irish music group The Chieftains
	1965	● Irish-American fiddler Eileen Ivers born (Bronx, New York)
Period of great political unrest and violence in Northern Ireland, especially in Belfast (through 1980s)	**1970s**	● Second generation of Irish music revival ● Planxty, Clannad, the Bothy Band, and De Danaan fuse Irish music with rock, jazz, other styles
	1971	● Sean Ó'Riada dies
	1973	● Planxty releases *The Well Below the Valley*
Revival initiatives benefiting Celtic languages and cultures emerge in Scotland and Wales	**1980s**	● Altan and other new groups established, preserving traditional styles while continuing to push Irish traditional music in new directions as well
	1982	● Seamus Ennis dies
Pan-Irish identity and culture become increasingly transnational and diversified	**1990s–present**	● *Riverdance* becomes an international sensation (fiddler Eileen Ivers featured) ● Eileen Ivers, Afro Celts, and other contemporary musicians and groups create highly innovative styles rooted in Irish traditional music ● Emergence of a truly international pan-Irish musical culture
	1990	● Altan releases *The Red Crow*
	1999	● Eileen Ivers releases *Crossing the Bridge*, featuring "Gravelwalk"

In this chapter, we trace a path through Irish music covering traditional, neo-traditional, and post-traditional styles. We will explore this progression in relation to a variety of vocal and instrumental genres from different historical periods, regions, and countries. Our principal focus will be on Irish dance tunes. The resilience of the Irish dance tune tradition and the malleability of dance tunes themselves make this an ideal topic for appreciating tradition and transformation in Irish music, and also for examining issues of traditionalism and modernity in Irish culture and society more broadly. Additionally, the Irish dance tune medium offers a revealing vantage point from which to view Irish music as a **pan-Irish** cultural phenomenon. Today, notions of what constitutes Irish identity and Irishness are perhaps defined as much by developments occurring outside of Ireland as by those occurring within Ireland itself: Irish culture has become transnational in the form of pan-Irish culture. Music, and dance music especially, is a prominent part of pan-Irish culture, and this is another topic we will explore.

■ ■ ■

A Preliminary Listening Experience

A good place to start our Irish music journey is with a listening-based comparison of three different performances of a characteristic melodic figure that occurs in many Irish traditional dance tunes. These performances may be heard back-to-back in **Online Musical Illustration #24** at the Online Learning Center (www.mhhe.com/bakan2e); each is about 15–20 seconds long. The first one is a solo Irish fiddle version with no accompanying instruments. The second is in a different style and features an ensemble of acoustic instruments. The third is a rock-influenced rendition. In the terms of this chapter, these three very different performances may be said to represent, in order, a traditional, a neo-traditional, and a post-traditional approach to the same type of melodic material.

Listen to all three of the performances now, one after the other. Make note of any similarities or differences you hear. On the basis of this exercise alone, what can you now say about style and identity in "Irish traditional music"?

Irish Music in Context

The story of Irish music told in this chapter unfolds against a backdrop of Irish national history and the modern history of the Irish people, both in Ireland and internationally. We therefore begin with the following overview, which provides a general background for understanding the different styles and examples of music addressed later in the chapter in cultural context.

Since 1920, the island of Ireland has been divided politically between the Republic of Ireland (Ireland) and Northern Ireland. The Republic of Ireland is an independent nation with its capital in Dublin. Northern Ireland, with its capital in Belfast, is a province of the United Kingdom (U.K.), which also includes England, Scotland, Wales, Cornwall, and the Isle of Man.

Northern Ireland covers Ireland's northeastern portion, accounting for about 15 percent of the island's landmass. It is an area whose people have suffered through a long history of often-violent struggle between the Irish Protestant majority of the province (accounting for

A group of Irish musicians performing in County Donegal, Ireland.

about two-thirds of the population) and its Irish Catholic minority (about one-third of the population). Persecution of Catholics, terrorism, conflicts between the Republic of Ireland and Britain (U.K.) over political control of the region, and failed British attempts to subdue the province through the imposition of martial law and other hard-nosed policies have been major factors accounting for Northern Ireland's troubled history. The 1970s and 1980s brought especially hard times, and though the situation is now improved (as of this writing), the provisional state of relative peace is tenuous and there remains much volatility.

In contrast to Northern Ireland, the Republic of Ireland, whose musical traditions are the main focus of this chapter, is host to a predominantly Catholic population. Approximately 93 percent of the nation's 3.6 million people identify themselves as Catholic. English and Irish (i.e., **Irish Gaelic**) are the two official languages, though English is dominant in 95 percent of the country, with Irish Gaelic mainly spoken in concentrated areas known as the Gaeltacht (see map, p. 157). The Republic of Ireland covers approximately 85 percent of the island's total landmass, including the entire southern and central region as well as the northwesternmost area, County Donegal, one of the Republic's 26 counties. Each county is known for its distinctive cultural traditions and character. Regional musical styles are key to the cultural identities of the different counties, much as the distinctive sound of Irish traditional music is a signature of Irish culture generally. The names of counties such as Donegal, Galway, Sligo, Limerick, Kerry, and Clare are well known to lovers of Irish traditional music through the styles and great musicians associated with them, both in Ireland itself and around the world.

Gaelic (GAH-lick [rhymes with "colic"])

Donegal (Dun-ee-GAHL)

The Republic of Ireland achieved full independence in 1949. Prior to that, from 1921–1949, it was known as the Irish Free State and was a quasi-autonomous, self-governing dominion within the British Commonwealth. The founding of the Irish Free State came in the wake of hundreds of years of struggle by Irish Catholics against British (Protestant) rule, domination, and repression. Pivotal to this history was the infamous **Irish potato famine,** which began in the 1840s. The famine and subsequent evictions led to the deaths of 1.5 million Irish people and massive (often fatal) attempts at emigration, resulting in the rapid reduction of the population from 8 million to 3.5 million. The Irish blamed the British for not doing enough to assist them during the famine, and this galvanized an Irish nationalist movement marked by violent resistance to British control of Ireland and calls for Irish self-rule. This movement would ultimately lead to the founding of the Irish Free State (later the Republic of Ireland) and the partition of Ireland into the Republic and the province of Northern Ireland.

It was the famine, too, that provided the main impetus for what would come to be known as the **Irish diaspora.** Millions of Irish people left Ireland for other lands during this and subsequent periods. A great many settled in American cities such as Boston and New York, establishing large Irish immigrant communities and making major contributions to the sustenance and transformation of Irish cultural traditions, including music.

The founding of the Irish Free State in 1921 marked a new chapter in the development of Irish nationalism. Eamon De Valera, the American-born first president of the country, envisioned an Ireland based almost entirely on a village economy. His well-intentioned policies led to the economic devastation of Ireland's inner cities, as described in books like Frank McCourt's *Angela's Ashes* (1996). Under the Irish Free State, government-sponsored

Irish-American women and men dressed up for an evening of social dancing, New York City, 1905.

initiatives were established to preserve Irish traditional culture, including rural oral/aural traditions of poetry, song, and instrumental music. The forces of modernization and urbanization were seen as major threats to the survival of these traditions. A national radio station, **Radio Éireann,** was founded in 1926. Irish traditional music became a powerful symbol of national identity and a tool of Irish nationalism, and nationwide radio broadcasts of performances featuring musicians from different counties all over the island played a very important role. The preservation, collection, and dissemination of Irish traditional music became priorities of Irish cultural nationalism. Yet despite such efforts and initiatives, traditional music held a relatively marginal status in Ireland during this period. It was seen as important, but was not widely popular among the general public.

The post-1949 era ushered in a period of massive urbanization, reliance on manufacturing rather than agriculture as the main basis of the economy, and large-scale industrialization of agriculture itself in the newly independent Republic of Ireland. These changes led to both increased prosperity and fears of culture loss. Both factors contributed to the **Irish music revival** of the 1960s, a phenomenon that would have profound implications on the future course of Irish music, both in Ireland and abroad. Growing interaction and cross-pollination between performers of Irish music in Ireland and in the United States, Canada, England, and other lands, from Italy to Japan, yielded many new musical innovations and musicultural developments, some of which had a major impact on music "back home" in Ireland. The internationalization of the Irish music **session** (*seisiún*), an informal gathering where musicians join together to play Irish tunes amidst socializing, was perhaps the most significant of these. This, together with developments such as innovative fusions of Irish traditional music with rock, jazz, and other international musical styles, led to the consolidation of a transnational musical culture rooted in Irish traditional music by the end of the 20th century, that is, to a pan-Irish musical culture.

A harp player performing a traditional Irish piece.

An Introduction to Irish Traditional Music

In terms of international popularity, Irish traditional music has the distinction of being "Europe's most commercially successful traditional music" (O'Connor 1999:170). The designation "Irish traditional music" is applied very broadly to an array of different types of music, from centuries-old folk tunes of rural Irish counties to more contemporary styles that may build from Irish musical stock while incorporating influences from outside the tradition. Historical documentation of Irish traditional music accounts for just the last two to three centuries of its development, but historians and Irish musicians alike believe that its roots are in antiquity.

The core identity of Irish traditional music, today as in the past, is to be found in a musical repertoire that was already well established prior to the 20th century. This repertoire consists of five main categories of music:

- The revered **sean nós,** or "old way," songs, which are sung in Irish Gaelic.
- Slow instrumental melodies called *airs,* which are often performed in free rhythm.
- Songs sung in English.
- The musical tradition of the Irish harp (the harp is the national symbol of Ireland).
- Instrumental dance tunes and medleys.

Sean nós is regarded by Irish music connoisseurs as the heart of Irish traditional music. It involves a style of singing that may feature either elaborate or subtle forms of melodic ornamentation, distinctive rhythmic phrasing, and deeply felt emotional expression. On all of these levels, the influence of sean nós is directly or indirectly apparent in most other types of Irish music, whether vocal or instrumental, traditional or modern. The texts of sean nós songs include nature poetry, love songs, and religious songs that express "a somewhat mystical brand of Irish Catholic belief" (Hast, Cowdery, and Scott 1999:60–61).

The Irish Gaelic sean nós song included on your CD set (**CD ex. #3-4**), "Ag an Phobal Dé Domhnaigh" (At the Congregation on Sunday), is best described as a love song, though it is a love song of a very dark hue and is anything but cheerful or innocent. In the opening verse (0:00–0:58), the narrator (i.e., the singer) is a man who expresses his longing for a woman he identifies simply as "the girl" (*chailín*). He tells of the great affection he lavished upon her at the congregation on Sunday and poetically praises her beauty. "Her little mouth was like roses and her gentle waist like snow," he proclaims, adding wistfully, "And God I wish my lodging was where she dresses her bed."

"Ag an Phobal Dé Domhnaigh" **("Egg un Fuh-bell Jey Dow-nee")**

This is a classic sean nós textual image of unattainable love, but as Irish music scholar Sean Williams has observed, such images often appear with "a bitter tinge" to them (Williams 2009:170). In this particular instance, that bitter tinge gets resolutely sour very quickly as we also learn that the love—or at least the lovemaking—was not so unattainable as we first assumed. The second verse (0:59–1:53) begins with an abrupt shift in tone and sentiment. "The rogue is seducing me and the sin is being committed," we now hear the singer intone. "He drew my heart inside and denied it thereafter." The woman—"the girl"—has suddenly become the narrator of the tale (even though the singer on the recording is still the same man), and clearly she is not happy. The root source of the problem is revealed in the next line: "But if you have your wife at home and your little child to coax, return again to them, you [home]wrecker, and I'll have nothing to do with you."

We come to understand now that this is a tale of adultery and betrayal, and suddenly the starry-eyed "mouth like roses" and "gentle waist like snow" references of the first verse appear tainted and decadent. In the end, the woman, after trying to rationalize the whole sordid affair to some extent during the song's middle verses (third verse, 1:55–2:52; fourth verse, 2:54–3:46), sends her two-timing, adulterous lover away for good, but she still holds affection for him and blesses him in parting. "My blessings upon you," she states in the closing line of the song's fifth and final verse (3:48–4:44), "and let each of us go home." (See Williams 2009, 170–72 and 248–50, for full song text, translation, and more detailed discussion.)

The singer on this recording is one of the recognized masters of the sean nós idiom in contemporary Ireland, Lillis O'Laoire. O'Laoire is a native speaker of Irish Gaelic from County Donegal in northwestern Ireland. He is a two-time winner of the nation's most prestigious sean nós singing award, the Corn Uí Riada, and is an Irish studies professor at the National University of Ireland in Galway. His performance here, with its gentle presentation and subtle ornamentation of the melody, is an exemplar of the northern Irish regional sean nós style as practiced in counties like Donegal (though it is at least as much an exemplar of his own unique artistry within that style); sean nós singers from Irish counties further south tend toward more elaborate forms of melodic ornamentation. O'Laoire's effective evocation of the text gains much from the melodic variations he introduces from one verse to the next (including variations in ornamentation) and from his understated yet expressive delivery of the lyrics.

Though it is far removed from the musical domain of sean nós, Noel McLoughlin's performance of "Song for Ireland" on **CD ex. #3-5** offers good examples of sean nós's pervasive influence on other genres and styles of Irish vocal music. The character and subtle ornamentation of the song's melody, the rhythmic phrasing, the understated yet emotionally powerful delivery of the text, and the melodic variations introduced in different verses all bring to mind stylistic features of sean nós performances like Lillis O'Laoire's version of "Ag an Phobal Dé Domhnaigh," albeit framed by a very different musical context. Here, rather than there being just a solo male vocalist, the singer (McLoughlin) is accompanied by an ensemble of musicians playing instruments such as the Irish harp, the **tinwhistle,** the **Irish wooden flute,** and the fiddle (we will learn more about Irish instruments later in the chapter). Moreover, the style, the musical arrangement, and the production values of the recording are all quite modern.

"Song for Ireland" is one of the best-known English-language Irish songs. It is sung everywhere, from the rural Irish countryside to New York City, and exists in well over a hundred recorded versions that feature artists as diverse as the Dubliners, Mary Black, the Celtic Angels, and the Three Irish Tenors. The song has become something of an Irish anthem; its celebration of Ireland's history, beauty, social solidarity, and freedom is poignantly juxtaposed to a lament on the ravages of war, struggle, and oppression that have affected Ireland for centuries. In the opening verse, the spirit of the Irish people is invoked in a metaphor of soaring falcons: "In silver wings they fly, for they know the call of freedom in their breasts" (0:32–0:41). This falcon metaphor of freedom returns in the last (fourth) verse, where it is paired with a personification of Ireland itself that captures the combined joys and sorrows, the hope and despair, that have long defined Irish existence: "Dreaming in the night, I saw a land where no one had to fight. But waking in your dawn, I saw you crying in the morning light. Lying where the falcons fly, they twist and turn all in your air-blue sky. Living on your western shore, saw summer sunsets, asked for more. Stood by your Atlantic sea, and sang a song for Ireland" (3:08–4:00).

If sean nós is indeed the heart of Irish music and powerful songs like "Song for Ireland" capture something of its soul, then instrumental dance tunes are the music's public and highly visible face. Music designed to accompany dancing has long been the most popular type in Ireland and throughout the Irish diaspora. Even as actual dancing has become increasingly divorced from dance music over the years, the dominant popularity of Irish dance tunes has endured.

The Musical Guided Tour for this chapter offers an introduction to foundational elements of Irish dance music style, focusing on basic dance rhythms, dance tune forms, and characteristics of melody and ornamentation. The fiddler is Lynnsey Weissenberger, an active performer of the music who lives in Florida. Lynnsey has studied and apprenticed with the renowned Irish fiddler James Kelly, won several fiddling competitions including the official State of Florida Fiddle Contest in 2005, and performed on one occasion with the leading Irish music group The Chieftains. Her mentor, James Kelly, who now also lives in Florida, is a major international figure in Irish traditional music. A former member of Planxty (an important Irish band discussed later in the chapter) who has performed with The Chieftains and other Irish music luminaries, he grew up in Dublin and is the son of fiddler John Kelly. John Kelly was a member of the highly influential Irish group Ceoltóirí Cualann (also discussed later in the chapter). From the age of three, James learned to play the fiddle from his father. His informal course of musical training also involved learning from the legions of renowned musicians from counties all over Ireland who would come to the Dublin home of the Kellys to visit, play music, and share tunes.

The transcript in the box on page 165 corresponds to the audio Musical Guided Tour. As you listen to this tour at the Online Learning Center (www.mhhe.com/bakan2e), follow along with this transcript.

Ceoltóirí Cualann (Kyol-TOR-ee KOO-lin)

Traditional Irish Dance Tunes and Medleys: Two Examples

Since at least the mid-20th century, Irish traditional dance tunes and medleys have usually been performed ensemble-style by groups of instrumentalists playing a variety of instruments. There are two main contexts for such performances. One is the **ceílí,** an informal social gathering that is normally held at a neighborhood pub or dance hall and involves dancing. The other is the aforementioned Irish music *session,* in which musicians playing different instruments come together to perform the older traditional tunes and newer ones modeled after them, but not to accompany dancing (at least not typically). Sessions are much more common than ceílís today, since fewer people actually dance to Irish dance tunes than in the past. Beyond their status as communal music-making events, sessions provide "a time for friendships to be validated,

ceílí (KAY-lee)

Irish Traditional Dance Tunes

Irish dance tune melodies are set to common dance rhythms such as the **jig** [♪], the **hornpipe** [♪], and, most popular of all, the **reel** [♪].

All of the tunes are based on three different types of scales. One of these, the Dorian scale, sounds like this [♪]. It is closely related to certain forms of the minor scale discussed in Chapter 4. Here is part of a reel based on the Dorian scale. In other words, it is a reel in a Dorian *key.* The title of the tune is "The Morning Dew" [♪].

Second, we come to the Mixolydian scale. It is essentially a major scale with a lowered seventh scale degree. It sounds like this [♪]. Lynnsey will now play part of a jig using the Mixolydian scale. The tune is called "Fraher's Jig" [♪].

Third, and finally, many Irish tunes use the familiar major scale. Here is a passage from a hornpipe in a major key called "Cronin's Hornpipe" [♪].

Ornamentation of melodies is an essential feature of Irish music performance. Indeed, Irish tunes are rarely performed without ornamentation. Listen to "Fraher's Jig" in a version with no ornamentation [♪]. Now here is "Fraher's Jig" again, the proper way, with ornamentation [♪].

Many different types of **ornaments** are used. Some embellish the basic melody; others add rhythmic interest to it. Five of the most common ornaments are the *roll,* the *cran,* the *treble,* the *cut,* and the *triplet.* Let's hear what these sound like.

First, here is an illustration of a roll, followed by a short section of a reel including several rolls [♪].

Next, we hear a cran, followed by a portion of a jig that has crans in it [♪].

Our third type of ornament is the treble, heard first in isolation and then in a musical context [♪].

Now, ornament number four, the cut, heard by itself and in the context of a tune [♪].

Fifth and finally, an illustration of the triplet: ornament first, followed by a musical example featuring triplets [♪].

Now that we have been introduced to some common dance rhythms, scales, and ornaments, we move on to a brief introduction to musical form. The form of an Irish dance tune usually consists of several sections, or *parts,* as they are known. When the tune is performed, it is common for each of these parts to be played twice in succession, the second time usually with variations. Lynnsey will now play a jig called "Paddy Clancy's." The form is AABB, probably the most common of all Irish dance tune forms. I will count the measures as Lynnsey plays and clap and call out the appropriate letter name (A or B) at the arrival of each part. Listen carefully, and you will notice how Lynnsey varies the melody and the ornaments each time she repeats a part. Notice also how the melodies of the A and B parts are different from one another; in other words, how they *contrast* [♪].

In performance, two or more tunes (typically three) are often strung together to form a set of tunes called a **medley.** All of the tunes in the medley are of the same tune type, for example, all reels, or all jigs. Now, as a musical conclusion, Lynnsey will play a medley consisting of two reels ("The Scholar" and "Sligo Maid"). This medley incorporates virtually all of the elements of Irish dance tune style we have discussed in this tour [♪].

for chat and fun . . ." (Moloney 1992:184). They occur in a wide range of social settings and contexts, as can be seen from the following reminiscences of Michael Moloney, a leading Irish session musician and scholar of Irish music:

As a musician myself I have participated in more sessions than I can count or remember over the past twenty-five years in Ireland, England, and America. As I write, images come to mind of sessions in small pubs in Ireland with musicians pressed tightly together in a corner in the familiar semicircle that Irish traditional musicians always form wherever they gather; with the sounds of the instruments struggling to break through a wall

An old-time Irish country dance.

of sound created by a babel of voices raised in consort around the bar. I remember similar sessions in little villages in County Clare where people "have great respect for the music[,]" when the pub patrons stopped their conversation and listened almost reverentially to the music for hours on end.

I remember sessions in villages on the coastline of west Clare or in little towns in County Kerry . . . where my mother's people came from, . . . in noisy pubs so densely crowded that it seemed almost impossible to push through to the bar to get a drink. It is a long way from the wild yells and whoops of such sessions to the quiet humid stillness of the campground area in White Springs, Florida, . . . where I have sat in the late night darkness with fiddler James Kelly from Dublin [and other musicians] . . . playing reels . . . while shadowy figures listened silently in the eerie gloom. (Moloney 1992:187–88)

Tinwhistle player Jim Cox and fiddler Lynnsey Weissenberger.

The playing of Irish dance tunes occupied a rather different social milieu in earlier times, especially before urbanization and modernization began to transform the social life of Irish dance music around 1920. During this earlier period, social dancing to music at rural domestic gatherings (the forerunners of the modern ceílí) was the main order of the day. At such events, a solo player or an *ad hoc* group of instrumentalists would typically provide music for the dancers. There was no real separation between the dance tune performance and the dancing itself, which were viewed as integral to one another, unlike today.

uilleann (ILL-inn)

The musicians played on instruments such as the fiddle, the tinwhistle (a small, end-blown flute with six fingerholes), and the **uilleann pipes** (a form of Irish bagpipe to which we will soon return). Stringing together two or more tunes in a single dance rhythm—a series of reels, or of jigs or hornpipes—musicians would generate impromptu dance tune medleys. A medley might continue for as long as the dancers wished to keep dancing, or for as long as the musician or musicians could think of more tunes to add, whichever came first. The music and the dancing, along with good and abundant food and drink, were key to fostering a spirit of camaraderie, solidifying communal bonds, and creating a joyful social environment. In good times and bad, through moments of celebration and hardship, music and dancing were fundamental to Irish social life.

In the face of modernity and massive urbanization, the old instrumental dance music styles fell into decline, but government-sponsored initiatives led to efforts to preserve and revitalize them in some instances. Key to these efforts was the important Irish musician and folklorist Seamus Ennis, the featured performer in the two very traditional-style solo Irish dance music selections of **CD ex. #3-6** and **CD ex. #3-7.**

Seamus Ennis playing the uilleann pipes.

guided listening experience

"The Cuckoo's Hornpipe," Seamus Ennis

- CD Track **#3-6**
- Featured performer(s)/group: Seamus Ennis (tinwhistle)
- Format: Complete track
- Source recording: *Two Centuries of Celtic Music,* by Seamus Ennis (Legacy)

**Seamus Ennis
(SHAY-muhs
EN-nis)**

"The Cuckoo's Hornpipe," as its title indicates, is a tune in the dance rhythm of the hornpipe. The hornpipe is a dance most closely identified with English traditional music, but it is also very popular in Irish and other **Celtic** traditions (see "Insights and Perspectives" box on Irish and Celtic music, p. 169). The standard hornpipe rhythm is in a two-beat (duple) meter and is performed at a medium to medium-fast tempo. It has a "lilting" rhythmic quality, which results from a steady alternation of notes of uneven length (with underlying triple subdivision of the beat) (Figure 9.1).

Celtic (KEL-tick)

In the example, Seamus Ennis is heard in a solo tinwhistle performance. This simple aerophone is usually made of metal (tin or other), though it also can be made of wood or plastic. Another common name for the instrument is *pennywhistle*. The tinwhistle is one of three popular flute-type aerophones used in Irish music, the other two being the larger, lower-pitched, and

FIGURE 9.1

Hornpipe rhythm.

1		2		1		2	
DAH	da	**DAH**	da	**DAH**	da	**DAH**	da

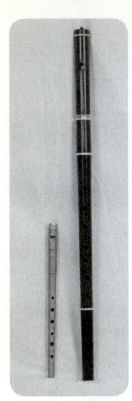

Tinwhistle and Irish wooden flute.

darker-toned Irish wooden flute and the more recently invented (in the 1970s) *low whistle,* a larger version of the tinwhistle with a lower range.

Virtually anyone can get a decent sound out of a tinwhistle, and its small size makes it a manageable instrument in tiny hands. It has therefore long been a favorite music learning instrument for Irish children. In the hands of master players like Seamus Ennis, however, it is transformed into a musical vehicle of surprising expressive range and subtlety.

The form of "The Cuckoo's Hornpipe" is the most standard one in Irish traditional dance music: AABB, with eight two-beat measures per part (i.e., per lettered section). Since varied repetition occurs throughout the performance, however, a representation of the form as AA′BB′ is most accurate. The AA′BB′ form is repeated once in its entirety, with an extra A section added on at the end to round things out. Thus, the complete form is: AA′BB′ AA′BB′ A.

Ennis performs "The Cuckoo's Hornpipe" with a high degree of ornamentation of the basic melody. The types of ornaments demonstrated earlier on the fiddle in the Musical Guided Tour are here transferred to the tinwhistle. Key elements of ornamentation, varied repetition, and other features are highlighted in the Guided Listening Quick Summary below.

guided listening quick summary

"The Cuckoo's Hornpipe," Seamus Ennis (CD ex. #3-6)

FIRST STATEMENT OF MELODY (AA′BB′):

0:00–0:11—A (First part: eight measures)

■ Melody mainly in lower register of tinwhistle's range.

0:11–0:21— A′ (Second part: eight measures)

■ Varied repetition of the **A** part: different opening melodic figure, use of different melodic ornaments.

0:21–0:31—B (Third part: eight measures)

■ New, contrasting melodic material introduced, mainly in higher register of the instrument.

■ Melodic ornamentation more elaborate here than in the **A** parts.

■ Louder and more boisterous than before.

0:31–0:40—B′ (Fourth part: eight measures)

■ Similar to the preceding part, but with some elements of varied repetition.

SECOND STATEMENT OF MELODY (AA′BB′):

0:40–0:49—A (First part: eight measures)

■ More breaths between notes than in the earlier **A** parts. (Possibly Ennis is getting tired, running out of breath.)

■ Similar to the earlier **A** parts, but with some melodic variation (e.g., at 0:45–0:47).

0:50–0:59—A′ (Second part: eight measures)

■ More notes with short articulations.

■ Melody jumps up to the higher octave range on the final note, adding excitement leading into the **B** section.

insights and perspectives

Irish Music and Celtic Music and Cultures

The identities of Irish music and culture, historical and contemporary, have always been importantly defined by their foundation in a *Celtic* cultural lineage. During ancient times and up through the early era of Christianity, so-called Celtic peoples ranged across much of Europe, from Britain to France and Spain and as far east as present-day Ukraine and Turkey. Today, the cultural legacy of these peoples survives mainly in Ireland, Scotland, Wales, and Brittany (westernmost France), as well as in certain regions of eastern Canada (especially in the provinces of Newfoundland and Nova Scotia) and other areas. The history of Celtic culture in Ireland, in particular, extends back to the 4th century BCE.

Celtic cultural survivals are most clearly evident in a family of related Indo-European languages known as the *Celtic languages.* There are two groups of languages within the Celtic languages family. The first is made up of Irish Gaelic, Scottish Gaelic, and Manx Gaelic. The second includes Welsh, Breton, and Cornish. These are minority languages wherever they are spoken and historically have been "victims of suppression by English and French authorities" (Kuter 2000:319). Since the 1920s in Ireland and the 1980s in Scotland and Wales, however, they have gained increased prominence and use as they have become associated in important ways with cultural revival initiatives belonging to larger nationalist movements in these countries. The growing stature and popularity of "Celtic music," both in specific association with these cultural revival movements and as a category of world music on an international scale (the latter being largely a music industry invention and marketing tool), has followed suit. Though there is no identifiable "set of sonic traits that can qualify or disqualify music as Celtic" (Kuter 2000:320), there are certain key unifying characteristics of musical style that are shared widely among the traditional musics of Celtic regions. These characteristics, all of which are displayed prominently in Irish traditional music, include:

■ Prevalence of melodies based on specific types of scales and modes (e.g., the major, Dorian, and Mixolydian types illustrated earlier in the Musical Guided Tour for this chapter).

■ Identifiable styles of melodic ornamentation (though there is much variation in types of ornamentation from one Celtic country or region to another).

■ Use of certain types of instruments (e.g., fiddles, bagpipes, flutes).

■ Dance tunes based on common dance rhythms (usually in duple or quadruple meters).

■ Standard forms for songs and dance tunes (e.g., AABB forms for dance tunes).

■ A close integration of music making with dancing, especially in connection with social gatherings that also feature uninhibited feasting and drinking (see Kuter 2000:320–22).

guided listening experience

"The First House in Connaught/The Copper Plate Reel"
(Medley), Seamus Ennis

- CD Track **#3-7**

- Featured performer(s)/group: Seamus Ennis (uilleann pipes)

- Format: Complete track

- Source recording: *Two Centuries of Celtic Music,* by Seamus Ennis (Legacy)

This second traditional-style dance music performance by Seamus Ennis consists of a medley of two tunes played on the uilleann pipes. The uilleann pipes are regarded as the most distinctively Irish of all Irish instruments. While the fiddle and the tinwhistle were originally brought to Ireland from other lands, the uilleann pipes—pipes, for short—were developed from imported continental European prototypes into a uniquely Irish instrument (Shields and Gershen 2000:384). This Irish variant of the bagpipe, which had evolved into its current form by about 1800, differs from the familiar Great Highland bagpipe of Scotland that most of us think of when the word *bagpipe* is used (**CD ex. #1-16**). It is distinct from the Bulgarian, Italian, Latvian, Indian, and other international variants of the bagpipe as well.

Compared to the Scottish bagpipes, the uilleann pipes are an instrument with a rather soft dynamic range and a more delicate, refined timbre. Additionally, they are designed to be played from a seated position rather than standing up. Though the person playing the uilleann pipes may look as if he is holding an octopus in his lap, all those pipes can be reduced to three functions, providing drones, melody, and chords (Figure 9.2).

Uilleann pipes of Ireland (left), Great Highland bagpipe of Scotland (right).

FIGURE 9.2

Uilleann pipes.

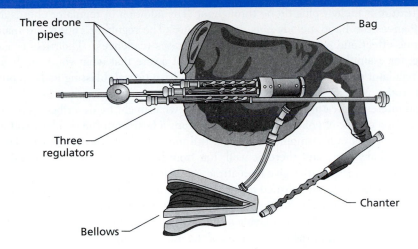

Three drone pipes

Bag

Three regulators

Chanter

Bellows

In common with its Scottish cousin, the uilleann pipes include three *drone pipes,* each of which plays the same tonic pitch in a different octave range (though the tonic pitch of the uilleann pipes is D, whereas that of the Scottish pipes is B♭). Sound is produced when air is forced through the pipes by a *bellows,* which is essentially a bag with collapsible sides. The bellows is inflated to capacity *before* the instrument is played. It is then held in the crook of the player's right arm and squeezed by the right elbow ("uilleann" means elbow in Irish Gaelic). This squeezing action forces sound-producing air through the three drone pipes attached to the instrument, as well as through a fourth pipe, the *chanter,* or melody pipe, and three additional ones, the *regulators,* which are used to generate chords. The *bag* serves as a reservoir of air.

The chanter is the only pipe on the uilleann pipes used for melodies. It is also the only one with *fingerholes,* which are pressed down in different combinations to produce the main melody notes and a variety of melodic ornaments. By covering or leaving open certain holes in certain combinations, the performer effectively changes the length of the pipe, and thus the pitch: the "longer" the pipe becomes, the lower the pitch produced. This same principle applies to the use of fingerholes on the tinwhistle, and on aerophones generally.

The three regulator pipes (regulators) are the only pipes on the instrument capable of producing chords. On each regulator are located four or five keys. Each produces a different pitch when it is pressed down. By pressing down different combinations of keys on the different regulator pipes, the player generates groups of notes. These may function as chords that underscore the melody (though typically only to a relatively limited degree) or they may provide rhythmic effects and punctuate the ends of melodic phrases. Both the drone and regulator pipes may be switched on or off by the player during the course of performance.

As can be imagined from the foregoing description, uilleann pipes players quite literally have their hands full just dealing with the instrument's practical logistics. Between moving one's fingers over the chanter, pumping the bellows, switching the regulators on and off and pressing their keys, and keeping all seven pipes going at once, there is much to keep track of. And those are just the rudiments. The real art of playing the uilleann pipes *musically* is another matter altogether, and Seamus Ennis stands as one of the great masters of all time in this regard.

The medley of two reels included on **CD ex. #3-7** provides a wonderful example of solo uilleann pipes music in the traditional dance tune style, as well as a fine display of Seamus Ennis's unique artistry on the instrument.

The dance rhythm featured throughout is that of the reel. The tempo of a reel is relatively fast (considerably faster than a hornpipe), making the music quite energetic in character.

The tune form is again AA′BB′. Both tunes of the medley adhere to this format, and both are played twice in their entirety.

The texture is melody-plus-drone throughout. The addition of regulator chords at certain points enhances the basic melody-plus-drone texture. The regulator chords are mainly used for rhythmic effect and punctuating the ends of phrases (cadences). Their use is sometimes surprising; for example, at 1:20–1:22, if you were not aware that what you were hearing was indeed a regulator chord, you might mistake it for an Irish taxicab blasting its horn outside the recording studio! Melodic ornamentation is again used profusely.

A final interesting feature of this performance is what might be described as its irregularities. There are a couple of points at which Ennis drops a beat from the regular two-beat meter pattern, and there is even a moment where a full measure seems to disappear. The rhythm sounds a bit "shaky" here and there as well. Far from being detrimental to the effect of the performance, these irregularities give it an attractive feeling of raw spontaneity that is a marked contrast to the more slick and polished musical productions we will encounter later on our journey. They are at the core of a traditional-style musical art that emphasizes creating music in the moment of performance and never playing a tune or part of a tune exactly the same way twice. This is an art of which Ennis (as well as some of the musicians mentioned earlier, such as John Kelly and James Kelly) was a true master.

guided listening quick summary

"The First House in Connaught/The Copper Plate Reel" (Medley), Seamus Ennis (CD ex. #3-7)

"THE FIRST HOUSE IN CONNAUGHT" (MEDLEY TUNE #1)

FIRST STATEMENT OF MELODY (AA′BB′):

0:00–0:10—A

- First we hear the drone, then the melody played on the chanter, then a regulator chord at the end of the section (at 0:09).
- Note the fast tempo and distinctive rhythmic character of the reel.
- Note the many melodic ornaments and different articulations (including many staccato [short] notes).

0:10–0:18—A′

- Regulator chords (0:14–0:15).
- Dropped beats near beginning and end of this part (e.g., at 0:16–0:18).

0:18–0:26—B

- "Shaky" rhythm in some passages.
- Melodic range higher than in the preceding **A** parts (as is common in the **B** parts of Irish dance tunes).

0:27–0:34—B′

- One full measure (two beats) is dropped at the end of this part.

SECOND STATEMENT OF MELODY (AA′BB′):

0:34–0:42—A

0:43–0:51—A′

- Note prominent use of regulator pipes.

0:51–0:59—B

0:59–1:07—B′

- The first couple of melody notes are played an octave *lower* than in earlier **B** parts (varied repetition).

"THE COPPER PLATE REEL" (MEDLEY TUNE #2)

FIRST STATEMENT OF MELODY (AA′ BB′):

1:08–1:15—A

- New tune begins (though this is not necessarily obvious for listeners new to the style!).

1:16–1:24—A′

- Listen for "car horn" regulator chord (1:20–1:22).

1:24–1:32—B

1:32–1:40—B′

SECOND STATEMENT OF MELODY (AA′BB′):

1:40–1:48—A

1:49–1:56—A′

1:57–2:05—B

2:05–end—B′

- The most elaborate ornamentation of the entire performance occurs in this final part (as was also the case in "Cuckoo's Hornpipe" and is common in Irish traditional music performances generally).

The life and legacy of Seamus Ennis

Beyond his stature as one of the great uilleann pipers of the 20th century, Seamus Ennis (1919–1982) was one of the most important figures in the preservation, cultivation, and dissemination of Irish traditional music (see the photo of a young Seamus Ennis, p. 167). He was born into a musical family in Jamestown, Ireland, near Dublin. His father, James Ennis, was a master uilleann pipes player, champion Irish dancer, and member of the famous Fingal Trio. This was one of the first Irish music groups to be featured on national radio broadcasts (on radio station 2RN, the forerunner of Radio Éireann). They had a major influence on later generations of Irish musicians. Falling asleep to the sounds of his father's piping was one of Seamus's earliest childhood memories, and the household in which he grew up was one of abundant musical riches. Local and visiting musicians would regularly come by to socialize and play music with his father, the music often accompanying dancing in the home.

Seamus began playing the uilleann pipes as a child and was a recognized master of the instrument by age 21, when he was featured on a series of Radio Éireann broadcasts in 1940. He never took formal lessons on the instrument, neither from his father nor anyone else, learning to play in the traditional oral/aural tradition way. His father was the only piper he ever credited as a major influence on his playing, especially for explaining how to deal with some of the "difficult bits" of piping technique and ornamentation. James also taught Seamus to read and write down music, skills that most other Irish traditional musicians of their time did not possess.

Seamus's music literacy aided him significantly in his professional career. It was an important qualification in his job as a folk music collector for the government's Irish Folklore Commission. This position gave him the opportunity to travel throughout Ireland, locating the best local musicians and singers and transcribing their songs, airs, and dance tunes. He spoke excellent Irish Gaelic, and this, combined with the fact that he himself was an outstanding musician, made for easy rapport with the musicians he met wherever he went. "He was clearly accepted and well-liked by those from whom he sought music," writes Irish music specialist Ronan Nolan, "and was able to instantly spot the genuinely good players and singers. Being a musician himself meant that he was in turn fully accepted by them—a case of like recognising like" (Nolan 2003).

Moving on from the Irish Folklore Commission, Seamus was appointed an Outside Broadcast Officer for Radio Éireann in 1947. The radio station had an already-established practice of bringing traditional singers and musicians from counties all over Ireland to perform for national broadcasts. The next venture was to devise a way that these musicians could be recorded in their home environments, in the villages and towns where they lived. For this, a special mobile recording unit was created. Seamus traveled the countryside with this unit, locating top local musicians and recording them for national broadcasts. These programs "increased public awareness of the richness of Irish traditional music, and a generation of older rural singers and musicians became known to, and admired by, the Irish public," both in rural and urban areas (Shields and Gershen 2000:391). They also made musicians from different Irish counties and regions familiar with the styles of one another. Now a musician from County Kerry in the south could listen to dance tunes and airs played by musicians of County Donegal in the north. As musicians in rural areas came to know and be influenced by each other's styles via radio, and as urbanization brought musicians from different places together in major cities like Dublin, a more pan-Irish approach to Irish traditional music began to emerge. Ennis was a key figure in this development, as in many others.

In 1951, Ennis moved to London to work for the British Broadcasting Corporation (BBC). He became part of a major BBC project devoted to the preservation on recordings of surviving folk culture traditions of Ireland, England, Scotland, and Wales: song, instrumental music, oral poetry, myths and legends, storytelling. Between 1951 and 1958, he made recordings and broadcasts throughout the United Kingdom and Ireland and also hosted a pioneering BBC folk music radio program (*As I Roved Out*).

Ennis returned to Ireland to live in 1958, doing freelance work for Radio Éireann as well as some shows in the new medium of television. He traveled the country playing music during the 1960s and became an important icon of the Irish music revival during that period. In 1964, he went to the United States to perform at the Newport Folk Festival, introducing traditional Irish music to a new, mass international audience. He died in 1982 at the age of 63. He continued to play right up to the end, and spent his final years living in a mobile home in the county where he was born. Today, his stature as a piper is almost legendary: "Seamus' playing of the uilleann pipes," writes Ronan Nolan, "was always instantly recognisable for his tone, technique and particular versions of tunes and the variations which he employed while playing them. Any tune, no matter how commonly played by musicians at sessions or elsewhere, became different when he played it and despite the amount of skill and technique which he used, the tune was never stifled or bent out of shape in any way and this was because Seamus had a great respect for the music and its idiomatic integrity" (Nolan 2003).

Neo-Traditional Irish Music and the Irish Music Revival

Through the 1950s, Irish society experienced profound socioeconomic changes. Large-scale industrialization in commercial areas such as food processing and beverage making led to massive urbanization and ultimately to an economy based principally on manufacturing rather than agriculture. Agriculture itself also became heavily industrialized, yielding major economic gains. Ireland prospered during the 1960s as an outcome of these changes. This prosperity, together with renewed fears of culture loss and a growing interest on the part of many younger Irish people in traditional Irish culture, sparked a major cultural revival movement.

The Irish music revival, which began in the 1960s, was a key component of this movement. Recordings of traditional musicians from counties all over Ireland were produced in record numbers and were broadcast and distributed nationwide. Many local, regional, and national traditional music competitions, such as the prestigious All-Ireland music competitions (called *fleadhs*) were established or revived, spurring great public interest in the music and inspiring many Irish youth to return to their "roots" by taking up traditional Irish instruments and learning the old musical styles.

fleadhs (flahs)

As the music was revived and revitalized, it also was transformed. It moved from the countryside and the home to the pub, the dance hall, and the concert hall. Approaches to the playing of dance tunes and medleys became more formal and structured, with well-planned musical arrangements often taking the place of the older, more spontaneous performance styles. In addition to traditional melodic instruments such as the fiddle, flute, tinwhistle, and uilleann pipes, the guitar and other chordal accompaniment instruments (along with drums and other percussion instruments) now became standard as well, and in many cases these newly added instruments even became the principal focal points of the new-style arrangements. Casual groups of musicians who had formerly gathered to play for dancing turned into established bands that performed, recorded, and toured professionally (Figure 9.3). With this move toward professionalism, the status of the old tunes themselves often was changed too. Traditional dance tunes that in the past had been regarded as common property now came to be increasingly identified with specific arrangements and recordings by specific performers and bands. This initiated a general trend toward the commodification of Irish traditional music, a trend that has only grown and intensified over the years. Finally, the performance of dance tunes and medleys became largely unhinged from dancing itself, as music's social function in Irish society came to reflect new social values and environments.

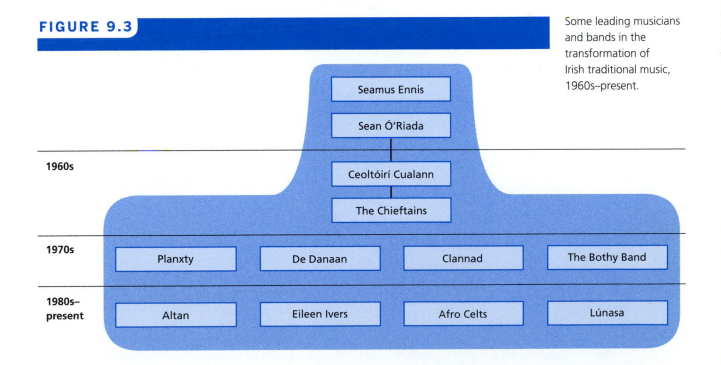

FIGURE 9.3

Some leading musicians and bands in the transformation of Irish traditional music, 1960s–present.

Sean Ó'Riada (left) and Ceoltóirí Cualann.

Sean Ó'Riada (SHAWN Oh REE-yah-dah)

bodhrán (BOH-rawn)

Sean Ó'Riada and the transformation of Irish traditional music

Key to the transformation of Irish music was Sean Ó'Riada (1931–1971). Seamus Ennis's status as an icon of Irish traditional music in the 20th century is matched, if not exceeded, by that of Ó'Riada. As important as Ennis was to the preservation and cultivation of older styles of Irish folk music, Ó'Riada was to their transformation and modernization. Both men were seminal figures during and leading up to the Irish music revival that crystallized around 1960, gained new momentum in the 1970s with the emergence of a new generation of outstanding musicians and bands, and continued henceforth into the 1980s and beyond (Figure 9.3).

In 1960, Sean Ó'Riada organized a group of leading Irish traditional musicians into the ensemble Ceoltóirí Cualann, or Musicians of Cualann (a region of Dublin). Together with these musicians, among them John Kelly, he essentially invented a fresh, neo-traditional Irish musical idiom that was soon absorbed into the Irish traditional music mainstream itself. Ó'Riada combined old-fashioned solo instrumental traditions and playing styles with sophisticated arranging techniques and an ensemble-based sound. Innovative use of chords, multiple-melody textures, changing combinations of instruments, and alternating solos on different instruments were among the features that defined his distinctive approach.

Ceoltóirí Cualann employed a core instrumental lineup of uilleann pipes, two fiddles, tinwhistle, button box accordion, and **bodhrán** (a hand-held frame drum with a goat skin head). The uilleann pipes, which, despite the valiant efforts of advocates like Seamus Ennis, had declined greatly in popularity during the preceding decades, were featured prominently in Ó'Riada's arrangements for Ceoltóirí Cualann. This restored a largely lost status to the instrument that endures to the present in Irish music. The group's contribution to the legacy of the bodhrán was perhaps even more impressive. Formerly a domestic utensil used by Irish homemakers to winnow grains, the bodhrán had traditionally led a double life as an occasional rhythmic accompaniment instrument used during rural ceremonial gatherings. With the promotion of the instrument by Ceoltóirí Cualann, however, it came to enjoy a new status as the main rhythmic accompaniment instrument of the new Irish traditional music ensemble style, a status it still retains today.

Bodhrán and button box accordion.

The Chieftains

Beyond its own historical importance, Ceoltóirí Cualann is also significant for a new group that emerged out of it, The Chieftains. Led by uilleann pipes master Paddy Moloney, The Chieftains are arguably the most widely influential and internationally renowned Irish traditional music group ever. Since the release of their first record album in 1963, they have become the premier international ambassadors of Irish

The Chieftains, with Paddy Moloney playing the uilleann pipes (front center) and guest fiddler Eileen Ivers (rear right). This photo is from a 1999 television broadcast.

traditional music. Their influence may be heard in the music of virtually all subsequent leading Irish groups—Clannad, Planxty, The Bothy Band, De Danaan, Altan, Lúnasa—and they have collaborated with members of all these groups on a variety of projects. They also have been inveterate boundary-blurring musical adventurers, undertaking collaborative projects with everyone from the Rolling Stones' Mick Jagger to reggae star Ziggy Marley.

Clannad (CLAHN-ad)

De Danaan (Day DAN-an)

Lúnasa (LOO-nuh-sah)

guided listening experience

"The Dingle Set" (Medley), The Chieftains

- CD Track #**3-8**
- Featured performer(s)/group: The Chieftains
- Format: Excerpt
- Source recording: "An Poc Ar Buile/The Dingle Set," from *The Essential Chieftains* (RCA Victor/Legacy).

This selection features a medley consisting of three reels: "Far From Home," "Gladstone," and "The Scartaglen." It was recorded live in County Kerry, Ireland, in 2000. Paddy Moloney, who is credited as the arranger, plays tinwhistle on the first tune ("Far From Home") and uilleann pipes on the last one ("The Scartaglen"). The other instruments in the ensemble are fiddles, Irish wooden flute, Irish harp, accordion, concertina (a smaller, accordion-like instrument), banjo, and bodhrán. From 1:51 to the end you will also hear the rhythmic footwork of guest artist and well-known fiddler Ashley MacIsaac (from Cape Breton Island, Nova Scotia, Canada) as he spontaneously breaks into dancing a reel.

Sean Ó'Riada's lasting influence on subsequent Irish music arrangers is evident here in Moloney's use of *changing textures* from one tune of the medley to the next. While the first and third tunes are played by the full ensemble, the middle tune ("Gladstone") is performed by the fiddlers alone. Altering the instrumentation in this way generates considerable musical variety and contrast in Moloney's arrangement.

In terms of form, "Far From Home" is in the standard AABB format already familiar to us. The tune is repeated once in its entirety (AABB AABB). "Gladstone" and "The Scartaglen" both have a formal design of AB, rather than AABB. (Reels with an AB form are called *single reels*, whereas those with an AABB form are called *double reels*.) "Gladstone" is played through twice (AB AB), while "The Scartaglen" is played through four times (AB AB AB AB).

In addition to offering an example of the consummate musicianship of an iconic Irish ensemble, this live recording also captures a special quality of exuberance in social celebration that is central to the Irish dance tune tradition overall.

guided listening quick summary

"The Dingle Set" (Medley), The Chieftains (CD ex. #3-8)

"FAR FROM HOME" (MEDLEY TUNE #1): AABB AABB

0:00–0:07—A

0:08–0:15—A

0:16–0:23—B

0:24–0:31—B

0:32–0:39—A

0:40–0:46—A

0:47–0:55—B

0:55–1:02—B

- Performed by full ensemble, including tinwhistle (Moloney), fiddles, Irish wooden flute, Irish harp, accordion, concertina, banjo, and bodhrán.
- Lively, up-tempo reel, with the bodhrán laying down a strong rhythmic foundation.

"GLADSTONE" (MEDLEY TUNE #2): AB AB

1:03–1:10—A

1:11–1:18—B

1:19–1:26—A

1:27–1:34—B

- Fiddles only throughout, with the rest of the ensemble laying out; instrumentation change creates interesting contrast in texture.

"THE SCARTAGLEN" (MEDLEY TUNE #3): AB AB AB AB

1:35–1:42—A

1:43–1:50—B

1:51–1:58—A (Ashley MacIsaac begins dancing here.)

1:59–2:06—B

2:07–2:14—A

2:15–2:22—B

2:23–2:30—A

2:31–end—B

- With the arrival of this final tune at 1:35, there is a return to a full ensemble texture (but with Paddy Moloney now playing uilleann pipes).
- The rhythms of the bodhrán and the rhythmic footwork of the dancer add energy and excitement as the performance drives to its conclusion.

The 1970s: Second generation of the Irish music revival

Though an ardent traditionalist throughout his life, Seamus Ennis was also an admirer of some of the newer sounds that came out of the post-Ó'Riada era of the Irish music revival in the 1970s. During that decade, Ennis developed a close friendship with Liam O'Flynn, a younger uilleann pipes virtuoso and member of one of the leading Irish bands of the time, Planxty. "When we travelled together," recalled O'Flynn many years later, "he always drove and that could be a fairly 'hairy' experience. The conversation always turned to music[,] with fascinating stories about places, tunes, songs, players and singers. I absorbed a great deal from him in this way. Planxty was in full flight at this time and he took a terrific interest in the group. He gave us songs and tunes in abundance" (O'Flynn, quoted in Nolan 2003).

Planxty was indeed in full flight. O'Flynn and his Planxty bandmates, including Andy Irvine, Christy Moore, Donal Lunny, and James Kelly, came together as products of the Irish revival generation. Many Irish musicians who emerged during this period had grown up with other kinds of music: rock, jazz, classical. Their re-embracing of cultural roots via Irish music in many cases came later. Moreover, their ideas about what Irish traditional music was becoming were as much informed by the already-modernized styles of Ceoltóirí Cualann and The Chieftains as by the older breed of traditional Irish musicians championed—and to some extent represented—by Seamus Ennis.

Donal Lunny of Planxty, 1970s.

This second wave of the Irish music revival, then, featured a new generation of musicians who approached the Irish tradition from a different, more cosmopolitan and commercial vantage point. Planxty, Clannad, the Bothy Band, and De Danaan were among its most important representative groups. On one level, these bands were significant for creating a new fusion of Irish traditional music, rock, jazz, and other international and popular styles. On another level, they were important for carrying on the songs, dance tunes, and performance traditions of their Irish forebears, albeit with an innovative approach.

A good example of the artistry of Planxty performing in this innovatively traditional vein is "Bean Pháidín" (Paddy's Wife) (**CD ex. #3-9**). This arrangement was originally released on the band's 1973 album *The Well Below the Valley,* which includes some of their best work. "Bean Pháidín" is an old, traditional Irish song from Connemara in County Galway. Like the sean nós song "Ag an Phobal Dé Domhnaigh" discussed earlier (**CD ex. #3-4**), "Bean Pháidín" tells a story about heartbreak, bitter jealousy, and adultery from the perspective of "the other woman." But unlike its sean nós counterpart, which is serious in tone and concludes with at least some measure of dignity and moral virtue as the heartbroken mistress blesses her lover and sends him back to his wife and child, "Bean Pháidín" is altogether a darkly comical and amoral send-up. The antiheroic narrator of this song tells us unabashedly that she is a woman having an affair with a married man named Paddy (Pháidín) and that she wishes Paddy's wife was dead so she could have him all to herself. "It is a bitter pity that I am not the wife of Paddy," our protagonist explains, "and [that] the wife he has is not dead." Should any doubts remain regarding her ill will toward the poor wife of Paddy, she follows up with a curse: "May your legs be broken, [Paddy's] wife . . . May your legs and bones be broken."

Certainly there is nothing inherently funny about the meaning or message of this lyric, but humor, the most culture-specific of all cultural domains, is in the eye, ear, and heart of the beholder. As Sean Williams explains of "Bean Pháidín," it is a song that "reflects a unique way of dealing with [extramarital] affairs and offers a window into bitter jealousy. . . . Men and women both sing this song with great enthusiasm, and it appears in contemporary song sessions, concerts, and recordings as a light-hearted respite from the intensity of *sean-nós.*" Its melody "responds to the potentially dark nature of the lyrics . . . by bouncing along in a major key. It is the juxtaposition of a major key with serious-seeming lyrics that make the song entertaining, together with the sentiment expressed by the lyrics" (Williams 2009:180).

Bean Pháidín
(Ban Faw-jeen)

In the Planxty performance of "Bean Pháidín" on your CD set, the bitter mistress's sentiments are voiced in Irish Gaelic by a male singer (Donal Lunny). The sung melody is doubled on the uilleann pipes by Liam O'Flynn, who also furnishes the accompanying drone; a bodhrán player joins in as well at 0:14 with a jig-like rhythm. Following the conclusion of the song proper at 1:47, the singing part drops out and "Bean Pháidín" gives way to a new tune ("Rakish Paddy") with an AABB-type form that is played solo on the pipes by O'Flynn over a lively reel dance rhythm in traditional style (1:48–2:23); the stylistic influence of Seamus Ennis on his protégé is most clearly in evidence here. After playing through the full form of the reel once, O'Flynn begins the tune again at 2:24. This time other instruments join the pipes on the melody and the bodhrán returns to provide a lively rhythmic accompaniment. The "Rakish Paddy" tune cycles back around one last time beginning at 3:01, with accompanying chords and harmonized melodies now giving it a more modern sound than before.

In the space of less than four minutes, Planxty's "Bean Pháidín" takes us on a journey through several phases of Irish musical development, from the original Connemara song of the title (0:00–1:47), to Liam O'Flynn's Seamus Ennis-like solo pipes rendition of the reel "Rakish Paddy" (1:48–2:23), to a second playing of that same tune with expanded instrumentation (2:24–3:00), and finally to its third playing with not only expanded instrumentation but chordal accompaniment as well (3:01–end). In this last guise especially, the foundational elements of the modern ensemble sound of Irish traditional music are already in place.

The modern ensemble sound of Irish traditional dance music

The innovative, cosmopolitan approach to playing standard Irish traditional dance tunes and medleys identified with bands like Planxty built on and extended the earlier innovations of Ceoltóirí Cualann and The Chieftains, while also adding novel elements. Planxty in particular has been credited for having ". . . really changed the way young Irish people looked on the old folk repertoire. Their arrangements of old airs and tunes, and Liam O'Flynn's wonderful uilleann piping, opened a lot of ears and inspired a lot of the new Celtic groups of [recent] decades" (O'Connor 1999:179). The Irish group Altan and bands led by the Irish-American fiddler Eileen Ivers, musical examples by both of whom we will explore shortly, are among the most important of these later groups.

The list that follows this paragraph summarizes some of the main features of the modern ensemble style of Irish dance music, which will be our focus throughout the remainder of this chapter. These features are characteristic of neo-traditional dance music styles, and also prefigure post-traditional styles. They essentially distinguish these modern approaches from traditional, instrumental dance music such as that heard in the Seamus Ennis recordings we listened to earlier. The modern ensemble sound here described crystallized in some of the music of Ceoltóirí Cualann and the early Chieftains during the 1960s. It developed in new ways with Planxty and other second wave Irish music revival groups of the 1970s. It has since been extended even further in the hands of more recent groups like Altan and Eileen Ivers' bands. Today, it is ubiquitous across many realms of Irish music performance, from concerts and recordings by professional groups to informal Irish music sessions held in pubs and other venues throughout Ireland, the Irish diaspora, and the world. All of the features included on this list have become standard in contemporary Irish dance music performance (especially as performed by professional groups), though it is important to note that not every *one* of them is necessarily present in any given performance. With all of this in mind, it may be stated that in the modern ensemble style:

- Performances typically feature groups (ensembles) of performers rather than just a solo performer. While some combination of traditional Irish melodic instruments (e.g., fiddle, flute, tinwhistle, uilleann pipes, accordion) is generally employed, the instrumentation is usually enhanced by the addition of chordal and rhythmic accompaniment instruments as well (see next page).

- Chordal accompaniment parts played on instruments such as the guitar and the Irish bouzouki (see "Insights and Perspectives" box below), which were not traditionally used in Irish music, often figure prominently; complex chord progressions and other nontraditional elements derived from jazz, rock, Spanish flamenco, or other international musical styles are used to modernize the sound of the music.

- Drums and other rhythmic accompaniment instruments are featured in many groups; these may include the bodhrán, drum set, conga drums (see Chapter 11, p. 244), or other percussion instruments.

- Traditional Irish dance rhythms, such as the reel, are often enhanced or transformed through the influences of jazz, rock, funk, and other musical styles, as well as by influences from musics of Africa, Latin America, the Balkans, or other world regions.

- Musical textures tend to be quite varied, even within a single performance. Rather than having the entire melody played on just a single instrument or performed in unison on all of the melodic instruments at the same time, the melody may instead be divided up among several instrumentalists who take turns playing in different parts of the arrangement, or it may be played simultaneously in two or more varied versions on different instruments, or it may even be replaced altogether by an improvised instrumental solo inspired by jazz- or rock-derived playing styles; additionally, the accompanying instruments may come in and out of the texture from one section to the next or perform in different styles during different parts of the arrangement, adding further variety to the music's texture.

- The former function of Irish dance music as music to be danced to is largely eclipsed by its new function as *music to be listened to but not danced to,* whether in the pub or the concert hall (though a modern revival of Irish dancing has been spurred by international theatrical productions such as *Riverdance*; for more information on that phenomenon, visit the Online Learning Center at http://www.mhhe.com/bakan2e).

insights and perspectives

The Irish Bouzouki

The Irish bouzouki is a flat-backed hybrid of the original Greek bouzouki (which is featured in **CD ex. #1-23**) and the mandolin. The bouzouki first came into Irish music through Johnny Moynihan in the late 1960s and became a signature element of groups like Planxty and the Bothy Band through the outstanding playing of Donal Lunny. It is now one of the standard chordal instruments used in Irish music, along with the mandolin and the guitar. With the introduction of the bouzouki into Irish music came other changes as well. Greek and other Balkan rhythms were incorporated into Irish dance music styles, and these, together with additional borrowed rhythms from rock, jazz, and other musicultural traditions, had a major impact on Irish music.

The Irish bouzouki.

"The Emyvale/Ríl Gan Ainm/The Three Merry Sisters of Fate" (Medley), Altan

- CD Track #3-10
- Featured performer(s)/group: Altan, with Mairéad Ní Mhaonaigh and Paul O'Shaughnessy (fiddles), Frankie Kennedy (flutes), Ciarán Curran (Irish bouzouki), and Mark Kelly (guitar)
- Format: Complete track
- Source recording: *The Best of Altan* (Green Linnet Records)

Altan is one of the most popular, widely respected, and influential Irish groups of the post-1970s era. The group formed in the mid-1980s and throughout the 1990s was recognized, along with other top bands like the Bothy Band and De Danaan, as the "flagbearers for the Irish traditional band scene" (O'Connor 1999:180). At once deeply rooted in Irish musical tradition and adventurously creative, Altan is a group that has garnered acclaim from traditionalists and modernists alike.

Mairéad Ní Mhaon-aigh (Mah–RAID Nah–WEE–nee)

Ciarán (Ky-EE-rawn)

Ríl Gan Ainm (Reel Gahn Ahm)

Altan was founded by Mairéad Ní Mhaonaigh of County Donegal, a fiddler and vocalist (and the daughter of a famous Irish fiddler), and her husband, the late Belfast-born Irish wooden flute and tinwhistle player Frankie Kennedy. Together with a second fiddler, Paul O'Shaughnessy; guitarist Mark Kelly; and Irish bouzouki player Ciarán Curran, Ní Mhaonaigh and Kennedy formed an outstanding quintet that produced several memorable albums, including 1990's *The Red Crow,* on which the dance tune medley of **CD ex. #3-10** first appeared. Subsequent years and albums witnessed a series of personnel changes (most notably following the tragic early death of Frankie Kennedy from cancer in 1994) and collaborations with a variety of guest artists.

Altan.

Altan's music has covered everything from Irish traditional dance medleys to Irish-rock fusion productions that combine diverse musical elements in unconventional ways. The medley of **CD ex. #3-10** falls squarely in the former category and provides excellent examples of many features of the neo-traditional, modern Irish ensemble sound outlined in the preceding section. It is comprised of three dance tunes, all reels. The first and third tunes are single reels, with alternating A and B parts (AB AB AB and AB AB AB A, respectively). The middle tune, "Ríl Gan Ainm," which literally means "Reel Without Name," is a double reel (AABB form) and is played through twice (AABB AABB). The two fiddles and Frankie Kennedy's Irish wooden flute provide the melodic layer of the music's texture. They play mostly in tight unison, right down to the melodic ornaments.

Much of the interest of the arrangement lies in its chordal accompaniment, which is provided by the guitar and Irish bouzouki. Sometimes they accompany the melody with simple chords reminiscent of the drone-based accompaniments of older styles, but there are also passages in which more intricate, jazz-influenced chord progressions are heard.

The guitar and Irish bouzouki also provide the music's rhythmic accompaniment layer (no percussion instruments are used in this arrangement). In some passages, the rhythmic treatment is quite straightforward; in others, influences of rock, jazz, bluegrass, and funk are evident in the syncopations of the guitar and bouzouki parts.

Overall, the playing of the ensemble is very clean technically. Rhythmic execution is strict and precise, meter and tempo constant and unwavering, phrases consistent in length. Clearly, Altan is operating from a rather different musical aesthetic than was Seamus Ennis in the uilleann pipes medley explored earlier in the chapter. This is because Altan has seemingly planned out virtually every move they make, whereas Ennis was more creating in the moment. Both selections (not to mention The Chieftains example we listened to) are excellent representatives of "Irish traditional music," but they represent different dimensions of that tradition, one neither better nor worse than the other. There is an old Irish Gaelic saying that translates as "It's not the same, but it's just as nice." That saying applies well here.

guided listening quick summary

"The Emyvale/Ríl Gan Ainm/The Three Merry Sisters of Fate" (Medley), Altan (CD ex. #3-10)

"THE EMYVALE" (MEDLEY TUNE #1—FORM: AB AB AB)

0:00–0:08—A

- Texture: unison melody (two fiddles, Irish wooden flute), chordal accompaniment (guitar, Irish bouzouki).
- Simple, drone-based chords.

0:08–0:16—B

- Chord progression becomes more jazz-like (though still moving overtop an implied drone).

0:16–0:24—A

0:24–0:32—B

0:32–0:40—A

0:40–0:48—B

- Rhythmic activity and dynamic level continue to grow as the music builds in intensity.

"RÍL GAN AINM" ["REEL WITHOUT NAME"] (MEDLEY TUNE #2—FORM: AABB AABB)

0:48–1:04—AA

- Change of key (from A Dorian to D Dorian) marks start of second tune. (Refer back to the Musical Guided Tour of this chapter for a musical illustration of a Dorian scale.)
- Funk-inspired, syncopated rhythmic pattern introduced in the chordal accompaniment.

1:05–1:19—BB

- Another change of key (modulation), this time to C major.
- Chordal accompaniment is less syncopated here (as compared to preceding "funky" style).

1:20–1:51—AABB

- Same sequence as before, but with more strummed chords on the guitar thickening the texture and with a more prominent Irish bouzouki part near the end.

"THE THREE MERRY SISTERS OF FATE" (MEDLEY TUNE #3—FORM: AB AB AB A)

1:51–2:00—A

- More changes of key.

The Post-Traditional World of Irish Music: Crossing Bridges with Eileen Ivers

The story of Irish music is only partially told through an exploration of music in Ireland itself. Equally significant is the history of Irish traditional music in the Irish diaspora. From the 1930s through the 1950s, there was a major decline in the support of Irish traditional music in Ireland. Political turbulence, a major economic downturn in the 1930s, and rapid modernization and urbanization all contributed to this decline. For many modern-minded Irish, the traditional music came to be associated with an antiquated and outmoded way of life that was out of step with the goals and aspirations of a modernizing Ireland.

Meanwhile, in Irish diasporic communities of the United States, Canada, England, and elsewhere, Irish traditional music was being tenaciously preserved and creatively developed as a touchstone of Irish ethnic identification with the homeland. Growing prosperity, ready access to international travel, tourism, mass media, and improved communication technologies on both sides of the Atlantic during the post-World War II era connected Irish music culture itself to the vibrant musical worlds of the Irish diaspora to an unprecedented degree. In particular, a number of early American recordings of the fiddlers Michael Coleman and James Morrison, both originally from County Sligo in Ireland, were highly influential in music circles "back home." Instruments, performance styles, and repertoires that had been kept alive in the diaspora while all but disappearing in Ireland were reintroduced to the homeland and revitalized. New musical styles and playing techniques cultivated by Irish diaspora musicians began to influence musicians in Ireland as well. Altogether, the vibrant new life of Irish music abroad galvanized musicultural life in Ireland itself, providing an important impetus for the Irish music revival of the 1960s. Since that time, the rich cross-pollination that has occurred between Irish music in the Irish diaspora and in Ireland has given rise to a truly transnational pan-Irish musical culture. If any one contemporary musician might be said to be representative of that transnational culture, it is the Irish-American fiddler Eileen Ivers.

Eileen Ivers.

The music and life of Eileen Ivers

Eileen Ivers has carved out a unique and important niche in contemporary, pan-Irish music. Her work spans a broad and eclectic range of musical styles, from neo-traditional Irish; to Irish-rock, Irish-Latin, and Irish-African fusion; to combinations of all of these and more. For Ivers, musical borders and boundaries are there to be broken. Yet the Irish traditional core that defines her extraordinarily diverse musical approach is always present. Irish traditional music is Eileen Ivers' home-base; she is just a frequent flyer.

Ivers was born to Irish immigrant parents in 1965 in the Bronx borough of New York City. She grew up in a large and vibrant Irish-American immigrant community where Irish music, dancing, and social and cultural values were a basic part of life. But the environment in which she was raised was also a diversely multicultural one, and this affected the formation of her musical and cultural identity as much as did her Irish heritage. She grew up listening to salsa, rock, jazz, Broadway show tunes, and classical music. All of these influenced her emergent and unique musical persona. As the Eileen Ivers admirer and Pulitzer Prize–winning author of *Angela's Ashes*, Frank McCourt, has written:

> She grew up in a boom box Bronx and she carries sounds from childhood that are surely embedded in her musical soul: the chirp and clank of an October radiator heating up; the rhythms of girls hopscotching on a nearby sidewalk; the sway and strut of a bodega beat; the roar of a baseball crowd at Yankee Stadium; mothers calling for their kids to come home; the rattle of a taxi; and, yeah, that lullaby of Broadway.
>
> She's Irish, she's American, she's international. She's the Bronx, Botswana, Balldehob [*sic*]. She's played solo and with groups in the noisiest of pubs and clubs, on cruise ships, in arenas and stadiums and Radio City Music Hall. I've seen her, heard her in all these venues and wondered, after you've been there and done that, Eileen, how are they going to keep you down on the farm? (McCourt 1999)

Ivers began playing Irish fiddle at the age of eight. Her principal mentor was the renowned fiddler Martin Mulvhill from County Limerick in western Ireland. Her talents were prodigious. She traveled to Ireland to compete in the All-Ireland Fiddle Championships and won—nine times! From there, she went from one success to another, performing with everyone from The Chieftains to the London Symphony Orchestra. She even found time to graduate *magna cum laude* in mathematics from Iona College.

In the late 1980s, Ivers began touring and recording as a solo fiddler and bandleader under her own name, crafting the unique and eclectic Irish-world music fusion sound with which she is now largely identified. Along the way came her starring musical role as featured fiddler in the Broadway production of *Riverdance* in the 1990s (for more information, visit the Online Learning Center at www.mhhe.com/bakan2e), and after that cofounding membership in the ground-breaking all-women's group Cherish the Ladies.

guided listening experience

"Gravelwalk" (Medley), Eileen Ivers

- CD Track #**3-11**
- Featured performer(s)/group: Eileen Ivers group, with Eileen Ivers (acoustic fiddle and electric violin), Jerry O'Sullivan (uilleann pipes), Seamus Egan (Irish wooden flute), Bakithi Kumalo (electric bass), and Steve Gadd (drum set)
- Format: Complete track
- Source recording: *Crossing the Bridge,* by Eileen Ivers (Sony Classical)

Crossing the Bridge is an album that fully demonstrates Eileen Ivers' eclectic, music-without-borders approach. In the CD's accompanying booklet, Frank McCourt describes the music of *Crossing the Bridge* as ". . . startling in its geographic variety: Spain, Africa, West Indies, Cuba, Ireland, always Ireland. And here you are digging jazz, jigs, hip hop, strains of reggae, flamenco, bluegrass. The Irish never stray far from country music. Who, after all, brought it to America?" (McCourt 1999).

The opening track of *Crossing the Bridge,* "Gravelwalk," is an innovative arrangement of a medley of three old-style Irish reels served up with hard-driving rock-Irish rhythmic grooves.

Ivers' scorching electric violin solos on "Gravelwalk" belie their instrumental source. They sound like they are being played on an electric guitar rather than a violin, and the influence of guitar greats like Jim Hendrix and Carlos Santana is apparent (see Chapter 11 for more on Santana).

Ivers is joined on "Gravelwalk" by an all-star international cast of musicians, including the uilleann piper Jerry O'Sullivan, Irish wooden flute player Seamus Egan, American drummer Steve Gadd, and South African electric bassist Bakithi Kumalo. The collaboration results in an interesting and highly effective blend of diverse musical traditions and approaches that strays from, yet never loses touch with, the work's Irish musical foundation.

The track begins with ambient electro-acoustic sounds, which build and lead into the opening tune of the medley, "Fermoy Lasses." This is a standard, AABB-form Irish double reel, though Ivers twists around the conventional form a little bit in the arrangement. The presentation of the tune starts out in a fairly traditional style, with Ivers playing the melody on acoustic fiddle, accompanied by a drone-like bass line and straightforward rhythms in the drum set part. The uilleann pipes soon join the fiddle in playing the melody as the bass playing gets more active and syncopated.

The mainly traditional sound of the opening of "Fermoy Lasses" gets a facelift at 0:32 when Ivers switches to electric violin and manipulates the timbre of the instrument further through use of a "wah-wah" electronic effects device. This change is matched in the drumming part, as Gadd moves to a more rock-like groove with backbeat accents. As the arrangement continues, there are many changes of key, as well as in instrumentation, musical texture, rhythmic accompaniment patterns, and overall style. Some portions of the medley sound resolutely Irish traditional, others like contemporary jazz, still others like hard rock, and quite a few like a seamless blend of all of the above. A wonderful improvised duet by Ivers (acoustic fiddle) and Seamus Egan (Irish wooden flute) that arrives in the middle of the second tune of the medley ("The Noisy Curlew") is a highlight of the performance. So too is Ivers' final electric violin solo in the last tune, "Gravelwalks to Granie," which builds and builds to an exciting climax.

"Gravelwalks to Granie" also takes us back full circle to the beginning of our journey. Listen carefully to the passage at 3:47 and you will recognize what you hear as the last of the three renditions of the characteristic Irish melodic figure featured in **Online Musical Illustration #24** (the second of these renditions, which immediately precedes the Ivers clip, is by Altan and can be located in *its* original musical context at 1:05 of **CD ex. #3-10**). Comparing Eileen Ivers' "Gravelwalk" to all of the music that came before it during the course of our journey, we are once again reminded of the old Irish saying, "It's not the same, but it's just as nice."

guided listening quick summary

"Gravelwalk" (Medley), Eileen Ivers (CD ex. #3-11)

INTRODUCTION

0:00–0:20

- Ambient opening: electronic timbres, cymbal roll with crescendo (0:15), Irish wooden flute (0:18).

"FERMOY LASSES" (MEDLEY TUNE #1)

0:21–0:28—A

- Key: E Dorian; melody played on acoustic fiddle (Ivers).
- Fairly traditional accompaniment, with drone-based chords and straightforward drum rhythms.

0:28–0:35—A′

- Uilleann pipes prominent; bass/drum accompaniment more syncopated.
- Ivers switches to electric violin with "wah-wah" effect at 0:32.

0:36–0:50—AA′

- Melody now played on electric violin (with "wah-wah" effects).
- Rock-style drumming with backbeats.

0:50–1:04—BB′

- Ivers switches back to acoustic fiddle as drumming intensifies, the key changes, and the electric bass anchors a chord progression (instead of drone-based harmonies).

1:05–1:47—A′A′BBA′A′

- Similar to before, but with addition of dramatic "orchestral" synthesizer chords and other electronic timbres at key points.

"THE NOISY CURLEW" [AKA "JACK McGUIRE'S"] (MEDLEY TUNE #2)

1:48–2:29—AA′BB′A′A′

- Fiddle (Ivers) and Irish wooden flute (Egan) duet, with clever interplay between the two instruments and much improvisation.

2:29–2:43—B′B′

- Call-and-response dialogue between the fiddle-flute duo and the full band, who trade four-measure phrases (i.e., "trading fours," a borrowing from jazz).

INTERLUDE (JAZZ-ROCK STYLE; NOT BASED ON ANY IRISH TUNE)

2:43–3:26

- Electric bass solo (Kumalo) over driving, rock-like drum groove, followed by electric violin solo (2:58) and building intensity.

"GRAVELWALKS TO GRANIE" (MEDLEY TUNE #3)

3:26–3:47—ABC

- More changes of key, relatively traditional sound and texture (acoustic instruments, straightforward rhythmic accompaniment), uilleann pipes become more prominent as intensity builds.

3:47–4:01—DD′

- **D** melody arrives triumphantly, along with a key change to C major; melodic instruments (fiddle, flute, pipes) continue as before; syncopated "shots" in bass and drums outline chord progression.
- (Same music as heard in final [third] segment of Online Musical Illustration #24.)

4:01–end—ABCDD′, then D′D′D′D′ vamp to end

- Varied reprise of the whole "Gravelwalks to Granie" tune, with more electric violin soloing.
- Ivers "takes over" through the vamp at the end, driving the performance to its climactic unison finish.

Summary

In this chapter, we journeyed a long distance, from sean nós singing and traditional dance tune performances of Seamus Ennis to Ceoltóiri Cualann, The Chieftains, Planxty, Altan, and Eileen Ivers. Along the way, we witnessed profound musicultural transformations of Irish traditional music on multiple levels, especially in terms of Irish dance tunes, which were the main focus. Despite their many differences, the various types of Irish dance music we listened to were all the same at a core level. The same kinds of tunes, instruments, dance tune forms, medley-based musical designs, and basic approaches to melodic ornamentation and variation were present in each. The styles of performing the old tunes, however, varied considerably from era to era and example to example. And the presence or absence of imported musical elements—as well as their degree of influence and musical use—were also important factors of difference.

Irish traditional music, like most traditional musics of the world, has endured and been transformed in response to the changing social, political, and cultural conditions that surround it. This chapter examined how Irish nationalism and transnationalism, modernization and urbanization, and musical and cultural revival have become inscribed on one particular domain of Irish traditional music: Irish dance tunes. As both a specifically Irish and an internationally pan-Irish phenomenon, the Irish dance tune symbolizes and serves as a medium for the performance of Irish identity and social life. It takes on different meanings in the home, the dance hall, the concert hall, and the recording studio. It says different things about its performers and audiences depending on who plays it, the instrument or instruments on which it is played, and the style and context in which it is performed. It also reflects very different social values and historical conditions by virtue of whether or not it is used to accompany dancing at all, and if so, what kind. Yet regardless of the musical surfaces to which they become attached or the historical or cultural realities they reflect, embody, and inform, Irish dance tunes—and by extension, Irish musics generally—always speak and respond to a core sense of what it is to be Irish, be that in Ireland, North America, or anywhere in the world.

Key Terms

Irish traditional music	session	reel
pan-Irish	sean nós	ornaments (roll, cran, treble,
Irish Gaelic (language)	tinwhistle	cut, triplet)
Irish potato famine	Irish wooden flute	medley
Irish diaspora	ceílí	uilleann pipes
Radio Éireann	jig	Celtic
Irish music revival	hornpipe	bodhrán

Study Questions

- Besides dance tunes, what are the other four main categories of Irish traditional music?

- What is sean nós, and why is it an important component of Irish traditional music? What themes and issues were addressed in the sean nós song discussed? Who was the singer of that song?

- What important concepts and metaphors emerge in "Song for Ireland"? Describe the performance of that song included on your CD set.

- What were some of the major developments of (and issues in) Irish traditional music during the Irish Free State period? What impact did the urbanization and modernization of Ireland during this and subsequent periods have on music?

- What instruments are conventionally used in Irish traditional music?

- How are the uilleann pipes constructed and played? What important uilleann pipers were discussed in this chapter?

- What is the difference between a ceílí and an Irish music session?

- What were the distinctive contributions of Seamus Ennis and Sean Ó'Riada to the preservation and development of Irish traditional music?

- How did The Chieftains first form and what is their historical (and contemporary) significance?

- What features have defined the modern, ensemble style of Irish music since the Irish music revival that began in the 1960s? (Summarize list from chapter.)

- Who were some of the leading proponents of Irish traditional music of the 1970s? The 1980s and 1990s?

- What is the song "Bean Pháidín" about? What makes it humorous?

- How have processes of diaspora and transnationalism impacted Irish traditional music? What are examples from the chapter that illustrate this impact?

Discussion Questions

- How might the historical development of Irish music traced in this chapter be shown to directly reflect the histories of Irish nationhood, urbanization, modernization, and transnational pan-Irish identity?

- While she is widely respected and admired for her artistry, Eileen Ivers also is regarded as a controversial representative of the Irish music tradition in certain circles. What case could be made in support of her inclusion as a representative of Irish traditional music? What case could be made against that status?

- Some of the songs included in this chapter dealt with challenging social and political issues, from adultery and malice to war and cultural resilience in the face of adversity. Identify and discuss some songs with which you are familiar that do likewise. Have these songs affected your own thoughts and views on the issues they address?

Applying What You Have Learned

- The Irish music session has become a common social institution in many parts of the world today. If you live in a city or college town, there is a good chance that you can find a session or other Irish music performance to attend in your local area. Try to locate a nearby session and go to it. Bring a notepad and jot down your observations: At what kind of a venue is the session held (pub, restaurant, nightclub)? What instruments do the musicians play? What can you say about the tunes played and the styles of performance on the basis of what you learned in this chapter? What kinds of social interactions go on between the participating musicians, and between the musicians and the audience? Is there any dancing? What does it feel like for you to be a part of this environment? Use your notes as the basis of a brief ethnomusicological report on the session and your experience of it.

- Locate several recordings or videos (e.g., on YouTube) of Irish or Irish-influenced music. Listen to each, applying your listening skills and what you have learned in this chapter to a compare-and-contrast exploration of the music. Identify any Irish instruments you hear. Note what other kinds of instruments they are combined with. Try to determine whether any of the music uses the standard tune forms (e.g., AABB) or medley forms of traditional Irish music, and whether these appear "as is" or mixed up with other kinds of forms (e.g., verse-chorus, 12-bar blues, ostinato-based). Listen to how the melodies are played or sung, noting whether the conventional types of melodic ornaments used in Irish music are employed.

Resources for Further Study

Visit the Online Learning Center at www.mhhe.com/bakan2e, as well as the author's personally maintained Web site at www.michaelbakan.com, for additional learning aids, study help, and resources that supplement the content of this chapter.

the river and the path:
conversation and **collective** expression in **West African musics**

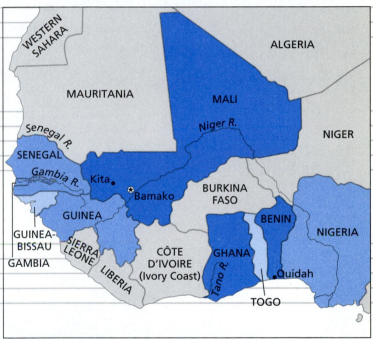

Related locations:

Brazil
Central African Republic
Cuba
Egypt
England
France
Haiti
The Netherlands
Jamaica
Libya
Morocco
Mozambique
Puerto Rico
South Africa

Trinidad and Tobago
Tunisia
Uganda
Zimbabwe

Bahia, Brazil
Mediterranean Coast
Sahara Desert

Athens, Georgia
Johannesburg
London
New York
Paris
Washington, D.C.

The river crosses the path,
the path crosses the river,
who is elder?

The path was cut to meet the river,
the river is of old,
the river comes from
"Odomankoma" the Creator.

Akan (AH-kahn)

This translated passage from an ancient proverb of the **Akan** people of Ghana, West Africa, sets the tone for our exploration of West African music. Its text speaks metaphorically to the key issues that underlie the musicultural journey of this chapter: intersections, pathways, relationships, interdependence, homage.

The proverb begins in the form of a riddle: Which is older, the river or the path? Then we learn the answer. It is the river that is older. The river comes from the divine source of creation. It provides the water that is the source of life and human sustenance, and it connects Akan people who find meaning in this proverb to Odomankoma, their Creator.

Yet it is the path, cut to meet the great Tano River by Akan ancestors of long ago, that connects the Akan to the Tano, marking the routes and

World events		Music events
Advanced civilizations and powerful empires across sub-Saharan Africa: Nok, Benin, Mande, Ghana, Songhay, Dahomey, Buganda	**Pre-15th century**	
Sunjata Keita unifies Mande (Mali) empire, centered in Bamako	**13th century** CE **(c. 1225–1252)**	Jeliya tradition dates from Sunjata period
Progressive colonization and foreign domination of sub-Saharan Africa	**15th–20th centuries**	
Decline, destruction, and collapse of traditional African nations, empires		
Transformation of African political and cultural map		
Slave trade, African diaspora	**17th–19th centuries**	
National independence movements emerge and develop throughout Africa in transitional period to Africa's postcolonial era	**Post-1945**	Sidiki Diabate and song "Kaira" closely identified with struggle for Malian independence beginning in 1940s
Ghana becomes independent nation (formerly a British colony)	**1957**	
Mali becomes independent nation (formerly a French colony)	**1960**	
Dahomey (renamed Benin in 1975) becomes independent nation (formerly a French colony)		Angélique Kidjo born in Ouidah, Benin
	1970s	American blues guitarist and world music pioneer Taj Mahal first encounters the kora, ultimately leading to travels in Mali and collaborations with Malian musicians (Toumani Diabate, Ali Farka Toure)
	1971	Release of *Ancient Strings* (Sidiki Diabate and Djelimadi Sissoko), first internationally distributed recording featuring the kora
	1987	Release of *Shaka Zulu*, by Ladysmith Black Mambazo, featuring "Unomathemba"; follows the 1986 release of Paul Simon's *Graceland*
Apartheid ends; Nelson Mandela elected president of South Africa	**1994**	
	1994–1996	Angélique Kidjo rises to world music stardom with dance single "Ayé" (1994), album *Fifa* (1996)
	1999	Release of *Kulanjan,* by Taj Mahal and Toumani Diabate, featuring "Atlanta Kaira"
	2001	Seckou Keita releases *Baiyo;* re-released by ARC Music Productions International Ltd. under the title *Mali* in 2002 (features "Dounuya")
	2002	Angélique Kidjo releases *Black Ivory Soul,* featuring "Iwoya" (with Dave Matthews) and "Okan Bale"

roots of human existence along the way. The path must meet the river to find its earthly purpose, yet the river must be met *by* the path to fulfill its own divine purpose, which is of utmost importance to the Akan. Both the river and the path are essential, indivisible. Human life relies upon their union and reciprocity.

The telling of this Akan proverb can be performed in different ways. It may be recited in spoken words or it may be recited in **drum speech.** This is because the language in which it is composed, a dialect of Twi, is a **tonal language.** The meaning of a word in a tonal language like Twi is determined not just by the actual sounds of its syllables, but also by the specific patterns of pitch, rhythm, and timbral inflection with which it is articulated. The exact "same" word can thus mean completely different things if the pitch, rhythm, and timbre with which it is uttered are altered. For example, *akonta,* if pronounced "a-kon-TA" (with the highest pitch and an accent on the last syllable) is understood to mean brother-in-law, while "a-KON-ta" (accent and highest pitch on the middle syllable) translates as mathematics. By replicating the pitch, rhythm, and timbre patterns of verbal speech, certain Akan drums such as the **atumpan** are literally capable of speaking themselves.

An example of drum speech on the atumpan is featured in **CD ex. #3-12.** This is an excerpt from a recording of the Akan proverb of the river and the path. Each text phrase is recited verbally and then reiterated in drum language. Listen to the example now, noting how the flow of pitches, rhythms, and timbres of each spoken part (the call) is replicated in the drum-speech part on the atumpan that follows it (the response). The portion of the proverb heard in the first 25 seconds of the example is included below in Twi and also in an English translation. Additional, shorter passages of call-and-response interaction between the voice and atumpan are heard in the final 30 seconds of the excerpt, where it is actually somewhat easier to hear that the voice and drum are "saying" the same words.

Atumpan drums (right) accompanying a dance performance by an Akan woman.

Twi (Chwee)

atumpan (AH-toom-pahn)

Twi text	English translation
Asuo twa okwan,	The river crosses the path,
okwan twa asuo,	the path crosses the river,
opani ne hwan?	who is elder?
Asuo twa okwan,	The river crosses the path,
okwan twa asuo,	the path crosses the river,
opani ne hwan?	who is elder?
Yeboo kwan no katoo asuo no,	The path was cut to meet the river,
Asuo no firi tete,	the river is of old,
Asuo no firi Odomankoma a oboo adee.	the river comes from "Odomankoma" the Creator.

Transcription and translation: Daniel Agyei Dwarko (in Vetter 1996:18–19).

The river and the path are literal parts of the Akan world. They are also metaphors with multiple levels of meaning. Just as the path must meet the river, the Akan must cut their own paths toward communion with the sources of their creation: divine, ancestral, familial, and natural. They also must aim to follow their individual pathways toward intersection with one another and mutual support. The ideal of mutual interdependence is of key importance for Akan people, as for people everywhere. We all have our individual paths and there is often the temptation to go it alone. Yet it is together, collectively, as members of communities

The kora, played by the late kora master Jali Mori Suso.

human and beyond, that we usually find ourselves best equipped to meet our needs, solve our problems, and pay homage to those to whom it is due. This Akan proverb encodes such messages and ideals in its literal and metaphorical depiction of the path and the river.

Much music in West Africa encodes similar ideals. Metaphorically, the artistry of West African music explored in this chapter *is* the meeting of the path and the river. Like the river, it flows to the pulse of many different rhythms, timbres, and layers that, on first impression, may suggest little sense of integrated coherence (that is, to the non-African listener). But, ultimately, the multidimensional musical flow reveals itself as an integrated collective of individual "voices" that are unified by shared values and a communal sense of purpose.

This chapter explores the musical element of polyphony, music of "many sounds," of "many parts." It might be more accurate, however, to describe this as a chapter about **polyvocality,** many *voices.* The music we will explore is not generally conceived of by its makers as existing solely for its own sake. Rather, it is a form of *conversation,* in which people alternately speak in turn and all at once. The ability of many voices to speak and be heard simultaneously, and in the process to express a unified diversity of views and perspectives, is valued in many modes of social and conversational interaction in West Africa. It resonates strongly in the social interaction of music making. Exploring how this works is our main musicultural focus.

The chapter begins by briefly situating West African musics within broader musical, cultural, and geographical contexts of the continent of Africa and beyond. We then explore polyvocality in a second Akan drumming-based piece. After that, the focus turns to three different pieces of music that all feature a particular instrument, the **kora.** This is a remarkable plucked chordophone of the **Mande** peoples of western Africa with a history dating back centuries. Today, the ancient legacy of the kora is preserved in the art of **jeliya,** the musical repertoire of the hereditary "praise singer," or **griot,** families among the Mande. The kora also has taken on a new life as a prominent musical instrument in a wide range of both African and international popular, intercultural jazz, and world beat music circles.

Mande (MAHN-day)

jeliya (jay-lee-uh)

griot (GREE-oh)

■ ■ ■

African Musics in Context

"Africa," writes Peter Fletcher, "gave birth to the first human beings and—we may assume—to the first human song" (Fletcher 2001:145). Indeed, Africa retains some of the world's oldest extant musical traditions. The origins of some of these may date back to tens of thousands of years ago.

But music in Africa, in many respects, is the heartbeat of modern, global musical expression as well. The rhythms and textures of just about every major international popular music phenomenon of the past century—from mambo to hip-hop and rock to reggae—have their roots in African soil, and African musicians continue to reshape and redefine contemporary world music expression right up to the present day. These include Angélique Kidjo and Toumani Diabate, whose music we will explore, as well as a host of other musical artists of global influence and international renown (some living, some now deceased): Salif Keita, Fela Anikulapo Kuti, Miriam Makeba, Thomas Mapfumo, Hugh Masekela, Youssou N'Dour, King Sunny Adé, and Papa Wemba, to name but a few. Probably the most famous African group of all internationally—and one of the most ubiquitous and influential music groups of any kind during the course of the past quarter century—is Ladysmith Black Mambazo (see "Insights and Perspectives" box, p. 195).

Toumani Diabate (Too-MAH-nee Jah-BAH-tay)

Youssou N'Dour (Yoo-soo En-DOOR)

N'Faly Kouyate (En-FAH-lee Koo-YAH-tay)

Isicathamiya and Ladysmith Black Mambazo

Under the direction of its longtime leader Joseph Shabalala, the brilliant South African vocal group Lady-smith Black Mambazo has been the dominant force in **isicathamiya** (ee-see-kah-tah-MEE-yah) music for decades. Isicathamiya is an a cappella (unaccompanied vocal) genre that emerged out of a synthesis of traditional music of Zulu peoples in southern Africa and Christian hymnody introduced by European missionaries; it was initially developed mainly by black South African migrant laborers who worked under oppressive conditions as miners. During the 20th century, isicathamiya became an important symbol and medium of cultural expression for Zulus and other black South Africans and formed the basis of a vibrant and exciting music competition tradition. The competitions showcased representative groups from different townships going head to head in musical battles that also highlighted intricate choreography and impressive showmanship.

Ladysmith Black Mambazo was already a top-tier championship isicathamiya group in South Africa when Shabalala and other group members first met the famous American musician Paul Simon in a Johannesburg recording studio during the 1980s. Simon featured the group, along with other iconic figures in the modern history of South African music such as Miriam Makeba and Hugh Masekela, on his 1986 album *Graceland*. They were also featured in international concerts and tours produced in association with the album's release (see photo, p. 196), including a historic concert in Zimbabwe that became the basis of a documentary film. The *Graceland* project had an extraordinary impact on many levels, thrusting South African music into the international spotlight while generating an unprecedented level of global public and media-based interest in "world music" more broadly. It also brought a great deal of attention, via international popular culture and the media, to the plight of black South Africans during the late apartheid era. South Africa's legalized system of racial segregation and oppression under apartheid had long been the subject of condemnation and official sanctions from the international community (e.g., the United Nations), but *Graceland* helped to galvanize a growing tide of public outrage and social activism against apartheid in mainstream popular culture by giving voice through the arts to people "speaking out" against it in both direct and indirect ways. The apartheid system finally collapsed in 1994, at which time a new, black majority government under Nelson Mandela was formed; Ladysmith Black Mambazo performed at Mandela's presidential inauguration.

The success of *Graceland* also helped to revive and redirect the career of Paul Simon and create new markets and professional opportunities for Ladysmith Black Mambazo and other South African musicians and groups. The year following *Graceland*'s release, 1987, witnessed the arrival of Ladysmith's own first U.S. release. The album, *Shaka Zulu,* which was produced by Paul Simon, won a Grammy Award and garnered widespread commercial success and critical acclaim. A string of popular and award-winning recordings and other projects have ensued in the intervening decades, and the group has been featured on everything from special performances for Queen Elizabeth II of England and Pope John Paul II, to the soundtrack of the *The Lion King Part II,* to Life Savers candy commercials, to a Michael Jackson music video ("Moonwalker") and an Academy Award–nominated documentary film (*On Tip Toe: Giant Steps to Freedom,* 2001).

The song "Unomathemba," from *Shaka Zulu,* provides a fine example of Ladysmith Black Mambazo's distinctive isicathamiya style. It is included as **CD ex. #3-13** of your CD set. As you listen, take note of the characteristic call-and-response texture (with Joseph Shabalala on the lead part), the intermittent clicking sounds in the voice parts that are inherent to the Zulu language in which the song is sung, the beautifully wrought harmonizations of the melody, and the music's compelling rhythms. The song is about an orphan child whose sadness leads to tears.

Ladysmith Black Mambazo (left, front) performing with Paul Simon during the *Graceland* tour in the late 1980s. Miriam Makeba and Joseph Shabalala are standing to the left of Simon (in white shirt) at the center of the stage. The great South African trumpet player Hugh Masekela is seen raising his fist in a gesture of power and solidarity at the back of the photo on the left side.

The African continent, sub-Saharan Africa, and the African diaspora

Africa is an enormous continent. Its landmass is second in size only to that of Asia, covering more than 11 million square miles and accounting for more than 20 percent of the earth's land surface. About one-sixth of the world's population resides in Africa itself, and millions of people of African descent reside throughout the world in the **African diaspora**, with especially large population concentrations in the United States, Brazil, the Caribbean (Cuba, Haiti, Jamaica, Trinidad and Tobago), and major European metropolises such as London and Paris.

The northern portion of the continent of Africa covers the vast Sahara Desert and is bordered along its northern coast by the Mediterranean Sea. This region includes Egypt, Libya, Tunisia, Algeria, Morocco, and other North African nations. Islam is the dominant religion of North Africa and Arab culture is pervasive throughout the region (see Chapter 12).

The majority portion of the African continent is located south of the Sahara and is known as sub-Saharan Africa. Selected musicultural traditions originating in western regions of sub-Saharan Africa, that is, in West Africa, form the main subject matter of this chapter. West African musical traditions are rich and varied in and of themselves and have had a profound impact on the course of musical developments worldwide over the past several centuries. This was the region of the continent from which most African slaves were brought to the Americas. In the Americas, African- and European-derived musics blended to form the foundations of many new types and styles of music. It is to this development that we trace the origins of ragtime, blues, jazz, rhythm-and-blues, soul, rock-and-roll, rap, hip-hop, salsa, Cuban *son,* Puerto Rican bomba, Trinidadian steel band, Jamaican reggae, Brazilian samba, and scores of other musical genres and subgenres too numerous to mention (several of the traditions just listed are covered in Chapter 11). In turn, elements of these and many other musics of the African diaspora have been reabsorbed back into newer styles of music in Africa, and from there have gone on to influence other international styles. In short, there is a continuous feedback loop between Mother Africa, the African diaspora, and global music making on a worldwide scale.

Music, culture, and history in sub-Saharan Africa

Sub-Saharan Africa comprises extraordinary ethnic, cultural, and musical diversity. For much of its history, large portions of the region were ruled by powerful kingdoms. The Nok, Benin, Mande, Ghana, Songhay, Dahomey, and Buganda empires that thrived centuries ago were

Benin
  (Bay-NEEN)

Songhay
  (Song-HIGH)

Dahomey
  **(Duh-HO-mee
  [or Dah-oh-MAY])**

Buganda
  (Boo-GAHN-dah)

among the world's most powerful during their respective eras. From the 15th century onward, however, European (and, later, U.S.) intervention and domination led to the dismantling of reigning African imperial powers, widespread destruction and brutality, and a transformation of the African political and cultural map. The most visible manifestations of this foreign encroachment were the slave trade of the 17th–19th centuries and the colonization of the majority of sub-Saharan Africa that occurred between the 19th century and well into the middle decades of the 20th century (and in South Africa and certain other nations, long after that as well). Beyond transforming Africa itself, colonization and the slave trade combined with other sociopolitical forces to initiate the African diaspora, which witnessed the forced or voluntary migration of millions of people from the African continent to other parts of the world, especially the Americas and certain parts of western Europe.

Since the end of World War II, the African continent has come to encompass many postcolonial, independent African nations. While great triumphs have been achieved in terms of sovereignty and civil rights in many modern African societies, struggles for freedom from colonial rule and for national independence were long, fierce, and costly on many levels. Political stability and economic prosperity have remained elusive for many African nations and peoples. Warfare, continued foreign exploitation of African lands and resources, and public health crises of catastrophic proportions such as the African AIDS pandemic have brought major challenges.

In African nationalist movements and African responses to modern sociopolitical challenges and opportunities alike, the revival, revitalization, and modernization of traditional forms of African music, dance, and ceremonial practice have figured prominently. So too has the development of new forms and styles of music aimed at responding to, reflecting, and affecting contemporary situations and circumstances. These new musical forms and styles frequently build from a combination of indigenous African and international elements, the latter most prominently influenced by U.S., Caribbean, and South American musics that evolved within the African diaspora (e.g., American popular musics and jazz, Cuban rumba and Brazilian samba—see Chapter 11). "Ingculaza (AIDS)" (**CD ex. #2-10**), a song by the Zimbabwean musician Dumisani "Ramadu" Moyo that was discussed in Chapter 6 (pp. 80–81), is a good example. It incorporates traditional African instruments (e.g., hand drums) and musical elements (e.g., singing style) into a setting that otherwise relies heavily on the instrumental and stylistic resources of African American popular music idioms such as soul and rhythm-and-blues. This syncretic mixture of elements serves as the musical backdrop for Ramadu to address, in his native language, Ndebele, the AIDS crisis in Africa.

**Ndebele
(IN-duh-bel-ee)**

Religion is a pervasive force in life throughout sub-Saharan Africa. Islam and Christianity are widespread, though their practice often represents a syncretism with indigenous forms of African religion that predated their arrival. There are hundreds, if not thousands, of religions practiced in sub-Saharan Africa. The diversity of religious belief and practice is immense. Paying homage and due respect—to deities, venerated ancestors, community leaders and elders, and the creative and sustaining forces of nature—is a major priority of religious practice and social life generally. Often this takes the form of communal rituals involving music and the active participation of all in attendance (whether through singing, playing instruments, dancing, clapping, or some other mode of participation). The collective expression of the community as a whole, diverse in its individual components, polyvocal in its articulation, unified in its totality, is highly valued in the act of paying homage. The spiritual/social values of paying homage and collective expression are strongly reflected in all of the music we will examine.

Drumming

The first thing that comes to mind for many non-Africans when they think about music in Africa is drumming, despite the fact that most African musics are not drumming-based and much of the music includes no drumming at all. Still, drums and drumming are prominent in the musical traditions of a large number of African cultures. This is certainly the case in West African countries like Ghana, from which the Akan drum proverb of **CD ex. #3-12** hails. **CD ex. #3-14** features another drumming-based example of Akan music. This time, however, rather than just one drummer, there is an ensemble of percussionists. All perform on drums with the exception of one, who plays a steady, repeating rhythmic pattern (ostinato) on an iron bell called a *dawuro*. This is music of the royal Akan drum ensemble known as **Fontomfrom**. It provides an excellent introduction to the concept of a conversation played out in musical tones between multiple participants "speaking" all together at once and in turn. Listen to it now as a prelude to the discussion that follows.

Fontomfrom: An Akan royal drum ensemble

The Akan are one of several West African ethnic groups who reside principally in the nation of Ghana, a former British colony that achieved national independence in 1957. English is the official language of Ghana, but about half of Ghanaians speak some version of the Akan language as well. Twi, the language of the river-and-path drum proverb, is the most widely spoken of these.

The Akan are principally a matrilineal people, which means that they trace their descent lines through the side of the mother. All Akan who can trace their ancestry back through their mother, maternal grandmother, and earlier generations of matriarchs to a common ancestress are considered blood relatives belonging to the same clan. All members of a clan are obligated to participate in rituals devoted to honoring their family ancestors, "a practice that is still central to Akan identity even among those who have converted to Christianity" (Vetter 1996:3).

In former times, Akan chiefs were the political leaders of Akan societies. Today, their leadership role has been overtaken to a significant degree by the Ghanaian government. Nonetheless, most small-scale claims involving land issues or domestic disputes are still mediated by village, district, or regional chiefs (Vetter 1996:12).

Akan chiefs, today as in the past, use certain types of traditional music and music instruments to symbolize their power and stature. Purchasing a royal set of drums such as a Fontomfrom and sponsoring Fontomfrom performances is a long-established chiefly tradition. These drums are played at events at which the chief makes a public appearance: processions, village ceremonies, funerals. The chief may dance at such occasions to the accompaniment of Fontomfrom music, often while brandishing a royal sword. An assistant stands close by throughout

Fontomfrom drums being carried in an Akan royal procession. The chief is also held aloft during the procession.

the dance, ready to catch the chief should he accidentally stumble and begin to fall. It is imperative that he not fall, since if he does, this is taken by the Akan as a sign that he is weak or vulnerable. In some instances, the drums of the Fontomfrom ensemble may be used to make specific utterances in the "speech mode" of drum language, such as *"Nana, bre bre"* ("Chief, walk majestically"). Additionally, call-and-response dialogue, with drummed linguistic content, may occur between the different drums of the ensemble.

The Musical Guided Tour and related Guided Listening Experience which follow collectively provide a musical introduction to the Fontomfrom tradition. Fontomfrom is used here to illustrate the principle of *musical conversation* as a fundamental element of West African music. The transcript below corresponds to the audio Musical Guided Tour. As you listen to this tour at the Online Learning Center (www.mhhe.com/bakan2e), follow along with this transcript.

musical guided tour

Instruments and Basic Rhythmic Patterns in Fontomfrom Music

The instrumentation of the Fontomfrom ensemble consists of the dawuro bell plus three pairs of drums. The first pair of drums is the *from* (frahm), the second is the atumpan, and the third is the *eguankoba* (ay-gwan-koh-bah) (see the photo below). All of the drums are barrel-like in shape and have a single drum head that is attached to the instrument with pegs. They are all played with wooden sticks.

The *from* is a very tall, heavy type of drum with a low pitch [♪]. The lead drummer of the Fontomfrom ensemble plays on the *from*. The atumpan are also large and heavy, though they are not nearly as tall as the *from* and are higher in pitch [♪]. The eguankoba are thin, relatively tall drums (taller than the atumpan, but significantly shorter than the *from*). Their pitch is higher than that of the other drums in the ensemble [♪].

Fontomfrom ensemble, left to right: eguankoba, atumpan, dawuro (difficult to see), and *from*.

Throughout the Fontomfrom piece we listened to earlier, a continually recurring rhythmic pattern was played on the dawuro bell. We will call this rhythm the *time-line*. It sounds like this [♪]. Now, try to clap out the time-line rhythm together with me as I play it on the dawuro. (Use the notation below as a guide.)

1	2	3	4	5	6	7	8	9	10	11	12	(1)
X	•	X	•	X	•	X	X	•	X	•	X	(X)

The time-line rhythm of the dawuro can be felt in several different ways. One way to feel it is as a four-beat pattern with three subdivisions per beat, like this [♪]. When this music accompanies dancing, the steps of the dancers often correspond to this way of feeling the rhythm.

The different drum parts line up with, and "cut across," the time-line rhythm of the dawuro in various ways. This creates a texture of *polyrhythms*: multiple layers of rhythm (in the different drum parts) that imply different beats and meters occurring all at the same time. A great range of different rhythmic variations—some set, some improvised—occur in each of the drum parts. The *from* and the atumpan parts tend to be especially varied in their rhythms. There are, however, certain standard, recurring Fontomfrom rhythmic patterns for each drum part that interlock with one another and with the dawuro time-line. Here, we focus specifically on one such set of rhythmic patterns.

To begin, here is a standard pattern played on the *from* [♪]. Against the dawuro time-line, it sounds like this [♪].

Next, a standard atumpan pattern [♪], which against the bell sounds like this [♪].

Finally, here is one standard eguankoba pattern [♪]. And now here it is again with the dawuro [♪]. Now the second eguankoba drum pattern [♪], and that pattern together with the dawuro [♪].

Now let's build up the full polyrhythmic texture one instrument at a time. Try to clap out the dawuro pattern continuously as the different drumming layers are gradually added in.

Here is the dawuro alone [♪]. Now we add the *from* [♪] and the atumpan [♪], the first eguankoba [♪], and the second eguankoba [♪]. A visual illustration of all the rhythms together is provided in Figure 10.1.

In this tour, we have only scratched the surface of the complexity of an actual Fontomfrom performance. Nonetheless, the tour provides a foundation for understanding and appreciating that complexity, and at least a rudimentary sense of how the principle of multipart musical conversation in West African music works.

Multiple layers of rhythm in Fontomfrom (Musical Guided Tour).

FIGURE 10.1

	1	2	3	4	5	6	7	8	9	10	11	12	(1)
Dawuro	X	•	X	•	X	•	X	X	•	X	•	X	(X)
Eguankoba 1	X	•	X	•	X	•	X	X	•	X	X	X	(X)
Eguankoba 2	•	•	X	•	X	•	•	X	•	•	X	•	(•)
Atumpan	X	X	X	X	X	•	X	X	X	X	X	•	(X)
From	•	X	•	X	X	•	•	X	•	X	X	•	(•)

Fontomfrom (Akan Royal Drum Ensemble Music)

- CD Track #3-14
- Featured performer(s)/group: Eyisam Mbensuon (group), led by Opanyin Yaw Amoah
- Format: Complete track
- Source recording: "Fontomfrom," from *Rhythms of Life, Songs of Wisdom: Akan Music from Ghana, West Africa* (Smithsonian Folkways)

We return now to the Akan performance of Fontomfrom music featured on the CD set. This recording was made in Ghana by the ethnomusicologist Roger Vetter. The first sounds you hear are rhythms played by the lead drummer on the *from* drums, which serve to announce the start of the performance. In his authority and leadership, the *from* drummer may be likened symbolically to the chief in whose honor the music is played.

The dawuro bell joins the *from* almost immediately (at 0:02), playing the same time-line rhythmic pattern illustrated earlier in our Musical Guided Tour. Note that the dawuro player "misses" the first note the first time he plays the pattern (Figure 10.2).

The atumpan and eguankoba drums enter at about 0:08–0:09 as the dawuro continues and the *from* plays one intricate rhythmic variation after another. The other drums introduce rhythmic variations as well here, and the overall effect is dizzying in its polyrhythmic complexity. The various drum parts flow into, around, and over each other like the rushing waters of a swift river, each changing course as needs be to accommodate the curves in the river's path.

At 0:27, there is a breath-length pause in the drumming, after which the drums reenter over the continuing pattern of the dawuro. Now the rhythms become more steady. Specific, recurring patterns (similar to the ones illustrated in the preceding Musical Guided Tour) come to be associated with each of the different drum parts and are layered atop one another and varied in different ways (i.e., layered ostinato texture with variations). These patterns are not mere musical utterances, but linguistic ones as well, "spoken" in the tonal language of the drums in this conversation between members of what is essentially a drum family.

The lead drummer directs the ensemble from the *from* with rhythmic cues and commands that mark transitions and different sections of the performance. The conversational element of the music becomes most clear in those sections where the *from* and the atumpan engage in a back-and-forth series of drummed statements and replies. The first two of these call-and-response dialogues occur at 0:33–0:47 and 1:03–1:32. Try to locate additional passages of *from*-atumpan call-and-response that occur during the remaining portion of the selection as you listen. Also attempt to tap out or clap along with the dawuro bell part (Figure 10.2).

In its totality, this music is far more than a mere drumming piece. It is also a multipart conversation and a musical model of idealized Akan social interaction.

FIGURE 10.2

Dawuro time-line, "Fontomfrom."

1	2	3	4	5	6	7	8	9	10	11	12	(1)
X*	•	X	•	X	•	X	X	•	X	•	X	(X)

*Note: First note of pattern is *not played* first time through cycle.

Unifying Features of Music in West Africa: Musical Africanisms

Despite popular misconceptions to the contrary, there is really no such thing as "African music" per se. Rather, as has already been alluded to, there are many different *African musics*. These musics collectively encompass a great range of musicultural diversity and are all unique and distinct in their own right. They span the gamut from traditional ritual and ceremonial musics of rural, village societies; to national musical forms associated with modern African nations; to regional genres that transcend ethnic or national affiliation; to transnational popular and experimental musics that creatively combine African traditional and myriad non-African musical elements.

Nonetheless, despite all of this diversity, many musics of sub-Saharan Africa, and of West Africa in particular, do exhibit certain key, readily identifiable features and musicultural characteristics that are widely shared (and that are prominent in many African diasporic musics as well). Ethnomusicologists identify these as musical **Africanisms**. We have encountered some of these already; others will come up in connection with selections still to be explored. The following list introduces and defines six of the most salient ones:

- **Complex polyphonic textures.** Textures featuring multiple layers of instruments/voices are common in sub-Saharan Africa. The Fontomfrom music of **CD ex. #3-14** and all of the other music we will explore later in the chapter exemplify this feature.
- **Layered ostinatos with varied repetition.** A standard device for creating polyphony in sub-Saharan African music is the layering of multiple, recurring patterns (ostinatos) one on top of another. This was well illustrated in **CD ex. #3-14,** in which, as is common,

the ostinato patterns tend to recur in varied forms rather than in the same form each time (varied repetition).

- **Conversational element.** Sub-Saharan African musics are frequently conversational in character, whether literally, figuratively, or metaphorically. The musical conversations come in many forms. They may have a call-and-response format, as in the river-and-path drum proverb and certain sections of the Fontomfrom piece; or they may be more in the mode of having many voices all speaking at once—complementing and commenting upon one another's utterances—again, as in some passages of the Fontomfrom piece (e.g., **CD ex. #3-14,** 0:10–0:26, 0:48–1:02). The relationship between music and dance that is so central to much sub-Saharan African performance also is frequently defined by a conversational character, a dialogue of sound and movement. (Resources on African music and dance may be found at the Online Learning Center at www.mhhe.com/bakan2e.)

- **Improvisation.** Improvisation is a hallmark of sub-Saharan African musical expression. Even in relatively "set" compositions that have been passed down through the generations or that are now transmitted via music notation, the incorporation of improvisation—sometimes subtle, sometimes pronounced—is usually expected. The lead drumming part of the *from* in **CD ex. #3-14** features much improvisation. The prominent place of improvisation in sub-Saharan African musics is likewise characteristic of African American musical traditions such as blues, jazz, and hip-hop.

- **Timbral variety.** Musicians in sub-Saharan Africa tend to exploit a wide range of timbral possibilities. Rather than aiming for a "pure" tone, African singers and instrumentalists may manipulate their voices and instruments to produce "buzzing" timbres and other timbral effects. The buzzing sound of the *mbira dzavadzimu* on **CD ex. #2-2** (produced by the rattling of bottle caps that are attached loosely to the instrument's frame—see photo, p. 68) is a good example of this.

- **Distinctive pitch systems and scales.** Certain types of scales, modes, and tuning systems are found widely and in varied forms throughout sub-Saharan Africa. Though these receive relatively little explicit attention in this chapter, it should be understood that they are integral to musical aesthetics and style on multiple levels.

mbira dzavadzimu (em-BEE-rah dzah-vah-DZEE-moo)

Timbila orchestra of the Chopi people, Mozambique.

More than Drumming: African Musical Diversity and the Kora

Thus far, the music we have examined in this chapter has been mainly drumming-based. Drums and drumming have undeniable importance in many African traditions, but it is important for us to remember that *drumming is **not** the basis of most music in Africa,* much of which does not include any drumming at all.

Highly developed forms of polyphonic music that are purely vocal, such as the traditional elephant hunting song of the Central African BaMbuti people heard on **CD ex. #2-4** (see pp. 76–77), are found throughout sub-Saharan Africa. The melodic complexity and sublime beauty of music played on the mbira dzavadzimu (**CD ex. #2-2,** pp. 66–68), an instrument of the Shona people of Zimbabwe that is one of many types of *plucked idiophones* in Africa, is another highlight of non-drumming-based African musical artistry. There are also large xylophone orchestras,

BaMbuti (BEH-em-boo-tee)

Mmen animal horn aerophones (right), Ghana.

Damascus Kafumbe playing endongo, a Ugandan chordophone.

such as the Chopi *timbila* ensembles of Mozambique (see photo, p. 203), as well as a great range of different kinds of aerophones, from animal horn trumpets and flutes to conch shells. Many imported instruments also have become part and parcel of the sound of much music in Africa. The acoustic guitar and the electric guitar are primary among these.

Chordophone-based traditions of many different types abound, from music of the one-stringed *nkokwane* "musical bow" of the Qwii people (Bushmen, San) of southern Africa (**CD ex. #2-8,** pp. 79–80) to *endongo* music of Uganda. Endongo, played by one of the instrument's leading exponents, Damascus Kafumbe, is featured on **CD ex. #3-15** (note the interesting "buzzing" timbre of this instrument). This is a solo performance in which Kafumbe sings and accompanies himself on endongo. The piece is a praise song in honor of an ancient Baganda king of the Buganda monarchy. It is sung in the Luganda language. Kafumbe, who wrote the song, is himself of Baganda royal lineage.

Another important African chordophone is the kora. This instrument of the Mande peoples of West Africa combines guitar- and harp-like features. It is probably the most widely known and appreciated nonpercussion instrument of sub-Saharan Africa on a worldwide scale. It has become an international symbol of "African music" in much the way that the sitar has become an international symbol of "Indian music" (see Chapter 8). Also like the sitar, it is an instrument whose sound has come to international attention both through the global exposure of its traditional musical repertoire and through its prominent use in intercultural popular, experimental, and jazz-based music styles.

**nkokwane
(en-koh-kwah-nay)**

**endongo
(ayn-doan-goh)**

The Kora and Its Musicultural World

The kora is a 21-string *spike harp chordophone* (see the labeled diagram of Figure 10.3). All spike harps have a neck (curved or straight) that pierces the resonator (body) of the instrument to form a post or tailpiece at the lower end. Spike harp chordophones are unique to West Africa.

The kora has a straight neck and a resonator made from a large calabash, or half gourd. A cowhide face stretches over the opening of the calabash and is attached to it with decorative tacks. A soundhole—circular, square, or triangular in shape—is cut into the right side of the resonator and a high *bridge* is mounted onto the face (leading some scholars to also classify the kora as a *bridge harp*—see Knight 2001). Two parallel rows of strings pass through notches that are carved into the bridge. The strings are made of nylon fishing line; prior to the introduction of nylon, they were made from thin strips of twisted antelope hide (King 1972:121). Each string is attached to its own rawhide tuning collar on the neck and passes to one side or the other of the bridge. All 21 strings meet at the bottom of the instrument, where they are attached to an iron ring in the tailpiece (Figure 10.3).

FIGURE 10.3   Kora.

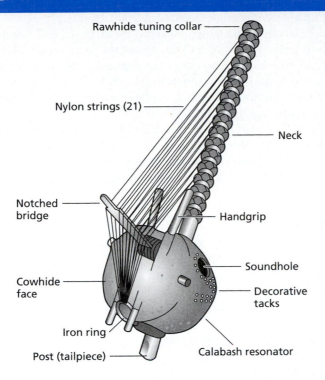

- Rawhide tuning collar
- Nylon strings (21)
- Neck
- Notched bridge
- Handgrip
- Soundhole
- Cowhide face
- Decorative tacks
- Iron ring
- Post (tailpiece)
- Calabash resonator

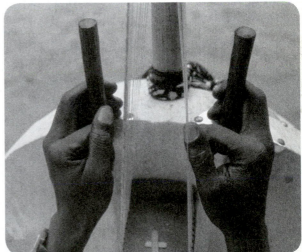

Right- and left-hand positioning on the kora.

When playing the kora, the performer holds the instrument by two handgrips mounted on either side of the neck and plucks the strings with only the thumbs and forefingers (see the photo). The traditional method of playing is from a seated position on the floor, with the tailpiece also in contact with the floor to add resonance to the sound. Playing while standing or moving about or while sitting in a chair are also possible (see photo, p. 212). Today, the use of amplification compensates for the loss of resonance that may occur when certain nontraditional methods of playing are employed.

Mande history and culture

The traditional homelands of the Mande span across the modern nations of Mali, Guinea, Guinea-Bissau, Senegal, and Gambia in western Africa. The great, ancient Mande civilization developed and spread along the three great waterways of this region: the western Niger River, the Senegal River, and the Gambia River (see map, p. 191).

In former times, the present homelands of the Mande were the domain of the powerful Mande empire, otherwise known as the Mali empire. This empire was unified by the legendary warrior and hero Sunjata Keita in the 13th century (sometime between 1225 and 1252). It was centered south of present-day Bamako, a city located on the banks of the Niger River in western Mali. Today, Bamako is the capital of the modern nation of Mali and remains the heartland of Mande culture.

Bamako (BAH-mah-koh)

Tales of the rise of the Mande empire from a small chiefdom ruled by great hunters to an expansive and powerful West African empire under Sunjata form a large body of oral and written Mande literature. Epic accounts of the founding of the empire (The Epic of Sunjata) constitute the texts of much of the traditional repertoire of Mande music. Pieces dedicated to Sunjata and chronicling his legendary achievements—from a child unable to walk, to a warrior in exile, to a great king—are numerous (see Charry 2000:40–43).

Traditional Mande culture and music, including the art of the kora, are preserved and continue to develop both within Mali itself and throughout the former realm of the Mande empire. The Mande ethnic group consists of two large, geographically defined subgroups: the Maninka of Mali and Guinea and the Mandinka of Senegal and Gambia (Senegambia). Collectively, both groups are referred to as the Mandenka, and their myriad of related languages and dialects fall within the Mande language group (i.e., Mande languages).

Colonial history also has left its strong mark on Mande culture, both linguistically and in terms of the modern map of Africa. Senegal, Mali, and Guinea are former French colonies where the official language is French. The tiny nation of Gambia, a former British colony, has English as its official language, while Guinea-Bissau was formerly colonized by Portugal and retains Portuguese as its official language.

The jeli and the art of jeliya

jeli (JAY-lee)

Kouyate (Koo-YAH-tay)

Diabate (Jah-BAH-tay)

Sissoko (See-soh-koh)

Kandia Kouyate (Kahn-jah Koo-YAH-tay)

The principal exponents of the kora and its art have always belonged to a hereditary class of professional Mande musicians known as **jeli** (pl. *jelilu*). The jelilu are the griots (praise singers, praise musicians) of Mande culture. Living members of the principal **hereditary jeli families**—Kouyate, Diabate, Sissoko (also spelled Cissokho)—can trace their lineage back across many generations, in some cases all the way to the original Mande court musicians patronized by King Sunjata himself.

A female jeli may be referred to as a *jelimuso* (pl. *jelimusolu*). While the men both sing and play instruments, the women normally specialize in singing exclusively. In modern times, several jelimusolu have emerged as major stars of both contemporary Mande and African pan-cultural music. The most revered and famous of these is Kandia Kouyate.

The jelilu are the purveyors of the hallowed Mande musical art of jeliya. People born into jeli families have the exclusive right—and are even bound by duty in many cases—to devote their lives to preserving and cultivating jeliya's classic repertoire. This repertoire centers on **praise songs**, which were formerly sung to honor royalty exclusively, but are now often performed in honor of modern politicians or other patrons wealthy enough to retain a jeli's services. An important new network of jeli patronage is the world music industry. Today, it is international music promoters and record producers, rather than Mande kings and princes, who often account for the livelihoods and prestige of the top exponents of jeliya musical artistry. Not surprisingly, many leading Mande kora players of the modern era have taken up residence—full or part time—in Paris, London, and New York, availing themselves of professional opportunities in these major commercial centers of the music industry that they would not have in the West African lands of their birth.

Kandia Kouyate.

Throughout the centuries, jelilu have served important roles not just as musicians, but also as historians, genealogists, and social and political commentators. Traditionally, they alone had the right to sing about certain sensitive issues of Mande social and political life. Moreover, only they have traditionally been permitted to perform on *designated jeli instruments,* including the kora and others. Even today, there is a stigma attached to musicians from non-jeli families who play such instruments.

bala (BAH-lah)

Besides the kora, the **bala** (or *balafon*) (see the photo on p. 207) is one of the principal designated jeli instruments. It is a xylophone constructed of between 17 and 21 hard wooden slats (keys) of different lengths that are suspended over a wooden frame in ascending pitch order.

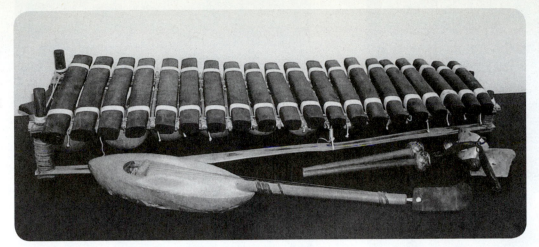

The range of the instrument spans up to three octaves, typically with seven notes per octave. Each slat is laid over its own calabash resonator. The larger (and thus lower-pitched) the slat, the larger the resonator. The player traditionally sits on the ground behind the instrument and strikes the keys with a pair of rubber-ended mallets. Alternatively, he may mount the instrument on a stand and play from a standing position, or even sling the bala around his neck with a long strap and play "marching band" style in processions.

Another important instrument of the jeli is the **koni** (*ngoni*). This is a plucked chordophone akin to the banjo. Some sources suggest, in fact, that the koni is the modern banjo's direct African ancestor. The body, or resonator, of the koni is made from a hollowed-out, canoe-shaped piece of wood covered by a tightly stretched animal hide (see the accompanying photo). The strings run along the neck, which consists of a round, fretless stick that is inserted directly into the instrument's body. The koni is held horizontally across the player's lap and played more or less like a guitar (or banjo). The size, pitch range, and number of strings vary. Some konis have four strings, others have five or even seven; some are quite small and have a high pitch range, others are rather large and function as bass instruments. In the modern era, the guitar has been adopted as a jeli instrument as well. Similarities between the koni and guitar in terms of construction and basic playing techniques likely account for the guitar's ready adaptation into the jeliya context.

koni (koh-nee)

You will soon be introduced to a musical example featuring kora, bala, koni, and guitar played together in an ensemble (along with traditional jeliya singing). First, however, we explore the solo kora and vocal artistry of the jeli Seckou Keita.

Seckou Keita (Say-koo KAY-tah)

Seckou Keita: Kora Master, Jeli, and Radical Royal

While it is generally frowned upon in Mande society for people of non-jeli families to play jeli instruments or otherwise practice the art of jeliya (e.g., as singers), disapproval is especially severe for persons of Mande royal lineage. According to Mande custom, anyone bearing the royal name Keita is forbidden from being a jeli, indeed from performing music professionally in any context. This custom endures to the present, but there have been individuals who have broken rank and defied it.

The best known of these radical royals is the Malian-born singer and world beat superstar Salif Keita (see photo, p. 208). His music blends traditional jeliya stylistic features, a cutting-edge contemporary popular sound, and strong doses of social and political commentary. Salif Keita has done much to bring international attention to Malian traditional music and to major social, cultural, and political issues affecting Mali in particular and Africa more broadly. He is arguably the best-known and most influential living "statesman" of this impoverished and troubled nation. In his homeland, however, Salif Keita is a figure surrounded by controversy, not so much for the boldness of his music, but rather on account of his decision to be a professional musician despite his noble lineage.

Salif Keita.

Seckou Keita.

"I am not shy to sing and play the kora"

Another Keita of royal lineage who broke rank for the sake of pursuing a musical career is the jeli and kora virtuoso Seckou Keita. We actually already heard examples of his music in Chapter 6. His composition "Founé" is included on your CD set as **CD ex. #2-7.** Listen to that selection again now. "Founé" features an ensemble of musicians singing and performing on drums from different regions of western Africa. The drums include the *sabar* of the Wolof people, the *bougarabou* of the Diola, the *djembe* of Guinea, and the Mandinka (Mande) *seourouba*. Traditionally, these drums would not all be played together, as they belong to different musical cultures, but in Keita's arrangement they blend very effectively in the lively, polyrhythmic accompaniment to the song, which is about twin sisters from a jeli family whose clairvoyance enables them to give advice to their elders on spiritual matters.

Though Seckou Keita is an outstanding drummer, he is far better known as a kora player. He was born into a "mixed heritage" family in southern Senegal in 1977. His father was a blue-blood Keita, his mother a descendant of the vaunted Sissoko family of jelilu. Seckou's mixed Keita-Sissoko lineage created ambiguity regarding his musical prospects. Properly, he should have eschewed any serious musical aspirations, at least professionally. But this was not to be his fate. He was raised principally by his mother's family rather than his father's, and this ultimately opened the door for him to pursue his musical passions toward the career path of a jeli while bringing relatively little disgrace to the Keita side of his pedigree.

Seckou's gratitude for being able to follow his musical destiny—his gratitude to his parents, to his grandfather, and to God—is eloquently expressed in "Sabu Nginma" (Good Help), a praise song featured on his international debut album *Baiyo* (2001), which was reissued under the title *Mali* by ARC Music Productions International Ltd. in 2002. In the English translation

"Sabu Nginma"
("Sah-boo
Nee-mah")

of the song's text included in the ARC CD booklet, Seckou recounts the fortuitous twists of fate that allowed him to practice the art of jeliya:

> It is not today that I have decided to be a musician and to sing. It is the luck of being born into the Griot [jeli] tradition through my mum's family, the Cissokho [Sissoko]. Oh mum! Oh dad! I am not shy to sing and play the *kora*.
>
> My mum and my dad like it. They agree that I am lucky to have this gift from God. Love has united my mum and dad despite the traditions [of social class exclusivity in marriage]. These traditions also do not allow a king such as somebody from the Keitas to become a musician, a griot. My grandfather always said to me, "If you leave well, you will arrive well." Everyone has luck from somewhere. (Keita 2002:4)

guided listening experience

"Dounuya," Seckou Keita

- CD Track #**3-16**
- Featured performer(s)/group: Seckou Keita (kora and voice)
- Format: Complete track
- Source recording: *Mali,* by Seckou Keita (ARC Music Productions International Ltd.)

A second track from the same Seckou Keita CD will serve as our musical introduction to the kora and to traditional jeliya musical style. The song is "Dounuya," meaning "The World." It was composed by Keita in an essentially traditional style and features him singing and accompanying himself on the kora.

**"Dounuya"
(Doo-noo-yah)**

In genuine jeliya tradition, "Dounuya" features a text that operates at several levels simultaneously. It is at once a praise song honoring the Creator (God), a critique of the shortcomings of people in their social lives, and a call for elevated virtue and integrity. In the true spirit of jeliya, too, it is a song deeply rooted in the Mande musical and cultural legacy, yet attuned to the contemporary milieu of the jeliya artist's situation. In the text, Seckou does not speak only to the Mande commuity, but to the global human community as a whole:

> I have seen something that scares me. There should not be any problems between ourselves and God. The problems come from the relationships we have with each other. All religions are the same. Anyone can pray, anyone can worship God. But we need to be circumspect in our own relationships with each other. God created the world with perfections and imperfections and gave us the choice between good and bad. Why should we choose the bad? (Keita 2002:5)

Or in other terms, as an Akan traditionalist might say, why should we follow the path that does *not* lead to the river, that takes us anywhere but to the eternal wisdom of the Creator?

In "Dounuya," Seckou's kora playing is the proverbial river that flows across and through the path of the message of his words. Following a brief introductory passage of solo kora playing delivered mainly in short (staccato), syncopated notes, the sound of the kora truly starts to flow like a river beginning at 0:10, where Keita begins playing in a style called **kumbengo**. This is the layered ostinato-based style on the kora that is normally used to accompany singing. Three kumbengo layers—one in the low-pitch register outlining a "bass line," the second occupying the instrument's middle range, and the third in the higher range—emerge and merge within seconds. They become a choir of three kora "voices" weaving in and out of one another.

**kumbengo
(koom-BAYN-go)**

Each layer of the kumbengo texture is at once fully itself yet completely dependent on the others for its identity and sustenance, like the interwoven drum parts in the Fontomfrom music of **CD ex. #3-14.** Here, though, a single musician is weaving together all the different layers on a single instrument and within a musical context largely defined by melodies and chords.

Though the overall kumbengo pattern recurs cyclically about every two to three seconds (0:10–0:13, 0:14–0:16, 0:17–0:19, 0:20–0:23), each recurrence is a variation on the others. No two statements of the pattern are precisely the same. They all differ in subtle nuances of rhythm, melody, ornamentation, and timbre.

birimintingo (beer-uh-men-TEEN-go)

Following the fourth statement of the pattern, Keita partially breaks from the kumbengo style momentarily to present an improvised melodic flourish called a **birimintingo** at 0:24. This anticipates the introduction of Keita's singing voice into the multipart musical conversation at 0:30. The continuing flow of the kumbengo part, now in an accompanying role, fills in the spaces between sung phrases. A return of the earlier birimintingo flourish occurs at 1:03, setting up the second sung verse of the song at 1:09. Then, a series of hammerlike, high-register kora chords (1:28–1:37) adds yet another musical layer as the singing and the kumbengo accompaniment continue. These chords have an almost disruptive effect on the smooth flow of the performance established up to that point. They also heighten its sense of musical drama, highlighting the key line of text meaning, "Why should we choose the bad [when the good is there for us to choose]?" When this rhetorical question comes back as a refrain near the end of the performance (beginning at 2:57), the hammerlike chords return as well.

From 1:41–2:14, following the completion of the second verse, the singing drops out to make way for a solo kora feature section in which the kumbengo pattern continues but is enhanced by birimintingo (melodic improvisation) passages and some clever call-and-response dialogue between the middle- and upper-range voices of the kora (starting at 2:02). This solo kora texture gives way at 2:15 to the return of Keita's singing voice, but the singing is now more improvisatory, extemporaneous, generally higher in pitch range, and sometimes even speechlike in character (e.g., at 2:47). This different style of vocalization is called **sataro**. The sataro section segues to the aforementioned refrain ("Why should we choose the bad?") at 2:57, replete with the hammerlike chords. The performance is rounded out by a return to the introductory solo kora material of the opening.

"Dounuya" is a song with a message. It tells us that we must improve our relationships with one another if we are to follow the path toward the good rather than the bad, the path toward rather than away from the divine source of creation. This message is stated explicitly in the text, but it is no less apparent on a symbolic, musical level in the integrated polyvocality of interaction between the voice of Seckou Keita and the multiple "voices" of his kora.

guided listening quick summary

"Dounuya," by Seckou Keita (CD ex. #3-16)

0:00–0:09

- Solo kora introduction featuring short (staccato) notes and syncopated rhythms.

0:10–0:23

- Solo kora continues, but now the playing style is kumbengo.
- Flowing, layered ostinato texture and interwoven kora lines in the low, middle, and high registers of the instrument.
- Ostinato patterns are varied each time they recur.

0:24–0:29

- Keita partially breaks from the kumbengo style momentarily at 0:24 to play a virtuosic, birimintingo flourish; this anticipates the arrival of the sung verse to follow.

0:30–1:08

- First verse of "Dounuya" song, sung by Keita as his kora playing now becomes the accompaniment; section concludes with a second birimintingo passage at 1:03.

1:09–1:40

- Second sung verse of "Dounuya" song (new text, varied melody).

- At 1:28, hammerlike chords in the kora's high register heighten the musical drama when the important line "Why should we choose the bad [when the good is there for us to choose]?" is sung.

1:41–2:14

- This section once again features the kora alone (solo); no singing.

- Texture highlights occasional birimintingo passages over continuing kumbengo accompaniment.

- Interesting call-and-response dialogue between middle- and upper-range kora "voices" beginning at 2:02.

2:15–2:56

- Keita now returns as vocalist, but performing in sataro style rather than singing as he did before.

2:57–end

- Final vocal refrain on the line "Why should we choose the bad?" once again enhanced by hammerlike chords in the upper register of the kora.

A Meeting of Musical Worlds: "Atlanta Kaira"

From the traditional-style, solo jeliya performance of "Dounuya," we now move to a more neo-traditional, ensemble jeliya performance entitled "Atlanta Kaira" (**CD ex. #3-17**). "Atlanta Kaira" features an ensemble of two singers (one male, one female), two koras, a bala, a koni, and an acoustic guitar. All but the guitarist are esteemed Mande musicians in the jeli tradition. Three of the most revered jeli families—Sissoko, Diabate, and Kouyate—are represented in the all-star lineup. The Kouyate clan is represented by koni maestro Bassekou Kouyate (playing a large, low-pitched version of the instrument), the Sissokos by the young kora star Ballake Sissoko, and the Diabates by the male vocalist Kassemady Diabate, the bala player Lasana Diabate, and the kora virtuoso Toumani Diabate. The female singer is Ramatou Diakite, who comes from another important Mande musical family.

The guitarist is the maverick American blues musician and intercultural music pioneer Taj Mahal. Mahal first discovered the kora in the 1970s and became immediately enamored of the instrument. He was initially struck by parallels he observed between kora playing techniques introduced to him by the Gambian jeli Alhaji Bai Konte (one of the first kora players to tour North America) and the down-home finger-picking guitar styles he had learned from Blind Jesse Fuller and other of his old-style blues mentors. At a deeper level, what Mahal heard in the kora artistry of Konte was something truly profound and personal, something that "was at the heart of his own music—perhaps even his own identity—the African roots of the blues" (Mahal 2004).

Mahal's kora epiphany and search for his musical roots eventually led him to Mali and a host of Malian musicians including guitarist Ali Farka Toure and kora player Toumani Diabate. In 1999, more than two decades after his initial encounter with the kora, he teamed up with Toumani to produce the album *Kulanjan*. The album included "Atlanta Kaira" and a number of other selections that paired Mahal with Toumani's all-star band of Mande jeli masters. For Mahal, *Kulanjan* represented the culmination of a long and fascinating musical roots odyssey, "bringing the blues and Malian music back together again, in one huge circle of 500 years" (Mahal, quoted in Duran 2000:5). For Toumani, it was perhaps less a search for roots than a logical extension of an ever-expanding and ever more complex web of Mande traditionalism and global modernity. The following passage from Eric Charry's excellent book

**"Kaira"
("Kai" rhymes
with "pie")**

**Bassekou Kouyate
(Bah-say-koo
Koo-YAH-tay)**

**Ballake Sissoko
(Bah-lah-kay
See-soh-koh)**

**Kassemady Diabate
(Kah-say-mah-dee
Jah-BAH-tay)**

**Lasana Diabate
(Lah-sah-nah
Jah-BAH-tay)**

**Ramatou Diakite
(Rah-mah-too
Jah-KEE-tay)**

**Alhaji Bai Konte
(Ahl-hah-jee Bie
Kohn-tay ["Bai"
rhymes with "pie"])**

**Ali Farka Toure
(Ah-lee Fahr-kah
TOO-ray)**

***Kulanjan*
(Koo-lahn-JAHN)**

Toumani Diabate.

Mande Music offers a revealing glimpse into Toumani's complex musicultural world (circa the 1990s):

> In the home given to his father by the first president of Mali, Toumani Diabate lives in a world of fax machines, cell phones, recording sessions, local nightclubs, international tours, electrified jelimuso-led ensembles performing at traditional celebrations, extended family and the extended obligations therein, high infant mortality, young kora apprentices, respect for the jelis of his father's generation, and the proud legacy of the Diabate lineage of jelis. Like many of his contemporaries, he uses modern technological tools to honor traditional commitments. Traditional musics are likewise put in modern contexts in his ensembles, mixing diverse instruments with new arrangements. Traditional and modern worldviews complement each other, meld together, and also remain distinct. . . . (Charry 2000:27)

Kulanjan manifests this complementary traditional/modern musical identity. The album was recorded not in Mali, but rather in Athens, Georgia (in the same studio where the rock band REM made many of their important albums). Some of the pieces are heavily oriented toward the blues or toward a relatively equal-parts syncretism of blues and jeliya elements. Others, most notably "Atlanta Kaira," are decisively slanted toward the pure jeliya side of the syncretic equation. "Atlanta Kaira" is less an example of cross-cultural fusion than it is a contemporary reinterpretation of the piece "Kaira" (Arabic for "peace"), a now-classic composition of the jeliya repertoire that is usually attributed to Toumani's late father, Sidiki Diabate, and is said to date from the 1940s, possibly earlier. Sidiki was known during his lifetime as the King of the Kora. He was, according to Charry, ". . . one of the greatest musical artists of his generation, whose death was cause for national mourning" in his adopted homeland of Mali (Charry 2000:27). (Sidiki was born in Gambia but moved to and settled in Mali early in life.) Beyond his renown in West Africa, Sidiki also played a seminal role in bringing the kora to broad international attention. His classic 1971 duet album with fellow kora master Djelimadi Sissoko, *Ancient Strings,* was the first internationally distributed recording to feature the instrument; the album achieved considerable commercial success.

Although Sidiki is often credited as the composer of "Kaira," he himself claimed merely to have "developed" it (Charry 2000:156). In any case, it is with him that the piece is mainly identified historically. Beginning in the 1940s, "Kaira" came to be closely associated with the Malian struggle for independence from French colonial rule. Its melody became well known and popular among the Malian people, inspiring many different texts reflective of different aspects of the nationalist struggle (Charry 2000:156). During this period, Sidiki traveled widely throughout Mali, performing "Kaira" and other jeliya pieces to galvanize the Malian nationalism movement. In true jeli fashion, he attuned the ancient jeliya repertoire to the needs, demands, and issues of his own time. In this way, he formed a link between the grandeur of the Mande's proud historical legacy and a vision of Mali's future as a modern Mande nation.

Sidiki's charisma and activism endeared him to the Malian people, but not to the French colonial authorities. For his efforts, he was eventually arrested by the French and imprisoned. But all this did was energize the independence movement, which then came to be known as the "Kaira Movement." When Mali achieved its independence in 1960, Sidiki was honored as a national hero. He counted among his close friends the nation's first president and became a cultural ambassador for the Malian nation and its great musical heritage within Mali, more broadly in Africa, and eventually throughout the world. "Kaira" became an emblem of himself, his musical legacy, and the country of Mali.

In the hands of his son Toumani Diabate, one of the greatest kora artists of his own generation, the development and cultivation of "Kaira" has continued. Toumani has recorded various versions of the piece, including one that served as the title track of his debut international album (*Kaira*). "Atlanta Kaira" adds to Toumani's recorded "Kaira" legacy, paying tribute to his father not just in music but also in words. The sataro portions of the piece, sung by Kassemady Diabate, pay homage to Sidiki: his signature song has been turned into a praise song in *his* honor.

In the many polyphonic layers that emerge in the performance—the singing, the kora playing, the parts of the bala and koni, Taj Mahal's guitar playing—the power of collective expression so characteristic of West African music becomes poignantly manifest. In its unified collage of sound, "Atlanta Kaira" is able to tell its many stories all at once. It is a tribute to Sidiki Diabate, an exemplar of traditional jeliya ensemble art, a chapter in Taj Mahal's roots musical odyssey, and a reflection of the contemporary "international jeli" culture to which Toumani Diabate belongs. All of these "voices" are allowed to speak, all at once, and none gets in the way of the expression of the other. It is the great power of music such as this to allow for such multiplicity and simultaneity of expression.

guided listening experience

"Atlanta Kaira," Toumani Diabate, Taj Mahal, and Ensemble

- CD Track **#3-17**
- Featured performer(s)/group: Toumani Diabate and Ballake Sissoko (kora), Taj Mahal (guitar), Kassemady Diabate and Ramatou Diakite (vocals), Bassekou Kouyate (koni), Lasana Diabate (bala)
- Format: Complete track
- Source recording: *Kulanjan,* by Taj Mahal and Toumani Diabate (Hannibal Records/Rykodisc)

"Atlanta Kaira" is played in a mode called **sauta**, which is one of the four principal modes in Mande music. Its scale sounds much like a major scale starting on the pitch F, but with a raised fourth degree, that is, F G A B C D E (F). This is only a rough approximation, however, since there are microtonal subtleties in sauta tuning that do not correspond to standard Western pitch intervals.

sauta (sow-tah)

Following a solo kora introduction played in free rhythm by Toumani Diabate, all of the other instrumentalists enter at 0:42, creating a texture of layered ostinatos with varied repetition that is embellished by full-fledged improvisation in certain parts. Each ostinato cycle is about three seconds long (0:42–0:45, 0:45–0:48, etc.), with eight beats per cycle. The vocalists enter at 0:53.

The piece shares many common features with Seckou Keita's "Dounuya" and illustrates many of the same musical Africanisms:

- Both pieces have complex polyphonic textures and feature layered ostinatos, varied repetition, and improvisation.
- Both include performance in the kumbengo, birimintingo, and sataro styles that are characteristic of jeliya music.
- Both are intensely "conversational" on multiple levels, with the various "voices" sometimes speaking all together at once and other times engaging in call-and-response dialogue.
- Both provide rich examples of timbral variety, especially through manipulation of the large range of timbres available on the kora.

The overall formal design of "Atlanta Kaira" consists of seven main parts:

1. *Solo Kora Introduction* (0:00–0:41). The introduction is played by Toumani Diabate, who establishes the sauta mode of the piece and demonstrates the full, virtuosic range of the instrument.

2. *Ensemble Introduction* (0:42–0:52). The bala, koni, guitar, and second kora join in and an eight-beat cycle of layered ostinatos with variations is established. The playing here is basically in the kumbengo, or accompaniment, style, though the bala is played by Lasana Diabate in the more soloistic, improvisational style of birimintingo. There are occasional flourishes of birimintingo in some of the other instrumental parts as well.

3. *"Kaira" Song* (0:53–1:28). The two vocalists (male, female) enter together at 0:53, singing the main melody and text of the "Kaira" song in a style that features rich and precisely coordinated ornamentation. This highly ornamented singing style is characteristic of jeliya. The instruments accompany with their varied kumbengo ostinatos.

4. *First Sataro Section* (1:29–2:50). At this point, the male vocalist, Kassemady Diabate, is featured performing in sataro style. The delivery becomes quite dramatic and almost speech-like, even oratorical, in character as Kassemady pays homage to the great Sidiki Diabate. There is also a conversational element, as Toumani Diabate "answers" Kassemady's various pronouncements with birimintingo kora passages interspersed between the vocal lines.

5. *Improvised Koni Solo* (2:51–3:32). The purely instrumental texture of the introduction (no singing) returns as the koni player, Bassekou Kouyate, who thus far has been essentially laying down the "bass line" of the piece, now moves to the forefront with an improvised koni solo. Some parts of the solo sound almost blues-like. As the section progresses, other instruments—kora, bala—break away from their kumbengo patterns at times to play in birimintingo style as well. The result is a texture of what might be described as collective improvisation, akin to similar kinds of textures that one hears in traditional jazz (e.g., Louis Armstrong) and other African American genres.

6. *Second Sataro Section* (3:33–4:21). Similar to the first sataro section, and again featuring the male vocalist, Kassemady Diabate.

7. *"Kaira" Song, Second Statement* (4:22–end). Reprise of the main song, performed as before to round out the performance.

---

guided listening quick summary

"Atlanta Kaira," Toumani Diabate, Taj Mahal, and Ensemble (CD ex. #3-17)

SOLO KORA INTRODUCTION (TOUMANI DIABATE)

0:00–0:41

- Played in the sauta mode.
- Good illustration of the musical range of the instrument and of Toumani Diabate's virtuosity.

ENSEMBLE INTRODUCTION TO "KAIRA" SONG

0:42–0:52

- Instrumentation: two koras, bala, koni, and guitar.
- Kumbengo texture with occasional birimintingo passages played on different instruments (bala plays birimintingo throughout this introduction).

"KAIRA" SONG

0:53–1:28

- The two singers, Kassemady Diabate (man) and Ramatou Diakite (woman) enter the texture and sing "Kaira" song.
- Melody highly ornamented and ornaments sung precisely together.
- Kumbengo accompaniment provided by instrumental ensemble.

FIRST SATARO SECTION

1:29–2:50

- Text pays homage to Sidiki Diabate.
- Dramatic, almost speechlike vocal delivery by Kassemady Diabate.
- Musical dialogue between vocal part (Kassemady) and birimintingo passages on kora (Toumani).

IMPROVISED KONI SOLO

2:51–3:32

- No singing.
- Koni player breaks away from "bass line" kumbengo to play an improvised solo.
- Passages where other instruments (kora, bala) break from their kumbengo patterns as well, creating a collective improvisation texture.

SECOND SATARO SECTION

3:33–4:21

- Kassemady's vocals again featured here.
- Similar to earlier sataro section.

"KAIRA" SONG, SECOND STATEMENT

4:22–end

- Sung as before by Kassemady and Ramatou with instrumental ensemble accompaniment.

Angélique Kidjo: West African Collective Expression in a Global Musical World

"Atlanta Kaira" offered us another example of the polyvocal, conversational approach to music that is so pervasive in West Africa. Its many "voices" were heard speaking all at once and in turn, all with their own distinctive things to say, all interacting with one another and supporting each other, all ultimately unified within the larger, collective expression of the greater whole. And what they were "saying," both in words and musical sounds, brought us back to another central theme of this chapter: the importance of paying one's respects to the sources of creation and wisdom—whether human or divine; parents, community elders, or master musicians; chiefs, kings, or sacred rivers.

The final work we explore in this chapter, Angélique Kidjo's "Okan Bale," extends these lines of polyvocality and homage into the realm of a style of mainstream international popular music that retains strong ties to its West African musical and cultural roots. In "Atlanta Kaira," the guitar artistry of Taj Mahal met the musical art of jeliya on its home turf and found a place of belonging there. In "Okan Bale," the kora artistry of Mamadou Diabate similarly finds its place of belonging in the cosmopolitan, pan-African, globally conscious musical world of Angélique Kidjo.

**"Okan Bale"
("Oh-kahn
BAH-lay")**

The diva from Benin

This final portion of our musical journey through West Africa takes us first to the nation of Benin, where Angélique Kidjo was born and raised. Benin is a tiny country with a population of about six million people. It is sandwiched between Ghana and Togo to the west and Nigeria to the east (see map, p. 191). Centuries ago, the Beninese city of Abomey was the capital of the great West African kingdom of Dahomey. The Dahomey empire achieved tremendous power during its precolonial era reign, rivaling the Mande empire in this regard. The 17th-century Dahomey rulers became heavily involved in supplying slaves to European slave traders. Many Dahomeans were shipped to the Americas as slaves, the majority to Brazil. The musical legacy of the Dahomey, whether directly or indirectly manifested, lives on in Brazil and throughout many other areas of the African diaspora.

With the end of the slave trade and the waning of the Dahomey empire in the 19th century, present-day Benin came under French colonial rule. An independent nation, Dahomey, was formed in 1960 following the ousting of the French. Dahomey was renamed Benin in 1975. During the 1970s and 1980s, it was governed as a socialist state. The early 1990s saw a shift to a multiparty democractic system of governance.

Yoruba (YOR-oo-buh)

The official language of Benin is French, but the traditional languages of the country's major ethnic groups, such as the Yoruba and the **Fon**, are widely spoken as well. Angélique Kidjo, a Fon, sings the majority of her songs in the Fon language. Despite the cosmopolitan internationalism of her music, this linguistic preference ties her and her artistry closely to her Fon heritage.

According to *The Rough Guide* to world music, Angélique Kidjo, the "diva from Benin," has "done more to popularise African music than any other woman" (Bensignor and Audra 1999:434). This claim is open to debate (a case could certainly be made for the late South African singer Miriam Makeba; see also Chapter 2, p. 19), but there can be little doubt that Kidjo ranks among the most talented and influential of all contemporary African musicians, female or male.

Ouidah (WEE-duh)

Kidjo was born in 1960 in the coastal city of Ouidah. She was raised in an artistic household by parents who belonged to an elite cultural community that helped establish Benin "as the seat of Africa's intellectual and creative avant garde" during that period (Bensignor and Audra 1999:434). She grew up listening to James Brown and Beatles records, singing along and making up her own words in Fon. From the age of six, she also danced and acted with her mother's theater company.

Angélique Kidjo.

Angélique had established herself as one of Benin's only professional female singers by the time she was 20. She faced limited professional prospects in Benin, however, and moved first to the Netherlands and then to Paris while in her twenties. In contrast to other expatriate African musicians she encountered on the vibrant Paris world music scene, she did not make a point of staying close to her homeland musical roots. Rather, she pursued a "crossover" approach right from the start, becoming part of a diverse community of French, Caribbean, African, and American musicians with broadly international musical tastes, sensibilities, and aspirations.

Her husband and producer, the French musician and record producer Jean Hébrail, was a key member of that community. The uniquely eclectic musical approach she and Hébrail developed drew on Angélique's Fon cultural roots, both in the language of her songs and her use of traditional Fon vocal techniques, but it was equally informed by a diversity of musical styles including American soul, rhythm-and-blues, funk, and jazz. "Throughout her career," it is written on Kidjo's Web site, "Angélique Kidjo has attempted to prove that the world is much smaller and far more culturally connected than it may appear. Her music glorifies individual cultures while also underlining their universal similarities" (Kidjo 2004).

Kidjo first hit the big time with her 1994 international dance hit "Ayé." It was her 1996 album *Fifa,* however, that truly launched her to stardom. Incorporating everything from authentic Beninese field recordings to hard-driving dance numbers and luscious ballads, *Fifa* was an instant world beat classic. Among other guest artists, it featured Latin rock guitar great Carlos Santana (see Chapter 11), one of Angélique's main musical inspirations during her formative years in Benin.

Following the success of *Fifa,* Kidjo embarked upon an ambitious undertaking: a trilogy of albums devoted to exploring the African roots of African-derived musics of the Americas. The first volume of this trilogy, *Oremi* (1998), drew mainly upon links between musics of Africa and the American rhythm-and-blues tradition. Part two, *Black Ivory Soul* (2002), explored the musical and cultural kinship of Africa and Brazil (especially between Benin and Bahia, the most Afro-Brazilian of Brazil's provinces). Part three, *Oyaya!* (2004), delved into the nexus of African and Afro-Caribbean musics (salsa, merengue, calypso, ska).

Today, Kidjo resides principally in New York, dividing her time between there, Paris, and London, and a busy schedule of international touring and recording. As the back-cover write-up of *Black Ivory Soul* rightly proclaims, she "is more than just one of the world's best-loved African singers—she is a musical ambassador for her country, Benin, and indeed, for the entire African continent."

guided listening experience

"Okan Bale," Angélique Kidjo

- CD Track **#3-18**
- Featured performer(s)/group: Angélique Kidjo group, with Angélique Kidjo (vocals), Mamadou Diabate (kora)
- Format: Complete track
- Source recording: *Black Ivory Soul,* by Angélique Kidjo (Columbia)

Though many of the selections on Kidjo's *Black Ivory Soul*—and the album itself—highlight musical links between West Africa and Brazil, some do not, at least not in any explicit or obvious way. These include the catchy, upbeat "Iwoya," in which Kidjo sings with guest artist Dave Matthews, and the moving and beautiful ballad "Okan Bale," a loving tribute to Kidjo's family.

"Okan Bale" (A Piece of My Heart) is a pop ballad in the conventional sense. It has a standard verse-chorus form, employs mainly Western instruments, and features melodies, harmonies, and chord progressions that sound entirely familiar to Western ears. But this is also a song of decidedly pan-African musicultural character on account of its Fon lyrics, the expressive style of Kidjo's singing, and, most important of all for our purposes, the featured role of the kora.

The kora player, Mamadou Diabate, is a younger cousin of Toumani Diabate. As a leading kora virtuoso in his own right, he is one of several prominent musicians carrying forth the proud, centuries-old legacy of the Diabate jeli clan. Mamadou was born in Kita, Mali, in 1975. His father, N'fa Diabate, was a well-known kora player and Mamadou's first teacher. Mamadou left school early to pursue a career as a kora player. After winning a regional kora competition at age 15, he moved to Bamako, where cousin Toumani took him under his wing. Within short order, he was performing regularly on the Bamako jeliya circuit, backing singers at weddings and baptisms and playing for tourists at posh hotels.

Mamadou Diabate.

Mamadou first traveled to the United States in 1996 as a member of a Malian touring troupe. He decided to stay, settling in New York. Since moving to the U.S., he has performed traditional Mande jeliya music at prestigious venues including the Kennedy Center and the Smithsonian Institution. He also has been featured on numerous jazz, pop, and cross-cultural fusion albums and projects. Besides Angélique Kidjo, he has worked with jazz trumpet great Donald Byrd, Zimbabwean pop legend Thomas Mapfumo, and many other luminaries.

Mamadou's playing on "Okan Bale" is florid and flowing. His cascading runs up and down the instrument and the free-floating rhythmic character of his style beg comparison with Toumani Diabate's performance in "Atlanta Kaira." The beauty of the kora is highlighted especially well in two soloistic birimintingo sections of "Okan Bale," the first beginning at 0:24, immediately before the opening (sung) verse, and the second beginning at 1:52, leading up to the second verse.

Also interesting is the way that the kora's role grows progressively throughout the performance within the verses and choruses themselves. During the first verse (0:36–0:57), the kora is largely absent, whereas it figures prominently in the second verse (2:14–2:35), weaving in and out of Kidjo's vocal phrases. Similarly, there is no kora soloing in the first chorus (1:19–1:51), while the kora is quite active in the second chorus (2:58–end) with its waterfall-like birimintingo runs interspersed between lines of Kidjo's singing. It is almost as though the kora, growing in "stature" through the course of the performance, is taking the listener on a journey back to Mother Africa, back to the homeland, family roots, the creative source.

The intimate musical dialogue that emerges between Kidjo's singing and Mamadou's kora playing on "Okan Bale" strongly evokes the jeliya musical art. Though Kidjo is neither a jeli nor any other kind of griot, and though the musical style of "Okan Bale" is oceans apart from jeliya proper, a jeliya essence pervades the performance throughout. The theme of the song's text—praising and expressing gratitude to one's family—also may be said to link "Okan Bale," at least in spirit, to core values of jeliya:

I know where I come from

From you, my family

Let me take a moment to thank you

Because you bring me joy and strength

If my moves are full of blessings

It comes from you, my family.

Kidjo's singing and Mamadou's kora may be the featured voices of "Okan Bale," but there are other notable contributions to the multipart musical conversation as well: synthesizer, guitar, electric bass, background vocals rendering ethereal harmonies in breathy tones (overdubbed by Kidjo herself), shifting musical textures, and changing timbral landscapes. They "speak" sometimes all at once and sometimes in turn, in monologues and in dialogues. And in the end, they contribute to a poignant realization of Angélique Kidjo's grand vision: to prove that the world is indeed smaller and more culturally connected than it seems; to glorify individual cultures while at the same time revealing the universality of human experience.

guided listening quick summary

"Okan Bale," Angélique Kidjo (CD ex. #3-18)

INTRODUCTION

0:00–0:35

- Ethereal synthesizer tones, acoustic guitar, electric bass (playing harmonics), harmonized voices (all Kidjo's, overdubbed)
- From 0:24–0:32, Mamadou Diabate plays kora solo in birimintingo style.

FIRST VERSE (VERSE I)

0:36–0:57

- Sung by Kidjo.
- Acoustic guitar is the main accompanying instrument; kora is largely absent.

FIRST BRIDGE SECTION (BRIDGE I)

0:58–1:18

- Different chord progression; guitar shifts to mainly staccato articulations.
- Brief kora birimintingo at 1:07–1:09 between vocal phrases.

FIRST CHORUS (CHORUS I)

1:19–1:51

- Dialogue between lead voice (Kidjo) and harmonized background vocals (also Kidjo, overdubbed).
- Beautiful, lush chord progression (outlined largely by the background vocals).
- Role of kora limited (no solo parts).

INTERLUDE ("REPRISE" OF INTRODUCTION)

1:52–2:13

- Solo kora (birimintingo) featured again.
- Kora solo more extended and florid in style than in introduction.

SECOND VERSE (VERSE II)

2:14–2:35

- Similar to first verse, but kora takes a more active role, weaving in and out of the lead vocal line with birimintingo flourishes.

SECOND BRIDGE SECTION (BRIDGE II)

2:36–2:57

- Similar to first bridge section, but this time it is a kora birimintingo, rather than a guitar lead-in, that provides the transitional material leading into the chorus.

SECOND CHORUS (CHORUS II)

2:58–end

- Similar to first chorus, except that the kora is now much more active than before, inserting several birimintingo flourishes.

Summary

In this chapter, we explored a range of different African musics in relation to a common theme: musical conversation. Traditions of West Africa south of the Sahara (sub-Saharan Africa), especially drumming-based traditions of the Akan people and the kora tradition of the Mande people, were the principal foci. Certain key musical Africanisms that link these particular traditions to each other and to musics of the African continent and the African diaspora more broadly were introduced. Beginning with the Akan drum proverb of the river and the path, we moved on to South African isicathamiya music and then to a discussion of Akan Fontomfrom royal drum ensemble music. From there, we shifted to the Mande world of the kora and the art of jeliya. A traditional-style solo piece for voice and kora by Seckou Keita, a neo-traditional ensemble piece featuring kora master Toumani Diabate with other Mande musicians and the American guitarist Taj Mahal, and a globally cosmopolitan pop ballad by Angélique Kidjo that placed the kora artistry of Mamadou Diabate in a resolutely post-traditional musical context were explored.

Throughout this journey, we encountered African musics as conversation and as polyvocal forms of collective expression. Whether speaking through their voices, through the voices of their instruments, all together at once, in call-and-response dialogues, or in some combination of different conversational modes, we discovered that certain unifying themes bridged the creators of the different types and styles of music encountered. Principal among these was a theme of communal expression of gratitude. In one way or another, all of the music in this chapter was music of homage, music performed by people out of respect for the human, natural, or divine sources of creation and support that sustain and inspire them: deities, rivers, chiefs, parents, musical elders, and mentors.

Through the musical conversations of African musics, rivers cross paths and paths cross rivers in the metaphorical expressions of musical sounds, and in the relationships these sounds embody. In the polyvocal expressions of the music are contained profound models of interaction and collective expression that manifest ideals of how people can live well together.

Key Terms

Akan	isicathamiya	bala
drum speech	African diaspora	koni
tonal language (e.g., Twi)	Fontomfrom	kumbengo
atumpan	Africanisms (musical)	birimintingo
polyvocality	jeli	sataro
kora	hereditary jeli families	sauta
Mande	(Kouyate, Diabate,	Fon
jeliya	Sissoko)	
griot	praise songs (in jeliya)	

Study Questions

- What is the Akan drum proverb of the river and the path about, literally and metaphorically?

- What aspect of West African languages such as Twi makes it possible for certain drums, like the atumpan, to literally speak? How are spoken and drum speech related?

- How is the term *polyvocality* applied in this chapter?

- Who are Ladysmith Black Mambazo and what did they contribute to South African musical and sociopolitical history?

- How has the jeliya tradition been significant in the history of Mande society and culture?

- What cultures and music traditions of the African diaspora were mentioned in this chapter?

- Traditionally, what was the function of the Fontomfrom ensemble and its music in Akan societies? Has modernization changed this? If so, how?

- What were the six musical Africanisms listed in the chapter? How do they apply to the various musical examples explored?

- Besides the kora, what other African chordophones were discussed in this chapter, and what countries/regions do these instruments come from? Who is Damascus Kafumbe and what is his cultural and musical lineage?

- Besides the kora, what other Mande instruments identified with jeliya were discussed?

- Who is Seckou Keita? Salif Keita? Who was Sunjata Keita? What does the last name Keita imply about a Mande person's family lineage? (Likewise, what do last names like Kouyate, Diabate, and Sissoko imply concerning family lineage?)

- Who was Sidiki Diabate? Who is Toumani Diabate? Mamadou Diabate? How are they related and what is the name of the instrument with which all of them are identified?

- What do the words *kumbengo, birimintingo,* and *sataro* mean relative to Mande musical practice? Where did you hear examples of these in the chapter's musical selections?

- What is the ethnicity of Angélique Kidjo, and how is this specifically reflected in her otherwise globally cosmopolitan music? What examples would you use to support the claim that her music *is* globally cosmopolitan?

- How may the growing presence of the kora over the course of "Okan Bale" be interpreted symbolically?

Discussion Questions

- An integral relationship between language and music is a feature of many styles and traditions of music worldwide. How do language and music combine and reinforce one another in the kinds of music you listen to? Can you think of instances in which the line between what constitutes speech and what constitutes music blurs?

- The so-called musical Africanisms discussed in this chapter are pervasive features of many music traditions outside of Africa as well, especially traditions that belong to or have been influenced by African diasporic culture. Listen to and discuss a range of music that is familiar to you. What Africanisms do you hear in the music, and what effect do they have on how the music sounds and makes you feel?

Applying What You Have Learned

- The American musician Taj Mahal has made a career of breaking down conventional musical boundaries and redefining world music as *worldly* music. Do some research on Mahal and locate recordings and videos of his that represent the range and diversity of his music. Write a report describing how Mahal has combined his musical foundation in blues music, his broad conception of "African" music as encompassing all forms of African and African diasporic musical expression, and his cosmopolitanism as a world music adventurer and pioneer. (You also could choose to focus on other musicians and groups discussed in this chapter in a report like this, such as Ladysmith Black Mambazo, Toumani Diabate, or Angélique Kidjo.)

- Locate recordings and videos representing several different African and African diasporic music traditions beyond those focused on in this chapter. Some possibilities: Brazilian samba, Trinidadian calypso, American funk and hip-hop, Ghanaian highlife, South African mbaqanga. What distinctive features do you hear in each? Are there any unifying elements that cut across some or all of them?

Resources for Further Study

Visit the Online Learning Center at www.mhhe.com/bakan2e, as well as the author's personally maintained Web site at www.michaelbakan.com, for additional learning aids, study help, and resources that supplement the content of this chapter.

'see how she moves':
musics of **Latin America** and the
"Oye Como Va" phenomenon

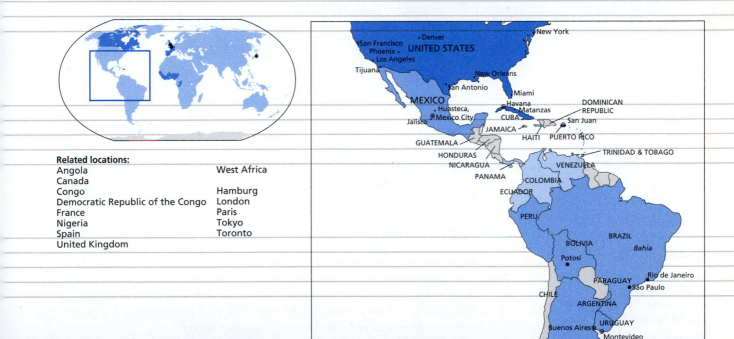

Related locations:

Angola	West Africa
Canada	
Congo	Hamburg
Democratic Republic of the Congo	London
France	Paris
Nigeria	Tokyo
Spain	Toronto
United Kingdom	

timbales
(teem-BAH-lays)

Tito Puente
(TEE-toh PWEN-tay)

Los Angeles. 1988. The lights dim. The curtain rises. A crowd of a thousand-plus Latin music fans cheers wildly, for there, standing center stage behind a battery of drums and other percussion instruments called the **timbales** is The King—*El Rey*—of Latin music: Tito Puente.

This is a king who wears many crowns: king of the timbales, king of **salsa** music, king of **Latin jazz**. Like Elvis Presley in rock-and-roll, Louis Armstrong in jazz, and Ludwig van Beethoven in Western classical music, Puente is an icon. He is a musician whose artistry and persona essentially define the musical tradition with which he is identified.

Tito immediately takes command of the band, locking in tightly with the other members of the **rhythm section** (pianist, bassist, percussionists)

Tito Puente playing the timbales.

and "kicking" the rhythms and **riffs** of the **horn section** (trumpets, trombones, saxophones) with a barrage of drum fills and accented shots. The energy his playing and presence generate is extraordinary, and the rest of the band rises to meet it.

Over the course of this magical night of music making, Tito Puente wows the audience with his dazzling timbales solos, his lyrical playing on the vibraphone (an instrument whose use he pioneered in Latin music), his bandleading skills, showmanship, charm, and humor. They take it all in, enjoying every minute, crying out "Tito, we love you!" at various points. There are many great moments, but there is one that unquestionably tops the rest as far as the response of the audience is concerned. When Tito and the band launch into an arrangement of "Oye Como Va," the most famous piece he ever wrote, the entire crowd rises from their seats as one, swaying and dancing to the **cha cha chá** beat of this classic **Latino/American** tune.

■ ■ ■

Introduction

samba (SAHM-bah)

tropicália (tro-pee-KAH-lee-ah)

mariachi (mah-ree-AH-chee)

rumba (room-bah)

danzón (dan-SOHN) [last syltable between "sun" and "sewn"])

son (sohn [between "sun" and "sewn"])

This chapter surveys a range of musicultural traditions from Latin America. It introduces **samba, bossa nova,** and **tropicália** from Brazil, **steel band** from Trinidad, **tango** traditions of Argentina and Uruguay, folk and folkloric musics of the Bolivian and Peruvian Andes, and Mexican **mariachi.** Its primary focus, however, is on a particular historical trajectory of **Latin music** that crystallized in Cuba out of a syncretism of West African and Spanish elements, experienced important developments in Puerto Rico, and was further cultivated and redefined in a myriad of ways in the United States. Out of this history have arisen a variety of dance-music genres including **rumba, danzón,** *son,* **danzón-mambo,** cha cha chá, **mambo,** Latin jazz, salsa, **Latin rock,** and a host of contemporary Latin popular music styles.

The primary focal point for viewing this trajectory of musical development emerging out of Cuba, Puerto Rico, and the United States will be a specific, well-known song, "Oye Como Va." According to ethnomusicologist and Tito Puente biographer Steven Loza, "Oye Como Va" is "an international anthem," "the most played Latin tune in the world," and a song which, in 1970, turned the worlds of rock and pop music upside down when it was recorded by the Latin rock band Santana and became a commercial mega-hit the likes of which had never been seen before in the domain of Latin music (Loza 1999:45, 73, 44).

The chapter begins by placing "Oye Como Va" in the contexts of Latin music and Latino/American culture. We then survey a variety of important genres from different Latin American nations and regions before focusing in on specific Cuban genres that prefigured the musical style and social significance of "Oye Como Va." The second half of the chapter builds around Guided Listening Experiences based on three important and influential recordings of that song:

■ The original Tito Puente recording from his 1963 album *El Rey Bravo.*

■ Santana's enormously popular, rock-infused version from the hit 1970 record *Abraxas.*

■ A hip-hop and techno-inspired dance mix version from a 2004 Tito Puente Jr. compilation entitled *Tito Puente Jr.: Greatest Club Remixes.*

Each of these recordings tells its own tale of the form and substance of *pan-Latino cultural identity* at a particular historical juncture. Each also reflects on a broader musicultural history of interrelationships between the United States, Puerto Rico, and Cuba. It is the musical products of this history that account for many of the major styles of popular Latin dance music: mambo, cha cha chá, salsa, Latin jazz, Latin rock, and a plethora of newer styles identified by umbrella labels like Latin pop and Latin hip-hop.

This chapter, then, takes a specific piece of music, "Oye Como Va," as its focus musical element, and looks at that piece in terms of the musicultural history of pan-Latino culture and society. A variety of topics and subjects emerge along the way. Five are of central importance:

- Latin music, both broadly defined and in the more specific terms of key developments in Cuba, Puerto Rico, and the United States.

- The Cuban cha cha chá: its musical and cultural roots and its historical transformation.

- Puerto Rican and **Newyorican** (New York/Puerto Rican) society and musicultural life.

- The life and career of Tito Puente (1923–2000).

- The commercial music industry.

"Oye Como Va" and Latin Music in Context

We begin with a deceptively simple question: Where does the song "Oye Como Va" (which basically translates as "See how she moves") come from? A simple answer: the United States, New York City specifically. New York is where Tito Puente was born and raised and where he based himself throughout his professional life. It is where the song was first performed and recorded. And it is almost surely where Puente wrote the tune in the first place.

So then, strictly speaking, "Oye Como Va" is an American song from New York (i.e., with "American" meaning "United States-ian" to be precise). That is not all there is to the matter, however. Though Puente was a lifelong New Yorker and a patriotic American citizen who served in the U.S. military during World War II, he identified himself, ethnically and culturally, as a Puerto Rican first and foremost. "Oye Como Va," and Puente's body of work overall, belongs to a grand legacy of Latino musical culture that developed principally among Puerto Ricans and Americans of Puerto Rican descent in both the United States (especially New York) and Puerto Rico. Perhaps, then, "Oye Como Va" is best described as an example of Puerto Rican music.

Alas, there is a catch to this theory, too. In terms of its fundamental *musical* identity—its core style, form, and structure—"Oye Como Va" is neither principally American nor Puerto Rican, but rather Cuban. It belongs irrefutably to the musical legacy of the cha cha chá, a Cuban dance-music genre that emerged around 1950 in the Cuban capital of Havana before being developed and gaining wide popularity in North America, Europe, and elsewhere. Furthermore, Tito Puente himself, throughout his life, insisted that his own musical identity was principally Cuban rather than Puerto Rican or American. By these measures, "Oye Como Va" would seem to be a Cuban song, or at least a song of Cuban musical extraction.

There is one more possibility to throw into the mix as well. "Oye Como Va" may have its musical basis in Cuba, its cultural essence in Puerto Rico, and its geographical point of origin in New York, but for millions upon millions of people around the world, it is, pure and simple, an American "classic rock" tune by Santana. Relatively few people who know and love "Oye Como Va" have any idea who Tito Puente was, let alone that he wrote and was the first to record this famous song. Nor do they know that Santana closely modeled his recorded version after the Puente original (though Santana never made any secret of that fact). Even among his legions of fans, Puente was not necessarily known as the composer of "Oye Como Va." Wherever in the world he would play, he used to report, people would come up to him and say, "Tito, could you please play Santana's tune, you know 'Oye Como Va'?" (Puente, quoted in Loza 1999:44). This brings us back full circle. Maybe "Oye Como Va" *is* an American song after all, but for different reasons than those outlined earlier.

The fact of the matter is that there is no single right answer to the question, Where does "Oye Como Va" come from? It comes from many different places, and in its eclectic

World events		Music events
European discovery of Cuba (Christopher Columbus) •·········	**1492**	
First Spanish settlers to Cuba •·········	**1511**	
Taino and other indigenous peoples all •········· but wiped out in wake of Spanish conquest		
Height of slave trade in Cuba •·········	**1790–1860**	
	Late 19th century	·········• Tango begins to develop in Buenos Aires, Argentina
		·········• Creolized dance-music forms develop in Cuba: contradanza, danzón
		·········• "Cielito Lindo"composed (1882)
	1920s	·········• Danzón essentially becomes national dance of Cuba
		·········• Urban mariachi begins to develop in Mexico City
		·········• Afro-Cuban *son* emerges and challenges danzón in both popularity and nationalistic significance
	1920s–1930s	·········• Golden age of tango
	1923	·········• Tito Puente born to Puerto Rican immigrant parents in Spanish Harlem, New York City
Film *The Four Horsemen of the* •········· *Apocalypse,* starring Rudolph Valentino, inspires an international tango sensation	**1926**	
	1930s	·········• Samba-enredo (theme samba) begins in Rio de Janeiro, Brazil
		·········• Xavier Cugat dominant figure in so-called Latin dance music in U.S.
	1940	·········• Formation of Machito and the Afro-Cubans
	1940s	·········• Steel drum invented, Trinidad
	1947	·········• Carlos Santana born in Mexico
	1949	·········• Pérez Prado's "Mambo #5" achieves major commercial success
	1950	·········• Cha cha chá originates in Cuba (Enrique Jorrin)

musicultural admixture brings to bear an even more complex question: Where does "Latin music" come from? And by extension, who, and what, does it represent?

Latin music defined

"Oye Como Va," in its many incarnations (at least the ones we deal with in this chapter), belongs to the realm of Latin music. This is one of those terms that can mean any or all of a number of different things, so let us establish from the outset what it is assumed to mean here.

The "Latin" in Latin music refers to Latin America. Geographically, Latin America is a large and culturally diverse region of the world encompassing all of South America and the various nations and territories of Central America, Mexico, and the Caribbean. (Some scholars offer a narrower definition limited to just those nations of the region in which Spanish or Portuguese are the predominant languages, but we will take the wider view.) In its broadest sense, Latin American music—or Latin music, for short—is any music originating from anywhere in

World events		Music events
	1950s	● Crystallization of modern mariachi style
		● Andean folkoric music becomes popular in Europe
		● Big band mambo and "mambo craze" in U.S. (Puente, Tito Rodríguez, Machito)
		● Latin dance music scene dominated by a combination of Cuban, Puerto Rican, and Newyorican bandleaders and musicians
		● Bossa nova develops in Rio de Janeiro, Brazil
Fidel Castro comes to power in Cuba, which becomes a socialist state ●	**1959**	
	1960	● Astor Piazzolla forms Quinteto Nuevo Tango
Pan-Latino movement emerges and develops in U.S., and eventually internationally ●	**1960s–1970s**	
Nationalist movements in South America (Peru, Bolivia) popularize Andeam folkloric music ●	**1963**	● Original Tito Puente recording of "Oye Como Va" released on *El Rey Bravo*
	1964	● "The Girl from Ipanema" becomes an international hit
	1968	● Peak of tropicália movement in Brazil (Os Mutantes)
	1970s	● Birth and rise to popularity of salsa music ("salsa explosion")
	1970	● Santana's Latin rock version of "Oye Como Va" released on *Abraxas*
	1971	● Tito Puente Jr. born in New York City
	1980s	● Mariachi revival (Linda Ronstadt)
	1990s	● Tropicália discovered by U.S. rock stars
	1996	● "Oye Como Va" released on *Guarachando*, by Tito Puente Jr. & the Latin Rhythm Crew
	2000	● Death of Tito Puente
	2004	● Tito Puente Jr. releases *Tito Puente Jr.: Greatest Club Remixes* (including remix version of "Oye Como Va") and *En Los Pasos de Mi Padre* (In My Father's Shoes)
	2008	● McDonald's commercial Featuring Os Mutantes' "A Minha Menina"

this vast region; and in this broad sense, too, musics of diasporic Latino communities in the United States, Canada, Europe, and elsewhere also may be included (e.g., salsa music, a genre of Latin music that was "invented" in New York City).

We will make use of this broad and inclusive definition of Latin music momentarily as we survey a range of traditions from South America, Mexico, and the Caribbean island of Trinidad. Following that introductory survey, however, our scope will become far more narrow. The principal sphere of Latin music addressed in this chapter encompasses *a host of popular dance-music genres that originated in or derived from the island of Cuba, have experienced significant histories of development in the United States and/or Puerto Rico, and have histories of transmission closely tied to the U.S./international commercial music industry and mass media distribution.* New York City has been the main U.S. hub for the development and popularization of such musics, though other cities—Miami, San Francisco, Los Angeles, and to some extent Paris, London, and even Tokyo—have played key roles as well.

The musicians responsible for shaping the history of this domain of Latin music encompass a diverse and confluent range of ethnic, national, and musical backgrounds. There are the

Enrique Jorrin
(En-ree-kay
Horr-EEN)

Mario Bauzá (MAH-
ree-o Bow-SAH)

Machito
(Ma-CHEE-toe)

Cuban and Cuban American pioneers: Israel "Cachao" López and Orestes López (the López brothers), Enrique Jorrin, Mario Bauzá, Machito (Frank Grillo), Pérez Prado, Arsenio Rodríguez, Mongo Santamaría, Francisco Aguabella, Celia Cruz. There are also the Puerto Rican and Puerto Rican–American bandleaders like Tito Rodríguez and Tito Puente, a musician whose impact, as we shall see, has been particularly decisive. African American jazz musicians including trumpet great Dizzy Gillespie have made seminal contributions too, as have a Panamanian salsa super-star, Rubén Blades, and a Mexican American (Chicano) rock guitarist, Carlos Santana.

Altogether, these musicians have been integral parts of a categorically multicultural and multidimensional mutual feedback loop between Latin American nations and the United States that constitutes a truly Latino/American phenomenon, the slash between "Latino" and "Ameri-can" implying "and/or" in the widest sense. We will return to this Latino/American realm of Cuban/Puerto Rican/U.S.-based music and to our principal case study of "Oye Como Va" later in the chapter. First, though, we survey a few of Latin America's many other rich musical cultures.

Latin Music Traditions and Transformations in South America, Mexico, and the Caribbean: A Selective Survey

In this section, we survey several Latin American musicultural traditions that originated in and are principally identified with nations and regions outside of Cuba, Puerto Rico, and the United States. This survey encompasses selected musics of Brazil, Trinidad, Argentina and Uruguay, Bolivia and Peru, and Mexico. It provides at least some sense of the immense diversity of musi-cal and cultural expression that has issued from the many historical streams of Amerindian, African, and European influence in the region. It also offers several different windows through which to view the complex processes of tradition and transformation that have shaped and con-tinue to shape musical life in this area of the world, and by extension internationally.

Brazil: Samba, Bossa Nova, and Tropicália

With the arguable exception of Cuba, Brazil has exerted a greater influence on the global land-scape of the contemporary musical world than any other country in Latin America. From the spectacular samba parades of Carnaval (Carnival) in Rio de Janeiro to the deeply African-rooted ritual musics of Bahia in the northeast and the modern, cosmopolitan sounds of MPB (*música popular brasileira*), Brazil, the largest country in South America, is and has long been a global juggernaut of musical richness and innovation.

Carnaval
(Car-nah-VAHL)

Bahia (Bie-YEE-uh)

música popular
brasileira
(Moo-see-kah
pah-pyoo-LAHR
brah-si-LAY-rah)

SAMBA Samba is the best-known Brazilian music internationally, having become almost synon-ymous with Brazil's musical culture in much of the world's eyes. Samba is actually an umbrella term for a number of distinct musical genres identified with different Brazilian regions, ethnic groups, and performance events. All share in common a host of musical elements that in one manner or another may be traced to African origins, though these take on different forms and characteristics in the different samba styles. Polyrhythmic textures built from layers of driving, percussive rhythmic patterns are characteristic of many samba forms, as are call-and-response singing, improvisational elements, and other features that collectively inscribe African musicul-tural lineage upon samba's varied Brazilian incarnations.

The form of samba that has the greatest global visibility is *samba-enredo* (theme samba), which originated in the 1930s and has long been identified with Carnaval in Rio de Janeiro (Rio). For the five days preceding Ash Wednesday, which marks the commencement of the Lenten season (Lent) in the Catholic cycle of rituals, Rio essentially shuts down for Carnaval. The city's Carnaval celebration vies for the title of world's largest street party (Mardi Gras in New Orleans, another pre-Lenten celebration, might be another contender). Millions of Brazil-ians participate actively in the festivities, joined by thousands of tourists who descend upon the city for the event every year. The highlight of Carnaval is the samba parade (*desfile*). The gargan-tuan "samba schools" (*escolas de samba*) that compete for glory in the parade showcase elaborate themed floats and costumes (see photo, p. 20), dancing, dramatic presentations, massive choruses singing songs composed especially for the occasion in call-and-response style (the lyrics of the songs reflect the annual Carnaval theme, e.g., Brazilian folklore, racial equality), and propulsive rhythms furnished by ensembles highlighting the talents of literally thousands of drummers. The resulting music is often described as the world's loudest!

Today, samba groups are found not only in Brazil but in many other countries as well. A number of ensembles have been formed in connection with ethnomusicology and world music programs at universities in North America. One such group, Jacaré Brazil, is based at the University of Florida in Gainesville. Jacaré Brazil is codirected by Larry Crook and Welson Tremura, who are music professors at the university and internationally renowned performers and scholars of Brazilian music. A small but surprisingly powerful samba percussion group consisting of Crook, Tremura, and seven student members of Jacaré Brazil performing live in concert is featured on **CD ex. #3-19,** "Evolução de Samba." This is a piece in the *samba de batucada* form, which emphasizes Brazilian percussion and Afro-Brazilian rhythms. It was arranged by Crook in the style of the giant samba school drumming performances heard on a much larger scale at Carnaval in Rio. Syncopated rhythms in the high-pitched drum and bell (*agogô*) parts create rich polyrhythmic textures overtop a booming, rock-steady beat played on the *surdo* bass drums. The vocalist (and whistle player) is Tremura; Crook is heard on the Brazilian *pandeiro* tambourine. Imagine music like this played by a thousand or so musicians rather than just nine and you begin to have a sense of what it would feel like to take part in an actual Carnaval celebration in Rio.

Jacaré (Jah-kah-RAY)

batucada (bah-too-KAH-dah)

agogô (ah-go-GO) surdo (SOOR-doh) pandeiro (pahn-DAY-ro)

BOSSA NOVA The elegant and intimate strains of Brazilian bossa nova would appear to represent the antithesis of the boisterous exuberance of Rio carnival-style samba, yet the two are related. Bossa nova originated in the late 1950s in the predominantly middle-class (and white) South Zone of Rio de Janeiro. Though not far geographically from the poor (and predominantly black) *favelas* (shantytowns, slums) located in the hills overlooking the wealthier southern areas, the cultural—and in turn musical—scene of the South Zone that gave rise to bossa nova was a world apart. The musical pioneers of bossa nova—composer and pianist Antonio Carlos (Tom) Jobim, lyricist Vinícius de Moraes, and singer and guitarist João Gilberto—adapted rhythmic and other musical elements from the samba styles of the favelas and combined these with influences from American jazz and popular music, as well as with *choro* and other styles from Brazil, to create a novel and cosmopolitan musical idiom.

favelas (fah-VAY-lahs)

João (Zhoe [like "Joe" but with a soft "j"])

The transformation of samba percussion rhythms into bossa nova guitar playing style developed by João Gilberto was especially ingenious. Gilberto cultivated a rhythmic approach to playing the guitar called *batida*. In batida, the accompanying chords were inserted between the syncopated notes of the sung (or played) melody while the upper and lower guitar strings were used both for chords and to reproduce the characteristic rhythms of high- and low-pitched samba percussion instruments such as those heard earlier in **CD ex. #3-19.** Though much of the rhythmic content of batida—and of the corresponding bass and drum set parts that were typically partnered with it—was adapted from samba, the aesthetic was profoundly different since the music was played at a soft dynamic level and in a very mellow, laid-back style. This same laid-back aesthetic applied to the understated, hushed, almost whispered tones of bossa nova singing that were developed by Gilberto and other bossa nova vocalists, whose approaches were influenced by those of American popular and jazz singers of the time such as Frank Sinatra and Sarah Vaughan.

The Brazilian bossa nova guitarist and vocalist João Gilberto.

Equally if not more influential on the bossa nova aesthetic overall were the interrelated cool jazz and West

On the Caribbean island of Trinidad, located just seven miles off the northeastern coast of Venezuela, Carnival celebrations of the pre-Lenten season leading up to Ash Wednesday rival those of Brazil in terms of their overall grandeur and spectacular musical offerings. The musical highlight of the Trinidadian version of Carnival (which is presented as a nationalized secular event rather than a Catholic observance) is Panorama, a competition featuring enormous *steel bands* that consist of hundreds of instruments and include upward of 100 musicians each. The pieces performed by the competing groups in Panorama are long, complex, and virtuosic—and exciting. The best groups whip the massive crowds in attendance into a frenzy, and the ability to do just that is indeed essential to competitive success.

The historical roots of the steel band date back centuries and encompass a fascinating and complicated lineage of cross-cultural interaction between African, Amerindian, Spanish, French, and British peoples and cultural institutions enmeshed in the island's colonial and postcolonial history. But the invention of the main type of instrument used in the modern ensemble, the *pan* (sometimes also referred to as the steel drum), dates only from the 1940s. During World War II, the United States had navy bases on Trinidad. They left behind thousands of discarded oil drums after the war. Resourceful Trinidadians, most of them belonging to Afro-Trinidadian communities, devised ingenious methods for hammering the unopened ends of these oil drums into a convex shape, then hammering circular protrusions of different sizes around the perimeter to produce notes of different pitch. Eventually, large, 55-gallon oil drums made of steel came to furnish the standard raw material for such instrument making.

Steel band performing at Panorama in Trinidad.

Coast jazz movements that emerged out of the United States (especially California) during this period. The influence was mutual. Bossa nova became all the rage in jazz circles and achieved immense popularity through collaborations of American jazz musicians like the tenor saxophonist Stan Getz and bossa greats such as João Gilberto and Tom Jobim. The three collaborated on the classic 1964 album *Getz/Gilberto,* which featured a performance of Jobim's "The Girl From Ipanema" in which João Gilberto sings the lyrics in Portuguese (Brazil's national language) and his wife, Astrud Gilberto, follows with an English-language rendition. Stan Getz's breathy-toned and intimate improvised saxophone solo forms the perfect complement to the suave Gilbertos, and all of this is elegantly supported by João's batida-style guitar playing and a topflight rhythm section also consisting of Jobim (piano), bassist Tommy Williams, and drummer Milton Banana.

Another West Coast jazz saxophonist identified with the cool jazz movement was Paul Desmond, who is most famous for his work with the Dave Brubeck Quartet (and who composed that group's hit tune "Take Five"). Desmond's laid-back playing style and breathy-toned sound on the alto saxophone suited the aesthetic of bossa nova beautifully. His recording of another Jobim classic song, "Wave" (**CD ex. #1-27**), to which we were first introduced in Chapter 4 (p. 54), provides a fine example of bossa nova style as filtered through the lens of the jazz idiom with which bossa was so closely identified from the start. The quartet assembled by Desmond for this 1974 recording was an all-star band. It included the preeminent Canadian master of the

Thus was born the pan, which is now the national instrument of the nation of Trinidad and Tobago (Tobago is Trinidad's much smaller neighboring island to the north).

Large and elaborate steel bands featuring pans of many sizes and accompanied by an "engine room" rhythm section of drum set, "irons" (usually automobile brake drums), **conga drums (congas)** (discussed later in the chapter—see photo, p. 244), shakers, cowbells, and additional miscellaneous percussion instruments would become an integral part of Carnival festivities and many other events henceforth. These bands include several instrumental sections of pans, each with its own pitch range and specific musical function within the ensemble. The highest-pitched instruments are the tenor pans (tenors), which serve as the main melodic instruments. One range lower are the double tenors and double seconds, which combine melodic and harmonic functions. Lower-pitched yet are the guitar pans and cello pans, instruments that mainly provide chordal accompaniment. The lowest-pitched sets, the bass pans, usually consisting of six or more large oil drums, lay down the anchoring bass lines for the music.

The steel band repertoire is highly varied. Local popular music traditions of the region—calypso, soca, Indo-Trinidadian chutney—are represented in instrumental pan arrangements or in arrangements featuring singers accompanied by steel bands. Arrangements of Western classical and jazz compositions are also common, as well as music based on or influenced by American pop, rhythm-and-blues, soul, rock, and hip-hop. The cosmopolitan internationalism of steel band music is mirrored by the global reach that pan has achieved in recent decades. Student steel bands have become fixtures of world music and percussion programs in many North American colleges and universities and professional steel band performers may be heard all over the world, from tourist restaurants and Disney theme parks in Florida to the major concert halls of Europe and international music festivals in Japan. Steel bands also perform at Carnival celebrations and Caribbean/Latin American festivals that are today held in North American cities like Miami, New York, and Toronto. The annual Miami Carnival often features Panorama-style performances by the steel band featured on **CD ex. #1-30,** the 21st Century Steel Orchestra, a South Florida–based group directed by Michael (Big Mike) Kernahan. As you listen, take note of the intricate interplay between the different sections of pans (including occasional passages of call-and-response musical dialogue), the infectiously danceable calypso groove, and the unique and extraordinary timbres of the instruments themselves.

jazz guitar, Ed Bickert; former Miles Davis Quintet bassist Ron Carter; and drummer Connie Kay of the Modern Jazz Quartet. Desmond's dulcet tones on the alto saxophone are aptly supported by the Bickert-Carter-Kay rhythm section here, and Bickert in particular offers a highly effective, jazz-inflected variant on the original batida style of playing originated by Gilberto and other Brazilian guitarists.

TROPICÁLIA During the same year that bossa nova was riding the crest of its wave of popularity with the unprecedented international success of "The Girl From Ipanema," 1964, other events playing out in both political and musical arenas were impacting the Brazilian musical landscape on many fronts. A military coup in that year resulted in the ousting of populist president João Goulart and the installation of a totalitarian regime in Brazil that was backed by the United States and multinational corporate interests. This development ushered in "a period of crisis for progressive forces that provoked a critical rethinking of nationally defined cultural imperatives that were articulated in several fields of artistic production, particularly in popular music" (Dunn 2001:73). Such rethinking of imperatives, or at least priorities, was also impacted with great force by the shockwaves of Beatlemania and the British Invasion in rock music that began to quite literally rock the world, and the world of Brazilian popular music specifically, beginning in 1964. The combined effects of the increasingly repressive and exploitative political situation in Brazil, debates over the liberatory versus destructive potential of rock music for Brazilian culture, and a host of competing intellectual and cultural movements that emerged to combat growing threats to social justice and progress collectively contributed to a radically transformed musicultural landscape for these new and troubled times.

One of the most important outcomes of this period of crisis in politics, popular music, and the arts more broadly was the emergence of tropicália. The founding fathers of the tropicália movement were Caetano Veloso and Gilberto Gil, two outstanding musicians from the northeastern province of Bahia, the country's epicenter of Afro-diasporic culture. The artistic and cultural sensibilities of Veloso and Gil were strongly defined by their Bahian roots. Both men were also devotees of João Gilberto and identified with the legacies of bossa nova and other genres of Brazilian song. But they were equally inspired by the Beatles, Jimi Hendrix, and James Brown, and sought to define a new expressive medium *and* sociopolitical stance in the combining of many seemingly disparate elements. "By using electric guitars in melodic compositions with elements of Argentine tango and African things from Bahia," explains Veloso, "we assumed a posture of 'being-in-the-world'—we rejected the role of the Third World country living in the shadow of more developed countries" (quoted in Dunn 2001:75).

Also foundational to the musical principles and philosophical orientations of Veloso, Gil, and other tropicalists was a concept derived from the *Manifesto Antropofágo (Antropofágico),* or Cannibalist Manifesto, by Brazilian author Oswald de Andrade. Summarizing the basic position of this influential 1928 publication, scholar Lorraine Leu explains that "[t]he manifesto attacked both a purist view of national culture and wholesale imitation of foreign models. Instead, Oswald advocated a selective devouring of elements of foreign cultures which would then be absorbed and transformed into Brazilian cultural products" (Leu 2006:86–87).

Such selective devouring, absorption, and transformation in music—musical cannibalism, in essence—found sublime forms of realization in the late 1960s work of Os Mutantes (The Mutants), the psychedelic, avant-garde rock band from the sprawling metropolis of São Paulo in southern Brazil to whom we were first introduced in Chapter 1 (see photo, p. 2). In his essay "Cannibals, Mutants, and Hipsters: The Tropicalist Revival," John J. Harvey asserts that cannibalism

> was the most important weapon in Os Mutantes' cultural arsenal. As the name suggests, it wasn't the group's faithful translation of American [or other foreign] pop for a Brazilian audience, but rather its "mutations" of the music that made it special. . . . The band's list of mutations is long. Its members reconfigured French pop, American psychedelic rock, *mode-de-viola* music of Brazil, bossa nova, the Beatles [as well as Bob Dylan, the Beach Boys, and Sly and the Family Stone], Brazilian carnival music, and mod rock . . . . the motifs were cannibalized, mutated, defected, and signified upon so that they were almost emptied of content until redeployed in the mix and impregnated with a new meaning belonging wholly to the group. (Harvey 2001:119–20)

Veloso and Gil regarded Os Mutantes as kindred spirits in the cannibalist project of tropicália. They admired, promoted, and were influenced by the band and performed and recorded with them on numerous occasions. Audiences did not necessarily share their enthusiasm, however, as is evident from the following evocative account by Harvey of the band's controversial performance with Veloso at the 1968 International Festival of Song in São Paulo, which you may recall was also discussed briefly in Chapter 1:

> Clad in surreal plastic outfits, the group settles in: Rita Lee Jones on vocals and the Baptista brothers, Arnaldo and Sérgio, on bass and guitar. The crowd eyes the longhaired, strangely dressed, foreign-looking Os Mutantes with suspicion. Backing Caetano Veloso on "É proibido proibir" [It's forbidden to forbid], the band launches into an amplified barrage of distorted noise that immediately elicits a hostile response from the audience, which begins to boo and hurl tomatoes, grapes, and wads of paper at the performers. Os Mutantes increases the distorted guitar attack in a defiant mocking of the

Caetano Veloso (Kae-TAH-noh Ve-LOH-SO)

spectators. The band members turn their backs to the crowd and continue the sonic assault. (Harvey 2001:107)

Tropicália in its initial bloom proved to be a potent but short-lived phenomenon. At the end of 1968, a year that had witnessed the majority of the movement's landmark moments, Gilberto Gil and Caetano Veloso were arrested, imprisoned, and ultimately exiled for two-and-a-half years, during which time they both resided mainly in London. Strong-armed but inconsistent policies of censorship and restrictions of freedom of expression ultimately quashed the burgeoning tropicália movement, though its long-term influence in Brazil and abroad would prove to be profound.

During the 1990s, Os Mutantes were "discovered" by the likes of the late Kurt Cobain (of Nirvana), Beck, and former Talking Heads lead singer David Byrne, the latter of whom reissued several of their recordings on his Luaka Bop label. Their classic, eponymous 1968 debut album *Os Mutantes,* which received the number-nine ranking in *Rolling Stone* magazine's list of the 100 greatest Brazilian albums of all time, was reissued in 1992 and achieved both popular success and critical acclaim. In an ironic twist, the band gained many new fans and admirers as a result of the use of one of the songs from that album, "A Minha Menina" (My Girl), on a popular 2008 McDonald's television commercial (see also Chapter 1, p. 2). They released their first new album in 35 years during the following year, 2009, and embarked upon a major North American tour that same year. How strange—yet cannibalistically appropriate—that Os Mutantes, pop culture icons of late 1960s Brazilian counterculture and subversive resistance to multinational corporate hegemony, should end up furnishing the soundtrack for a commercial produced by the dominant force in multinational corporate fast-food culture some forty years later (though certainly no more ironic than the Beatles' song "Revolution" serving as the soundtrack for a Nike athletic shoes commercial a few years ago).

We return now to the classic, original 1968 recording of "A Minha Menina" included as the opening track on your CD set (**CD ex. #1-1**) for a more detailed exploration. The song is a joyful proclamation of youthful love and bliss ("She's my girl and I'm her boy; she's my love and I'm her love completely") devoid of some of the weightier tones and experimental elements of many of the band's other productions. The signature spirit of tropicalist cannibalism is nonetheless evident in "Minha's" carnivalesque collage of distorted electronic timbres and effects, folksy chordal accompaniment, Jimi Hendrix-like electric guitar soloing, doo-wop vocal licks, Beatles and Beach Boys–inspired vocal harmonies, and samba-infused rock grooves. The samba-rock element, in particular, owes much to the featured guest artist on this track, composer and guitarist Jorge Ben (from Rio de Janeiro), who actually wrote "A Minha Menina" and was a pioneer of the samba-rock style in Brazilian music beginning in the late 1960s. Ben is most famous as the composer of another song, "Mas Que Nada" (No Way), which ranks with "The Girl from Ipanema" as one of the best-known pieces of music ever to come out of Brazil. He grew up playing samba in the carnavals of Rio, and like Caetano Veloso and Gilberto Gil, found significant inspiration in the music of João Gilberto and the bossa nova movement during his early career.

Another guest performer on "A Minha Menina" was the Brazilian percussionist Dirceu, whose enlivening drumming brought rock and samba elements together in a unique and highly compelling way. A year earlier, in 1967, Dirceu and Os Mutantes had appeared together backing Gilberto Gil in a historic performance that helped to launch the tropicália movement. Dirceu performed on a traditional Brazilian musical bow-type chordophone called the *berimbau* on that occasion. This instrument, which is closely identified with the Brazilian dance/sport/martial art form called *capoeira* (which originally developed in Brazil among slaves brought to the country from present-day Angola and other regions of western, central, and southern Africa) is regarded as the most quintessentially Brazilian of all Brazilian instruments. Gil's conscious juxtaposition of the berimbau and Os Mutantes' electrified rock music was perceived as both a powerful and controversial expression of complexly multifaceted Brazilian identity at the time

Jorge (HOR-hay)

"Mas Que Nada" ("Mash Ke NAH-dah")

berimbau (BEE-rum-bow [rhymes with "now"])

capoeira (kah-po-AY-rah)

(Galm 2010:57). In recent years, the berimbau has found its way into an eclectic range of musical styles within and beyond Brazil. A. R. Rahman's Bollywood-style Indian film song "Barso Re" (**CD ex. #3-3** and pp. 150–154) offers one interesting example of a novel use of this instrument.

Argentina and Uruguay: Tango

Tango is a highly sensual form of dance and music from Argentina. It has been poetically described as "the vertical expression of a horizontal desire" on account of its often overtly sexual character. Tango emerged from the hard streets, bars, and brothels of the port district of Argentina's capital city, Buenos Aires, during the latter part of the 19th century. The *porteños* (people of the port) who worked the docks or otherwise provided the requisite goods and services for the area were a diverse lot, comprising Europeans, people of African descent, and *criollos* (creoles) of mixed ancestry. The varied ethnicities and heritages of the porteños prefigured the eclectic musical influences that came to bear in the early development of tango: Spanish flamenco and *contradanse*, Italian song traditions, Central European polka, African-derived rhythms, and dance-music styles from Cuba. On a more local level, rural music from the Argentine countryside, and most especially the *milónga* song tradition of the *gaucho* cowboys, became central to the emergent style of tango. The predominant tango instrument by the end of the 19th century was the **bandoneón,** a box-shaped button accordion originally brought to Argentina from Germany (see photo, p. 235).

bandoneón (bahn-doh-nee-YONE)

By the early 1900s, tango had eclipsed its lowbrow porteño origins and become an integral component of Buenos Aires popular culture at large. There was vocal resistance to the embrace of tango amongst the city's middle and upper classes, who regarded it as a potentially corrupting influence—especially for youth—but this ultimately just proved to be fuel for tango's growing fire. The alluring appeal of the dance and its music won out, and soon the tango was not only being danced and played throughout Buenos Aires and in nearby cities such as Montevideo (the capital of neighboring Uruguay), but was storming Europe as the first of a series of 20th-century Latin dance crazes as well. It caught on with a vengeance in Paris, and this international recognition had the effect of making the tango not just more popular but also more credible and legitimate back home in Buenos Aires.

The legendary singer Carlos Gardél was both an agent and beneficiary of tango's transformation and vastly increased stature in Argentina and around the world. He was the leading superstar during tango's golden age of the 1920s–1930s. This period witnessed the progressive consolidation of tango dancing's "contradictory mix of earthly sensuality and middle class kitsch," which arose within "an almost violent and dangerous friction of bodies, colliding often in a passion which seems controlled by the dance itself. A glittering respectability hid darker undercurrents in the obvious macho domination of the male over the female in a series of intri-

Rudolph Valentino dressed in stylized gaucho attire.

cate steps and close embraces, which were highly suggestive of the sexual act" (Peiro and Fairley 2000:306–07). All of these features of the dance were embodied in the tango songs and musical styles of the golden age period, and Gardél himself came to embody them in his alternately suave and aggressive macho-romantic image and lifestyle. His stardom rose with the ascent of radio, recordings, and film, and his permanent legend status was ensured by his tragic death in an airplane crash in 1935.

Gardél's influence on the development and legitimization of tango was immeasurable, but another heartthrob, the Hollywood movie star Rudolph Valentino, may have had an even greater impact on the phenomenon of tango as an international pop culture sensation. In 1926, Valentino was featured wearing a stylized Argentine gaucho costume and dancing a tango in the film *The Four Horsemen of the Apocalypse*. (The fact that gauchos had never danced the tango was conveniently ignored.) Valentino's tango was the hit of the film and launched the international tango craze to new and unprecedented heights, from Paris to London and throughout the Americas. Now even Carlos Gardél was forced to perform tangos in gaucho garb during his shows in Paris and elsewhere, perpetuating an incongruous conflation of the rural gaucho and the urban tango that would permeate stereotypical representations of Argentines henceforth.

The dominant figure in tango music through the second half of the 20th century was the classically trained composer, bandleader, and bandoneón virtuoso Astor Piazzolla. Even today, some two decades after his death (in 1992), his music and legacy continue to shape and define the musicultural world of tango internationally. Piazzolla was born in Argentina in 1922 but moved to New York with his family as a child, returning to his native Argentina to live in 1937. He showed prodigious talent on the bandoneón from a young age and while still in his teens had already performed with both Carlos Gardél and Anibal Troilo, the foremost master of the bandoneón in the pre-Piazzolla era.

**Piazzolla
(Pee-ah-TZOH-lah)**

In the 1950s, Piazzolla received a scholarship to study in Paris with the famous composition teacher Nadia Boulanger. She encouraged him to develop a new compositional style that at once built on the foundations of traditional tango and transformed it through the infusion of elements borrowed from Western art music, jazz, and other traditions. This Piazzolla did with relish, most notably with the famous Quinteto Nuevo Tango (New Tango Quintet) that he founded in 1960. With boundless energy and innovation, Piazzolla composed and performed tango in a manner that turned the traditions and conventions of the music upside down and inside out. His use of complex and unusual chords and harmonies, dissonant melodies, and extended solo improvisations and new approaches to ensemble playing inspired by jazz and experimental Western art music garnered many admirers, while at the same time enraging tango purists who regarded his music as a desecration of tango tradition. Piazzolla continues to have his detractors even today, but the overall arc of tango history has led to a broad acceptance of his music and to his undeniable status as the most influential tango musician of his era.

**Boulanger
(Boo-lahn-ZHAY)**

Astor Piazzolla performing on the bandoneón.

The legacy and creative spirit of Astor Piazzolla have been carried forward and extended in contemporary times by younger South American musicians such as the Uruguayan bandoneón player Hugo Diaz. Diaz was born and raised in the capital city of Uruguay, Montevideo, which rivals Buenos Aires as a center of tango development and activity in South America. His musical approach continues in the vein of the *nuevo tango* of Piazzolla, drawing liberally from different tango styles and eras and also from jazz, Western art music, and diverse international traditions. Like Piazzolla, Diaz learned the bandoneón at an early age and began playing professionally while still in his teens. Like Piazzolla, too, he developed a special passion for the music of Johann Sebastian Bach and also studied the works of contemporary Western composers. He aspires to create music that combines the natural flow of traditional tango with the sophisticated compositional procedures of classical chamber music, and he undertakes this entire endeavor using approaches to improvisation, ensemble organization, and musical interaction that are closely akin to those of modern jazz. This compelling synthesis of elements within the contemporary tango milieu is well displayed in Diaz's recording of Charlo Manzi's tango "Fueye" (**CD ex. #4-1**). Here, the two melodic instruments, the bandoneón and the guitar, engage in an intimate and ever-changing musical dialogue that parallels the rich dynamics of interaction between male and female tango dancers. The bandoneón leads this musical dance, forming the "male" dimension of the partnership with its strident tone and directive role. The guitar, in the "female" role, follows the bandoneón's lead with skill and grace and moves with a sound of refinement and elegance that

Fueye (FWAY-yay)

often seems to outclass the dominant bandoneón. One can almost imagine just from listening to this music how a couple might dance the tango to it.

Folkloric Andean Music of Bolivia and Peru (and Paris and Buenos Aires, Too)

The Andes mountains of South America extend for more than 4,500 miles from the northernmost regions of the continent in Venezuela and Colombia to its southernmost reaches in Chile. For thousands of years, these mountains have been home to indigenous, Amerindian peoples. The largest populations and groups reside in mountainous regions of Bolivia, Peru, and Ecuador. These are the primary traditional centers of what has come to be known generically in modern times as Andean culture, a phrase that acknowledges common ancestries, languages, and other cultural formations which to some extent unify the region, but that fails to account for the great cultural diversity that distinguishes the various Andean peoples one from the other.

**Quechua
(KE-choo-ah)**

The two principal languages other than Spanish that are spoken by members of Andean communities are Quechua and Aymara. Quechua was the language of the great empire of the Inca civilization during pre-conquest times, to which many Andean peoples trace their ancestry. It is currently spoken by some six million people. Aymara has more than two million speakers today and is identified historically with the ancient Aymara civilization. While outsiders (including the governments of nations in which they reside) have tended to group and distinguish the different peoples of the rural Andean highlands under broad rubrics like Andean, Quechua, Aymara, indigenous, or Indian, the people themselves—at least those in remote, rural areas who have largely preserved their traditional cultural lifeways—typically self-identify principally in terms of their **ayllu,** or native community. The ayllu is defined by extended family lineages, particular locations of residence and ancestry, and unique cultural practices—including musical ones—that foster social solidarity and facilitate harmonious relationships with the natural world and the spirit realm.

ayllu (ie-yoo)

Music is an essential component of ritual and daily life on all levels in the ayllu. Particular instruments, traditions, and styles of music have specific associations with seasonal observances, agricultural rituals, life-cycle events (births, marriages, funerals, etc.), and religious ceremonies (which in modern times encompass both indigenous belief systems and Catholicism, often in syncretic forms). For example, in Peru, traditional double-row panpipes called *siku* (see photo, p. 78) are associated with ayllu rituals and activities of the dry season, which lasts from April to October, whereas end-blown *tarka* and *pinkullu* cane flutes are played specifically for festivals held during the rainy season (November–March). Through such exclusive associations between seasons and instruments, ayllu communities in the Andes essentially orchestrate the year through their annual cycles of music performances (Stobart 2006:47).

Both in specific instances and general use, music encodes core values of *egalitarianism* that inform traditional social and cultural life in the Andean highlands. As the ethnomusicologist Thomas Turino explains, the concept of egalitarianism does not imply that all people of the ayllu are regarded as equal in all ways. Some families have more land than others, some people have specific skills that others lack, women and men have different modes of interaction, and so on. All of this is recognized and acknowledged, but there is an overarching application of egalitarian principles in the conspicuous absence of what Turino (2008:7) calls "formal structures or institutions of coercion or control through which certain individuals can force their will on others." Decision making, adds Turino, "requires group consensus . . . . everyone has to agree with a particular decision or project if full participation is needed. In keeping with egalitarian principles, individuals do not like to stand out in group settings and the group is emphasized over the individual" (Turino 2008:8).

The egalitarian ideal of the ayllu has profound musical manifestations on many levels. One of the clearest examples is to be found in the interlocking parts of paired panpipe instruments such as the siku and the **julajula,** the latter of which are played by members of the Quechua-speaking Kalankira community of the ayllu of Machu in North Potosí, Bolivia, for harvest season (*kusicha timpu*) rituals. This community has been the focus of ethnomusicologist Henry Stobart's research on music and culture in the Bolivian Andes. A julajula actually consists of two "half" instruments, each played by a separate player. One player performs on a panpipe with four tubes (pipes) that are tuned to four of the seven pitches of the scale used in julajula music; his partner plays on a panipe of three tubes tuned to the scale's three remaining pitches. The four-tube panpipe is called the *yiya* (from the Spanish word *guia,* meaning "leader"); its three-tube counterpart is called the *arka* (Aymara/Quechua for "follower"). The total range of the yiya and the arka combined covers just over an octave. From low to high, at least in some Kalankira julajula music, the yiya plays the notes D, G, B, and (high) E, while the arka supplies the notes in between the successive yiya pitches, namely, E, A, and (high) D. The composite sequence of yiya and arka pitches from low to high, then, with the yiya notes marked in boldface, is **D** E **G** A **B** D **E.** This scale is reproduced across multiple octave ranges by pairs of julajula that come in five or six different sizes and are played by ensembles that may comprise up to 25 or 30 men. Unlike most other traditional Andean ensembles that feature panpipes or flutes, the julajula ensemble is not normally accompanied by drums.

CD ex. #4-2 is a field recording (made by Stobart) of a group of Kalankira men performing on julajula panpipes in Machu during a corn beer making ritual. The timbres of the yiya and arka pipes are quite distinct from one another on this recording, so that it is relatively easy to hear how the melody is created through interlocking (the first two notes are played on the yiya, the next two on the arka, the next four alternate yiya-arka-yiya-arka, and so on; try to hear how the parts interlock as you listen). Playing julajula melodies like this one requires close coordination between the yiya and arka players. The interlocking parts and instruments are analogized to older and younger brothers (Stobart 2006:150). Neither part makes any sense alone; they are completely interdependent and both are essential. A variety of metaphors are used to describe this integral partnership, such as *qhespinakunku,* meaning "one without the other would die out" (Stobart 2006:150–52).

Julajula ensemble performing at a communal event in the Andes.

Performing julajula music requires skills *of* cooperative interdependence on the part of the players; at the same time, it powerfully demonstrates *how* cooperation and mutual dependence are essential to the proper functioning of the integrated, communal whole, providing through music an aural analog of the egalitarian ideal that pervades virtually every aspect of life in the ayllu. From pairs of brothers working together while harvesting potatoes to large-scale communal celebrations, the values of egalitarianism and collective endeavor cut across all levels of social engagement in the ayllu, and music serves as a potent embodiment and symbol of those values.

Musical and cultural traditions of the Andes such as those described above have been well documented in ethnomusicological publications, ethnographic films, and music recordings. The dominant medium of representation of Andean music and culture on a global scale, however, and even in countries like Bolivia and Peru, is only tangentially related to the actual lives and musical practices of indigenous people in ayllu communities. This dominant medium is the domain of so-called **Andean folkloric music,** which first developed not in the Andes but in the urban environs of Buenos Aires, and which crystallized in the "folk" clubs of Paris in the 1950s before ultimately being reappropriated by Bolivians and other South Americans in connection with several nationalist movements that swept the continent beginning in the mid-1960s.

Thomas Turino, inspired by the classic sociological theories of Max Weber, characterizes the phenomenon of Andean folkloric music as a "modernist-cosmopolitan cultural formation"

Promotional photograph of an Andean folkloric musician. Images like this one, along with Andean folkloric music itself, are used to market "Andean authenticity" to tourists and other international consumers.

kena (KAY-nah)

charango (cha-RAHN-go)

and identifies "belief in technological 'progress,' scientific method, capital accumulation, occupational specialization, and 'rational' bureaucratic organization and control" as core modernist values (Turino 2008:128). "When the cosmopolitan value of eclecticism—say, an interest in exotic Andean music and imagery—is combined with the fundamental modernist values," writes Turino, "the result is the transformation, or 'reform,' of the original tradition in light of modernist values" (Turino 2008:128). Adding an interesting if bizarre twist to this common transformative process is a certain sleight-of-hand trick of cultural appropriation that allows for the reformed, modernized cultural product (e.g., Andean folkloric music) to be presented and validated as the genuine article: for most people in the world who live beyond the confines of isolated ayllu communities of the Andes, it is assumed that the carefully crafted sounds and associated idyllic images (e.g., the photo on this page) of folklorized Andean music such as that heard on **CD ex. #2-6** are authentic representations of the raw, real thing—that this is the kind of music you would hear being played if you trekked to some remote, pristine ayllu way up in the Andes that had magically remained impervious to modern influences. The marketing strategies for such music ensure that these kinds of illusory assumptions are maintained to the greatest extent possible, since the selling of "authenticity" is key. In contrast to tango or bossa nova or tropicália, which celebrate the modernist-cosmopolitan spirit that pervades them, Andean folkloric music is essentially modern, cosmopolitan music that is often disguised as an authentic expression of roots indigeneity.

The *real* roots of Andean folkloric music such as that heard on **CD ex. #2-6** are to be found in 1940s Buenos Aires. It was here that a band called the Abalos Brothers (Los Hermanos Abalos) formed and began to play a mixed repertoire of cultivated Andean music, tangos, and gaucho songs. They used Andean instruments such as the *kena* (*quena*) flute and the *charango* (a mandolin-like instrument with an armadillo body that had been developed by Andean highlanders after Spanish models), as well as the standard guitar and the Argentine version of the Andean *bombo* drum. This instrumental lineup of kena, charango, guitar, and bombo established the standard for Andean folkloric groups internationally henceforth. Moreover, the polished performance style and aesthetic of the Abalos Brothers—which occupied a musical space light years removed from the rough-hewn, communal sensibilities of the ayllu (e.g., the julajula music of **CD ex. #4-2**)—transformed the traditional melodies and textures of Andean highland music into something entirely (or at least very radically) new, and that something became the new aesthetic yardstick by which "Andean music" was measured in its modernist-cosmopolitan incarnation.

The reformed style of music introduced by the Abalos Brothers gained wide popularity in Europe in the 1950s through the performances of Paris-based Latin American music groups such as Los Incas, which included Argentine and Venezuelan musicians and specialized in playing Abalos Brothers arrangements of Andean tunes. Los Incas would eventually (in 1963) record a landmark Andean folkloric album called *Amérique du Sud* that included an arrangement of the song "El Condor Pasa," itself the product of an earlier era of indigenous Andean musical appropriation (the *indigenismo* movement of early 20th century Peru) composed half a century before. Paul Simon acquired a copy of *Amérique du Sud* and was much taken with it, especially by "El Condor Pasa." He added English lyrics, and with his partner Art Garfunkel, dubbed vocals over the original Los Incas instrumental track. The result was Simon & Garfunkel's hit song "I'd Rather Be a Hammer Than a Nail," which became an anthem of the 1960s folk music movement in North America.

Returning now to the Andean music scene of Paris in the late 1950s and early 1960s, an explosion of Andean flute music ensembles occurred in the wake of the success of Los Incas and other pioneering groups. The cosmopolitan folkloric style crystallized in a more or less standardized form with an instrumental lineup of one or two kenas, charango, guitar, and bombo. Eventually, double-row panpipes such as the siku and other traditional instruments were added for novelty and variety. In many instances, instrumental combinations that defied traditional ayllu norms and conventions occurred; for example, sikus might be combined with pinkullus or tarkas, contorting the traditional calendrical distinctions between dry season and rainy season instruments.

In the mid-1960s, a variety of left-leaning political and social movements in South American countries that rallied around the championing of indigenous groups and causes created new markets "back home" for folklorized forms of Andean music. Gilbert Favre, an expatriate Swiss kena player who had settled in Bolivia, collaborated with Bolivian musicians to form a folkloric ensemble called Los Jairas (The Lazy Boys) that became the leading group of its kind and helped to popularize the Bolivian style of Andean folkloric music that has largely dominated the scene during the intervening years. As Turino observes of contemporary times, "the folkloric style is so prominent in Bolivia that it has become the preeminent national emblem and popular commercial music. In spite of the facts that the folkloric style derived from cosmopolitan roots in Buenos Aires and Paris and was largely initiated in Bolivia by a European, Bolivians could claim special ownership of it since it featured instruments and certain genres indigenous to their country" (Turino 2008:136).

Jairas (HAI-rahs)

The ensemble Ukamau, which is featured on **CD ex. #2-6,** is representative of the modern Bolivian stream of Andean folkloric music. This recording of the song "Ratita" was drawn from a CD entitled *Magic Flutes & Music from the Andes*. The original CD booklet cover includes an image of two siku players and a bombo player attired in colorful ponchos and woven wool hats performing on a mountain plateau in front of a primitive-looking thatched roof hut. It is reasonable to assume that this photo was not shot on site at the recording studio in Hamburg, Germany, where "Ratita" was produced. The instrumentation reflects the standard format for the genre, with interlocking siku panpipes, kena flutes playing harmonized melodies, chordal and rhythmic accompaniment provided by charango and guitar, percussion parts, and vocal shouts and interjections presumably intended to create a "fiesta" environment akin to what one might expect to experience in an Andean ayllu. The playing is uniformly clean and well executed, consistent with the high aesthetic standards and production values of modernist-cosmopolitan music of this type. The opening passage of melody provides a clear illustration of siku interlocking textures, with the two panpipes alternating notes in customary fashion. The stereo separation of the recording places the two parts in separate channels (left and right), making it easy to hear how they interlock to generate the opening melody. After a charango interlude, the main melody of the kena flutes, played in pristine harmony, is introduced at 0:22. The alternation of siku sections and kena sections continues through the remainder of the track, with the charango and the guitar occasionally coming to the fore as well. This is not authentic music of the highland ayllu, but it *is* authentic modernist-cosmopolitan Andean folkloric music in the Bolivian style, and a good example of the genre at that.

Mexico: Mariachi

Listen to **CD ex. #1-20.** You may or may not know the name of this famous song, "Cielito Lindo." Whether or not you do, there is a good chance that you have heard it before, that you know or assume that its country of origin is Mexico, and that the style of music being played is called mariachi.

"Cielito Lindo"
("SEE-eh-lee-toh
LIN-doe")

Mexico is home to a great variety and rich history of diverse musical traditions, from *corridos, banda* music, and *norteño* (known as Tex-Mex north of the Mexican-U.S. border) to Mexican-style *cumbia* and *rocanrol* (Mexican rock). The best-known type of Mexican music, however, certainly beyond Mexico itself, is mariachi. For Mexicans, Mexican Americans, and diasporic Mexican communities worldwide, mariachi is more than just music; it is a national symbol. Los Angeles-based mariachi bandleader José Hernández has stated that playing mariachi "is like waving the Mexican flag. The mariachi is the flag wherever it

cumbia
(KOOM-bee-yah)

goes" (quoted in Sheehy 2006:54). During World Cup matches, Mexican fans regale their beloved soccer team with mass renditions of "Cielito Lindo." And in the Chicano (Mexican American) *movimento* that followed in the wake and spirit of the African American Civil Rights movement, mariachi was promoted and performed as "a proud symbol of Mexican identity" (Sheehy 2006:87–88).

traje (trah-hay)

There is a darker side to mariachi's social history as well. For many people in Mexico and beyond, the sound of the music, the stylized *traje de charro* "Mexican cowboy suit" donned by the musicians who play it (see photos, pp. 40 and 243), and the seemingly inescapable presence of mariachi music and imagery in virtually any movie, television show, commercial, or tourist-shop trinket that bears an identification with "Mexico" is deemed offensive. Throughout its modern history, mariachi has long been exploited in aid of the perpetration of negative, condescending Mexican stereotypes. Mass-media portrayals of Mexican people as fun-loving but not too bright, or as lazy, hapless, bumbling, corrupt, or shiftless, have too often been projected, and more often than not, the music and culture of mariachi have been invoked through sound and image in such portrayals.

One of the most infamous examples of such stereotyping was the Frito Bandito, the cartoon mascot of a popular series of Frito's corn chips commercials that were produced in the United States between 1967 and 1971. Voiced by Mel Blanc (also the voice of another stereotypical "Mexican" cartoon character, Speedy Gonzales), the Frito Bandito spoke in broken English with a highly exaggerated Mexican accent and had a penchant for stealing corn chips from people he encountered. The prototype for this character was to be found in earlier stereotypical portrayals of "Mexican bandits" that had been featured in Hollywood Westerns. The Frito Bandito's theme song was a mariachi-style performance of "Cielito Lindo" equipped with silly English lyrics ("Ie, yie yie yie. I am a Frito Bandito," etc.). Cultural perceptions of Mexico and Mexicans have been ineluctably affected—and not for the better—by the Frito Bandito phenomenon and related stereotypical representations, demonstrating once again that musicultural products of the modernist-cosmopolitan world are very often problematic and rife with complexities and contradictions.

The mariachi musical style that is known throughout Mexico and the world today is *mariachi moderno* (modern mariachi). The standard musical format and instrumental lineup of this style crystallized around 1950 among bands in Mexico City, the central location of the music's development since its emergence there around 1920. That lineup consists of trumpets (usually two or more), violins (typically three or more), *vihuela*, guitar, and *guitarrón*. The trumpet, violins, and guitar are of the standard type. The vihuela and the guitarrón, which appear in the photo in Chapter 3, page 40, were developed in Mexico from Spanish prototypes and are unique in origin to certain areas of western Mexico.

vihuela (vee-HWAY-lah)

guitarrón (gee-tahr-RONE)

The vihuela has five strings and is smaller than a standard guitar. Like the guitar, it is used for chords and rhythmic accompaniment and sometimes for the playing of melodies as well. The guitarrón is similar to the vihuela in appearance but is much larger; indeed, it is huge (imagine a guitar on steroids). It serves as the bass instrument of the mariachi ensemble. The vihuela, guitar, and guitarrón together constitute the *armonía* section of the ensemble, with the name "armonía" referencing the primarily harmonic (chordal accompaniment) function of this set of instruments. The singers, violinists, and trumpet players furnish most of the melodic material (note that most mariachi musicians both sing and play instruments). Harmonization of melodies in the violin, trumpet, and vocal parts is also characteristic of the mariachi style. In some forms of mariachi, ensembles of smaller size are employed. A case in point is the recording of "Cielito Lindo" on **CD ex. #1-20,** which was performed by a popular mariachi group from Mexico called Mariachi Sol. We return to that recording now for a closer listen.

armonía (ahr-mo-NEE-ah)

"Cielito Lindo" (*lindo* means "beautiful"; *cielito* may mean either "sweetheart" or "sky" and can also be a woman's name) is a traditional Mexican verse-chorus song that was reportedly composed by Quirino Mendoza y Cortés in 1882. It has been performed and recorded in many different styles and settings and is probably the most well-known Mexican song ever written. When played by mariachi groups, it most commonly takes the form of the version heard here, with a medium tempo and triple meter waltz-style rhythm.

The lyrics of the first verse (here summarized in English translation) are highly metaphorical and enigmatic: "They come down from the Sierra Morena mountains, a pair of black eyes, [my] beautiful sweetheart, which is contraband." Interpreters of a historical bent have suggested that these words reference armed bandits and drug runners of the 1600s who lived in these mountains. It also has been posed that Cortés adopted this opening verse from a song about such bandits written during that earlier historical period. Romantics hear in these words a plainer message of adoration for the heaven-sent, virginal (ergo forbidden/"contraband"), black-eyed beauty that is the serenader's muse. The chorus and subsequent verses offer more straightforward fare in which the serenader tries to woo his would-be young lover. The chorus implores the maiden to "sing and not cry, for singing gladdens the heart." Its opening "Ie, yie yie yie" refrain is without doubt one of the most familiar—and most often parodied—musical phrases ever created.

The instrumentation used by Mariachi Sol on this track consists of a single trumpet, vihuela, guitar, and guitarrón, plus a lead male vocalist and a male chorus (*coro*). There are no violins. All of the instrumentalists sing as well as play. We first hear the trumpet intoning the familiar "Ie, yie yie yie" melody over a straightforward armonía accompaniment in which the guitarrón plucks out the bass notes of the chord progression on the first beat of each three-beat measure and the vihuela and guitar reply with strummed chords on beats two and three (refer to Figure 3.10 on p. 39 of Chapter 3). The bass-chord-chord, triple meter accompaniment pattern of the introduction continues uninterrupted throughout the entire song. The first verse, featuring the lead vocalist singing in a romantic *bel canto* (operatic) style, commences at 0:20, and is followed directly by the uplifting first chorus at 0:53, where everyone joins in on the richly harmonized "Ie, yie yie yie" melody. The same alternation of lead singer and harmonizing chorus recurs in the subsequent verses and choruses of the form. One other notable feature of this performance is the presence of what are known as *gritos* at key points. Gritos may take the form of spoken vocal interjections, shouts, yells, or hoots, and occur as responses to emotional moments in the music; gritos are characteristic of mariachi style. Several occur during the trumpet solo commencing at 1:58.

gritos (GREE-tose)

The roots of urban mariachi moderno are to be found in rural traditions of the Mexican countryside, especially those of Jalisco in the west of Mexico. From Jalisco came the *son jaliscience,* one of many regional genres of *son* (Spanish for "song"; the plural form is *sones*) that were adopted and adapted into mariachi. The Jalisco tradition of *son* is regarded as the bedrock of the mariachi repertoire. (Note: Mexican and Cuban *son,* the latter of which is discussed elsewhere in the chapter, are separate traditions.) Distinctive forms of *son* from other regions of Mexico (*son jarocho, son huasteca*) became mariachi staples early on as well, as did the songs and styles of three other traditions: the *huapango,* which is believed to have roots in dance-music styles of the Náhuatal Indians indigenous to the Huasteca region of northeastern Mexico; the *canción ranchera* ("ranch song"), an urban, stylized form of "country music" that developed mainly in connection with the thriving film and radio industries of Mexico City beginning in the 1930s; the *bolero ranchero,* a suave, romantic style of Mexican song that was originally derived from the Cuban *bolero*; and the polka, a popular dance of 19th-century Europe that spread to Mexico and throughout the world—from Poland to Paraguay and Chicago to Sweden— acquiring a plethora of national and regional variants in the process.

jaliscience (ha-lis-kee-EN-say)

jarocho (hah-RO-cho)

Huasteca (Hwah-STAY-kah)

canción ranchera (kahn-see-YONE rahn-CHAY-rah)

bolero ranchero (bo-LAY-ro rahn-CHAY-ro)

According to mariachi scholar and performer Daniel Sheehy, the huapango, the canción ranchera, the bolero ranchero, the polka, and the various regional genres of Mexican *son* "are so characteristic of the mariachi that they help define the essence of its sound," with *son* in particular having defined that sound "more than any other form of music" (Sheehy 2006:28–29). But these five important genres represent just the tip of the iceberg relative to the many, many different types and styles of music that have been absorbed into mariachi's unfathomably diverse and eclectic repertoire: cumbia from Colombia, *joropo* from Venezuela, waltzes and classical favorites from Europe, Broadway show tunes, bluegrass, rock-and-roll, and hip-hop from the United States. There appears to be virtually no limit to either the mariachi appetite for novel musical styles or the resourcefulness of mariachi musicians in casting different types of music in the mariachi mold.

The motivations for such cosmopolitan eclecticism are closely tied to mariachi economics. The stock in trade of most bands is playing songs requested by customers at restaurants, bars, or other venues. Customers pay by the song, and if the band does not know the song being requested this equates to a potential loss of income. Top mariachi bandleaders are reported to have repertoires of 1,500 or more songs, and there is a saying among professional mariachi musicians that if you only have 200 songs, you might as well stay home in the village.

The origin of the term *mariachi* is not clear. The earliest known written use of the word in connection with music appears in an 1852 letter written by a Catholic priest who was based near the present-day Jalisco region. In that letter, he describes entertainments "that generally are called in these parts *mariachis*," in which music is played and "many crimes and excesses are committed" (see Sheehy 2006:15). Some speculate that the term *mariachi* may be a corruption of the similar-sounding French word for marriage, *mariage,* which seems at least plausible given the music's historical associations with wedding ceremonies and varied romantic functions, such as serenading lovers or would-be lovers.

The urban transformations that would ultimately lead to the familiar mariachi moderno style embodied in performances like the version of "Cielito Lindo" heard earlier began to take shape around 1920. It was in that year that a guitarrón player named Cirilo Marmolejo from the town of Tecolotlán, Jalisco, traveled with his sextet to Mexico City and began to perform in the area. This group eventually came to be known as Mariachi Coculense (Cocul is a town in Jalisco that has produced many of the finest mariachi musicians). They, along with a host of similar groups based in the city around the same time, helped to establish the urbanized, professional musical style and culture that within short order had become widely known as mariachi.

By 1925, Mexico City was awash in mariachi music. Hundreds of musicians would gather daily at the city's famous Plaza Garibaldi to serenade passersby with hopes of enticing potential clients to hire them for events. The tradition continues to the present day. The emergence of a recording industry in Mexico City in the 1920s was a major development affecting mariachi musicians. Many of them made records that helped to popularize the music beyond its local environs and brought a much-needed source of new income. The advent of radio in 1930 had an even greater impact on the dissemination and profitability of mariachi. By the early 1930s, a bourgeoning film industry had been established in the capital as well, and this boosted mariachi's fortunes all the more. Cirilo Marmolejo and his group appeared in the first Mexican sound film, *Santa* (1931), and soon appearances by mariachi bands in films coming out of Mexico City, and eventually Hollywood too, were commonplace.

"Over the next three decades," writes Sheehy (2006:20), "the media—radio and film in particular—would amplify the mariachi's impact throughout Mexico and beyond, and would transform its image and sound into those of the mariachi we know today." It was through the Mexican cinema that solo vocalists singing in the operatic, bel canto style rose to star status in the mariachi culture and that a mass marketing niche was opened for mariachi music as a major "brand" of popular culture, first throughout Mexico and ultimately throughout the rest of Latin America. According to Sheehy, Colombia, Venezuela, Guatemala, Bolivia, Nicaragua, and El Salvador are just a few of the many Latin American countries in which scores of local professional musicians regularly put on their mariachi cowboy suits and hire themselves out to play the latest sones, rancheras, and boleros for enthusiastic audiences (Sheehy 2006:64–65). Like salsa and other popular Latin genres, mariachi has become a key component of pan-Latino identity. It has also achieved popularity in Europe, Japan, and elsewhere internationally.

The biggest mariachi markets outside of Mexico are found in major cities of the United States, especially in the Southwest (e.g., Denver, Phoenix, San Antonio). Los Angeles is arguably the largest and most important stateside center for mariachi. On many levels, the city's vibrant mariachi scene has been inextricable from that of Mexico since the 1930s, not least of all through mutual influences between the Mexican film industry and Hollywood. It is noteworthy, too, that several Los Angeles mariachi bandleaders—Pedro Hernández, José Hernández, and Natividad (Nati) Cano—have Jalisco roots. Cano, who was born and raised in Jalisco, directs the foremost U.S.-based mariachi band, Mariachi Los Camperos. For some fifty years, they have performed at Los Angeles's La Fonda Restaurant, where they have presented their spectacular mariachi dinner show for an estimated three million patrons and become a major cultural institution. In the late 1980s, Cano's group played on the Grammy Award–winning Linda Ronstadt album *Canciones de Mi Padre* (Songs of My Father), on which the popular vocalist sang renditions of traditional songs of her Mexican heritage. The album became a milestone in the revival and popularization of mariachi worldwide. Also featured on this album was Mariachi Vargas de Tecalitlán, a Mexican group of international prominence that, according to ethnomusicologist Steven Loza, "has generally been recognized as the most long-standing and successful group in the history of mariachi music" (Loza 1993:92).

Linda Ronstadt and Mariachi Vargas de Tecalitlán.

From the sones of Jalisco to the Frito Bandito, mariachi's history encompasses a veritable cornucopia of musicultural traditions and transformations that might be seen as a microcosm of the compelling and sometimes confounding mixture of linkages, contradictions, and incongruities that have defined the modern musical world at large for a century and more. Sometimes it's enough to make you just want to throw your hands up and say, "Ie, yie yie yie."

Cuba, Creolization, and the Roots of Latin Dance Music

Having surveyed other musical traditions of Latin America, we return now to our principal focus on the musicultural matrix of Cuba, Puerto Rico, and the United States.

The roots of the Cuban dance-music styles that gave rise to the cha cha chá and, in turn, to the song "Oye Como Va," take us back to Spain and West Africa. Centuries ago, Spain colonized Cuba (as well as Puerto Rico) and instituted slavery there, bringing millions of African slaves to the island. It was through the blending of musical elements of Spanish and West African derivation—their syncretization or *creolization,* in the hands of first African slaves and then their African-derived and *mulatto* ("mixed race") descendants especially—that the distinctive forms of Afro-Cuban music that form the basis of all of the popular Latin dance music genres we will discuss were born.

An understanding of Cuban dance music and the popular Latin music styles that grew from it begins with an understanding of the creolization of African-derived (principally West African) and European-derived (principally Spanish) musical culture in Cuba.

Afro-Cuban roots of Latin dance music

The European discovery of Cuba occurred in 1492, when Christopher Columbus and his Spanish fleet arrived on the island. The indigenous population was comprised of Amerindian peoples such as the Taino, who, tragically, were all but wiped out in the wake of the Spanish conquest. Spanish settlers began arriving in Cuba in 1511. They established large sugar cane plantations. African slaves were brought to the island in huge numbers—an estimated five million in all—to work the plantations. They came from many different African nations and ethnic heritages, but most were of either Yoruba or Congolese descent (*Note*: Today, the Yoruba are West Africa's largest ethnic group; the majority of their population is based in Nigeria. The

Congolese presence in modern Africa is reflected in the names of two nations, Congo and the Democratic Republic of the Congo; the name for conga drums also is related.)

A very large majority of the slaves brought to Cuba arrived between 1790 and 1860, much later than their counterparts in British colonies of the Caribbean and in the United States. (Importation of slaves to the British Caribbean colonies ceased in 1804, and the U.S. slave trade also greatly declined around that time.) This relatively late arrival of slaves in Cuba helps to explain why, even today, much Cuban music sounds distinctly more "African" (and, more specifically, Yoruba- or Congolese-derived) than other African-derived musics of the Americas (e.g., American blues, Jamaican reggae).

Other factors account for this difference as well. Due to differing approaches and attitudes toward the institution of slavery on the part of slave owners, traditional African-rooted forms of worship, music, and dance were retained in Spanish colonies such as Cuba to a much greater extent than they were in British colonies (e.g., Jamaica, Trinidad) or in the United States. Additionally, compared to their counterparts in Jamaica, Trinidad, or the U.S., a relatively large proportion of Cuban slaves were able to buy or seize their freedom. Thus, sizable communities of free blacks were established in Cuban towns and cities by the early 18th century, and they, together with slaves in these same areas, celebrated religious and social occasions in ways that were largely consistent with the practices of their African forebears. These conditions fostered an environment that "favored the dynamic flourishing of neo-African music in Cuba" (Manuel 1995:20).

Two types of traditional, neo-African music in Cuba would prove especially influential to the later development of Latin dance music: ritual drumming associated with the Afro-Cuban religion of **Santería** (Regla de Ocha) and the secular, social dance music of traditional Cuban rumba.

Santería
(San-te-REE-yah)

batá (bah-TAH)

Santería ritual drumming is traditionally performed on a set of three drums called **batá** (see the photo on page 22, in which two of the three drums are visible). Each drum is of a different size and pitch (low, medium, high). Stringed bells attached to the lowest-pitched, lead drum enhance its timbre, providing an idiophonic element to the sound. The drums are played in an intricate, interlocking style of complex polyrhythms (see Hagedorn 2001, Amira and Cornelius 1992). The lead drummer's part involves much improvisation, whereas the two other drummers' parts are mainly based on recurring rhythmic patterns (ostinatos). In ritual contexts, the batá drums often accompany sacred songs, such as the one heard on **CD ex. #4-3.**

clave (KLAH-vay)

The music of rumba also features a set of three drums—low-, medium-, and high-pitched—played in a complex, polyrhythmic style. The modern, barrel-shaped conga drums used by many contemporary Latin and popular music groups are descendants of the original rumba drums (called *ngoma*). Rumba drummers today usually play the music on congas.

Conga drums and claves.

All of the rhythms in rumba music in a sense derive from a single rhythm called **clave,** which is played on an instrument, the **claves,** that consists of a pair of thick, round sticks that are struck together. Indeed, the clave rhythm, of which there are actually four variants (see Figure 11.1 on p. 245, corresponding to **Online Musical Illustration #25**), is the rhythmic basis of virtually all forms of Latin dance music, including cha cha chá tunes like "Oye Como Va." Clave is so fundamental to Latin dance music that it is often not even actually played; rather, its presence is simply *felt,* by the musicians, dancers, and listeners alike.

In traditional rumba performances, the percussion instruments (the three conga drums, the claves, and an additional wooden idiophone called *palitos* that usually plays an

FIGURE 11.1

The four versions of the clave rhythm.

Son 3-2   X • • X • • X • • • X • • X • • • •   *Son 2-3*   • • X • X • • • X • • X • • X • • •

Rumba 3-2   X • • X • • • X • • X • • X • • • •   *Rumba 2-3*   • • X • X • • • X • • X • • X • • • X

embellished version of the clave rhythm) accompany songs sung by a lead singer and a group of background singers (the *coro*, or chorus). The singers interact with each other in call-and-response style. The music accompanies dancing. The dance associated with the style of rumba music heard in **CD ex. #4-4,** called *rumba guaguancó,* is performed by a man and a woman who engage in what ethnomusicologist Peter Manuel has characterized as "a pantomime game of coy evasion on the woman's part and playful conquest on the man's" (Manuel 1995:25).

Spanish-Cuban roots of Latin dance music

The other half of the story of traditional, creolized forms of Cuban dance music that preceded modern Latin styles as represented in songs like "Oye Como Va" has to do with European, especially Spanish, musical influences.

Creolized dance-music styles blending African (especially Yoruba and Congolese) and European (especially Spanish) elements became highly prominent beginning in the latter part of the 18th century. Prior to that, white urban Cuban society had relied mainly on European genres such as the waltz, the minuet, and the mazurka for their dance entertainment. Increasing disenchantment on the part of the white Cuban establishment with economic restrictions and governmental corruption and inefficiency issuing from Spain led to a rejection of these cultural symbols of the European past. New, distinctly Cuban hybrid dance-music forms emerged as Cuban musicians—primarily of Afro-Cuban or mulatto descent—grafted rhythmic and other elements of African-derived traditions onto adapted European dance-music forms. These new, creolized styles, such as the *contradanza* and the danzón, became important symbols of an emergent Cuban national identity that arose in the late 1800s in connection with a strong, anti-Spanish rule nationalist movement. They reflected a shift toward a more inclusive notion of what constituted Cuban identity, one in which whites, blacks, and mulattos all had a place (though full racial equality was by no means achieved). Some of the creolized dance-music styles also gained international popularity, setting the stage for the dominance of Cuban-derived musics in the international Latin music culture of later periods.

By the 1920s, the danzón had essentially become the national dance of Cuba. Danzón music was mainly performed on a type of "sweet-sounding" ensemble called a **charanga.** Charanga instrumentation usually featured a wooden flute and two or more violins backed by a piano, a string bass, a *güiro* (wooden scraper idiophone—see photo, p. 246), and a pair of drums that were the forerunners of the modern timbales. Maracas (shakers) were often used as well.

guaguancó (wah-wahn-KOH)

charanga (cha-RAHN-gah)

güiro (WEE-ro)

A couple dancing to the accompaniment of the Cuban group Rumba Morena.

Güiro and maracas.

Around this same time, however, in the 1920s, the dan-zón's status as the reigning form of Cuban national dance music was challenged by the emergence of a new, more heavily African-influenced style called *son.* Yet despite the dramatic ascent of *son,* both in popularity and as a symbol of Cuban national consciousness (see Moore 1997; Manuel 1995, for more on this subject), the danzón and the charanga did not fade away. Rather, they rallied to meet the challenge. The charanga danzón groups, "with their quaint yet soulful flute-and-violin sound, were surviving by changing with the times and making their music hotter and more Afro-Cuban" (Manuel 1995:41). This led to the emergence of a new dance-music style, the danzón-mambo (Gerard 2001:68), and in turn to the Cuban cha cha chá style in which the direct musical ancestry of "Oye Como Va" is rooted.

The Danzón-Mambo

The danzón-mambo was a highly Afro-Cubanized version of the earlier danzón. The principal charanga group responsible for its development was Arcaño y sus Maravillas (or Maravillos). This group was led by the flutist Antonio Arcaño, but two other members of the band, the brothers Orestes López and Israel "Cachao" López, were the principal innovators of the danzón-mambo style.

Elements of Afro-Cubanization were present at multiple levels in the danzón-mambo. Conga drums were added to the standard charanga percussion section of timbales, güiro, and maracas. The complex and syncopated rhythms played on the congas added a strong imprint of Afro-Cuban rhythmic character to the music. (This imprint reflected influences from *son* especially.) Additionally, a cowbell was added to the percussive arsenal of the timbales player (*timbalero*), paving the way for the development of the standard "drum kit" setup of modern timbaleros like Tito Puente (consisting of two or more metal-sided timbale drums, cowbells, woodblock, one or more cymbals, and sometimes additional instruments—see the photo on p. 224).

These various elements of Afro-Cuban musical influence were most prominent in the so-called *mambo sections* of danzón-mambo arrangements. These highlighted rhythmically exciting music with lots of repetition and textures featuring layered ostinatos. Even the violins, whose function in earlier danzón styles had been almost entirely melodic, took on a largely rhythmic function in the danzón-mambo, playing syncopated ostinato figures that complemented the Afro-Cuban character of the percussion parts. Soaring, improvised flute solos were another signature element of the style.

The historical importance of the danzón-mambo is twofold, since its influence fed directly into the two most successful and influential Latin dance-music phenomena of the early 1950s, **big band mambo** and cha cha chá. These two genres, in turn, would coalesce in the original Tito Puente version of "Oye Como Va."

Enrique Jorrin and the Cuban Cha Cha Chá

While the López brothers moved the danzón in an increasingly Afro-Cuban, *son*-influenced direction through the late 1940s, another alumnus of Arcaño y sus Maravillas, the violinist and bandleader Enrique Jorrin, took the music in another direction altogether beginning in 1950. It was in that year that Jorrin recorded a composition entitled "La Engañadora" (The Beguiler) with his own charanga group, Orquesta América. This was the first cha cha chá ever recorded.

It represented a fusion of older danzón sensibilities with the retention of certain elements that had come into the music via the danzón-mambo, such as the use of conga drums.

As interesting as the musical synthesis itself in cha cha chá was its underlying motivation. More than anything, Jorrin wanted to devise a Cuban dance-music style that would appeal to non-Cuban dancers, especially Americans. He was reportedly first inspired to compose "La Engañadora" after watching a group of American dancers struggle to keep up with complex Cuban rhythms on the dance floor (Fairley 2000:389).

The key to creating accessible Cuban dance music, Jorrin reasoned, was rhythmic simplification. Thus, he dispensed with the syncopated rhythm of the timbales part heard in danzón and danzón-mambo arrangements and replaced it with a "four-square rhythm" in which the steady beat was crystal clear (at least by Latin music standards). Tempos were kept in a comfortable, medium range, so as not to tax the dancers' feet or aerobic conditioning too much. Even inexperienced, non-Cuban dancers were able to keep pace with the relatively simple "one-two-cha-cha-chá" footwork required. The rhythmic foundations of cha cha chá music are illustrated and explained in the Musical Guided Tour for this chapter. The transcript on page 248 corresponds to the audio Musical Guided Tour. As you listen to this tour at the Online Learning Center (www.mhhe.com/bakan2e), follow along with this transcript.

Another distinctive feature of the Jorrin-style Cuban cha cha chá was the role of the singers. Singing, which had either been entirely absent or used sparingly in the danzón-mambo style, became an identifying feature of the cha cha chá. However, the harmonized vocal textures and involved patterns of vocal call-and-response found in earlier Cuban musics such as rumba and *son* were here substituted for by simpler, mainly unison singing textures.

Following the success of "El Engañadora," Jorrin released other popular cha cha chá recordings. One of these was "El Bodeguero" (The Grocer). **CD ex. #4-5** is an excerpt from a recording of "El Bodeguero" performed in a modern charanga arrangement that for the most part remains true to the original Jorrin style (though electronic keyboard instruments are used and there are no violins). A contemporary Cuban group, Grupo Cimarrón de Cuba, is featured. As you listen, take note of the accessible dance rhythm (which is anchored by the same types of percussion instruments and rhythmic patterns demonstrated in the Musical Guided Tour), the unison group singing texture (up until 1:20, after which the vocal parts are harmonized), and the prominent role played by the flute.

"El Bodeguero"
("El Bo-day-GAY-ro")

The "Cuban light" appeal of the cha cha chá, as represented by the music of Enrique Jorrin and a host of other musicians influenced by him, proved highly marketable internationally. The dance swept across North America and Europe in the 1950s, aided greatly by the advent of two new technologies, television and the LP (long-playing) record. By mid-decade, it "had become the vogue among aficionados of Latin music in the United States and abroad" (Loza 1999:142).

Cha cha chá fizzled out after a few years, however, at least as an international mass culture phenomenon. Its decline was most certainly hastened by the rock-and-roll explosion of the mid- to late 1950s (e.g., Elvis Presley, Chuck Berry, Jerry Lee Lewis, Little Richard), but cha cha chá was also a victim of its own unabashedly populist, commercial appeal; its "commercialization and Arthur Murray-style dilution . . . guaranteed its decline" (Manuel 1995:41). "A few years of lumpy rhythm sections, mooing sax section [*sic*], and musicians raggedly chanting CHAH! CHAH! CHAH! were enough" (Roberts 1979:133).

Couple dancing the cha cha chá in the 1950s.

Bongó drums being played.

In a standard cha cha chá, the timbalero (timbales player) marks out a basic beat of steady quarter notes in a four-beat meter on a small cowbell, like this [♪]. Sometimes extra notes are added between the main cowbell beats to embellish the rhythm. Here is an example of what that sounds like [♪]. This embellished version of the cowbell rhythm is reinforced by the wooden scraper-type idiophone called the güiro, whose part sounds like this [♪]. Another timbral layer is often provided by the maracas (shakers), which play a rhythm of steady eighth notes, like this [♪]. The cowbell, güiro, and maracas together, then, create this rhythmic texture [♪].

Another percussive layer of cha cha chá rhythm is furnished by the conga drums, with their signature, syncopated rhythmic pattern called *tumbao* (toom-BAH-oh). Tumbao is a rhythm that can be traced back to traditional rumba styles (and that also finds parallels in ritual batá drumming). It came into the cha cha chá via the influences of *son* and the danzón-mambo. Alone, tumbao on the conga drums sounds like this [♪]. Together with the cowbell, güiro, and maracas, it sounds like this [♪]. An additional layer of rhythm furnished by a small pair of drums called the **bongó** (bon-GO [as opposed to the English pronunciation BAHN-go]) may be incorporated as well [♪], resulting in this overall sound and rhythmic texture [♪].

Though the clave rhythm is often not actually played in a cha cha chá performance, its presence is clearly implied by the tumbao rhythm of the conga drums. We will now play tumbao on the congas together with clave rhythm played on a pair of claves; notice how the conga part seems to trace the shape of the clave rhythm while at the same time filling in the rhythmic spaces between clave strikes [♪].

Finally, here is the full percussion section—including the claves—playing as they would in a standard cha cha chá arrangement [♪].

Yet the cha cha chá did not die. In fact, it took on new life and a new sound in the hands of the same great New York–based Latin bandleaders who had blazed the trails of the other Cuban-derived Latin dance craze of the early 1950s, big band mambo. For these bandleaders and their audiences, cha cha chás provided a nice contrast to the hot rhythms, fast tempos, heavy syncopations, and trenchant Afro-Cubanisms of the mambos that otherwise dominated their set lists. The four-square rhythm of the cha cha chá possessed an elegantly funky quality all its own and gave the denizens of the Latin dance ballrooms of New York and other places a chance to slow down and get acquainted between tear-it-up mambo numbers. Yet while it represented a contrast to the big band mambo style, the new style of the cha cha chá that yielded tunes like "Oye Como Va" was musically influenced in important ways by big band mambo, to which we now turn our attention.

Mambo (Big Band Mambo)

The musician commonly credited with the "invention" of the mambo (from a Congolese word meaning "chant") was the Cuban bandleader Pérez Prado, who spent the majority of his career touring and recording in Mexico and elsewhere outside of Cuba. It was Prado who had the first international mambo hit, "Mambo #5," in 1949 (which would later form the basis of Lou Bega's 1999 hit song of the same title).

Yet while Prado may have crystallized the mambo into a distinctive genre, it was the bands of a group of bandleaders in New York City known as the **mambo kings**—Machito and the Afro-Cubans and groups led by Tito Puente and Tito Rodríguez—who took mambo to its most sublime heights. Fusing the Prado-style mambo with a deeper entrenchment in Afro-Cuban percussion and rhythm, as well as abundant use of borrowed elements from American jazz and popular music of the day, they created something profoundly new and different. "For the first time," writes Cuban music scholar Charley Gerard, "a new Cuban style originated outside of the island" (Gerard 2001:2).

Mambo, as developed by the big New York Latin dance bands of Tito Puente and his contemporaries in the early 1950s, was a musical genre defined by the following features:

- **Big band instrumentation.** This was adapted from the model of American big band swing and jazz of the era. The typical lineup included trumpet, trombone, and saxophone sections; plus a rhythm section of piano, bass, and three or more percussionists (with singers possibly in addition, depending on the arrangement). The percussion section featured the three types of drums also used in Cuban *son* bands: the timbales, the conga drums, and the bongó drums, along with additional Latin percussion instruments (cowbells, claves, güiro, maracas, etc.).

- **Musical textures featuring layered ostinatos throughout the band.** The parts of all of the instrumentalists—the percussionists, pianist, bassist, saxophonists, trombonists, and trumpet players—featured ostinatos, or *riffs*, that were repeated over and over, often with variations, and layered one atop the other. The resulting layered ostinato textures, inspired by Cuban *son* and danzón-mambo, created "a tight, composite rhythm that had a unique drive and an electrifying appeal to dancers" (Manuel 1995:37).

- **Driving, Afro-Cuban percussion rhythms.** The syncopated, interlocking rhythms of the percussion section in mambo, all growing from the root rhythm of clave and reflecting the characteristic Cuban styles of rumba and *son*, served as the engine that drove the music.

- **Jazz influences.** Beyond the big band instrumentation, influences from American jazz were reflected in the harmonies (chords and chord progressions), rhythms, and arrangements of mambos, and also in the highlighting of extended, improvised instrumental solos.

- **Fast tempos and highly energetic playing.** The tempos of the mambos were upbeat and the music was exciting and eminently danceable (though not *easy* to dance to, unlike the cha cha chá).

- **Absence, or at least limited use, of singing.** Compared to related Cuban forms like *son*, there was relatively little focus on singing—and in turn on song texts—in mambo. "With its emphasis on short, often meaningless vocal interjections, it was the perfect style for an audience who didn't speak Spanish" (Gerard 2001:2–3). This was important, since mambo was designed to appeal to Latino and non-Latino audiences alike (and succeeded in doing so).

The big band mambo sound outlined above is well illustrated by the mambo "Sambia" (**CD ex. #4-6**), a classic recording by Machito and the Afro-Cubans. Listen especially to the section that begins at 0:19, which follows the jazz-inspired opening. First the saxophones present a riff (0:19–0:26), then they repeat it with the trumpets and trombones "answering" between phrases in call-and-response fashion (0:27–0:35), and finally an intricate texture of layered riffs is created by saxophones, trumpets, and trombones together (0:36–0:52). All the while, the driving Afro-Cuban rhythmic base of the rhythm section pushes the music along with propulsive force and energy.

Tito Puente, the Newyorican Connection, and Latino/American Music Culture in New York City

Despite its principally Cuban musical lineage, the culture of Latin music in New York in the 1950s and beyond represented a complex mixture of ethnicities and cultures. Of the leading mambo bandleaders, Machito and Mario Bauzá were from Cuba, but Tito Rodríguez was from Puerto Rico, and Tito Puente, as was mentioned earlier, was a Newyorican, born and raised in New York of Puerto Rican descent. The personnel of the bands were likewise ethnically diverse. The percussion section of Machito and the Afro-Cubans, for example, featured drummers from Cuba as well as Newyorican percussionists who were intensely devoted to mastering the Afro-Cuban styles (these included a young Tito Puente at one point—see pp. 251–252). All of this reflected larger demographics of Latino/American society during this period. As Gerard explains, "Afro-Cuban music developed its stateside [U.S.] home not in Cuban neighborhoods, which . . . were primarily white, but in Puerto Rican neighborhoods, where Afro-Cubans mixed with dark-skinned Puerto Ricans" (Gerard 2001:13). Primary among these Puerto Rican neighborhoods in both size and cultural influence was Spanish Harlem in New York City, otherwise known simply as the *barrio* (neighborhood).

Tito Puente was born in the barrio of Spanish Harlem in 1923 to Puerto Rican immigrant parents. He grew up there, absorbing the myriad influences of traditional Puerto Rican music, Afro-Cuban music, American popular song, African American jazz, big band swing, even Western art music. All of these were integral parts of the rich, living soundtrack that surrounded him in his native musical environment and formed the fabric of his eclectic and syncretic musical range.

"The background of the perennial bandleader," Gerard says of Puente, "is a perfect metaphor for what made him a central figure in stateside Cuban music. He grew up speaking English on the street and Spanish at home. As a young man, he learned big band [jazz] drumming.

Machito and the Afro-Cubans in the History of Latin Dance Music

Machito and the Afro-Cubans, the band featured in "Sambia" (**CD ex. #4-6**), was one of the most important and influential of all Latin dance bands. It was this group, more than any other, that formed the seminal link between Cuban dance music in Cuba and Cuban-derived dance music in New York, ultimately leading to the profusion of modern, international styles of Latin dance music that would emerge.

Machito and the Afro-Cubans formed in 1940, two years after Machito moved to New York from his native Cuba at the invitation of his longtime musical collaborator (and brother-in-law) Mario Bauzá. Bauzá had settled in New York several years earlier. In the late 1930s, so-called Latin dance music in the United States was dominated by the syrupy, sanitized Latin sound of the Spanish-born, Cuban-raised popular musician Xavier Cugat. Like Enrique Jorrin with the cha cha chá, Cugat opportunistically set out to create a style of Latin music that would have broad popular appeal beyond the Latino market, but he went considerably farther in this direction than did Jorrin with the original cha cha chá. "To succeed in America," Cugat once said, "I gave the Americans a Latin music that had nothing authentic about it" (Roberts 1979:87).

Cugat's formula proved immensely successful. He became a perennial New York high-society favorite, playing "for Anglos in swanky lower Manhattan ballrooms" (Manuel 1995:69). He and his orchestra also appeared in numerous Hollywood films, introducing mainstream America to the ostensibly "Latin" dance-music sound. Cugat's popularity paved the way for later popular Latin bandleaders who worked in an essentially similar idiom, such as Desi Arnaz of television's *I Love Lucy* fame.

Bauzá and Machito, "disgruntled with the watered-down rhythms of Latin society bands" like Cugat's, launched Machito and the Afro-Cubans in response. They forged an innovative musical approach that was rooted in the classic *son* style of Cuban masters like Arsenio Rodríguez, but that also incorporated the sonic force of the jazz big band and the influences of jazz improvisers like Dizzy Gillespie and Charlie Parker, the future founders of bebop jazz. "With powerful horns and a hell-fired rhythm section, the band immediately captured the attention of the Latino community in New York" (Leymarie 2002:4).

Publicity shot of Desi Arnaz.

As a teenager, he joined Machito's orchestra and learned how to play Cuban popular rhythms. Later, he made it his business to acquaint himself with Afro-Cuban culture. A trained musician [in Western art music] who read music fluently, he took the study of the oral tradition of Afro-Cuban folkloric music seriously at a time when many musicians thought that if you weren't from an Afro-Cuban *barrio* you could never master the idiom" (Gerard 2001:2).

This multicultural upbringing and eclectic musical background would profoundly shape Tito Puente's multifaceted conceptions of his own identity throughout his life. As we learned earlier in the chapter, he identified himself principally as a Puerto Rican even though he was born and raised in New York:

> Wherever I go . . . they ask me, "What are you?" I say "I'm Puerto Rican" . . . But I am international, too. I play for all kinds of people, and they dance to my music and I have all kinds of a following; so I don't want to tag myself . . . but when they ask me who I am, I represent Puerto Rico. (Puente, quoted in Loza 1999:224–25)

The vibraphone.

Yet when asked about his *musical* identity, his standard response, despite his greatly varied musical experience, was simply, "I play Cuban music" (Puente, cited in Manuel 1995:74).

These different types of self-identification may seem paradoxical, but they are completely consistent with the larger history of Latin music culture in New York City. According to Manuel, Newyorican and Puerto Rican immigrant musicians who had mastered and in a sense reinvented traditional Cuban music styles were dominating the city's Latin music scene by the 1940s (Manuel 1995:67).

Tito Puente joined Machito and the Afro-Cubans in 1942 but was drafted into the U.S. Navy shortly therearter. (He played drums and saxophone with the Navy band.) Returning to New York in 1945, he reestablished his career as a dance band musician and also enrolled at the prestigious Juilliard School. He studied conducting, orchestration, music theory, and percussion at Juilliard, and became especially interested in playing the vibraphone during this period.

The post–World War II era brought massive migration of Puerto Ricans to the U.S. mainland, the majority coming to New York. This created a growing market for dance bands that played Cuban-derived Latin music, which had long been popular in Puerto Rico. An influx of important new arrivals from Cuba, including the great percussionists Chano Pozo (who developed an important association with Dizzy Gillespie), Mongo Santamaría, and Francisco Aguabella, altered the musical landscape as well. They brought with them the authentic rhythms of Cuban batá drumming and rumba, and these were absorbed into the musical fabric of bands like Machito's. Puente became an avid protégé of Aguabella and Santamaría, in particular, soaking up all he could about Afro-Cuban drum styles, music, and culture.

The year 1949 proved to be a pivotal one for Puente and Latin music. It was in this year that Pérez Prado's first big hit, "Mambo #5," launched what would soon come to be known as the *mambo craze* of the 1950s. It was also in 1949 that Max Hyman purchased New York's Palladium Ballroom and quickly transformed it into the epicenter of the burgeoning mambo world. Riding the wave of mambomania, Tito Puente formed his first Latin dance band that same year, and within short order was playing the Palladium and other top venues and rivaling the likes of Machito and Tito Rodríguez for top billing as the reigning king of mambo. His bands were as hot and as innovative as any, and included percussionists such as Mongo Santamaría, Francisco Aguabella, Ray Barretto, Manny Oquendo, and Willie Bobo alongside Puente on the timbales in what today are remembered as some of the greatest Latin rhythm sections of all time.

Buoyed by his star status at the Palladium, Tito Puente went from success to success, touring widely with his band and making many records. By the time he released his most popular song, "Oye Como Va," on the 1963 album *El Rey Bravo,* he had almost 40 albums as a bandleader to his credit, including big sellers like *Dance Mania* (1958). By this time also, "mamboized" cha cha chás like "Oye Como Va" were a staple of his repertoire. We now turn our attention to this classic recording.

guided listening experience

"Oye Como Va," Tito Puente (1963)

- CD Track #**4-7**
- Featured performer(s)/group: Tito Puente band, with Tito Puente (timbales)
- Format: Complete track
- Source recording: *El Rey Bravo,* by Tito Puente (Tico/Sonido)

The Palladium Ballroom

The Palladium must have been an amazing place to be during the heyday of the mambo. Battles of the bands between top groups like Puente's and Machito's were a highlight of the entertainment format, and audiences delighted in the sizzling results of these informal contests as each band tried to outdo the other. The Palladium was also interesting as a hotbed of multicultural interaction, its audiences often casting off the shackles of racial and ethnic division to meet out on the dance floor. "The audiences that began to form in the Palladium and other dance halls," explains Steven Loza, "were, like those of jazz, highly integrated, notwithstanding the elements of discrimination and segregation that still existed in a large part of the society" (Loza 1999:222). For Latin music historian Max Salazar, the mambo and the Palladium scene were nothing less than agents of profound social change in American society: "The Palladium was the laboratory. The catalyst that brought Afro-Americans, Irish, Italians, Jews. God, they danced the mambo. And because of the mambo, race relations started to improve in that era. What social scientists couldn't do on purpose, the mambo was able to accomplish by error" (Salazar, quoted in Loza 1999:68). The Palladium was also a great venue for celebrity watching. Entertainer Sammy Davis Jr., painter Jackson Pollock, beat poet Allen Ginsberg, and movie stars Marlene Dietrich and Marlon Brando were all patrons. Brando was even known to sit in on the bongó drums with Machito on occasion!

Tito Puente and his band performing at the Palladium.

The original Tito Puente recording of "Oye Como Va" is essentially a cha cha chá with big band mambo instrumentation, textures, and stylistic elements. Comparing it to the more traditionally Cuban cha cha chá style of "El Bodeguero" (**CD ex. #4-5**), one discovers both similarities and differences. While the basic groove and feel of the conventional cha cha chá dance rhythm are present in both, the tempo of "Oye Como Va" is slightly faster, giving it an edge and intensity that contrasts with the more relaxed feel of "El Bodeguero." Additionally, and more importantly, the organ and bass riffs of "Oye Como Va" that swirl around the foundational cha cha chá percussion groove (which is first introduced just by clicked sticks and handclaps and is then reinforced by the full complement of timbales, congas, and güiro from 0:15 on) offer the Puente performance a deliciously funky and syncopated rhythmic flair, generating a kind of swagger that finds no parallel in "El Bodeguero." (The use of the organ itself was a novel feature introduced into Latin dance music with this recording.)

The minor key of "Oye Como Va" (A minor) also creates a contrast with "El Bodeguero," which, in common with the majority of traditional Cuban cha cha chás, is a tune in a major key. Compared to the cheerful, lighthearted quality of brightness created by "El Bodeguero," "Oye Como Va" comes off as a bit more hard-nosed and gritty, an effect at least partially attributable to its minor key.

At 0:15, the entrance of a big band–style horn section (saxophones, trumpets, and trombones) along with the full Latin percussion section puts the instrumentation squarely in the camp of big band mambo. The improvised, solo playing of the flute, however, forms a clear link to the charanga instrumentation of Cuban-style cha cha chá. Reminiscent of traditional cha cha chá, too, is the singing in "Oye Como Va" (0:46 –1:04, 1:56-2:18), which features a group of male vocalists who are also the instrumentalists in the band (as opposed to designated

FIGURE 11.2

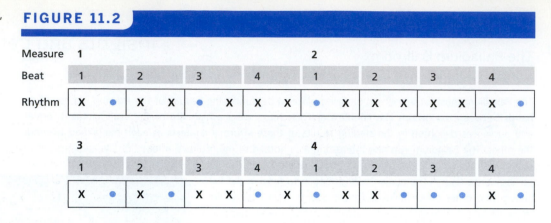

Measure	**1**				**2**			
Beat	1	2	3	4	1	2	3	4
Rhythm	X •	X X	• X	X X	• X	X X	X X	X •

	3				**4**			
	1	2	3	4	1	2	3	4
	X •	X •	X X	• X	• X	X •	• •	X •

singers) singing a short and simple tune with a single-line Spanish text in which a *macho* protagonist boasts about the potency of his "groove" to a *mulatta* dancer.

At 0:38, just before the singing begins, the entire band joins together in the playing of a syncopated, unison figure that is highly compelling (the rhythm is charted out in Figure 11.2). This unison figure, which returns intermittently at different points in the arrangement, has over time become a recognizable musical signature of this famous song.

Following a partial return of the signature unison figure at 1:01, the band launches into the first of two instrumental mambo sections—that is, mambo sections set to a cha cha chá rhythmic groove—beginning at 1:05. Layered riffs (ostinatos) in the horn section grow progressively overtop a continuing cha cha chá groove in the rhythm section. As in Machito's "Sambia" (**CD ex. #4-6**), the saxophones start things off, repeating their riff over and over from 1:05 forward. Next come the trombones at 1:20 and then the trumpet riff at 1:36. Occasional vocal interjections like "uh-huh," along with a whistle or two and sporadic moments of flute improvisation, are thrown into the mix as well.

Following a partial return of the signature unison figure, a second singing of the "Oye Como Va" tune, and an exciting crescendo that builds through the whole band, the second mambo section arrives at 2:19. In this mambo, the saxophone, trombone, and trumpet riffs are more syncopated and complex than in the first mambo. The flute soloing is more animated here, too, and sporadic singing, vocal shouts, and whistling create a party-like atmosphere. Then, like a precision knife cutting through thick brush, the signature unison figure returns at 3:06 to close out the section. At this point, the band stops playing and there is cheering, whistling, and applause. But just when you think it's all over, Tito and company kick it up one last time for an encore mambo at 3:26, then finish up for real with a final statement of the signature unison figure at 4:19.

guided listening quick summary

"Oye Como Va," by Tito Puente (CD ex. #4-7)

INTRODUCTION (INSTRUMENTAL)

0:00–0:45

- Piece begins with syncopated organ riff over straight cha cha chá rhythm (the latter initially marked out just by clicked wooden sticks and handclaps).
- Full percussion section and horn section enter at 0:15 (following a lead-in played on the timbales): timbales, congas, and güiro play standard cha cha chá rhythmic patterns; horns (saxophones, trombones, trumpets) double organ riff rhythm.

- Flute takes main melody beginning at 0:23 (charanga-esque).
- Signature unison figure played at 0:38.

SINGING OF MAIN TUNE, FIRST TIME

0:46–1:04

- "Oye Como Va" tune sung by group of male singers (unison/harmonized vocal texture; cha cha chá groove).
- Partial return of signature unison figure at 1:01.

FIRST MAMBO SECTION (MAMBO I)

1:05–1:55

- Saxophone riff (1:05), trombone riff (1:20), trumpet riff (1:36).
- Another partial return of signature unison figure (1:51).

SINGING OF MAIN TUNE, SECOND TIME

1:56–2:18

- As before, but ends with big instrumental crescendo (2:11) leading up to second mambo section.

SECOND MAMBO SECTION (MAMBO II)

2:19–3:13

- More syncopated and complex horn riffs than in first mambo section; building intensity.
- Flute, vocal shouts, and whistling create party-like atmosphere.
- Section concludes with full statement of the signature unison figure at 3:06.

ENCORE MAMBO SECTION (MAMBO III)

3:14–end

- Music stops; cheering, applause suggest we have reached the end, but then band launches into an encore mambo at 3:26 to conclude. Final signature unison figure at 4:19 brings performance to a close.

New Sounds, New Times: "Oye Como Va," the Santana Version

When "Oye Como Va" was released in 1963, Tito Puente was already well established as the king of Latin music. He was as famous and as respected as any Latin bandleader and was credited with numerous important innovations and achievements, musical and otherwise. "Oye Como Va" helped make *El Rey Bravo* Puente's second best-selling album up to that point (after *Dance Mania*) and became an audience favorite everywhere he played. But no one, least of all Puente himself, could have predicted the impact that "Oye Como Va" would ultimately have on the future of Latin music and Puente's own career.

In 1970, Santana, a San Francisco–based rock band with a Latin dance band twist, recorded a rock-infused cover version of "Oye Como Va" and included it on their second album, *Abraxas*. The album became a mega-hit, selling millions of copies. "Oye Como Va" was one of two hit singles to come out of *Abraxas* (the other was "Black Magic Woman"). It rose to #13 on the *Billboard* rock charts, an unprecedented achievement for a recording of a tune that had been taken "right out of the Latin catalog" of standard dance band numbers (Loza 1999:65). With "Oye Como Va" and *Abraxas*, Latin rock, a genre invented almost single-handedly by Santana and one that remains even today principally identified with that band and its leader,

Cover of Santana's *Abraxas.*

guitarist Carlos Santana, was cemented into the lexicon of Latin music. Beyond its own success, Santana's "Oye Como Va" also would have far-reaching effects on the career of Tito Puente, the "salsa explosion" of the 1970s, and the consolidation of a new and cosmopolitan pan-Latino identity that was closely tied to Latin music.

The rise of Santana and Latin rock

Carlos Santana was born in Mexico in 1947. He grew up listening to various kinds of music, especially American rock-and-roll and the recordings of Chicano (Mexican American) musicians such as Ritchie Valens, who had the first major Latino rock crossover hit with "La Bamba."

Santana took up the guitar as a child and by his early teenage years was gigging regularly in Tijuana area nightclubs. When he was 15, he moved to San Francisco. There he encountered and became enamored of an array of musics that were new to him. This was the early 1960s, and San Francisco was host to a booming, multicultural music scene. The closest thing to a West Coast New York (albeit with a very different cultural mix and urban flavor), San Francisco teemed with concert venues, nightclubs, and record stores. The city also was taking shape as ground zero for the youth counterculture movement that would revolutionize the American cultural, societal, and political landscape in the late 1960s (see also Chapter 8).

In this urban cauldron of cultural richness, Santana discovered the new jazz sounds of Miles Davis and John Coltrane (**CD ex. #3-1**). He got deeply into the blues of Muddy Waters and B.B. King, and indeed had already established himself as "an avid exponent of the blues before his Latin-rock innovations" (Loza 1993:282). As the decade progressed, he witnessed and became an integral part of San Francisco's own thriving rock music scene, where he shared the spotlight with the likes of Janis Joplin, Jimi Hendrix, and Sly and the Family Stone.

All of these experiences shaped Santana's musical vision and his unique and ultimately influential approach to the electric guitar. But the two elements that largely set him and his music apart were his Latino identity and the pervasive influence of Latin music on his musical style. This Latino musical imprint was present in the influences he had absorbed from his childhood in Mexico. Even more important, however, were the influences of leading New York–based Latin dance bands that he became familiar with through recordings by Tito Puente, Machito, Willie Bobo, and others.

insights and perspectives

Carlos Santana and Prince

As an innovator on the electric guitar, Carlos Santana has been a major influence on legions of younger guitarists, including Prince. Rock critics have often noted a close similarity between Prince's guitar style and that of Jimi Hendrix, implying that Hendrix was Prince's main influence on the guitar. Prince himself denies this, however.

"It's only because he's black," Prince has said regarding such comparisons with Hendrix. "That's really the only thing we have in common. He plays different guitar than I do. If they really listened to my stuff, they'd hear more of a Santana influence than Jimi Hendrix" (Starr and Waterman 2003:400).

Santana, featuring guitarist Carlos Santana (right), performing at Woodstock, 1969. The band's bassist, Dave Brown, is on the left.

SANTANA, THE BAND In 1968, Carlos Santana joined forces with several other up-and-coming young San Francisco–area musicians to form the band Santana. They came from working- and middle-class backgrounds and collectively represented something of a microcosm of American cultural diversity at the time: Latino, African American, Euro American. Their musical range was at least equally diverse. The group's unique sound coalesced as a synthesis of rock, blues, jazz, rhythm-and-blues, soul, Mexican, Chicano, Afro-Cuban, and contemporary Latin dance musics.

Santana's big break came when they were invited to perform at Woodstock, the historic 1969 rock festival that would come to define an era and a generation. Santana was a little-known, upstart band at the time, but their Woodstock performance created a sensation. It launched their ascent to rock superstardom and also established their compelling Latin rock sound as a staple of American youth counterculture identity at a decisive historical moment. Tens of thousands of people moved to the groove of Santana at Woodstock, and millions more soon came to know the band through the film version of the festival, *Woodstock,* which was released not long after the actual event. As Ben Fong-Torres explains,

> [Santana] turned an also-on-the-bill stint at the Woodstock festival into a mesmerizing mini-set, and when they appeared in the Woodstock film, they galvanized audiences the way Janis Joplin had at Monterey Pop [another major rock festival of the late 1960s; see also Chapter 8]. On tour, town by town, they exposed fans to their revolutionary fusion of Afro-Latin rhythms and rock and roll and got them dancing—and running off to the record store. And it got fellow musicians and producers listening—and taking notes. (Fong-Torres 1998:2)

Santana played Woodstock in August 1969. The band's debut album, *Santana,* was released on Columbia Records in the fall of that same year. It was a major commercial hit, thanks largely to Santana's Woodstock triumph. *Santana* sold more than two million copies and produced a major hit single, "Evil Ways." "Evil Ways" was, in essence, a rocked-up version of a standard Latin dance band–style cha cha chá that had been composed and first recorded by the New York Latin bandleader, and former Tito Puente band percussionist, Willie Bobo. Santana mixed the traditional Latin percussion instruments (timbales, congas, güiro) and conventional cha cha chá groove of Bobo's original with elements of rock-style drumming (played on a drum set) to create the song's distinctive Latin rock rhythmic foundation. Above this rhythmic base, the tune was delivered in a highly electrified style, with the signature solo voice of Carlos Santana's electric guitar soaring atop the texture. The rock-ified cha cha chá sound of "Evil Ways," with its prominent electric guitar part and fused Latin and rock rhythms, introduced to the world the sound of Latin rock. It also set the stage for "Oye Como Va," in which Santana applied a similar musical formula in their treatment of the Tito Puente original.

***ABRAXAS* AND "OYE COMO VA"** *Abraxas,* Santana's second album, was released a year after their debut album, *Santana.* It produced the two hit singles mentioned earlier, "Oye Como Va" and "Black Magic Woman," and became the band's best-selling album ever. It is often described as the finest album Santana ever made and regularly appears on "greatest rock records of all time" lists.

Abraxas was created "under the stress of success" (Fong-Torres 1998:1). In the wake of Woodstock and *Santana,* Carlos Santana would recall many years later, "you had a bunch of kids who, next thing you know, were going to New York and hanging out with Miles Davis and all these incredible musicians, coexisting with Jim Hendrix, Janis Joplin, and The Who" (quoted in Fong-Torres 1998:2).

Such notoriety certainly had its upside, but it came with the price of pressure to follow up with an album that was not just as good as *Santana,* but even better. *Abraxas* met the challenge. It sold millions of copies and spent 88 weeks on the *Billboard* charts, holding down the #1 spot for six weeks. The singles it yielded, "Oye Como Va" and "Black Magic Woman," have both become enduring classics of the American popular music repertoire.

guided listening experience

"Oye Como Va," Santana (1970)

- CD Track #**4-8**
- Featured performer(s)/group: Santana, with Carlos Santana (electric guitar), Gregg Rolie (Hammond B-3 electric organ)
- Format: Complete track
- Source recording: *Abraxas,* by Santana (Columbia/Legacy)

In most respects, Santana's "Oye Como Va" is a straight-up cha cha chá modeled after the Tito Puente original version of 1963. In comparing the two, Steven Loza states: "Santana replaced the flute and horn riffs with his guitar to great effect. Otherwise, however, Santana's arrangement is basically a duplicate (minus some extra *coro* [chorus] and horn sections in Puente's arrangement) with a different instrumental texture and a fused rhythmic base of rock-R&B and cha-cha" (Loza 1999:196). Loza is correct, at least technically. Here is a list of basic musical features that remained intact from Puente's version to Santana's:

- The "Oye Como Va" tune itself.
- The key (A minor).
- The tempo.
- The simple, one-line, Spanish-language song text.
- The singing style (unison/harmonized vocal texture; group of male singers).
- The underlying cha cha chá groove.
- The basic form of the arrangement.

The main areas where Santana departs from Puente are in

■ The absence of the solo flute part and the horn section, both of which are essentially replaced by, and in some cases absorbed into, Carlos Santana's rock- and blues-inspired electric guitar playing.

■ The embellishment of the traditional cha cha chá rhythmic groove with rock-style drumming (played on a drum set).

■ The highly prominent role of the Hammond B-3 electric organ (played by Santana keyboardist Gregg Rolie) as a solo instrument, and the heavily blues- and rock-influenced style of the improvised organ solo.

■ The substitution of the horn riff–dominated mambo sections of the Puente original by improvised electric guitar and Hammond B-3 organ solos in the Santana arrangement.

Listed dryly on the printed page, the preceding list of differences between Puente's and Santana's versions of "Oye Como Va" may not seem like they would add up to much, but the whole is greater than the sum of its parts in terms of distinctive musical effect. These differences largely explain the rock anthem–like character of Santana's version, which is quite a dramatic departure from the mamboized cha cha chá character of Puente's rendition.

Listen now to Santana's "Oye Como Va" and make your own subjective comparison to the Tito Puente original explored earlier. How would you describe the similarities and differences, not just in terms of instrumentation and such, but also in terms of how they make you *feel,* what thoughts and images they bring to mind, perhaps even the different ways they make your body want to move? This is an excellent exercise for exploring how seemingly "technical" musical elements—changes in instrumentation, use of different technologies, modifications in rhythm, different approaches to solo improvisation—can combine to transform a composition into something very different than it once was.

On your second listening, follow along with the timeline of the Guided Listening Quick Summary in the box below and listen for the elements and features identified.

---

guided listening quick summary

"Oye Como Va," Santana version (CD ex. #4-8)

INTRODUCTION

0:00–0:37

■ Opens with the standard "Oye" organ riff (as in Puente original), but with the distinctive Hammond B-3 organ timbre creating a very different effect; also, no clicked sticks/clapping groove here, and the bass part is more prominent in the mix.

■ Standard cha cha chá groove established with entry of percussion section at 0:08; no horns; electric guitar (played by Carlos Santana) replaces the flute of Puente's version on the melody and bluesy guitar licks give the music a different character as well.

■ Signature unison figure arrives at 0:30.

SINGING OF MAIN TUNE, FIRST TIME

0:38–0:56

■ Singing is similar to that heard in the Puente version, though the vocal timbre is different.

■ Partial return of signature unison figure at 0:53.

FIRST IMPROVISED SOLO (ELECTRIC GUITAR)

0:57–1:44

- Played by Carlos Santana; electronic distortion enhances the basic timbre of the instrument.

- Replaces the first mambo section (Mambo I) of the Puente arrangement.

- Though horn section is absent, Carlos Santana's guitar solo actually builds mainly from lines adapted *from* the original Puente horn riffs (enhanced by occasional bluesy riffs at the ends of phrases).

- Percussion instruments played more freely here than in Puente (e.g., improvised drum fills in conga and timbales parts) and more of a rock feel is evident in the rhythmic groove, though a cha cha chá foundation still predominates.

INTERLUDE/TRANSITION #1

1:45–2:06

- First, return to opening organ riff (over cha cha chá rhythmic groove).

- Second, contrasting section (1:53) with very different mood and style.

- Third, dramatic crescendo at 2:04 (akin to the big crescendo at the comparable point in the Puente arrangement).

SECOND IMPROVISED SOLO (HAMMOND B-3 ELECTRIC ORGAN)

2:07–2:47

- Played by Gregg Rolie; note distinctive timbre of the Hammond B-3.

- Replaces second mambo section (Mambo II) of Puente arrangement.

- Rolie immediately rips into a heavy, rock- and blues-style solo that takes the piece far from its Latin roots and into new musical territory.

INTERLUDE/TRANSITION #2

2:48–2:58

- Shorter than first Interlude/Transition section.

- Partial return of signature unison figure at 2:56.

SINGING OF MAIN TUNE, SECOND TIME

2:59–3:21

- Sung as before.

- Singing followed by an extended crescendo build-up at 3:14 (again reminiscent of the Puente recording).

THIRD IMPROVISED SOLO (ELECTRIC GUITAR)

3:22–end

- Played by Carlos Santana.

- Begins like the first guitar solo, but then ventures further afield into rock-blues territory; as solo progresses, Santana shifts back and forth between Latin, rock, and blues styles, creating a highly effective and fluid blend of stylistic elements.

- Performance concludes with a final full statement of the signature unison figure at 4:06.

The Hammond B-3 Organ and "Oye Como Va"

The Hammond B-3 organ, as heard in Santana's "Oye Como Va," was one of the emblematic sounds of rock music of the 1960s and 1970s. (Another band of the period that featured the instrument prominently was The Doors.) The original Hammond electric organ, the Model A, was invented by Laurens Hammond in 1935. That led to the popular B-3, which was manufactured from 1955 to 1975 and became a staple of not only rock music during that period, but of jazz, blues, and gospel as well. Comparing the very different organ sounds of the Puente and Santana recordings of "Oye Como Va" we have listened to (only the latter features a B-3) offers a good example of the Hammond B-3's powerful musical effect.

Beyond the Music: Santana, "Oye Como Va," and Pan-Latino Identity

For Carlos Santana, the decision to include "Oye Como Va" on *Abraxas* was "a natural." In his own words, "I thought, this is a song . . . that when you play it, people are going to get up and dance, and that's it" (quoted in Fong-Torres 1998:6).

That *was* it, and perhaps still *is* it, but there is more to consider as well. Santana's "Oye Como Va" did not only turn the rock world upside down. It also helped to galvanize Latin dance music and its culture; became a symbol of an emergent pan-Latino identity; and brought new-found renown, wealth, and professional opportunities to Tito Puente himself.

Santana's "Oye Como Va" and Tito Puente

Tito Puente, as the composer of "Oye Como Va," made more money from Santana's recording of the tune than he did from any of his own recordings, much more in fact. "That was the one recording that Puente could have retired on," Latin music producer and radio personality Lionel "Chico" Sesma told Steven Loza in an interview. "He probably made more money off the royalties of that Santana recorded success than he had made in his entire life before that. That must have galled him to no end" (Sesma, quoted in Loza 1999:98).

Galled him perhaps, but it also revitalized Puente's career and the Latin music scene more broadly. Prior to Santana's "Oye Como Va," Latin music had been in a state of progressive decline in terms of mainstream commercial popularity. The rock-and-roll explosion of the mid-1950s had squashed the mambo and cha cha chá crazes in the United States and internationally. Beatlemania and the flourishing of a plethora of new rock and pop styles in the 1960s pushed Latin music even further out of the spotlight. The Latin dance bands of Tito Puente and others managed to stay in business and even to thrive, but their market narrowed, being confined mainly to sectors of Puerto Rican–dominated Latino communities and some other areas. Even within U.S. Latino communities, members of the younger generations gravitated away from the Latin bands and toward rock. Exacerbating the situation was the United States' tense relationship with Cuba, which had become a socialist state under Fidel Castro in 1959 and had been largely shut off from the U.S. since the early 1960s. Though Latin dance music was rarely being marketed as Cuban music by this time, the fact of its core Cuban root identity remained. The dint of Latin music's historical association with Cuba did little to advance its cause in the United States in a tense political climate.

The success of Santana's "Oye Como Va" helped swing the pendulum of commercial viability back in the direction of Latin music. It brought youth culture and Latin dance music back together in a unique transformation and opened the door to a new age of Latin music culture beyond Santana's distinctive brand of Latin rock itself. In a review of *Abraxas* in *Rolling Stone* magazine, reviewer Jim Nash wrote, prophetically, "The major Latin bands in this country gig for $100 a night, and when you see them, you can't sit still. If Santana can reach the pop audience with *Abraxas,* then perhaps there will be room for the old masters like . . . Puente to work it out at the ballrooms" (Nash, quoted in Fong-Torres 1998:6).

In the wake of Santana's hit, Puente did indeed get to "work it out" as never before, not only at the ballrooms, but eventually at major music festivals and on concert stages worldwide as well. Nevertheless, the scope of his fame never approached Santana's own. As Puente told Steven Loza in a 1994 interview, Santana's "Oye Como Va" recording "really helped me a lot to get that recognition with the people, because when he does his interviews, you know he mentions it, and his interviews are twenty times bigger than mine. All over the world, and the people that he caters to, they're twenty, thirty, forty thousand people in a stadium. I cater to a few hundred people in a ballroom. It's quite different than the music that I play" (Puente, quoted in Loza 1999:45).

The king of salsa and Latin jazz

In another of the seemingly endless paradoxes that define the modern history of Latin music, Tito Puente's revitalized image as a Latin music icon occurred in connection with neither the mambo, the cha cha chá, nor any other style key to his initial rise to fame. Rather, he was reconfigured as the king of a "new" kind of Latin dance music that took shape in the 1970s, *salsa,* itself a New York (largely Newyorican) musical "invention" with decidely strong musical roots in the Afro-Cuban *son.*

Salsa, Loza explains, "basically adheres to the traditional structure and instrumentation of Afro-Cuban dance forms, but with significant embellishments, adaptations, and new formats and influences. Among the various artists spearheading this movement were Eddie Palmieri, Johnny Pacheco, Ray Barretto, and Willie Colón. Artists such as Tito Puente and Mongo Santamaría, who had been performing the same basic musical forms for the previous thirty years, adapted well and opportunistically to the new popular format . . ." (Loza 1999:16).

The timing of the "salsa explosion" of the 1970s was not a coincidence. Though it was by no means the whole story or even necessarily the main part of it, the success of Santana's "Oye Como Va" in 1970 had a significant impact. The huge spotlight of international attention that burned down on Santana was large enough to cast its light on the emerging stars of salsa as well, and the catchy marketing term *salsa* itself made for a more commercially viable product than, say, "Latin dance music."

Tito Puente had little use for the name salsa per se, but he recognized its promotional value and pragmatically accepted his title as the music's *de facto* king. "Salsa," he once told an interviewer, "means sauce, literally; it's just a commercial term for Afro-Cuban dance music which was used to promote the music. My problem is that we don't play sauce, we play music, and Latin music has different styles; cha-cha, mambo, guaguancó, and son. Salsa doesn't address the complexities and the rich history of the music that we play. But it's accepted now and it helped get the music promoted" (in Loza 1999:16; cf. Sanabria and Socolov 1990:23).

Puente's royal status extended to the realm of salsa's close musical relative, Latin jazz, as well. There is much overlap between the genres and it is often difficult, if not impossible, to clearly delineate one from the other. In general, however, it can be said that salsa emphasizes singing, is geared toward providing music for dancing, and is most popular among Latino audiences; and that Latin jazz emphasizes fully (or almost fully) instrumental textures, extended solo improvisations, and jazz-inspired musical forms and textures, while catering more to non-Latino audiences.

Tito Puente was and remains, even after his death, the leading figure in both areas. "An inspection of any contemporary major record store," wrote Steven Loza in 1999, will reveal that "the bins of Puente's recordings will predominate the various Latin jazz artists included in the collection; additionally, Puente will predominate the collection of the salsa artists. Two worlds and two markets have thus largely become associated with Tito Puente's music: the English-speaking and Spanish-speaking Americas. Added to this cultural matrix are the extended geographies of Puente's popularity, including Africa, Asia, and Europe" (Loza 1999:xvi). The record stores may have largely disappeared, but Loza's claims about Puente's enduring marketability remain relevant still today.

Deep Cuban Tradition Meets Salsa and Latin Jazz: Francisco Aguabella's "Nena"

Listen to **CD ex. #4-9.** This piece, "Nena," might be said to walk precisely down the middle line where salsa and Latin jazz meet. It is also a track that brings to bear the artistry of a musician of most impressive pedigree and deep Cuban roots who had a profound impact on the history of Latin music on many levels for more than 50 years, Francisco Aguabella (1925–2010). As was mentioned earlier in the chapter, Aguabella was one of several outstanding percussionists from Cuba who moved to New York in the 1950s and performed with the great Latin dance bands of Tito Puente. This is just one of the highlights of his illustrious résumé. He also performed and recorded with the likes of Dizzy Gillespie, Frank Sinatra, Peggy Lee, Machito, Tito Rodríguez, and Carlos Santana; and with fellow luminaries of the Latin percussion world including Mongo Santamaría and Poncho Sánchez. He additionally made important contributions as a Latin bandleader and composer, as represented by albums like *H20,* on which the track "Nena" was originally released, and as a teacher of international renown.

Francisco Aguabella was born and raised in Matanzas, Cuba, the heartland of Afro-Cuban sacred *batá* drumming and traditional Cuban rumba. He grew up surrounded by the sounds of batá and the rituals of Santería and other Afro-Cuban religions, as well as rumba played in the streets and at parties and other social events. Aguabella started studying the sacred traditions of batá drumming at the age of twelve and eventually rose to the rank of an *olubatá,* a master sacred drummer "sworn to the drum." Beyond mastering the musical traditions of Santería, he also became proficient in other sacred Afro-Cuban musics including Abakuá, Iyesá, and Arará, all of which had close ties to parallel religions of Yoruba, Ewe, and other West African cultures (Fernandez 2006:116–17).

As a young man, Aguabella moved from Matanzas to Havana, where he became an active part of the city's vibrant sacred and secular music scenes. There he came to know other great drummers including Mongo Santamaría and Carlos "Patato" Valdes, who would later move to New York and help to revolutionize both Latin music and jazz through their deep infusions of Afro-Cuban styles and rhythms into the repertoires of leading artists like Tito Puente, Machito, and Dizzy Gillespie.

When Aguabella himself made the move to the United States in 1957, he was immediately sought out by Puente, Gillespie, and others not just for his superb skills as a *conguero* (conga player) but also because of his deep knowledge of batá and other sacred Afro-Cuban drumming forms. He quickly gained recognition as the leading authority in this area residing in the United States. He collaborated during the year of his arrival on the Tito Puente album *Top Percussion,* which would attain instant classic status on account of its all-star cast of percussionists—Puente, Santamaría, Bobo, Aguabella, and others—and even more so due to its deep connection to the extraordinarily complex rhythms and forms of authentic batá drumming, which proved to be a major and compelling revelation for Latin and Latin jazz musicians and aficionados in the United States and elsewhere outside of Cuba. On the more popular, secular side, Aguabella not only performed with Puente's band, but also contributed two guaguancó tunes to Puente's hit album *Dance Mania.*

By 1958, Aguabella had grown weary of the fast pace and intensity of New York and relocated to the West Coast, residing mainly in Los Angeles and San Francisco during different periods. In addition to maintaining an active career as a bandleader, composer, and percussionist, he did perhaps more than any other individual to advance understanding of Afro-Cuban musical and cultural traditions as a teacher, especially in the area of batá drumming. His students included leading percussionists such as John Santos and Michael Spiro, as well as the ethnomusicologist Katherine Hagedorn, whose award-winning 2001 book *Divine Utterances: The Performance of Afro-Cuban Santería,* provides a fascinating account of the author's engagement with the tradition that is deeply indebted to Aguabella's teaching, performance, and influence. Aguabella was also the subject of an outstanding 1995 documentary film by Les Blank, *Sworn to the Drum*, which chronicles his life and lineage and includes invaluable performance footage.

Aguabella's album *H20* was originally released in 1986 by a small record label but received wider dissemination a few years later when it was rereleased by CuBop, one of the top labels historically for Latin jazz, comparable in impact to Fania Records on the salsa side. (The CuBop catalog is now available

through new reissues produced by Ubiquity Records.) The various selections on *H20* cover a broad range of styles and influences across the Latin jazz spectrum, with some tracks leaning to the salsa side, others residing dead center in the hard-driving Latin jazz mold, and still others displaying explicit resonances and rhythms of batá, rumba, *son,* and other traditional Cuban styles. Like Tito Puente and other greats, Aguabella didn't play sauce, he played music; the various elements from the plethora of styles and forms in which he was versed flow together with a fluidity that often belies clear identification in terms of one genre or another, though the classification for this album overall is Latin jazz.

"Nena," with its heavy emphasis on singing and highly danceable rhythm, is one of the most salsa-oriented tracks on *H20.* The complexly syncopated and beautifully harmonized vocal lines of the melody are performed by a coro consisting of Agua-bella, Orlando Lopez, and singer and timbalero Humberto "Nen-gue" Hernandez, who also supplies a tasteful timbales solo in the latter part of the track (3:15–4:00). The timbales feature section is preceded by a saxophone solo (2:24–2:59) in the mambo section of the form. The saxophonist builds to ever greater intensity over the accompaniment of first just the rhythm section and then layered riffs in the horn section as well. Finally, the saxophone gives way to the power of the horn section *en masse* for about 15 seconds at the 3:00 mark before the horns in turn give way to the aforementioned timbales solo. In the final part of the arrangement, a solo lead singer is heard for the first time, alternating phrases with the coro. In a standard salsa tune, this alternating call-and-response texture would first occur near the beginning of the arrangement. Here, in the innovative twists and turns of its salsa-inclined Latin jazz milieu, it arrives as a welcome and appealing climax to the tune but also as a bit of an afterthought to the overall musical design. Innovative, perpetually grooving, and steeped in the deep roots of Afro-Cuban tradition and all that has emerged from it, "Nena" is a fine example of pluralistic Latin jazz of the salsa persuasion.

"Oye Como Va" and the emergence of pan-Latino identity

Santana's "Oye Como Va" not only launched the band to new heights of fame and popularity, revived and redirected the career of Tito Puente, and helped ignite the salsa explosion of the 1970s, but also played an important role in the forging of a new Latino social consciousness rooted in the concept of pan-Latino identity. Santana's symbolic eradication of the boundaries between Latin music and rock served as a powerful symbol of a conception of Latino/American-ness that insisted on inclusion while demanding distinctiveness of identity, and that recognized the uniqueness of different "Latin" (Latino) nationalities and cultures while building bridges between them.

And Tito Puente, both as the composer of "Oye Como Va" and as an iconic figure of Latin music generally—of a music that was now being held up as a unifying symbol of pan-Latino culture—also found himself at the center of the pan-Latino social movement. His fame and notoriety, combined with his multiplex identity, musical and otherwise—Puerto Rican,

Newyorican, master of Cuban music, innovator of Latin music, fervent traditionalist and tireless experimenter, savvy and industrious entrepreneur, World War II veteran—made him an obvious choice as a symbol of pan-Latino pride. At a time when there was little Latino representation in U.S. political institutions, star musicians like Puente, not to mention Carlos Santana, became flashpoints around which to galvanize political mobilization and ethnic pride movements. As Loza explains,

> Throughout the midseventies, another factor that profoundly affected Puente's role as a master musician was that of a growing and expanding pan-Latino identity in the United States. Young Puerto Ricans, Chicanos, Cubans, Dominicans, Central Americans, and other Latin Americans who were living in the country began to unite in a political, social, and cultural momentum that constantly sought symbols, leaders, and common expression in the arts. The salsa movement was in full drive, and younger musicians and artists, as had Carlos Santana, looked to Puente for inspiration and leadership. (Loza 1999:175–76)

The roots of this pan-Latino movement that crystallized in the 1970s had already begun to take shape in the 1960s, and Puente was an important figure then, too. While many Latino youth were moving away from Latin music in favor of the Beatles and other popular non-Latin bands, some, like Carlos Santana himself, were "discovering" the likes of Puente and Machito at the *same* time that they were discovering the Beatles and the blues, and seeing no need for selecting one over the other. For progressive-minded young Latinos like Santana, it was hip, not backward, to be into the "old" music of an artist like Tito Puente. This was the logical entry point for the formation of a new, pan-Latino musical—and in turn social, cultural, and political—identity.

In the post-1970s era, Puente and Santana have remained enduring emblems of pan-Latino identity on many levels, their distinct personae bound together by the single song with which *both* of them are arguably most closely identified, "Oye Como Va." Santana, in keeping with the tenor of his times, has been more overt in his political activism as a musical statesman of pan-Latino causes than Puente was. But Puente's role was no less important, and the longevity of his significance as both a musical and social figure has been quite remarkable.

"Perhaps one of the most significant aspects of Puente," Steven Loza wrote shortly before Puente's death, "is that he became enmeshed with various generations—the adults, the children, and the babies of the forties through the nineties. Race and intercultural relations have taken different courses during these years, but Puente has attempted to adapt to each era. It can be said that he has taken more of the multicultural versus nationalistic course, consistently emphasizing the international popularity and charisma of his music and himself. At the same time, however, he has often been active in the artistic and political solidarity of the Latino community in the United States" (Loza 1999:224).

The pan-Latino movement that arose in the United States in the 1960s and 1970s now encompasses not just diverse Latino communities in the U.S., but nations throughout Latin America, from northern Mexico to southern Chile and throughout the Caribbean. Salsa, a Cuban-derived music developed in New York, has become an international Latino music and identity emblem. The Latin rock phenomenon intitiated by Santana has inspired or given rise to a myriad of commercially oriented popular Latin dance music styles. Perhaps no artist has so fluidly bridged the gap between musical artistry and activism on behalf of pan-Latino causes than the Panamanian salsa star Rubén Blades. Beyond being an exceptional musician with a

Rubén Blades in performance.

rare gift for infusing his songs with poignant social commentary, Blades is also a lawyer, a politician, and an actor who has appeared in several Hollywood films (*The Milagro Beanfield War, The Super*).

Directly or indirectly, the legacies of Tito Puente, Santana, and "Oye Como Va" are carried on in a great many spheres of the Latino/American musicultural world. Their convergence, however, is nowhere more clear than in the music of our final Guided Listening Experience, Tito Puente Jr.'s version of "Oye Como Va."

"Oye Como Va": The Next Generation

Since 1970, "Oye Como Va" has been recorded by everyone from muzak maestro Percy Faith to rapper Mr. Capone-E (Table 11.1). Of all the many renditions, the one that has probably generated the most public attention is that of Tito Puente's own son, Tito Puente Jr., the self-anointed Prince of Latin Dance music.

Tito Puente Jr. was born in New York City in 1971, just as Santana's "Oye Como Va" was climbing the charts. He is 24 years younger than Carlos Santana, 48 years the junior of his late father. He grew up "feeling the rhythms of [Latin] music before he could walk or talk" (Puente Jr. 2004). His first instrument was percussion. As he writes on his Web site, "I had no choice; there were 50 sets of timbales in the garage" (Puente Jr. 2004). He would later study piano, songwriting, and record producing as well—mostly under the tutelage of his famous father—and performed from an early age with his dad and with other Latin music legends, including the late, great Cuban American singer Celia Cruz.

As a young adult, Puente Jr. moved from New York to Miami. This move took him closer, culturally and geographically, to the source of the Latin music traditions that made his father famous, Cuba. It also placed him in the milieu of a city that today rivals New York as the Latin music capital of the United States, if not the world. With the possible exception of New York, Miami is the most ethnically and culturally diverse "Latin American city" anywhere. The Cuban presence—culturally, politically, and musically as well—is especially pervasive, but it is just one large piece of the city's very large pan-Latino cultural pie. "I'm thrilled with the many faces and sounds of Miami," says Tito Puente Jr. "The opportunity to listen to music from Mexico, South America, the Caribbean and other parts of the world has allowed me to expand my own musical horizons, so my music can reach more people" (Puente Jr. 2004). The pan-Latino mosaic of Miami is embedded in his music, much as the rich multicultural mosaic of New York City was embedded in his father's.

Guarachando (Wa-ra-CHAN-doh)

Puente Jr. acknowledges his father as his single greatest musical influence. The year 1996 saw the release (on EMI Latin) of *Guarachando,* the debut album of Tito Puente Jr. and the

TABLE 11.1	A sampling of other recordings of "Oye Como Va."	
Artist	**Year**	**Description**
Percy Faith	1971	Easy listening, orchestral ("muzak")
The Ventures	1971	Straight cover of Santana version
Fattburger	1996	Smooth jazz, melody played by flute
Michel Camillo	1997	Progressive jazz
Kinky	2004	Electronic/Latin Dance
Groove Society	2005	A cappella (unaccompanied vocal group)
Mr. Capone-E	2005	Rap/hip-hop

Latin Rhythm Crew. The album featured an innovative arrangement of "Oye Como Va" by Puente Jr. The sound of this "Oye Como Va," and of *Guarachando* generally, was at once eclectically (and electrically) contemporary and solidly grounded in the Latin dance music tradition of the elder Puente. Puente Jr. identified the style of this music as **Latin Dance** (not to be confused with the generic label "Latin dance music" used elsewhere in this chapter). Latin Dance is essentially a hybrid of diverse contemporary music styles—pop, rock, hip-hop, techno, Latino pop—"laced with influences of Mambo, Cha Cha and [Dominican] Merengue" (Puente Jr. 2004). This is a music that is pan-Latino—Latino/American—in a very broad sense. Puente Jr. describes Latin Dance as "a new explosion of authentic music created from the streets," but it is just as surely a novel synthesis of modern dance club music and earlier styles of Latin music. Echoes of his father's legacy resonate powerfully in Tito Puente Jr.'s work, as do the influences of later Latin music icons such as Carlos Santana.

Tito Puente Jr. in performance.

guided listening experience

"Oye Como Va," Tito Puente Jr. (2004)

- CD Track #**4-10**
- Featured performer(s)/group: Tito Puente Jr. group, with Tito Puente Jr. (timbales, percussion, vocals), Tito Puente (Sr.) (timbales), La India and Cali Aleman (vocals)
- Format: Complete track
- Source recording: *Tito Puente Jr.: Greatest Club Remixes* (TPJR Productions)

Tito Puente Jr.'s *Guarachando* performed well on the *Billboard* dance music charts, largely on account of the popularity of "Oye Como Va." The album also was honored with a prestigious Latin Music Award at the Grammys. The version of "Oye Como Va" included on your CD set is not the original 1996 recording from *Guarachando,* but is, rather, a remix version of that recording that was released on *Tito Puente Jr.: Greatest Club Remixes* (2004). This later version is the one preferred by Tito Puente Jr. himself (personal correspondence with the author, 2006). Among other differences, it puts the virtuosic timbales artistry of his father on more prominent display. Also featured here are the singers Cali Aleman and La India. La India is regarded as one of the top Latin female vocalists of the post–Celia Cruz era.

In Tito Puente Jr.'s "Oye Como Va," the traditional cha cha chá rhythmic groove and many other features of both the original Tito Puente and Santana recordings are present. They undergo various types of transformations in this novel, Latin Dance musical context, however. For example, there are instances where synthesized or digitally sampled reconfigurations of the sounds of traditional Latin percussion instruments, a mambo horn section, and even a Hammond B-3 organ (sampled directly from Santana's "Oye Como Va" recording) replace the original instruments. On the rhythmic level, a relatively conventional cha cha chá groove established at the beginning (0:07) is first embellished by the simple addition of off-beats, "played" on electronic hi-hat cymbals beginning at 0:15. But from 1:06 on, the basic cha cha chá feel, while never disappearing entirely, is subjected to a variety of rhythmic and timbral transformations that move the music in a progressively more funky and techno-influenced direction.

A new melody that provides an interesting counterpoint to the main "Oye Como Va" tune is introduced by La India at 1:19 and becomes a central feature of the arrangement henceforth. Many of the horn riffs from the original Tito Puente version are incorporated as well, but mainly in the form of digitally synthesized tones that give the music a very different character. Topping everything off is some brilliant timbales soloing that features both the elder and the younger Tito Puente playing together and trading licks. The dueling timbales increasingly become the driving force of the music from 2:44 to the end.

Altogether, Tito Puente Jr.'s "Oye Como Va" is a fun and creative take on this classic Latin dance tune. It succeeds in balancing tradition, transformation, and innovation, at once remaining grounded in the historical legacy from which it springs and pushing that legacy forward toward new musical vistas reflective of the time of its making (see Table 11.2, p. 269). Listen to it now, while following along with the Guided Listening Quick Summary in the box below.

guided listening quick summary

"Oye Como Va," Tito Puente Jr. version (CD ex. #4-10)

INTRODUCTION

0:00–0:06

- Begins with the standard "Oye" organ riff, this time in the form of a heavily processed digital sample of the Hammond B-3 organ from the Santana recording (*Note:* The key is A♭ minor, in contrast to the Puente [Sr.] and Santana versions, which are both in A minor).
- Electronically processed güiro timbre, along with other digitally sampled and synthesized Latin percussion sounds.

SINGING OF MAIN TUNE, FIRST TIME

0:07–0:24

- Standard singing style (unison/harmonized texture; male singers); electronically enhanced cha cha chá groove (especially from 0:15).
- Partial statement of "Oye" signature unison figure at 0:22.

FIRST MAMBO SECTION (MAMBO I)

0:25–0:43

- Melodic material based on horn riffs from Tito Puente's original version (sometimes including bluesy embellishments, *à la* Santana), but with simpler, shorter riffs and use of synthesizer timbres in place of actual horns.
- Section concludes with partial statement of signature unison rhythmic figure; call-and-response vocal exclamation "Everybody say WHOA-paaa!" laid over top (0:39–0:43) as groove continues underneath.

SINGING OF MAIN TUNE, SECOND TIME

0:44–1:05

- Off-beat electronic hi-hat cymbal rhythm (like that heard earlier, at 0:15) fortifies cha cha chá groove; some solo timbales improvisation interspersed.
- Return of signature unison figure (complete) at 0:58.

FUNK/CHA CHA CHÁ SECTION

1:06–2:17

- Cha cha chá groove radically transformed by funky, electronic percussion/bass groove.

- New melody introduced by female vocalist, La India, at 1:19 ("Ritmo Latino") becomes counter-melody to the main "Oye" tune.

- Main "Oye" tune sung again as heavy funk/cha cha chá groove continues at 1:35; syncopated interjections by La India between phrases.

- From 1:49, mambo-like riffs from synthesized "horns," group of male singers; La India continues.

- Short, improvised timbales solo (2:04–2:10), leading directly back to the signature unison figure (complete) at 2:11.

2:18–2:43

- Contrast provided by introduction of new "bass" synthesizer ostinato, then heavy, steady-beat bass drum pattern under a return of the main sung tune (at 2:25); texture changes again briefly at 2:33.

2:44–end

- Improvised timbales soloing (Tito Puente and Tito Puente Jr. together) adds energy and excitement as the music builds to a climactic unison ending.

- Puente Sr. heard exclaiming "That's it!" at the end.

TABLE 11.2 Summary comparison of Tito Puente, Santana, and Tito Puente Jr. arrangements of "Oye Como Va."

	Tito Puente	Santana	Tito Puente Jr.
Year	1963	1970	2004
Album	*El Rey Bravo*	*Abraxas*	*Tito Puente Jr.: Greatest Club Remixes*
Instrumentation	Big band horn section (saxophones, trumpets, trombones); layered ostinato horn riffs	No horn section, though horn riff figures are worked into electric guitar solo	Simplified horn riffs played on synthesizers
	Male voices	Male voices	Male voices plus female solo vocalist (singing contrasting melody)
	Main solo instrument: flute	Main solo instruments: electric guitar, Hammond B-3 organ	Main solo instrument: timbales (no melodic instrument solos)
	Organ	Different type of organ (Hammond B-3)	Digitally sampled B-3 with heavy electronic processing
	Acoustic bass	Electric bass	Synthesized/electric bass
	Latin percussion; cha cha chá groove	Drum set plus Latin percussion; cha cha chá groove reinforced by rock-style drumming	Timbales, etc., plus digitally sampled/synthesized percussion; funk/electronic grooves mixed with cha cha chá
Style	Mamboized cha cha chá	Latin rock/cha cha chá	Latin Dance/cha cha chá

Tito Puente Jr.: Into the future, back to the past

Since the death of Tito Puente in 2000, Tito Puente Jr. has dedicated much of his career to honoring his late father by carrying on his musical legacy. A second album of his from 2004, *En Los Pasos de Mi Padre* (In My Father's Shoes), was the most explicit tribute to his father's memory to date. It included classic Puente tunes from the mambo kings days of the 1950s and the salsa explosion years of the 1970s.

"I am now performing the music of Tito Puente," explains Puente Jr. "I think it's very important that the youth of today understand the music of my father, la música de ayer [the music of yesterday], la música del Palladium. It's timeless music—music that makes you dance . . . Carrying the torch and the tradition of my father's music to a whole new generation of fans has been a lifelong dream of mine" (Puente Jr. 2004).

This carrying of the torch took an interesting twist in the early 2000s when Tito Puente Jr. became co-director of a band called The Big 3 Palladium Orchestra. His collaborators in this venture were none other than "Machito" Grillo and Tito Rodríguez. No, not the famed mambo kings of the 1950s, but their musician sons who bear their names. Puente Jr., Grillo, and Rodríguez, all fine musicians in their own right, joined forces to initiate "a lush and fiery rebirth of the music made famous by their fathers" via this most interesting project (Puente Jr. 2004). More recently, Puente Jr. has been heading up his own large Latin dance band, The Tito Puente Jr. Orchestra, a group he formed for the explicit purpose of introducing the music of his father to new generations of listeners and reintroducing it to earlier generations of Tito Puente admirers.

Summary

This chapter surveyed a diverse range of Latin American musicultural traditions from South America, Mexico, and the Caribbean. Its primary focus was on particular Latin dance musics that originated in Cuba and experienced important developments in Puerto Rico and the United States. The central case study was of a particular song representative of that historical musicultural trajectory, "Oye Como Va." We chronicled its path from Afro-Cuban ritual music, to Afro-Cuban rumba, to creolized Cuban dance-music styles such as the danzón and the danzón-mambo, to the cha cha chá and big band mambo styles of the 1950s, to the original 1963 Tito Puente recording of "Oye Como Va," to "Oye Como Va" as re-created by Santana (1970) and Tito Puente Jr. (1996/2004).

Comparing and contrasting the three versions of "Oye Como Va" explored in the later part of the chapter offered a revealing view of processes of musical tradition and transformation. Musically, commercially, socially, and even politically, each of these distinct yet related interpretations of the same song speaks both to the times and conditions of its own emergence and the historical and cultural legacy to which it belongs. "Oye Como Va" *is* an article of tradition, and like all articles of tradition, it is at once both perpetually ripe for creative transformation and possessed of the inherent capacity to remain resolutely itself regardless of the types of change to which it is subjected. Like the legacy of Afro-Cuban music, or the legacy of Tito Puente, "Oye Como Va" endures at the core of its many surfaces and interpretations.

As for Tito Puente himself, his spirit and legacy are being carried forward today by many great musicians, including his own talented son. Though promotional in nature, the following passage from Tito Puente Jr.'s Web site captures a quality that is, in essence, real and true. It offers a fitting point of closure for this chapter's musicultural journey:

> Natural heir to the throne of El Rey, he is unmistakably the son, physically, spiritually and musically of Tito Puente, seminal bandleader, percussionist and legendary good will ambassador of Latin music.
>
> Young Tito's heart is rooted deep in the musical soul of his father. But he is staking out a future in the affectionate response of those who want a modern edge added to the sensuous music that runs

through all Latin lives. Puente Jr. is taking his own eclectic sound and like his father before him—is making history and moving generations.

Certainly his father is there in the wide grin, the wild timbales and the charisma that rushes past the footlights and tells the world that this is the music that moves your feet, your soul and your spirit. (Puente Jr. 2004)

Key Terms

timbales
salsa
Latin jazz
rhythm section (piano, bass, percussion)
riffs
horn section (saxophones, trombones, trumpets)
cha cha chá
Latino/American
samba
bossa nova
tropicália
steel band

tango
mariachi
Latin music (1. generic; 2. as Cuban-derived tradition)
rumba
danzón
son (Cuban)
danzón-mambo
mambo
Latin rock
Newyorican
conga drums (congas)
bandoneón
ayllu

julajula
Andean folkloric music
Santería
batá
clave (rhythm)
claves (instrument)
charanga
big band mambo
bongó (bongo drums)
mambo kings (Machito, Tito Puente, Tito Rodríguez)
Latin Dance (as contemporary dance-music genre)

Study Questions

■ What three recordings of "Oye Como Va" were explored in this chapter? Who was the featured artist/ band on each? What years were they recorded and on what albums did they originally appear? What similarities and differences were there between them? How was each a reflection of Latino/American music and identity at the time it was recorded?

■ What styles and traditions of Latin American music (Latin music) from South America, Mexico, and the Caribbean were surveyed in this chapter? What are the countries of origin, main musical features, and key historical and cultural features of each? Create a study chart to list and organize this information.

■ In what senses might Tito Puente be described as an individual of complex, multiple ethnic/musical identities?

■ What are batá drums? In what type of religious ritual context are these drums used? What was Francisco Aguabella's significance in the dissemination of batá drumming?

■ What is involved in the performance of rumba and what kinds of instruments are used?

■ Describe the following instruments: timbales, congas, bongó, claves, güiro, maracas.

■ What is the clave rhythm and why is it important?

■ Define and discuss the following dance-music genres: danzón, danzón-mambo, *son,* cha cha chá, salsa. Note musical features and important historical points.

■ Who were the mambo kings?

■ What were the six defining features of big band mambo listed in the chapter?

■ What were defining features of Santana's Latin rock style? How were these manifest in the Santana version of "Oye Como Va"?

■ How are salsa and Latin jazz similar to and different from one another? How might Francisco Aguabella's "Nena" be heard as a synthesis of both, as well as a musical embodiment of their common Cuban roots?

■ In what ways has Tito Puente Jr. carried on his father's musical legacy? In what ways has he introduced innovations that extend the range of Latin dance music? How is his recording of "Oye Como Va" representative of this merging of tradition and transformation?

Discussion Questions

- Latin American music is integral to the basic fabric of musicultural life throughout the Americas. Outside of what you have studied in this chapter, what kinds of Latin music have you encountered in your daily life? How is this music used to reflect and express ethnic and cultural identity, and how has it shaped your own impressions or experiences of Latino culture?

- How might any three (or four or five) of the musicultural traditions discussed in this chapter (e.g., tropicália, mariachi, salsa) be collectively understood in relation to the theoretical concept of modernist-cosmopolitan musical traditions?

Applying What You Have Learned

- Do a YouTube keyword search of "Latin music". Take note of what you discover and document a representative sample of the different musical styles, artists, countries, and cultures represented. Write a brief report chronicling your experiences. What did you learn about the diversity of Latin American music? About musical tradition and transformation? What kinds of images and impressions does viewing Latin American culture through the lens of this experience generate for you?

- Numerous theatrical movies and documentary films featuring Latin musics of the kinds discussed in this chapter are readily available for viewing. Access a copy of *El Cantante, The Mambo Kings, Buena Vista Social Club, Calle 54*, or episodes of the documentary series *Latin Music USA*. Write a review, integrating your observations of the film with what you have learned from this chapter and the listening skills you have developed.

- Beyond the recordings of "Oye Como Va" included in this chapter, there are dozens of other ones available. Do an Internet search to find different recorded versions. Listen to as many as you can. Create an annotated list describing the styles and other notable features of the different versions you hear. What does this exercise teach you about tradition and transformation in Latino/American music? In music generally? You may also want to include videos available on YouTube or elsewhere online.

Resources for Further Study

Visit the Online Learning Center at www.mhhe.com/bakan2e, as well as the author's personally maintained Web site at www.michaelbakan.com, for additional learning aids, study help, and resources that supplement the content of this chapter.

chapter twelve

from **baladi** to **belly dance:**
rhythm, dance, and music in
Egypt and beyond

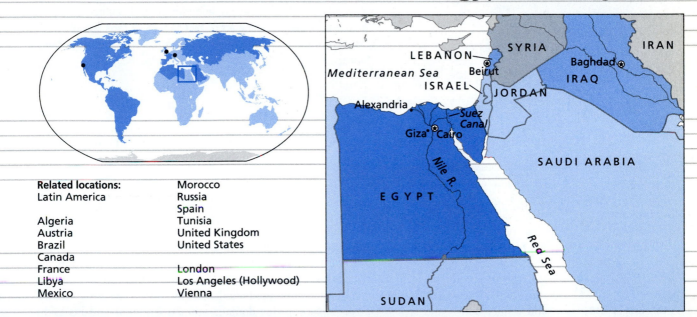

Related locations:

Latin America	Morocco
	Russia
	Spain
Algeria	Tunisia
Austria	United Kingdom
Brazil	United States
Canada	
France	London
Libya	Los Angeles (Hollywood)
Mexico	Vienna

Racy (Rah-See)

The lights dim as the musical performance begins. The ensemble on stage is under the direction of Dr. A. J. Racy, a leading scholar, performer, and composer of Middle Eastern (aka Near Eastern) music. He is joined by the drummer Souhail Kaspar and several other highly accomplished instrumentalists. I am on the gig, too, as the second percussionist, though I hardly deserve to be in such company. This is my first professional job performing with an Arab music ensemble. I am nervous, but everything seems to go just fine so long as I keep my eyes glued on Souhail and follow his every cue and gesture.

The event is a $1,000-per-head black-tie affair at a grand ballroom in one of Los Angeles's finest hotels. It is a big occasion, with the Lebanese ambassador to the United States in attendance, along with radio and television personality Casey Kasem (who is of Middle Eastern descent) and a host of other celebrities and luminaries of the Arab American world.

Dancer Aisha Ali performing.

**raqs sharqi
(ra[k]s shar[k]ee)**

Initially, the mood is quite subdued. Then there is a sudden burst of energy as an elegant female dancer, Aisha Ali, flows past us to the front of the stage. (At this point, turn on **CD ex. #4-11** and continue reading.) Souhail's playing becomes more animated from the moment of her entrance. The other musicians and I follow suit. Ms. Ali's dancing is truly enchanting: fluid and strong yet sublimely graceful. Every part of her body seems to follow its own rhythm, and also to correspond to different dimensions of Souhail's drumming. Her hips sway to the pulse of his low drum strokes. Her shoulders shimmy at the call of piercing, high-pitched rolls and accents. Her arms flow fluidly around the beat. And for all of its many layers, this entire symphony of bodily movement is a model of perfect balance and unity. Dance and music become mutual manifestations of a single expressive gesture while dancer, musicians, and audience merge as one within the collective pulse of movement, melody, and rhythm. It is beautiful, profound, and deeply moving. It is the art of Middle Eastern **raqs sharqi,** or, as it is known in the English-speaking Western world, the art of **belly dance.**

■ ■ ■

Introduction

This chapter is about women's solo dance traditions of the Middle East and their music. It centers on certain traditions of, or associated with, the country of Egypt. The principal musical focus is on Egyptian dance rhythms. We will explore such rhythms mainly through the music of Hossam Ramzy, a leading international proponent of Egyptian dance music and a master of Arab percussion. We will also learn about and listen to dance music by other important artists, such as the revered 20th-century Egyptian composer Muhammad 'Abd al-Wahhab and the contemporary Lebanese musician Emad Sayyah (now based in Vienna, Austria). Additionally, we will be introduced to musics not associated with dance, such as the high art tradition of the Middle Eastern **takht** ensemble, with its intricate melodic modes, distinctive instruments, and refined forms and styles. Our exemplars in this domain, Ahmed Mukhtar and his takht ensemble, hail from Iraq rather than Egypt. A heavy metal band from Iraq that is now based in the United States, Acrassicauda, will be discussed as well.

**Hossam Ramzy
(Hoes-SAM
RUM-zee)**

**takht
(tah-kht [press
tongue back and
up to roof of
mouth for "kh"
sound])**

tabla (TUB-lah)

**dumbek/doumbec
(DOOM-bek)**

Hossam Ramzy was born and raised in Egypt and now lives in London, England. He plays many different Middle Eastern percussion instruments, including the Egyptian **tabla** (not to be confused with the Indian instrument of the same name—see Chapter 8). This is a goblet-shaped, single-headed drum that is also known by several other names (e.g., *darabukkah, dumbek, doumbec*). It is held under one arm, usually the left, and played with both hands (see the photo, p. 275). The tabla is the lead drum in Egyptian dance music.

Ramzy has produced a large catalog of recordings of Egyptian dance music and related styles for ARC Music Productions International Ltd. These are used by "belly dancers" worldwide as accompanying soundtracks for their dance routines. Some are educationally oriented and used by student dancers and musicians as learning resources. Beyond his own productions, Ramzy has performed and recorded with Robert Plant and Jimmy Page (of Led Zeppelin fame), on Peter Gabriel's soundtrack for the film *The Last Temptation of Christ*, and with everyone from the Rolling Stones to the late Luciano Pavarotti.

We will travel via recordings by Ramzy and others from the heartland of the rural Egyptian countryside to the nation's cosmopolitan capital city, Cairo, and outward from there to the world of international belly dance. Three distinct yet interrelated domains of Middle Eastern and Middle Eastern–derived women's dance are examined. It is important from the outset to learn their names and familiarize yourself with them (see also the photos, p. 278). The three domains are:

- **Raqs baladi.** "Folk dance," implying associations with rural culture or origins. This encompasses the traditional dance styles associated with women's social gatherings and rituals, as well as with certain types of folk rituals and ceremonial performances not restricted to women. While not exclusive to Egypt, **raqs baladi,** like its more modern countepart raqs sharqi (see below), is "regarded as preeminently Egyptian" (Saleh 2002:624–25).

- **Raqs sharqi.** "Oriental dance." This is the professional entertainment medium of women's dance, associated with Egyptian weddings, nightclub and cabaret performances (usually for predominantly male audiences), and films and other mass media (e.g., music videos that are broadcast on Egyptian television stations). It combines a root identity of raqs baladi with various imported elements, most notably adopted or adapted features of European ballet and Hollywood movie musical dance numbers. The music of raqs sharqi tends to be more cosmopolitan and modern in orientation than that associated with raqs baladi. In general, raqs sharqi dancing privileges showmanship and entertainment over communal ritual and celebration. It is mainly an urban phenomenon, identified especially with the city of Cairo.

Hossam Ramzy playing the Egyptian tabla in a recording studio.

- **Belly dance.** This is the generic, all-encompassing, English-language term used in the West to refer to *all* Middle Eastern and Middle Eastern–derived forms of women's dance. Here, however, it is used specifically in referenc e to Western/international derivatives and offshoots of Egyptian and other Middle Eastern raqs baladi and raqs sharqi forms. Belly dancers tend to draw upon many different traditional styles—Egyptian, Turkish, Moroccan, Lebanese—to create their own forms of dance expression, though some specialize exclusively in one style or another. The belly dance phenomenon also has given rise to new idioms, such as *American tribal* (which emphasizes improvised group dancing and the women's community) and *cabaret* (which, as its name implies, tends toward the seductive and exhibitionistic side of the continuum). In keeping with their internationalist character, belly dancing and belly dance music (as well as the dancers' costumes) may draw upon just about anything: ballet, modern dance, hip-hop, music videos. At some level, however, a traditional raqs baladi/raqs sharqi core identity is always present in the dance movement vocabulary. This is characterized by *an emphasis on circular and undulating movement generated from the hips and pelvic region and by maintenance of a low center of gravity in the body.*

raqs baladi (ra[k]s bah-lah-dee)

In exploring these three domains, we will track several popular, traditional Egyptian dance rhythms through a series of diverse dance-music contexts. These contexts include an ancient form of ritual called **zaar** (*zar*), the professional dance routines of raqs sharqi and belly dance performers, musical compositions originating in Egyptian commercial film, and the global sphere of contemporary, international belly dance. The structures of the individual rhythms, the instruments on which they are played, and the traditional, neo-traditional, and post-traditional musicultural contexts and meanings with which they are associated are all discussed.

zaar (zahr)

Egyptian and Egyptian-derived forms of women's dancing represent a significant yet controversial marker of Egyptian identity. Public women's dancing is a social practice that often has been criticized, both in Egypt and throughout the rest of the Arab world, as excessively sensual and at odds with Arab-Islamic mores. Though many figures of modern Arab literature

World events		Music events
Ancient Egyptian civilization ●	**3rd millennium** BCE	● Depictions of female dancers and dance performances in ancient Egyptian tombs suggest ancient lineage of Egyptian dance tradition
One of the most advanced cultures of ● antiquity, with major advances in sciences, arts, technology, religion, architecture, politics		
Decline of Ancient Egypt begins, following ● some 2,000 years as dominant power of region	**1070** BCE	
Egypt becomes part of Arab-Islamic empire ●	**7th century** CE	● Islamic mores concerning public female dancing and dancers have major cultural impact; status of music relative to Islam also complex
Profound cultural transformations with ● adoption of Islam, Arabic language		
Ottoman conquest of Egypt ●	**1517**	● Ghawazi female dance tradition in Egypt may date from this time
Egypt ruled by Ottoman Turks for ● centuries (officially until 1914)		
French occupation of Egypt (Napoleon ● Bonaparte)	**1798–1801**	● Egyptian-Western encounter had important implications for developments in Egyptian dance, music
Though occupation short-lived, major ● implications for Westernization of Egypt (especially Cairo)		
French encounter with Egypt inspired ● Orientalism, exoticization in 19th century West		
French driven out of Egypt by British ●	**1801**	
Britain becomes the major power in the ● region through mid-20th century (until 1952)		
Muhammad Ali appointed governor of ● Egypt by Ottomans (with strong British support)	**1805**	● Ali institutes sweeping social reforms, including expelling all ghawazi from Cairo
Egyptian nationalism emerges under Ali ● (though he himself was not an Egyptian)		
	Late 19th/ early 20th century	● Egyptian *musical* nationalism emerges ('Abduh al-Hamuli, Sayyid Darwish)
	1910	● Birth of Muhammad 'Abd al-Wahhab, Egyptian modernist composer

and cinema have been dancers, and though characterizations of dance and dancers appear in traditional Middle Eastern poetry as well (usually as metaphors of beauty and allure), female dancers and their art have very often been marginalized, or omitted altogether, in the official annals of Egyptian/Middle Eastern heritage and cultural history.

Adding to the complexity is the history of Western portrayals. The figure of the alluring and mysterious female Middle Eastern dancer has been a predominant feature of an invented, **Orientalist** image of the Middle East since the 19th century. The Orientalist fantasy has figured prominently in everything from 19th-century European paintings (see p. 279) to Hollywood movies and so-called exotic dance (striptease). It also underlies a confounding cultural paradox, which is articulated in the following comments of Wendy Buonaventura in the book *Serpent of the Nile: Women and Dance in the Arab World:*

World events		Music events
	1920s	● Emergence of Cairo commercial film industry, flourishing of casino/dance-theaters (Badiaa Masabni, central figure)
Provisional Egyptian independence under constitutional monarchy of King Faruq	**1922**	
	1930–1960	● Golden age of Egyptian media stars (Muhammad 'Abd al-Wahhab, Farid al-Atrash, Umm Kulthum, Samia Gamal, Tahia Carioca)
Declaration of the Jewish state of Israel	**1948**	
Defeat of Egypt in war with Israel		
	1950	● Egyptian film *Zannouba,* starring Samia Gamal, with music by Muhammad 'Abd al-Wahhab ("Zeina")
Egypt gains full national independence as Arab Republic of Egypt following "bloodless revolution"	**1952**	
Presidency of Gamal 'Abd al-Nasser	**1954–1970**	
	1954	● Dancer Samia Gamal featured in international films *Ali Baba and the Forty Thieves* and *Valley of the Kings*
	1959	● Formation of Reda Troupe (Farida Fahmy)
	1964	● Legendary concert of Muhammad 'Abd al-Wahhab and Umm Kulthum
Presidency of Anwar Sadat	**1970–1981**	
	1970s	● Dancer Nagwa Fu'ad and drummer Ahmed Hammouda create *Tabla Solo* dance form
Hosni Mubarak becomes president of Egypt	**1981**	
	1990s–2000s	● Hossam Ramzy releases numerous recordings on the ARC label, including *Zeina: Best of Mohammed Abdul Wahab, Sabla Tolo,* and *Latin American Hits for Bellydance.*
	2009	● Release of Emad Sayyah's *Modern Bellydance: Lebanese Nights,* including "Hou Hou Hou"
	2010	● Release of Acrassicauda's *Only the Dead See the End of the War*

Scantily clad entertainers who, in the commercial world, are compelled to highlight the more provocative elements of their dance are not a good advertisement for Arab womanhood. Yet their high public profile, in contrast to that of the majority of women in Muslim society, makes them the best known of Arab women outside their own country [and has rendered the art with which they are associated] the best-known manifestation of Arabic dance in the West. (Buonaventura 1989:154, 21)

Raqs baladi performers in Egypt.

American belly dancer.

Raqs sharqi dancer performing at an Egyptian nightclub.

Given the controversial status of women's dance in Egypt and elsewhere in the Arab world, the decision to focus this chapter primarily on musical traditions associated with such dance at the expense of more extensive coverage of highly regarded traditions such as those of the takht ensemble may likewise be seen as controversial. Yet whatever might be said about it, positive or negative, the art of Egyptian women's dance and the music with which it is associated are integral to both Egyptian musicultural heritage and the impact of that heritage on the broader world. They are worthy of our attention and consideration.

Egypt: An Overview

Our exploration of Egyptian and Egyptian-derived dance and dance music is framed in important ways by key developments in Egyptian political, social, and cultural history, as well as by the larger history of music in the Arab-Islamic world. We therefore begin with the following historical overview, which also includes the chapter's first Guided Listening Experience.

The Arab Republic of Egypt (Egypt) is located in northeastern Africa. With more than 70 million people, it has the second-largest population of any African nation (after Nigeria). The vast majority of the Egyptian landmass is dominated by desert, and almost the entire population lives either in the Nile River Valley and its fertile delta or along the Suez Canal, which was built in the late 1800s to create a connecting waterway between the Mediterranean and Red Seas. The highest population concentration is in the region of Cairo, a metropolis of some 17 million people.

Geographically, culturally, economically, and politically, Egypt—and its capital city, Cairo, in particular—has long stood as a major center of both the region known as the Middle East (or Near East) and the Arab-Islamic world. The Arab world extends from the Arabian peninsula (including Saudi Arabia) and Iraq in the east through the Levant nations of Syria, Lebanon, and Jordan; to Egypt; and across northern Africa west of Egypt from Libya to Morocco. Sandwiched between the Levant nations and Egypt is the principally Jewish state of Israel, which is identified throughout much of the Arab world as Palestine.

The Arabic language and the religion of Islam (based on the worship of Allah as the single supreme deity, recognition of the Prophet Muhammad as Allah's messenger, and the holy book the Qur'an) are unifying features of this vast region. Broad similarities in cultural practices, values, beliefs, and political convictions across the diverse societies of the Arab world also are significant, though they are counterbalanced by profound cultural and political differences. Religious divisions within Islam, political and social injustices, and long histories of tension and conflict between different nations and ethnic groups within the Arab Middle East have been sources of divisiveness. Large diasporic Arab communities in North America, Europe, and elsewhere connect Middle Eastern nations culturally—and often politically—to other world regions. Moreover, the vast spread of Islam beyond the Arab world links the Arab Middle East to Turkey, Iran, Central Asia (Kazakhstan, Uzbekistan, Turkmenistan, Kyrgyzstan, Tajikistan),

South Asia (India, Pakistan, Bangladesh), Southeast Asia (Malaysia, Indonesia), and even northwestern China (see "Insights and Perspectives" box, Chapter 13, p. 346).

Ancient Egypt and the rise of Arab-Islamic culture

Egypt's Nile Valley gave rise to one of the world's first great civilizations, Ancient Egypt, which was founded some 5,000 years ago and flourished for more than 2,000 years at the center of a succession of powerful empires. Many of the foundations of modern societies—agricultural cultivation, city-states, writing, arithmetic, geometry, astronomy, architecture—have roots in Ancient Egypt. Additionally, the archaeological record chronicles a rich culture of music making and ritual dancing. Thanks to Egypt's dry climate, many of the great temples, sculptures, and pyramids of ancient times have survived to the present day. These are some of the priceless treasures of human history.

The decline of Ancient Egypt commenced around 1070 BCE. The empire eventually succumbed to a series of foreign invaders: first the Nubians, Assyrians, and Persians; later the Greeks under Alexander the Great (after whom the Egyptian city Alexandria is named); and then the Romans/Byzantines. Beginning in the 7th century CE, Egypt became part of a large Arab-Islamic empire that flourished for many centuries through the succession of many different dynasties (caliphates). At its height, this empire stretched from the westernmost reaches of the Indian subcontinent in the east to Spain and Morocco in the west. Egypt became an important and powerful part of the imperial Islamic world, and, during certain eras, Cairo was the capital of major Islamic empires. Islam was gradually adopted as Egypt's majority religion through the centuries, and Arabic as the country's principal language.

Islam and the Arabic language served as the catalysts for new cultural formations and developments, in Egyptian religion, sciences, politics, and literature, as well as in music.

maqam (mah-KAHM)

Qur'anic (Koar-AH-nik)

The great modal musical system of *maqamat* (singular, **maqam**—see the next section) was introduced to and developed in Cairo and other centers such as Baghdad (Iraq), as were the revered traditions of **Qur'anic recitation** (**CD ex. #1-4**) and different forms of Islamic religious chant. According to Islamic custom, Qur'anic recitation and Islamic chant were regarded as entirely separate from music itself, despite having maqam-like "musical" characteristics (see "Insights and Perspectives" box, p. 298). Negative attitudes toward female dancers who danced in public also emerged in connection with the rise of Islam, and such attitudes were to have profound implications on future cultural developments, as we shall see in several later sections of the chapter.

The Sphinx, framed by one of the great pyramids of Egypt.

guided listening experience

Arab Music and the Art of Maqam ("Iraqi Café," by Ahmed Mukhtar)

- CD Track #**1-15**
- Featured performer(s)/group: Takht ensemble under the direction of Ahmed Mukhtar, featuring Ahmed Mukhtar ('ud), Hassan Falih (qanun), Alaa Majeed (nay), Wasseem Faris (joza), Shaker Hassan (percussion)
- Format: Complete track
- Source recording: *The Road to Baghdad: New Maqams from Iraq,* by Ahmed Mukhtar (ARC Music Productions International Ltd.)

The modal system and musical art of maqam, which developed in Egypt and throughout the Arab-Islamic world from the era of the Islamic dynasties forward, has fundamentally shaped the musical landscape of the region for many centuries and continues to do so even today.

Like an Indian raga (see Chapter 8, p. 132), a maqam is built from a specific sequence of ascending and descending pitches (i.e., a scale), but it encompasses much more as well. Specific melodic patterns and ornaments, procedures for moving from one pitch to another, microtonal nuances, and other features define each maqam and distinguish it from all other maqamat. Each maqam is also defined by rules of *modulation,* that is, how to change from that maqam to one or more other ones during the course of a performance or composition. Additionally, a given maqam may be defined by a host of extramusical features, such as specific emotions, geographical locations, organs of the body, psychological states, or even healing properties.

As in the Indian raga system, the system of maqamat draws from a palette of pitches that is much larger than that used in standard Western music. As many as 24 distinct pitches, separated by microtonal intervals of a **quarter tone,** are commonly identified within the octave in Arab music theory (compared to just twelve pitches in Western music—see Chapter 4), and in actual musical practice many additional microtonal pitches are used as well (Racy 2003:106).

Musical performances typically begin and end in the same maqam, but there are often modulations to one or more different maqamat in between. The ability of soloists or ensembles to skillfully modulate from one maqam to the next while capturing and expressing the appropriate mood and sentiment of each is appreciated as a measure of their ability, especially in forms and styles that highlight improvisation.

An important type of ensemble for performances based on maqamat is the *takht,* which in its classic formation consists of five instruments: the **'ud,** the **qanun,** the **nay,** and the violin, discussed below; and the **riqq,** or Arab tambourine, which serves as the rhythmic accompaniment instrument and is discussed in more detail later in the chapter (see pp. 291–293). Photos of all of these instruments are found on page 282. For dance accompaniment or other lively musical styles, the tabla drum, to which you have already been introduced (and to which we will return) is sometimes added to the takht instrumental lineup as well.

'ud (ood)

qanun (kah-NOON)

nay (nah-EE)

riqq (ri[k])

The 'ud is the most popular traditional instrument in the Middle East and the lead instrument of the takht ensemble. It has a body in the shape of a half pear and a short neck with no frets, along which runs five courses (pairs) of strings made from gut or nylon. It is played with a quill *plectrum* (a plucking or strumming implement; an eagle feather plectrum is the most traditional type). This instrument was the progenitor of the European lute.

The qanun is a plucked zither with a trapezoidal shape. The number of strings may vary, but the most common form of the instrument has 24 courses of three strings (for a total of 72), with the three strings of each course tuned to the same pitch. Special metal bridges may be inserted under the strings to alter their tunings and allow for the playing of different maqamat. The instrument is held across the lap of the player during performance (or placed on a wooden stand) and plucked with tortoise shell (traditionally) or plastic plectra that are attached to rings on the player's index fingers.

The violin is the other chordophone of the takht ensemble. It is usually held under the chin and played in the conventional Western manner by Arab musicians, though there is a tradition in Morocco of balancing it vertically on the left knee and bowing it like a cello (see Touma 1996:116). This same, cello-like playing position is also used on the *joza,* a traditional bowed chordophone with four strings that sometimes replaces the violin in the Iraqi version of the takht ensemble.

The nay is a type of end-blown flute. It is usually made of a bamboo or cane tube and has seven finger holes, six on the front and one on the underside. The player produces sound by blowing against the edge of the open end at the top of the tube and may cover a melodic

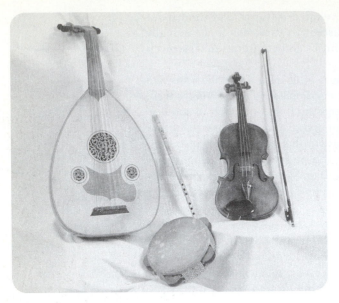

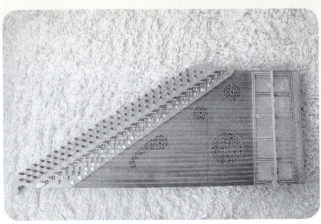

Instruments of the takht ensemble. Left-side photo, clockwise from left: 'ud, nay, violin, and riqq. Right-side photo, qanun.

range of three octaves or more. The nay comes in a number of different sizes, all of which are designed for playing in specific maqamat.

Ahmed Mukhtar playing the 'ud.

CD ex. #1-15, which we first listened to in Chapter 2, provides an excellent example of maqam-based music performed by a takht ensemble. The performance is led by the 'ud player Ahmed Mukhtar, a leading modern representative of the Iraqi tradition of Arab art music. Though distinct from its Egyptian counterpart in certain key regards, the Iraqi tradition of takht is closely related to that of Egypt, as well as to the traditions of other Arab nations and regions. Noteworthy on this recording is the use of the joza in place of the violin, which, as we learned earlier, is characteristic of the Iraqi takht tradition specifically.

Ahmed Mukhtar has toured and performed throughout the world and been featured on numerous recordings, including a CD for the benefit of victims of terrorism and war that was produced under the auspices of the United Nations. He counts among his musical mentors the late Munir Bashir (see photo, Chapter 5, p. 57), an Iraqi musician who many regard as the greatest 'ud master of the 20th century. Mukhtar's fellow musicians on this recording are all recognized masters of their respective instruments as well.

The principal maqam featured in this performance is called Bayati (or Bayat). According to some scholars, it is associated with qualities and emotional states such as vitality, femininity, and joy (Touma 1996:43). Normally, Bayati is performed with a tonic note of D, but there are other possibilities as well. Here, for example, the tonic note is C instead of D (this is common in the Iraqi style). A Western approximation of the resulting basic scale is as follows: C D♭ E♭ F G A♭ B♭ C. Note that the "D♭" pitch is actually *higher* by a microtonal interval (about a quarter tone) than its standard Western pitch counterpart, meaning that it sounds like a "sharpened" Db or a "flattened" D to Western ears. There are numerous other microtonal subtleties as well, but the main point for our purposes is simply to recognize and appreciate the complexity and sophistication of the maqam pitch system, with its many microtonal nuances and inflections.

The performance begins with a **taqsim** played by Mukhtar on the 'ud (0:00–1:34). A taqsim (pl. *taqasim*) is a form of instrumental improvisation that is heard in many maqam-based styles. Sometimes, as in the opening portion of this recording, a taqsim features the soloist alone, without any rhythmic accompaniment, performing in what might be described as a free rhythmic style (although the rhythmic regularity increases progressively in the latter portion of this taqsim, especially after 1:16). At other times, including several later portions of this same recording (i.e., at 2:09, 2:47, 3:34, and 4:22), the soloist performs a taqsim *with* rhythmic accompaniment, in this case provided by the riqq tambourine and subtle reinforcement on a tabla drum, which together outline a repeating metric cycle (meter) of six beats from the 1:35 point forward.

taqsim (tak-SEEM)

It is at this same point of the recording, 1:35, that the three other melodic instruments of the ensemble—qanun, joza, and nay—enter the musical texture for the first time. The main composed melody of the piece (as opposed to improvised melody) is introduced in its entirety here (1:35–2:08), having been foreshadowed just prior by Mukhtar during the final portion of his 'ud taqsim. The melody unfolds in Maqam Bayati overtop a recurring six-beat metric pattern marked out by the riqq and tabla: || Dum – tek – tek – Dum – tek – tek – || ("Dum" is a low-pitched drum stroke; "tek" is a high-pitched drum stroke—more on these later in the chapter, pp. 291–293).

While all of the melodic instruments play the same melody together, they do not exactly play in unison. Rather, each instrumentalist adds his own unique variations and embellishments to the melody as it takes shape. This results in a texture called *heterophony*: varied versions of a single melody played simultaneously. Mukhtar's contribution on the 'ud is especially florid in its ornamentation and elaboration of the basic melodic line, as is befitting of the 'ud's status as the lead instrument of the ensemble.

The ensemble passage from 1:35–2:08 is followed by a brief 'ud taqsim with rhythmic accompaniment (i.e., a *rhythmic taqsim*) from 2:09–2:22. In this passage, Mukhtar skillfully modulates from the original maqam, Bayati, to another popular maqam called Hijaz (which is sometimes identified with "distant desert" locales and imagery—see Touma 1996:43). When the full ensemble reenters at 2:23, their rendition of the original Maqam Bayati melody is transformed by its new Maqam Hijaz incarnation (2:23–2:46).

A second rhythmic taqsim (2:47–3:05) yields a modulation to yet another maqam (called Segah), which becomes the basis of the next full ensemble passage from 3:06–3:33. This pattern of alternation—a rhythmic taqsim featuring a modulation to a new maqam followed by an ensemble passage played in the new maqam—continues throughout the rest of the performance. The maqam featured in the fourth ensemble section (3:53–4:21), Maqam Ajam, is especially striking on account of its close similarity to the Western major scale.

Following the "major"-sounding Ajam section, Mukhtar modulates one final time during his last rhythmic taqsim (4:22-4:39), taking us back to the Maqam Bayati home base. From 4:40 to the end, the main melody in Bayati is played once again by the full ensemble. Here, it sounds very much like it did the first time we heard it (i.e., at 1:35). One striking moment of difference occurs with the big 'ud chord played by Mukhtar at 4:49, which gives a momentary Western-influenced flourish to this otherwise traditional-style, maqam-based takht performance.

"Iraqi Café," Ahmed Mukhtar (CD ex. #1-15)

TAQSIM

0:00–1:34

- Played on the 'ud by Ahmed Mukhtar.

- Mukhtar explores the various dimensions of Maqam Bayati in this opening section, gradually introducing all of its pitches and other key features through his solo improvisation.

- The final portion of the taqsim, from 1:16–1:34, becomes increasingly rhythmic and also foreshadows the arrival of the full-ensemble main melody at 1:35.

MAIN MELODY PLAYED BY FULL ENSEMBLE

1:35–2:08

- Following the taqsim, the main melody is presented in its entirety by all of the takht melodic instruments: 'ud, qanun, nay, and joza (the latter used in place of a violin).

- The melodic texture is heterophonic.

- Rhythmic accompaniment is provided by the riqq (reinforced by the tabla); the foundational metric cycle is six beats long: || Dum – tek – tek – Dum – tek – tek – ||.

RHYTHMIC TAQSIM #1

2:09–2:22

- Again, the solo 'ud is featured, minus the other melodic instruments, but this time with continuing rhythmic accompaniment (i.e., this is a rhythmic taqsim).

- Modulation to Maqam Hijaz.

FURTHER ENSEMBLE SECTIONS, RHYTHMIC TAQASIM, AND MODULATIONS

2:23–2:46

- Main melody recast in Maqam Hijaz, played by full ensemble.

2:47–3:05

- Rhythmic taqsim #2 ('ud plus percussion), with modulation to Maqam Segah.

3:06–3:33

- Ensemble melody in Maqam Segah.

3:34–3:52

- Rhythmic taqsim #3 ('ud plus percussion), with modulation to Maqam Ajam.

3:53–4:21

- Ensemble melody in Maqam Ajam (sounds like Western major scale).

4:22–4:39

- Rhythmic taqsim #4 ('ud plus percussion), modulating back to Maqam Bayati.

CONCLUDING SECTION

4:40–end

- Final ensemble section, played in Maqam Bayati, rounds out the form with a performance of the main melody that is essentially identical to that heard at the outset (i.e., at 1:35), but for the unexpected 'ud chord at 4:49.

Iraqi Rock: Acrassicauda's
Only the Dead See the End of the War

Refined, maqam-based art music in the Iraqi tradition such as that exemplified by Ahmed Mukhtar and his takht ensemble (**CD ex. #1-15**) finds its musicultural opposite in the work of the contemporary heavy metal band Acrassicauda. Accrassicauda was formed in war-torn Baghdad, Iraq, and first rose to international attention as the subject of the 2007 documentary film *Heavy Metal in Baghdad*. The film was produced by Spike Jonze and chronicled the band's struggles in their ravaged homeland. They were more recently featured in a 2010 article in *Newsweek* magazine. As the article's author, Lorraine Ali, writes, "Acrassicauda isn't your average group of head-bangers. The foursome, whose name means 'black scorpion' in Latin, played their first real show behind blast walls and barbed wire, had their rehearsal space destroyed by a missile, and received death threats from fundamentalists for playing 'Western devil music'—all before ever stepping into a recording studio. You might say they picked a rough neighborhood for launching a music career" (Ali 2010:60).

The Iraqi heavy metal band Acrassicauda (now based in the United States).

In 2006, the members of Acrassicauda fled Iraq, leaving everything behind and eventually settling in the United States. They released their first-ever recording, the EP *Only the Dead See the End of the War,* in March 2010. It immediately began receiving favorable reviews and considerable media attention. Regarding the band's quick ascent to prominence, Lorraine Ali astutely notes in her *Newsweek* piece that "Acrassicauda does have one advantage over most heavy-metal groups—its members have actually lived the words they scream and growl. War is common fodder among thrash [metal] bands, but when [lead singer Faisal Talal] Mustafa rails in 'Message From Baghdad,' 'Is it God's will or just a lie?/People live and others die/Never had the chance and they never will/Forever doomed as I wonder why,' it's full of an urgency and realism rarely heard in rock music today" (Ali 2010:61).

Foreign rule, nationalism, and nationhood in Egypt

In 1517, Egypt was conquered by the Turkish Ottoman Empire. The Ottomans were Muslims, but they were not Arabs, and they spoke Turkish rather than Arabic. Officially, Ottoman rule continued in Egypt until 1914, though the country was invaded and briefly controlled by the French (under Napoleon Bonaparte) from 1798–1801. Then, after defeating the French in alliance with the Ottomans, the British established themselves as the dominant power in the region from the early 19th century through to the establishment of Egypt as a fully independent nation in 1952. Resentment toward the Ottomans and foreign rule generally was strong in many sectors of Egyptian society throughout the Ottoman period. Opposition toward foreign domination inspired the rise of **Egyptian nationalism** beginning in the 19th century. The nationalist movement was characterized by three major currents:

- **Localism.** Pride in Egyptianness as the antithesis of "foreignness".
- **Pan-Arabism.** Identification with other Arabic-speaking peoples and with Arab-Islamic history and culture.
- **Islamism.** Principal identification with the Muslim religion, and more specifically that of the Arab world.

From the 19th century onward, Egyptian music and various forms of musical folklore and theater (and later film) involving diverse styles of music and dance would play key roles in the forging of Egyptian nationalism and new conceptions of Egyptian identity.

Also integral to Egyptian nationalism from the 19th century forward was a fervent current of *modernism*. Paradoxically, this modernist current led to the large-scale appropriation of Western cultural influences and resources in many areas, including music and dance. Thus, "foreignness" was simultaneously embraced and frowned upon in the modern construction of Egyptian national identity. Though French rule of Egypt in the late 19th century had been short-lived, it was this French-Egyptian encounter that first fueled Western fascinations with Egyptian "exoticism" and antiquity, on the one hand, and Egyptian interests in Western-style modernity, on the other. This cross-cultural exchange would have ramifications in later periods on everything from Egyptian cinema and folk culture to exotica in Hollywood films and the international belly dance craze, all of which we will explore.

It is paradoxical, too, that a foreigner, Muhammad Ali, the Ottoman-appointed governor of Egypt who came to power (with strong support from the British) in 1805, is the individual often credited as the father of modern Egyptian nationalism. Ali instituted ambitious reforms aimed at modernizing and Westernizing Egypt, and in the process fostered the emergence of what El-Hamamsy has characterized as a class of Egyptians "imbued with a new national consciousness which expressed itself in a desire to improve society and to secure for themselves a greater share in its control and development" (quoted in Danielson 1997:39). This new national consciousness would ultimately permeate cultural developments in Egyptian music and related arts (including dance, theater, and film).

Faruq (Fah-roo[k])

Following a revolutionary struggle, Egypt achieved provisional independence as a constitutional monarchy under the British Crown in 1922. The country officially came under the leadership of King Faruq, though in reality the British retained a high measure of control. The Faruq era also saw the rise of the Egyptian film industry, which became a major engine of new developments in music and dance, as well as a repository of images of Egyptianness that influenced both Egyptian nationalism and *inter*nationalism.

Gamal 'Abd al-Nasser (Gah-mal Ahb-del-NAH-sir)

Full Egyptian independence was achieved in 1952 following the "bloodless revolution" of that year (discussed later in the chapter). Since that time, Egypt's modern era of political history has been defined by the regimes of three important leaders: Gamal 'Abd al-Nasser, who ruled from 1954 until his death in 1970; Anwar Sadat, the Egyptian president from 1970 until his 1981 assassination; and Hosni Mubarak, who became president in 1981. Changing attitudes and policies toward dance and dance music have reflected larger-scale changes in Egyptian society and conceptions of identity throughout the nation's modern, post-independence era.

The Foundations of Egyptian Women's Dance

In the West, what people know about Middle Eastern women's dance is defined mainly by the performances of professional or semiprofessional dancers in nightclubs, films, videos, public shows, concerts, and demonstrations. The principal domain of women's dancing in the Arab world, however, is neither the nightclub, the concert stage, nor the silver screen. It is, rather, the domestic women's gathering. From time immemorial, family-based communities of Arab women have gathered, out of the sight of men and in the privacy of their own homes, to socialize, eat together, share stories, sing songs, provide mutual support to one another, and teach their daughters and granddaughters important lessons about life and womanhood. Dancing has always been central to such occasions, and the forms of dance still performed at Arab women's gatherings today may derive from dances that originated in antiquity. These dances also share much in terms of style and substance with their more professionalized counterparts, raqs sharqi and belly dance, despite their very different context and social function.

Rosina-Fawzia Al-Rawi (Roe-zeena Fow-ya Ahr-RAH-wee)

Often it is through a display of dancing at a women's gathering that a girl marks her "initiation" into the women's community. Dancer and writer Rosina-Fawzia Al-Rawi, author of the engaging book *Grandmother's Secrets: The Ancient Rituals and Healing Power of Belly Dancing* (1999), offers the following autobiographical account of her own initiation through dance as a child in Iraq:

> My aunt gave me a scarf, which I tied around my hips. I listened to the music for an instant, and in I walked. All the guests turned to me and smiled encouragingly. I started moving slowly, getting in harmony with the rhythm. I felt stiff and clumsy. I suffered from all the concentrated attention.
>
> Then my eyes fell upon my grandmother. She was sitting quietly among the guests and her eyes stroked me briefly. Her calm gave me confidence and I glided deeper into the circling movements. Slowly, the audience disappeared and soon I didn't even notice my grandmother any longer. I heard my heartbeat give me the rhythm and I felt my body dissolve in movements much older than me. Happiness and pride overwhelmed me and a deep inner knowledge curled my lips into a smile. I don't know how long I danced, because my sense of time had melted into the heat of my dancing. The inner and the outer worlds were touching. At that moment, I was neither young nor old. Eternity beckoned inside me and I gave in to the call of Life and danced with the intensity and fervor of Life itself. When I stopped and ran out of the room, I heard the guests clap and I knew that I had completed my initiation successfully. I was nine years old: a woman and a child at the same time. (Al-Rawi 1999:24)

Speculations on ancient roots

Exactly where, when, and how the ancient forms of Middle Eastern women's dance originated and evolved is largely a matter of speculation. Al-Rawi suggests that these root forms may have emerged several thousand years ago during an age that predated the great civilizations of Ancient Egypt. She portrays the cultures in which such dances first developed as ones in which matriarchal goddess cults and societies worshipped a Great Mother goddess as the source of all creation. Women belonging to such societies, she writes, would gather together during the nighttime to honor the earth, the moon, the goddesses of fertility and maternity, and the benign and malevolent spirits of nature and the netherworld through dance. Al-Rawi goes on to propose that since these ancient dances revolved around fertility, the belly and the hips—moving in circular motions that symbolized the process of giving birth and the cycle of life—played a major part in the dance movement vocabulary, as they continue to do in present-day Middle Eastern women's dance styles (thus the moniker "belly dance," at least according to some theories). In her evocative (albeit highly speculative) rendering, these ancient dances "were used to strengthen sexual energy, to awaken joy, and to praise the mysteries of life. The women danced their dance, a dance that corresponded to their body and expressed all the moods and feelings, all the longings, sufferings, and joys of being a woman. Through their dance, they came into harmony with the universe, abandoning themselves to life and to the divine. . . ." (Al-Rawi 1999:33).

The Ghawazi tradition

The tradition of professional, public women's dancing in Egypt that formed the foundation for modern Egyptian women's dance and its international derivatives is associated with hereditary families of dancers called **ghawazi** (*ghawazee*). Ghawazi dance lineages trace back many generations. There are various theories concerning the origins of the ghawazi and their art in Egypt. Edward Lane, in his classic 19th-century book *An Account of the Manners and Customs of the Modern Egyptians,* claims that "In many of the tombs of the ancient Egyptians we find representations of females dancing at private entertainments, to the sounds of various instruments, in a manner similar to the modern Ghawázee [ghawazi]. . . . It is probable, therefore, that [this tradition] has continued without interruption; and perhaps the modern Ghawázee are descended from the class of female dancers who amused the Egyptians in the times of the early Pharaohs" (Lane 1978[1895]:374–75).

ghawazi (gha-WAH-zee)

Ancient Egyptian tomb painting of female dancers and musicians performing at a banquet (circa 1400 BCE).

Other theories place the beginning of ghawazi dance culture in Egypt in more recent historical times, suggesting that the original ghawazi may actually have belonged to families of Roma ("Gypsy") descent who came to Egypt beginning in the 16th century in the wake of the Ottoman invasion (Saleh 2002:625). According to such theories, these immigrants brought with them their distinctive traditions of dance and music, which in turn came both to influence and to be influenced by local Egyptian music and dance styles. The Roma also filled a commercial niche. In Muslim Egypt, dancing by women was something to be done in the company of women only. Dancing in public in front of men was considered shameful, and dancing for money reprehensible. Nevertheless, a large market for female dancers existed, and the ghawazi met the market demand, becoming the principal class of professional dancers, and in turn the direct progenitors of modern raqs sharqi and belly dance.

The designation "ghawazi" originally referred to the specific hereditary class of professional dancers described above, but it is now applied to virtually *all* professional female dancers in Egypt and throughout the Middle East, regardless of their family lineage or ethnic derivation. Translation of the term *ghawazi* itself sheds light on the low social status of the professional female dancer. The word means "outsider" or "invader," implying that in the Arab-Egyptian worldview, the female dancer who dances in the company of men for profit is a figure tied fundamentally to foreignness, to marginality, to aggressive intrusion.

In the early 19th century, Muhammad Ali officially expelled all ghawazi from the city of Cairo and exiled them to provincial towns far removed from the country's major urban centers (though a good many of them managed to stay in Cairo and profitably carry on their businesses in secrecy). This was done in the midst of Ali's sweeping reform efforts. Cairo by this time had become the cultural, political, and economic hub of the Arab world and the main nexus between the Arabic "East" and the European "West." The conspicuous presence of ghawazi culture did not conform well to the governor's aspirations for Cairo as the stellar symbol of modern Egypt. But while the expulsion of the dancers may have advanced Ali's public relations campaign on behalf of Egypt, it hurt Cairo's economy considerably, since the ghawazi, according to Lane, had accounted for more than 10 percent of city tax revenues (Buonaventura 1989:68).

Witness to a ghawazi performance

To be sure, the ghawazi were a major Cairo attraction for foreign visitors, many of whom, "if given the choice, would rather have seen the dancing than the pyramids," according to at least one report from that period (see Buonaventura 1989:61). The following account by the English

Muhammad Ali Street

Many years after Muhammad Ali's death, the ghawazi would be granted legal permission to return to Cairo (in 1866). Ironically, the center of the Egyptian dance entertainment industry today is located on the very street that bears his name, Muhammad Ali Street.

painter and Egyptophile James Augustus St. John of a dance performance he witnessed near Cairo in 1840 provides a sense of the Orientalist fascination that the ghawazi inspired:

> Suddenly the musicians, who had hitherto gratified us only with fantasias of various kinds, and Arab melodies, struck up a dancing measure: the door was opened, and two Arab dancers entered. They were girls between the ages of 16 and 30, tall and admirably proportioned. . . .
>
> Their eyes shot fire . . . and their bodies assumed the most varied attitudes and inflexions. They twined round each other snake-like, with a suppleness and grace such as I had never seen before. Now, they let their arms drop, and their whole frames seemed to collapse in utter exhaustion. . . . All this while the music continued to play, and in its very simplicity was like a pale background to the picture, from which the glowing figures of the girls stood out in so much the stronger relief. (St. John, quoted in Buonaventura 1989: 64–65)

Zaar: Egyptian Women's Dance in a Healing Ritual

Another type of cultural performance that inspired fascination among foreign visitors to Egypt was the *zaar* (see photos, pp. 24 and 290). Zaar is an ancient healing ritual rooted in ages-old shamanistic practices and involving spirit possession and trance. Its practice extends from Egypt south into Sudan. It is mainly a domain of women (though men may participate, especially as musicians). The practice of zaar is officially prohibited among Egyptian Muslims, but it continues to be practiced nonetheless, usually in secretive ceremonies.

Despite its officially "banned" status, zaar is paradoxically *embraced* as an integral element of Egyptian **baladi,** or folk culture heritage. Folklorized dramatizations of zaar rituals are produced in Egypt, and elements of the zaar ceremony, including its ecstatic dances and music, appear frequently in raqs baladi, raqs sharqi, and belly dance performances. In these appropriations, zaar serves as a powerful symbol of Egyptian folk roots and cultural authenticity.

The zaar ritual

Zaar centers on the power of the *jinn,* a form of magically empowered spirit being. Jinn (from which the English word "genie" derives) are believed to have the capacity to cause evil among humans by entering their souls. Women are viewed as especially susceptible to their malevolent powers (Saleh 2002:632). If a woman is possessed by a jinn, she will be afflicted by illness. She may suffer from any of a variety of physical ailments, as well as from neurotic conditions, psychotic episodes, or psychosomatic symptoms. If possession by a jinn is suspected as the cause of the illness, a zaar may be performed in order to neutralize the jinn's power and convince it to depart the woman's soul. The afflicted woman is cured if this goal is achieved.

Dealing with a jinn is a delicate matter and requires the utmost care, deference, and diplomacy. The afflicting jinn is referred to during the ceremony as *asyad,* or "master," rather than by Arabic equivalents of terms such as "spirit" or "devil," which are considered derogatory and suggest irreverence (Saleh 2002:632). Negotiation with the asyad is mainly the job of the woman who leads the ceremony. She is often elderly and is believed to have powers of clairvoyance. She is known by names such as "the old mistress" and "the one who knows." During the ritual, she strikes her spiritually empowered *duff* (a large frame drum—see photo, p. 290) and beats it against her body to put herself into a state of trance. In that state, she is addressed by the afflicting asyad, who reveals to her "the wishes and conditions under which it will leave the patient and restore peace" (Al-Rawi 1999:147).

Music is absolutely crucial to the efficacy of a zaar. Each asyad is associated with specific ritual songs. The correct songs must be selected and performed in the afflicting asyad's honor in order to placate it and convince it to depart. The songs are sung and accompanied by rhythms played on an ensemble of drums and other percussion instruments such as finger cymbals (**sagat**—see photo, p. 292) and a rattle made of goats' hooves.

asyad (ahs-sigh-yed)

duff (dahf)

sagat (sah-gaht)

A zaar ritual in Cairo, 2001.

A dancer executing a "writhing bow" back bend.

Customizing the musical presentation to the ritual needs of the afflicted person is also critical. As the ritual progresses, the musicians experiment with different rhythms, searching for the one that best suits the needs of the affected individual. The link between healing and rhythm is profound and decisive. It is the correct rhythm of the drums, once identified, that directs and inspires the afflicted and her cohort of ritual supporters to dance their way to ecstasy and ultimately a cure. The zaar is usually a multiday affair. On the climactic, final Great Night, the afflicted woman, dressed as a bride on her wedding day, is paraded around an altar erected in honor of the asyad. Blessings are intoned and passages of the Qur'an are recited. A variety of rites, from animal sacrifices to the ritual burning of incense, may be performed.

Then the ritual dancing begins. It is "violent and unrestrained, peaking in crises and subsiding when the dancers become exhausted. The convulsive movements include tripping in a tight circle, running in place, stamping, bending and plunging forward and backward, and jerking and twisting the torso and head from side to side with arms held close to the body or swinging back and forth. Emotion reaches a height as constraints are removed and repressed impulses are released" (Saleh 2002:633). Impressive feats of dexterity are involved. An eyewitness account of a zaar ceremony in Cairo written by the British expatriate James McPherson in 1920 describes how the participants would bend their bodies "till they formed a vibrating and writhing bow, resting on the ground by the heels and back of the head, whilst the muscles of their bodies carried on the dance with unbelievable contortions" (quoted in Buonaventura 1989:162). Finally, breathing deeply to the mesmerizing beat of the rhythm, the dancers enter a state of trance and collapse to the floor, unconscious. In this moment of cathartic release, the asyad finally liberates the afflicted individual from the clutches of spirit possession so that she may return to a state of health and wholeness.

If you have ever been to a belly dance performance yourself, some of the movements described above may seem familiar. This is because much of the movement vocabulary of zaar ritual dancing has been integrally absorbed into the movement vocabularies of belly dance and raqs sharqi. Similarly, the percussive rhythms of zaar music have become a common feature of belly dance and raqs sharqi performances in which the spirit and character of the traditional zaar ritual are evoked. We will encounter such rhythms in three very different dance-music contexts in the course of this chapter (**CD exs. #4-12, 4-16,** and **4-20**). We begin with a Guided Listening Experience of **CD ex. #4-12,** an excerpt from a Hossam Ramzy recording that features a composition based entirely on traditional zaar rhythms.

FIGURE 12.1

Basic pattern of the zaar rhythm.

Beat:	1		2		1		2	
Strokes:	**Dum**	tek	**Dum**	tek	**Dum**	tek	**Dum**	tek

guided listening experience

Traditional Zaar Rhythms, Hossam Ramzy

- CD Track #**4-12**
- Featured performer(s)/group: Hossam Ramzy (Ramzy plays all of the instruments; the different percussion parts were overdubbed in a multitrack recording studio)
- Format: Excerpt
- Source recording: "Alla Hai," from *Baladi Plus,* by Hossam Ramzy (ARC Music Productions International Ltd.)

While many percussive rhythms may be performed during the course of a zaar, a large number of these represent variant forms of a single rhythm known as *ayyoub* or, alternately, simply as *zaar.* This is a straightforward rhythm with a duple meter that may be played at many different tempos and levels of intensity, from slow and subdued to rapid and frenzied. The tempo and energy of zaar music follow the pace and intensity of the dancing or singing it accompanies and tend to reflect the overall mood of the ceremony at any given moment as well.

The zaar rhythm, like all Arab dance rhythms, is defined by a skeletal ostinato rhythmic pattern built upon two fundamental kinds of drum strokes: the low-pitched **Dum** and the high-pitched **tek.** Dum strokes mark the two main beats of the pattern, while tek strokes fill in with syncopations. Listen to the portion of **CD ex. #4-12** beginning at 0:18 and try to clap out the basic *zaar* rhythmic pattern (as outlined in Figure 12.1 above) with the drummers. Use a deep, full-handed clap for the Dum strokes and a sharp, fingertips-on-the-palm clap for the tek strokes. (You are encouraged to clap out the basic rhythmic patterns along with the recordings in this manner throughout the rest of the chapter as well.)

CD ex. #4-13 consists of a brief Musical Guided Tour in which Hossam Ramzy demonstrates the basic drum strokes and explains how they are produced. A transcript of Ramzy's presentation is included in the Musical Guided Tour box on page 292. Follow along with this transcript as you listen to the recording.

Continuing now with our discussion of **CD ex. #4-12,** we turn to instrumentation. The zaar rhythms in the example are performed and embellished by an ensemble featuring the following percussion instruments (membranophones/idiophones—see the photos, p. 292):

- The *mazhar,* a large, deep-toned tambourine with large jingles (cymbals).
- The duff, a mazhar without jingles.
- The riqq, a medium-sized, higher-pitched tambourine with jingles (the head of which is traditonally made from a fish skin).
- The tabla (darabukkah, dumbek), which functions as the lead drum of the ensemble.
- The doholla, a larger, "bass" version of the tabla.
- The sagat, or finger cymbals.

doholla (doe-hole-lah)

Now I will introduce you to the [drum] sounds. Basically there are two, the Dum and the tek. The Dum is the bass beat in any Egyptian drum; the tek is the treble. On the tabla and the *doholla* [an oversized version of the tabla], the Dum is produced by striking the middle of the skin with the hand's four fingers close together, and moving the hand away as if one has touched a hot iron by accident. Here is an example of some tabla Dums [♪]. The tek on the tabla and the doholla is produced by striking the rim of the drum with one or more fingers from the right hand. In using the left hand, the tek is produced from striking the rim with the hand's third finger alone. Here is an example of some tabla teks [♪].

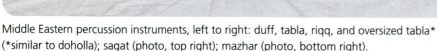

Middle Eastern percussion instruments, left to right: duff, tabla, riqq, and oversized tabla* (*similar to doholla); sagat (photo, top right); mazhar (photo, bottom right).

These are the standard percussion instruments used in Egyptian dance music, whether for raqs baladi, raqs sharqi, or belly dance. Some or all of them are featured in each of the pieces explored in this chapter. (*Note:* In traditional ritualistic contexts such as zaar, other "folk" percussion instruments may be used in place of the standard ones listed.)

Hossam Ramzy introduces and illustrates the sounds of several of these instruments—in order, the mazhar (0:14), duff (0:31), doholla (0:43), and tabla (1:03)—on **CD ex. #4-14.** Listen to that example now and familiarize yourself with the different instrument names and timbres. The two other percussion instruments on the list at the bottom of page 291 are demonstrated by Ramzy on **CD ex. #4-15:** first the riqq (0:00–0:15), then the sagat (0:16–0:29).

Now that you have some points of orientation, listen again to **CD ex. #4-12.** It begins with an introductory series of Dum strokes. Then, at 0:18, following a lead-in by the tabla, the full "group" begins to play the standard zaar rhythm at a slow tempo. Notice how the basic rhythm is maintained by the doholla and the duff, while the tabla moves between outlining this basic rhythm and playing in a characteristic Arab style that involves "filling out the beat" with "a rich filigree of timbral and accentual nuances" (Racy 2003:116). Meanwhile, the sagat and the tambourines (riqq, mazhar) flesh out the texture with faster, ornamental rhythms. The more ornate passages of tabla playing (heard mainly from about the 1:00 point on) nicely exemplify the improvisatory art of Arab percussion performance, which is especially identified with the tabla and the riqq.

At 1:49, the tabla plays a syncopated rhythm that serves as a transition to the second part of the piece. This second part begins at 1:53, where the tempo is doubled and the energy increases accordingly. This faster-tempoed rhythm is the type one would expect to hear in the later portion of a zaar ritual, when the dancers begin to move toward ecstasy.

---

guided listening quick summary

Traditional Zaar Rhythms, Hossam Ramzy (CD ex. #4-12)

INTRODUCTION

0:00–0:17

- Series of unison Dum strokes in slow, sparse rhythm; same rhythmic pattern is repeated four times.

SLOW ZAAR SECTION (PART I)

0:18–1:52

- Doholla and duff lay down the basic zaar rhythm, while tabla embellishes this rhythm with improvisational elaborations (especially from the 1:00 point on) and tambourines (riqq, mazhar) and sagat add an ornamental rhythmic layer.

- Tabla cue at 1:49 signals transition to second, faster part of piece that follows.

FAST ZAAR SECTION (PART II)

1:53–end

- Tempo is doubled and energy of music intensifies; faster tempo and more energetic character reflective of what one would expect to hear during the later portions of a zaar ritual.

Music, Dance, Nationalism, and Mass Media Entertainment in 20th-Century Egypt

In 1920, the year of James McPherson's earlier-cited eyewitness account of a zaar ritual in Cairo, the Egyptian people were engaged in the first major phase of their ultimately successful revolutionary struggle for independence from British rule. Egyptian music and musical theater played an important role in this struggle, and the music and theatrical productions of one composer, Sayyid Darwish, were especially significant.

Grafting Egyptian nationalistic themes onto a base of Western-influenced Arab music that drew upon the symbolic images and musical and choreographic resources of Egyptian

Sayyid Darwish (Saiyid Der-WEE-sh)

folk music and devotional song, Sayyid Darwish pioneered a new Egyptian music that became closely identified with Egyptian nationalism. He essentially established a new aesthetic ideal for music and other arts. This ideal hinged on achieving an elusive balance between:

asil (ah-SEEL)

- That which was *asil,* that is, authentically Arab-Egyptian in a manner that reasserted Egyptian cultural traditions and values.

hadith (hah-DEETH)

- That which was *hadith,* that is, "new, useful, and, if necessary, imported," typically from the West (Danielson 1997:40).

- That which succeeded, through its synthesis of asil and hadith elements, in living up to the political and cultural challenges of its time (Racy 1981:11).

Muhammad 'Abd al-Wahhab (Mooham-mad Ahb-del Wah-HAAB)

During his short life, Darwish achieved the status of a musical legend and hero of the Egyptian nation, and this status has endured. He also became a mentor and inspiration for the musical leaders that followed him, most notably the composer and singer Muhammad 'Abd al-Wahhab (see the photo on p. 296), who rose to prominence as a member of Darwish's theatrical troupe in the late 1910s. In carrying Darwish's musical legacy forward (especially in the 1950s and later), 'Abd al-Wahhab and his contemporaries formed the vanguard of the so-called new heritage (*turath jadid*) of Egyptian music.

'Abduh al-Hamuli (Ahb-doo el-Hah-MOO-lee)

For many Egyptians, Egyptian music proper, *purely* Egyptian music, did not even emerge until the era of Darwish and his immediate predecessors, such as the famous late-19th-century Egyptian singer 'Abduh al-Hamuli. Its purported nonexistence prior to that was attributed to the insidiousness of foreign influences. One prominent Egyptian intellectual, for example, professed in 1972 that "The Arab listener did not rid himself from Ottoman, Persian and gypsy musical gibberish . . . until less than a hundred years ago [when the singer 'Abduh al-Hamuli] began to Egyptianize and Arabize the singing of Egypt, and to depart from the lingering remnants of Ottoman singing and gypsy screaming which our country was subject to during the epochs of national and social decadence" (Kamāl al-Najmī, quoted in Racy 1981:9). It remained for Darwish to perfect the Egyptian national music idiom and tailor it to the nationalist climate of a new era, and for his protégé Muhammad 'Abd al-Wahhab, the great singer Umm Kulthum, and others to extend its range into the evolving nationalist climate of subsequent decades.

Umm Kulthum (Ohm Kahl-SOOM)

The contributions of Badiaa Masabni

Badiaa Masabni (Bed-ee-ya Mah-sab-nee)

Equal in significance to Sayyid Darwish's contributions to the art of Egyptian music were the contributions of Badiaa Masabni to the art of Egyptian women's dance. During the constitutional monarchy era under King Faruq that began in 1922, lavish casino-theaters, or *salas,* brought in huge profits and fostered creative developments that gave rise to a burgeoning popular entertainment industry with Egyptian dance and music at its center. Foremost among these salas was Badiaa Masabni's Casino Badiaa. Masabni, like her musical counterparts Darwish and 'Abd al-Wahhab, was a great syncretizer and modernizer. Her innovations were put on prominent display in Casino Badiaa productions. "Her choreographers," explains Barbara Lüscher (aka Aischa), "came from abroad and her stage shows and dance theater had heavy foreign, and especially western influence" (Lüscher 2000:18). In the new style that coalesced under Masabni's watch, the arms and torso of the dancer were used much more prominently than before, with the arms often swaying in "flowing, serpentine patterns of movement" (Buonaventura 1989:149). Dances came to cover large territories of floor space, rather than being rooted to a single spot on the floor.

The look of the dancers also was transformed in a manner reflective of the influence of Hollywood glamor. "Hollywood," writes Buonaventura (1989:148–49), "exerted the greatest influence . . . and its fantasy of Oriental dance filtered through and was taken up and unconsciously parodied by Arab dancers in their desire to emulate Western behaviour and modes of fashion." Hollywood's version of the "Oriental" dance costume—sequined bra, bare midriff, and a low-slung gauzy skirt—itself a fantasy elaboration on the traditional ghawazi regalia theme (which had first created a sensation in the United States when dancers from the Middle East performed at the Chicago World's Fair in 1893) became the new dance attire of choice in Casino Badiaa. A general air of Hollywood-esque glitz and glamor pervaded the new medium as well and was appropriated as definitively "Egyptian." Music followed suit, incorporating larger ensembles combining Western and Arab instruments with song styles, rhythms, and arrangements of an increasingly Western-influenced, cosmopolitan hue. "It was in this cultural melting pot," writes Lüscher (2000:18), "that today's *Raks Sharki* [raqs sharqi] style of oriental dance, with glittering costumes and glamorous stage-show, began," moving on from there to the world of Egyptian film and eventually out into the global phenomenon of belly dance.

In the 1930s and 1940s, Badiaa's sala was *the* place to be and be seen in Cairo, and it was on her stage "that stars were born" (Lüscher 2000:18). For Egyptian dancers such as Samia Gamal (see the photo, p. 296), to whose life and career we will soon return, membership in the Casino Badiaa dance-theater troupe was a virtual prerequisite to stardom in Cairo's booming film industry.

Dance, music, and the Egyptian film industry

The Egyptian film industry emerged in Cairo in the late 1920s and quickly became the lynchpin of the city's huge and vibrant mass media entertainment industry (which, by that time, also hosted large radio and music recording industries). Egyptian film was heavily influenced by Hollywood cinema. The films built from romantic plot lines and featured "glamorous characters, exotic settings from Arab history, clearly drawn lines of good and evil, and resolutions in favor of goodness and justice" reflective of Arab-Egyptian social values of the time (Danielson 1997:88). Grand and dramatic dance spectacles featuring beautiful dancers accompanied by lively, thickly orchestrated music were a highlight of many Egyptian films.

Hollywood-esque "Oriental" dance costume modeled by the American dancer Gitana de la Rosa.

From the 1930s onward, virtually all prolific and highly respected performing artists in Egypt—the musicians Muhammad 'Abd al-Wahhab, Farid al-Atrash, and Umm Kulthum; the dancers Samia Gamal and Tahia Carioca—were stars of both the stage and the silver screen. Conventional distinctions between "high art" and "popular entertainment" cultures, distinctions that carried considerable weight in many other societies (India, the West), had relatively less overall significance in Egypt (see Racy 1981). The modern film star, the nationalist symbol, and the icon of Egyptian cultural heritage were all rolled together into one in the figure of the Egyptian media star. In an emerging nation heir to a great ancient civilization but subject for many centuries to foreign subjugation, the "new" traditions that emerged with Egyptian mass media entertainment effectively moved to the core of what Egyptian people conceived of as their own cultural heritage.

Farid al-Atrash (Fah-reed ahl-At-rush)

Samia Gamal (Sa-mee-ya Gah-MAHL)

Muhammad 'Abd al-Wahhab and Samia Gamal

The golden age of the Egyptian media stars spanned from the 1930s to the 1960s. The stars of this era endure strongly in the collective consciousness of Egyptians even today, and their legacy continues to inform prevalent notions of modern Egyptianness.

In the worlds of music and dance, two stars, the composer Muhammad 'Abd al-Wahhab and the dancer Samia Gamal, occupied somewhat parallel positions as great modernists of their era. 'Abd al-Wahhab continued the line of Sayyid Darwish, the main pioneering figure of modern Egyptian music; Gamal was a protégé of Badiaa Masabni, the main pioneering figure of modern Egyptian women's dance (raqs sharqi). Each extended the progressive vision of their

The composer Muhammad 'Abd al-Wahhab.

mentor, and each, thanks to the power of mass media, achieved a level of fame and notoriety in Egypt and beyond that was unparalleled by the luminaries of prior generations. They were the quintessential progressive modernists of Egyptian arts and entertainment, each in their own way representing a particular vision of what constituted Egyptianness in the minds and hearts of the Egyptian people. Collectively, their personalities, public personae, and modes of artistic expression came to encompass the aspirations and ideals, as well as the contradictions and ambiguities, of Egyptian society during a defining period in its modern history.

Samia Gamal was a true innovator. She was reportedly the first Egyptian dancer to dance with a veil (though it should be noted that veil dancing is not nearly as prominent in Egyptian raqs sharqi as in international belly dance), the first to dance in high heels rather than barefoot, and one of the most influential figures involved in the syncretization of Middle Eastern and Western dance elements in raqs sharqi. As Lüscher comments, Gamal's dance style "has influenced generations of students, and continues to do so today. Her vivid and fluent veil work, her gracious arm movements and her elegant attitude combined with a real Hollywood smile made her one of the most glamorous dancers of the so-called Golden Age of Egyptian dance history" (Lüscher 2000:22).

Beyond her starring roles in many Egyptian films and stage appearances all over the Middle East, Gamal was additionally featured in European and American films of the 1950s, including

The dancer Samia Gamal in the film *Valley of the Kings* (1954).

Accidental Innovations

It is humorous to note that some of Samia Gamal's dance innovations came less from the realization of an artistic vision than from happenstance. She reportedly first danced with a veil at the suggestion of a Russian ballet teacher, who felt that practicing her stage entrance while holding a veil in both hands behind her might improve her arm carriage. Gamal tried this out in a performance, the audience loved it, and soon everyone was emulating her. As for wearing high heels on stage, Gamal, who was raised in poverty, claimed that she started doing that by virtue of the simple fact she could afford the shoes and wanted people to know it.

Ali Baba and the Forty Thieves and *Valley of the Kings* (see the photo, p. 296), both of which were released in 1954. She also was famous throughout the Arab world for her professional and romantic partnership with composer, musician, and singer Farid al-Atrash, who produced and co-starred in several of her films and was inspired in the writing of some of his most beautiful songs by his love for her.

Muhammad 'Abd al-Wahhab was born into a religious family in a working-class area of Cairo in 1910. His father was the religious leader (*imam*) of the neighborhood mosque. As a child, 'Abd al-Wahhab was educated at a religious school, where he studied the complex art of Qur'anic recitation (see "Insights and Perspectives" box, p. 298). He also attended and participated in Sufi religious rituals, where he was lauded for having the voice of an angel. This early training and experience would influence his music throughout his career; many of his songs and compositions reflect influences of Qur'anic recitation style and Sufi music.

imam (ee-MAHM)

While still a child, 'Abd al-Wahhab disgraced his family by running away from home to join a traveling circus. He soon moved on to a theater troupe, dressing up in drag and impersonating a girl singer between the main acts of the show. He eventually landed a position in the theater troupe of Sayyid Darwish, and this turn of events proved decisive in setting his future course. Though 'Abd al-Wahhab was not with Darwish for long (Darwish died of a cocaine overdose at age 32), Darwish's influence on the impressionable younger musician was an enduring one. Throughout his life, 'Abd al-Wahhab credited Darwish as a mentor.

'Abd al-Wahhab rose to fame first as a singer and later as a film actor, composer, and producer. Some of his most famous and revered songs were composed for Umm Kulthum (see photo, p. 302), though the two great stars and rivals avoided collaboration for decades until finally joining forces for a legendary concert in 1964. 'Abd al-Wahhab is widely regarded today, as he was in his own time, as "the greatest Arab modernist of the twentieth century" in the area of music (Danielson 2002:600). His compositions form the backbone of the modern Egyptian musical repertoire. The following comments from Umm Kulthum biographer and ethnomusicologist Virginia Danielson attest to his greatness, musical range, and influence:

> An accomplished musical classicist, 'Abd al-Wahhāb was at the same time an inveterate innovator. He probed the possibilities of all musics that came his way, borrowing from the nineteenth-century European symphonic literature; Spanish, Latin American, North American, and local Middle Eastern dance rhythms; and instruments from everywhere, including the Hawaiian guitar. . . . From the perspective of the twenty-first century, 'Abd al-Wahhāb's legacy is inestimable. His grasp of international musical styles is unparalleled. His songs are a cherished part of people's memories of home and childhood [for Arabs everywhere]. (Danielson 2002:600)

Qur'anic Recitation versus Musical "Enchantment" in Islamic Society

The Arabic word for "singer" (*mutrib* [moet-rib]) translates as "one who enchants" (i.e., creates *tarab*), whereas the Arabic word for one who chants the Qur'an (*qari'*) means "one who recites." While the musical art of "enchantment" and the sacred vocal art of recitation may sound remarkably similar due to their common "musical" features (modes and scales, pitch contours, ornamentation, articulations), conservative Muslims reject the very idea of a musical identity for Qur'anic recitation or other forms of sacred Islamic vocalization. To identify an individual who recites the Qur'an as a singer (mutrib) would be offensive. The words of the Qur'an are sacrosanct for Muslims. Qur'anic recitation (**CD ex. #1-4** is an example) represents the highest expression of religious devotion to Allah (God), while "singing" and "music" per se are seen contrastingly as potential threats to Islamic piety. They have the capacity to "enchant," and thus to tempt people away from their principal sacred duties of devotion to Allah.

The clear theoretical distinction between music and nonmusic implied above is not always so clear in actual practice and individual attitudes. The mystical Sufi sects of Islam and certain other Muslim groups offer a contrasting view, sometimes claiming that music—and even dance—are important paths to spiritual transcendence, ecstasy, and communion with the divine. Additionally, there are forms of "popular Islam" in which certain types of devotional song and other kinds of music are considered to be religious or semireligious.

All of these paradoxes are underscored by, on the one hand, a "suspicion toward music because of its secular and even profane associations" that dates back many centuries (Nelson Davies 2002:158) and, on the other, a recognition (by many, at least) that sacred forms of vocal Islamic art do indeed possess musical qualities. "The prevailing impression among scholars and laypeople alike," writes ethnomusicologist Michael Frishkopf, "is that Islam forbids music in religious ritual and frowns on music in any context; the use of singing in Sufi (mystic) orders is often cited as a rare exception. But in fact melodious use of the voice is seldom absent, even in mainstream Islam" (Frishkopf 2002:165).

guided listening experience

"Zeina," by Muhammad 'Abd al-Wahhab (Arrangement by Hossam Ramzy)

- CD Track #**4-16**
- Featured performer(s)/group: Hossam Ramzy and ensemble, with Hossam Ramzy (Egyptian percussion instruments), Magid Serour (qanun), Mahmoud Effat (nay), Farouq Mohammed Hassan (quarter-tone accordion)
- Format: Excerpt
- Source recording: *Zeina: Best of Mohammed Abdul Wahhab,* by Hossam Ramzy (ARC Music Productions International Ltd.)

"Zeina"
("Ze-hee-NAH")

Zannouba
(Zahn-NOO-bah)

firqa musiqyya
(fir-[k]AH
moo-si-ki-YAH)

Composing dance music for films was one of the many areas in which Muhammad 'Abd al-Wahhab not only thrived but essentially defined the musical idiom. An example of his work in this area is "Zeina," which was originally composed for a dance number featuring Samia Gamal in the 1950 Egyptian film *Zannouba*. Like much of 'Abd al-Wahhab's music, "Zeina" employed the resources of a relatively large ensemble called a **firqa (firqa musiqyya)**. The firqas heard on

Egyptian film soundtracks of the era typically combined instruments of the traditional Arab takht ensemble with Western orchestral string instruments (violins, cellos), a full complement of Arab percussion instruments, and sometimes additional Western instruments as well. Solo singers and choruses were also often featured, as in the final portion of the original *Zannouba* version of "Zeina" danced by Samia Gamal, which at the time of this writing was viewable at www.youtube. com/watch?v=ouCtyxwhPRk.

In dance pieces especially, 'Abd al-Wahhab was inclined to much experimentation with novel instruments and exciting rhythms, some drawn from the stock of traditional Egyptian folk music (baladi), others from American popular music of the day or Latin styles like the rumba and the bolero. He used Western harmonies with maqam-based melodies, explored innovative compositional and arranging techniques, and employed new approaches to instrumentation that highlighted the accordion, electric guitar, bass clarinet, and "exotic" percussion instruments of various kinds. The late 1940s and early 1950s, however, saw a stylistic shift in his music, with greater emphasis placed on distinctly Arab-Egyptian–derived elements.

"Zeina," represented here in an arrangement by Hossam Ramzy from his tribute album to 'Abd al-Wahhab (**CD ex. #4-16**), is a good example. It has a maqam-based melody (in Maqam Hijaz, roughly D Eb F# G A Bb C [D]) featuring standard Arab-Egyptian forms of melodic ornamentation. The firqa instrumentation includes Western instruments but gives most prominent voice to traditional Arab instruments like the qanun, the nay, and Arab percussion. Most importantly for our purposes, Egyptian dance rhythms played on the standard Arab percussion instruments provide the rhythmic foundation throughout.

The arrangement begins with an introduction featuring a syncopated melody played on the qanun. Each qanun phrase is "answered" by the string section (four violins and two cellos); during the second statement of the melody (0:11–0:20), the riqq (Arab tambourine) doubles the qanun's rhythm. At 0:21, the main melody arrives in the form of a sultry, heavily ornamented performance on the nay (flute), with swooping melodic answers provided by the string section together with the qanun. The strings and the qanun also take the melodic lead at some points (0:42–0:46, 0:56–1:06).

The percussion section comes in at 0:21 too, led by the tabla. The first rhythm heard is one of the most popular and important in raqs baladi, raqs sharqi, and belly dance. It is called **masmoudi** (or *masmudi*) and features the ostinato pattern of dum and tek strokes illustrated in Figure 12.2.

masmoudi
(mas-MOO-dee)

The masmoudi rhythm and the medium-slow tempo at which it is played provide a perfect match for the sensuous melody of the nay. Indeed, masmoudi (aka "slow maqsoum"—see "Insights and Perspectives" box, p. 300) is very appropriate for dances requiring an especially intimate character. For example, when a woman marries, she may perform a special dance for her husband that reveals, to quote Al-Rawi (1999:141), "the full bloom of her femininity." Masmoudi is often the accompanying rhythm for such dancing, and likewise for segments of raqs sharqi and belly dance routines and cinematic dance numbers that invoke a similarly sensuous mood and character.

At 1:07 of "Zeina," the nay flute melody is repeated (i.e., with varied repetition) over the continuing masmoudi groove. This time, however, the accompaniment is enhanced by the rhythms played on a *quarter-tone accordion*, which is basically a standard accordion modified to accomodate the microtonal intervals of Arab music.

FIGURE 12.2

Masmoudi rhythmic pattern.

Beat:	1			2			1			2		
Strokes:	**Dum**	Dum	tek	**Dum**		tek	**Dum**	Dum	tek	**Dum**		tek

The names assigned to the various Egyptian dance rhythms can vary. For example, masmoudi comes in several forms other than the one charted out in Figure 12.2, including this one:

Beat:	1			2			1			2		
Strokes:	**Dum**	Dum	tek	**Dum**		tek	tek	**Dum**	Dum	tek	**Dum**		tek	tek

and this longer one:

Beat:	1		2			3			4		
Strokes:	**Dum**	Dum	**Dum**	tek	tek	**Dum**	tek	tek		tek	tek

Moreover, the rhythm identified in the Guided Listening Experience for "Zeina" as masmoudi, that is:

Beat:	1			2			1			2		
Strokes:	**Dum**	Dum	tek	**Dum**		tek	**Dum**	Dum	tek	**Dum**		tek

is sometimes identified by a different name, **maqsoum** (or *maqsum*) [mak-SOOM], though this is a rhythm that more usually takes the following form:

Beat:	1			2			1			2		
Strokes:	**Dum**	tek	tek	**Dum**		tek		**Dum**	tek	tek	**Dum**		tek	

Accounting for variance and ambiguity in the terminologies surrounding music is a common challenge faced by ethnomusicologists. This is but one of many possible examples.

Then, at 1:52, there is a dramatic transformation. A sudden upward jump in tempo occurs, the rhythm changes, sagat (finger cymbals) enter the texture prominently, and (beginning at 1:55) the quarter-tone accordion, playing a new melody, replaces the nay as the lead melodic instrument. The rhythm here may sound familiar to you, since it is the same one, zaar (ayyoub), that was featured in **CD ex. #4-12.** It is played at an upbeat tempo, with the percussion instruments reinforced by an electric bass part. Compare this to the fast-tempoed zaar rhythm heard at 1:53 of **CD ex. #4-12.** Aside from the presence of the electric bass and the accordion, the two are virtually identical in rhythm, tempo, and instrumentation.

Ramzy's rhythmic treatment of the zaar section is somewhat different than that employed by 'Abd al-Wahhab in his original *Zannouba* arrangement of the song. In both cases, however, an effective merging of traditional and modern sensibilities is achieved in the recontextualization of zaar-based rhythms. Emphasis is placed on "Zeina's" baladi essence, in other words, its Egyptian folk root. Describing "Zeina" in the CD booklet, Ramzy states that "It sounds like a classical [Arab] song to the uneducated ear but it is a 100% Baladi and traditional piece, hence the ZAAR part (the Ayyoub rhythm) in the middle . . ." (Ramzy 1995:2).

As the zaar section unfolds, it does so in an AA'BB' AA'BB' form (eight measures per lettered section), with the A sections dominated by accordion melody and the B sections led by the nay flute and the string section together (see the Guided Listening Quick Summary). Then, at 3:00, there is a sudden break, followed by a flourish on the qanun and a return to the original "Zeina" melody and the slow, masmoudi rhythm. The melody this time is played by the accordion and the other melodic instruments of the ensemble (nay, qanun, violins, and cellos) as the excerpt fades out.

guided listening quick summary

"Zeina," by Muhammad 'Abd al-Wahhab, Arranged and Performed by Hossam Ramzy and Ensemble (CD ex. #4-16)

INTRODUCTION

0:00–0:20

- Syncopated melody, qanun; strings (violins, cellos) "answer" qanun between phrases; riqq (tambourine) doubles qanun rhythm in second half (0:11–0:20).
- Melody maqam-based (Maqam Hijaz, roughly D E♭ F♯ G A B♭ C [D]).

"ZEINA" MELODY, FIRST STATEMENT

0:21–1:06

- Percussion instruments (tabla, riqq, etc.) enter here, establishing slow-tempoed masmoudi rhythmic groove: || D D - t D - t - ||.
- Highly ornamented main melody played by nay (flute), with string section (violins, cellos) and qanun answering between nay phrases.
- Violins, cellos, and qanun take over lead melody in some parts (0:42–0:46, 0:56–1:06).

"ZEINA" MELODY, SECOND STATEMENT

1:07–1:51

- As before, but with variations and rhythmic reinforcement from the quarter-tone accordion.

FAST ZAAR SECTION

1:52–2:59

- Zaar rhythm || D - - t D - t - || in percussion section played at a much faster tempo than the preceding masmoudi rhythm. Sagat (finger cymbals) prominent.
- Quarter-tone accordion takes lead melody for **A** sections (1:55–2:11, 2:28–2:43); melodic call-and-response between nay-plus-strings and accordion in **B** sections (2:12–2:27, 2:44–2:59).

REPRISE OF "ZEINA" MELODY

3:00–end

- Following brief pause and qanun flourish, the masmoudi rhythm is reestablished.
- Melody now played by accordion and other instruments as the music fades out at end of excerpt.

The Post-Independence Era

The political climate in Egypt in 1950 that surrounded the release of films like *Zannouba* was a tense one. Many Egyptians had grown increasingly weary of King Faruq (whose favorite dancer, incidentally, was Samia Gamal) and what they regarded as his puppet monarchy. Britain's continuing stronghold over Egypt fostered ever-greater resentment and resistance among the Egyptian population. The declaration of the Jewish state of Israel in 1948 proved especially inflammatory in both regards. The British had supported the founding of Israel, and Faruq's ineffectiveness in blocking this development, combined with Egypt's dismal failure in the 1948 war against Israel, had a devastating impact.

The eventual outcome of all of this was the "bloodless revolution" of 1952, which was led by an Egyptian military commander named Gamal 'Abd al-Nasser. 'Abd al-Nasser and his secretly organized Revolutionary Command Council (RCC) orchestrated a largely peaceful takeover of Egypt. They marched into government offices, national radio stations, and the headquarters of major utility providers and took control of these institutions with little resistance. They were greeted with broad popular support. Faruq and the constitutional monarchy fell, British troops left the country in large numbers, and the Arab Republic of Egypt was declared an independent nation in that same year (1952). 'Abd al-Nasser ascended to the presidency in 1954 and remained in that position until his death in 1970.

Cultural nationalism and the baladi folk ideal in post-revolutionary Egypt

'Abd al-Nasser's cultural nationalism agenda placed emphasis on the support and promotion of Egyptian baladi, or "folk" culture. Ambitious initiatives aimed at preserving and cultivating "authentic folk culture" were undertaken. Baladi became an important symbol of both the new nationalist Egyptian identity and the roots of that identity in the Egyptian past. This applied to music, dance, and folk rituals and ceremonies of all kinds.

Contrastingly, the raqs sharqi world of professional female dance entertainment suffered under 'Abd al-Nasser. Growing anti-Western sentiment and the institutionalization of Arab-Islamic mores in the new Egyptian nationalist ideology contributed to the closing or destruction of many of Cairo's major casinos, nightclubs, cinemas, and places of Western entertainment. Casino Badiaa shut down, and Badiaa Masabni herself left Egypt and returned to her native Lebanon. Summarizing the situation, anthropologist Karin van Nieuwkerk explains that "['Abd al-]Nasser's postrevolutionary Arab nationalism and Islamic socialism prompted a reappraisal of Arabic culture. Folk art, folk music, and folk dance, all of which glorified traditional Arabic culture, were revived. Belly dancers [i.e., Egyptian raqs sharqi dancers] were seen as a bad advertisement for Arabic Muslim womanhood" (van Nieuwkerk 1995:48).

**fallahin
(fah-la-HEEN)**

Singer Umm Kulthum, "The Voice of Egypt."

Musicians, at least the leading media stars of the Egyptian music world, fared much better than raqs sharqi dancers. Both Muhammad 'Abd al-Wahhab and Umm Kulthum benefited from 'Abd al-Nasser's patronage. In 'Abd al-Nasser's Egypt, 'Abd al-Wahhab became an icon of Egyptian musical modernity done right (though not one devoid of controversy) while Umm Kulthum was canonized as the embodiment of traditional Egyptian virtues and contemporary pan-Arab ideals.

The 'Abd al-Nasser–Umm Kulthum connection was especially close. Each cultivated a charismatic public persona emphasizing humble roots in the rural countryside and an abiding commitment to the common Egyptian people. Especially central in both cases was identification with the peasant classes, or **fallahin,** who were romantically idealized as authentic (asil) Egyptians of *un*common virtue and held up as models to be emulated by Egyptians of all classes. Umm Kulthum both promoted herself and was promoted by others as an icon of "peasant" virtues. Regarding her work ethic, for example, a longtime collaborator fondly recalled how, during recording sessions, she "was the first to arrive and the last to leave. . . . She had the tirelessness of the peasant . . . and exerted the effort of [one] if the case required it" (see Danielson 1997:131).

Farida Fahmy and the Reda Troupe

In the late 1950s and especially through the 1960s, one performer, Farida Fahmy, transcended the conventional "erotic and disdained image of the female dancer" in Egypt (Franken 1998:265) to become a national symbol and a heroic figure of Egyptian virtue almost on a par with the legendary Umm Kulthum herself. Farida was the lead dancer of the famed Reda Troupe, a pioneering folkloric group formed by her father, Mahmoud Reda, in 1959. The performance medium of the Reda Troupe built from the roots of peasant (fallahin) and other folk dances of Egypt. These were combined in formally staged performances with modern elements, Western influences, and a strong current of Egyptian nationalistic pride. Two films made by the Reda Troupe, *Igazat nuss al-sana* (Mid-Year Holiday) of 1961 and *Gharam fi al-Karnak* (Love in Karnak) of 1964, were especially influential.

Farida Fahmy performing with the Reda Troupe in peasant costume.

'Abd al-Nasser actively promoted the Reda Troupe and showcased them on major state occasions that aimed to emphasize "the integrity, validity, and artistic worth of indigenous Egyptian culture, free in Egyptian eyes from Western themes and ideals" (Franken 1998:277). There was a certain irony in this, in that Western influences and aesthetics were prevalent in the Reda Troupe's approach, and Farida and other performers of the troupe were in fact people quite far removed from the indigenous, rural baladi world of which they became official representatives. Yet this was also a large part of the appeal for Egyptians from many walks of life:

> Farida Fahmy, daughter of a university professor, graduate of the elite English School and Cairo University, whose mother was English and paternal grandfather an estate manager for King Faruq, married to a film director—Farida Fahmy danced in the dress of a Delta peasant girl, covered her head with traditional veils, wore her hair in long plaits that whirled as she danced like any village girl. This was a spectacle indeed, and Egyptians of all ranks were drawn by curiosity, wonder, admiration, and above all a sense of affinity, to see Farida and the Reda dancers. (Franken 1998:278)

Farida Fahmy (Fah-RI-da Fah-MEE)

Reda (Re-DAH)

***Igazat nuss al-sana* (Ah-gah-zaht nos-ahs-sana)**

***Gharam fi al-Karnak* (Ghah-ram fil karrnuk [roll the double r])**

Folk dance rhythms in raqs sharqi and belly dance: Fallahi and Saaidi

The popular entertainment worlds of raqs sharqi and international belly dance came strongly under the influence of the Reda Troupe and other folkloric groups that issued in its wake. Raqs sharqi dancers in Egypt and elsewhere in the Arab world, as well as belly dancers worldwide, now incorporate "folkloric dances" of different kinds into their nightclub acts and stage routines. As Egyptian dance historian Marjorie Franken notes, "What began as an elevation of the folk dance of Egypt by a Westernized elite in the nationalism of the postrevolutionary period has ended in the spread and adoption of this dance into various popular entertainments" (Franken 1998:279).

This popular interest in folklore has resulted in the adoption and adaptation of certain dance rhythms identified with Egyptian folk culture. These include **fallahi** (from *fallahin,* "peasant"), an upbeat rhythm that is traditionally used in accompaniment of songs and dances of celebration performed during agricultural rituals of Nile Delta farmers. It is lively and played at a quick tempo in a simple two-beat (duple) meter (Figure 12.3, p. 304). (*Note:* The basic rhythmic pattern of fallahi is identical to that of the standard maqsoum [see the "Insights and Perspectives" box, p. 300]; fallahi is played much faster, however.) **CD ex. #4-17** is an illustration of the fallahi rhythm played by a full Arab percussion section. The recording features Hossam Ramzy.

fallahi (fah-la-HEE)

Fallahi rhythm.

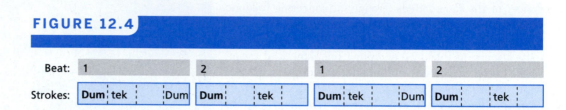

FIGURE 12.3

Beat:	1		2		1		2	
Strokes:	**Dum**	tek	tek	**Dum**	tek	**Dum**	tek	tek	**Dum**	tek

Saaidi rhythm.

FIGURE 12.4

Beat:	1		2		1		2	
Strokes:	**Dum**	tek	Dum	**Dum**	tek	**Dum**	tek	Dum	**Dum**	tek

Saaidi (Sah-ayi-DEE)

tahtib (tah-TEEB)

Another very popular folk dance rhythm is **Saaidi** (*Saidi*). Where the fallahi rhythm connotes rural, folk roots of the Nile Delta region, the Saaidi rhythm connotes the traditional baladi culture of other rural areas of Egypt. This rhythm is closely linked to **tahtib,** an Egyptian martial art that has existed for several thousand years and is represented on tomb paintings from Ancient Egypt. Tahtib opponents wield a long, thick bamboo or wood stave called an *'asaya* (see the photo, p. 305). The 'asaya is about 45 inches in length and three to four inches around. It is grasped firmly in one or both fists and is a formidable and dangerous weapon in the hands of a skilled practitioner when used in actual fighting. Most commonly, however, tahtib is practiced as a pastime rather than as a form of true combat. Strict rules are enforced in the recreational version to ensure avoidance of serious injury or death on the part of the tahtib "players." In this respect, tahtib might be compared to fencing in the West, in that both derive from potentially fatal forms of fighting but have been transformed into relatively benign forms of sporting combat.

raqs bil-'asaya (ra[k]s bil ah-SAH-yah)

Beyond the two contexts of actual fighting and sportlike sparring, there is a third type of tahtib called *dance with stick* (*raqs bil-'asaya*). This dance is usually performed prior to or following a tahtib match. It "allows a player to demonstrate skill, inventiveness, and musicality in the manipulation of his weapon, alone or in an ensemble [including other stick players]" (Saleh 2002:631). A large number of movements and maneuvers are used as the player issues a sequence of blows (stick strikes) and parries (deflections of strikes). These include a variety of leaps, hopping motions, and stances and poses intended to protect different parts of the body from attack (Saleh 2002:631). The sequence of blows, parries, and maneuvers between opponents is delivered in a quasi-choreographed, quasi-improvised manner to the accompaniment of music grounded in the energizing, medium-tempoed groove of the Saaidi rhythm. In traditional contexts, this rhythm is performed on a drum called a *tabl baladi,* which is struck with a stick. (In other contexts, the tabla or other drums are used in substitution.) The two Dum strokes in the middle of the pattern (see Figure 12.4 above) give Saaidi rhythm its signature sound. Melodies played on one or more aerophones called *mizmar* are often performed overtop a Saaidi rhythmic accompaniment. The mizmar has a strident, wailing tone that is very characteristic of Egyptian folk music of certain regions.

mizmar (miz-MAHR)

The same type of mizmar-plus-percussion texture set to Saaidi rhythm is also used to accompany ceremonies and entertainments in some parts of Egypt that feature the "dancing" of Arabian stallions. **CD ex. #4-18,** an excerpt of a Hossam Ramzy piece called "Arabian Knights" (a reference to the stallions), offers an illustration of Saaidi rhythm, which is performed here on the standard Arab percussion instruments in accompaniment of a mizmar melody.

raqs 'al-asaya (ra[k]s al-ah-SAH-yah)

Like fallahi, Saaidi has become a staple rhythm of raqs baladi, raqs sharqi, and belly dance. The traditional baladi form of the women's **cane dance** (*raqs 'al-asaya*), which originated long

Tahtib.

The cane dance.

ago, derives from tahtib. As dancer and dance scholar Shira explains, the martial art of tahtib inspired Egyptian women "to create their own 'stick' dance. The women's cane dance is a playful parody of the men's martial art. The women's raks al assaya ['asaya] movements are playful, feminine, and flirtatious" (Shira 2000:82). This folk dance, in turn, gave rise to the ubiquitous cane dance, or stick dance, of raqs sharqi and belly dance routines, in which the phallic symbolism of the cane may be played up to humorous effect.

The *Tabla Solo* Dance

An important neo-traditional innovation of the modern era of raqs sharqi and belly dance has been the genre of solo dance known as **Tabla Solo.** The *Tabla Solo* dance was "invented" and first popularized by the Egyptian dancer Nagwa Fu'ad and her long-time tabla accompanist Ahmed Hammouda in the 1970s. (Ahmed's brother, Mahmoud Hammouda, was Hossam Ramzy's Egyptian drumming mentor.) Nagwa Fu'ad was a famous, albeit notorious, dancer. Like Samia Gamal and Tahia Carioca, she was one of the star dancers and actresses of Egyptian film. The persona she cultivated on screen was an especially licentious one, however. She often was cast as a prostitute who used the allure of her dancing to seduce another woman's husband. As Franken explains, Nagwa Fu'ad "made explicit the contrast between acceptable female social dance and dangerous, seductive, illicit dance" that has long been articulated in public perceptions of female dancers in Egypt (Franken 1998:268).

Following its introduction by Nagwa Fu'ad and Ahmed Hammouda, the *Tabla Solo,* which is an exciting dance suite set to a series of different rhythms played on one or more percussion instruments (sometimes just a single tabla), achieved tremendous popularity in the raqs sharqi and belly dance worlds. Today, inclusion of a *Tabla Solo* number is a standard

FIGURE 12.5

Beat:	1		2		1		2	
Strokes:	**Dum**	tek		tek	**Dum**	tek		tek

feature of raqs sharqi and belly dance performances. It is, in fact, typically the climactic number of a dance routine.

Tabla Solo in a raqs sharqi dance routine

malfuf (mahl-FOOF)

In a standard, Egyptian-style raqs sharqi performance, the *Tabla Solo* is usually the second-to-last item on the program. The show normally begins with a quick-tempoed introductory dance set to music featuring a lively, two-beat rhythm called **malfuf** (**CD ex. #4-19** and Figure 12.5). As she comes onto the stage, the dancer wears some version of a Hollywood-type raqs sharqi costume—sequined bra, low-slung skirt, bare midriff. She may hold in both hands a diaphonous veil, which trails behind her in the air as she enters. (This feature of the dance is one of many that was first introduced by Samia Gamal—see "Insights and Perspectives" box, p. 297.) Walking and spinning as she swirls the veil around her, she dances for about a minute before discarding it. At this point, malfuf generally segues into a different rhythm, such as maqsoum or masmoudi. The dance becomes highly virtuosic and the music complex, with abundant changes in rhythm, breaks, and stops that show off the dancer's expertise.

Following this opening dance, the dancer leaves the stage and returns in a folkloric costume for a more traditional number. The cane dance is a popular choice, and the music usually features the Saaidi rhythm. The cane dance is followed by two or more additional dance numbers. Each contrasts with the others in terms of style, character, costuming, and music. A variety of tempos and moods, from slow and sultry to fast and feisty, accompanies a diverse array of dance movements: hip circles, shoulder shimmies, figure eights, snake arms (see photo), head slides, and stomach rolls. (Visit the Online Learning Center at www.mhhe.com/bakan2e to see additional illustrative photographs.) Then the dancer leaves the stage and returns once more, this time for the *Tabla Solo* dance, "the final climax in a series of dance climaxes" (Buonaventura 1989:191).

For the *Tabla Solo*, the dancer and a solo tabla player (or an ensemble of percussionists led by a tabla player) engage in a playful and mutually reflective duet of rhythmic movement and percussive sound (see the photo, p. 307). The music moves from one rhythm to another to create a kind of rhythmic suite that usually lasts for between two and four minutes. The dancer stands right beside the tabla player throughout the performance, covering little if any floor space while moving all the different parts of her body in a complex polyphony of motion that forms a near-exact visual match to the sonic complexities of the musical rhythm. Every percussive timbre is highlighted by specific movements and bodily gestures as the dance evolves. The virtuosity of expression and the integration of dance and rhythmic sound in a first-rate *Tabla Solo* dance are marvels to behold.

There is no true leader or follower in the *Tabla Solo*. At its best, it is an idiom in which movement and sound, dancer and drummer, merge as dual manifestations of a single artistic expression. The music is "full of syncopation and offbeat accents, providing an opportunity for playfulness and intense

Gitana de la Rosa strikes a "snake arms" pose.

[shoulder] shimmies" on the part of the dancer (Donald 2000:176). Rhythmic accents and flourishes come at a fast and furious pace, and the drummer will often play a single figure several times in a row to give the dancer "a better chance of catching the accents with [her] hips" (Donald 2000:177).

The dancer and tabla player appear almost as two lovers, enticing and wooing each other at one moment, chiding and cajoling one another the next. A humorous, flirtatious atmosphere is generated between the two as they coax and challenge each other through the sequence of rhythmic changes.

The audience is no silent partner in the affair either. As Buonaventura explains,

> This is one of the most popular parts of a dance for the audience, which responds instinctively to the hard-hitting, playful rhythms. The drum solo [*Tabla Solo*] is outgoing and bold, and if a dancer has a good rapport with her *tabla* player it can be the most enjoyable part of the dance for her. When the audience is clapping along and the music is good, she can be inspired by their support and feedback to bring out that aspect of the dance which is uniquely concerned with sharing its humour and playfulness directly with the audience. (Buonaventura 1989:191)

A *Tabla Solo* performance.

guided listening experience

"Belhadawa Walla Belshaawa?" (*Tabla Solo*), Hossam Ramzy

■ CD Track #**4-20**

■ Featured performer(s)/group: Hossam Ramzy (all parts)

■ Format: Complete track

■ Source recording: *Sabla Tolo: Journeys into Pure Egyptian Percussion,* by Hossam Ramzy (ARC Music Productions International Ltd.)

In the year 2000, Hossam Ramzy produced a CD on the ARC label featuring 13 original *Tabla Solo* compositions, several of them inspired by and dedicated to great dancers such as Samia Gamal and Tahia Carioca. The title of the album is *Sabla Tolo* (a play on "Tabla Solo"). It is used by belly dancers worldwide to accompany their *Tabla Solo* dance numbers. (Dancers do not always have the luxury of performing with their own percussionists "live.") On this album, Ramzy plays all of the instruments: the various Middle Eastern percussion instruments as well as a host of others. All of the parts were overdubbed in a multitrack recording studio.

One of the pieces featured on *Sabla Tolo* is "Belhadawa Walla Belshaawa?" In the CD booklet, a translation of "Rough or Cool?" is given. "Belhadawa Walla Belshaawa?" features most of the Egyptian dance rhythms introduced in this chapter (Figure 12.6, p. 308), as well as several others. It offers an excellent opportunity to hear the different rhythms we have been exploring combined together in an exciting, all-percussion format. As you listen, follow the timeline of the Guided Listening Quick Summary (p. 308) and try to identify these rhythms as they come up. Wherever you can, clap the basic rhythmic patterns of Figure 12.6 along with the recording.

Dance rhythms featured in "Belhadawa Walla Belshaawa?"

FIGURE 12.6

Masmoudi (0:19–0:38)*	**Dum**		Dum				tek		**Dum**				tek			
Malfuf (0:55–1:02, 1:09–1:16)	**Dum**			tek			tek		**Dum**			tek			tek	
Fallahi (1:02–1:09, 1:16–1:23)	**Dum**	tek		tek	**Dum**		tek		**Dum**	tek		tek	**Dum**		tek	
Fast zaar (2:09–2:23)	**Dum**			tek	**Dum**		tek		**Dum**			tek	**Dum**		tek	
Saaidi (2:23–3:18)†	**Dum**	tek		Dum	**Dum**		tek		**Dum**	tek		Dum	**Dum**		tek	

* The section labeled masmoudi here is identified in the *Sabla Tolo* CD liner notes as maqsoum (as per the varied terminologies for different rhythms discussed in the "Insights and Perspectives" box, p. 300). The rhythm is notated in "half-time" tempo (compare to Figure 12.2, p. 299) to better illustrate how it relates to the other dance rhythms in the context of this performance.

† The Saaidi passages feature call-and-response dialogue between the solo tabla and the other instruments, and also present complex variants of the standard Saaidi rhythm notated above.

guided listening quick summary

"Belhadawa Walla Belshaawa?" (*Tabla Solo*), Hossam Ramzy (CD ex. #4-20)

0:00–0:19: Introduction

- Starts with call-and-response between the tabla and the rest of the ensemble (0:00–0:10).
- Call-and-response opening is followed by a solo on the tabla (0:11–0:19) that sets up the slow tempo and dance rhythm groove of what immediately follows.

0:19–0:38: Masmoudi (aka slow maqsoum)

- Full ensemble re-enters here.

0:39–0:55: Reprise of Introduction

- Starts with same call-and-response material as at beginning; this time, though, the solo tabla (starting at 0:49) sets up a fast tempo for the malfuf section that follows and is quite flashy and virtuosic.

0:55–1:02: Malfuf

1:02–1:09: Fallahi

1:09–1:16: Malfuf

1:16–1:23: Fallahi

1:23–2:09: Several sections featuring other dance rhythms

2:09–2:23: Fast zaar

2:23–3:18: Saaidi

- Includes some passages with "basic" Saaidi rhythm, as well as others featuring Saaidi rhythmic variants.
- Some sections with full ensemble, others with call-and-response between tabla and rest of ensemble.

3:18–end: Ending section

- Like the first part of the Introduction, but at a considerably faster tempo.

From Cairo to Mexico, Lebanon, and Beyond: Contemporary Belly Dance Music

Listen to the brief excerpt of **CD ex. #4-21.** Can you recognize the rhythm from this short snippet? It is malfuf. How about the instruments? They include the standard membranophones and idiophones of the Arab-Egyptian percussion section: tabla, doholla, sagat, and so on. We are clearly in familiar musical terrain for this chapter.

Now listen to CD **ex. #4-22,** which begins exactly like the preceding track but then continues from there. You arrive at 0:09. Surprise! The malfuf groove carries on, but now it is surrounded by the sounds of South American panpipes, a chord progression played on guitar, a melody in a major key. There is not a maqam, an Arab-style melodic ornament, or an Egyptian melodic instrument anywhere to be found. And when you get to 0:25, you discover that everything leading up to this point has actually been an elaborate setup for a clever arrangement of a famous *Mexican* tune, "La Cucaracha" (The Cockroach).

You would expect this song to be played by a group like the mariachi band featured on **CD ex. #1-20,** but you would not likely think of it as a musical accompaniment to a belly dance routine. Yet, with its malfuf rhythmic foundation and Egyptian percussion-grounded texture, that is exactly what this arrangement of "La Cucaracha" is intended for. It is one of 20 such numbers featured on one of Hossam Ramzy's most popular recordings, *Latin American Hits for Bellydance* (ARC Music Productions International Ltd).

This version of "La Cucaracha" provides a fitting point of entry into a world of international belly dance music that is populated by musical numbers such as our final Guided Listening Experience example, "Hou Hou Hou," by Emad Sayyah.

guided listening experience

"Hou Hou Hou," Emad Sayyah

- CD Track #**4-23**
- Featured performer(s)/group: Emad Sayyah and ensemble
- Format: Complete track
- Source recording: *Modern Bellydance: Lebanese Nights,* by Emad Sayyah (ARC Music Productions International Ltd.)

The popularity and extraordinary productivity of Hossam Ramzy have helped to leverage ARC Music Productions International to a prominent position in the world of international belly dance. Though Ramzy dominates the ARC catalog, the company's list also features a number of other leading musicians in this area, including Emad Sayyah, whose recordings are likewise very popular among belly dancers worldwide.

Sayyah was born in Beirut, Lebanon, a city that has traditionally rivaled Cairo for leadership status among cosmopolitan, urban cultural centers in the Middle East. Both the music and the raqs baladi and raqs sharqi dance traditions of Lebanon are widely known and admired. Lebanese dances and the distinctive regional and modern musical styles with which they are associated have been highly influential in shaping the global culture of modern belly dance. Debates about which is the more important tradition—Egyptian or Lebanese—form the basis of lively discussions among Middle Eastern dance aficionados.

Growing up in Beirut, Sayyah studied both music and business administration. He moved from Lebanon to Vienna, Austria, in 1978, while in his twenties. There, he established himself as a central musical figure in the international belly dance movement. He has toured, recorded, and performed extensively throughout the Middle East and Europe for more than 20 years. He is principally a singer, but also plays several instruments including the accordion and the bass, and is a prolific composer, lyricist, arranger, and producer as well. Like his fellow ARC recording artist Hossam Ramzy, Sayyah has a hand in most every aspect of his musical productions, both on the creative side and the business side.

Sayyah's music is explicitly intercultural, combining traditional Middle Eastern instruments (e.g., qanun, nay, tabla, and riqq) with a wide array of Western instruments (saxophone,

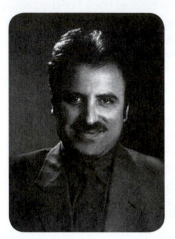

Emad Sayyah.

flute, oboe, clarinet, accordion, violin, cello, and bass) and sophisticated use of musical electronics (synthesizers, digital samplers, and electronic percussion). Elements of regional folk music styles from Lebanon, Egypt, and elsewhere in the Middle East blend seamlessly with art and popular music influences spanning from Beirut and Cairo to Hollywood and Bollywood (see Chapter 8). Traditional Middle Eastern dance rhythms such as malfuf and masmoudi are ever present, but they are woven into rock, jazz, funk, and Latin-tinged grooves in which Middle Eastern percussion instruments join forces with the drum set, Latin percussion, and electronics. Though the foundations of maqam-derived melodies and traditional styles of melodic ornamentation are pervasive, they are couched in a cosmopolitan dance-music idiom that largely eschews microtonal subtleties and celebrates catchy pop hooks and Western-style harmonies. Sayyah is an unapologetic champion of music that sounds "modern" and is readily accessible. He wants to appeal to as broad an audience as possible, and most especially to provide a user-friendly medium of expression for the belly dancers around the globe who constitute much of his market.

"Hou Hou Hou," from Sayyah's 2009 ARC release *Modern Bellydance: Lebanese Nights*, provides a fine example of his distinctive style. Following a bouncy, rhythmic opening with sweeping "harp" glissandos, Sayyah and his band launch into a sensuous instrumental introduction played on synthesizers and backed by a driving, zaar-based rhythmic groove that combines a tabla lead drum part with drum set, electronic percussion, other electronic effects, and "orchestral" strings (0:00–0:19).

The singers (actually just one singer, Sayyah, harmonizing with himself on multiple tracks) enter at 0:20, delivering the catchy hook of the title over the continuing zaar groove. The song's straightforward message, "Love will keep you young," is set forth in this section as well. Later, this message is expanded to encompass Sayyah's seemingly ecumenical philosophy on love, with lines (in translation) like "Love the blonde, love the brunette," "Love them in the morning, love them in the evening," "Love the short one, love the tall one; love the big one, love the skinny one"; it would seem that Mr. Sayyah is an avid proponent of equal opportunity where matters of the heart are concerned.

The rhythm and mood change dramatically at 0:48, where a sultry melody accompanied by a half-tempo masmoudi groove comes to the fore. Here, the music becomes more explicitly maqam-like and traditional, akin to what one might expect to hear in a Samia Gamal dance number of an Egyptian film with a score by Muhammad 'Abd al-Wahhab; the addition of sagat finger cymbals at 0:56 is especially evocative.

The arrival of another new section (1:04–1:20) marks a further shift in style that moves us away from traditional Arab rhythms and toward a more sentimental, melodramatic mood. Then it is back to the "Hou hou hou, ha ha ha" hook over fortified zaar groove (1:21–1:36), a brief reprise of the introduction (1:37–1:48), a return of the masmoudi section with its sultry melody and finger cymbals (1:49–2:04), a second statement of the sentimental material (2:05–2:20), and more "Hou hou" (2:21–2:38), all in quick succession.

A final, new section that contrasts with the others arrives somewhat unexpectedly after this (2:39–3:15). It takes a decidedly Latin turn with its clave-like rhythmic base, rumba-esque improvisations in the tabla part, and call-and-response vocals (see Chapter 11). Here again, echoes of Muhammad 'Abd al-Wahhab's legacy—he of the pioneering efforts in integrating Latin rhythms into Arab music—may be reasonably inferred. The track concludes with final reprises of the "Hou hou hou" hook (3:16–3:31) and the instrumental opening material of the introduction (3:32–end).

Belly dance recording artists like Emad Sayyah and Hossam Ramzy are catering to a huge international market of dancers. They and their audiences represent a diverse lot, coming from a wide range of backgrounds and musical tastes. Some want to dance to the most ardently traditional baladi music, others to the more orchestrated sounds of pieces like "Zeina," others to lighthearted transcontinental romps like "La Cucaracha," others still to slick contemporary productions such as "Hou Hou Hou," and a good many more to all of these. There are the high-profile professional dancers who earn their livelihoods from their craft and the pop superstars like Beyoncé ("Naughty Girl") and Shakira ("Hips Don't Lie") who have drawn upon the visual, choreographic, and musical elements of belly dance in some of their hit tunes and music videos. But most people who belly dance—whether in France or Finland, Caracas or Canada—do so for two main reasons: to express themselves and to have fun. On these levels, Rosina-Fawzia Al-Rawi regards the global phenomenon of modern belly dance as having come full circle back to its ancient roots:

> In this [modern] historical phase of searching and testing, dancing has regained its role, long lacking, in the official body of socially acknowledged forms of physical expression. It is a sensual instrument that wants to enjoy life in the here and now. By intensifying the moment, dancing facilitates the development and finding of the self beyond any anxieties about the future or burdens from the past. . . . Dancing has thus completed its transformation from the realm of the sacred to the aesthetic and artistic and back to a joyful, sensual, and playful instrument for self-discovery. (Al-Rawi 1999:53)

So enjoy "Hou Hou Hou," and "La Cucaracha" and "Zeina" and all of the other enticing dance numbers featured in this chapter as well. And if the spirit moves you, get up and dance!

---

guided listening quick summary

"Hou Hou Hou," Emad Sayyah (CD ex. #4-23)

INTRODUCTION

0:00–0:19

- Bouncy, rhythmic opening with sweeping "harp" glissandos (0:00–0:03).
- Sensuous synthesizer melody accompanied by "orchestral" strings, electronic effects, and fortified zaar rhythmic groove (tabla, drum set, and electronic percussion) (0:04–0:19).

MAIN TUNE ("HOU HOU HOU")

0:20–0:47

- Catchy "Hou hou hou, ha ha ha" hook sung in harmony by male vocalists. (*Note:* This is actually one vocalist, Sayyah himself, overdubbed on multiple tracks.) Message: Love will keep you young.

MASMOUDI SECTION

0:48–1:03

- New, sultry, more maqam-like and traditional melody presented over half-tempo, masmoudi-like groove; sagat (finger cymbals) enter at 0:56.

Summary

In this Egypt-centered musicultural journey through the world of Middle Eastern and Middle Eastern-derived women's dance and the music that accompanies it, we focused on three domains of dance—raqs baladi, raqs sharqi, and international belly dance—and on common percussion rhythms and instruments used in dance accompaniment. The music we encountered was mainly by a single musical artist, Hossam Ramzy, though the selections of his that we surveyed encompassed a wide range of genres and styles: a zaar-inspired percussion piece, an arrangement of a Muhammad 'Abd al-Wahhab dance composition originally created for Samia Gamal in the film *Zannouba*, a *Tabla Solo* composition, and a belly dance arrangement of "La Cucaracha" with Egyptian rhythms and percussion. Beyond the Ramzy productions, we also explored maqam-based art music in the Iraqi tradition performed by Ahmed Mukhtar and his takht ensemble, were introduced to the Iraqi-American heavy metal band Acrassicauda, and finished off with the cosmopolitan belly dance sounds of the Vienna-based Lebanese musician Emad Sayyah.

Though we ventured widely, our principal focus remained on Egypt. Situating the history of Egyptian women's dance in the context of Egyptian cultural and political history, we explored the controversial status of women dancers and their art in Egyptian society and in the Arab-Islamic world more broadly. We also saw how this status has been complicated by Orientalist representations of Middle Eastern dancers in the West, and how agendas of nationalism, internationalism, traditionalism, modernism, folklorization, Arabization, and Westernization have impacted the reputations and the rights and opportunities of dancers during different periods and under different circumstances.

Women's dance and the music that accompanies it are important parts of Egyptian cultural heritage and conceptions of Egyptianness on an international scale, yet their status has traditionally been marginal. This chapter has attempted to both celebrate this great cultural legacy and examine some of the issues and complexities that surround it.

Key Terms

raqs sharqi
belly dance
takht
tabla (Egyptian)
raqs baladi
zaar
Orientalist (Orientalism)
maqam
Qur'anic recitation
quarter tone
'ud

qanun
nay
riqq
taqsim
Egyptian nationalism
ghawazi
baladi (folk heritage)
sagat
Dum, tek (drum strokes)
firqa (firqa musiqyya)
masmoudi

maqsoum
fallahin
fallahi
Saaidi
tahtib
cane dance
Tabla Solo (genre)
malfuf

Study Questions

■ What are raqs baladi, raqs sharqi, and belly dance? In what ways are these three domains of dance related? In what ways do they differ?

■ What are the standard drums and other percussion instruments used in the accompaniment of Egyptian women's dance music? What is the name of the lead drum? What were the main dance rhythms discussed and illustrated in the chapter?

■ Who is Hossam Ramzy? What accounts for his significance—and controversial status—as a representative of Egyptian musical tradition?

■ Why might the choice of Egyptian women's dance and dance music as the basis for an introductory textbook chapter on music of the Middle East be regarded as controversial?

■ According to Al-Rawi, when and in what form did the ancient forerunners of modern Middle Eastern women's dance likely emerge? How is the legacy of ancient dance rituals carried on in women's gatherings today?

■ What is a maqam? A taqsim? What are the instruments of the takht ensemble?

■ How is a firqa similar to and different from a takht ensemble?

■ What country do both Ahmed Mukhtar and the band Acrassicauda come from? What kinds of music do they play?

■ What religion and language are dominant throughout the Arab Middle East?

■ What foreign powers successively dominated Egypt over the course of many centuries through to the mid-20th century? How did this history of foreign domination ultimately influence the attitudes and cultural values of Egyptian nationalism?

■ What is a ghawazi? What are the main theories concerning how the ghawazi first came to Egypt? What is the literal meaning of the word *ghawazi* and how is this significant in terms of understanding the perception of professional female dancers in Egypt?

■ What occurs during a zaar ritual? What function does the ritual serve? How does music contribute and what kind of music is played?

■ What was the aesthetic ideal for Egyptian music forged by Sayyid Darwish? How did this ideal connect to broader currents of Egyptian nationalism?

■ When did the Egyptian film industry emerge and what was its impact?

■ What were the significant contributions and innovations of Muhammad 'Abd al-Wahhab, Badiaa Masabni, Samia Gamal, Umm Kulthum, Farida Fahmy, and Nagwa Fu'ad to Egyptian music, dance, culture, and national identity?

■ What is a *Tabla Solo* dance and where does it usually occur during a typical raqs sharqi dance routine?

- What is distinctive about the rhythmic approach in the recording of the Mexican song "La Cucaracha" featured in this chapter?

- What are some of the traditionally Middle Eastern musical features of Emad Sayyah's "Hou Hou Hou"? What are some of its nontraditional features?

Discussion Questions

- The image of the "belly dancer" has become a significant international emblem of Western popular culture. In what contexts have you encountered belly dance images or references in your own life? What, in your opinion, have such images and references been used to symbolize, and what cultural impressions do they engender?

- Beyond its specific subject matter, a fundamental issue explored in this chapter is the relationship between dance and musical rhythm. How do dancing and the rhythms of music animate one another and define cultural meaning in dance/music contexts with which you are familiar?

- Many forms and styles of music and dance are regarded as controversial in their respective cultures. Identify some relevant examples and research and discuss factors that may account for their controversial status. Do these seem reasonable to you? Why or why not?

Applying What You Have Learned

- Even today, stereotypical "Orientalist" depictions of the Middle East abound in popular culture: on television, in movies, in "Middle Eastern"–influenced pop tunes. Spend some time over the course of a week watching TV and films, listening to the radio, surfing the Internet. Document what kinds of "Middle Eastern" images you encounter (if any). Describe what these reveal about contemporary Western representations of, and attitudes toward, Islamic and Arab cultures. Discuss how what you observe and hear in doing this project relates to, or perhaps contradicts, what you have learned in this chapter.

- Go back and listen to the musical examples from this chapter in random order. Try to identify the different rhythms you hear by name and try to mark out their basic rhythmic patterns as you listen. Play with creating your own *Tabla Solo*–like composition by stringing together a series of different dance rhythms one after the other without pause.

- The Iraqi heavy metal band Acrassicauda (now based in the United States) presents an interesting case study in heavy metal as a global phenomenon. Research this phenomenon and write a brief report on heavy metal bands based in countries beyond North America and Europe.

Resources for Further Study

Visit the Online Learning Center at www.mhhe.com/bakan2e, as well as the author's personally maintained Web site at www.michaelbakan.com, for additional learning aids, study help, and resources that supplement the content of this chapter.

chapter thirteen

a **musicultural** history of the **Chinese zheng**

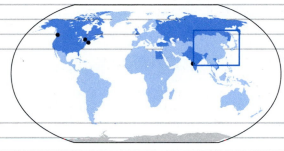

Related locations:

Canada	Mundgod, India
Egypt	New York
Pakistan	Ottawa
Singapore	Toronto
Turkey	Vancouver
United States	
United Kingdom	
Vietnam	

Deng Haiqiong
   (Dung High-chee-ong)

zheng (jung [rhymes
   with "lung"])

The entertainment portion of the musicology conference banquet is about to begin. The program indicates that there will be a short concert featuring a performer named Deng Haiqiong playing the **zheng.** Amidst the clatter of dishes and the chatter of music professors, few of us digging into our just-arrived chicken *cordon bleu* take much notice as an elegant young lady attired in a full-length red dress is introduced. She walks purposefully to the center of the hall and sits down behind her instrument. (At this point, listen to **Online Musical Illustration #26** as you continue reading.) She begins to play, filling the room with a rich, harp-like sonority. In an instant, the audience is captivated, fully attentive, focused in on this wondrous sound and the charismatic performer behind its creation. Tones rise out of the zheng like

World events		Music events
Earliest Chinese dynasties; emergence of ancient Chinese civilization	**16th century** BCE	
Lifetime of Confucius (551–479 BCE)	**5th century** BCE	Earliest known progenitors of the modern zheng (archaeological evidence)
Unification and imperial expansion of China under the Qin dynasty	**3rd century** BCE	Zheng spreads and becomes a popular instrument in many regions of China
	237 BCE	Earliest known written reference to the zheng (Qin era manuscript)
Han dynasty era: Chinese imperial expansion	**202 BCE–220 CE**	Zheng gains in popularity
Confucianism established as foundation of Chinese social order		Qin becomes instrument of noble and educated classes
Buddhism first practiced in western China (1st century CE) and spreads eastward		
Tang dynasty	**618–907**	Huge government music ministry (over 30,000 musicians and dancers from throughout the empire and beyond employed)
Vast imperial expansion; Silk Road		Apogee of zheng
		Pipa introduced into Chinese music, becomes closely associated with zheng
Nara period, Japan (710–784)		Koto and gagaku in Japan, Nara period
Ming dynasty	**1368–1644**	Regional Chinese opera forms flourish
Emergence of large Chinese middle class		Zheng: favored among middle classes (especially young females); important regional opera ensemble instrument
Edo period, Japan (1615–1868)		
Qing dynasty	**1644–1911**	Beijing Opera (from 18th century)
Final period of Chinese dynastic era		Westernization (musically, culturally, politically)
Meiji Restoration, Japan (1868)		Regional solo zheng styles (19th century)
		Modern solo koto repertoire, Japan (from 1868)
Republican era	**1912–1949**	Major cultural reform efforts, including musical reform; Western music as model
Declaration of the Republic of China	**January 1, 1912**	
	1936	"Return of the Fishing Boats," by Lou Shuhua, defines new idiom of solo zheng music
Initial communist period	**1949–1965**	
Chinese communism, under Mao Zedong: People's Republic of China declared	**1949**	
Beginning of Chinese occupation of Tibet	**1950**	First full-fledged zheng curriculum in Chinese music conservatory

World events		Music events
	1952	Zheng programs at most conservatories, including Beijing, Shanghai
	1955	"Celebrating the Harvest" (important zheng piece)
Persecution of Tibetans	**1956**	
	1958	Piano-influenced zheng compositions and performance styles (Shanghai); "Spring on Snowy Mountains," by Fan Shang'e representative.
Dalai Lama flees Tibet under threat of Chinese persecution	**1959**	
International council accuses China of genocide against Tibetans	**1961**	
	1964	*The Red Lantern* (Revolutionary Chinese Opera)
Cultural Revolution era	**1966–1976**	Censorship of music and most other forms of artistic expression
Period of severe oppression and repression		Stagnation in zheng's development
"Ethnic minorities" (Tibetans, Uighurs) persecuted		
Death of Mao Zedong, followed by period of political instability	**1976**	
Period of Openness	**Late 1970s–present**	Zheng renaissance (especially in conservatory style): new compositional styles, organizations, international attention for zheng artists
Deng Xiaoping comes to power; introduces new, "open" policy on the arts	**1979**	
	1980s	"New Wave" movement in Chinese composition: increasing modernization, Westernization, interest in reviving ancient Chinese musical traditions
	1980	Beijing Zheng Association founded
	1986	National Zheng Symposium established
	1988	"Music from the Muqam" composed
Tiananmen Square uprising and massacre	**1989**	Cui Jian, "Nothing to My Name"
	1995	Deng Haiqiong wins National Zheng Competition of China
	2002	Deng Haiqiong releases CD *Ning*
	2004	Japanese pop band Rin releases "Sakitama"
	2010	Release of *Into the Wind*, by Bei Bei He and Shawn Lee, featuring "Hot Thursday"

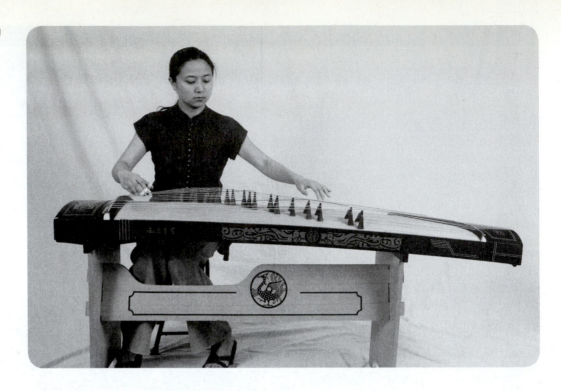

Deng Haiqiong playing the zheng.

strings of pearls, then rush back down like waterfalls. Delicate melodies and subtle ornamental touches evoke an air of exquisite refinement as all of us in attendance are transported to a realm of profound beauty and elegance.

■ ■ ■

Introduction

The musicultural focus of this chapter is a particular instrument, the zheng, which we will discuss through the lens of Chinese history and the political movements and ideologies that have shaped it. Though the history of the zheng since ancient times will be surveyed, primary attention is devoted to the virtuosic tradition of solo zheng playing that has developed in state-sponsored music conservatories of mainland China since the 20th century. This is a tradition of which Deng Haiqiong is representative, and several of the recordings we will listen to and discuss feature her artistry.

The conservatory solo zheng style was predated and influenced by a number of important **regional styles of solo zheng music** in the 19th century, and these are discussed as well. Other traditional Chinese instruments such as the **pipa** and the **qin** are also introduced in the course of the discussion, along with related forms of music and drama such as **Beijing Opera** (aka Peking Opera). We will additionally explore **koto, gagaku,** and popular music of Japan, Tibetan Buddhist chant, Uighur traditional music, and Chinese and Chinese American rock. Overall, though, we will center mainly on the zheng. The range and diversity of Chinese musical culture is immense, as one would expect of a country that is so vast, has a population of well over a billion people (the world's largest), and is host to a civilization whose documented history dates back several millennia. By focusing on a single, important Chinese music instrument, we will be able to appreciate the richness and complexity of Chinese music, culture, and history within a manageable scope.

pipa (pee-pah)

qin (chin)

Uighur (Wee-gur)

China: An Overview

The musicultural world of the zheng in mainland China is framed by the Chinese nation and its long historical and cultural development from antiquity to the present. We therefore begin with the following overview to establish a context for the main body of the chapter that follows it.

The nation-state of modern China

The People's Republic of China (PRC) is the most populous nation on earth, with an estimated population of 1.3 billion. It is also the world's third-largest nation in geographical size. Only the landmasses of Russia and Canada are larger. Along its massive border, China meets up with nations of five major world regions (North Asia, Central Asia, East Asia, South Asia, and mainland Southeast Asia). These nations include Russia, Mongolia, Kazakhstan, Vietnam, India, Nepal, and Korea (see map, p. 315). The histories of all these countries—as well as others including Japan, the United Kingdom, France, the United States, and Canada—intertwine with China's own at multiple levels, and this is reflected in histories of politics, religion, arts and culture, and trade. Ancient Chinese cultural traditions that disappeared from China long ago live on in Japan and Korea. These include the great court orchestra traditions gagaku (Japan) and *aak* (Korea) and the religion Zen Buddhism. The histories of Taiwan, an island located off the eastern coast of China, and Hong Kong, a tiny island located just to the south of the Chinese mainland, are also complexly entwined with China's own. The modern histories of both Taiwan and Hong Kong are marked by tensions with the People's Republic of China, though much is shared between all three culturally.

The capital of the People's Republic of China (henceforth, also China) is Beijing (formerly Peking). It was here that Communist China's founding father, Mao Zedong, declared the People's Republic in 1949. Since that time, China has been governed, in effect, as a single-party communist republic.

Several hundred miles south of Beijing is the coastal city of Shanghai. Beijing, with an estimated population of 14 million, and Shanghai, with some 17 million people, are China's two largest metropolises. Both are vibrant and cosmopolitan economic and cultural centers that host active musical scenes encompassing everything from symphony orchestras and traditional Chinese ensembles to hip-hop dance clubs, karaoke bars, and thrash metal bands. There are many other large cities as well. In fact, at least 35 Chinese cities have populations of a million people or more.

The east-central and southeastern portions of China are very densely populated and heavily urbanized and industrialized, though agriculture remains the principal source of livelihood for the majority of Chinese people even today. The urbanized eastern coast and the cities along major waterways, especially the great Yangtze River (Chang Jiang), collectively account for a very large portion of China's total population, despite covering a relatively small geographical area within this vast land. The mountainous southwest of the country (including significant portions of the Himalaya Mountains along the western border), by contrast, is sparsely populated, as are the steppe (high plateau) and mountain regions of the northwest, where the majority of China's 55 recognized "ethnic minority" populations reside.

Mandarin Chinese is China's official language, though many other languages and regional dialects are spoken as well. This great linguistic diversity is reflected in tremendous cultural diversity, whether expressed through music, belief systems, or culinary practices. Ethnically, China is dominated by its majority **Han Chinese** population, who account for approximately 92 percent of the populace. The remaining 8 percent of the population (about 100 million people) is mainly made up of "ethnic minority" groups, including the Uighur (Uygur, Uyghur) and Tibetan peoples. Though regarded as Chinese minorities by the Han-dominated political authorities, many of these so-called minority groups regard themselves as occupied peoples and have been engaged in long struggles for independence from China. As the Chinese music scholar Alan Thrasher notes, "Among the many non-Han peoples, ethnic minorities who

Mao Zedong (Mao Dse[r]-dong ["Mao" rhymes with "how"; "Ze" to rhyme with "sir," but stop before you reach the "r"])

Yangtze/Chang Jiang (Yaang-tzee/ Chaang Jee-ang)

An enormous statue of Mao Zedong dominates the scene at a patriotic rally in China.

have been pushed into the mountains, deserts and other less desirable space, the more usual response to Han unification [than acceptance] has been resistance and often bloody rebellion." Moreover, musical traditions among these minority groups "share few roots with the 'great tradition' of the Han," and China's appropriation of minority traditions for the sake of projecting a desired image of multicultural diversity and national unity is often resented by minority populations (Thrasher 2005). This issue figures significantly in the discussions of some of the music explored in this chapter.

From antiquity to the present

The civilization of China is one of the world's oldest, dating back more than 3,500 years. It is to the Chinese people of ancient times that we owe such inventions as paper, wheel-carts, grid maps, accurate time-measurement devices, guns, gunpowder, and cannons. In the area of medical science, the Chinese had developed a full understanding of the body's blood circulation system, circadian rhythms ("biological clocks"), and the dietary causes of deficiency diseases some two thousand years before such foundational features of human biology were "discovered" by Europeans. Even the equal-tempered, chromatic scale of Western music, with its 12 equally spaced pitch intervals (see Chapter 4, pp. 48–50), has Chinese roots. It was reportedly worked out by a Chinese music scholar using bamboo pitch pipes in the 16th century before being adopted into the mainstream of Western music during the 17th century (Fletcher 2001:325). Institutions such as government music ministries and state music conservatories and research institutes were likely also inventions of the ancient Chinese.

For the vast majority of its history, China was ruled by imperial dynasties. A long succession of dynasties—including the Zhou, Qin, Han, Tang, Song, Ming, and Qing—rose and ultimately fell during the course of the dynastic period. Some of these ranked among the largest and most powerful and culturally influential empires ever. Throughout virtually the entire history of imperial China, music was regarded as an important component of political life. Rulers recognized, respected, and exploited what they perceived as music's special capacity to reflect, influence, and model an idealized Chinese social order. The history of imperial music ministries and other official music institutions such as conservatories covers a span of more than 3,000 years.

Zhou (Joe)
Qin (Chin)
Han (Hahn)
Tang (Tahng)
Qing (Cheeng)

China's long dynastic era came to an end with the collapse of the Qing dynasty (1644–1911). This was followed by the declaration of the Republic of China (established on January 1, 1912), which eventually came under the rule of former general Jiang Jieshi (better known in the West as Chiang Kai-shek) and his Chinese Nationalist Party regime. The Nationalists' agenda centered on modernizing China and developing a new Chinese nationalism rooted in economic, social, and cultural reform. Music was key to the reform effort.

Jiang Jieshi's rule, however, was chronically unstable. Invaded by Japan, which progressively occupied large parts of China throughout much of the first half of the 20th century, Jiang also was confronted by the challenges of Western imperialism and the emergence and ascent of the **Chinese Communist Party (CCP)** under Mao Zedong.

Mao and the Communists gained political control of China in 1949, founding the People's Republic of China as a socialist (communist) state. From the inception of the PRC to the present, Chinese socialism has placed great emphasis on the importance of state patronage and control of music in efforts to encode and promote official state ideology. National music conservatories and research institutes have figured prominently.

The history of the People's Republic of China may be divided into three principal periods. In each, the relationship of politics and music has been highly significant, though in somewhat different ways. These periods are:

- The initial communist era of Mao Zedong's regime, 1949–1965, which saw the profound reformation of Chinese society and culture under Communist rule.

- The **Cultural Revolution** era of 1966–1976, which witnessed unprecedented levels of intolerance for deviation from state ideology and a concomitant movement toward extreme restrictions on cultural and artistic expression, both for Han and minority populations.

- The **Period of Openness,** which began to take shape in the turbulent years of the late 1970s following Mao Zedong's death in 1976 and fully crystallized around 1980 under the rule of Deng Xiaoping. Deng brought about major economic reforms with the introduction of free enterprise, increased the involvement of China in global economic and cultural markets, and loosened existing constraints in a variety of civil, cultural, social, artistic, and religious spheres, though not without problems or costs.

With the above historical overview in mind, we now turn our attention to the musicultural life of the zheng in the context of Chinese history.

Jiang Jieshi (Jee-ang Jee-yeh-shir)

Deng Xiaoping (Dung Hsee-ow-ping)

An Introduction to the Zheng

The zheng is a Chinese *board zither chordophone*. As with other instruments of this type, its construction features a series of strings laid lengthwise across a wooden frame (the "board") that is attached to its own resonating chamber. The zheng is historically related to several other Asian board zither chordophones, including the Japanese koto (**CD ex. #2-1**), the Korean *kayagum,* the Mongolian *jatag,* and the Vietnamese *dan tranh.* The koto's impact on musical developments both in Japan and internationally has been especially profound, as is discussed in the "Insights and Perspectives" box on Japanese music found on pp. 322–324.

The archaeological record suggests that the ancestral version of the modern zheng was invented more than 2,500 years ago, possibly in southeastern China (Lawergren 2000:80–83). Thus, the historical legacy of the zheng, or *guzheng* ("ancient zheng"), as it is also known, traces back to the age of the great Chinese philosopher Confucius (551–479 BCE). Today, the zheng is a tremendously popular instrument in the PRC, as well as in Taiwan and Hong Kong and among Chinese musicians and music enthusiasts worldwide. (The zheng and its culture beyond mainland China, however, are for the most part beyond the scope of this chapter.)

There are numerous theories and legends concerning when and under what circumstances the koto became an integral part of Japanese musical culture, but it is at least well established that the original instrument that gave rise to it was brought to Japan from China more than a millennium ago. This probably occurred during the first few years of the Nara period (710–784), when the court orchestra traditions of China and Korea that formed the basis of Japanese gagaku were brought to Japan. The koto's legacy as a gagaku instrument dates back to this time.

The word *gagaku* may be translated as "elegant music," a reference to its refined aesthetic and courtly lineage (see photo, p. 5, and listen to **CD ex. #1-3**). Since the 9th century CE, there have been two main repertoires of gagaku: *togaku* and *komagaku*. The togaku repertoire descends from China; the komagaku repertoire descends from Korea. The word *togaku* means "music from Tang dynasty China." As we will learn later in the chapter, the Tang dynasty era represented a golden age for China, both in terms of political power and cultural development. Tang court music was not preserved as a continuous living tradition in China, but it was preserved as such in Japan to a large extent through togaku. Therefore, togaku offers the modern world a window through which to view not only the vestiges of an ancient Japanese musicultural tradition, but an ancient Chinese one as well by extension.

The oldest gagaku pieces were created to accompany dance performances. Such works belong to the category of *bugaku,* or dance compositions. It is usually possible to distinguish bugaku compositions of Chinese origin from those of Korean origin by the costumes of the dancers. The costumes for the Chinese (togaku) pieces are typically red, while those for the Korean (komagaku) pieces are typically green. Beginning in the 10th century, another category of pieces designed for musical performance alone, that is, not to accompany dance, developed as well. These are known as *kangen.*

In togaku, the koto is used in kangen pieces but not in bugaku pieces. Indeed, a basic distinction between these nondance and dance repertoires, respectively, is that chordophones such as the koto are not used in the pieces that accompany dancing, whereas they are used in the pieces that do not accompany dancing. The *biwa,* a pear-shaped lute with four strings that is historically related to the Chinese pipa (see pipa photo, p. 329), is the other standard chordophone of togaku. There are usually two koto players and two biwa players in the ensemble. Other togaku instruments include a variety of traditional drums and aerophones; the aerophone section features a distinctive mouth organ called the *sho* that is also of Chinese derivation (and is related to the Chinese *sheng,* which is shown on p. 344). Unlike the chordophones, the drums and aerophones are used in dance compositions as well as nondance pieces.

In addition to its important historical role in gagaku, the koto has been an indispensable instrument in many other contexts as well over the course of its long history in Japan. It was included in ensembles that accompanied ancient vocal genres such as *saibara* and has long been a fixture of a popular type of small instrumental ensemble called *sankyoku,* which consists of three instruments: koto, *shamisen,* and *shakuhachi.* The

Sankyoku ensemble featuring Mariko Kezuka (koto), Satomi Fukami (shamisen), and Christopher Yohmei Blasdel (shakuhachi).

shamisen, like the biwa, is a lute-type chordophone, but it has only three strings (rather than four) and is equipped with a box-shaped (rather than pear-shaped) resonator—it looks almost like a square-bodied banjo. It has been a very important instrument in many styles of Japanese folk and popular music historically and also has been integral to the ensembles used to accompany traditional Japanese theatrical forms such as *kabuki.* The shakuhachi, to which you were introduced in earlier chapters, is a long, end-blown flute made of thick, strong bamboo. In addition to its role as an ensemble instrument, it also has a long tradition as a solo instrument. The excerpt of the solo shakuhachi piece "Daha" (The Beating of the Waves) heard on **CD ex. #1–14** demonstrates the instrument's great expressive range. This is a 19th-century adaptation of a composition dating back some 800 years. The breath pulsations on certain long-held notes musically evoke the beating waves of the title.

The tradition of solo music for the koto, like that of the shakuhachi, goes back many centuries. The classic solo koto repertoire dates mainly from the Edo period (1615–1868), while the modern repertoire is identified with the post-Meiji Restoration era. The Meiji Restoration of 1868 marked the commencement of Japan's era of modernization, characterized by myriad forms of Westernization, industrialization, and escalating technological development. In music, Meiji reform involved the wholesale adoption of Western art music—symphony orchestras, operas, ballets, Western instruments—as part of the Japanese national culture. In another dimension, it featured new developments in Japanese traditional music (*hogaku*), though this musical realm was generally regarded as inferior to its imported, Western counterpart (similar developments would come to mark the modern history of music in China as well, as we shall see). In the case of solo koto music in particular, the new, post-Meiji style featured elements and aesthetics adapted from Western instrumental repertoires such as those of the piano and the harp. New playing techniques, standardization of tuning, and the adoption of melodic and harmonic approaches and compositional procedures from Western music were fused with earlier koto techniques and styles to form a new musical vocabulary and virtuosic idiom for the instrument.

The foremost composer for the koto in post-Meiji Japan was Miyagi Michio (Michio Miyagi) (1894–1965); his successor, Sawai Tadao (Tadao Sawai) (1937–1997), was recognized as the primary koto composer—and one of the preeminent koto performers as well—of the late 20th century. "Tori no Yo ni" (Like a Bird) is one of Sawai Tadao's best-known solo koto compositions. It may be heard on **CD ex. #2–1** in a performance by the composer. This piece was inspired by a dream in which Tadao saw himself transformed into a bird. "If I could fly in the sky like a bird. . . everyone has had a dream like this," he wrote in describing the piece. "Ordinarily, this is when you're asleep and your consciousness is low, but occasionally you open your eyes. When you're yearning, when you're happy, when your heart is content, you float in the sky. Like a bird" (translated from Japanese by Anne Prescott). The perpetual rhythmic motion, frequent changes in dynamics, and varied timbres and melodic ornaments heard in "Tori no Yo ni" collectively contribute to the music's evocative impression of a bird in flight.

In recent years, the koto has been embraced by Japanese and international popular musicians as well as traditionalists. Japanese pop music, or J-pop, is an extraordinary phenomenon of both Japanese national culture and international popular culture. Some J-pop groups and artists skillfully combine contemporary pop and rock sounds and styles with instruments and musical elements drawn from Japanese traditional music. One such band is Rin, a group that was formed in 2003 by three young women who were graduates of Tokyo's National University of Fine Arts and Music. (As of this writing, the group had recently disbanded.) All three are highly accomplished performers of traditional Japanese instruments. Two of them, Chie Arai and Mana Yoshinaga, play both the koto and the shamisen; the third, Tomoca Nagasu, plays the shakuhachi and the biwa. All three are vocalists as well.

On Rin's first hit single, "Sakitama" (**CD ex. #4–24**), originally released in 2004, the Japanese instruments and powerful vocals render melodies wrought in the tones and scales of Japanese traditional music, but the production overall is heavily oriented toward rock and pop sensibilities. Ample use of electronic and electro-acoustic timbres, along with rich vocal harmonizations, hard rock grooves, and a verse-chorus-type pop song form, envelop the traditionally Japanese core of instrumental and vocal melody to create a compelling musical tapestry of considerable emotional power. Koto playing is prominent throughout the track. The distinctive timbre and character of

Mana Yoshinaga, formerly of Rin, playing the koto in concert.

koto melody first come to the fore at 0:19, and as the performance unfolds we hear the koto alternately taking the role of lead melody instrument (e.g., 0:19–0:31), acting as an accompanying instrument to the vocal parts (e.g., 1:07–1:28), and contributing to rich multipart musical dialogues also involving other traditional Japanese instruments (e.g., 3:12–3:29). In this highly post-traditional musical milieu, then, the koto actually displays many faces of its traditional identity: solo instrument, vocal accompanying instrument, and ensemble instrument.

Moreover, the tradition and repertoire of the solo zheng has contributed as much to our notions in the West of what Chinese instrumental music is and what it sounds like as any other musical idiom (Jones 1995:80).

The oldest forms of the zheng consisted of five silk strings mounted on a bamboo frame. Later developments yielded a wooden-framed zheng with 12 or 13 strings that was similar in construction to another ancient Chinese board zither, the 25-string *se*. Over time, the zheng evolved into its various modern forms, which typically feature a wooden frame and either 16 strings (three-octave range) or 21 strings (four-octave range). The 21-string instrument is the one most commonly used today.

Zheng strings, which are now usually made of metal-wound nylon (silk, copper, and steel strings were used in earlier times, and steel strings are still used for more traditional styles), are laid horizontally across a slightly rounded wooden soundboard that is mounted directly over the instrument's frame/resonator and attached to pegs at both ends. The strings are supported by *movable bridges*, which may be made of wood, ivory, plastic, or other materials. The positioning of the bridges is adjusted for different tunings. The frame rests on a wooden stand with four legs, behind which the performer plays from a seated position. (See Figure 13.1 and the photo, p. 318.)

The Musical Guided Tour for this chapter provides an introduction to the zheng, illustrating basic scales, techniques, melodic ornaments, and playing styles that we will encounter in Guided Listening Experience selections later on. Deng Haiqiong (or Haiqiong Deng, as she is known in the West) is the performer. She is among the leading zheng players of her generation from mainland China. Haiqiong was born in 1975 and started playing the zheng at age eight. She is a graduate of the Shanghai Conservatory of Music and also studied at the Chinese Conservatory in Beijing. In 1995, she won first prize in the prestigious National Zheng Competition of China. Since that time, she has concertized in China, Japan, Singapore, Canada, and the

se (like "sir," but stop before you reach the "r")

Labeled diagram of a zheng.

FIGURE 13.1

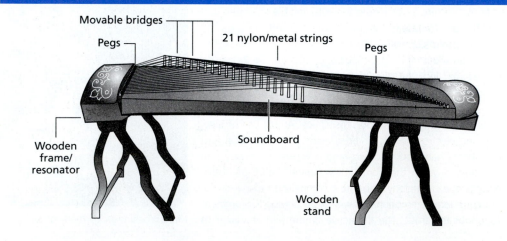

Movable bridges

Pegs

21 nylon/metal strings

Pegs

Wooden frame/resonator

Soundboard

Wooden stand

United States, including a recital at New York's famed Carnegie Hall. She also has studied ethnomusicology at the graduate level in the United States.

The transcript below corresponds to the audio Musical Guided Tour. As you listen to this tour at the Online Learning Center (www.mhhe.com/bakan2e), follow along with this transcript.

musical guided tour

The Zheng

(The tour begins with Deng Haiqiong performing the final portion of a solo zheng piece called "Fighting the Typhoon.")

The 21-string zheng which you just heard has a range of four octaves [♪]. Altering the positions of the movable bridges on the instrument allows for several different pentatonic [five tone per octave] tunings of the 21 strings. The most commonly used tuning on the zheng produces a scale of D E F♯ A B (D), which sounds like this [♪]. This scale is essentially identical in structure to the Western pentatonic scale to which you were introduced in Chapter 4. Two other zheng tunings are very common as well. These produce the following scales: D E G A B (D), which sounds like this [♪]; and D E G A C (D), which sounds like this [♪].

In traditional zheng playing styles, only the thumb, index finger, and middle finger of the right hand are used to pluck and stroke the strings. The performer usually attaches small, plastic plectra (which are like miniature guitar picks) to the fingertips to produce a clear, bright timbre. Listen now as Haiqiong illustrates a single-line melody using the traditional, one-hand plucking style [♪].

Here is another example of one-hand plucking technique, but this time Haiqiong simultaneously plucks two strings that are an octave apart on most of the melody notes; in other words, she plays the melody in octaves (*da cuo*). This is common in zheng music [♪].

Since the 1950s, techniques involving plucking and stroking the strings of the zheng with both hands, rather than with just the right hand, have become standard. To a significant degree, such techniques reflect Western musical influences, especially influences from Western piano music. Here are a few illustrations of two-hand plucking techniques on the zheng:

- First, a melody harmonized in two-note chords (*xiao cuo*) [♪].

- Second, a melody embellished by arpeggiated chords (*payin*) [♪].

- Third, a melody played in the right-hand part with accompanying chords and arpeggios in the left-hand part [♪].

In the last musical illustration, Haiqiong sustained the notes of the right-hand melody part using a tremolo, or "roll," technique called *yao zhi*. Here's what the tremolo sounds like on its own [♪]. A more rhythmic technique for sustaining notes (*da zhi yao*) is used in many older zheng pieces; it involves a quick back-and-forth thumb motion and sounds like this [♪]. Also popular is the "four-point fingering" technique (*si dian*), which features a quick alternation of middle finger (M), thumb (T), and index finger (I) plucks, in the following pattern: M T I T M T I T, etc. Here is an illustration of what that sounds like [♪].

Melodic **ornamentation** is very highly developed in zheng performance and there are many different kinds of ornaments. Especially striking is the large variety of **gua-zou** (goo-wa-zoh), or *glissandos*. These are rapid ascending or descending sweeps across the strings. Here are four of the main types:

- First, the short gua-zou, consisting of a sweep of a few notes that lands on a main melody note [♪].

- Second, the long gua-zou, which is often described by Chinese musicians as the "falling water" ornament, for reasons that will likely be apparent to you from the following musical illustration [♪].

- Third, the strong gua-zou, which is heavily accented and almost attack-like [♪].

- Fourth, the gua-zou played on the left-hand side of the strings (that is, to the left of the movable bridges), which creates this very distinctive effect [♪].

A host of other zheng ornaments are created by pressing into the string with the fingers of the left hand while the right hand plucks. The main types of left-hand ornaments are:

■ First, the up-glide (*shang hua-yin*) [♪].

■ Second, the down-glide (*xia hua-yin*) [♪].

■ Third, the round-glide (*hui hua-yin*), which may go either up and then down [♪], or down and then up [♪].

■ Fourth, a narrow vibrato (*xiao chan-yin*) [♪].

■ Fifth, a wide vibrato (*da chan-yin*) [♪].

■ Sixth, harmonics, or overtones (*fan yin*) [♪].

There are several distinct regional styles of zheng playing in China. Unique approaches to melodic ornamentation are characteristic of each of these. For example, in the regional style of Shandong province, a narrow vibrato is generally preferred over a wide vibrato, whereas in the regional style of Henan (He[r]-nahn) province, the opposite is true. Thus, if you were to hear a zheng piece that sounded like this [♪] and another one that sounded like this [♪], you could make an educated guess, just on the evidence of the vibrato alone, that the first piece was in Shandong style and the second piece was in Henan style. Here again, we find an example of purely musical style serving as an index of *cultural* style as well.

The Zheng in Imperial China

The origin of the name *zheng* is not known. One theory is that it is onomatopoeic, reflecting the timbre of the instrument when its strings are plucked. Another theory has to do with the possible relationship of the instrument's name to a different translation of the word *zheng,* which is "dispute." Legend has it that during the ancient era of the Qin dynasty (3rd century BCE), two sisters in the imperial palace got into a heated argument over a 25-string se zither and broke the instrument in half. This yielded two instruments, one with 12 strings, the other with 13. Amused by the incident, the emperor named these new "half" instruments "zheng" in acknowledgement of the "dispute" that had given rise to them. According to some versions of the story, the 13-string instrument was eventually given as a gift by the Qin emperor to the imperial house of Japan, giving rise to the 13-string Japanese koto. The 12-string model, meanwhile, ended up in Korea, where it became the prototype of the 12-string Korean kayagum. With respect to at least the koto origins side of this legend, however, the historical record suggests a different interpretation, namely, that the koto likely arrived in Japan in the 8th century CE as part of the gagaku orchestra (see "Insights and Perspectives" box, p. 322).

The earliest written document containing a reference to the zheng is from a Qin era manuscript of 237 BCE, which describes groups of musicians in rural areas of China who "beat clay drums and earthen jars, play *zheng* and slap their thighs to accompany songs" (Han Mei 2005). This ancient zheng seemingly made a favorable impression on Qin imperialists. It was quite loud and portable and could be adapted to different musical situations. It became a favored Qin instrument, and as the Qin's dynastic realm expanded, so too did the zheng's geographical and musical diffusion. It was incorporated into ensembles, became a popular instrument for accompanying singing of various types, and was employed in a wide range of entertainment and ritual contexts, from imperial banquets to village ceremonies and sacrificial rites.

With Qin imperial expansion came the emergence of what has been described by some scholars as the advent of the first "popular music" culture in China (Lawergren 2000:83). Musical styles whose uses transcended their specific places and cultures of origin, and which blended together elements from different regions and idioms to create new forms of musical expression, began to proliferate as contact between formally separate cultures and traditions increased. The

Painting of a court dance performance from the Tang dynasty era. The dancers in the center are accompanied by a women's court orchestra (rear left and rear right) performing on a variety of traditional Chinese instruments. Elaborate entertainments such as the one depicted here were also produced during the earlier Han dynasty era.

zheng was a key instrument in this emergent, ancient "popular music" culture. As it took root in different areas of Qin China, regional styles began to emerge. Some zheng regional styles today (for example, in Shaanxi, Henan, and Chaozhou) are believed, by local musicians in those areas and by Chinese music historians alike, to retain musical elements passed down through the millennia from the Qin era. Members of the Shaanxi zheng school in particular refer to their regional tradition as "Qin zheng style" as a way of claiming links to this historical legacy.

Shaanxi (Shahn-hsee)

Chaozhou (Chow-joe)

The Han dynasty era

During the Han dynasty (202 BCE–220 CE), a grand epoch of Chinese civilization during which **Confucianism** was established as the foundation of the Chinese social order (see "Insights and Perspectives" box, p. 328), the zheng continued to develop and gain popularity as an instrument of entertainment and public ritual. It was played at weddings, banquets, and funerals, sometimes even on horseback (Cheng 1991:9). Archaeological evidence indicates that music played on the zheng and other ancient instruments was used to accompany elaborate entertainments and rituals that also involved singing, acrobatics, and dance. Though the accompanying painting of such an event dates from the later dynastic period of the Tang (see p. 329), the elaborate entertainments of Han court life were likely of a similar spirit and character.

The zheng during Han times was played by professional court musicians, women, slaves, and common folk and favored by members of diverse social classes—courtesans and poets, soldiers and servants. Though cast as a "vulgar" instrument by some Han poets and literati, it was hailed by others as embodying a high moral character befitting of gentlemen and heroes (Rault-Leyrat 1987:35). Moreover, though it appears that the zheng was mainly an ensemble instrument used in entertainment contexts in Han China, it is possible that a solo tradition of zheng playing also dates back this far. The solo zheng tradition may have developed in association with Confucian practices of using music for purposes of self-cultivation, practices that have been more extensively documented in the history of another Chinese board zither chordophone, the qin (see "Insights and Perspectives" box, p. 328). Disciplined self-cultivation and self-refinement at the individual level were seen as key to the development and maintenance of a morally virtuous social order on the larger scale of society, which was in turn the hallmark ideal of Confucian social and political philosophy.

insights and perspectives

The teachings of Confucius, only moderately influential during his lifetime (551–479 BCE) and largely ignored for over 200 years of political instability and frequent warring following his death, became the cornerstone of Chinese society and social policy under the rule of the Han dynasty. Another important influence on Chinese social and cultural developments during this period was Buddhism, which originated in India and entered China from the west, gradually spreading eastward throughout much of the country beginning in the 1st century CE.

Confucianism insisted upon the need for social control and direction at every level. Hierarchical social stratification, deference to authority, codification of behavior across the full range of social classes, and the primacy of fulfilling one's duty to society above all other considerations underscored its fundamental goal: the establishment, preservation, and perpetuation of a morally virtuous social order. All facets of society—from family dynamics and political administration to the arts, religious belief and ritual, and cultural and intellectual life—were bound up in the Confucian code of moral virtue as "right" social order.

Confucius had claimed that music, properly employed, had great value as a medium for establishing and sustaining a good and moral society. He believed that music had an inherent capacity to cultivate inner character, to mold people's minds and hearts in ways that would make them more committed to—and better capable of—serving the common good. This was true for emperor, sage, and peasant alike. For each social class, certain types of music were regarded as being most appropriate and beneficial. Governmental regulation, control, and institutionalization of music and musical activities were deemed essential for matching the right kinds of music to the right kinds of people. Under the Han, a large governmental music bureau was established to oversee such regulation.

At the top of the Confucian social hierarchy were the *junzi* (jün-dse), or "superior individuals." These were men from the ruling and educated classes thought to possess the requisite moral propriety, intellect, and practical wisdom to guide Han society (and music) along the proper path to order and virtue. (Notably, education offered opportunities for upward social mobility for intellectually gifted Chinese males.) The junzi instrument *par excellence* was the seven-string *qin,* a board zither chordophone with no bridges that is smaller than the zheng and has a much softer dynamic range. The qin was an instrument of the gentleman scholar. It was usually played solo, often in solitude. Playing the qin was seen as an aid to enlightenment, disciplined thinking, and self-reflection. Many Chinese works of art and poems depict the figure of a junzi with qin engaged in quiet contemplation. Confucius himself is believed to have played the qin.

CD ex. #4–25 features a portion of a solo performance played on the qin. The melody of this piece is based on an ancient Buddhist chant. With its slow and contemplative style and the use of signature qin musical techniques such as the bell-like harmonics heard from 0:39–0:56, this is a good example of the traditional qin musical art. The performer is Tao-Chu-Sheng, a qin master from Taiwan.

Painting of two junzi playing music together in an idyllic natural setting. The seated musician on the left is playing a qin. A photograph of Deng Haiqiong playing the qin may be seen at the Online Learning Center at www.mhhe .com/bakan2e, where photos of other Chinese instruments are included as well.

The Tang dynasty era

The zheng reached its apogee in imperial China during the period of the Tang dynasty (618–907 CE), another golden age in China's cultural history (Rault-Leyrat 1987:80). At its height, the Tang government music ministry employed 30,000 musicians and dancers from throughout the Chinese empire and beyond (South Asia, Central Asia, Southeast Asia). The popular and adaptable zheng thrived in this era of musical experimentation and cosmopolitanism. It was incorporated into many different kinds of ensembles and used in a wide range of contexts. New features were added (e.g., additional strings) and novel playing techniques were introduced. The zheng's increased stature in this era of opulence was symbolized in features of its decoration and design, from silver-engraved wooden frames to jade bridges. The earliest known examples of notated zheng music also date from this era (Cheng 1991:16).

The zheng was combined with a variety of other instruments in Tang court ensembles. Some of these instruments, including the qin, were of ancient Chinese origin. Others, which also gained popularity in regional folk music traditions outside of the court, had come to China from foreign lands the imperial Chinese had encountered through trade and conquest. Especially important in this regard was the **Silk Road,** or Silk Road trail, which connected China to peoples and lands as distant as Central Asia, India, Egypt, and Turkey.

It was via the Silk Road that the *pipa,* a pear-shaped, plucked chordophone with four strings, was introduced into Chinese musical culture, ultimately becoming one of the most important of all Chinese instruments. From Tang times forward, the pipa and the zheng were closely associated with one another, accompanying sung poetry, performing instrumental duets, and playing together in different types of ensembles and various performance contexts.

The pipa, here played by Yiyi Wang.

CD ex. #4-26 is an excerpt of a duet for zheng and pipa. The performers are Deng Hai-qiong (zheng) and Hou Yuehua (pipa). The excerpt begins with the pipa, which has an almost banjo-like timbre. Note the dramatic tremolo "rolls" (*yao zhi*). (This technique was originally associated with the pipa, and was later adapted for the zheng; the zheng version was demonstrated earlier in the Musical Guided Tour.) The zheng makes its entrance at 0:17 with a short, descending gua-zou (glissando). From 0:45 until the music fades out at the end of the excerpt, the two instruments are featured playing together.

Hou Yuehua (Ho Yoo-e-hwah)

Women began playing the zheng in greater numbers during the Tang period, yielding a cultural association of gender to instrument that continues in modern times. Whereas female zheng players of earlier eras had typically been of low social status (prostitutes, concubines, servants), girls and women of the upper classes now started playing the zheng too—often solo—for both entertainment and self-cultivation (Rault-Leyrat 1987:83). Along with the new gendered identity came an identification of the instrument with romantic subjects: the beauty of nature, the beauty of women, sentimental feelings of love, and memories of sadness and longing.

The Tang emperor Xuanzong played an important role in cultivating the zheng as a "women's instrument," and in promoting women's performance on other instruments, such as the pipa, as well. Under his patronage, hundreds of women in the imperial palace were given expert training on the zheng by leading (male) court musicians. Ensembles of well-trained female musicians entertained guests at royal banquets and in other contexts (see the painting on p. 327).

Xuanzong (Hsü-en-dsong)

The Ming and Qing dynasty eras

Following a period after the Tang and subsequent Song dynasty eras when it declined in popularity, the zheng became very popular again in the 14th century during the Ming dynasty (1368–1644). The Ming witnessed the rise of a large Chinese middle class, and a zheng was a standard item to have in the home. There was even a popular saying in Ming times that claimed: "Almost every household has a painted drum and a silver *zheng* can be found everywhere" (Cheng 1991:11). Girls and young women were especially encouraged to study and play the instrument.

The Ming was also an era when various regional styles of *Chinese opera* (*xi, xiqu,* or *xiju*) flourished in different areas of the country. The zheng was an important instrument in the ensembles that accompanied regional opera performances, from Shandong and Henan in the north to Chaozhou and Hakka in the south. This was true during the consequent Qing dynasty as well, which saw a continued efflorescence of Chinese opera forms (see "Insights and Perspectives" box). Distinctive zheng playing techniques and styles of melodic ornamentation were developed in each region to capture the nuances of regional languages and dialects, especially in connection with local forms of opera and song and their related instrumental styles. These developments were important to the eventual emergence of identifiable regional styles of *solo* zheng playing, which would in turn help to shape the conservatory style of solo zheng performance in the modern era.

**xi, xiqu, xiju
(hsee, hsee-chew, hsee-jü)**

insights and perspectives

Chinese Opera and Beijing Opera in Dynastic and Post-Dynastic China

Common to the different styles of traditional Chinese opera was a format in which a dramatic story was enacted by costumed performers wearing makeup who combined heightened speech, song, dance, mime, acting, and acrobatics in their presentation. The use of stage props was minimal, and the action tended to be highly stylized (as opposed to realistic). Traditional, regional Chinese opera styles featured four standard character types: male (*sheng*), female (*dan*), painted-face male (*jing*), and clown (*chou*). The parts of the female characters were often played by boys or adult female impersonators.

The most widely known type of Chinese opera is Beijing Opera (or Peking Opera), which had its origins in the capital in the late 18th century but did not fully crystallize until the 19th century. Like other forms of traditional Chinese opera, Beijing Opera is highly stylized. There are 26 ways to laugh, 20 different types of beard, and 39 ways of manipulating the beard (Han and Mark 1980:21). The accompanying instrumental ensemble in traditional Beijing Opera features a small, two-string fiddle with a piercing timbre called the *jinghu* (meaning "Beijing fiddle"), as well as other chordophones including the pipa. Additional melodic instruments (chordophones and aerophones) are also included, and there is a percussion section (gongs, cymbals, wooden clappers). The leader of the ensemble performs on a drum called a *danpi gu,* which creates a unique clicking sound.

Beijing Opera experienced its golden age in the early decades of the 20th century, spanning the decline of the Qing dynasty and the early years of the Republican era. Indeed, Beijing Opera served as a powerful vehicle of social and political change during that transitional period of Chinese history (see Mackerras 1997).

During the Communist era, especially in the 1960s and early- to mid-1970s, Beijing Opera and other Chinese opera genres were either discredited or else radically transformed in accordance with the stringent political priorities and agendas of Chinese socialism. Contemporary themes, plots, and costumes, as well as realistic staging, were used to modernize the look of the performances and to advance socialist propaganda. The heightened speech of the old dramas was replaced by ordinary Mandarin speech. The traditional division of the characters into four types and most of the conventional stylized and symbolic gestures were removed. In the new style, traditional Beijing Opera melodies alternated with revolutionary songs espousing the virtues of Chinese communism. The music also was modified through the addition of Western instruments and imported elements such as Western harmony.

A classic example of this type of Revolutionary Chinese Opera that derived from the original Beijing Opera form was *The Red Lantern* (1964), the plot of which concerns three generations in a family of Chinese revolutionaries during the China–Japan war of 1937–1945. Productions of *The Red Lantern* were common during the Cultural Revolution era of 1966–1976. After that period, it was not performed for many years. It was revived, however, in 1995. **CD ex. #1-5,** which we listened to earlier in connection with Chapter 2, features an excerpt from a 1997 recording of a song from *The Red Lantern* sung by the vocalist Wei Li. Although this is an example of a Revolutionary Opera song rather than a song from a traditional Beijing Opera, the musical style of the arrangement is essentially traditional. The melodic instruments (there is no percussion in this excerpt) are led by the *jinghu* fiddle and the pipa also is heard.

Traditional Beijing Opera images are now seen in pop music videos, such as Leehom Wang's "Hua Tian Cuo" (Mistake in the Flower Field), in which the pop star's own fictionalized romantic trials and tribulations are visually analogized to scenes from a Beijing Opera he is seen viewing on his iPod. This video had received more than 200,000 YouTube hits at the time of this writing.

Scene from a traditional Beijing Opera.

Scene from a Revolutionary Chinese Opera.

Regional Styles: Traditional Solo Zheng Music

During the later Qing dynasty era, a number of distinct regional styles of solo zheng music and performance practice crystallized in different parts of China. These developed out of existing regional traditions of folk opera, sung poetry, musically accompanied storytelling, and instrumental ensemble music involving the zheng; they also reflected a long history of mixing between folk, popular, and court music traditions. By the mid- to late-19th century, distinctive regional solo zheng styles were recognized in areas including Shandong, Henan, Shaanxi, Chaozhou, Hakka, and Zhejiang. These regional styles still exist today, though in many respects they have been absorbed into or eclipsed by the "national" style of the conservatories.

Each regional style has its own, distinctive **yun,** or "regional character." The yun of Henan zheng, for example, is known for its liveliness, short descending melodic phrases, and, as was demonstrated earlier in the Musical Guided Tour, a preference for wide rather than narrow vibrato. The dramatic vocal rises and falls of Henan spoken dialect (especially as reflected in Henan folk opera) are mirrored by similarly dramatic up- and down-glide ornaments in Henan zheng playing.

Common to the various regional zheng styles is a shared basis in pieces that are in a form called **baban.** In the Guided Listening Experience that follows Table 13.1 on page 332, we explore one such piece.

yun (yün)

baban (bah-bahn)

TABLE 13.1 Major developments of the zheng and its musical culture during the dynastic era (pre-1912).

Qin Dynasty Era (3rd century BCE)

- 237 BCE: First written documentation of zheng
- Zheng prominent in emergent "popular music" culture of China
- Possible origin of regional zheng styles

Han Dynasty Era (202 BCE–220 CE)

- Zheng played in many different contexts and types of ensembles
- Possible origin of regional traditions of solo zheng performance

Tang Dynasty Era (618–907)

- Zheng reaches its apogee
- Played in many new ensemble contexts, introduction of new features of instrument design and construction, elaborate instrument decoration (silver engraving, jade bridges), new playing techniques
- Earliest known examples of music notation for zheng
- Close association with the pipa established
- Women zheng players and women's court ensembles (Emperor Xuanzong)

Ming Dynasty Era (1368–1644)

- Reemergence of zheng in popularity after a period of post-Tang decline; girls and young women especially encouraged to play
- Zheng becomes important instrument in regional Chinese opera ensembles

Qing Dynasty Era (1644–1911)

- Continued importance of zheng in regional Chinese opera ensembles
- Crystallization of regional solo playing styles and traditions in Shandong, Henan, etc.
- Pieces in baban form central to solo zheng traditions

guided listening experience

"Autumn Moon over the Han Palace," Deng Haiqiong

- CD Track #4-27
- Featured performer(s)/group: Deng Haiqiong (zheng)
- Format: Excerpt
- Source recording: *Ning,* by Hai-qiong Deng [Deng Haiqiong] (Celebrity Music)

"Autumn Moon over the Han Palace" is one of the best-known traditional zheng pieces in the baban form. The version heard here, performed by Deng Haiqiong, is representative of the

Shandong regional zheng style. Archaeological evidence indicates that the zheng has been a part of musical life in Shandong since at least the 3rd century CE (Cheng 1991:88).

Haiqiong plays the piece on a 16-string zheng with steel strings, rather than on the more common 21-string zheng with metal-wound nylon strings that we heard in the Musical Guided Tour. The smaller zheng with steel strings is generally preferred for traditional pieces like this one because:

■ Plucked tones on steel strings are able to resonate (sustain) longer than plucked tones on metal-wound nylon strings, allowing for subtle nuances in melodic ornamentation that the traditional pieces demand.

■ These compositions do not exceed the three-octave range of the 16-string instrument, unlike many modern compositions that employ the full, four-octave range of the 21-string zheng.

Though not a representative of the Shandong zheng tradition herself, Haiqiong learned "Autumn Moon over the Han Palace" from one of the most revered 20th-century Shandong zheng masters, Gao Zicheng (b. 1918). She first learned to play the piece on her own with the aid of a cassette recording by Gao. She would listen to this recording on her portable tape player through headphones over and over again and try to emulate what she heard. Later, while a student at the high school for performing arts in Xi'an, she got an opportunity to work on the piece directly with Gao. But in teaching Haiqiong "Autumn Moon," Gao did not so much teach her to play the piece as simply play it *for* her in between lengthy discourses on various aspects of the life, culture, and musical world of Shandong. And what music "teaching" there was per se consisted mainly of Gao playing the piece straight through from start to finish, then listening to Haiqiong play it back for him in the same manner. He had little to say to her at all in the way of specifics concerning her performance or interpretation.

"He would listen to me play through the piece," Haiqiong recalled to me during an interview, "and then say, 'No, something's totally incorrect.' Then he would play the whole piece again, but I really couldn't hear the difference and he wouldn't explain [laughs]. . . . I really didn't understand at that age. My other teachers [at the conservatory] were much more systematic and analytical. It was so different. But later, when I was older, I realized what he was trying to teach me. That it's not about technique. It's about where the music comes from, its feeling and its cultural background. . . . When I was little [i.e., a teenager], I thought, 'This is such a simple piece. It's boring, not challenging.' But as I grow older I realize you can never get bored playing this piece. There's always something more. It's not always necessary to be complicated and technical for [good] musical expression. Just being simple is sometimes more effective. That's what I learned from playing this piece and, looking back, from studying with Gao Zicheng."

Haiqiong's love of the piece "Autumn Moon over the Han Palace" extends to a deeper appreciation of the baban tradition to which it belongs. "These baban pieces are just so perfect, though they are very simple," she explains. "You cannot imagine a single note being added or taken away." The standard formal design of a baban piece consists of a melody with eight phrases (Figure 13.2, p. 334). The basic unit of measurement for each phrase is called a *ban*. Each *ban* is essentially a measure of two beats, with a strong beat (*ban*) followed by a weak beat (*yan*). Seven of the eight melodic phrases have a length of eight *ban*, while a single phrase (the fifth) has an extended length of 12 *ban*. One baban cycle, then, has a total length of 68 *ban*. This 68-*ban* form is typically played twice in succession in the performance of a baban composition (Figure 13.2).

The baban form serves as a framework for many different melodies. Varied approaches to melodic ornamentation and embellishment may be applied to any one of these. How the melody is treated is determined both by the music's regional character (yun) and the unique style and interpretation of the individual performer.

In interpreting "Autumn Moon over the Han Palace," Haiqiong aimed to capture both the yun of traditional Shandong zheng playing and the unique stylistic approach of Gao Zicheng within that Shandong tradition. Beyond that, she simply allowed her musical personality to come through. "The more I play the piece, I don't worry about the style anymore," she explains. "It's just there."

Gao Zicheng (Gow Dser-chung)

Xi'an (Hsee-ahn)

Baban form outline.

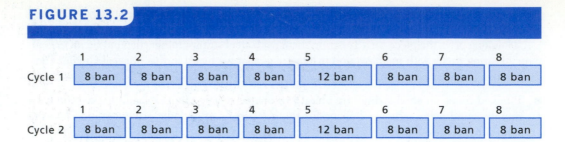

FIGURE 13.2

	1	2	3	4	5	6	7	8
Cycle 1	8 ban	8 ban	8 ban	8 ban	12 ban	8 ban	8 ban	8 ban

	1	2	3	4	5	6	7	8
Cycle 2	8 ban	8 ban	8 ban	8 ban	12 ban	8 ban	8 ban	8 ban

yijing (ee-jing)

Haiqiong is, however, guided significantly in her playing by the desire to capture the culturally designated emotional quality, or **yijing,** of the composition. This piece is identified with an yijing of "sadness," but Haiqiong is quick to emphasize that this is a different brand of emotion than is generally implied by that word in the English language.

"The yijing is of a sadness that's in your heart, that you keep inside yourself," she explains. "It's very gentle, moderate, and controlled. This sense of moderation is what has to come through when you play the piece. More important than expressing 'sadness' through the music for me is expressing this mood of moderation, of a certain sense of peacefulness and restraint."

Listen now to the excerpt of Deng Haiqiong's rendition of "Autumn Moon over the Han Palace" on **CD ex. #4-27,** which includes one full cycle of the 68-ban baban form (on the original recording, the entire form is repeated once). Follow along with the Guided Listening Quick Summary. Use the summary's timeline to track the eight phrases of the baban form, noting that it is sometimes difficult to hear where the new phrases begin. Also, take note of the many different kinds of melodic ornaments that occur, the first few of which are charted out. Listen carefully, and you will hear that virtually every note of the melody is ornamented in one way or another.

guided listening quick summary

"Autumn Moon over the Han Palace," Deng Haiqiong (CD ex. #4-27)

The piece is in the standard 68-*ban* baban form and uses the tuning of one of the three standard zheng modes: D E G A B (D).

0:00–0:20: Phrase 1 (Length of phrase = 8 ban)
Examples of melodic ornaments in Phrase 1:

- 0:00: gua-zou (glissando)
- 0:02: up-glide (*shang hua-yin*)
- 0:03: down-up round-glide (*hui hua-yin*)
- 0:05: down-glide (*xia hua-yin*)
- 0:12: vibrato "shake" (*rou*)

0:21–0:38: Phrase 2 (Length of phrase = 8 ban)

0:39–0:55: Phrase 3 (Length of phrase = 8 ban)

0:56–1:12: Phrase 4 (Length of phrase = 8 ban)

1:13–1:36: Phrase 5 (Length of phrase = 12 ban)

1:37–1:53: Phrase 6 (Length of phrase = 8 ban)

1:54–2:08: Phrase 7 (Length of phrase = 8 ban)

2:09–2:25: Phrase 8 (Length of phrase = 8 ban)

Emergence and Development of the Conservatory Solo Zheng Style in Mainland China

The conservatory tradition (*xueyuan pai*) of solo zheng playing of which Deng Haiqiong is representative has its direct roots in the Republican era of Chinese history, 1912–1949. This era covers the years following the collapse of the Qing dynasty at the end of 1911 through to the establishment of the People's Republic of China as a communist state under the leadership of Mao Zedong in 1949. During this period, China experienced great political instability and massive social and cultural reform. Modernization was seen as key to reform efforts on all levels, and modernizing China equated largely with appropriating Western technological, economic, and cultural systems and resources for purposes of Chinese nationalism and economic growth.

Music, which had been used for explicitly political purposes throughout Chinese dynastic history, became a major focus of reform efforts during the post-dynastic Republican period too. Chinese traditional musics were essentially cast as backward and regressive, while Western music (especially that of European Classical and Romantic era composers of the 18th and 19th centuries) was prized as an adopted icon of Chinese modernity and progressiveness. Some reformers believed that wholesale replacement of Chinese music by Western music was the proper path for modern Chinese musical nationalism. This attitude was fueled by a prevalent notion that Western music was inherently superior to Chinese music, a notion that still persists even today, according to ethnomusicologist Stephen Jones. Conservatory "students of traditional Chinese instruments are plainly considered inferior to students of Western music," Jones writes. "For many urban Chinese, their traditional music is 'backward', less 'scientific' than Western music" (Jones 1995:62).

Buoyed by such prejudices, music conservatories, symphony orchestras, and other institutions devoted to the cultivation of Western music were established in Chinese cities such as Shanghai and Beijing during the first half of the 20th century. Expatriate Western musicians, as well as Chinese musicians who had studied at major music schools in Europe, North America, and Japan, taught at the conservatories.

There was another important school of thought in the music reform arena of Republican China, however. Members of this school, led by Liu Tianhua, argued that traditional Chinese musics and instruments should not be discarded, but rather should be reformed in accordance with modern, nationalistic ideals to become the basis of a new, national Chinese music. (See Stock [1996] on musicultural life in China during this period of reform.) Many leading representatives of this camp, like their counterparts on the other side of the music reform debate, had studied Western music abroad. They sought to "improve" the quality of traditional Chinese music by modernizing it, which largely equated with incorporating Western elements: standardized tunings, Western-style harmonies and textures, and modifications to traditional Chinese instruments inspired by the modern technologies of Western instruments (e.g., the piano). Collecting, transcribing, and publishing traditional folk music from different regions of China were regarded as key to the reform effort. Folk music was to provide the base upon which a new Chinese national music would be created with the aid of more "advanced" (i.e., mainly Western-derived) musical resources. This was to be a music imbued with Chinese "national characteristics," a music that would ideally evolve to be "the equal of Western music" in the aspirations of its most ambitious advocates (Wong 2002:382). One significant outgrowth of this branch of reform was that regional masters of instruments like the zheng and pipa were hired as part-time music instructors at some urban conservatories, institutions that had initially been devoted almost exclusively to Western music.

Meanwhile, musical life outside the cities continued much as it had before, and regional music traditions such as those associated with the solo zheng continued as part of local musicultural scenes. Some regional zheng players straddled both worlds, continuing to function as local musicians in their home communities while also teaching part-time at the urban conservatories, where their "folk art" was passed on and developed by a new generation of

xueyuan pai (hsoo-e-yoo-en pie)

Liu Tianhua (Lee-oo Tee-en-hwah)

conservatory-trained musicians. These formally trained conservatory musicians, with backgrounds in both Chinese and Western music, developed and ultimately published a body of traditional and neo-traditional solo zheng repertoire. Collections of notated zheng pieces representing different regional styles were compiled. Also, new pieces based on traditional tunes and forms but modified in ways that reflected the new musical values and approaches of the reform movement were created.

Lou Shuhua
(Lo Shoo-hwah)

The most important and influential of these neo-traditional compositions was "Return of the Fishing Boats" (1936), by Lou Shuhua. This was the first solo zheng piece to break away from reliance on the baban form. Additionally, it introduced a variety of new techniques and stylistic elements to zheng playing, such as an approach to melodic ornamentation that was clearly inspired by Western piano and harp music. Another innovation was the work's highly literal use of *programmaticism,* that is, the employment of instrumental music to tell a story, illustrate an idea, or evoke visual images or scenes. In the last part of the piece, acceleration of the tempo, melodic repetition, and ornamentation of the melody with sweeping glissandos (gua-zou) were used to paint a vivid sonic portrait of fishermen rowing their boats toward home at the end of the work day. While programmatic elements had existed in Chinese music for centuries, this kind of *literal* programmaticism was something entirely new, and here again the presence of Western influences—especially those of 19th-century European composers of programmatic music such as Franz Liszt and Hector Berlioz—were unmistakable.

Music and the conservatory solo zheng tradition in Communist China, 1949–1965

With the rise to power of Mao Zedong and the Chinese Communist Party in 1949, efforts to reform Chinese music continued, but now with a thick overlay of explicit political content tied to the doctrines of Chinese socialism. According to Mao Zedong, all music and arts in the "New China" were to expressly serve the goals of the socialist state: to elevate and valorize the peasantry and proletarian masses, promote revolutionary ideals, and glorify the revolution, communism, and Mao himself. Communist songs for the masses like "On the Golden Hill in Beijing" (sung by Deng Haiqiong's mother, Li Xiuqin, with zheng accompaniment by Haiqiong, on **CD ex. #4-28**) were created in abundance and used to propagate Chinese state ideology and policies. With its melody based, at least ostensibly, on a Tibetan folksong, the text of "On the Golden Hill in Beijing" invokes several standard themes of Chinese communist rhetoric. These include:

A mass children's choir and orchestra perform a song entitled "We Are Successors to Communism" in Beijing (1965).

- The literal and metaphorical glorification of Mao Zedong and the CCP.

- The rationalization of CCP policies regarding China's "ethnic minorities" (in this case, Tibetans, many of whom regarded this song as "an offensive official reaction to the threatening antagonism" they felt toward the Chinese state [Baranovitch 2003:65]).

- The "emancipation" of the peasant masses.

- The ideal of building socialism for China.

"On the Golden Hill in Beijing" (partial text translation, adapted from Baranovitch 2003:62) (CD ex. #4-28)

> *Rays of light from the golden hill in Beijing illuminate the four directions.*
> *Nurtured by the thought of Mao Zedong, we grow up.*

The emancipated peasants have good morale, and new Xijang [Tibet] is building socialism. Songs of praise are offered to Chairman Mao, songs of praise are offered to the Chinese Communist Party.

Under Mao's rule, the government gradually became the sole official patron and controller of the arts, artistic activities, and arts-related institutions in Communist China. Organizations including the Chinese Musicians' Association, centered in Beijing, were established "to develop a body of music for the masses (peasants, workers, and soldiers) that . . . would reflect China's national aspirations and its achievements under communism" (Wong 2002:386). Regional and national music conservatories and research institutes played a major role in cultivating and promoting the new, official musical culture of the Chinese communist state. By 1952, conservatories were being established throughout the mainland, with the flagship institutions in Beijing and Shanghai.

As during the preceding Republican era, both Western and Chinese music were taught at the conservatories. Western music and instruments (especially the violin and the piano) continued to have the highest prestige, but Chinese music and instruments, including the zheng, made gradual advances in prominence and stature. The first full-fledged conservatory curriculum in zheng was established at the Shenyang Conservatory in 1950. A year later, in 1951, the prestigious Shanghai Conservatory instituted a major in zheng performance, and in the years that followed full-time zheng instructors were appointed at conservatories throughout China.

Extensive collection, research, and "development" of folk, minority, and historical traditions constituted a major component of the communist agenda for Chinese music. Government-sponsored music research institutes sent scholars, composers, and "music workers" out to towns, villages, and rural areas throughout China to collect data on traditional music genres so that they could be "preserved, studied, reformed, and modernized to serve the state and the people" (Wong 2002:387–88).

Within the new, socialist musical environment of the urban conservatories and music institutes, the zheng was promoted as a "genuine folk instrument" (Zheng 1983) and many new works for solo zheng were composed. These new pieces were generally based (or at least said to be based) on traditional folk music. The influences of technical and stylistic elements from Western music were even more pronounced than in "Return of the Fishing Boats," however, and the programmatic elements of the music now became explicitly political. Musical works were equipped with titles and *programs* (i.e., descriptions of what the music was properly supposed to represent and evoke) informed by the dominant themes of socialist ideology: celebration of the proletariat, glorification of the revolution and communism, homage to Mao Zedong and the CCP. Especially important and influential among the new solo zheng compositions of the period was "Celebrating the Harvest" (1955), which made extensive use of a piano-inspired, two-hand technique that would become a standard feature of much later zheng music.

In 1958, a government initiative to increase the official stature of Chinese music led several talented pianists at the Shanghai Conservatory to switch to the zheng as their main instrument. Among these was Fan Shang'e, who was also significant as a representative of a new generation of female zheng players who soon came to replace the older, male regional masters as the most renowned

Fan Shang'e (Fan Shaang-uh)

The composer and zheng player Fan Shang'e.

players of the instrument. The virtuosic, "pianistic" potential of the zheng was greatly developed by this new generation of performers. Solo zheng pieces became increasingly demanding technically, requiring new, flashier playing techniques. The zheng itself was modified to meet the new musical demands. It was during this period that the 21-string zheng, with its expanded four-octave range, replaced its three-octave, 16-string predecessor as the standard form of the instrument in the conservatories.

guided listening experience

"Spring on Snowy Mountains," by Fan Shang'e

- CD Track #**4-29**
- Featured performer(s)/group: Xiao Ying (zheng)
- Format: Excerpt
- Source recording: *The Art of the Chinese Harp: Guzheng,* by Xiao Ying (ARC Music Productions International Ltd.)

The virtuosic, piano-inspired approach to solo zheng composition that emerged out of Shanghai and other conservatories in the post-1958 era is well represented by the piece "Spring on Snowy Mountains," by Fan Shang'e (who now lives in Toronto). Here again, a Tibetan folksong is cited as the source of the piece's melody, but aside from the possible connection of the "Spring on Snowy Mountains" main melody to an actual Tibetan tune, the piece has little, if anything, to do with traditional Tibetan folk music. (Visit the Online Learning Center at www.mhhe.com/bakan2e for references to Tibetan music recordings and resources.)

The socialist program linked to "Spring on Snowy Mountains," which describes a scene of Tibetans happily singing and dancing in their beautiful, mountainous land in a spirit of welcome toward Chinese communist rule, has even less bearing on Tibetan realities. Tibetans during this time were severely oppressed under Chinese occupation. Through instrumental music like this and propaganda songs such as "On the Golden Hill in Beijing," the Chinese government, via its music-based initiatives, endeavored to invent and promote an image of national harmony and inclusiveness that was starkly at odds with political realities (see "Insights and Perspectives" box, p. 339).

What is most interesting and novel about this piece in comparison to earlier solo zheng music is the highly developed two-hand playing technique, which reflects the composer's background as a pianist. Especially striking in this regard are passages in which the right hand plays the melody in notes sustained by tremolos (*yao zhi*) overtop arpeggiated left-hand chords in the accompaniment part. The section of the piece included on **CD ex. #4-29** begins with an example of this type of texture (0:00–0:44), which is embellished by abundant glissandos (gua-zou). This is followed by a short, lovely passage featuring harplike, descending arpeggios (0:45–1:01). The final portion of the excerpt is in a lively dance rhythm meant to evoke images of "happy Tibetans" performing their traditional folk dances (1:02–end).

The novel zheng style represented by "Spring on Snowy Mountains" and other works of this period, including the very famous solo zheng composition "Fighting the Typhoon" (1965; passages from this piece were featured in both Online Musical Illustration #26 and the chapter's Musical Guided Tour), was considered extremely difficult to master in terms of its technical demands when it was introduced in the late 1950s and early 1960s. However, in the hyper-virtuosic environment of contemporary zheng playing, mastery of pieces of this level of difficulty has become just a basic requirement of performance competence on the instrument.

The Guided Listening Quick Summary for "Spring on Snowy Mountains" is located on page 340. As you listen to the piece, follow the summary's timeline and listen carefully for the musical features highlighted. After that, return to page 339, where the "Insights and

The Chinese Occupation of Tibet and the Plight of Tibetan Buddhists

Communist China's gradual takeover and occupation of Tibet, beginning in 1950 and intensifying after 1956, led to brutal persecution of Tibetans, especially monks of Tibetan Buddhist monastic orders. It was this persecution that led the Dalai Lama, the renowned spiritual leader of Tibetan Buddhism (and winner of the 1989 Nobel Peace Prize), to flee Tibet for exile in India in 1959. In the wake of his departure, upwards of a hundred thousand Tibetan Buddhists fled Tibet to escape persecution so brutal that China was accused of committing genocide against the Tibetan people by an international council in 1961.

Still today, the Dalai Lama and multitudes of Tibetan Buddhists remain political refugees from their homeland, now China's so-called Autonomous Region of Tibet. Their chants and music have been the subject of much interest among ethnomusicologists and scholars of religion (see references at the Online Learning Center: www.mhhe.com/bakan2e). An example of Tibetan Buddhist chant performed by monks of the Drepung Gomang Monastery is featured on **CD ex. #4-30.** The original Drepung Gomang Monastery was founded near Lhasa, the capital of Tibet, in 1416. In the wake of the destruction of Tibetan Buddhist monasteries during the Chinese communist invasion, some 300 monks of the Gomang order escaped China, fleeing to neighboring India to live in exile. Under the sponsorship of the Dalai Lama, the Drepung Gomang Monastery was rebuilt in Mundgod, India, in 1969.

This recording of the Drepung Gomang monks features an extraordinary type of chant called *gyü-ke*, in which the monks manipulate their voices to produce an extremely low-pitched and powerful vocal sound rich in overtones. In gyü-ke, each voice produces multiple tones (multiphonics), so that both the super-low notes described and also high-pitched, almost bell-like overtones sound together to produce a sound that is not only unique in the world of music, but also profoundly spiritual from a Tibetan Buddhist perspective. From that perspective, gyü-ke is perceived as a sonic realization of everything that exists in the universe.

Though unique in sound and cultural meaning, Tibetan Buddhist chant such as that heard in **CD ex. #4-30** involves "overtone singing" techniques similar to those from Mongolia (**CD ex. #1-6**) and Tuva (**CD ex. #1-18**) that were discussed in earlier chapters.

Monks of the Drepung Gomang Monastery.

Perspectives" boxed feature will introduce you to a *real* Tibetan musicultural tradition, Tibetan Buddhist chant.

The Cultural Revolution era

The Cultural Revolution (1966–1976) is generally depicted as a dark period in China's modern history. The purported aim of the Cultural Revolution was to rid Chinese culture of anything "alien to the egalitarian spirit of [Chinese] socialism" (Fletcher 2001:344). In effect, this translated into brutally oppressive policies aimed at many sectors of Chinese society. Freedom of intellectual and artistic expression was severely constrained. Individuals and groups accused of going against the grain of state ideology were sent off to work camps in the country to be "reformed." (Many were tortured or even executed.) Beijing Opera and other Chinese opera and theater forms were placed in a virtual stranglehold. Most Beijing Opera productions were banned outright, and those that were allowed were so profoundly saturated with Cultural Revolution–inspired politicization that they barely resembled the operas of earlier periods. Religion (or "superstition," as it was known), already subject to severe repression prior to the Cultural Revolution, was now squelched to unprecedented degrees. Oppression of ethnic minority groups also escalated, devastating peoples such as the Uighurs and the Tibetans in their Chinese-occupied homelands.

For all of its atrocities, however, the Cultural Revolution was not quite the cultural vacuum that popular accounts often make it out to have been. Musical life, though restrained, continued. People sang revolutionary songs. They were allowed to learn and play instruments (though only certain approved pieces). There was considerable activity in the domains of both amateur and children's music making. In rural areas far from the centers of bureaucratic power, cultural life in some cases went on much as it always had, existing largely beyond the scrutiny of the centralized political authorities.

With respect to the zheng in conservatory music culture, Te-yuan Cheng, an authority on the instrument and its history, claims that the Cultural Revolution "choked off new composition" and that activities related to the zheng essentially "came to a halt" (Cheng 1991:192, 249). This is perhaps an overstatement, though it does seem clear that the evolution of the zheng was severely impeded. A relatively small number of new solo zheng compositions were composed, and the titles and programs linked to these pieces, not surprisingly, were defined by an especially intense political character. These included "Molten Iron Pouring in a Stream" (a disturbing title if ever there was one) and "Little Sister Hero of the Plains." The latter of these programatically depicts a Mongolian child protecting her commune's sheep in the midst of a blizzard while singing songs in praise of the Cultural Revolution (Cheng 1991:191).

The Rise of Deng Xiaoping and the Period of Openness

The death of Mao Zedong in 1976 and the fall of the Gang of Four, a group of ultraradical CCP leaders (including Mao's wife, Jiang Qing, who had been a catalyst in the effort to place extreme constraints on artistic expression during the preceding decade), brought to an end the Cultural Revolution. In its wake came a period of major social upheaval and instability. Rampant persecution, widespread poverty and disease, and large-scale societal frustration with China's increased international isolation and resultant economic failures led the Chinese populace to call for major political, economic, and social reforms. Deng Xiaoping, a CCP senior official who had been demoted during the Cultural Revolution, reemerged to become the new leader of China and ushered the troubled nation into the so-called Period of Openness era that crystallized in the early 1980s.

Deng's regime was in effect a high-wire act of radical political experimentation. His goal was to maintain the communist political order amid an environment of free enterprise and engagement with global markets of which China had not previously been a part. In many respects, his experiment achieved great successes, its continuing legacy still evident in China's remarkable ascent as an international economic power in recent decades. In other respects, it failed miserably, the most notorious example being the Tiananmen Square massacre of 1989, where the old draconian tactics of authoritarian rule that lurked beneath the public facade of a more liberal and tolerant government were brutally exposed (see "Insights and Perspectives" box below). The shockwaves of change initiated by Deng resonate still today, as China's balancing act between capitalist enterprise and communist ideology grows ever more complex.

Rocking the Zheng on the New Long March: Cui Jian and Bei Bei He

The Chinese rock star Cui Jian (Tsway Jee-en) has been described by author and musician Dennis Rea as "Bob Dylan, John Lennon, and Kurt Cobain all rolled into one, a one-man rock and roll revolution whose poignant songs of alienation spoke volumes to a generation searching for meaning in a rapidly changing and increasingly globalized China." His best-known song, "Nothing to My Name" ("Yi Wu Suo You"), was adopted as an unofficial anthem of the Chinese democracy movement that reached its climax in a massive hunger-strike protest at Beijing's Tiananmen Square in 1989. Cui Jian and his band ADO performed this song and others at the protest. The image of him defiantly rallying the protesters with his music, in Rea's words, "symbolized a generation's struggles and aspirations." The Tiananmen Square uprising began as a peaceful protest led by college students and other alienated Chinese youth who were frustrated by the institutionalized corruption, rampant materialism, widening social stratification, and "bankrupt ideology" of late 1980s "open" China under Deng Xiaoping and the CCP. It ended in bloodshed and tragedy when army tanks rolled into the Square and opened fire on the assembled masses, killing many. More than any other single incident, this tragic event came to symbolize the troubling vestiges of old, authoritarian rule in the ostensibly new and open society of post-1970s China (Rea 2006; see also Baranovitch 2003).

Cui Jian.

The same year as the Tiananmen Square uprisings, 1989, also witnessed the release of Cui Jian's most successful and influential album, *Rock 'n' Roll on the New Long March*. It is usually described as the first Chinese rock album. "Nothing to My Name" was the featured track on *New Long March*, which also included several other standout Cui Jian songs including "Fake

Monk." The instrumentation of "Fake Monk" combines standard rock band instruments (saxophone, electric guitar, drum set, etc.) with traditional Chinese instruments. The zheng, in particular, is highlighted in the introduction and in several other parts of the arrangement (at the time of this writing, a live performance of Cui Jian and his band performing "Fake Monk," with close-ups of the zheng player, was viewable at www.youtube.com/watch?v=iXbC2f1BV_Y).

Since the time of Cui Jian's innovations in the late 1980s, the zheng has been incorporated into a variety of other rock and popular music contexts, both in China and internationally. *Into the Wind,* a 2010 release from Ubiquity Records featuring the zheng virtuoso Bei Bei He and the American-born, London-based multi-instrumentalist Shawn Lee, offers a compelling example. One of the tracks from *Into the Wind,* "Hot Thursday," is included on your CD set (**CD ex. #4-31**). On that selection, the driving soul-funk-rock grooves and textures created by Lee are integrated with Bei Bei's alternately refined and hard-rocking zheng part in a highly synergistic way. Elements of jazz, rock, and funk are woven through Bei Bei's improvisations, but so too is traditional Chinese zheng playing style. There is even a direct musical quotation from a well-known solo zheng composition, Xu Xiao-lin's "Moon of Jian-Chang," at 1:55–2:10.

Bei Bei He was born in Chengdu, China. She started playing the zheng at age seven and quickly rose through the ranks of the Chinese conservatory system, eventually majoring in zheng and graduating from the performing arts high school division of the Central University of Nationalities in Beijing in 2000. Later that same year, she moved to Hong Kong to study zheng at the Academy of Performing Arts, but while there switched majors to focus on music recording and sound design, graduating in 2003.

The next move for Bei Bei was a big one, taking her all the way to Southern California, where she has lived since 2003. Her American/international musical life is as rich as it is diverse, with activities ranging from an appearance on the *Oprah Winfrey Show* to studio sessions as a zheng player for *Battlestar Gallactica* soundtracks and concert performances at the National Arts Center of Canada in Ottawa, Ontario.

The collaboration with Shawn Lee that yielded "Hot Thursday" and *Into the Wind* did not originate or develop in China, Hong Kong, California, or London; rather, it emerged and took shape on the Internet. Lee discovered Bei Bei and her music on MySpace. Impressed by what he heard, he contacted her and asked if she would be interested in collaborating with him on a new recording project. She replied that she would. *Into the Wind* was the eventual result. Different tracks on the album were approached in different ways, but the entire production was essentially conceived and realized online: Lee and Bei Bei met only one time (in California) during the entire process.

As Bei Bei recounted to me during an October 2010 telephone interview, "When I got to California, I started getting more into jazz, hip-hop, all kinds of stuff that I had been introduced to in Hong Kong but in a fairly limited way. I had studied drum set in Hong Kong, too, but in California I got much more deeply into that. So I began experimenting with putting all these different types of things together in my home recording studio, and after a while I thought to myself, 'It would be so cool to play zheng in something like that.' Then Shawn contacted me and asked if I might want to work with him, and that sounded great. But four years went by without anything happening, and then one day, out of the blue, I received a whole bunch of [instrumental] tracks from him. Those became the basis of 'Hot Thursday.' I laid improvised zheng tracks over his tracks in my studio, then sent what I had done back to him; then he added more tracks and back and forth it went like that. It was great, and I think it ended up being the most spirited, improvisational piece on the album. At first, I was kind of self-conscious, but Shawn was very encouraging. So I committed myself to doing this [project] and it came out pretty well. It's really been like a rebirth for me musically, and it's helped me to grow a lot artistically."

Left to right: Bei Bei He (zheng), performing with Joey Reina (electric bass) and Judson McDaniel (guitar).

The arts, the zheng, and musicultural life in post-1970s China

In 1979, Deng Xiaoping introduced his policy for the arts in a new, more "open" China as part of a sweeping agenda for the modernization of the country and Chinese socialism. Framing his words in relation to the preceding era of severe governmental control and censorship of the arts, he stated that

> our nation has a long history, a vast domain, a huge population, many different peoples, a great range of occupations . . . and a variety of customs, cultural traditions and artistic interests. If only we can educate and enlighten the people and enable them to enjoy beauty and recreation, then they will find their own place in the sphere of the arts. . . . In their leadership of artistic and literary work, the [communist] party will not simply issue orders and commands, nor will it demand that literature or art submit to political work on a temporary, a concrete or a direct basis. . . . The complex spiritual labor of artistic and literary creation truly requires that writers and artists give free rein to their individual creative endeavors. Whatever they write or create can only be investigated and resolved by artists. There will be no interference in these matters. . . . (Deng Xiaoping, quoted in Cheng 1991:194)

The new policies of openness, combined with the release of the pressure valve of controls on artistic freedom that had held Chinese musicians in its grip during the preceding era, yielded a Chinese musical renaissance. International mass media entertainment—popular music, music videos, commercial films, and television shows—flooded into mainland China from Hong Kong, Taiwan, the West, and elsewhere. A booming local Chinese popular music culture and industry emerged as well, producing superstar figures such as the rock musician Cui Jian (see "Insights and Perspectives" box, pp. 341–342). Traditional, pre-revolutionary Beijing Opera and other styles of regional drama were revived and flourished. Formerly suppressed folk, ritual, religious, and minority music traditions, as well as court music traditions of the dynastic period that had been roundly condemned under earlier communist regimes, were allowed to reemerge and were officially embraced as integral dimensions of China's multicultural society. Extensive research on living rural traditions and music and dance of China's ethnic minorities was conducted at state music institutions (Witzleben 2002:90). Conservatory-trained virtuoso performers on both Western instruments (piano, violin) and Chinese instruments (zheng, pipa) appeared on concert stages worldwide and were featured on internationally distributed recordings.

**Tan Dun
(Tahn Doo-en)**

erhu (err-hoo)

**sheng (shung
[rhymes with
"lung"])**

Attitudes toward Western art music (the "classical" music traditions of the West) relative to Chinese music also underwent a transformation. The works of experimental Western composers of the 20th century, formerly censored or at least frowned upon in official Chinese cultural circles, now came to be appreciated and to exert a significant influence on the Chinese conservatory culture. Numerous gifted, young Chinese composers were sent abroad to study at major university music schools and conservatories, where they learned the techniques and methods of Western new music composition. The integration of diverse Chinese, Western, and other musical elements in the works of these composers yielded the "New Wave" movement in modern Chinese music. Tan Dun, the Academy Award–winning composer of the musical score for the film *Crouching Tiger, Hidden Dragon,* is the best-known of the New Wave composers to come out of China. His composition "Desert Capriccio" (**CD ex. #4-32**) is a quite lovely work from that film. The soloist is the American cellist (of Chinese descent) Yo-Yo Ma. He is accompanied by an ensemble of Chinese instruments including the pipa, the *erhu* two-stringed fiddle, and a fascinating ancient instrument that was mentioned earlier, the sheng, which is a mouth organ with 17 bamboo pipes arranged in an incomplete circle formation (see photo, p. 344).

Composer Tan Dun receiving his Academy Award for the score of *Crouching Tiger, Hidden Dragon.*

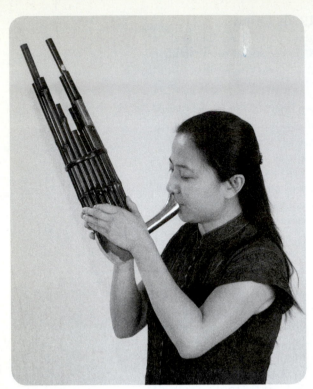

Sheng being played.

The zheng and its conservatory-based musical tradition blossomed in post-1970s China. The founding of the Beijing Zheng Association in 1980 and the establishment of the National Zheng Symposium in 1986 (at which Deng Haiqiong performed "Autumn Moon over the Han Palace" in a tribute concert for Gao Zicheng) were important institutional benchmarks of the instrument's ascent. The emergence of novel compositional styles representing entirely new levels of virtuosity, experimentalism, and cosmopolitanism (especially in the incorporation of adapted, modern Western compositional techniques) was a major development. So too was a revival of interest in researching, preserving, and cultivating older regional styles of zheng music. Gifted female zheng artists, the majority of them associated with the Shanghai Conservatory, increasingly came to dominate the zheng performance world. New, experimental instruments, such as the 49-string "butterfly zheng"—named for its distinctive shape—were invented (though they generally did not achieve wide popularity). Collectively, these many and varied developments marked the arrival and evolution of a post-traditional age for the zheng in mainland China (see Table 13.2).

Yet while the musical renaissance of the Period of Openness, in the zheng world and beyond, brought many positive and exciting developments in the wake of the Cultural Revolution, it was by no means devoid of problems. As in virtually every other era of Chinese history, close links between musical and political life underscored both the good and the bad. On the one hand, China's increasing integration into the global economy afforded new opportunities for musicians from the PRC to study and perform abroad, widening their musical horizons and providing abundant new professional opportunities. On the other hand, as China moved aggressively toward its own version of a free market economy, government support of state institutions such as music conservatories generally decreased. This compelled many talented, conservatory-trained musicians to pursue international careers not only out of a desire to seek new opportunities but also out of economic necessity.

Another problem has had to do with a new variation on the old theme of cultural appropriation of folk and minority musics by the state conservatory music culture. "The People's Republic of China, a multi-ethnic state that takes pride in its wealth of diverse traditions," writes Sabine Trebinjac, an ethnomusicologist who specializes in music of the Uighur people of northwestern China, "is also anxious to affirm the existence of a national musical tradition, which involves manufacturing heavily sinicized [i.e., Chinese-ified] versions of the products of other cultures," in particular, cultures such as the Uighurs and Tibetans, who are much less likely to view themselves as Chinese people than as people living against their will under Chinese rule (Trebinjac 2005). Ethnic groups such as the Tibetans and Uighurs have suffered greatly at the hands of Chinese authorities. While their contemporary situations are perhaps better than they were, say, during the Cultural Revolution, acute tensions, troubling civil rights issues, and struggles for national sovereignty and independence continue.

A significant portion of the repertoire of solo instrumental music of the modern conservatory tradition, including solo zheng music, consists of heavily sinicized/Westernized compositions "based on" minority music traditions of peoples such as the Uighurs and the Tibetans. Many of these pieces are extremely well crafted and very effective on a purely musical level. They project a positive image of a unified, inclusive, multicultural Chinese

TABLE 13.2 Major developments of the zheng and its musical culture during the modern era (post-1912).

Republican Era (1912–1948)

- Zheng taught at urban conservatories

- Neo-traditional musical style for solo zheng pieces ("Return of the Fishing Boats," Lou Shuhua, 1936): new techniques, explicit programmaticism, music of a more dramatic character, departure from baban form

Initial Period of Communist Era (1949–1965)

- Establishment of zheng programs in most major conservatories, including Beijing and Shanghai (early 1950s)

- Significant Western influences (especially piano-derived) on zheng music and playing styles; pianistic two-hand playing techniques; titles and programs of pieces linked to communist ideology ("Celebrating the Harvest," 1955)

- Increasingly pianistic, virtuosic style of solo zheng playing post-1958 (Fan Shang'e, "Spring on Snowy Mountains"); 21-string zheng replaces 16-string zheng as standard instrument around the same time; Shanghai Conservatory leads the way

Cultural Revolution Era (1966–1976)

- Development of zheng stifled during this oppressive period; new pieces that emerge are exceedingly ideological ("Molten Iron Pouring in a Stream," "Little Sister of the Plains")

Period of Openness (Late 1970s–Present)

- Modern zheng renaissance: new techniques, playing styles, and compositional styles ("Music from the Muqam," discussed in next section of chapter); openness to contemporary Western music influences and experimentation among "New Wave" and other composers (e.g., Tan Dun)

- Major professional organizations founded and conferences established (Beijing Zheng Association, 1980; National Zheng Symposium, 1986)

- Women zheng artists dominant (especially out of Shanghai Conservatory)

- Major new instrument innovations and experiments (e.g., 49-string "butterfly zheng"), though standard 21-string zheng remains predominant

- Numerous leading conservatory-trained zheng players establish international careers (e.g., Deng Haiqiong)

- Zheng used in rock and other popular music contexts (Cui Jian, Bei Bei He)

nation that is very much in keeping with the public image the Chinese government endeavors to promote to both its own citizenry and the broader world. Alas, the positive image projected still contradicts much harsher sociopolitical realities. The peoples ostensibly represented through music of this kind—Uighurs, Tibetans, members of other minority groups in China—typically resent having their musical traditions, and by extension themselves, cast in this light. This is important to keep in mind as we turn now to a final Guided Listening Experience focusing on a Uighur-inspired Chinese zheng piece entitled "Music from the Muqam."

"Music from the Muqam," by Zhou Ji, Shao Guangchen, and Li Mei

- CD Track #**4-33**
- Featured performer(s)/group: Deng Haiqiong (zheng), Quek Ling Kiong *(dap)*
- Format: Excerpt
- Source recording: *Ning,* by Hai-qiong Deng [Deng Haiqiong] (Celebrity Music)

Li Mei (Lee May)

muqam (moo-KAHM)

"Music from the Muqam" is a composition for solo zheng with drum accompaniment. It was created in 1988 by three Han Chinese composers from the far northwestern region of China called Xinjiang (East Turkistan or Uighuristan by Uighur nationalists), where the majority of Uighur people live. One of the composers, Li Mei, was a teacher of Haiqiong.

The piece takes its inspiration and key elements of its style and design from a Uighur tradition known as the Dolan Muqam. This is one of several regional traditions of **muqam** that collectively constitute the core foundation of Uighur musical art. Some of these, like the venerable Twelve Muqam (*On Iqqi Muqam*) are believed to descend from the Uighur royal courts of olden times and are repositories of rich cultural lore and symbolism. For example, Muqam Raq, one of the Twelve Muqam, is symbolically tied to a Uighur legend in which the protagonist wanders through the labyrinth of a network of a thousand caves, each of which presents him with some treasure and mystery. The "wanderer" is considered to be on the way to discovering new treasures of traditional Uighur wisdom (Czekanowska 1983:104).

In contrast, the Dolan Muqam is pure village style, representing the rough, raw end of Uighur music. The Dolan were traditionally the poorest, most despised class of Uighurs. Under Chinese imperial rule, they served the Chinese administration as indentured servants, and they were well-known for their enthusiasm for rebellion.

Muqam is a local pronunciation of the Arabic term *maqam*. In Arab music, *maqam* essentially means "mode" and the term is integrally linked to a wide range of music traditions (see Chapter 12, p. 281). In the Uighur context, however (and in Central Asia generally), *muqam* has a different meaning, referring to a particular type of large-scale, precomposed suite of songs and instrumental music.

insights and perspectives

Uighur History and Culture

More than six million Uighurs live in the so-called Xinjiang-Uighur Autonomous Region of northwestern China, accounting for some 45 percent of the region's total population. The Uighur are Muslims who long ago converted from Buddhism and before that practiced shamanistic religions. They speak a Turkic language and their cultural and musical traditions draw more from Persian (Iranian), Arabic, and Turkic (including Uzbek and Tajik) sources than from Chinese ones. In ancient times, the Uighur occupied a strategic position along the Silk Road and prospered greatly through favored trade relations with imperial China during some dynastic eras. It was in the ancestral homelands of the Uighur that Chinese traders crossed paths with the likes of European imperialists and explorers such as Alexander the Great and Marco Polo. It was also along the Silk Road through Uighur lands that Central Asian prototypes of instruments such as the pipa and erhu first came to China. Uighur music ensembles are documented as having resided and performed at the Chinese imperial courts during dynastic times.

A muqam performance begins with a free rhythm introduction (with or without singing) followed by a series of pieces performed in different meters at progressively faster tempos. The instrumentation is not standardized, but generally features either a solo vocalist accompanying himself on a plucked chordophone (e.g., a *rawap*; see the photo above) or a lead vocalist accompanied by a small chorus of singers and a small ensemble of instrumentalists. The rhythmic accompaniment is provided by a frame drum called a **dap** (see photo). The head of the dap is made of donkey hide or snake skin.

Though they are not Uighurs themselves, Li Mei and the two other composers of "Music from the Muqam" have all studied and researched the muqam traditions extensively. Li Mei grew up in Xinjiang and was trained as a zheng player in the Chinese conservatory system. She eventually went on to advanced musicological studies of Uighur music at the graduate level. Haiqiong believes that Li Mei's life experiences in Xinjiang and her extensive record of musical and scholarly study of Uighur music set her apart from many other Chinese composers—especially composers of earlier eras—who have composed modern-style pieces based on "minority" source music materials.

"The earlier pieces based on minority music," states Haiqiong, "always have a similar kind of 'happy' feeling. They all describe the beauty of nature and scenery and people living a happy life with much singing and dancing. When I was little, that was what I believed [the lives of members of China's ethnic minority groups were like]. But 'Music from the Muqam' is different. It's a really great piece. Li Mei and her collaborators brought some deeper feeling and expression to it, and new ways of performing on the zheng. It completely changed my perceptions of the possibilities of zheng performance."

"Music from the Muqam" employs an unusual zheng tuning: D F♯ G A C. According to Haiqiong, this tuning reproduces the melodic character of a traditional Uighur mode. She also explains that certain rhythmic patterns, melodic ornaments, and elements of formal design in "Music from the Muqam" likewise represent direct Uighur influences. Of particular interest on the rhythmic level is the prominent use of meters with five beats per measure. Meters of five and seven are common in Uighur music, where they generate what the Uighur refer to as *aksak,* literally "limping," rhythms (Rachel Harris, personal correspondence with the author, 2006).

Despite these identifiable Uighur influences, "Music from the Muqam" is firmly centered in the virtuosic style of contemporary, conservatory zheng music, and therefore reflects a high level of Western influence as well. Even the Uighur-inspired tuning of the zheng is evidence of this, since the "Uighur mode" employed is recast in equal-tempered (evenly spaced) intervals unrelated to traditional Uighur musical practice.

"Music from the Muqam" is a lengthy composition. The excerpt of **CD ex. #4-33** features the second half of the piece. It begins with a hauntingly beautiful zheng melody that builds through several phrases (0:00–1:54). Many of the melodic ornaments, such as the various forms of gua-zou (glissandos), are standard to Chinese zheng style and familiar to us from earlier examples; others are not. Especially distinctive is an ornament in which strings tuned to the pitch A are bent slightly upward (almost to the pitch B) on certain notes (e.g., at 0:06). This, according to Haiqiong, is an inflection inspired by traditional melodic ornamentation in Uighur music. Haiqiong also explains that the ostinato, duple-meter rhythmic pattern of the dap frame drum in this section is characteristically Uighur. Noteworthy, too, but for a different reason, are the chords played on the zheng. Many of these consist of four different pitches, rather than the customary three- or two-pitch chords of earlier zheng styles. This exemplifies the presence of more modern streams of Western influence than we have encountered previously in the chapter's musical examples. Moreover, in Haiqiong's assessment, these more complex chords represent a distinctively innovative feature of this piece.

There is a change in style and mood at 1:55. Following a transitional moment of free rhythm, during which time seems to hang suspended in mid-air (1:55–2:04), aksak rhythms come to the fore, replacing the steady duple-meter rhythms of the preceding section. From 2:05, the music moves along mainly in a five-beat, aksak meter with unpredictable accents. It builds progressively—in volume, tempo, and overall intensity—to a dazzling, glissando-laden climax at 3:10. This kind of dramatic buildup has no parallel in traditional Uighur music, though it has many in standard zheng pieces and in Western music. Throughout this second part of the example, the zheng and the dap proceed in lock-step rhythmic unison, and the precise synchrony of their playing is impressive. So too is the flair of Haiqiong's performance here, which puts the expressive range of the zheng on brilliant display. Following this climactic moment, the piece concludes with soft, sparse, solo playing on the zheng from 3:16. The mood in this last part is calm and introspective, even meditative.

guided listening quick summary

"Music from the Muqam," Deng Haiqiong (CD ex. #4-33)

Zheng tuning: D F♯ G A C (D) (nontraditional)

0:00–1:54

- Steady, duple-meter rhythm; rhythm of dap (frame drum) characteristically "Uighur."

- Many standard zheng melodic ornaments used (e.g., gua-zou), but so too are a variety of other ornaments that are not conventional for the zheng and reflect traditional Uighur musical practices (e.g., the upward bend of the pitch A heard at 0:06 and elsewhere in the piece).

- Chords often include four pitches, suggesting more modern Western influences than are evident in earlier zheng pieces.

1:55–end

- Transitional moment of free rhythm creates momentary impression of suspension of time; aksak ("limping") rhythms replace the steady, duple-meter rhythms of the earlier portion of the piece.

- From 2:05, five-beat meter is established and maintained (except for two measures of six-beat meter at 2:21), though the rhythmic accents are varied and unpredictable.

- Progressive, gradual acceleration and intensification leading to an exciting climax at 3:10.

- Impressive rhythmic synchrony between the zheng and dap, and dazzling displays of zheng virtuosity by Deng Haiqiong.

- Following climax (3:10), piece concludes with a soft, sparse, solo zheng passage, which starts at 3:16.

Summary

In the course of this chapter, we tracked the history of the zheng and its music from the Qin dynasty of the 3rd century BCE to contemporary times. Primary attention was devoted to the history of the zheng during the modern era, especially to the tradition of solo zheng playing associated with the government-sponsored, conservatory music culture of mainland China in the 20th century and since. Deng Haiqiong, the featured performer in several of the chapter's musical examples, was cast as a representative of that tradition. The integral historical link between regional solo zheng traditions and the conservatory style these traditions fed into was examined. So too was the important relationship between Chinese traditional and Western musics, a relationship that has influenced the development of zheng music on many levels. Additional topics covered included Japanese koto, gagaku, and popular music, Beijing Opera, the Uighur muqam tradition, and Chinese and Chinese American rock.

The approach of the chapter was essentially historical, linking well-known zheng compositions of different eras to significant musical, political, and cultural events and movements. In tracking the evolution of zheng music from one period to the next—from traditional styles ("Autumn Moon over the Han Palace"), to neo-traditional styles ("Return of the Fishing Boats," "Spring on Snowy Mountains"), to post-traditional styles ("Music from the Muqam," "Hot Thursday")—we saw how continuity and change in music may be seen to reflect continuity and change much more broadly at societal, political, and cultural levels. Issues of ethnicity, gender, ideology, cultural appropriation, censorship, human rights, political agency, provincialism versus internationalism, and artistic freedom and constraint were all shown to be implicated in the particular course of development that the zheng has followed over the more than two thousand years of its existence.

Music, from antiquity to the present, from China to Chile, and from Henan to hip-hop, can teach us essential lessons about who we are and what really matters. It is imperative that we take the time to listen and to think deeply about how we might better tune our world.

Key Terms

zheng	Mandarin Chinese (language)	gua-zou
regional styles of solo zheng music	Han Chinese (majority ethnic group)	Confucianism
pipa	Chinese Communist Party (CCP)	Silk Road
qin	Cultural Revolution	yun
Beijing Opera	Period of Openness	baban
koto	ornamentation	yijing
gagaku	(different types)	muqam
		dap

- Who is Deng Haiqiong? What instrument does she play? What have been some of her significant professional accomplishments?

- What are China's two most populous cities (also the locations of the country's leading music conservatories)?

- What type of instrument is the koto? How is it related to the zheng? What types of Japanese music discussed in the chapter featured this instrument?

- What kind of a song is "Sakitama," by Rin? What traditional Japanese instruments does it employ? How are Japanese traditional music and Western popular music elements combined?

- Which of the many imperial dynasties of China were discussed in this chapter? What developments in zheng music and culture were associated with each?

- How is the zheng constructed? What were some of the main zheng playing and ornamentation techniques discussed?

- What other zither-type chordophones besides the zheng are found in China and other nations of East and Southeast Asia (Japan, Korea, Mongolia, Vietnam)?

- What were the principal regional styles of solo zheng playing discussed in the chapter? Of what regional style is "Autumn Moon over the Han Palace" representative? What is the name of the musical form of this piece (and most other traditional zheng compositions)?

- What was the Silk Road? What was its significance to the development of Chinese music and culture during the dynastic era?

- What musical innovations were introduced and/or developed in the following compositions: "Return of the Fishing Boats," "Spring on Snowy Mountains," "Music from the Muqam"? Who were the composers of these important works?

- What have been the three main historical periods of the People's Republic of China (est. 1949)? What major political developments were associated with each period and what developments in Chinese musical culture (and the conservatory-based culture of the zheng especially) occurred during each?

- How does the history of Beijing Opera since the 19th century reflect larger social and political movements in Chinese history?

- What was the historical significance of Cui Jian's "Nothing to My Name" in Chinese political history?

- What is innovative about Bei Bei He's use of the zheng on recordings like "Hot Thursday"?

- Who is Tan Dun and what is his significance as a composer?

- How has the appropriation of Uighur, Tibetan, and other "minority" musics into the musical culture of the Chinese conservatories been approached during different periods? What sorts of issues and controversies surround such appropriations, both musically and sociopolitically?

Discussion Questions

- A major issue explored in this chapter is the relationship between musical developments and political movements in Chinese history. Relationships between music and politics run deep in societies throughout the world. Where do you see instances of music being used in political contexts in your own society? Are the political uses of music of which you are aware explicit or implicit, obvious or subtle? Why do you think music has been closely aligned with so many political regimes and institutions in so many societies throughout history?

- In this chapter, a single instrument, the zheng, was taken as a lens through which to view large currents in the history of Chinese society, culture, and politics. A similar approach might be productive in studies of American or other Western societies. What might a historical, ethnomusicological approach to the study of the electric guitar reveal about larger issues in American social history? What could we learn about the cultures and histories of Europe or the Americas through a sociopolitically informed history of the piano?

■ Research and discuss other instances in which popular music and politics have intersected in impactful ways, as happened when Cui Jian performed at Tiananmen Square in 1989.

Applying What You Have Learned

■ The People's Republic of China today is a nation in the midst of tremendous economic, political, social, and cultural transformation. Contemporary Chinese musicultural life reflects this climate of change profoundly, with burgeoning movements in rock, punk, hip-hop, avant-garde, and other musical styles that were formerly proscribed. Use Internet keyword searches (e.g., "Chinese rock," "Chinese punk," etc.) to research the contemporary music scene in mainland China. Write a report chronicling your findings. Conclude with some general comments in which you apply what you have learned about historical processes of tradition and transformation in Chinese music in this chapter to your assessment of current musical trends and directions in China.

■ Research and write a report on Chinese American/Asian American rock, pop, jazz, or hip-hop. Describe how traditional Asian elements are combined with other musical elements, instruments, and styles in the examples you encounter.

Resources for Further Study

Visit the Online Learning Center at www.mhhe.com/bakan2e, as well as the author's personally maintained Web site at www.michaelbakan.com, for additional learning aids, study help, and resources that supplement the content of this chapter.

glossary

accents: (Ch. 3) Notes in music that are given special emphasis, usually by being played louder than other notes surrounding them.

acoustic: (Ch. 5) Not amplified, as in acoustic guitar (versus electric guitar).

aerophones: (Ch. 5) Instruments in which the sounds are generated from vibrations created by the action of air passing through a tube or some other kind of resonator (e.g., flute, trumpet, *didgeridoo,* human voice).

African diaspora: (Ch. 10) The dispersal of millions of people from Africa (the majority from West Africa) to other parts of the world, especially the Americas (the United States, Brazil, the Caribbean, etc.); largely a result of the Euro-American slave trade, at least initially. Today, the African diaspora is global in scope and its worldwide musical impact cannot be overestimated.

Africanisms (musical): (Ch. 10) Identifiable musicultural characteristics that are widely shared across sub-Saharan Africa and are prominent in musics of the *African diaspora* as well.

Agama Tirta [Ah-gah-muh TEER-tuh]: (Ch. 7) Balinese *Hindu religion,* representing a syncretism of Hindu, Buddhist, and indigenous Balinese elements; literally means "Religion of Holy Water."

Akan [AH-kahn]: (Ch. 10) A large ethnic group of West Africa concentrated principally in the modern nation of Ghana.

alap [ah-LAHP]: (Ch. 8) The nonmetric, improvisatory exploration of a *raga* that constitutes the opening portion of a typical *Hindustani raga* performance; an exploratory journey through the raga's melodic essence and range of possibility.

amplitude: (Ch. 3) The loudness of a tone; basis of dynamics in music.

Andean folkloric music: (Ch. 11) Modern, urban, cosmopolitan transformation of the musical traditions of rural, indigenous Andean peoples. Features instruments like the kena (flute), siku (double-row panpipe), charango (strummed chordophone), and bombo in stylized and polished arrangements that promote a kind of constructed, folklorized form of Andean authenticity.

arpeggio [ahr-PEH-jee-oh]: (Ch. 4) A chord in which the pitches are performed in sequence (one after the other) rather than all at once. An arpeggio (arpeggiated chord) also may be referred to as a "broken chord."

arranging: (Ch. 2) The craft of taking an existing musical work and transforming it into something new, while still retaining its core musical identity.

articulation: (Ch. 4) The way in which a given tone or series of tones is played or sung, for example, with short notes (*staccato*) versus with sustained notes (*legato*).

atma: (Ch. 7) Human soul (in Hinduism, Balinese *Agama Tirta*).

atumpan [AH-toom-pahn]: (Ch. 10) A set of two large drums used by the *Akan* for drum speech and also in other contexts (such as in *Fontomfrom* music).

ayllu [ie-yoo]: (Ch. 11) Indigenous term for "native community" of the South American Andes. Shared family lineages, locations of residence and ancestry, and cultural practices (including musical and religious practices) define ayllu membership.

baban [bah-bahn]: (Ch. 13) Chinese musical form with eight melodic phrases; most traditional solo *zheng* pieces are in this form (e.g., "Autumn Moon over the Han Palace").

Bahasa Indonesia [Bah-HAH-suh In-doh-NEE-see-uh]: (Ch.7) The national Indonesian language.

bala [BAH-lah]: (Ch. 10) Xylophone of the *Mande* people of West Africa; one of several instruments historically identified with the musical traditions of *jeliya.*

baladi [bah-lah-dee]: (Ch. 12) Folk heritage (Egypt).

Bali Aga: (Ch. 7) The indigenous people of Bali, whose culture and religion predate the arrival of Hinduism and Buddhism. Bali Aga mainly live in remote Balinese villages (e.g., Tenganan) and have distinctive, ancient forms of *gamelan* (e.g., gamelan selonding).

bandoneón [bahn-doh-nee-YONE]: (Ch. 11) Box-shaped accordion of German ancestry that typically serves as the lead instrument in an Argentine or Uruguayan *tango* band; Astor Piazzolla was a master of this instrument.

banjar [BAHN-jahr]: (Ch. 7) Balinese village ward, hamlet, neighborhood organization; responsible for core communal, religious, and social activities of its membership, including cremations and other mortuary rituals; most *gamelan* clubs (sekehe gong) are organized at the banjar level.

barhat [bar-hut]: (Ch. 8) Growth, specifically referring to the musical growth that occurs during a *Hindustani raga* performance.

batá [bah-TAH]: (Ch. 11) Sacred drums used in rituals of the *Santería* (Regla de Ocha) religion.

beat: (Ch. 3) Underlying pulse; fundamental unit of rhythmic organization.

Beijing Opera: (Ch. 13) Best-known type of Chinese opera. Like other types, it features heightened speech, song, dance, mime, acting, and acrobatics. The socialist "revolutionary operas" of the 1960s and 1970s (e.g., *The Red Lantern*) represented a radical transformation of the genre during that period.

belly dance: (Ch. 12) Generic term in English for virtually all forms of Middle Eastern and Middle Eastern–derived women's dance; in this text, refers more specifically to Western/international derivates and offshoots of *raqs sharqi* and *raqs baladi.*

bhajan [BUH-jin]: (Ch. 8) A particular class of Hindu devotional songs and hymns with close ties to the historical development of Indian classical music.

bhangra [BHAHNG-rah]: (Ch. 8) Originally a folk music tradition of the Punjab region; now more widely known in its contemporary popular style; often featured in Indian "Bollywood" films.

big band mambo: (Ch. 11) The highly syncretic *mambo* style of the 1950s indentified with New York–based bandleaders such as Tito Puente, Machito, and Tito Rodríguez (see also *mambo kings*). Incorporated more Afro-Cuban and American jazz and popular music elements than did the earlier Cuban mambo style.

birimintingo [beer-uh-men-TEEN-go]: (Ch. 10) The improvisational, soloistic style of instrumental performance used on instruments like the *kora, bala,* and *koni* in Mande *jeliya* music.

blues scale: (Ch. 4) A distinctive type of *scale* associated with blues and blues-derived musics that combines elements of major, minor, pentatonic, and traditional African scales.

bodhrán [BOH-rawn]: (Ch. 9) Irish hand-held frame drum with a goat skin head. (Synthetic heads are sometimes used in place of goat skin today.)

bongó [bon-GO]: (Ch. 11) Pair of small, single-headed drums used in percussion sections of many types of Latin bands. Held between the knees and played with the fingers.

bossa nova: (Ch. 11) Brazilian genre that emerged in the late 1950s and achieved great popularity both in Brazil and internationally in the 1960s; combined elements of *samba* and jazz in a cool, laid-back style.

call-and-response: (Ch. 6) Back-and-forth alternation between different instrument or voice parts.

cane dance: (Ch. 12) Popular Middle Eastern women's dance form in which the dancer perfoms with a cane. Different variants found in *raqs baladi, raqs sharqi,* and *belly dance.* Historically related to the Egyptian *tahtib* martial art.

ceílí [KAY-lee]: (Ch. 9) Informal social gathering involving dancing, usually held at an Irish pub or dance hall.

Celtic [KEL-tick]: (Ch. 9) A complex of historically related cultures that today mainly survive in Ireland, Scotland, Wales, Brittany, and certain regions of eastern Canada. This cultural complex is principally defined by the Celtic family of languages, though other shared aspects of culture, including musical ones, are significant as well.

Central Javanese court gamelan: (Ch. 7) The *gamelan* traditions associated with the royal courts of the cities of Yogyakarta and Surakarta; along with Balinese *gamelan gong kebyar,* the best-known type of gamelan internationally.

cha cha chá: (Ch. 11) A Cuban dance-music genre characterized by relatively simple dance rhythms and singing; originated with Enrique Jorrin around 1950 and eventually gained international popularity. In the hands of Tito Puente and other New York bandleaders, the cha cha chá took on a new musical identity, leading to the style of arrangements like Puente's original recorded version of "Oye Como Va" (1963).

charanga [cha-RAHN-gah]: (Ch. 11) "Sweet-sounding" Cuban ensemble associated with the *danzón, danzón-mambo,* early Cuban *cha cha chá,* and other dance-music styles. Usually includes flute, violins, piano, bass, and percussion (plus singers).

Chinese Communist Party (CCP): (Ch. 13) The ruling party of the People's Republic of China from 1949–present. Originally led by Mao Zedong until his death in 1976, the party and its policies experienced profound transformations under the leadership of Deng Xiaoping beginning in the late 1970s.

chord: (Ch. 4) A group of two or more notes of different pitch that are sounded simultaneously (or that are perceived as belonging to a single unit even when not sounded simultaneously—see *arpeggio*).

chord progression: (Ch. 4) The sequence of movement from one chord to another in a musical work or performance.

chordophones: (Ch. 5) Instruments in which the sound is activated by the vibration of a string or strings over a resonating chamber (e.g., guitar, violin, piano, *zheng*).

clave [KLAH-vay]: (Ch. 11) Fundamental rhythm of *Latin music;* comes in four different varieties; often played on *claves,* but even if not actually played its presence is always implied.

claves: (Ch. 11) Instrument consisting of a pair of thick, round sticks that are struck together. Identified with the *clave* rhythm.

composition: (Ch. 2) A musical work; the process of creating a musical work; the process of planning out the design of a musical work prior to its performance.

Confucianism: (Ch. 13) The sociopolitical doctrine and philosophy originating with the writings of Confucius, which stressed rigid social hierarchy, civic responsibility, and a particular conception of morally virtuous social order. Basis of Chinese society for many centuries from the Han dynasty era forward.

conga [KOAN-gah] **drums (congas):** (Ch. 11) Large, barrel-shaped drums of Afro-Cuban origin and West African (Congolese) derivation. Usually played in sets of three, either by three separate players or by just one player. Used in *rumba* and in most styles of *Latin music.*

crescendo: (Ch. 5) Getting louder.

Cultural Revolution: (Ch. 13) Final period of Mao Zedong's leadership of China, 1966–1976. Unprecedented levels of intolerance for deviation from communist state ideology; extreme restrictions on cultural and artistic expression.

culture: (Ch. 2) As defined in 1871 by anthropologist Edward Tylor, "that complex whole which includes knowledge, belief, art, law, morals, custom, and any other capabilities and habits acquired by man [humankind] as a member of society."

cultures: (Ch. 2) Social entities that are defined by particular complexes of ideas, beliefs, and practices: religions, ideologies, philosophies, sciences, moral and ethical principles, artistic creations, ritual performances.

cycle: (Ch. 6) A recurring musical unit (pattern, sequence), but typically longer than an *ostinato*; basis of cyclic musical forms like the *gong cycles* of Indonesian *gamelan* music and the *talas* of *Hindustani raga*.

danzón [dan-SOHN]: (Ch. 11) Creolized Cuban dance-music genre that essentially became the national dance of Cuba in the 1920s; important forerunner of the *danzón-mambo* and the *cha cha chá.* Closely identified with the *charanga* ensemble.

danzón-mambo: (Ch. 11) More Afro-Cubanized version of the earlier *danzón*; created and popularized by Arcaño y sus Maravillas. Maravillas band members the López brothers ("Cachao" and Orestes) were the true innovators of the style, which ultimately influenced both *cha cha chá* and later forms of *mambo*.

dap: (Ch. 13) Traditional Uighur frame drum. Drum head is usually made of donkey hide or snake skin.

decrescendo: (Ch. 5) Getting softer.

diaspora: (Ch. 2) An international network of communities linked together by identification with a common ancestral homeland and culture. People in diaspora exist in a condition of living away from their "homeland," often with no guarantee, or even likelihood, of return.

didgeridoo [DIJ-er-ee-DOO]: (Ch. 5) Aboriginal Australian aerophone; traditionally constructed from a termite-hollowed eucalyptus branch.

digital sampling: (Ch. 5) Technology that allows for any existing sound to be recorded, stored as digital data, and then reproduced either "verbatim" or in electronically manipulated form.

drone: (Ch. 6) A continuous, sustained tone.

drum speech: (Ch. 10) Linguistic use of certain types of West African drums (e.g., *atumpan*) in certain contexts (e.g., reciting proverbs), which is made possible by the use of *tonal languages*.

drum set: (Ch. 5) Compound instrument consisting of a combination of *membranophones* (drums) and *idiophones* (cymbals).

Dum, tek: (Ch. 12) The syllables for the two principal drum strokes used on the Egyptian *tabla* and other Middle Eastern percussion instruments. The *Dum* is low-pitched and deep; the *tek,* high-pitched and piercing.

duration: (Ch. 3) The length of a tone; basis of *rhythm* in music.

dynamic range: (Ch. 5) The range of volume (*amplitude*) between the softest and loudest *tones* in a piece of music or a musical performance.

Egyptian nationalism: (Ch. 12) Nationalist movement that crystallized beginning in the 19th century and gained momentum through the 20th century. Inspired by Egyptian opposition to foreign domination and defined by currents of Egyptian localism, pan-Arabism, and Islamism. Musicians such as Sayyid Darwish, Muhammad 'Abd al-Wahhab, and Umm Kulthum, as well as the dancer Farida Fahmy, were prominent nationalist icons.

eighth notes: (Ch. 3) Notes played at the level of rhythmic *subdivision* at which there are two evenly spaced notes per *quarter note.*

electronophones: (Ch. 5) Instruments that rely on electronic sound generation/modification to produce their timbres.

ensembles: (Ch. 5) Music groups comprising instrumentalists, vocalists, or a combination of instrumentalists and vocalists.

ethnocentrism: (Ch. 1) Imposition of one set of culturally grounded perspectives, biases, and assumptions (e.g., Western) on peoples and practices of other cultures.

ethnomusicology: (Ch. 2) An interdisciplinary academic field that draws on musicology, anthropology, and other disciplines in order to study the world's musics; ethnomusicologists are interested in understanding music as a *musicultural* phenomenon.

fallahi [fah-la-HEE]: (Ch. 12) Upbeat dance rhythm traditionally used in accompaniment of Egyptian rural folk dances; also used to evoke "peasant" image in *raqs sharqi, belly dance,* and Egyptian folkloric dance.

fallahin [fah-la-HEEN]: (Ch. 12) Literally, peasant; refers also to a metaphorical, romanticized cultural ideal of authentic (asil) Egyptianness.

fieldwork: (Ch. 2) In *ethnomusicology,* a hallmark of research involving living for an extended period of time among the people whose lives and music one studies; often encompasses learning and performing their music as well.

firqa (firqa musiqyya) [fir-[k]AH moo-si-ki-YAH]: (Ch. 12) Large ensemble, involving both traditional Middle Eastern instruments of the *takht* ensemble and Western instruments.

five propositions (about music): (Ch. 1) In this text, the propositions that music is based in sound, that the sounds of music are organized in some way, that music is a form of humanly organized sound, that it is a product of human intention and perception, and that the term music itself is inescapably Western.

Fon: (Ch. 10) One of the major ethnic groups in the West African nation of Benin; Angélique Kidjo is of Fon heritage and many of her songs are in the Fon language (e.g., "Okan Bale").

Fontomfrom [Fon-tom-frahm]: (Ch. 10) *Akan* royal drum ensemble featuring several drums (*from, atumpan, eguankoba*) and the *dawuro* iron bell.

form: (Ch. 6) The sequential ordering of a piece of music; the resultant shape and design of the music; a specific, conventional type of musical design (e.g., *12-bar blues, verse-chorus form*).

free rhythm: (Ch. 3) Musical rhythm in which there is no discernible *beat* or *meter.*

frequency: (Ch. 3) The highness or lowness of a note; basis of pitch in music.

Gaelic [GAH-lick]: (Ch. 9) See *Irish Gaelic.*

gagaku [ga-GAH-koo] (Ch. 13): Ancient, traditional court orchestra music of Japan.

gamelan [gah-muh-lahn]: (Ch. 7) Generic Indonesian term for "ensemble," "orchestra"; used in reference to a diverse class of mainly percussion-dominated music *ensembles* found on Bali, Java, and several other Indonesian islands.

gamelan beleganjur [buh-luh-gahn-YOOR]: (Ch. 7) Balinese processional ensemble consisting of multiple gongs, drums, and cymbals, played in ritualistic contexts (e.g., cremation processions) and in modern music contests.

gamelan gong kebyar [kuh-BYAHR]: (Ch. 7) Best-known type of Balinese *gamelan.* Instrumentation features *gangsa* metallophones; gongs of many types, sizes, and functions; drums, cymbals, and other instruments. Associated with virtuosic kebyar musical style.

gangsa [GAHNG-suh]: (Ch. 7) Keyed metallophone instrument of a Balinese *gamelan.*

gat [like English "gut"]: (Ch. 8) The main part of a *Hindustani raga* performance following the *alap*; a *tala* (metric cycle) serves as its metric/rhythmic foundation; the entry of a rhythmic accompaniment part (usually played on *tabla*) marks the commencement of the gat.

gerak [GUH-rahk]: (Ch. 7) Literally means "movement"; specifically in this text, refers to the choreographed movements performed by the musicians in beleganjur contests; associated with *kreasi beleganjur.*

gharana [gha-RAH-nah]: (Ch. 8) A "musical family" or lineage that preserves, cultivates, and develops a particular tradition of *raga* performance, often over the course of many generations.

ghawazi [gha-WAH-zee]: (Ch. 12) Specifically, a hereditary class of professional female dancers in Egypt; more broadly, a designation for all professional female dancers in Egypt and throughout the Middle East; term literally means "outsider" or "invader."

gilak [GEE-lahk]: (Ch. 7) Common, eight-beat *gong cycle* used in *gamelan beleganjur* and other Balinese music traditions.

gong ageng [gohng ah-GUHNG]: (Ch. 7) "Great gong"; the largest gong (or gongs, if two) in a *gamelan.*

gong cycle: (Ch. 7) A recurring sequence of gong strokes (usually employing two or more gongs) that provides the musical foundation of a *gamelan* piece.

griot [GREE-oh]: (Ch. 10) Generic term (from French) covering a diverse range of African hereditary praise song/ music traditions, including that of the Mande *jeli.*

gua-zou [goo-wa-zoh]: (Ch. 13) General term for a variety of glissando-type ornaments used in *zheng* and other Chinese instrumental traditions.

guru: (Ch. 8) Teacher, mentor (in this text, specifically of Indian classical music).

Han Chinese: (Ch. 13) Chinese ethnic majority, accounting for approximately 92 percent of the population of the People's Republic of China.

harmonics: (Ch. 5) The overtones, or partials, of a tone (as distinct from the fundamental of that tone).

harmonization: (Ch. 4) In this text, the procedure (and result) of building *chords* from the individual notes of a melody.

harmonized texture: (Ch. 6) Texture resulting when notes of different pitch occur together to form *chords,* or "harmonies."

harmony: (Ch. 4) A *chord* that "makes sense" within the context of its musical style.

hereditary jeli families: (Ch. 10) Family lineages of professional musicians (Kouyate, Diabate, Sissoko), many dating back centuries, who are exclusively associated with the *griot* traditions of Mande *jeliya* in West Africa.

Hindustani raga [Hin-dus-TAH-nee RAH-gah (or RAHG)]: (Ch. 8) The *raga* tradition of North India.

Hindu religion: (Ch. 8) The principal religion of India and one of the world's oldest religions. A related but distinct form of Hinduism, *Agama Tirta*, is practiced in Bali, Indonesia.

HIP (human intention and perception) approach: (Ch. 1) An approach to the study and exploration of world music (advocated in this text) that privileges inclusiveness over exclusiveness and emphasizes the idea that music is inseparable from the people who make and experience it.

Hornbostel-Sachs classification system: (Ch. 5) Music instrument classification system (originally published in 1914) that classifies the world's instruments into four main categories: *chordophones, aerophones, membranophones,* and *idiophones.* A fifth category, *electronophones,* has since been added.

hornpipe: (Ch. 9) Commonly used dance rhythm in Irish music.

horn section: (Ch. 11) The trumpet, trombone, and saxophone players in a Latin or jazz band.

identity: (Ch. 2) Defined by people's ideas about who they are and what unites them with, or distinguishes them from, other people and entities: individuals, families, communities, institutions, *cultures, societies, nations,* supernatural powers.

idiophones: (Ch. 5) Instruments in which the vibration of the body of the instrument itself produces the sound (e.g., shaker, cymbal, xylophone).

improvisation: (Ch. 2) The process of composing in the moment of performance; takes different forms in different music traditions (e.g., jazz, *Hindustani raga*).

instrumentation: (Ch. 5) The types of instruments and the number of each employed in a given musical work or performance. Potentially includes voices.

interlocking: (Ch. 6) Division of a single melodic or rhythmic line between two or more instruments/voices.

interpretation: (Ch. 2) The process through which music performers—or music listeners—take an existing composition and in a sense make it their own through the experience of performing or listening to it.

interval: (Ch. 4) The distance in pitch between one note and another.

Irish diaspora: (Ch. 9) The dispersal of millions of people from Ireland to other countries, especially the United States and Canada, where large diasporic communities ultimately formed. The Irish diaspora commenced in response to the *Irish potato famine*.

Irish Gaelic [GAH-lick]: (Ch. 9) The traditional *Celtic* language of Ireland; mainly spoken in the Gaeltacht areas of the country. The Gaelic language subfamily also includes Scottish Gaelic and Manx Gaelic. *Sean nós* songs are sung in Irish Gaelic.

Irish music revival: (Ch. 9) Major musicultural phenomenon of the 1960s and henceforth that both preserved and transformed *Irish traditional music* on many levels, in Ireland itself and internationally.

Irish potato famine: (Ch. 9) Devastating famine that began in the 1840s. Led to decimation of the Irish population, the *Irish diaspora,* violent resistance to British control of Ireland, and the beginnings of Irish nationalism.

Irish traditional music: (Ch. 9) Umbrella term for a wide range of musics—traditional, neo-traditional, and post-traditional—that share a common basis in rural, Irish folk music.

Irish wooden flute: (Ch. 9) A relatively large and low-pitched *aerophone* with a distinctive *timbre* that is a standard instrument in *Irish traditional music.*

isicathamiya [ee-see-kah-tah-MEE-yah]: (Ch. 10) South African a cappella vocal genre; largely identified with the iconic group Ladysmith Black Mambazo.

jeli [JAY-lee] (pl. jelilu): (Ch. 10) A Mande *griot.* Most of the leading jelilu are descended from a *hereditary jeli family* (Kouyate, Diabate, Sissoko). Those who are instrumentalists play specific jeli instruments such as *kora, bala,* and *koni.*

jeliya [jay-lee-yuh]: (Ch. 10) The artistic culture of the *jeli,* including its *praise songs* and instrumental music traditions.

jhala: (Ch. 8) Concluding section in the form of a standard Hindustani raga performance, characterized by fast tempos, tempo accelerations, and great rhythmic intensity.

jig: (Ch. 9) Commonly used dance rhythm in Irish music.

jor: (Ch. 8) Transitional section in the form of a Hindustani raga performance, linking the *alap* to the *gat.*

julajula: (Ch. 11) Andean panpipe instruments (*aerophones*) that are played in pairs within ensembles; interlocking parts between pairs of julajula generate the music's melodies.

Karnatak [Kar-NAH-tuck]: (Ch. 8) The culture of South India; in this text, specifically refers to the South Indian classical music tradition.

Kecak [ke-CHAHK]: (Ch. 7) Balinese dance-drama that employs a gamelan suara (*gamelan* of voices) as its sole musical accompaniment; music features complex interlocking rhythms derived from the *kilitan telu.*

keeping tal: (Ch. 8) Practice of outlining the metric cycle of a *tala* using a combination of claps, waves, and finger touches to mark the various beats.

key: (Ch. 4) Term that indicates the fundamental *scale* from which a piece of music is built (e.g., a piece in the key of C major is based on a C-major scale).

kilitan telu [kee-lee-TAHN tuh-LOO]: (Ch. 7) Set of three interlocking rhythmic patterns that are an integral component of much Balinese music; basis of the interlocking cymbal patterns in *gamelan beleganjur* music and of the interlocking vocal patterns in *Kecak.*

koni [koh-nee]: (Ch. 10) Banjo-like plucked chordophone of the *Mande; jeli* instrument. Bassekou Kouyate is one of its best-known exponents.

kora: (Ch. 10) 21-string *Mande* spike harp chordophone; *jeli* instrument. Sidiki, Toumani, and Mamadou Diabate represent one of the great lineages of kora players.

koto: (Ch. 13) Japanese board zither chordophone with 13 strings. Historically related to the Chinese *zheng.*

kreasi beleganjur [kray-YAH-see buh-luh-gahn-YOOR]: (Ch. 7) Modern, contest style of beleganjur music; first developed in 1986 in Denpasar, Bali.

kumbengo [koom-BAYN-go]: (Ch. 10) The accompaniment style of instrumental performance used on instruments like the *kora, bala,* and *koni* in Mande *jeliya* music.

Latin Dance: (Ch. 11) Dance-music genre that is a hybrid of diverse contemporary music styles—pop, rock, hip-hop, techno, Latino pop—and *mambo, cha cha chá,* and Dominican merengue. Identified specifically with Tito Puente Jr. in this text.

Latin jazz: (Ch. 11) Umbrella term for a variety of musical styles that combine elements of Latin dance and popular musics (mainly of Cuban/Puerto Rican derivation, such as the Cuban *son*) with jazz; considerable overlap with *salsa* in many instances.

Latin music: (Ch. 11) Musics of Latin America (South America, Central America, Mexico, and the Caribbean) and of Latino/American communities of the United States and elsewhere as well. The chapter focused mainly on a Latin music trajectory centered on developments in Cuba, Puerto Rico, and the U.S.

Latin rock: (Ch. 11) Hybrid of *Latin music* styles (*rumba, cha cha chá, mambo,* etc.) and rock. Term is most closely identified with the music of Santana.

Latino/American: (Ch. 11) The slash between the words implies "and/or" in the widest sense; that is, it points to the fluidity and multiplicity of Latino and American identities, musiculturally and otherwise.

layered ostinatos: (Ch. 6) "Stacking" of two or more *ostinatos* one atop the other.

legato [le-GAH-toe]: (Ch. 4) Italian term for a type of articulation in which the notes are sustained; opposite of *staccato.*

major scale: (Ch. 4) A common type of *scale* in Western music with seven pitches per octave. The ascending and descending forms of the scale employ the same set of pitches.

malfuf [mahl-FOOF]: (Ch. 12) Lively, quick-tempoed Egyptian dance rhythm often heard in the opening numbers of *raqs sharqi* and *belly dance* routines.

mambo: (Ch. 11) Highly Afro-Cubanized form of *Latin music* that was crystallized by Pérez Prado but is today principally identified with 1950s New York Latin big bands like Machito and the Afro-Cubans and the bands of Tito Puente and Tito Rodríguez.

mambo kings: (Ch. 11) The leaders of the top Latin dance bands of New York in the 1950s, who were responsible for the "mambo craze" of that era: Machito, Tito Puente, Tito Rodríguez.

Mandarin Chinese: (Ch. 13) China's official national language.

Mande [MAHN-day]: (Ch. 10) Major ethnic group of western Africa, concentrated in areas of Mali, Senegal, Guinea, Guinea-Bissau, and Gambia. Principal subgroups are the Maninka (Mali, Guinea) and Mandinka (Senegal, Gambia).

maqam [mah-KAHM]: (Ch. 12) Term essentially meaning *mode* in Arab music; part of a large modal system comprising many maqamat (plural of maqam).

maqsoum [mak-SOOM]: (Ch. 12) Popular rhythm used in the accompaniment of certain forms of Egyptian women's dance.

mariachi [mah-ree-AH-chee]: (Ch. 11) Popular music of Mexico that developed mainly in Mexico City through the synthesis of regional forms from rural areas (such as the *son* forms of Jalisco) and an eclectic range of Mexican and international musical styles.

masmoudi [mas-MOO-dee]: (Ch. 12) Very commonly used Egyptian dance rhythm; comes in several different varieties and may be played at different tempos.

measure: (Ch. 3) One unit, or group, of beats in music that has *meter* (i.e., in metric music).

medley: (Ch. 9) A musical form in which two or more pieces (e.g., Irish dance tunes) are performed one after the other without pause.

melody: (Ch. 4) A sequence of pitches that defines the identity of a song or other piece of music as it unfolds; a "tune." Every melody has distinctive features including range, direction, and contour.

membranophones: (Ch. 5) Instruments in which the vibration of a membrane (natural or synthetic) stretched tightly across a frame resonator produces the sound (e.g., drums).

meter: (Ch. 3) The systematic grouping of individual *beats* into larger groupings; a specific pattern of grouped beats (e.g., duple meter, triple meter).

metric cycle: (Ch. 3) Like a *meter,* but longer (e.g., *gong cycle* in Indonesian *gamelan* music, *tala* cycle in *Hindustani raga*).

microtones: (Ch. 4) Tiny pitch *intervals,* as found in the pitch systems of Middle Eastern, Indian, and other music traditions that recognize more than the 12 divisions of the *octave* identified in the Western chromatic *scale* (and/or that divide the *octave* into different proportions).

minor scales: (Ch. 4) Like the *major scale,* minor scales have seven pitches per octave, but they differ in that the *interval* between the second and third scale degrees is always smaller than in the major scale. Additionally, the ascending and descending forms of a minor scale may use different sets of pitches.

mode: (Ch. 4) A comprehensive, multidimensional musical system—based on but not limited to a specific *scale* of pitches—that guides composers/performers on how to generate musical works and performances *in* that mode. May encompass both musical dimensions (pitches, ornaments, melodic procedures) and extramusical dimensions (associations with particular times of day, seasons, emotions).

modulation: (Ch. 4) Changing *key* (or changing *mode*) in the course of a composition.

mrdangam [mir-DUNG-ahm]: (Ch. 8) Double-headed South Indian drum used in *Karnatak* music.

multiple-melody texture: (Ch. 6) Texture in which two or more essentially separate melodic lines are performed simultaneously.

multitrack recording: (Ch. 5) Involves technologies that make it possible to layer dozens upon dozens of separate musical tracks one atop the other using computers or other equipment.

muqam [moo-KAHM]: (Ch. 13) In Uighur music (and Central Asian traditions more broadly), a large-scale, precomposed suite of songs and instrumental music.

music director: (Ch. 8) In Indian cinema (e.g., Bollywood), the individual responsible for all of a film's musical components, including background music, songs, and dance compositions.

music instrument: (Ch. 5) Any sound-generating medium used to produce tones in the making of music.

musical syncretism: (Ch. 2) The merging of formerly distinct styles and idioms into new forms of musical expression.

musicultural: (Ch. 2) Conception of music in which music as sound and music as culture are regarded as mutually reinforcing and essentially inseparable.

Nada Brahma: (Ch. 8) "The Sound of God" (Brahma); the divine source of all sound and thus of all ragas. *Raga* performance, at its highest level, is ultimately a pursuit of the ideal of Nada Brahma.

nation-state/nation: (Ch. 2) A nation-state is defined by a national society and culture *and* a national homeland (e.g., Canada); a nation may be defined in an identical manner, but some nations do not have political autonomy over the geographical area they claim as their homeland (e.g., as of this writing, Palestine).

nationalist music: (Ch. 2) Music tied to movements of nationalism and to concepts of and ideas about national identities.

nay [nah-EE]: (Ch. 12) End-blown bamboo or cane flute with seven finger holes that is a standard instrument of the Arab *takht* ensemble.

Newyorican: (Ch. 11) New York resident of Puerto Rican descent; includes both New York natives (e.g., Tito Puente) and Puerto Rican immigrants to New York (e.g., Tito Rodríguez).

octave [OCK-tiv]: (Ch. 4) The phenomenon accounting for why the "same" pitch may occur in multiple—that is, higher and lower—versions (e.g., why a note on the pitch C sung by a woman sounds higher than a note on the pitch C sung by a man).

ombak [OAM-bahk]: (Ch. 7) Means "wave"; refers to the acoustical beating effect generated by instruments with *paired tuning* in a Balinese *gamelan.*

Orientalist (Orientalism): (Ch. 12) Exoticized (and often marginalizing) representations of "Eastern" (i.e., "Oriental") people and cultures. Orientalist characterizations of Egypt spanned from 19th-century French paintings to 20th-century Hollywood movies, and the image of the Middle Eastern female dancer (belly dancer) was consistently prominent.

ornamentation: (Ch. 4, 13) Decoration, or adornment, of the main notes in a *melody* by additional notes and ornamental figures (e.g., pitch bends, glissandos).

ornaments: (Ch. 9) A general term relating to the decoration of melodies in music traditions worldwide (see *ornamentation*); in the chapter, relates specifically to

ornaments used in Irish music such as the roll, cran, treble, cut, and triplet.

ostinato [ah-sti-NAH-toe]: (Ch. 6) A short, recurring musical figure; may be repeated exactly or with variations as the music unfolds. Generally, the smallest unit of musical organization upon which formal musical designs are built (as in ostinato-based forms).

overdubbing: (Ch. 5) The process of separately recording and then combining multiple recorded tracks using *multitrack recording.*

paired tuning: (Ch. 7) The tuning of the pitches of the "male" and "female" instruments of a Balinese *gamelan* to slightly different *frequencies;* striking the "same" pitch simultaneously on a male-female pair creates *ombak;* female instruments of each pair are tuned lower than their male counterparts.

pan-Irish: (Ch. 9) Pertaining to Irish identity and culture (including music) in Ireland itself, transnationally throughout the *Irish diaspora,* and worldwide across the expansive range of Irish and Irish diasporic influence.

pentatonic scale: (Ch. 4) Five-tone *scale* (five tones per *octave*). The version discussed in the chapter is closely related to the *major scale,* though there are many different forms of pentatonic scales in other world music traditions as well.

Period of Openness: (Ch. 13) Modern period of Chinese socialism, initiated by Deng Xiaoping in late 1970s/early 1980s. Yielded profound transformations of Chinese society, including introduction of free enterprise economy, China's immersion in global markets, and liberalization of policies on the arts.

pipa [pee-pah]: (Ch. 13) Pear-shaped, plucked chordophone with four strings. Chinese instrument of Central Asian heritage; close historical association with the *zheng.*

playback singer: (Ch. 8) In Indian cinema (e.g., Bollywood), a vocalist who sings the songs that are included in films, but who does not appear on screen. Playback singers are voice surrogates for on-screen actors and actresses, who typically lip-synch their parts.

polyphonic: (Ch. 6) Music with two or more distinct parts.

polyrhythm: (Ch. 6) Multiple layers of rhythm occurring simultaneously in a musical context; rhythmic polyphony.

polyvocality: (Ch. 10) Comprising "many voices"; in the chapter, relates to the conversational dimension of much West African music, wherein many voices—vocal and/or instrumental—may speak and be heard all at once, expressing a unified diversity of views and perspectives.

praise songs: (Ch. 10) In the *jeliya* tradition of the *Mande* and in other African *griot* traditions, a class of songs that were traditionally sung to honor royalty exclusively, but that are now often performed in honor of modern politicians or other wealthy patrons who are not of royal lineage as well.

qanun [kah-NOON]: (Ch. 12) Trapezoidal, plucked zither used in Arab music; standard instrument of the *takht* ensemble.

qin [chin]: (Ch. 13) Ancient Chinese zither-type chordophone with seven strings, no bridges; quintessential instrument of the Chinese gentleman/scholar (junzi) during the dynastic era. Confucius is said to have played this instrument.

quarter notes: (Ch. 3) Notes whose duration often defines the *beat* in music; see also *eighth notes* and *sixteenth notes.*

Qur'an [Koar-AHN]: (Ch. 1, 12) The holy book of Islam; principal sacred text of that religion.

Qur'anic [Koar-AH-nik] **recitation:** (Ch. 12) The melodious art of reciting the Qur'an. Though it sounds musical to Western listeners and uses *maqam*-like melodies similar to those found in Middle Eastern music, it is categorically *not* music according to most Muslims.

quarter tone: (Ch. 12) Microtonal interval that falls halfway between the smallest intervals (semitones) in the conventional Western pitch system (i.e., halfway between consecutive keys on a piano). Quarter-tone intervals are used in *maqam*-based music of the Middle East.

Radio Éireann [AIR-ahn]: (Ch. 9) Ireland's national radio station.

raga: (Ch. 8) In Indian classical music, a complete and self-contained melodic system that serves as the basis for all the melodic materials in any composition or performance created *in* that raga.

ranges: (Ch. 4) The different octave registers (pitch ranges) in which particular instruments and voices perform (e.g., the range of a tuba is much lower than the range of a flute).

raqs baladi [ra[k]s bah-lah-dee]: (Ch. 12) Egyptian (and other Middle Eastern) "folk dance"; the term implies rural culture or origins; encompasses traditional dance of women's gatherings and certain types of folk rituals and ceremonial performances.

raqs sharqi [ra[k]s shar[k]ee]: (Ch. 12) The professional entertainment medium of women's dance, associated with Egyptian weddings, nightclub and cabaret performances, and commercial film and other mass media.

reel: (Ch. 9) The most commonly used dance rhythm in Irish music.

regional styles of solo zheng music: (Ch. 13) A complex of distinctive playing styles, repertoires, and performance traditions on the *zheng* that crystallized in the late 19th century in regions of China including Shandong, Henan, Shaanxi, Chaozhou, Hakka, and Zhejiang.

reyong: (Ch. 7) In the *gamelan beleganjur,* a set of four small, hand-held gongs (each played by a separate performer) played in interlocking style; main function is to elaborate the music's core melody. The reyong of the *gamelan gong kebyar* is a related but distinct instrument.

rhythm: (Ch. 3) In music, the organization of sounds and silences in time.

rhythm section: (Ch. 11) The pianist, bassist, and percussionists in a Latin dance band.

riffs: (Ch. 11) Short, recurring patterns (ostinatos) that are repeated over and over, often with variations, and layered one atop the other. Important feature of arrangements in *mambo, salsa,* and other *Latin music* styles.

riqq [ri[k]]: (Ch. 12) Arab tambourine.

rituals: (Ch. 2) Special events during which individuals or communities enact, through performance, their core beliefs, values, and ideals.

rumba [ROOM-bah]: (Ch. 11) Traditional Afro-Cuban secular dance music featuring singing and music played on *conga drums* and other instruments.

Saaidi [Sah-ayi-DEE]: (Ch. 12) Egyptian dance rhythm associated with certain forms of *baladi* culture and with the martial art of *tahtib.*

sagat [sah-gaht]: (Ch. 12) Finger cymbals used in *raqs baladi, raqs sharqi,* and *belly dance.*

salsa: (Ch. 11) Major form of *Latin music* that emerged in New York in the 1970s. Strongly rooted in Cuban *son.*

sam [like English "some"]: (Ch. 8) The first beat of a *tala* cycle (and, simultaneously, the last beat of the preceding cycle).

samba [SAHM-bah]: (Ch. 11) Umbrella term for a wide range of musical traditions of Brazil that share in common Afro-Brazilian musical and cultural ancestry; energetic percussion, call-and-response singing, improvisation, and grand spectacle including dance and dramatic presentations characterize many samba performance styles.

Santería [San-te-REE-yah]: (Ch. 11) Afro-Cuban religion based on traditional West African religious practices of the Yoruba people syncretized with Catholicism. Sacred ritual music employing the *batá* drums is central. (Also known as Regla de Ocha.)

sataro: (Ch. 10) Improvisatory, speechlike style of singing in *jeliya* vocal art. Kassemady Diabate is a master of sataro.

sauta [sow-tah]: (Ch. 10) An important musical mode in *Mande* music, using a *scale* that is roughly equivalent to F G A B C D E (F) in Western music.

scale: (Ch. 4) An ascending and/or descending series of notes of different pitch. Songs and other pieces of music are typically "built" from the notes of particular scales. The chromatic, major, pentatonic, minor, and blues scales are important types in Western and related music traditions.

sean nós [SHAWN nohs]: (Ch. 9) The "old way" songs , sung in *Irish Gaelic;* revered as the cornerstone of *Irish traditional music.*

session (Irish music session): (Ch. 9) Informal gathering at which musicians playing different instruments come together to perform traditional Irish tunes and newer tunes modeled after them, but not generally to accompany dancing.

Silk Road: (Ch. 13) Expansive trade route of antiquity that connected China to lands as distant as Central Asia, India, Egypt, and Turkey.

single-line texture (monophony): (Ch. 6) Music with only a single part, for example, a single melody. Note that this one part may be performed by multiple performers, and may involve different voices, instruments, and octave *ranges*. (See also *unison*.)

sitar [si-TAHR]: (Ch. 8) North Indian plucked chordophone; one of the main melodic instruments in Hindustani music; principal instrument of Ravi Shankar; iconic symbol of "Indian music" internationally.

sixteenth notes: (Ch. 3) Notes played at the level of rhythmic *subdivision* at which there are four evenly spaced notes per *quarter note*.

social institutions: (Ch. 2) Institutions (governmental, economic, legal, religious, family-centered, activity- or interest-based, service-oriented, etc.) whose functions and interactions largely define the structure of a *society*.

society: (Ch. 2) A group of persons regarded as forming a single community of related, interdependent individuals; defined largely by *social institutions*.

son [sohn]: (Ch. 11) Afro-Cuban dance-music style that gained popularity from the 1920s onward, influencing related styles such as *danzón, danzón-mambo,* and *mambo* and prefiguring later developments like *salsa* and *Latin jazz*. Also historically important as a symbol of Cuban nationalism. Central historical figure was Arsenio Rodríguez. Distinct from the various Mexican genres of *son*.

staccato [stah-KAH-toe]: (Ch. 4) Italian term for a type of articulation in which the notes are performed in a short, clipped manner; opposite of *legato*.

steel band: (Ch. 11) Large percussion orchestra of Trinidad and Tobago, featuring pans (steel drums) of many different sizes and ranges; the pans are made from oil drums.

subdivision: (Ch. 3) The dividing of beats into smaller rhythmic units.

syncopation: (Ch. 3) An *accent* or other note that falls in-between main *beats*.

tabla [TUB-lah] (Egyptian): (Ch. 12) Lead drum in Egyptian dance music. This single-headed, goblet-shaped drum should not be confused with the Indian instrument of the same name. The Egyptian tabla is also known by several other names (darabukkah, dumbek, doumbec).

tabla [TUB-lah] (Indian): (Ch. 8) The principal percussion instrument in North Indian music (not to be confused with the Egyptian tabla, an entirely different instrument). Consists of two drums—the higher-pitched dahina and

lower-pitched bayan. Master performers include the late Alla Rakha and his son Zakir Hussain.

Tabla Solo: (Ch. 12) Neo-traditional dance genre "invented" in the 1970s by Nagwa Fu'ad and her tabla accompanist Ahmed Hammouda; involves close coordination and interaction between dancer and drummer(s); often the highlight of a *raqs sharqi* or *belly dance* routine.

tahtib [tah-TEEB]: (Ch. 12) Traditional martial arts form/dance of Egypt. The *Saaidi* rhythm and the various forms of the women's *cane dance* all have their origins in tahtib.

takht [tah-kht]: (Ch. 12) Main instrumental ensemble for Arab art music. Includes the *'ud, nay, qanun,* violin, and *riqq,* sometimes supplemented by *tabla* (i.e., Egyptian). In the Iraqi takht, a joza may substitute for the violin.

tala [TAH-lah (or TAHL)]: (Ch. 8) Metric cycle in Indian music.

tambura [tum-BOO-rah]: (Ch. 8) *Chordophone* used to provide drone in Indian music; Hindustani and Karnatak versions are distinct.

tango: (Ch. 11) Sensuous dance-music style of Argentina (also Uruguay) that achieved great international popularity in the 1920s–1930s and was developed and transformed in later years by the innovations of modern masters such as Astor Piazzolla.

taqsim [tak-SEEM]: (Ch. 12) Solo, instrumental improvisation in *maqam*-based Arab music, performed either in *free rhythm* or with rhythmic accompaniment.

tek: (Ch. 12) See *Dum/tek*.

tempo: (Ch. 3) The rate at which the beats pass in music.

texture: (Ch. 6) Musical element defined by the relationships and interactions between the different parts in a musical work or performance.

theka [TAY-kah]: (Ch. 8) The basic pattern of drum strokes (e.g., on the Indian *tabla*) that outlines a *tala* in its most skeletal form.

tihai [ti-HA-EE]: (Ch. 8) Rhythmic cadence (ending), in which the same rhythmic pattern is played three times in succession, generating complex rhythmic relationships with the underlying *tala* cycle in the process.

timbales [teem-BAH-lays]: (Ch. 11) Latin "drum set" featuring two or more relatively high-pitched metal-sided drums (the timbales), plus cowbells, woodblock, cymbal(s), and sometimes additional drums and other percussion instruments.

timbre [TAM-ber]: (Ch. 3) Sound quality, or "tone color"; what particular notes, instruments, or voices "sound like."

tintal [TEEN-tahl]: (Ch. 8) A 16-beat metric cycle (i.e., *tala*) used in *Hindustani raga* and other types of North Indian music.

tinwhistle: (Ch. 9) Small, end-blown flute with six finger-holes used in Irish music. Usually made of metal (tin or other), but may alternately be made of wood or plastic. Also known as the pennywhistle.

tonal languages: (Ch. 10) Languages in which the meaning of words is determined not just by the actual sounds of their syllables, but also by the specific patterns of pitch, rhythm, and timbral inflection with which they are articulated. Many West African languages (such as the Akan language Twi) are tonal; so too are other languages, including *Mandarin Chinese*.

tone: (Ch. 1) A sound whose principal identity is a musical identity, as defined by people (though not necessarily all people) who make or experience that sound.

tonic: (Ch. 4) The first, fundamental pitch of a *scale* (e.g., the pitch C relative to a C-major scale or a piece in the *key* of C major).

tradition: (Ch. 2) In this text, a process of creative transformation whose most remarkable feature is the continuity it nurtures and sustains.

tropicália [tro-pee-KAH-lee-ah]: (Ch. 11) Radical and innovative movement in Brazilian arts, culture, and social activism of the late 1960s that privileged an aesthetic of so-called cannibalism, the selective devouring of elements of foreign cultures for absorption and transformation into Brazilian cultural products (Leu 2006:86–87); in music, Os Mutantes, Caetano Veloso, and Gilberto Gil were central figures of the tropicália phenomenon.

12-bar blues: (Ch. 6) Cyclic form defined by a standard-length *cycle* (12 measures) and *chord progression*. Employed in most blues tunes and in many other blues-derived musical contexts as well.

'ud: (Ch. 12) Pear-shaped, short-necked, lute-type plucked *chordophone* of Arab music; lead instrument of the *takht* ensemble and progenitor of the European lute.

uilleann [ILL-inn] **pipes:** (Ch. 9) The Irish version of the bagpipe, regarded as the most distinctively Irish music instrument.

unison: (Ch. 6) The same part performed by two or more instruments/voices.

Unity in Diversity: (Ch. 7) The national slogan of the Republic of Indonesia; important relative to Indonesian policies of cultural diversity, preservation and development of indigenous cultural traditions, and nationalism.

vadi [VAH-dee]: (Ch. 8) The tonic, or fundamental pitch, of a *raga*.

Vedas [VAY-dahs]: (Ch. 8) The four ancient Sanskrit scriptures of Hinduism, believed by Hindus to be of divine origin; some (including Ravi Shankar) claim that Vedic chant was the original basis of Indian classical music (though this claim is widely disputed).

verse-chorus form: (Ch. 6) Very common formal design in Western popular music and many other world music traditions. Features two main types of formal sections—verse and chorus—often with additional sections as well (introductions, interludes, bridges, transitions, ending sections).

vina [VEE-nah]: (Ch. 8) South Indian plucked *chordophone;* one of the main melodic instruments in *Karnatak* music.

virtual communities: (Ch. 2) Communities forged in the electronic sphere of cyberspace (e.g., on the Internet) rather than in more conventional ways.

vocables: (Ch. 2) Nonlinguistic syllables that are used in vocal performances (singing, rapping, etc.) in many musical styles, including Native American/First Nations powwow songs.

yijing [ee-jing]: (Ch. 13) Designated emotional quality of a musical work (e.g., yijing of "sadness" for "Autumn Moon over the Han Palace"). Usually complex and multifaceted rather than simple and straightforward.

yun [yün]: (Ch. 13) Distinctive regional character of a piece of music or particular musical style (e.g., Shandong yun versus Henan yun in *zheng* music).

zaar [zahr]: (Ch. 12) Ancient healing ritual (performed mainly for and by women) rooted in shamanistic practices and involving spirit possession and trance. In modern times, the ritual has been folklorized, and zaar-derived rhythms and dance elements are commonly used in *raqs baladi, raqs sharqi,* and *belly dance.*

zheng [jung]: (Ch. 13) Chinese board zither chordophone of ancient heritage. Most common form of instrument today has 21 strings and movable bridges; historically related to several other Asian zither-type chordophones (Japanese *koto,* Korean kayagum, Mongolian jatag, Vietnamese dan tranh).

references cited in the text

Al-Rawi, Rosina-Fawzia. 1999. *Grandmother's Secrets: The Ancient Rituals and Healing Power of Belly Dancing.* Translated by Monique Arav. Brooklyn, NY: Interlink.

Ali, Lorraine. 2010 (March 22). "Acrassicauda: Iraq 'n' Roll." *Newsweek*, pp. 60–61.

Amira, John, and Steven Cornelius. 1992. *The Music of Santería: Traditional Rhythms of the Batá Drums.* Crown Point, IN: White Cliffs Media Company.

Anderson, Benedict. 1991. *Imagined Communities: Reflections on the Origin and Spread of Nationalism.* 2nd ed., revised and extended. London and New York: Verso. First edition published 1983.

Arnold, Alison (ed.). 2000. *South Asia: The Indian Subcontinent.* Vol. 5 of *The Garland Encyclopedia of World Music.* New York and London: Garland Publishing, Inc.

Bakan, Michael B. 1999. *Music of Death and New Creation: Experiences in the World of Balinese Gamelan Beleganjur.* Chicago and London: University of Chicago Press.

———. 2009. "The Abduction of the Signifying Monkey Chant: Schizophonic Transmogrifications of Balinese *Kecak* in Fellini's *Satyricon* and the Coen Brothers' *Blood Simple.*" *Ethnomusicology Forum* 18(1):83–106.

Baranovitch, Nimrod. 2003. *China's New Voices: Popular Music, Ethnicity, Gender, and Politics, 1978–1997.* Berkeley and Los Angeles: University of California Press.

Barnard, Alan. 2000. *History and Theory in Anthropology.* Cambridge and New York: Cambridge University Press.

Bensignor, François, and Eric Audra. 1999. "Benin and Togo." In *World Music: The Rough Guide.* Vol. 1. New edition, ed. Simon Broughton, Mark Ellingham, and Richard Trillo. London: The Rough Guides, pp. 432–36.

Blacking, John. 1973. *How Musical Is Man?* Seattle: University of Washington Press.

———. 1995. *Music, Culture, & Experience: Selected Papers of John Blacking.* Chicago and London: University of Chicago Press.

Booth, Gregory D. 2008. *Behind the Curtain: Making Music in Mumbai's Film Studios.* New York: Oxford University Press.

Buonaventura, Wendy. 1989. *Serpent of the Nile: Women and Dance in the Arab World.* London: Saqi Books.

Charry, Eric. 2000. *Mande Music.* Chicago and London: University of Chicago Press.

Cheng, Te-yuan. 1991. *Zheng, Tradition and Change.* Ph.D. dissertation, University of Maryland, Baltimore County.

Czekanowska, Anna. 1983. "Apects of the Classical Music of Uighur People: Legend versus Reality." *Asian Music* 14(1):94–110.

Danielson, Virginia. 1997. *The Voice of Egypt: Umm Kulthūm, Arabic Song, and Egyptian Society in the Twentieth Century.* Chicago and London: University of Chicago Press.

———. 2002. "Stardom in Egyptian Music: Four Case Studies." In *The Middle East,* ed. Virginia Danielson, Scott Marcus, and Dwight Reynolds. Vol. 6 of *The Garland Encyclopedia of World Music.* New York and London: Routledge, pp. 597–601.

Dibia, I Wayan. 1996. *Kecak: The Vocal Chant of Bali.* Denpasar (Bali): Hartanto Art Books Studio.

Donald, Mary Ellen. 2000. "Basic Rhythms for a Cabaret Belly Dance Routine." In *The Belly Dance Book: Rediscovering the Oldest Dance,* ed. Tazz Richards. Concord, CA: Backbeat Press, pp. 176–77.

Dunn, Christopher. 2001. "Tropicália, Counterculture, and the Diasporic Imagination in Brazil." In *Brazilian Popular Music & Globalization,* ed. Charles A. Perrone and Christopher Dunn. Gainesville: University Press of Florida, pp. 72–95.

Duran, Lucy. 2000. *The Rough Guide to the Music of Mali & Guinea.* CD booklet. World Music Network/Rough Guides RGNET 1048 CD.

Eiseman, Fred B. 1990. *Sekala and Niskala,* Vol. II of *Essays on Society, Tradition, and Craft.* Berkeley, CA, and Singapore: Periplus Editions.

Ephland, John. 1991 [1976]. *Shakti, with John McLaughlin.* CD booklet. New York: Columbia/Legacy CK 46868.

Fairley, Jan. 2000. "Cuba: Son and Afro-Cuban Music." In *World Music: The Rough Guide.* Vol. 2. New edition, ed. Simon Broughton and Mark Ellingham. London: The Rough Guides, pp. 386–407.

Farrell, Gerry. 1997. *Indian Music and the West.* New York: Oxford University Press.

———. 2000. "Music and Internationalization." In *South Asia: The Indian Subcontinent,* ed. Alison Arnold. Vol. 5 of *The Garland Encyclopedia of World Music.* New York and London: Garland Publishing, Inc., pp. 560–69.

Fernandez, Raul A. 2006. *From Afro-Cuban Rhythms to Latin Jazz.* Berkeley and Los Angeles: University of California Press.

Fletcher, Peter. 2001. *World Musics in Context.* New York: Oxford University Press.

Fong-Torres, Ben. 1998. *Abraxas.* CD booklet. New York: Sony Music Entertainment, Inc.

Franken, Marjorie. 1998. "Farida Fahmy and the Dancer's Image in Egyptian Film." In *Images of Enchantment: Visual and Performing Arts of the Middle East,* ed. Sherifa Zuhur. Cairo: American University in Cairo Press, pp. 265–81.

Frishkopf, Michael. 2002. "Islamic Hymnody in Egypt: *Al-Inshād al-Dīnī.*" In *The Middle East,* ed. Virginia Danielson, Scott Marcus, and Dwight Reynolds. Vol. 6 of *The Garland Encyclopedia of World Music.* New York and London: Routledge, pp. 165–75.

Galm, Eric A. 2010. *The Berimbau: Soul of Brazilian Music.* Jackson: University Press of Mississippi.

Gerard, Charley. 2001. *Music from Cuba: Mongo Santamaría, Chocolate Armenteros and Other Stateside Cuban Musicians.* Westport, CT and London: Praeger.

Gerard, Charley, and Marty Sheller. 1989. *Salsa! The Rhythm of Latin Music.* Crown Point, IN: White Cliffs Media Company.

Hagedorn, Katherine J. 2001. *Divine Utterances: The Performance of Afro-Cuban Santería.* Washington, DC: Smithsonian Institution Press.

Han, Kuo-huang, and Lindy Li Mark. 1980. "Evolution and Revolution in Chinese Music." In *Musics of Many Cultures: An Introduction,* ed. Elizabeth May. Berkeley and Los Angeles: University of California Press, pp. 10–31.

Han Mei. 2005. "Zheng." *Grove Music Online,* ed. L. Macy, www.grovemusic.com (accessed April 1, 2005).

Harvey, John J. 2001. "Cannibals, Mutants, and Hipsters: The Tropicalist Revival." In *Brazilian Popular Music & Globalization*, ed. Charles A. Perrone and Christopher Dunn. Gainesville: University Press of Florida, pp. 106–22.

Hast, Dorothea E., James Cowdery, and Stan Scott. 1999. *Exploring the World of Music.* Dubuque, IA: Kendall/Hunt.

Hornbostel, Erich M. von, and Curt Sachs. 1992 [1914]. "Classification of Musical Instruments." English trans. version. In *Ethnomusicology: An Introduction,* ed. Helen Myers. New York: W.W. Norton & Co., pp. 444–61.

Jackson, Margaret Ruth. 2010. *The Poets of Duisburg: Risk and Hip-hop Performance in a German Inner City.* Ph.D. dissertation, Florida State University.

Jones, Stephen. 1995. *Folk Music of China: Living Instrumental Traditions.* Oxford: Clarendon Press.

Kaufmann, Walter. 1968. *The Ragas of North India.* Bloomington and London: Indiana University Press.

Keita, Seckou. 2002. *Mali.* CD booklet, with liner notes by Jalikunda/Diz Heller. ARC Music Productions International Ltd. EUCD 1779.

Khan, Ali Akbar, and George Ruckert (editors). 1998. *The Classical Music of North India.* Vol. 1. New Delhi: Munshiram Manoharlal Publishers Pvt. Ltd.

Khan, Hafez Inayat. 1991. *The Mysticism of Sound and Music.* Boston: Shambhala.

Kidjo, Angélique. 2004. Angélique Kidjo official Web site, www.angeliquekidjo.com (accessed 2004).

King, Anthony. 1972. "The Construction and Tuning of the Kora." *African Language Studies* 13:113–36.

Knight, Roderic. 2001. "Kora." ed. Stanley Sadie and John Tyrrell. In *The New Grove Dictionary of Music and Musicians.* Vol 13. London: Macmillan, pp. 796–99. (Also in *Grove Music Online,* ed. L. Macy, www.grovemusic.com.)

Kuter, Lois. 2000. "Celtic Music." In *Europe,* ed. Timothy Rice, James Porter, and Chris Goertzen. Vol. 8 of *The Garland Encyclopedia of World Music.* New York and London: Garland Publishing, Inc., pp. 319–23.

Lane, Edward William. 1978 [1895]. *An Account of the Manners and Customs of the Modern Egyptians (Written in Egypt During the Years 1833–1835).* The Hague and London: East-West Publications. (Orig. pub: Cairo: Livres de France, 1836.)

Lavezzoli, Peter. 2006. *The Dawn of Indian Music in the West: Bhairavi.* New York and London: Continuum.

Lawergren, Bo. 2000. "Strings." In *Music in the Age of Confucius,* ed. Jenny F. So. Washington, DC: Freer Gallery of Art and Arthur M. Sackler Gallery, Smithsonian Institution, pp. 65–85.

Leu, Lorraine. 2006. *Brazilian Popular Music: Caetano Veloso and the Regeneration of Tradition.* Aldershot, UK: Ashgate.

Leymarie, Isabelle. 2002. "Latin Jazz." *Latin Jazz: La Combinación Perfecta.* CD booklet. Washington, DC: Smithsonian Folkways Recordings SFW 40802.

Loza, Steven. 1993. *Barrio Rhythm: Mexican American Music in Los Angeles.* Urbana and Chicago: University of Illinois Press.

———. 1999. *Tito Puente and the Making of Latin Music.* Urbana and Chicago: University of Illinois Press.

Lüscher, Barbara (Aischa). 2000. "The Golden Age of Egyptian Oriental Dance." In *The Belly Dance Book: Rediscovering the Oldest Dance,* ed. Tazz Richards. Concord, CA: Backbeat Press, pp. 18–23.

Mackerras, Colin. 1997. *Peking Opera.* Hong Kong: Oxford University Press.

Mahal, Taj. 2004. Taj Mahal official Web site, www.taj-mo-roots.com/kulanjan.html (accessed 2004).

Manuel, Peter (with Kenneth Bilby and Michael Largey). 1995. *Caribbean Currents: Caribbean Music from Rumba to Reggae.* Philadelphia: Temple University Press.

McCourt, Frank. 1996. *Angela's Ashes: A Memoir.* New York: Scribner.

———. 1999. "Crossing the Bridge." CD booklet essay. In *Crossing the Bridge,* Eileen Ivers. Sony Classical SK 60746.

Metting, Fred. 2001. *The Unbroken Circle: Tradition and Innovation in the Music of Ry Cooder and Taj Mahal.* Lanham, MD, and London: Scarecrow Press.

Molloy, Michael. 2002. *Experiencing the World's Religions: Tradition, Challenge, and Change.* 2nd ed. New York: McGraw-Hill.

Moloney, Michael. 1992. *Irish Music in America: Continuity and Change.* Ph.D. dissertation, University of Pennsylvania.

Moore, Robin. 1997. *Nationalizing Blackness:* Afrocubanismo *and Aristic Revolution in Havana, 1920–1940.* Pittsburgh: University of Pittsburgh Press.

Moyo, Dumisani "Ramadu," and Diz Heller. 2002. *Izambulelo: Traditional and Contemporary Music from Zimbabwe.* CD booklet. ARC Music Productions International Ltd. EUCD 1704.

Nelson Davies, Kristina. 2002. "The Qur'ān Recited." In *The Middle East,* ed. Virginia Danielson, Scott Marcus, and Dwight Reynolds. Vol. 6 of *The Garland Encyclopedia of World Music.* New York and London: Routledge, pp. 157–63.

Nettl, Bruno. 2006. *The Study of Ethnomusicology: Thirty-one Issues and Concepts.* Urbana and Chicago: University of Illinois Press.

Nolan, Ronan. 2003. "Seamus Ennis 1919–1982." Rambling House (Irish music Web site), www.iol.ie/~ronolan/ennis.html (accessed 2005).

O'Connor, Nuala. 1999. "Ireland." In *World Music: The Rough Guide.* Vol. 1. New edition, ed. Simon Broughton, Mark Ellingham, and Richard Trillo. London: The Rough Guides, pp. 170–88.

Olsen, Dale A. 1996. *Music of the Warao of Venezuela: Song People of the Rain Forest.* Gainesville: University Press of Florida.

Peiro, Teddy, and Jan Fairley. 2000. "Argentina: Tango." In *World Music: The Rough Guide.* Vol. 2. New edition, ed. Simon Broughton and Mark Ellingham. London: The Rough Guides, pp. 304–14.

Porter, Lewis. 1998. *John Coltrane: His Life and Music.* Ann Arbor: University of Michigan Press.

Puente, Tito Jr. 2004. Tito Puente Jr. official Web site, www.titopuentejr.net/biography.html (accessed 2004).

Racy, A. J. 2003. *Making Music in the Arab World: The Culture and Artistry of Tarab.* Cambridge and New York: Cambridge University Press.

Racy, Ali Jihad. 1981. "Music in Contemporary Cairo: A Comparative Overview." *Asian Music* 13(1):4–26.

Radano, Ronald, and Philip V. Bohlman (editors). 2000. *Music and the Racial Imagination.* Chicago and London: University of Chicago Press.

Ramzy, Hossam. 1995. *Zeina: Best of Mohammed Abdul Wahab.* CD booklet. ARC Music Productions International Ltd. EUCD 1231.

Rault-Leyrat, Lucie. 1987. *La Cithare Chinoise* Zheng, *Un Vol D'oies Sauvages Sur Les Cordes de Soie . . . .* Paris: Le Léopard D'Or.

Rea, Dennis. 2006. "Live at the Forbidden City." www.dennisrea.com/cuijian.html (accessed 2006).

Rice, Timothy. 1994. *May It Fill Your Soul: Experiencing Bulgarian Music.* Chicago and London: University of Chicago Press.

Roberts, John Storm. 1979. *The Latin Tinge: The Impact of Latin American Music on the United States.* New York: Oxford University Press.

Ruckert, George, and Richard Widdess. 2000. "Hindustani Raga." In *South Asia: The Indian Subcontinent,* ed. Alison Arnold. Vol. 5 of *The Garland Encyclopedia of World Music.* New York and London: Garland Publishing, Inc., pp. 64–88.

Saleh, Magda. 2002. "Dance in Egypt." In *The Middle East,* ed. Virginia Danielson, Scott Marcus, and Dwight Reynolds. Vol. 6 of *The Garland Encyclopedia of World Music.* New York and London: Routledge, pp. 623–33.

Sanabria, Bobby, and Ben Socolov. 1990. "Tito Puente: Long Live the King." *Hip: Highlights in Percussion for the Percussion Enthusiast* 5, pp. 1–7, 22–23.

Shankar, Ravi. 1968. *My Music, My Life.* New York: Simon and Schuster.

———. 1999. *Raga Mala: The Autobiography of Ravi Shankar,* ed. George Harrison. New York: Welcome Rain Publishers.

Sheehy, Daniel. 2006. *Mariachi Music in America: Experiencing Music, Expressing Culture.* New York: Oxford University Press.

Shields, Hugh, and Paulette Gershen. 2000. "Ireland." In *Europe,* ed. Timothy Rice, James Porter, and Chris Goertzen. Vol. 8 of *The Garland Encyclopedia of World Music.* New York and London: Garland Publishing, Inc., pp. 378–97.

Shira. 2000. "Props for Oriental Dance." In *The Belly Dance Book: Rediscovering the Oldest Dance,* ed. Tazz Richards. Concord, CA: Backbeat Press, pp. 80–92.

Shubhash. 2010. "Biography for A.R. Rahman." The Internet Movie Database, www.imdb.com/name/nm0006246/bio (accessed 2010).

Slawek, Stephen. 1991. "Ravi Shankar as Mediator between a Traditional Music and Modernity." In *Ethnomusicology and Modern Music History,* ed. Stephen Blum, Philip V. Bohlman, and Daniel M. Neuman. Urbana: University of Illionis Press, pp. 161–80.

Spiller, Henry. 2008. *Focus: Gamelan Music of Indonesia.* 2nd ed. New York: Routledge.

Srinivasan, Gopal. 2002. "The Complete Biography of A.R. Rahman." http://gopalhome.tripod.com/arrbio.html (accesed 2010).

Starr, Larry, and Christopher Alan Waterman. 2003. *American Popular Music: From Minstrelsy to MTV.* New York: Oxford University Press.

Stobart, Henry. 2006. *Music and the Poetics of Production in the Bolivian Andes.* Aldershot, UK: Ashgate.

Stock, Jonathon P. J. 1996. *Musical Creativity in Twentieth-Century China: Abing, His Music, and Its Changing Meanings.* Rochester, NY: University of Rochester Press.

Tenzer, Michael. 1998 [1991]. *Balinese Music.* Berkeley, CA, and Singapore: Periplus Editions.

———. 2000. *Gamelan Gong Kebyar: The Art of Twentieth-Century Balinese Music.* Chicago and London: University of Chicago Press.

Thrasher, Alan. 2005. "China." *Grove Music Online,* ed. L. Macy, www.grovemusic.com (accessed April 1, 2005).

Touma, Habib Hassan. 1996. *The Music of the Arabs.* New expanded ed. Translated by Laurie Schwartz. Portland: Amadeus Press.

Trebinjac, Sabine. 2005. "China (Minority Traditions: North and West China)." *Grove Music Online,* ed. L. Macy, www.grovemusic.com (accessed April 1, 2005).

Turino, Thomas. 2008. *Music in the Andes: Experiencing Music, Expressing Culture.* New York: Oxford University Press.

van Nieuwkerk, Karin. 1995. *"A Trade Like Any Other": Female Singers and Dancers in Egypt.* Austin: University of Texas Press.

Vetter, Roger. 1996. *Rhythms of Life, Songs of Wisdom.* CD booklet. Smithsonian Folkways SF CD 40463.

Williams, Sean. 2009. *Focus: Irish Traditional Music.* New York: Routledge.

Witzleben, J. Lawrence. 2002. "China: A Musical Profile." In *East Asia: China, Japan, and Korea,* ed. Robert C. Provine, Yosihiko Tokumaru, and J. Lawrence Witzleben. Vol. 7 of *The Garland Encyclopedia of World Music.* New York and London: Routledge, pp. 87–93.

Wong, Isabel K. F. 2002. "Nationalism, Westernization, and Modernization." In *East Asia: China, Japan, and Korea,* ed. Robert C. Provine, Yosihiko Tokumaru, and J. Lawrence Witzleben. Vol. 7 of *The Garland Encyclopedia of World Music.* New York and London: Routledge, pp. 379–90.

Zemp, Hugo. 1978. "'Are'are Classification of Musical Types and Instruments." *Ethnomusicology* 22(1):37–67.

———. 1979. "Aspects of 'Are'are Musical Theory." *Ethnomusicology* 23(1):5–48.

Zheng, Cao. 1983. "A Discussion of the History of the Guzheng." Translated by Yohana Knobloch. *Asian Music* 14(2):1–16.

credits

Preston/Corbis; **244**: © The McGraw-Hill Companies, Inc./Michael Redig, photographer; **245**: © Peter Turnley/Corbis; **246**: © The McGraw-Hill Companies, Inc./Michael Redig, photographer; **247**: © Hulton Deutsch Collection/Corbis; **248**: © The McGraw-Hill Companies, Inc./Michael Redig, photographer; **250**: © Frank Driggs Collection/Getty Images; **251**: © Everett Collection; **252**: © C Squared Studios/Getty Images; **253**: Courtesy, Margaret Puente **256**: © The McGraw-Hill Companies/ John Flournoy, photographer; **257**: © Tucker Ransom/Getty Images; **264**: © Malcolm Ali/WireImage/Getty Images; **265**: © AFP/Getty Images; **267**: © AP Images/Dean Cox

Chapter 12

Page 274: © Ali Al Gabry, Courtesy Aisha Ali; **275**: Courtesy, ARC Music Productions International Ltd.; **278**: (clockwise, from top left) © Bettmann/Corbis, © The McGraw-Hill Companies, Inc./Michael Redig, photographer, © Alfred/Sipa Press;

279: © Gavin Graham Gallery, London, UK/The Bridgeman Art Library; **280**: © The McGraw-Hill Companies, Inc./Michael Redig, photographer; **282**: (clockwise, from top left) © The McGraw-Hill Companies, Inc./ Michael Redig, photographer, Courtesy, J.C. Sugarman, Courtesy, ARC Music Productions International Ltd.; **285**: © Chris Hondros/Getty Images; **288**: © The Art Archive/Dagli Orti; **290**: (top) © AP Images/STR, (bottom) © The McGraw-Hill Companies, Inc./ Michael Redig, photographer; **292**: (left) © The McGraw-Hill Companies, Inc./ Michael Redig, photographer, (top right, bottom right) © Michael Redig; **295**: © The McGraw-Hill Companies, Inc./Michael Redig, photographer; **296**: (top) © AFP/Getty Images, (bottom) © Everett Collection; **302**: © Bettmann/ Corbis; **303**: © Mahmoud Reda, Courtesy, Aisha Ali; **305**: (left) © Eliot Elisofon/Time Life Pictures/Getty Images, (right) © The McGraw-Hill Companies, Inc./ Michael Redig, photographer; **306**, **307**: © The McGraw-Hill Companies,

Inc./Michael Redig, photographer; **310**: Courtesy, ARC Music Productions International Ltd.

Chapter 13

Page 318: © The McGraw-Hill Companies, Inc./Michael Redig, photographer; **320**: © Chine Nouvelle/Sipa Press; **322**: From "The Shakuhachi—A Manual for Learning," Christopher Yohmei Blasdel and Yuko Kamisango, Printed Matter Press, Tokyo, 2008. Photo courtesy of the author; **323**: © avex trax; **327**: © Bridgeman Art Library; **328**: © Christie's Images/The Bridgeman Art Library; **329**: © Dale A. Olsen; **331**: (left) © Imaginechina, (right) © Sovfoto/Eastfoto; **336**: © Sovfoto/ Eastfoto; **337**: Courtesy, Madam Fan Shang'e; **339**: Courtesy, Drepung Gomang Monastery; **341**: © Patrick Zachmann/Magnum Photos; **342**: Courtesy, Bei Bei He. www.beibeizheng.com. Photo by Michael Clark; **343**: © Reuters/ Corbis; **344**: © The McGraw-Hill Companies, Inc./Michael Redig, photographer; **347**: © Miradil Hassan/Fausto Caceres

index